# The European Union and Peacebuilding

## Policy and Legal Aspects

T.M.C. ASSER INSTITUTE UNIVERSITY OF LEUVEN

# The European Union and Peacebuilding

## Policy and Legal Aspects

edited by

Steven Blockmans
Jan Wouters
Tom Ruys

T•M•C• Asser press

Published by T·M·C·ASSER PRESS
P.O. Box 16163, 2500 BD The Hague, The Netherlands
<www.asserpress.nl>

*Cover photograph*: Council of the European Union

ISBN 978-90-6704-329-8

# FOREWORD

Dear Reader,

You have in your hands the last part of a trilogy exploring the European Union's approaches to conflicts and crisis. The titles of these books present well the evolution of the international policy debate and thinking during the first decade of the 21$^{st}$ century from a relatively narrow pre-conflict perspective to a wider approach which encompasses all phases of the crisis. The first part published in 2004 was called 'The European Union and Conflict prevention', reflecting how conflict prevention was high on the agenda as a response to the Balkan Wars. In 2008 the second part, 'The European Union and Crisis Management', was published as the European Security and Defence Policy (ESDP)-missions had been operational for some years. Finally the series is completed in 2010 with "The European Union and Peacebuilding".

Peacebuilding is a somewhat flexible concept, of which there is currently no officially agreed international definition. However, this descriptive phrase is perhaps most useful in its most comprehensive sense – efforts aiming at a solid and lasting peace. For the European Union, peacebuilding requires bringing together a variety of external policy tools which include security aspects, mediation and preventive diplomacy, development cooperation and trade relations, in order to make an impact, be coherent and achieve sustainable results.

The European Union has made systematic efforts to ensure an integrated approach to peacebuilding. In this regard, the decisions adopted on the security and development nexus and on fragility in 2007 were a strategic step forward. We are engaged in various activities across the globe, such as for example supporting conflict resolution processes and ensuring the engagement of women in these, as well as building the peacebuilding capacities of regional organisations.

Successful peacebuilding requires taking on a preventive focus. Conflict prevention continues to lie at the heart of all European Union activities, as it is the most cost effective and life saving approach. Conflict prevention implies providing early and sustainable assistance to countries under stress and it is the best measure to avoid a relapse into conflict. While building for the future, we must strive to put an end to the suffering caused by legacies of conflicts, such as the scourge of landmines and other inhumane weapons, which continue to create a burden even decades later and delay development and prosperity goals.

Moreover, peacebuilding is also a joint effort in which the international community needs to work together. In this regard the United Nations, international and regional organisations and especially civil society are all vital partners for the European Union. However, international efforts need to involve local communities early on in order to create a nationally owned process, which is a requisite for lasting peace. Only through partnership with local actors can international norms be combined with a respect and understanding of local context, and promote the transfer of responsibilities and ownership to the populations concerned. In this work we need to engage with local civil society as well as representatives of media and local business communities.

The link between peace, security and development has been widely recognised by the international community, and as a response, the United Nations Peacebuilding Commission (PBC) was created in 2005. The European Union is committed to actively supporting the work of the Peacebuilding Commission on the basis of its experience, resources and worldwide operability.

During the first five years the PBC has brought together all key players on the ground to enable a comprehensive approach to peacebuilding in selected post-conflict states. In 2010 the progress of the PBC so far will be examined in order to take on board lessons learned for the next steps, ensuring that it can discharge its mandate more effectively and better deliver real progress on the ground. 2010 is also the year for the Review Summit of the UN Millennium Development Goals (MDG) aiming at eradicating poverty. The link between countries affected by fragility and conflict and those lagging most behind in attaining the MDGs indicates clearly the need for stronger ties between security and development efforts.

I congratulate the authors of this informative and well-written book, who are not afraid of taking a critical approach. From the point of view of the EU institutions, it is published at a particularly timely moment, as we embark upon a new era in the European Union's external relations through the implementation of the Lisbon Treaty. I hope that you as a reader will find enriching this thorough and wide ranging description of the various aspects of peacebuilding, a concept that we will undoubtedly keep on discussing in the coming years and a goal at which we will continue to aim.

March 2010

Catherine ASHTON

*High Representative of the Union for Foreign Affairs and Security Policy / Vice-President of the European Commission*

# PREFACE AND ACKNOWLEDGEMENTS

The present volume constitutes the last part of a triptych, with earlier works dealing with conflict prevention (V. Kronenberger and J. Wouters, eds., *The European Union and Conflict Prevention: Policy and Legal Aspects* (The Hague, T.M.C. Asser Press 2004)) and crisis management respectively (S. Blockmans, ed., *The European Union and Crisis Management: Policy and Legal Aspects* (The Hague, T.M.C. Asser Press 2008)). The obvious implication is that we aim at focusing on the final phase of peacemaking efforts to break conflict cycles, on *The European Union and Peace-building*.

Leading practitioners and prominent academics have been invited to explore the wide variety of policy and legal aspects of the European Union's contribution to building durable peace in countries ravaged by violent conflict. The book is testimony to the enormous complexity of international efforts to break conflict cycles, which requires both long-term commitment and a multi-faceted approach, combining the re-establishment of basic security with the promotion of respect for human rights, the rule of law, good governance and economic recovery.

Given the intricacies and dynamics of the editorial process, some of the contributions were completed prior to the entry into force of the Lisbon Treaty. Where appropriate, these contributions nonetheless refer to the impact expected from the new Treaty. Other chapters have integrated the institutional developments since the Lisbon Treaty became operational. In any event, the editors are convinced that this divergence does not detract from the value of the analyses, nor from the lessons drawn from years of inter-institutional practice and which should be taken to heart to make the Union's efforts in the field of peacebuilding more efficient and more effective.

We would like to express our sincere gratitude to the practitioners and academics who contributed to this volume. Thanks to their unique insights and high quality contributions, the book offers the first comprehensive and in-depth treatise of the role of the EU in the international peacebuilding endeavour. Special thanks also go to the T.M.C. Asser Instituut for financially supporting the production of this book, to Suzanne Habraken for her sub-editing and language-editing of the manuscript and to Steffen van der Velde for compiling the index and the list of abbreviations. This volume is the result of a fruitful cooperation between the Centre for the Law of EU External Relations (CLEER) and the Leuven Centre for Global Governance Studies.

March 2010 — The editors

# SUMMARY OF CONTENTS

# TABLE OF CONTENTS

Part III. ***Peace and security***

# LIST OF ABBREVIATIONS

**A**

| | |
|---|---|
| AA | Association Agreement |
| ACHPR | African Charter on Human and People's Rights |
| ACP | African, Caribbean and Pacific countries |
| AFET | Committee on Foreign Affairs of the EP |
| AIA | Afghan Interim Authority |
| AIDCO | EuropeAid Cooperation Office |
| AMIS | African Union Mission in Sudan |
| AMISEC | African Union Mission of Securisation of the Elections in the Comoros |
| AMISOM | African Union Mission in Somalia |
| AMM | Aceh Monitoring Mission |
| ANA | Afghan National Army |
| ANP | Afghan National Police |
| AP | Action Plan |
| APF | African Peace Facility |
| APSA | African Peace Security Architecture |
| ARTF | Afghanistan Reconstruction Trust Fund |
| ASEAN | Association of South East Asian Nations |
| ASF | African Standby Force |
| AU | African Union |
| AUC | African Union Commission |
| AUP | Aid to Uprooted People |

**B**

| | |
|---|---|
| BiH | Bosnia and Herzegovina |
| BST | Border Support Team |

**C**

| | |
|---|---|
| CAAC | Children Affected by Armed Conflict |
| CAR | Central African Republic |
| CARDS | Community Assistance for Reconstruction, Development and Stabilisation |
| CAS | Country Assistance Strategy |
| CEDAW | Convention on the Elimination of all forms of Discrimination Against Women |
| CEEC | Central and East European Countries |
| CENI | Commission Electorale Nationale Indépendante |
| CEPS | Centre for European Policy Studies |
| CESDP | Common European Security and Defense Policy |
| CFSP | Common Foreign and Security Policy |
| CHOPA | Chain of Payments Project |
| CIAT | Comité Internationale d'Accompagnement de la Transition |
| CiO | Chairman in Office of the OSCE |
| CIS | Commonwealth of Independent States |
| CIVCOM | Committee for the Civilian Aspects of Crisis Management |
| CMD | Crisis Management Division |
| CMI | Crisis Management Initiative |
| CNDP | Congrès National pour la défense du Peuple |
| CoHA | Cessation of Hostilities Agreement |
| COHOM | Council Working Group on Human Rights |
| CONOPS | Concept of Operations |
| CONUN | Council Working Group of the United Nations |
| COSA | Commission of Security Arrangements |
| COST | European Co-operation in Science and Technology |
| CPC | Conflict Prevention Centre |
| CPCC | Civilian Planning and Conduct Capability |
| CPPB | Conflict Prevention and Peace Building |

| | |
|---|---|
| CPRDC | Commission Permanente de réforme du droit Congolais |
| CPRW | Convention on the Protection of the Rights of Women |
| CRCT | Crisis Response Coordination Team |
| CRIS | Common RELEX Information System |
| CRT | Civilian Response Team |
| CSDP | Common Security and Defence Policy |
| CSM | Country-Specific Meeting |
| CSP | Country Strategy Paper |
| CSTC-A | Combined Security Transition Command Afghanistan |
| Cts | Carats |

**D**

| | |
|---|---|
| DAC | Development Assistance Committee |
| DACDF | Diamond Area Community Development Fund |
| DCAF | Geneva Centre for the Democratic Control of Armed Forces |
| DCI | Development Cooperation Instrument |
| DDR | Disarmament, demobilisation and reintegration |
| DEI | Directorate for European Integration |
| DfID | Department for International Development |
| DG | Directorate General |
| DG AIDCO | Directorate General Aid Coordination Office |
| DG DEV | Directorate General Development |
| DG ELARG | Directorate General for Enlargement |
| DG JLS | Directorate General Justice, Freedom and Security |
| DG RELEX | Directorate General for External Relations |
| DiCOSA | District Level Commission of Security Arrangements |
| DIS | Détachement Integré de Sécurité |
| DO | District Office |
| DPA | Dayton/Paris Peace Accords |
| DPA | Department of Political Affairs |
| DPKO | United Nations Department of Peacekeeping Operations |
| DRC | Democratic Republic of Congo |

**E**

| | |
|---|---|
| EaP | Eastern Partnership |
| EASBRIG | East African Standby Brigade |
| EBRD | European Bank for Reconstruction and Development |
| EC | European Commission (or, when indicated, European Community) |
| ECCAS | Economic Community of Central African States |
| ECHO | European Commission Humanitarian Aid Office |
| ECHR | European Convention on Human Rights |
| ECJ | European Court of Justice |
| ECOWAS | Economic Community of West African States |
| ECRI | European Commission against Racism and Intolerance |
| EDF | European Development Fund |
| EEAS | European External Action Service |
| EIDHR | European Initiative for Democracy and Human Rights |
| EMMA | Executing, Monitoring, Mentoring and Advising Mission |
| EMP | Euro-Mediterranean Partnership |
| ENP | European Neighbourhood Policy |
| ENPI | European Neighbourhood and Partnership Instrument |
| EOM | Election Observation Mission |
| EP | European Parliament |
| EPLO | European Peacebuilding Liaison Office |
| ERD | European Report on Development |
| ESDP | European Security and Defence Policy |
| ESS | European Security Strategy |
| EU | European Union |
| EU COPPS | EU Coordinating Office for Palestinian Police Support |
| EUFOR | European Union Force |
| EULEX | European Union Rule of Law Mission in Kosovo |
| EUMC | European Union Military Committee |

| | |
|---|---|
| EUMM | European Union Monitoring Mission |
| EUMS | European Union Military Staff |
| EUNAVFOR | European Union Naval Force |
| EUPM | European Union Police Mission |
| EUPOL | European Union Police Mission |
| EUPT | European Union Planning Team |
| EUR | Euro |
| EUSEC | European Union advisory and assistance mission for security reform |
| EUSEC FIN | EUSEC Finance Mechanism |
| EUSR | European Union Special Representative |
| **F** | |
| FAFA | Financial and Administrative Framework Agreement |
| FAO | Food and Agriculture Organization |
| FARDC | Forces Armées de la République Démocratique du Congo |
| FATF | Financial Action Task Force |
| FBiH | Federation of Bosnia and Herzegovina |
| FDLR | Forces Démocratiques pour la Libération du Rwanda |
| FOC | Full Operating Capability |
| FSC | Forum for Security Cooperation |
| FYROM | Former Yugoslav Republic of Macedonia |
| **G** | |
| G8 | Group of Eight |
| GAERC | General Affairs and External Relations Council |
| GAM | Free Aceh Movement |
| GMRRR | Groupe Mixte de Réflexion de la Police Nationale Congolaise |
| GNI | Gross National Income |
| GoI | Government of Indonesia |
| GPPO | German Police Project Office |
| GRAPAX | Groupe de Recherche en Appui aux Politiques de Paix |
| GTZ | Deutsche Gesellschaft für Technische Zusammenarbeit |
| **H** | |
| HCNM | High Commissioner on National Minorities |
| HPCR | International Association for Humanitarian Policy and Conflict Research |
| HQ | Headquarters |
| HR | High Representative |
| HRD | Hoge Raad voor Diamanten (Antwerp World Diamond Centre) |
| HR/SG | High Representative for CFSP/Secretary General of the Council |
| HR/VP | High Representative of the Union for Foreign Affairs and Security Policy/Vice-President of the European Commission |
| **I** | |
| IBM | Integrated Border Management |
| ICC | International Criminal Court |
| ICCPR | International Covenant on Civil and Political Rights |
| ICERD | International Convention on the Elimination of Racial Discrimination |
| ICESCR | International Covenant on Economic, Social and Cultural Rights |
| ICG | International Crisis Group |
| ICO | International Civilian Office |
| ICONS | Impending Crisis Online News System |
| ICR | International Civilian Representative |
| ICRC | International Committee of the Red Cross |
| ICTY | International Criminal Tribunal for the former Yugoslavia |
| IDEA | Institute for Democracy and Electoral Assistance |
| IDP | Internally displaced person |
| IEC | Independent Election Commission |
| IfS | Instrument for Stability |
| IHL | International Humanitarian Law |
| IMF | International Monetary Fund |
| IMP | Initial Monitoring Presence |

| | |
|---|---|
| IO | International Organisation |
| IOM | International Organisation for Migration |
| IPA | Instrument for Pre-Accession Assistance |
| IPBS | Integrated Peacebuilding Strategies |
| IPTF | International Police Task Force |
| IPU | Integrated Police Unit |
| IRFFI | International Reconstruction Fund Facility for Iraq |
| ISAF | International Security Assistance Force |
| ISI | Inter-Service Intelligence |
| ISPA | Instrument for Structural Policies for Pre-Accession |
| ISSAT | International Security Sector Advisory Team |
| ITA | Indirect Tax Administration |
| **J** | |
| JAES | Joint Africa-EU Strategy |
| JCC | Joint Control Commission |
| JMCE | Jean Monnet Centre of Excellence |
| JTF | Joint Task Force |
| **K** | |
| KDOM | Kosovo Diplomatic Observer Mission |
| KFOR | Kosovo Force |
| KLA | Kosovo Liberation Army |
| KP | Kimberley Process |
| KPCS | Kimberley Process Certification Scheme |
| KPS | Kosovo Police Service |
| KVM | Kosovo Verification Mission |
| **L** | |
| LOGA | Law on the Governing of Aceh |
| LOTFA | Law and Order Trust Fund Afghanistan |
| LRA | Lord's Resistance Army |
| LSMS | Legal System Monitoring Section |
| **M** | |
| MDG | Millennium Development Goal |
| MDTF | Multi-Donor Trust Fund |
| MEDA | Euro-Mediterranean Partnership (Technical Assistance Regulation) |
| MINURCAT | United Nations Mission in Central African Republic and Chad |
| MMA | Monitoring, Mentoring and Advising |
| MoI | Ministry of the Interior |
| MONUC | United Nations Organisation Mission in DR Congo |
| MoU | Memorandum of Understanding |
| MRIS | Management Reporting Information System |
| **N** | |
| NAM | Non-Aligned Movement |
| NARC | North Africa Regional Capability |
| NATO | North Atlantic Treaty Organization |
| NCA | National Chadian Army |
| NDC | NATO Defense College |
| NGO | Non-governmental Organisation |
| NIP | National Indicative Programme |
| NPAA | National Programme for the Adoption of the *Acquis* |
| NTM-A | NATO Training Mission Afghanistan |
| **O** | |
| OAS | Organization of American States |
| OAU | Organisation of African Unity |
| OCHA | Office for the Coordination of Humanitarian Affairs |
| OCT | Overseas Countries and Territories |
| ODA | Official Development Assistance |

| | |
|---|---|
| ODIHR | Office for Democratic Institutions and Human Rights |
| OECD | Organisation for Economic Co-operation and Development |
| OHCHR | Office of the High Commissioner for Human Rights |
| OHR | Office of the High Representative |
| OIC | Organization of the Islamic Conference |
| OJ | Official Journal |
| OPLAN | Operations Plan |
| OPT | Occupied Palestinian Territory |
| OSCE | Organization for Security and Co-operation in Europe |
| OSINT | Open Source Intelligence |
| **P** | |
| PAS | Programme d'Accompagnement à la Stabilisation |
| PBC | United Nations Peace Building Commission |
| PBF | United Nations Peace Building Fund |
| PbP | Peacebuilding Partnership |
| PBSO | United Nations Peace Building Support Office |
| PCA | Partnership and Cooperation Agreement |
| PCD | Policy Coherence on Development |
| PCNA | Post-Conflict Needs Assessment |
| PESC | Politique étrangère et de Sécurité commune |
| PHARE | Poland and Hungary Assistance for Reconstructing the Economy |
| PIC | Peace Implementation Council |
| PIFWC | Person Indicted for War Crimes |
| PIR | Rapid Intervention Police |
| PISG | Provisional Institutions of Self-Government |
| PJCCM | Police and Judicial Cooperation in Criminal Matters |
| PN | Police Nationale |
| PNC | Police Nationale Congolaise |
| PR/HR | Personal Representative of the High Representative |
| PRC | Police Reconstruction Commission |
| PRI | Police Research and Intervention |
| PRT | Provincial Reconstruction Team |
| PSC | Political and Security Committee |
| PSO | Peace Support Operation |
| PSOD | Peace Support Operations Division |
| **Q** | |
| QIP | Quick Impact Project |
| **R** | |
| RCC | Regional Cooperation Council |
| REC | Regional Economic Community |
| RECOM | Regional Commission for Truth-seeking and Truth-telling About War Crimes |
| REJUSCO | Justice Reform Project in the Congo |
| REPI | Recherche et Enseignement en Politique Internationale |
| RoC | Republic of Congo (Brazzaville) |
| RS | Republika Srpska |
| **S** | |
| SAA | Stabilisation and Association Agreement |
| SADC | Southern African Development Community |
| SADR | Sahrawi Arab Democratic Republic |
| SALW | Small Arms and Lights Weapons |
| SAP | Stabilisation and Association Process |
| SAPARD | Special Accession Programme for Agriculture and Rural Development |
| SASE | Safe and Secure Environment |
| SDP | Social Democratic Party |
| SEC | European Commission document which cannot be classified in any of the other series |
| SFOR | Stabilisation Force |
| SFRY | Socialist Federal Republic of Yugoslavia |
| SG/HR | Secretary General/High Representative |

| | |
|---|---|
| SIGMA | Support for Improvement in Governance and Management |
| SIPA | State Information and Protection Agency |
| SitCen | Situation Centre |
| SOP | Standard Operation Procedure |
| SPA | Strategic Partnership Agreement |
| SRO | Sub Regional Organisation |
| SRSA | Swedish Rescue Service Agency |
| SRSG | Special Representative of the Secretary General |
| SSR | Security Sector Reform |
| SVEZ | Government Office for Development and European Affairs (Slovenia) |

**T**

| | |
|---|---|
| TA | Technical Assistance |
| TACIS | Technical Assistance for the Commonwealth of Independent States |
| TAIEX | Technical Assistance and Information Exchange instrument |
| TEC | Treaty Establishing the European Community |
| TEU | Treaty on European Union |
| TJ | Transitional justice |
| TOR | Terms of Reference |

**U**

| | |
|---|---|
| UDHR | Universal Declaration of Human Rights |
| UK | United Kingdom |
| UN | United Nations |
| UNAMA | United Nations Assistance Mission in Afghanistan |
| UNAMID | African Union - United Nations Hybrid Operation in Darfur |
| UNDP | United Nations Development Programme |
| UNGA | United Nations General Assembly |
| UNHCR | United Nations High Commissioner for Refugees |
| UNICEF | United Nations International Children Emergency Fund |
| UNIDIR | United Nations Institute for Disarmament Research |
| UNMIK | United Nations Interim Administration Mission in Kosovo |
| UNODC | United Nations Office on Drugs and Crime |
| UNOMIG | United Nations Observer Mission in Georgia |
| UNOPS | United Nations Office for Project Services |
| UNRWA | United Nations Reliefs and Works Agency |
| UNSC | United Nations Security Council |
| UNSCR | United Nations Security Council Resolution |
| UNSC Res | United Nations Security Council Resolution |
| UNSG | United Nations Secretary General |
| UNSRSG | United Nations Special and Personal Representative of the Secretary General |
| US | United States |
| USD | United States Dollar |

**V**

| | |
|---|---|
| VP | Vice-President of the European Commission |

**W**

| | |
|---|---|
| WB | World Bank |
| WDC | World Diamond Council |
| WFP | World Food Programme |
| WG | Working Group |
| WGLL | Working Group on Lessons Learned |
| WGM | Monitoring Working Group |
| WGS | Working Group on Statistics |
| WHO | World Health Organization |
| WTO | World Trade Organization |

# MAKING PEACE LAST. THE EU'S CONTRIBUTION TO PEACEBUILDING

**Steven Blockmans*, Jan Wouters** and Tom Ruys*****

## 1. INTRODUCTION TO THE BOOK

It is common knowledge that states which are most prone to societal violence are those with a recent past of internal conflict and gross human rights abuse. Despite several decades of experience, the international community can boast few genuine successes in terms of post-conflict peacebuilding. Examples where efforts to break the cycle of conflict eventually failed regrettably hold the upper hand. This finding is fully corroborated by the report of the UN Secretary-General of June 2009 on peacebuilding in the immediate aftermath of conflict.[1] Far too often has the international community missed the window of opportunity after the guns fell silent: 'Time and again, we have failed to catalyse a response that delivers immediate, tangible results on the ground.'[2]

Assisting states recovering from violent conflict in their quest for sustainable peace is and remains a very complex endeavour. It requires continued commitment, based on the recognition that military intervention alone cannot in itself prevent a country from sliding back into conflict, and extending beyond the immediate aftermath of the conflict. It also requires a multi-faceted approach, combining the re-establishment of basic security with the promotion of respect for human rights, the rule of law, good governance and economic recovery. The afore-mentioned UN report identifies the following 'building blocks' that should, as a minimum, be addressed:

---

* Dr. Steven Blockmans is Senior Research Fellow in EU law at the T.M.C. Asser Institute in The Hague and academic coordinator of the Centre for the Law of EU External Relations (CLEER).

** Prof. Dr. Jan Wouters is Jean Monnet Chair EU and Global Governance, Professor of International Law and International Organisations and Director of the Leuven Centre for Global Governance Studies and Institute for International Law at the University of Leuven.

*** Dr. Tom Ruys is attorney at law at Stibbe in Brussels and Substitute Lecturer and Senior Member of the Leuven Centre for Global Governance Studies at the University of Leuven.

[1] Report of the UN Secretary-General on peacebuilding in the immediate aftermath of conflict, 11 June 2009, UN Doc. A/63/881 – S/2009/304, at 3.

[2] Ibid.

*S. Blockmans, J. Wouters & T. Ruys, eds., The European Union and Peacebuilding*

- Support for basic safety and security, including mine action, protection of civilians, disarmament, demobilisation and reintegration (DDR), strengthening the rule of law and security sector reform (SSR);
- Support to political processes, including electoral processes, promoting inclusive dialogue and reconciliation;
- Support to the provision of basic services, such as water and sanitation, health and primary education, and support to the safe return of internally displaced persons (IDPs) and refugees;
- Support to restoring core government functions, in particular basic public administration and public finance; and
- Support to economic revitalisation, including employment generation as well as rehabilitation of basic infrastructure.[3]

Finally, while national ownership is a key ingredient, peacebuilding efforts are most likely to succeed when they involve a wide variety of actors at the international, regional and non-governmental level, each bringing to the field their own expertise and resources.

The EU's contribution to the peacebuilding domain is, admittedly, fairly novel and originally constituted a response to, by and large, the Balkan Wars on its own doorstep. Since then, however, parallel to the rapid development of the Common Foreign and Security Policy (CFSP), the European Union has gone a long way in improving the instruments at its disposal and has generated considerable pools of civilian capabilities, including police officers, judges and prosecutors, and civil administration experts. Even though the European Security and Defence Policy (ESDP) was only declared operational in December 2001,[4] the EU has so far already launched over 20 EU operations around the globe, including police missions, security sector reform missions, rule of law missions as well as military stabilisation operations. At the same time, from Colombia to Iraq, and from Afghanistan to Sri Lanka, the European Union has, in various other ways, contributed to a wide range of peacebuilding activities, ranging from the promotion of independent media to tackling the proliferation of small arms and light weapons, addressing the exploitation of natural resources and reintegration of ex-combatants into society.

In previous years, it appeared that the European Commission focused primarily on conflict prevention, whereas the Council was mainly involved in crisis management. More recently, however, and especially since the (EU-sponsored) genesis of the UN Peacebuilding Commission, there seems to be a growing awareness among policy makers in both the Commission and the Council Secretariat of the importance and specific challenges of peacebuilding. Even if the concept itself remains far less omnipresent in EU jargon than that of, for instance, 'conflict prevention',

---

[3] Ibid., at 6.

[4] Presidency Conclusions, Laeken European Summit, 14 and 15 December 2001, para. 6 and Annex II.

and even if cross-departmental coordination is probably less developed than in the United Nations, several indicators attest to this evolution. Examples are the existence within DG RELEX's Directorate A (Crisis Platform) of a separate unit for 'Crisis Response and Peacebuilding', as well as the organisation of specific courses on the topic. Another interesting element concerns the establishment of a separate funding instrument, drawing on the Instrument for Stability (IfS), namely the Peacebuilding Partnership (PbP).[5] The PbP provides funding, mainly to specialised NGOs, but also to international and regional actors as well as EU Member State agencies, for a variety of peacebuilding activities, such as training or the evaluation of operations.[6]

All in all, it is safe to say that, like conflict prevention and crisis management, post-conflict peacebuilding has come to form an integral part of the EU's external policy *sensu lato*. This is illustrated by the attention paid by the 2003 European Security Strategy to the need to break 'the cycle of conflict, insecurity, poverty'.[7] More explicitly, the Lisbon Treaty, which entered into force on 1 December 2009, expands the scope of the so-called 'Petersberg tasks' to cover 'joint disarmament operations, humanitarian and rescue tasks, military advice and assistance tasks, conflict prevention and peacekeeping tasks, tasks of combat forces in crisis management, including peace-making *and post-conflict stabilisation*' (Article 43(1) Treaty on European Union).[8] Peacebuilding is thus fully included in the tasks which the EU can perform in the implementation of (what is now called) Common Security and Defence Policy (CSDP).

Given its potential contribution in financial and logistic terms, the EU's advance in this field has been universally welcomed by other relevant peacebuilding actors, both intergovernmental and non-governmental. At the same time, the EU has been

---

[5] See Art. 4(3) of Regulation (EC) No 1717/2006 of the European Parliament and of the Council of 15 November 2006 establishing an Instrument for Stability, *OJ* 2006 L 327/1.

[6] See on the PbP: S. Bayne and P. Trolliet, 'Stocktaking and Scoping of the Peacebuilding Partnership' (study commissioned by DG RELEX), August 2009, available at: <http://ec.europa.eu/external_relations/ifs/pbp/docs/study_en.pdf>.

[7] *A Secure Europe in a Better World – A European Security Strategy*, adopted by the European Council on 12 December 2003 (available at: <http://www.consilium.europa.eu/uedocs/cmsUpload/78367.pdf>) and complemented by the High Representative's *Report on the Implementation of the European Security Strategy – Providing Security in a Changing World*, doc. 17104/08 (S407/08), 11 December 2008, as endorsed by the European Council, Presidency Conclusions, doc. 17271/08 (CONCL 5), 12 December 2008, point 30.

[8] Consolidated version of the Treaty on European Union, *OJ* 2008 C 115/13 [emphasis added]. With the entry into force of the Lisbon Treaty, the 'European Community' has disappeared together with the '3-Pillar' structure of the EU. It is hoped that thereby previous interinstitutional conflicts will also disappear. But until the dust over the creation of the EEAS settles, there is no way of telling for sure. What is clear is that there is potential confusion in historical accounts of EC and EU policy making, for some of the terms used have no meaning in the post-Lisbon framework. 'EC', for instance, will from now on be the more logical abbreviation for the 'European Commission', instead of the 'European Community', Likewise, 'CSDP', 'Common Security and Defence Policy', has replaced 'ESDP', 'European Security and Defence Policy'. In this volume, where it is relevant to do so, the terms are employed as legally valid at the time of their usage.

confronted with the incredible complexity of the broader peacebuilding endeavour. Thus, despite billions in aid to the Western Balkans and a plenitude of projects, some countries in the region still suffer (to a greater or lesser degree) from widespread poverty, unemployment and corruption, coupled with a considerable number of internally displaced persons and a lingering potential for inter-ethnic tension. These and other experiences have forced the EU to evaluate its lessons learned and to strive for a more efficient and more integrated approach.

## 2. Scope and objective

The book thus starts from the assumption that within a relatively short time frame the EU has established itself as a valuable peacebuilding partner and that the tools at its disposal merit further scrutiny and development. Itself having been created as a project designed to secure peace and prosperity after the Second World War, the European Union has a moral duty to employ its considerable financial and logistic resources to assist states recovering from violent conflict, whether or not they border on the EU's own frontiers. Furthermore, in today's globalised world, as recognised by the European Security Strategy, the chaos resulting from failed states or regional instability does not stop at national or regional borders. Conflicts' centrifugal forces export flows of refugees, trafficking of various kinds, and/or terrorist activities. Such spill-over effects are unavoidable absent a concerted and sustained effort of the international community to counter these ills. Finally, it may be noted that at a time when the pace and objectives of horizontal and vertical European integration are increasingly called into question, Eurobarometer reports indicate that European citizens by and large support a stronger role for the EU in promoting peace and security around the globe.[9]

Against this background, the book aims at providing a broad and in-depth overview of the various facets of EU peacebuilding by means of a series of contributions written by EU officials – both desk officers and officials with extensive field experience –, national diplomats, representatives from other international organisations and academic experts.

The present volume constitutes the last part of a triptych, with earlier works dealing with conflict prevention (V. Kronenberger & J. Wouters, eds., *The European Union and Conflict Prevention: Policy and Legal Aspects* (The Hague, T.M.C. Asser Press 2004)) and crisis management respectively (S. Blockmans, ed., *The European Union and Crisis Management: Policy and Legal Aspects* (The Hague,

[9] According to an opinion survey published in December 2006, 'European public opinion remains very positive on issues relating to ESDP. On average, three out of four citizens are in favour of a common security and defence policy.' These figures have remained relatively stable (never falling below 60%) in all Eurobarometer surveys since 1999. See European Commission, Eurobarometer 66: 'Public Opinion in the European Union', December 2006, available at: <http://ec.europa.eu/public_opinion/archives/eb/eb66/eb66_highlights_en.pdf>, at 25.

T.M.C. Asser Press 2008)). The obvious implication is that we aim at focusing on the final phase of peacemaking efforts to break conflict cycles. Nonetheless, as several of the contributing authors acknowledge, there still exists a considerable degree of conceptual confusion as to the precise purport of the term 'peacebuilding'. The term was first incorporated into UN strategy with the publication, in 1992, of UN Secretary-General Boutros-Ghali's *Agenda for Peace*.[10] The 2008 'Principles and Guidelines' for UN Peacekeeping Operations (the so-called 'Capstone Doctrine') refer to

> 'a range of measures targeted to reduce the risk of lapsing or relapsing into conflict by strengthening national capacities at all levels for conflict management, and to lay the foundation for sustainable peace and development. Peace-building is a complex, long-term process of creating the necessary conditions for sustainable peace. It works by addressing the deep-rooted, structural causes of violent conflict in a comprehensive manner.'[11]

What is clear from this description is that peacebuilding involves more than the achieving of 'negative' peace – viz. the halting of armed conflict. Instead, it also aims at tackling the root causes of the conflict so as to create an environment of 'positive' peace. In addition, peacebuilding is not merely concerned with the immediate aftermath of armed conflict. The goal is to create a sustainable peace – in other words: to make peace last. On the other hand, there is no clear demarcation where peacebuilding ends and is taken over by the regular channels of development assistance and politico-military cooperation. Conversely, it cannot be excluded that low-intensity violence flares up again after peacebuilding efforts have been initiated. This is illustrated by the outbreak of violent conflict in Kosovo in March 2004, leading to the killing of over thirty persons and the wounding of several hundreds.[12] Although the lines between the various phases may be blurred, the chapters compiled in this book in principle deal with post-conflict societies and only to a lesser extent touch upon classical cases of prevention of (entirely new) conflicts, peacekeeping or peace enforcement.

The book examines EU peacebuilding from a twofold perspective, one being essentially descriptive, the other more critical/evaluative. From a primarily descriptive angle, the book examines, amongst others, the evolution of the concept of peacebuilding, the evolution of the role of the European Union as a global peacebuilder, and the array of instruments at its disposal. Yet, the objective is also to draw up an interim balance of the EU's progress in this field: what is the added value of EU peacebuilding; what are its strengths, weaknesses and challenges; and

---

[10] *Agenda for Peace*, Report of the Secretary-General, 17 June 1992, UN Doc. A/47/277 – S/24111.

[11] United Nations Department of Peacekeeping, Department of Field Support, *United Nations Peacekeeping Operations: Principles and Guidelines*, January 2008, available at: <http://pbpu.unlb.org/pbps/Library/Capstone_Doctrine_ENG.pdf>, at 18.

[12] E.g., 'Kosovo clashes "ethnic cleansing"', *BBC News*, 20 March 2004.

what mechanisms and aspects can be improved? The editors firmly believe that these analyses come at a proper time, now that the new actors, services and instruments provided for by the Lisbon Treaty are being put in place.

The two sets of questions are in turn examined from a double perspective, which is *grosso modo* reflected in the structure of the book. First, EU peacebuilding is considered from a more institutional angle in order to identify the relevant players and instruments involved and to evaluate the extent to which they act in an efficient and coordinated manner. Second, it is examined how the EU has been able to make a difference on the ground, by identifying some core themes of EU peacebuilding and by providing an in-depth review of several case studies. While the book does not claim to offer an exhaustive analysis of all of the EU's peacebuilding efforts past and present, the various contributions do cover a broad array of thematic issues, without being limited to specific geographic areas.

## 3. Overview

*Part One* of the book brings together a number of chapters dealing with the EU's contribution to peacebuilding from a more general perspective. Simon Duke and Aurélie Courtier not only analyse how the term 'peacebuilding' is defined in the UN and EU contexts. They also provide a comprehensive overview of the relevant instruments at the EU's disposal – both CFSP-related tools as well as others, such as the European Development Fund, the Instrument for Stability and the African Peace Facility. Furthermore, their chapter identifies the different players within the EU's institutional framework as well as the external partners in peacebuilding. Specific attention is also paid to the possible impact of the Lisbon Treaty on the efficiency and coherence of the EU's efforts in this field. This chapter is the first-ever comprehensive overview of concepts, players and instruments in EU peacebuilding.

While Duke and Courtier look at EU peacebuilding from an institutional angle, Nathalie Tocci does so from an 'actorness' perspective: what role does the Union play on the international scene of peacebuilding? She identifies a twofold manner in which the EU may contribute to stability in post-conflict societies. One mechanism is support for the restoring of adequate administrative, judicial, security or economic *capacities* to engage in peaceful change through targeted financial or technical assistance. Second, the EU may tackle the lack of *political will* in favour of conflict transformation by creating certain incentives. Depending on the coercive or consensual character of these incentives, Tocci distinguishes between socialisation, conditionality and passive enforcement. While conceding that, on both counts, the EU may bring significant added value, she cautions that its efforts are sometimes hampered by credibility problems.

Steven Blockmans subsequently looks at the EU enlargement process as a peacebuilding tool. As noted above, the European integration process started out as a post-war rehabilitation process. In the wake of the Cold War and the armed conflicts in the Balkans, the enlargement policy of the Union continues to extend the peacebuilding philosophy throughout the entire continent. Blockmans observes that the European Union has put 'Member State-building' at the centre of its enlargement policy. He identifies three building blocks of such 'Member State-building': legal approximation, institution building and constituency building. While concluding that EU enlargement may be a formidable peacebuilding tool, the author nonetheless cautions that a balanced application of the conditionality principle, e.g., taking account of the particularities of the countries involved, is central to success.

Keeping in mind that effective peacebuilding requires a concerted approach on the international plane, *Part Two* of the volume addresses the cooperation between the European Union and other concerned actors. Catriona Gourlay assesses the widespread assumption that the EU and the UN are 'natural partners' in peacebuilding. After analysing the implications of the two organisations' different concepts of peacebuilding, Gourlay paints a nuanced picture of two particular fields of cooperation. On the one hand, she analyses the development dimension of the EU-UN partnership, primarily by identifying funding trends and operational challenges. On the other hand, she explores the extent to which ESDP has contributed directly or indirectly to UN peace operations. Two specific case studies (DRC and Kosovo) are used to illustrate the added value of, but also the obstacles to, EU-UN cooperation.

A separate chapter is devoted to the UN Peacebuilding Commission (PBC). This body, established in December 2005 in the wake of the September 2005 UN World Summit, brings together all key players in order to enable a comprehensive approach to peacebuilding in selected post-conflict states (four countries are currently on the PBC's agenda: Burundi, Sierra Leone, Guinea-Bissau and the Central African Republic). Offering an insightful account of the EU's relationship with the PBC, Stefano Tomat and Cesare Onestini examine the creation of the PBC, its mandate, its instruments and its activities so far. In addition, they look at the active and positive role played by the European Union in the creation and the functioning of the PBC, including at how the European institutions are represented therein. The chapter concludes with an assessment of the PBC's effectiveness from an EU perspective.

Two other international organisations are addressed in Part Two. In light of the adoption of the Joint Africa-EU Strategy in Lisbon in December 2007, EU Special Representative Koen Vervaeke sheds light on the emergence of a peace and security partnership between the EU and the African Union (AU). The chapter describes the institutional ties between both organisations, as well as the EU's contribution to the AU in terms of capacity building (vis-à-vis the operationalising of the African Peace and Security Architecture) and predictable funding (through the African Peace Facility). A number of future challenges are also examined, including the need to develop a productive relationship between the AU, the EU and the UN.

David Galbreath subsequently addresses the development of the relationship between the EU and the Organisation for Security and Cooperation in Europe (OSCE) in relation to peacebuilding. Observing that the agendas and functions of the two organisations are converging to a growing extent, the author looks at three relevant areas of mutual interest and cooperation: peacekeeping, democracy promotion and human rights protection. Furthermore, drawing on interviews performed in Brussels and Vienna, the chapter provides an insight into the perception of their respective role and tasks on the part of EU and OSCE officials.

*Parts Three to Five* of the book turn away from the more institutional perspective and attempt to provide an overview of the EU's contribution on the ground. In accordance with the *In Larger Freedom* Report of UN Secretary-General Kofi Annan (2005),[13] a broad distinction is made between three interrelated aspects of sustainable peace, namely security ('freedom from fear'), rule of law, democracy and human rights ('freedom to live in human dignity'), and economic development ('freedom from want'). These domains are addressed in three separate chapters, which combine thematic contributions with a number of case studies of specific countries.

Thus, *Part Three* starts with a thematic analysis of the EU Policy Framework for Security Sector Reform (SRR). David Spence provides an account both of the evolution of the EU's concept of SRR and of the policies concerning SSR implementation in partner states. In addition, the chapter reflects on whether the Lisbon Treaty is likely to end existing inter-Pillar and interinstitutional disputes so as to allow a more efficient and coherent approach to SSR.

Subsequently, a first case study illustrates the added value of EU SSR by looking at the EU's efforts in the Democratic Republic of Congo. Following an overview of the security situation on the ground, Marta Martinelli evaluates the country-specific approach to SSR applied by the Commission and the Council and implemented through operations EUPOL Kinshasa, EUPOL RD Congo and EUSEC DR Congo. The author discerns several strengths of the afore-mentioned ESDP missions, such as the integration of a gender dimension, but also points to various lingering weaknesses. Examples of the latter include the different institutional cultures informing Council and Commission interventions in crisis areas, but also the fact that the issue of national ownership is sometimes overlooked.

Ambassador Michael Humphreys and Jasna Jelisić subsequently offer a fascinating – albeit somewhat gloomy – picture of the complexity of state building and the difficulty of remedying mistakes committed in the early stages of peacebuilding at a later stage. The authors examine the efforts of the international community, and the EU in particular, in Bosnia and Herzegovina between 2002 and 2006. Despite the presence of several promising factors – e.g., the strong desire for EU membership on behalf of all constituent peoples and the positive contribution by the Office of the High Representative – they observe how the state-building process effectively came to a halt, *inter alia*, as a result of unrealistic timeframes for reform, growing EU disunity and political developments on the ground.

---

[13] *In Larger Freedom: Towards Development, Security and Human Rights for All*, Report of the UN Secretary-General, 21 March 2005, UN Doc. A/59/2005.

Cees Wittebrood and Christophe Gadrey turn their attention to Chad, where, against the background of a broader regional crisis, the EU has engaged in humanitarian assistance and participated in the political dialogue (*inter alia*, through the activities of the EU Special Representative). The main focus of their chapter concerns the deployment, from March 2008 to March 2009, of EUFOR Chad, which was the first EU autonomous military operation of such scale and acted as a 'bridge' pending the full deployment of MINURCAT. In light of the operation's recent conclusion, the two authors offer a critical appraisal and an elaborate list of lessons learned.

Closer to home, Michael Merlingen and Rasa Ostrauskaitė examine how the EU has proceeded from a 'hands-off' to a 'hands-on' engagement vis-à-vis Georgia following the August 2008 war with Russia. Their chapter looks at, amongst others, the role of the EU Special Representative for the Southern Caucasus, the rule of law mission EUJUST THEMIS and the ongoing EU Monitoring Mission in Georgia. The authors applaud the EU's posture during and in the wake of the conflict as a signal of growing assertiveness in the external relations field. At the same time, if the aftermath of the war is said to have added to the EU's foreign policy stature, experience also suggests there is a need to further develop the EU's mediation capacities.

*Part Four* touches upon the promotion of democracy, human rights and the rule of law in post-conflict societies. Within this context, the first chapter deals with a somewhat under-researched – and perhaps undervalued – activity that forms part of the broader peacebuilding process, namely electoral support. Patrick Dupont, Francesco Torcoli and Fabio Bargiacchi identify two distinct aspects, namely election observation – viz. the impartial assessment of the actual electoral event – and electoral assistance – viz. the technical or material support given to the broader electoral process. In each of these areas, it is observed, the EU has made significant progress, both in terms of activities, funding, development of methodology and good practices, and as regards cooperation with other actors (most notably UNDP and the OSCE).

Subsequently, Hadewych Hazelzet illustrates how human rights and gender issues have been mainstreamed into the European Security and Defence Policy since 2003. While acknowledging that there has been a steady increase in the paper trail underlining the importance of these issues as well as in the number of human rights and gender advisors deployed in ESDP missions, she stresses that further implementation is needed. The positive experience of the EU Monitoring Mission in Georgia is considered as a useful precedent for moving forward.

Stephan Keukeleire and Robin Thiers offer an in-depth account of the history, background and activities of the largest and most ambitious civilian ESDP mission launched so far, namely the European Union Rule of Law Mission in Kosovo (EULEX Kosovo). Special consideration is given to EULEX Justice, which the authors regard as the most problematic component of the mission. Although it is too early to pass judgment on the success of the operation, Keukeleire and Thiers explain how EULEX Kosovo illuminates some of the general dilemmas which the EU is facing in peacebuilding operations as well as the daunting challenge of interiorising rule of law principles within a society ravaged by ethnic conflict.

The chapter by Justin Davies provides a positive appraisal of the Aceh Monitoring Mission (AMM). Apart from elaborating on the mandate of the operation and the political climate on the ground, the author stresses the innovative character of AMM: not only was it the first occasion where the EU cooperated (in a mutually beneficial manner) with ASEAN states, it was also the first ESDP operation to be officially tasked with human rights monitoring. It is illustrated how, despite cumbersome legislative procedures and a lack of readily available logistics, AMM nonetheless succeeded in creating a positive setting in which human rights and democracy could flourish.

In his chapter on transitional justice, Thomas Unger addresses a field of action which long languished in obscurity – the phrase 'transitional justice' did not figure in any official EU document prior to 2004 –, but which has recently emerged as a political and financial priority for the EU. In this context, Unger offers a definition of the term and its main mechanisms (e.g., criminal prosecutions and truth commissions) as well as an overview of the current EU policy in this area. In addition, the author sets out an ambitious list of recommendations for the EU as a whole, for the Council and for the Commission, which could serve as a basis for a framework document on transitional justice, or at least a set of institutional guidelines.

Finally, *Part Five* deals with economic recovery and good governance as an integral part of the effort of breaking the conflict cycle in the longer run. Tonny Brems Knudsen and Christian Nielsen provide a thorough analysis of the international community's engagement in international trusteeship and administration of post-conflict countries, as well as the concomitant challenges. Two key dilemmas are tackled in particular: first, the need to impose democracy from the outside (e.g., should international administrators have the authority to remove democratically elected officials?); second, the need to combine interim administration with delicate questions concerning the future political status of the territory concerned (can the two be tackled simultaneously, should one have precedence over the other?). By reference to the EU's experience in Bosnia and Herzegovina and in Kosovo, the authors evaluate how the EU and its partners have handled these dilemmas and what lessons learned may be identified.

In his contribution, Philippe Darmuzey argues that while the European Commission's development assistance to post-conflict countries and countries in a state of fragility had been a prominent part of the EU package for some time, explicit recognition of the key linkage between security and development only came in 2005 with the adoption of the European Consensus on Development. He provides an overview of the main tools for immediate crisis responses, such as the Instrument for Stability, humanitarian aid and civil protection, as well as the medium to longer-term instruments geared to developing and aiding post-conflict countries (EDF, APF, etc.). Darmuzey concludes his chapter with an analysis of the

European Commission's and the Council's ongoing efforts to develop practical ways for EU actors to address, in a more coherent – 'Whole-of-the-Union' – manner, issues of development cooperation in situations of fragility and (post-)conflict.

The next chapter turns to the international community's efforts to tackle the exploitation of natural resources in conflict and post-conflict countries, and more particularly to the Kimberley Process (KP) and its impact on the trade in so-called 'conflict diamonds'. Stéphane Chardon describes the functioning, the evolution and the implementation of the KP. While praising the mechanism's flexibility, the author draws attention to a number of challenges to its effectiveness, most notably the limited institutional capacity of some of its participants. At the same time, the chapter examines whether the KP could serve as a model to fight illegal trade in other 'conflict resources'.

Last but definitely not least, the final chapter by Eva Gross offers an overview of the EU's peacebuilding efforts in the conflict setting of Afghanistan, following the US-led intervention in 2001. Whereas the engagement in Afghanistan holds a number of lessons for the EU and Member States involved in the country's reconstruction, such as challenges of civil-military coordination and the sequencing, or simultaneous provision, of security and development in a deteriorating security environment, Gross focuses on good governance and the rule of law as two of the central challenges to the success but also the sustainability of collective efforts. While conceding that efforts have gradually become more coherent and targeted and while drawing a positive balance of the EU's involvement in such a difficult and insecure environment, Gross suggests that greater attention should be paid to issues of legitimacy and accountability.

# Part I
# *EU peacebuilding – general perspectives*

# Chapter 1
# EU PEACEBUILDING: CONCEPTS, PLAYERS AND INSTRUMENTS

**Simon Duke and Aurélie Courtier***

## 1. Introduction

The goal of this chapter is to look at the concept of peacebuilding, in general but also in the context of the European Union (EU), as well as to consider the key players and instruments engaged in various facets of EU peacebuilding. As will be seen, the notion of peacebuilding remains one that is notoriously difficult to pin down in terms of not only meaning but also differentiation from other similar, and linked, terms such as conflict prevention and post-conflict stabilisation. The absence of a peacebuilding strategy *per se* suggests that it is easiest to think in terms of peacebuilding as synergy rather than strategy since it links together different threads from conflict prevention, crisis management, peacemaking and post-conflict stabilisation. However, the lack of a clear definition or accompanying strategy means that the final objective or outcome is often challenged by efficiency, coordination and sustainability issues.

This contribution will first look at the multiplicity of existing concepts and definitions of peacebuilding and try to clarify the understanding of peacebuilding from an EU perspective. The overview of concepts and definition will consider some of the difficulties in understanding the notion of peacebuilding not only within the EU but also at the more general international level. It will be argued that the EU's understanding of peacebuilding is multi-faceted and that this, in turn, has implications for the manner in which peacebuilding is implemented in the context of the EU's external relations. Drawing from this conceptual overview, we shall then set out to identify and portray the players, instruments and policies that embody the EU's peacebuilding. Particular attention will be paid to the distribution of role and competences in an attempt to portray the current peacebuilding architecture within the EU. The role of the respective Pillars of the Union will be examined and although there are obvious complications for peacebuilding that stem from the EU's complicated architecture, it is nonetheless too simplistic to attribute the challenges

* Prof. Dr. Simon Duke and Aurélie Courtier are both working at the European Institute of Public Administration (Maastricht). The authors would like to thank Charles-Michel Geurts and his colleagues at the European Commission (DG RELEX) for their invaluable comments and suggestions. The usual disclaimer applies. Research on this chapter was closed before the entry into force of the Lisbon Treaty.

*S. Blockmans, J. Wouters & T. Ruys, eds., The European Union and Peacebuilding*

in the peacebuilding domain to this alone. It will therefore be argued that the sheer scope and complexity of peacebuilding, as understood in the EU context, implies formidable coordination between not only the Pillars (*institutional consistency*) but also within the Pillars themselves (*horizontal consistency*) as well as with the relevant international partners.

The overview of the concepts and definitions, followed by the players and instruments, cannot hope to be comprehensive but the aim is nevertheless to provide not only a general introduction to the topic but also context for the following chapters offering in-depth analyses of specific aspects of peacebuilding.

## 2. Concepts and definitions

### 2.1 **Introduction**

The term 'peacebuilding' is difficult to define in the EU context. As a concept, it is amorphous and the difference between aspects of conflict prevention, crisis management and post-conflict stabilisation is often hard to spot. It is perhaps easiest to think of peacebuilding as part of a continuum aimed at achieving a specific goal ('to build peace'), involving different players and utilising different instruments towards that common end. The goal is thus constant, but the means by which this goal is reached will depend very much on the specifics of the scenario in question. The initial post-war usage was linked to the idea of post-conflict stabilisation aimed at preventing a relapse into war. It was, however, gradually expanded to refer to integrated approaches to address violent conflict at different phases of the conflict cycle. Thus, many consider conflict prevention and peacebuilding as two sides of the same coin. As Necla Tschirgi reminds us:

> 'At its core, peace-building aims at the prevention and resolution of violent conflicts, the consolidation of peace once violence has been reduced and post-conflict reconstruction with a view to avoiding a relapse into violent conflict. Peace-building seeks to address the proximate and root causes of contemporary conflicts including structural, political, socio-cultural, and economic and environment factors.'[1]

The association with conflict prevention, conflict resolution and post-conflict stabilisation is therefore clear and implies that peacebuilding is best conceived of as a basket of activities directed towards a shared goal. The essence of this is nicely caught in the definition provided by the Peacebuilding Initiative, on their informative website, as 'rebuilding the institutions and infrastructures of nations torn by

---

[1] N. Tschirgi, *Strenghtening the Security – Development Nexus: Conflict Peace and Development in the 21$^{st}$ Century: Peacebuilding as the Link between Security and Development: Is the Window of Opportunity Closing?*, International Peace Academy Studies in Security and Development, December 2003, New York, at 2.

civil war and strife; and building bonds of peaceful mutual benefit among nations formerly at war; and in the largest sense, to address the deepest causes of conflict.'[2]

In the intellectual sphere, the term is often attributed to Johan Galtung who, in 1975, coined the term in his pioneering work *Three Approaches to Peace: Peace-keeping, Peacemaking, and Peacebuilding.*[3] He argued that 'peace has a structure different from, perhaps over and above, peacekeeping and ad hoc peacemaking (...) More specifically, structures must be found that remove causes of wars and offer alternatives to war in situations where wars might occur.'[4] These observations constitute the intellectual antecedents of today's notion of peacebuilding as an endeavour aiming to create sustainable peace by addressing the root causes of violent conflict and eliciting indigenous capacities for peaceful management and resolution of conflict.

John Lederach, another key scholar in the rapidly growing peace studies field, called for an expanded understanding of peacebuilding. To him it was more than 'post-accord reconstruction' and should be seen as:

> (...) 'a comprehensive concept that encompasses, generates, and sustains the full array of processes, approaches, and stages needed to transform conflict toward more sustainable, peaceful relationships. The term thus involves a wide range of activities that both precede and follow formal peace accords. Metaphorically, peace is seen not merely as a stage in time or a condition. It is a dynamic social construct.'[5]

Lederach refers to *conflict transformation* as a holistic and multi-faceted approach to managing violent conflict in all its phases. The term signifies an ongoing process of change from negative to positive relations emphasising the conflict triangle (contradiction, attitude and behaviour).[6] To Lederach, the integrated approach to peacebuilding must take into account the complex and multi-dimensional nature of the human experience and rely on broad social participation where 'the key lies in the relationship of the involved parties, with all that the term encompasses at the psychological, spiritual, social, economic, political and military levels.'[7] Cultivating an infrastructure for peacebuilding, as he called it, means that 'we are not merely

---

[2] HPCR International, *Introduction to Peacebuilding: History: A UN History of the Notion*, The Peacebuilding Initiative, New York, USA, available at: <http://www.peacebuildinginitiative.org> (last accessed 5 May 2009).

[3] J. Galtung, 'Three Approaches to Peace: Peacekeeping, Peacemaking, and Peacebuilding', in J. Galtung, ed., *Peace, War and Defense: Essays in Peace Research,* Vol. II (Copenhagen, Christian Ejlers 1976), at 297-298.

[4] See *supra* n. 2, HPCR International, *History: The Conceptual Origins of Peacebuilding.*

[5] J. Lederach, *Building Peace: Sustainable Reconciliation in Divided Societies* (Washington, D.C., U.S. Institute of Peace Press 1997), at 20, see *supra* n. 2, HPCR International, *Introduction to Peacebuilding: History: The Conceptual Origins of Peacebuilding, The Peacebuilding Initiative.*

[6] J. Lederach, 'Conflict Transformation in Protracted Internal Conflicts: The Case for a Comprehensive Framework', in Kumar Rupesinghe, ed., *Conflict Transformation* (New York, St. Martin's Press; Basingstoke: Macmillan 1995) at 201-222, *supra* n. 2, HPCR International, *History: The Conceptual origins of peacebuilding.*

[7] J. Lederach, *Building Peace: Sustainable Reconciliation in Divided Societies* (Washington, D.C.: U.S. Institute of Peace Press, 1997), 75, see *supra* n. 2 and n. 5.

interested in "ending" something that is not desired. We are oriented toward the building of relationships that in their totality form new patterns, processes, and structures.'[8] Utilising a building metaphor, Lederach described peacebuilding as a long-term commitment to a *process* that includes investment, gathering of resources and materials, architecture and planning, coordination of resources and labour, laying solid foundations, construction of walls and roofs, finish work and ongoing maintenance. Lederach also emphasises that peacebuilding is fundamentally concerned with the transformation of relationships. Catherine Morris reflects this when she argued that sustainable reconciliation requires both structural *and* relational transformations.[9]

In practical terms, though, much of the conceptualisation of peacebuilding, which has informed EU thinking on the topic, was shaped by the United Nations (UN) and it is to this that we now turn.

## 2.2 The UN's understanding of peacebuilding

Much of the current context for the EU's understanding of the concept derives from the UN. Boutros-Ghali used the term in his *Agenda for Peace* in 1992 as 'an action to identify and support structures which will tend to strengthen and solidify peace in order to avoid a relapse into conflict.'[10] This conceptualisation of peacebuilding was then developed in a series of reports such as *An Agenda for Development* (1994),[11] *An Agenda for Democratization* (1996),[12] the *UNDP Report on Human Security* (1994)[13] and *An Inventory of Post-Conflict Peace-Building Activities* (1996),[14] which all put more stress on the fundamental link between security and development. Peacebuilding was seen as not only instrumental in achieving peace in the post-conflict phase, but also as central to preventive diplomacy.

The *Supplement to an Agenda for Peace*,[15] which appeared in 1995, put more emphasis on creating structures for the institutionalisation of peace. By 2000, in the *Report of the Panel on United Nations Peace Operations* (often referred to as the *Brahimi Report*),[16] peacebuilding was defined as 'activities undertaken on the far side of conflict to reassemble the foundations of peace and provide the tools for building on those foundations something that is more than just the absence of war.'[17]

---

[8] Ibid.

[9] C. Morris, *What Is Peacebuilding? One Definition* (2000), available at: <http://www.peacemakers.ca/publications/peacebuildingdefinition.html> [emphasis added]

[10] *Agenda for Peace*, Report of the Secretary-General of 17 June 1992, UN Doc. A/47/277-S/24111.

[11] *An Agenda for Development,* Report of the Secretary-General of 6 May 1994, UN Doc. A/48/935.

[12] Boutros-Ghali, *An Agenda for Democratisation,* A 51/761, United Nations, New York, 1996.

[13] *UNDP Report on Human Security* (New York, Oxford University Press 1994).

[14] *An Inventory of Post Conflict Peace-Building Activities*, ST/ESA/246.

[15] *Supplement to an Agenda for Peace*, Report of the Secretary-General of 3 January 1995, UN Doc. A/50/60 – S/1995/1.

[16] *Report of the Panel on United Nations Peace Operations*, 21 August 2000, UN Doc. A/55/305 – S/2000/809.

[17] See *supra* n. 2.

The conceptual development of peacebuilding within the UN family was accompanied by corresponding institutional development to address the need for further integrated and coordinated strategies in the field.[18]

The Peacebuilding Commission, Peacebuilding Fund and Peacebuilding Support Office were established within the UN in December 2005.[19] The Peacebuilding Commission's mandate was described as follows:

> 'Countries emerging from conflict face a unique set of challenges and unless they are identified and effectively addressed, these countries face a high risk of relapsing into violence. The Commission was therefore created to serve as a dedicated institutional mechanism to address the special needs of countries emerging from conflict towards recovery, reintegration and reconstruction and to assist them in laying the foundation for sustainable peace and development.'[20]

The Peacebuilding Commission's mandate did not really clarify the definition of peacebuilding as such but set up an institutional framework and formulated guidelines on post-conflict peacebuilding which significantly contributed to strengthening international thinking and awareness of conceptual and practical peacebuilding. The next significant conceptual leap forward in the understanding of peacebuilding occurred thirteen years after An Agenda for Peace in the form of the *United Nations Peacekeeping Operations: Principles and Guidelines*, which defined peacebuilding as involving:

> '(...) a range of measures targeted to reduce the risk of lapsing or relapsing into conflict by strengthening national capacities at all levels for conflict management, and to lay the foundation for sustainable peace and development. Peace-building is a complex, long-term process of creating the necessary conditions for sustainable peace. It works by addressing the deep-rooted, structural causes of violent conflict in a comprehensive manner. Peace-building measures address core issues that affect the functioning of society and the state. In this regard, they seek to enhance the capacity of the State to effectively and legitimately carry out its core functions. Peace-building is undertaken by an array of UN and non-UN actors, including the UN Agencies, Funds and Programmes, the International Financial Institutions and NGOs.'[21]

In spite of the apparent clarity, the same document noted that the boundaries between conflict prevention, peacekeeping, peacebuilding and peace enforcement are becoming increasingly blurred:

---

[18] The Peacebuilding Commission, Peacebuilding Fund and Peacebuilding Support Office were launched within the UN in 2005, see: <http://www.un.org/peace/peacebuilding/>.

[19] United Nations General Assembly Resolution 60/180: The Peacebuilding Commission, of 30 December 2005, UN document A/60/L.40.

[20] United Nations General Assembly/Security Council, *Report of the Peacebuilding Commission on Its First Session, June 2006 -June 2007*, A/62/137-S/2007/458, 4.

[21] UN Department of Peacekeeping Operations, *United Nations Peacekeeping Operations: Principles and Guidelines*, March 2008, at 18, available at: <http://www.unhcr.org/refworld/docid/48455 9592.html> (last accessed 7 May 2009).

'While United Nations peacekeeping operations are, in principle, deployed to support the implementation of a cease-fire or peace agreement, they are often required to play an active role in peacemaking efforts and may also be involved in early peacebuilding activities. United Nations peacekeeping operations may also use force at the tactical level, with the authorization of the Security Council, to defend themselves and their mandate, particularly in situations where the State is unable to provide security and maintain public order.'[22]

If the meaning of peacebuilding is complex, so too is what qualifies as a peacebuilding *activity*. Again, drawing upon the same source as above, peacebuilding activities constitute the achievement of sustainable peace which requires progress in at least the four critical areas:[23]

'a) Restoring the State's ability to provide security and maintain public order;
b) Strengthening the rule of law and respect for human rights;
c) Supporting the emergence of legitimate political institutions and participatory processes;
d) Promoting social and economic recovery and development, including safe return or resettlement of internally displaced persons and refugees uprooted by conflict.'

The UN activities that support what are peacebuilding activities are therefore often multi-faceted and might include disarmament, demobilisation and reintegration of combatants (DDR); anti-mine actions; security sector reform (SSR) and other rule of law-related activities; the protection and promotion of human rights; and electoral assistance and support to the restoration and extension of (legitimate) state authority. Unsurprisingly, the complexity in terms of both the conceptual understanding of peacebuilding and its practical implementation is mirrored in the EU context.

Most recently, the *Report of the UN Secretary-General on peacebuilding in the immediate aftermath of conflict* of June 2009 approached the notion of peacebuilding in the specific context of 'the immediate aftermath of conflict,' defined as 'the first two years after the main conflict in a country has ended.'[24] According to the report:

'The immediate post-conflict period offers a window of opportunity to provide basic security, deliver peace dividends, shore up and build confidence in the political process, and strengthen core national capacity to lead peacebuilding efforts. If countries succeed in these core areas early on, it substantially increases the chances for sustainable peace and reduces the risk of relapse into conflict. In too many cases we have missed this early window (...) Seizing the window of opportunity requires that international actors are, at a minimum, capable of responding coherently, rapidly and effectively to support these recurring priorities.'[25]

---

[22] Ibid., at 19.
[23] Ibid., at 25.
[24] *Report of the Secretary-General on Peacebuilding in the Immediate Aftermath of Conflict*, UN General Assembly, A/63/881–S/2009/304, 11 June 2009, at 3.
[25] Ibid., at 2.

In the context of the report, peacebuilding relates to a list of 'core peacebuilding priorities,' further detailed as follows:

'• Support to basic safety and security, including mine action, protection of civilians, disarmament, demobilization and reintegration (DDR), strengthening the rule of law and initiation of security sector reform (SSR);
- Support to political processes, including electoral processes, promoting inclusive dialogue and reconciliation, and developing conflict-management capacity at national and sub-national levels;
- Support to the provision of basic services, such as water and sanitation, health and primary education, and support to the safe and sustainable return and reintegration of IDPs and refugees;
- Support to restoring core government functions in particular basic public administration and public finance, at national and sub-national levels;[26]
- Support to economic revitalization, including employment generation and livelihoods particularly for youth and demobilized former combatants, as well as rehabilitation of basic infrastructure.'

The report is of note since it puts the emphasis upon a relatively short time period: up to two years after the conflict took place. Furthermore, the emphasis is upon deploying fast integrated and coordinated peacebuilding capacities since there is a critical moment, or 'window of opportunity', in the early post-conflict situation that may decisively influence the chances of sustainable peace or a relapse into conflict.

Even if a precise definition of peacebuilding remains elusive, its goal, that of sustainable peace, is clear. The progression of thought in the UN context on peacebuilding shows a gradual shift in emphasis from various forms of long-term support designed to underpin stability to a more focused examination of the likely preconditions for sustainable peace. The identification of the 'window of opportunity' is an interesting and logical development, but it remains to be seen what the practical implications of this are for the UN and the EU alike.

## 2.3 The EU's understanding of peacebuilding

### 2.3.1 *Introduction*

Peacebuilding is a term that is increasingly present in the EU lexicon but it remains an imprecise notion. Notwithstanding this, it has crept into the EU's lexicon in a variety of ways and forms. For instance, reference is made to the EU's Peacebuilding Partnership as a component of the Commission's Instrument of Stability (addressed in more detail below); in Directorate-General Development reference is made to Conflict Prevention and Peacebuilding; and the Commission's Directorate General for External Relations, Directorate A (or the so-called 'Crisis Platform' for policy

[26] Ibid., at 6.

coordination in CFSP), includes a unit dedicated to Crisis Response and Peacebuilding. In each case though, the term peacebuilding is used in a slightly different manner. It would, though, be unrealistic to expect the EU to have a precise definition of the term, given the general conceptual variance in understanding the notion.

In the absence of any common definition, the EU institutions have had to find their own way of defining and understanding the term. In the EU context, the understanding of peacebuilding is complicated by the more general debate surrounding the nature of security in the post-cold war era. Under the general security rubric we find within the EU reference to human security (another term in increasing use in the Commission), environmental security, energy security, the civilian aspects of crisis management, conflict prevention, post-conflict reconstruction and stabilisation, and sustainable peace and development. In spite of the lack of precision it is possible to ascertain some general characteristics of peacebuilding in the EU context. As was discussed in the UN context, the term peacebuilding tends to be used as a framework term that includes a number of sub-themes. As with the UN, peacebuilding is part of an overall EU conflict prevention strategy related to the prevention or reoccurrence of the outbreak of conflict and those activities aimed at creating the conditions for sustainable peace. In the UN case, however, peacebuilding is increasingly associated with post-conflict peacebuilding aimed at stopping the reoccurrence of conflict and to create the conditions necessary for sustainable peace in war-torn societies.[27]

If we look beyond the general conceptual discussions to the treaties, any precise understanding of peacebuilding is again evasive. The first and most obvious problem is the general lack of explicit reference to peacebuilding in the treaties. However, a number of terms or concepts related to peacebuilding or to peacebuilding operations/activities, as outlined above in the UN context, are in regular use. For instance, Article 11 of the Treaty on European Union (TEU) refers to the objectives of CFSP as: 'To safeguard common values (...) in conformity with the principles of the UN Charter (...)'; 'to strengthen the security of the Union in all ways (...)'; 'to preserve peace and strengthen international security in accordance with the principles of the United Nations Charter'; 'to promote international co-operation'; and 'to develop and consolidate democracy and the rule of law, and respect for human rights and fundamental freedoms.'[28] It could be argued that although peacebuilding is not explicitly mentioned, it is certainly an implicit aspect of the TEU and the rationale of the Second Pillar.

In the areas of Community competence, the notion of peacebuilding is also implicit. For instance, in accordance with Articles 177-181 of the Treaty establishing the European Community (TEC), Development Policy, Economic, Financial and

---

[27] 1999 Annual report on the Work of the Organization, at para. 101; DPA Departmental Retreat on Post-Conflict Peace Building, 9-11 December 1999 – Summary Report; see also *supra* n. 24.

[28] Art. 11 of the consolidated versions of the Treaty on European Union and of the Treaty Establishing the European Community, 29 December 2006, *OJ* 2006 C 321 E/1.

Technical Cooperation is intended to 'contribute to the general objective of developing and consolidating democracy and the rule of law, and to the objective of respecting human rights and fundamental freedoms.' In a similar vein, the Common Commercial Policy states, in Article 131, that, 'By establishing a customs union between themselves Member States aim to contribute, in the common interest, to the harmonious development of world trade, the progressive abolition of restrictions on international trade and the lowering of customs barriers.' More generally, reference is made to the 'solidarity which binds Europe and the overseas countries and desiring to ensure the development of their prosperity, in accordance with the principles of the Charter of the United Nations.'[29] Although it can be debated whether or not these general references amount to peacebuilding *per se*, the general framing is nevertheless important since it forms the normative base for the EU's authority in its relations with third parties and thus its credibility as an international peacebuilding partner.

The above reference to the UN Charter is also significant since peacebuilding in the EU context cannot be considered in isolation. Any attempt to understand peacebuilding must take account of the direct links with the UN when it comes to representation (through the two permanent and the non-permanent members of the Security Council, the Commission and Council Secretariat offices in Geneva and New York and the coordination that goes on prior to meetings of the General Assembly) and to seeking legitimacy for a variety of peacebuilding tasks, notably those falling under the Petersberg tasks.[30] More often than not a UN mandate is sought or evoked to underpin the legality of a proposed crisis management operation and thus to enhance its status and authority. More generally, the 'primacy of the UN Security Council in the maintenance of international peace and security' is recognised in the *European Security Strategy* (ESS), as well as by the Member States, and it is therefore unsurprising that EU understanding and practice is heavily influenced by that of the UN.[31]

If the TEC only gives the general context for Community peacebuilding activities, a closer examination of specific Community documents is far more illuminating regarding the meaning and application of the term. For instance, the Commission's 1996 document *The European Union and the Issue of Conflicts in Africa: Peace-Building, Conflict Prevention and Beyond* deliberately adopts a comprehensive approach whereby 'Activities of conflict prevention in a wider sense should be summarized under the term peacebuilding.'[32] Conflict prevention thus applies mainly in a situation of tensions where the outbreak of violence is imminent

---

29 Ibid., Preamble, Treaty Establishing the European Community.

30 The tasks were originally adopted by the Western European Union in 1992 and then assumed by the European Union in the Amsterdam Treaty. They are described in Article 17 (2), Treaty on European Union as, including (but not being confined to) 'humanitarian and rescue tasks, peacekeeping tasks and tasks of combat forces in crisis management, including peacemaking'.

31 *European Security Strategy: A Secure Europe in a Better World*, Brussels, 12 December 2008, at 9.

32 *The European Union and the Issue of Conflicts in Africa: Peace-Building, Conflict Prevention and Beyond*, Brussels, 6 March 1996, SEC (96) 332 final, at 5.

but also in activities to prevent the occurrence of such a situation. The Commission also considers conflict prevention to constitute those actions 'in the *short term* to reduce manifest tensions and/or to prevent the outbreak or recurrence of violent conflict.'[33] Conflict management is considered to extend to 'actions undertaken with the main objective to prevent the vertical (intensification of violence) or horizontal (territorial spread) escalation of existing violent conflicts.' Finally, conflict resolution is construed as 'action undertaken over the short term to end violent conflict.'[34]

One critical distinction drawn by the Commission is therefore the time frame of the envisaged action, with conflict resolution being short term in nature, whereas conflict management and peacebuilding are mid to longer term. Conflict prevention, as laid out in the 2001 European Commission *Communication on Conflict Prevention*, includes both short and longer-term aspects, the latter stressing efforts to address the root causes of conflict utilising development, trade, arms control, human rights and environmental policies.[35] Conflict management, which is different from the Council's *crisis* management, is aimed at preventing the spread of violence and appears to be a general instrument – in other words, there is the assumption that conflict management applies to violent situations. Peacebuilding, by way of contrast, could apply in 'all phases of conflict and peace. However, as peacebuilding measures will generally embrace projects and programmes with the longer-term aim of the stabilization of societies, their impact will be greatest in non-violent situations.'[36] With this in mind, peacebuilding is often understood as *post-conflict peacebuilding* or, more specifically, 'actions undertaken over the medium and longer-term to address root causes of violent conflicts in a targeted manner.'[37]

Root causes, in turn, are considered to constitute one of more of the following: an imbalance of political, socio-economic or cultural opportunities among different identity groups (ethnic, religious, regional, social, etc.); a lack of democratic legitimacy and effectiveness of governance; the absence of effective mechanisms for the peaceful conciliation of group interests (including democratic structures) and for bridging dividing lines between different interest groups; and the lack of a vibrant civil society.[38] Root causes are further detailed in the *European Commission Checklist for Root Causes of Conflict*, clustered around eight main headings: the legitimacy of the state; rule of law; respect for fundamental rights; civil society and media; relations between communities and dispute-solving mechanisms; sound economic management; social and regional inequalities and; the geopolitical situation.[39] The checklist is shared with other international partners, such as the United

---

[33] S. Duke, *The EU and Crisis Management, Developments and Prospects* (Maastricht, European Institute of Public Administration 2002), at xiv-xv [emphasis added].

[34] Ibid., *Loc cit.*

[35] Communication from the Commission on Conflict Prevention, COM (2001) 211 final, Brussels, Commission of the European Communities, 11 April 2001, at 6.

[36] See *supra* n. 32, at 6.

[37] See *supra* n. 33, at xiv.

[38] See *supra* n. 32, at 3, *The Importance of the Political Analysis of Structural Root-Causes of Conflicts*.

[39] See: <http://ec.europa.eu/external_relations/cfsp/cpcm/cp/list.htm>.

Nations, so that they may develop their own checklists or supplement that of the European Commission.

The adoption by the European Commission of a *Communication on Conflict Prevention* in April 2001, later complemented by the ESS, placed the emphasis upon conflict prevention.[40] The ensuing *Programme for the Prevention of Violent Conflicts* calls for a 'co-operative approach to facilitate peaceful solutions to disputes and implies addressing the root-causes of conflicts,' under the rubric of conflict prevention.[41] The programme cannot, however, be considered an exclusive Community preserve since the ESDP has, from the outset, also been intended to strengthen the EU's capacity for action in the crucial field of conflict prevention.

The December 2003 ESS, referred to briefly above, evolved in response to 9-11 and was designed to reinforce transatlantic relations at a time of considerable differences over military intervention in Iraq. Although conspicuously modelled on the US National Security Strategy of September 2002,[42] it nevertheless differed notably from the Bush administration's concept of pre-emption. Solana wrote in the ESS that 'we should be ready to act before a crisis occurs. Conflict prevention and threat prevention cannot start too early.'[43] The context of the remarks indicated that the EU should use its tools and instruments to bring about the conditions for stability. The same theme reappeared in the follow-up to the European Security Strategy, the *Report on the Implementation of the European Security Strategy: Providing Security in a Changing World*, of December 2008:

> 'Preventing threats from becoming sources of conflicts early on must be at the heart of our approach. Peace-building and long-term poverty reduction is essential to this. Each situation requires coherent use of our instruments, including political, diplomatic, development, humanitarian, crisis response, economic and trade co-operation, and civilian and military management. We should also expand our dialogue and mediation capacities. EU Special Representatives bring EU influence to bear in various conflict regions. Civil society and NGOs have a vital role to play as actors and partners (…).'[44]

The types of security challenges facing the EU have expanded appreciably beyond those identified in the 2003 ESS to include crime, illegal immigration, piracy, nuclear proliferation, threats to critical infrastructure as well as energy supplies and the macro challenges posed by global poverty, environmental degradation and climate change. These challenges and the tools at hand to respond to them result in what the report calls a 'distinctive European approach to foreign and security policy.'[45] The

---

[40] See *supra* n. 35.

[41] *European Union Programme for the Prevention of Violent Conflicts*, Council of the European Union, 9537/1/01, 7 June 2001, para. 3.

[42] *The National Security Strategy of the United States of America*, Washington, 17 September 2002, available at: <http://georgewbush-whitehouse.archives.gov/nsc/nss/2002/index.html>.

[43] *European Security Strategy*, at 7.

[44] *Report on the Implementation of the European Security Strategy – Providing Security in a Changing World*, S407.08, Brussels, 11 December 2008, at 9.

[45] Ibid., at 2.

distinctiveness of the EU's approach lies in the potential, nascent or realised, to respond to a variety of challenges. Some reflect a conflict prevention orientation while others, specifically through the ongoing development of ESDP, put the emphasis on post-conflict or crisis stabilisation. Conceptually, therefore, we may conclude that peacebuilding in the EU context includes both the conflict prevention role as well as the ability to immediately respond to conflict or crises. By way of contrast, the UN appears to now be placing more emphasis on the post-conflict stabilisation role and in particular the 'window of opportunity' following the cessation of hostilities. The 'distinctive' European approach is though fully compatible with the UN's peacebuilding activities and on several occasions, such as the ESDP military operation in the Democratic Republic of the Congo in 2003 or the contemporary rule of law mission in Kosovo, has demonstrated this in a practical manner.

### 2.3.2 *Internal and external, shorter and longer-term peacebuilding*

If we now look beyond the treaties and the key documents at the actual practice of peacebuilding, we are immediately faced with the fact that European integration is, in essence, a giant peacebuilding project that arose from the ashes of World War II and the Marshall Plan. The aims of these initiatives centred on the unification and pacification of the continent and establishing a community of stability, prosperity and democracy. Arguably, the idea of European integration as a peacebuilding project informs the outlook of the EU in its external peacebuilding efforts since the EU sees itself as exemplar. The idea of the EU as a peacebuilding project *par excellence* also raises the issue of time frame since there were clearly shorter-term dimensions, such as the Marshall Plan, as well as longer-term dimensions involved in building sustainable peace in Europe. It may therefore be useful to sharpen the distinction along two lines. The first is to distinguish between the internal and external dimensions of EU peacebuilding, while the second involves distinguishing between short and longer-term aspects of peacebuilding.

If we avoid the temptation to navel-gaze and to avoid further deliberation about the extent to which the EU itself is about peacebuilding, the internal dimensions of peacebuilding are primarily confined to the EU's enlargement policy. As will be argued in more detail below, the European Neighbourhood Policy (ENP) might superficially be associated with this category but the lack of a membership prospect and the presence of predominantly 'soft' influence, as opposed to the enlargement context in which the Commission is unambiguously in the driver's seat, make it more akin to other areas of the EU's external relations. It will therefore be argued below that although ENP has peacebuilding dimensions to it, they belong primarily to the external dimensions since the type of negotiating environment, the relationship of the third parties with the EU and its institutions, as well as the funding on offer and the potential stakes of success or failure, mark the EU's enlargement policy as a distinct form of internal peacebuilding. The other areas of EU peacebuilding, including ENP, therefore belong to the external dimensions of peacebuilding.

The second distinction is that between shorter-term peacebuilding and longer-term peacebuilding. Generally speaking, the Second Pillar, or CFSP, is more oriented towards short-term stabilisation efforts while the Community's policies and programmes are more oriented towards longer-term sustainable peace. As will be explored below, this cannot be considered a rule since there are important exceptions, especially when it comes to emergency or short-term funding instruments which tend to be found on the Community side rather than in the Second Pillar. Similarly, a number of ESDP operations, such as some in the Western Balkans or the Great Lakes Region of Africa, are assuming a more long-term character, especially where initial military operations give way to police and other civilian operations.

Ideally, these distinctions should not be apparent to the observer since internal and external peacebuilding should be treated alike in the sense that the EU should promulgate the same principles and values to candidates or non-candidates. Similarly, the shorter and longer-term aspects of peacebuilding are designed to form a continuum, emphasising the importance of early response as well as having the correct follow-up programmes and funding in place to reinforce the prospects for sustainable peace.

### 2.3.3 *Short-term dimension of EU peacebuilding (CFSP and ESDP)*

It was argued above that the short-term dimensions of the EU's peacebuilding efforts tend to be found primarily in the Second Pillar (CFSP-ESDP) area. Article 17 of the TEU states that CFSP shall include '*all* questions relating to the security of the Union including the progressive framing of a common defence policy' [emphasis added]. The 'questions' referred to include 'humanitarian and rescue tasks, peacekeeping tasks and tasks of combat forces in crisis management, including peacemaking.' These tasks commonly referred to as the Petersberg tasks, serve as the framework for a broad range of activities associated mainly with the short-term aspects of peacebuilding. The European Security and Defence Policy (ESDP), as an integral part of CFSP, through which the players and instruments that implement the Petersberg tasks collaborate, includes both military and civilian crisis management capabilities. Although the military operations tend to grab the headlines, they represent a minority of the operations conducted thus far. The civilian aspects of crisis management have been developed around four priority areas which were successively defined at the Feira European Council (June 2000) and in the Civilian Headline Goals of 2008 and 2010;[46] these are police and security sector reform, strengthening the rule of law, strengthening civilian administration and civil protection.[47]

---

[46] *Final Report on the Civilian Headline Goal 2008*, 19 November 2007, doc. – 14823/07 and *Civilian Headline Goal 2010*, 19 November 2007, doc. – 14807/07.

[47] Council of the EU, 'European Security and Defence Policy: The Civilian Aspects of Crisis Management', June 2008, Civ/02.

The evolution of ESDP saw the development of battlegroups of around 1,500 armed combat personnel. There are currently fifteen battlegroups, some of which are national and others multinational in composition, of which two are on stand-by during any six month period. The battlegroups are designed to be deployed within 5-10 days of approval by the Council, sustainable for at least thirty days, which can be extended to 120 days if resupplied. Aside from the Petersberg tasks mentioned above, the battlegroups also have a range of tasks stemming from the ESS, such as joint disarmament operations, support for third parties in counter-terrorism and some aspects of security sector reform. The limited size of the groups and their limited deployment period naturally restricts the type of tasks that they may be called upon to perform and three typologies have been suggested: to offer temporary support to existing operations; preparation for larger and longer-term deployments; and, finally, rapid response missions restricted in terms of size and duration.[48]

It would however be a misconception to portray all of the short-term peacebuilding capacities as those of the Second Pillar. The European Community also has a number of valuable short-term response tools, most notably the Instrument for Stability (discussed in more detail below). The Instrument actually has both short and longer-term dimensions but, in the case of the former, the main emphasis is upon securing the necessary conditions to permit the implementation of longer-term Community development assistance. According to the Commission's own website, the focus is upon 'situations of urgency, crisis and emerging crisis, situations posing threats to democracy, law and order, the protection of human rights and fundamental freedoms, the security and safety of individuals, or on situations threatening to escalate into armed conflict or severely to destabilise the third countries or country concerned.'[49] The Instrument for Stability is designed to deal with emerging or actual crisis scenarios of a non-humanitarian nature (there are separate provisions for this contingency) and to last for no longer than eighteen months. It should be noted that both the ESDP battlegroups and the Instrument for Stability fit rather nicely into the UN thinking on the implementation of post-conflict peacebuilding and 'window of opportunity' contingencies.

### 2.3.4 *Longer-term dimension of EU peacebuilding (EC)*

As with the above discussion, the general association of the longer-term aspects of peacebuilding with the Community side should not be assumed as a hard and fast rule. As has been observed, the Community's peacebuilding instruments tend to be longer term in nature but a number are of shorter-term duration (see above). The overarching emphasis tends to be upon longer-term peacebuilding since the connection between poverty and insecurity is not only one that is complex but also one that does not lend itself to immediate solutions. The sources of instability often

---

48 G. Lindstrom, *Enter the EU Battlegroups*, Chaillot Paper No. 97 (Paris, European Institute of Security Studies, February 2007), at 17-19.

49 See: <http://ec.europa.eu/europeaid/where/worldwide/stability-instrument/short-term_en.htm> (accessed 15 May 2009).

stem from a complex mix of factors such as environmental factors, competition for scarce resources, radical ideologies, economic collapse or exploitation, state failure, and also call for long-term approaches to peacebuilding. Although any of these challenges could lead to the outbreak of conflict, the tools to address them are generally found in the Community areas of competence such as the common commercial policy or development aid and assistance.

The Community's emphasis is increasingly on integrated approaches to the cause of conflicts as well as to post-conflict state building. Naturally, any such integrated approach is often complex and the timing and balance of the various components involved may be difficult to reach. The components range from economic development, the bolstering of civil society and the principles of good governance, and the observance of human and minority rights and environmental factors – all present in the European Consensus on Development.

The use of the term peacebuilding in the long-term sense should be considered as a general term covering a wide variety of sub-themes. The European Commission also frequently uses a number of related terms such as conflict prevention defined as 'the activities aiming not only at easing a situation where an outbreak of violence is imminent (conflict prevention in a narrow sense) but also at preventing the occurrence of such a situation (conflict prevention in a wider sense).'[50] Reference is also made to reconstruction and rehabilitation which means the 'reestablishment of a working economy and the institutional capacities needed to restore social and political stability in developing countries that have suffered serious danger through war, civil disorder.'[51]

Peacebuilding is moreover increasingly seen as the process of addressing the post-conflict transition phase and building reconciliation and peace. In this context, peacebuilding could cover everything from peacekeeping operations (emphasising local ownership wherever possible); capacity building in various guises; planning and training of peace support operations; disarmament, demobilisation and reintegration; the fights against illegal arms and organised crime; governance reform (including justice, civilian and military organisation); human rights and democracy; border management; police and penitentiary issues; as well as parliamentary oversight. The growing 'nexus' between security and development goes to the heart of peacebuilding, which is why peace and security are often seen as the foundations for progress and sustainable development. In practice, peacebuilding is built into the EU's relations with the ACP countries in the first of the five pillars of the Cotonou Agreement, signed on 23 June 2000 for a period of twenty years. The first pillar addresses the political dimension, which includes peacebuilding policies, conflict prevention and resolution with the overall aim of promoting regional initiatives and

[50] *The European Union and the Issue of Conflicts in Africa: Peace-Building, Conflict Prevention and Beyond*, Commission of the European Communities, SEC(96) 332, Final, Brussels 6 March 1996, at 5-6.

[51] Council Regulation (EC) No 2258/96 on rehabilitation and reconstruction, quoted in *Civilian Instruments for EU Crisis Management*, European Commission Conflict Prevention and Crisis Management Unit, April 2003, at 29.

approaches as well as building local capacities. Other aspects of this pillar, such as good governance and the promotion of democratic rights based on the rule of law, are also connected in a general way with peacebuilding

The challenge for the Community is to apply the right mix of tools at the correct time. Many post-conflict scenarios, like that in the Central African Republic, will involve an intricate mix of security sector reform, including disarmament, demobilisation and reintegration; governance and the rule of law; as well as economic expansion aimed at regional growth. Effective peacebuilding therefore depends upon its permeation into all areas of not only EU external relations but also those of the Member States. Long-term peacebuilding, as suggested, is a holistic activity. This was made clear in the recent G8 Report on Peacekeeping/Peacebuilding:

> 'Overcoming conflict requires a strategic vision and an integrated approach, from peacekeeping to post-conflict stabilization, involving, as necessary, military, police, judicial and other civilian components that are fully interoperable and possess a common mandate and objectives. Upholding the rule of law, international humanitarian law and human rights are essential components of this approach. In recent years, the challenges with regard to conflict prevention, peacekeeping, peacebuilding and post-conflict reconstruction have grown significantly.'[52]

## 3. Competence and role distribution: policies, instruments, players

### 3.1 Introduction

The multi-faceted nature of peacebuilding means that the competences are attributed to the different Pillars of the EU, primarily the 'First' Pillar, the European Community, and the Second Pillar, CFSP/ESDP. Many peacebuilding activities fall into 'grey areas' of competences, especially those relating to peacebuilding operations (such as civil protection, civilian aspects of crisis management and various aspects of human rights). Consequently, the distribution of roles and tasks within the EU is not always very understandable and the sometimes apparent institutional disconnect between the Commission and the Council means that the necessary tools are not brought to bear in an integrated manner to the crisis prevention, crisis management and peacebuilding activities of the Union.[53]

It should also be borne in mind, as mentioned in the introduction to this volume, that the development of peacebuilding in the EU context was primarily spurred by the Balkan crisis of the 1990s. Aside from any institutional disconnects within the EU, peacebuilding remains a relatively new departure for the Union and it is still feeling its way. It would therefore be unfair to present any competence issues or other shortcomings as evidence of a more general systemic problem.

---

[52] *G8 Summit 2009, From La Maddalena to L'Aquila,* para. 2.

[53] EPLO, *A European Peacebuilding Office*, Policy Paper, January 2006.

The broad understanding of peacebuilding within the EU, discussed at length above, means that a broad range of instruments and programmes have some form of applicability. The overview that follows will consider the set of policies, instruments and players in the Community context, followed by those in the CFSP/ESDP domain. Attention will also be paid to the implications of the Lisbon treaty for EU peacebuilding.

## 3.2 Peacebuilding activities under the Community Pillar

The emphasis on the Community side, as observed earlier, was until recently upon conflict prevention. The EU instruments for conflict prevention were discussed in an earlier volume in this series but it is nevertheless helpful to recap the procedures for identifying a threat to peace and stability since this is obviously key to a timely and effective response.[54] The *European Commission Checklist for Root Causes of Conflict*, touched on briefly above, is used as the first stage of the conflict prevention effort.[55] Information and analysis of intelligence from a variety of sources will be compiled in conjunction with the Council Secretariat, and those with the highest 'score' on the list of indicators will be brought to the attention of the General Affairs and External Relations Council. The list is compiled on the basis of a detailed checklist of conflict indicators.

The checklist is of considerable importance since it serves as the template for conflict assessment on the part of desk officers based in Brussels, as well as for the staff in the 134 Commission delegations around the world. The routine reporting from the delegations as well as within Brussels will also shape awareness about which country or region is most at risk of an outbreak, continuation or re-emergence of conflict. The delegations pay particular attention to areas such as human rights, minority rights, non-proliferation (of weapons of mass destruction) and other critical indicators. The countries or regions assessed to be most at risk are placed on a confidential 'watch list' which is subject to constant updating. Within the Commission, the 'Crisis Platform' (Directorate A in DG External Relations, under Richard Wright) will complement incoming information with open source information (OSINT) and also, when appropriate, involve ECHO's disaster monitoring system, the Impending Crisis Online News System (ICONS).

The watch list also serves as an important coordination device between the Council Secretariat and the Commission. It is shared with the General Affairs and External Relations Council and, at a more operational level, forms the basis for the Situation Centre's (SitCen) monitoring on a 24-7 basis. The SitCen brings together the intelligence divisions of the Policy Planning and Early Warning Unit (Policy Unit), the EU Military Staff as well as a number of seconded national intelligence officials.

---

[54] See J. Pérez, 'EU Instruments for Conflict Prevention', in V. Kronenberger and J. Wouters, eds., The *European Union and Conflict Prevention: Policy and Legal Aspects* (Cambridge, Cambridge University Press 2004).

[55] For an overview of the checklist, see: <http://ec.europa.eu/external_relations/cfsp/cpcm/cp/list.htm>.

The Commission is also associated with the work of the SitCen and in particular with drawing up or amending the EU watch list of those countries most at risk of imminent instability or crisis. The actual identification of the root causes of conflict is therefore the result of information and analysis of intelligence from many different sources resulting in a composite picture of the challenge at hand. This, in turn, will inform those who have to make the basic choices regarding the appropriate response to any given crisis scenario.

The Communication on Conflict Prevention of 11 April 2001 noted that 'development policy and cooperation programmes provide the most powerful instruments at the Community's disposal for treating the root causes of conflict.'[56] This could apply either in the context of an emerging crisis scenario or, with equal relevance, to a post-conflict stabilisation scenario. As indicated above, the emphasis is now increasingly upon post-conflict stabilisation as well as conflict prevention. The same need for accurate information is present in either case since it will help to determine what is needed on the ground.

The Community's peacebuilding policies and instruments cannot be considered exclusive in nature; instead, they are more general policies and instruments that have broad peacebuilding applicability. A non-exhaustive overview of those policies and instruments with peacebuilding applicability includes the following:

### 3.2.1 *Policies*

*External Relations*: The Commission will engage in political dialogue at numerous levels and formats, including those occurring in the CFSP 'troika' format in which the Commission is represented alongside the High Representative for CFSP, Javier Solana, the Presidency of the Council and, if need be, the following Presidency. The exact scope and nature of the dialogue will depend very much upon the specific legal agreements with the country or regional actors, as well as the agendas placed on the table. The political dialogue in conflict prevention or post-crisis stabilisation cases has become increasingly crowded, including a range of other actors, such as Special Representatives, Personal Representatives of the High Representative, as well as European Parliamentary delegations all of whom are involved in liaison with other regional or international actors (discussed in more detail below). In those scenarios where a peacebuilding perspective is appropriate, the key aim from the EU side is to ensure inclusiveness of all parties to an actual or potential conflict, including representatives of civil society. The importance of the latter is underlined by the self-proclaimed normative nature of EU external relations where the 'fundamental rights and needs of people are just as important as the "security of states", therefore, the EU supports good governance practices and attempts to lay a viable democratic, international order.'[57] At the political level, the political dialogue con-

---

[56] See *supra* n. 35, at 4.

[57] European Commission, External Relations, at <http://ec.europa.eu/external_relations/peace_security/why_en.htm >.

ducted through the First and Second Pillars plays an important role in peacebuilding as well as in the implementation of peacebuilding strategies through the use of the appropriate mix of instruments. A further dimension worthy of mention is the involvement of national diplomatic representations with the EU Heads of Mission (that is, the heads of the 135 EU delegations located in countries and international organisations) in coordination in the field. This is particularly important in conducting political dialogue under Article 8 (addressing political dialogue) of the Cotonou Agreement in which 'Broadly based policies to promote peace and to prevent, manage and resolve violent conflicts shall play a prominent role';[58]

*Common Commercial Policy/External Trade*: Trade policies at the EU's disposal can contribute actively to peacebuilding by promoting economic development (economic incentives) and regional integration. Peacebuilding instruments in this area include the Generalised System of Preferences, including the 'Everything But Arms' Regulation of 2001 allowing for duty-free access to all imports from the lesser developed countries except arms and ammunition,[59] and the EU Aid for Trade Strategy.[60] The Community has a particularly strong role to play in this policy area owing to its exclusive competence stemming from Articles 131 and 133 of the Treaty Establishing the European Community. As with development policy, discussed below, the precise interlinkage between trade policy and peacebuilding is not entirely obvious other than in the general sense of measures to enhance security and peace. At the general level, both trade and development make the link between economic and political stability. The support given to private sector development has become a priority in many countries in order to reinforce this link. The Community can also utilise trade-related tools in a punitive sense, especially through specific trade sanctions and embargoes. In many cases, the UN is the prime sanctioning actor and the restrictive measures of the EU normally follow suit. The Council's general guideline on the use of sanctions mentions that

> 'Sanctions should be targeted in a way that has maximum impact on those whose behaviour we want to influence. Targeting should reduce to the maximum extent possible any adverse humanitarian effects or unintended consequences for persons not targeted or neighbouring countries. Measures, such as arms embargoes, visa bans and the freezing of funds are a way of achieving this.'[61]

It is far from clear that there is an EU sanctions policy *per se* and even their patterns of use indicate selective targeting. In the case of the EU's vicinity, sanctions have tended to be imposed in response to direct security concerns while elsewhere in the

---

58 Cotonou Agreement, Article 8(5).

59 Council Regulation (EC) No 416/2001, February 2001, *Official Journal of the European Communities*, L60/43, 1 March 2001.

60 On the EU Aid for Trade Strategy, see: <http://trade.ec.europa.eu/doclib/docs/2007/october/tradoc_136452.pdf>.

61 *Basic Principles on the Use of Restrictive Measures (Sanctions)*, Council of the European Union, 10198/1/04 PESC 450 "I/A" ITEM NOTE, Rev. 1, Brussels, 7 June 2004, para. 6.

world they have tended to follow UN recommendations in response to challenges to the rule of law or value-based considerations. The majority of sanctions have been imposed 'to protect democracy and human rights.'[62] As with the UN, the EU has shown increasing interest in 'smart' sanctions, targeting specific groups or even individuals. The problem remains, however, of the extent to which sanctions constitute a specific peacebuilding policy or, indeed, how the common commercial policy generally relates to peacebuilding. As Joakim Kreutz suggests, it is perhaps best to think of EU restrictive measures as 'part of peace-making initiatives in conflict and attempts to protect civilians from government repression rather than an aggressive policy tool to pursue EU interests.'[63] As such, restrictive measures deserve inclusion in the general policy tools available to support EU peacebuilding efforts;

*Development Cooperation*: The EU and its Member States provide over 50% of all Official Development Assistance (ODA) worldwide and, as such, this provides the EU with a potent but general policy for promoting sustainable peace. The general goal of eradicating poverty and of meeting other challenges such as sustainable development, HIV/AIDS, forced migration and so forth, is implicit in development instruments, either generally or more specifically. The European Consensus on Development and the Millennium Development goals associate the EU with wider international efforts at peacebuilding and stability through development tools. The goals are however oriented to factors that certainly underpin sustainable development, but they are not necessarily targeted towards peacebuilding other than in the most general sense. The right balance of development assistance is obviously important for the consideration of the prospects for sustainable peace beyond the UN 'window of opportunity' referred to earlier. One of the most vexatious issues associated with development is its association with security and the nexus thereof. The understanding of 'security' has broadened, notably since the cold war, as also has the notion of development, thus creating considerable overlap between the two, the precise amount of overlap and the implications thereof depending upon the stance of the observer. On the one hand, as Christian Bueger and Pascal Vennesson suggest, we have a narrow conception of peacebuilding following the logic of Boutros-Ghali's *Agenda for Peace*.[64] In this case, peacebuilding refers to the activities in between conflict and the use of peacekeeping force on the one side and broader development strategies on the other. The second type, following Galtung's lead, is broader in nature and focuses on wider strategies and instruments that can prevent and manage conflict and sustain peace. The narrower conception will tend to privilege security-led instruments and policies while the broader conception will favour a development-led lead. The former will tend to be applied to actual conflict situa-

[62] J. Kreutz, *Hard Measures by a Soft Power? Sanctions Policy of the European Union 1981-2004* (Bonn, Bonn International Center for Conversion 2005), at 20.

[63] Ibid., at 42.

[64] C. Bueger and P. Vennesson, *Security, Development and the EU's Development Policy*, European University Institute, Florence, April 2009, at 15-18, available at: <http://erd.eui.eu/media/vennesson2.pdf>.

tions or situations soon after the cessation of conflict, while the latter has been applied more to preventive scenarios where there is a non-imminent risk of violence.

The narrower model typifies the EU, while the broader version reflects current UN thinking which has tended to expand the notion of peacebuilding towards human or comprehensive security outlooks. The EU's current adoption of the narrower variant is best explained by evolution rather than by conscious choice since development policy within the EU is well-established while the security dimensions are far more recent and are still being developed. The onus has therefore been on the defining security in relation to development and not vice versa. So far, this has not been an easy process, especially given the early emphasis on developing the military aspects of crisis management which tended to polarise issues rather than highlight complementary aspects. One prominent example of this was the alleged use of development-tagged funding for the Africa Peace Fund for ostensibly security-oriented purposes. As the security dimensions develop further within the EU, it is reasonable to expect further tensions in the security-development nexus, with the strong likelihood that the EU will be pulled to broader (and hopefully comprehensive) conceptions of the relationship between the two.

*Enlargement Policy*: The EU's enlargement policy is, in a loose sense, a peacebuilding exercise. Candidates for EU membership have to meet a number of criteria, including the political elements of the Copenhagen criteria,[65] as well as satisfy the Commission that they are capable of effectively implementing the *acquis communautaire*. Although often presented as a negotiation process, the accession 'negotiations' are more one-sided with the onus being on the candidates satisfying the European Commission and the Member States of their ability to accede to the Union. For the candidates the emphasis is on confirming and not on negotiation. The assumption is that the candidates, when ready to accede, will meet all of the criteria for membership, and this includes general political stability. The ability of the EU to use the accession process for peacebuilding ends can be called into question in the case of Cyprus where in December 1999 the EU members chose not to make a settlement of the Cyprus problem a precondition for membership. This has led to the unfortunate situation where two of the parties to the dispute, Cyprus and Greece, are full members of the EU while Turkey is a candidate. In the case of the latter, it is inconceivable that it could be a member without a solution to the Cyprus problem. Thus, in a rather loose but ambiguous sense, enlargement could be portrayed as a peacebuilding policy. Another case of a dispute between a member and a candidate (Slovenia and Croatia), over a maritime boundary, also calls into question the strength of the peacebuilding credentials of the enlargement process. Indeed, it could be argued that once one of the candidates to a dispute has acceded, the dispute becomes more difficult to handle and will become a barrier to member-

---

[65] The Copenhagen criteria, adopted in 1993, include political, economic and social criteria. In the first category this includes stability of institutions guaranteeing democracy, the rule of law, human rights and respect for and protection of minorities

ship for the remaining party. The existing Member States also have little interest in internalising serious territorial disputes. The effect of enlargement on intra-state disputes is also difficult to assess since, more often than not, such matters invoke subsidiarity claims. The possibility of 'enlargement fatigue' may blunt the utility of enlargement as a peacebuilding exercise, especially with potentially challenging cases like Bosnia-Herzegovina in mind;

*European Neighbourhood Policy* (*ENP*): The ENP, whose original objective is 'to avoid the emergence of new dividing lines' between the EU-27 and its neighbours by 'consolidating a ring of prosperity, stability and security' on the EU's periphery can also be considered as part of the EC's peacebuilding policy portfolio in a general sense. In particular, by promoting political reform leading to better respect of human rights and the rule of law, economic reform in favour of greater economic prosperity, regulatory convergence with EU norms as well as security cooperation, the ENP reflects and exports the principles and values that have inspired the EU's creation and thus can positively contribute to promoting stability and sustainable peace in its neighbourhood. It should, however, be recalled that unlike enlargement policy, the ENP does not offer the carrot of EU membership, although, as noted above, this carrot has not always been sufficient to avoid crises in accession or pre-accession countries. Since the policy is based on the principle of joint ownership, the extent to which the EU can influence existing or emerging conflicts in the neighbourhood depends very much upon the willingness of the party in question to put the issue on the table. A cursory glance at the map of the countries covered by the ENP[66] raises legitimate doubts about any specific peacebuilding attributes offered by the policy. The evidence from the events of August 2008 in Georgia, as well as from the other so-called 'frozen conflicts' in Nagorno-Karabakh which is *de facto* independent from Azerbaijan, Transniestria which is *de facto* independent from Moldova, and the often forgotten plight of the Western Sahara which is still the object of dispute between the Kingdom of Morocco and the Polisario Front independence movement (and the government of the Sahrawi Arab Democratic Republic or SADR) is that the ENP has a marginal impact on these disputes. Given the difference in the EU's position vis-à-vis the candidates for EU membership and the ENP participants, some of whom are more engaged than others, it is best to think of the former as essentially part of the EU's internal peacebuilding efforts while the ENP is more closely associated with the EU's external efforts. The EU also remains a rather insignificant actor in the resolution of the Israeli-Palestinian imbroglio, nor did it prove effective in preventing or curtailing the bombing of Gaza in December 2008. These arguments do not seek to suggest that the ENP cannot have a generally beneficial and stabilising effect in the neighbourhood, but the presence of an actual peacebuilding dimension can be questioned.

---

[66] Algeria, Armenia, Azerbaijan, Belarus, Egypt, Georgia, Israel, Jordan, Lebanon, Libya, Moldova, Morocco, Occupied Palestinian Territory, Syria, Tunisia and Ukraine.

### 3.2.2 *Instruments*

*The European Development Fund*: The EDF is the main funding instrument for Community development assistance to the African, Caribbean and Pacific States (ACP) and the Overseas Countries and Territories (OCT). The Community is currently in its tenth EDF, each lasting for around five years. The current one represents €22,682 million over the period 2008-13. Within the EDF, which is not part of the Community's general budget but is funded via the Member States, there are many instruments that have some conflict prevention or peacebuilding applicability although they are not designed as targeted peacebuilding instruments;

*External assistance programmes*: There are many external assistance instruments, such as those run through EuropeAid, the European Commission's Humanitarian Aid Office (ECHO), DG Trade, DG ELARG and DG RELEX, that have general peacebuilding applicability. Assistance includes economic, financial and technical cooperation with third countries and this may vary widely in terms of its actual content, but the use of various forms of conditionality (positive and negative) can be used to reinforce stability and to avoid conflict or sustain peace in a country or regional setting;

*Humanitarian aid*: This refers primarily to short-term assistance and relief to the victims of natural disasters or armed conflict outside the EU, but can also be utilised to foster the conditions for re-establishing peace or avoid relapse into conflict (often in conjunction with longer-term development tools);

*The Instrument for Stability (IfS)*: This instrument is a successor to the Rapid Reaction Mechanism which, again, is not an exclusive peacebuilding instrument but refers in its objectives and applicability to a wide range of activities related to peacebuilding. The instrument is worth €1.822 billion over the current financial perspective (2007-13) and is designed to offer short-term non-humanitarian financial assistance to alleviate emerging crises or crisis situations.[67] The objectives include conflict prevention measures, support for post-conflict political stabilisation, the abatement of situations threatening to escalate into armed conflict or to severely destabilise the country or region involved. The instruments include Exceptional Assistance Measures and Interim Response Programmes with a maximum duration of eighteen months, through to longer-term measures designed to build the capacity to address specific global threats of a destabilising nature and to ensure preparedness to address pre and post-crisis situations. The 'threats' include those pertaining to weapons of mass destruction, to law and order and to more general risk mitigation.[68] Although the Instrument for Stability includes conflict prevention, crisis

---

[67] For more information, see: <http://europa.eu/scadplus/leg/en/lvb/l14171.htm>.

[68] For further details, see Regulation (EC) No 1717/2006 of the European Parliament and of the Council of 15 November 2006 establishing an Instrument for Stability, *Official Journal of the European Communities*, L327/1, 24 November 2006.

preparedness and crisis management elements, it is one of the first in the EU context to have consciously tried to include peacebuilding aspects.

An integral component of the IfS is the Peacebuilding Partnership (PbP). The PbP was designed as a long-term measure to 'improve communication with key partners in crisis response' focusing on the Commission's implementing partners. The PbP is part of the IfS and is consciously designed to assist in the development and dissemination of best practice, and in rapid access to qualified human resources, as well as to provide adequate logistical and technical support. The PbP draws upon Article 4.3 of the IfS (the crisis preparedness component) to include work on 'conflict prevention, policy dialogue and other related issues.'[69] The PbP has three principal programme components: the Peacebuilding Partnership support (aimed at civil society capacity building; 'Track II' diplomacy and mediation expertise; early warning and field-based expertise analysis; pro-active policy advice and the fostering of expertise and synergies among civil society partners); second, the cooperation with international, regional and sub-regional organisations on, *inter alia*, early warning and recovery, mediation, national resources and conflict; and finally, training for civilian stabilisation missions. The PbP draws upon the Instrument for Stability and in 2008 this amounted to a modest €8 million, split between three principal programme components. The first, peacebuilding partnership support, includes civil society capacity building; civil society early warning and field-based analysis activities on conflict prevention; and pro-active advice from civil society. The second, addressing cooperation with IOs on early warning and recovery, includes the development of post-conflict and disaster needs assessment frameworks and the development of a natural resources management and conflict policy framework, guidelines and training. Finally, the training for civilian stabilisation missions includes the delivery of training to civilian and police experts in civilian missions.[70] The funds, provided through the Instrument for Stability, can be used to support the EU's cooperation with the UN, regional organisations (like the African Union) and related Member State agencies. It can also be used to provide training, to evaluate operations, to develop and circulate best practices and to assist in the development of early warning systems as well as to provide mediation services and facilitate reconciliation processes.[71] Although most of the funding is targeted at specialised NGOs, it has also been used to support EU cooperation with the UN (UNDP) as well as regional organisations like the African Union and EU Member State agencies.[72] The Commission has established a portal in order to encourage non-state and specialist organisations to provide information on ongoing practices and operations.[73]

---

[69] See: <https://webgate.ec.europa.eu/tariqa/pub/fck/File/PBPcsmtg270608cncln_Amended.pdf> (registration required).

[70] For full details, see *Crisis Preparedness – Annual Action Programme* 2008 (also constituting the Annual Work Programme) covering the 'Strategy paper 2007 -2011' and the 'Indicative Programme 2007-2008' at: <http://ec.europa.eu/external_relations/cfsp/doc/si_action_prog_2008.pdf>.

[71] See: <http://ec.europa.eu/external_relations/ifs/pbp_en.htm>.

[72] For an overview of the activities of the PbP, see: <http://ec.europa.eu/external_relations/ifs/pbp_en.htm>.

[73] The webgate may be consulted at: <https://webgate.ec.europa.eu/tariqa/PeaceBuilding/>.

The PbP is a relatively young programme (the first activities were implemented under the 2007-8 Annual Action Programme) but the initial indicators suggest that the process of intensified dialogue and consultation with selected partners has provided value-added, although more linkages between the activities of the different target groups have yet to emerge.[74]

More emphasis is now being accorded to the civil society sector since this is where much of the peacebuilding field experience lies, and it is therefore seen as essential to link these actors up with the policy makers at national and regional levels;

*Targeted Community programmes* focus on: democratic policing; disarmament; demobilisation disarmament, reintegration and rehabilitation (DDRR) of combatants; security sector reform (SSR); de-mining; civilian administration and good governance; democratisation; rule of law; children-related post-conflict assistance; degradation and export of natural resources; the proliferation of small arms and light weapons (SALW); and reconstruction and rehabilitation related to development assistance;

*Relations with international organisations*: Relations with the UN family are particularly important but the association with other international organisations (Council of Europe, OSCE, etc.) with broadly-based human rights mandates, as well as a number of prominent NGOs, are also relevant to the EU's peacebuilding efforts;

*The European Union's external action in human rights matters*: The observation of human rights and the reinforcement of the rule of law go hand in hand. Human rights are reinforced in many different ways, such as: the use of 'essential elements' clauses in development cooperation; support from the European Initiative for Democracy and Human Rights (EIDHR); and backing for the International Criminal Court and international or mixed 'ad hoc' criminal tribunals. Other related programmes include regional, country and local-level initiatives aimed at strengthening the human rights infrastructure, information campaigns, election observation and the development of civil society;[75]

*Targeted geographical instruments*: These include largely ACP-related programmes such as the Africa-EU Strategic Partnership, the African Peace Facility (APF) and Africa's Peace Security Architecture.[76] Typically, these programmes are designed

---

[74] The Indicative Programme on the Crisis Preparedness Component (Art. 4.3) of the Instrument for Stability, Peace-Building Partnership is available at: <http://webgate.ec.europa.eu/tariqa/pub/fck/File/draftelements1008.doc> (registration required). An assessment of the PbP is being conducted during 2009 to further reflect on the implementation of the crisis preparedness component of the IfS. Consequently, no fund is being allocated to the programme component under the 2009 Annual Action Programme, but it is envisaged that a financial amount proportionate to the sum of the individual amounts for 2009-2010 will be included in the 2010 Annual Action Programme.

[75] For a more comprehensive overview, see: <http://ec.europa.eu/external_relations/cfsp/news/memo05_313.htm>.

[76] See, respectively, <http://europa.eu/scadplus/leg/en/lvb/r12540.htm> and <http://ec.europa.eu/world/peace/geographical_themes/africa/african_peace/index_en.htm>.

to encourage local ownership of the peace process, as well as to enhance the role of regional actors or organisations in attaining stability. The APF is an example of this since it is owned, staffed and operated by Africans;

*The Kimberley Process*: The EC is a participant in the Kimberley Process, designed to introduce transparency and regulation in the trade in diamonds and to halt diamond-fuelled conflicts in places such as Sierra Leone, the Democratic Republic of the Congo or Angola;

*Small Arms and Light Weapons (SALW)*: The EU has adopted a number of policies, such as the 1997 EU Programme for Preventing and Combating Illicit Trafficking in Conventional Weapons and the 1998 Code of Conduct on Arms Exports,[77] as well as specific projects financed through the EDF, to halt the manufacture and spread of SALW;[78]

*De-mining*: The EU partners, with many international organisations in support of mine action, regularly fund anti-mine activities within the context of the EC Mine Action Strategy.[79] De-mining assistance has been given to a number of countries, such as Afghanistan, Colombia and Sri Lanka;

*Rule of law support*: The EC has supported a number of programmes to increase the transparency and effectiveness of the legal system. One such programme is that in Bunia in the Democratic Republic of the Congo.

The 'players' in EU peacebuilding are varied and, due to the multifaceted meaning of the term, numerous. It is notable, though, that the EU generally is not yet at the point where peacebuilding is given a specific bureaucratic space. Instead, it is subsumed under a variety of different roles and functions.

### 3.2.3 *Players*

At the most generic level, the key players have a general interest in peacebuilding, commencing with the Commission Presidency and, on the Council side, the High Representative of the Union for CFSP. As discussed above, the Commissioners for External Relations, Trade and Development also have important general responsibilities. The more general functional levels are within the Directorates-General, most notably DG RELEX and DG ELARG. The 'Crisis Platform' (RELEX DDG1.A under Richard Wright) with overall responsibility for policy coordination in CFSP,

---

77 *EU Programme for Preventing and Combating Illicit Trafficking in Conventional Arms – Second Annual Report*, 19/01/2000, *OJ* C15/1, and Council of the European Union, *European Union Code of Conduct on Arms Exports*, 5/06/1998, 8675/2/98.

78 *EU Strategy to combat illicit accumulation and trafficking of SALW and their ammunition*, Council of the European Union, 5319/06, Brussels, 13 January 2006.

79 *The European Roadmap towards a Zero Victim Target –The EC Mine Action Strategy and Multi-Annual Indicative Programming 2005-2007*, Brussels, 18 October 2004 (not published in the Official Journal).

is divided into four units addressing, respectively, the duties of the European Correspondent; crisis response and peacebuilding; CFSP operations; and security policy.

The presence of a unit dealing with crisis response and peacebuilding might seem to imply that the relevant aspects are dealt with within this unit but, given the multifaceted nature of EU peacebuilding, the associated roles are spread throughout the Directorate-General. For instance, it was argued above that effort to halt the spread of SALW has an active peacebuilding component, yet this is addressed within the security policy unit. The former unit reflects the emphasis accorded to crisis management and, from the Community side, to crisis response and only more recently to peacebuilding.

To return to the peacebuilding element specifically within RELEX DDG1.A, it was framed originally as part of the Instrument for Stability or, more particularly, the crisis preparedness component of the Stability Instrument. This has now been reframed as the Peacebuilding Partnership (PbP) discussed in detail above. Elsewhere in RELEX's Directorate A, the units, broadly speaking, are the main counterparts for the CFSP personnel, and the RELEX staff will liaise frequently with their Council colleagues on a variety of CFSP issues, many of which will be crisis management-related. As has been seen, however, the emphasis since April 2001 has been upon crisis prevention which has become a 'fixed priority' for the EU.

The Commission also has strong peacebuilding interests represented by DG Development since the EU, like other actors, has concluded that there is a strong link between armed violence and poverty. Although the link between poverty and insecurity is tremendously complex, and beyond the immediate scope of this chapter, there is consensus that the EU and the Member States need to harness increasingly complex and sophisticated instruments to attain peace and stability. The linkage between security and development is explicit in a number of Commission documents such as the Cotonou Agreement, regulating the EU's relations with the African, Caribbean and Pacific partners, and the European Consensus on Development.

The challenge for DG Development, as well as for DG Trade, is how to harness general instruments and make them more efficient in the peacebuilding context. In 2005, the EU agreed to the *Policy Coherence on Development* (PCD), which recognises that many policies other than development have a strong impact on developing countries. The PCD was also framed with the Millennium Development Goals in mind. It was established at a time when the EU had the intention of increasing development aid, thus making the need for maximum coherence between the different policy areas a priority.[80] The ultimate aim of the PCD is to consider the implications for the developing countries of every single policy decision. The PCD has no less than twelve 'priority areas,' one of them being peace and security and many of the themes within this area are pertinent to peacebuilding. It remains early days for the PCD, but it at least has the beneficial effect of strengthening

80 Commission Communication on 'Policy Coherence for Development – Accelerating Progress towards Attaining the Millennium Development Goals', COM(2005)134 final of 12 April 2005, and May 2005 General Affairs and External Relations Council (GAERC), Conclusions on the Millennium Development Goals (Doc. 9266/05).

thinking about the important linkages between security and development. In spite of progress, a 2007 report on the security dimensions of the policy noted:

> '(...) improved coordination between security and development is still needed. This implies strengthening organisational mechanisms in the Commission and the Council to better take account of development concerns in security decisions, conducting systematically security-related analyses when informing and guiding development cooperation, improving the transition between the different financial instruments and continuing to build and sustain partnerships with the different international and regional organisations and civil society.'[81]

The PCD is implemented through a rolling work plan which includes questionnaires sent to the Member States to assess the implementation of the policy. The Netherlands was the first to respond to the latest questionnaire (in 2009) and its assessment was that 'the Work Programme has not been translated into operational terms and its relevance for setting up concrete PCD projects is limited.' For the Netherlands, it would be rather useful 'if the EC would select a few priorities, instead of the twelve selected themes.' It would lead to 'more cooperation between Member States and the Commission to implement the Work Programme.'[82] As a result of the feedback, a revision of the PCD will now focus on five areas only, of which security is one.

Finally, the External Service of the Commission plays a critical role in peacebuilding since it is the eyes and ears of the delegations on the ground. The ability of the EU to respond in an appropriate and timely manner will depend heavily upon having access to the right information at the right time. In some specific cases, most notably the African Union, the EU has actively promoted peacebuilding and conflict prevention with the appointment of Koen Vervaeke as EU Special Representative and Head of the European Commission Delegation to the African Union. Part of the ambitious mandate accorded to Vervaeke is to 'predict, prevent, manage, mediate and resolve conflict, support efforts to promote peace and stability, support post-conflict reconstruction.'[83] The significance of his appointment also lies in the deliberate, if somewhat awkward, fusing of Commission and Council duties.

## 3.3 Peacebuilding activities under the Second Pillar

Peacebuilding in the CFSP and ESDP contexts is similarly problematic to distinguish from conflict prevention and some aspects of crisis management. Much attention has been paid to the emergence of ESDP and the increasing demand for EU

---

[81] Commission Working Paper, *EU Report on Policy Coherence for Development*, Brussels, 20 September 2007, COM(2007) 545 final, section 2.4.

[82] 'Netherlands Reveals Results of 2009 PCD Questionnaire', available at: <http://www.eucoherence.org/renderer.do/clearState/false/menuId/313375/returnPage/227304/itemId/606508/instanceId/313389/pageId/313375/>.

[83] Council Joint Action 2007/805/CFSP of 6 December 2007 appointing a European Union Special Representative to the African Union, *OJ* 2007 L 323/45, 8 December 2007.

involvement in a variety of peacekeeping operations. The initial emphasis, with the experience of the Western Balkans in mind, was upon the military dimensions of crisis management while, more recently, the EU has embarked upon an increasingly complex range of civilian operations, ranging from rule of law, to police operations and civilian administration missions.

The overlap between the Pillars has already been touched upon above. Generally speaking, there is much coordination between the Community aspects and CFSP, but there is also continuing friction. In some specific areas, such as conflict prevention, there remains a certain amount of unhealthy duplication, resulting in the need) to improve the Community and Second Pillar efforts in this domain. One of the pressing needs is therefore to find agreement on joint strategies and frameworks under which all of the institutional and Member State efforts can be placed. Whether the Lisbon Treaty will facilitate efforts to this end remains an open question. It is also important to remember that ESDP, in particular, remains a relatively young policy area with not even a decade of operational experience. The challenge for the interested observer is therefore to make sense of a fast-changing and dynamic environment.

Two general reservations can be made though at the outset. First, as has been observed, ESDP tends to emphasise the short term since crisis management remains to the fore (although this is gradually changing), whereas the Community is more suited to longer-term peacebuilding since the policy perspectives and lead-in times are inherently longer. Second, the funding instruments in the CFSP area remain limited. Community support for funding CFSP is primarily for administrative expenditure and some operational expenditure, as well as the Instrument for Stability in general terms (although this remains very much a Community instrument). In the crisis management domain, the Member States are the main funders of military operations and, for this reason, the emphasis is very much on the shorter term and upon creating the conditions in which longer-term stabilisation efforts may flourish. Although not a rigid rule, Community efforts tend to emphasise the longer term, while CFSP and ESDP instruments tend to stress the shorter term. The main role of the Second Pillar in peacebuilding terms is therefore primarily that of creating the conditions in which peacebuilding efforts can flourish.

The broad division of the economic and security dimensions of peacebuilding between the Pillars is often seen as one of the root causes for lack of coordination, or even for competition. Seidelmann makes this point as follows:

> '... placing the economic dimension of foreign and security policies including peace-interventions at the Commission, and the military dimensions at the Council creates on the one side competitive institutions and contradictions between economic and military measures, and prevents on the other side the formation of an effective, cohesive, and consistent grand strategy, which effectively combines sanctions with incentives, economic with military means, and negative security- with positive peace-building.'[84]

---

[84] R. Seidelmann, *Problems and Prospects of the Common Foreign and Security Policy (CFSP) and European Security and Defence Policy (CESDP): A German View*, available at: <http://www.desk.c.u-tokyo.ac.jp/download/es_1_Seidelmann.pdf>.

He is, however, careful not to attribute the differences between the Pillars to rivalling personalities but to institutional structures and the lack of clear political subordination. The case though is probably more nuanced, with a number of ESDP operations, such as the monitoring mission in Aceh, demonstrating more of a peacebuilding role than a crisis management one. Similarly, it could be argued that many of the Special Representatives, appointed through a Council Joint Action, play an active peacebuilding role. As will be seen in the following section, a number of CFSP policies and instruments support peacebuilding, making it a responsibility that falls neither to the Community nor to CFSP explicitly.

### 3.3.1 *Policies*

CFSP covers all areas of foreign and security policy and, like the Community, has general responsibilities towards the rule of law and respect for human rights. Peacebuilding activities under the CFSP umbrella therefore appear under one or both of these rubrics. The respective responsibilities between the Pillars for peacebuilding are ill-defined (this is discussed in more detail above, under competences). Efforts in the CFSP realm are normally complemented by Community-led programmes and funding. Since the ESDP elements of CFSP are relatively young, there has been a certain amount of duplication of effort with the Community, most notably in civilian aspects of crisis management. The question of whether a monitoring mission is an ESDP or Community one, or whether a rule of law mission should fall under the Second Pillar, are all issues that will require further attention and thought. In this regard, the coordination efforts of the Council Secretariat and their counterparts in the Commission's DG RELEX are of particular importance.

The importance of linking cross-Pillar efforts in peacebuilding was illustrated in the case of the Western Balkans. The initial efforts at peacebuilding were made through the Member States (and the Contact Group in particular, involving France, Germany, Italy and the United Kingdom from the EU side) and the relatively new CFSP. The diplomatic clout of the High Representative for CFSP, backed by growing crisis management capabilities, undoubtedly played an important role. It would nonetheless be incorrect to claim that peacebuilding in the Western Balkans was primarily or exclusively part of CFSP. It is unlikely that peacebuilding would have proceeded as it did without external assistance (bearing in mind the relative newness and fragility of CFSP) and the extensive use of Community instruments. The provision of institutions, commencing with the Stabilisation and Association Process (SAP), was also critical in providing for long-term peace and stability. The use of the SAP as a tool to gradually transpose the *acquis communautaire* and to prepare the countries in the region for membership was, arguably, a significant factor in the relative success of peacebuilding efforts in the Western Balkans. It was, however, the ability of the High Representative and the Special Representative to use conditionality and potential membership of the EU as a potent tool that was perhaps one of the most influential factors for stability. At the same time, it is premature to talk of peacebuilding as an accomplished mission in the Western Balkans, or many other parts of the world, since the eventual aim should be to foster inclusive and self-sustaining governance at the domestic level. The continuation of a quasi-trusteeship in parts of the Western Balkans means that peacebuilding cannot be considered complete.

Elsewhere in the world, most notably in Africa, the emphasis accorded to local ownership of the crisis management and peacebuilding processes is notable. The African Peace Facility is a striking example of this, as is the strong EU support for the African Union and EU efforts in this domain. The EU provides a variety of support for peacebuilding efforts in the Great Lakes Region of Africa and elsewhere, as well as crisis management involvement, but with the specific recognition that without local ownership, long-term peace is unattainable. The contrast between the two regions is marked; in the case of the Western Balkans, the EU has taken a level of 'local ownership' itself, especially through active involvement in assisting the countries in the region to become members of the Union. On the other hand, the lack of any membership prospect for African countries has led to different dynamics and approaches in the peacebuilding process.

### 3.3.2 *Instruments*

The instruments available in the CFSP context are similarly hard to define as in the Community context. The CFSP instruments are varied and differ from Community instruments since, with one exception (concerning questions of inter-Pillar competence[85]) the European courts do not have any formal powers. The CFSP instruments, such as joint actions, common positions and declarations, should therefore be seen as primarily political obligations undertaken by the Member States. At the most general level, the general guidelines and common strategies are laid down by the European Council. In spite of their general nature, the guidelines can be useful as a means of ensuring that the Union itself extols the values and principles that it wishes to apply in peacebuilding elsewhere in the world. Joint actions are often used to appoint Special Representatives and to launch ESDP operations. Common positions are often adopted to enforce punitive sanctions (either targeting a country, group or even an individual). Economic sanctions are complex and controversial in terms of whether they attain their desired effects or not, but are often not a peacebuilding tool since they are coercive rather than conditional (positive) in effect. Declarations, issued either by the Presidency or the Council, may also serve to reinforce the normative basis for any subsequent peacebuilding activities.

---

[85] The EU's competences in foreign policy are shared between the European Community and CFSP including, in particular, a number of 'grey areas' of competences falling in between the two Pillars, such as: human rights, civil protection, civilian aspects of crisis management, SALW, and defence industrial issues. Although in principle the ECJ is excluded from CFSP, in case of the adoption of a measure with implications for both Pillars, it is competent to delimit the right legal basis for adoption of this action, as illustrated in the ECOWAS case. See on this topic, S. Duke, 'Areas of Grey: Tensions in EU External Relations Competences', 1 *Eipascope* (2006) 21-27.

The lack of major funding instruments is a crucial contrast with the Community-led efforts and this is one of the main reasons that many tend to portray the CFSP contributions to peacebuilding as short-term. The TEU, Article 28, states that for CFSP

> 'Administrative expenditure (…) and operating expenditure to which the implementation of those provisions gives rise shall also be charged to the budget of the European Communities, except for such expenditure arising from operations having military or defence implications and cases where the Council acting unanimously decides otherwise.'

And, 'in cases where expenditure is not charged to the budget of the European Communities, it shall be charged to the Member States in accordance with the gross national product scale, unless the Council acting unanimously decides otherwise.'

The funding question becomes even more obtuse when considering civilian crisis management operations, when the legal basis and the source of financing is determined in part by the purpose of the proposed action. Generally, humanitarian aid, food aid, securing the livelihoods and safety of refugees, civilian emergency assistance, rehabilitation, reconstruction, infrastructure development, de-mining, economic aid, consolidation of democracy and the rule of law, institution building and some human rights-related expenditure will fall under the Community budget line. The civilian Petersberg tasks, which are not covered by Community competence (such as non-proliferation, disarmament, security, monitoring, certain executive police missions, and fact-finding missions preceding an envisaged operation), will be attributed to the CFSP part of the Union's budget. The military aspects of the Petersberg tasks (that is, peacekeeping tasks and tasks of combat in crisis management including peacemaking) are charged to the Member States on a sliding GNI scale. There is provision for some specific common costs to be covered by the Community's Athena mechanism established on 23 February 2004. The mechanism can cover items such as the funds for the Operations Headquarters (in Europe), the Force Headquarters (in theatre), the Component Headquarters and the necessary infrastructure for the force as a whole, including items such as communication and camps. The Council can also approve other costs such as transport and the lodging of forces, satellite imagery or airborne surveillance.[86]

The question of which financial instrument to use and, indeed, which Pillar should take the lead, will vary from case to case. The demands of conflict prevention and peacebuilding are likely to involve longer-term instruments whereas crisis management, by definition, tends to emphasise the ability to respond quickly and appropriately.

The development of crisis management tools through ESDP has also introduced some instruments that may have wider peacebuilding relevance. The original Petersberg tasks were supplemented by a variety of civilian instruments such as

---

[86] See EU Council Factsheet, *Financing of ESDP operations*, June 2006, available at: <http://consilium.europa.eu/uedocs/cmsUpload/Factsheet_Financing2.pdf>.

those in the field of police, strengthening the rule of law, civilian administration, civil protection and monitoring missions. Often the missions are mixed and complex in nature. Although primarily designed with crisis management role in mind, a number of the ESDP instruments have obvious applicability for peacebuilding missions. This could include niche capabilities that may be of particular importance for SSR or DDR missions, especially those that require specialist knowledge or input. EU police and rule of law missions have been used to instil 'best practice' in a number of parts of the world, which, again, it could be argued. has an important peacebuilding component. The integrated rule of law mission in Kosovo (EULEX) is a case in point where, in contrast to past missions, a deliberate attempt has been made to be inclusive and to actively engage civil society.

### 3.3.3 *Players*

The players in Second Pillar peacebuilding are difficult to define due to the overlap between the crisis management elements of CFSP and those that may assume a variety of peacebuilding roles. Thus, in a general way, the High Representative for CFSP has an obvious role since he will be the central coordinating point for all peacebuilding and related activities. The Political and Security Committee, consisting of ambassadors appointed to the committee from the permanent representations of the Member States, will also have an important role to play through the political and strategic direction of crisis management operations.

The support and advisory elements of the Petersberg tasks are also likely to assume a peacebuilding role, such as those currently involved in EULEX Kosovo. This would include, from the Council side, the Committee for the Civilian Aspects of Crisis Management (CIVCOM), the Situation Centre (SitCen), the EU Military Committee (EUMC) and the EU Military Staff (EUMS). More recently, the Civilian Planning and Conduct Capability (CPCC), with responsibility for the planning and conduct of civilian operations under the political and strategic guidance of the PSC, has rounded off the list of players. The CPCC director will act as the EU Civilian Operations Commander, whereas the military operations can be headed by either an EU commander, via the EU Operations Centre, or a national command operating as a 'framework nation' or, finally, via NATO's planning and command facilities (under the Berlin Plus Agreements).

The point of interest to note for the purposes of this chapter is that most of the players are designed with a crisis management role in mind. It was out of this role and the first few missions from 2003 onwards that the peacebuilding efforts evolved in, for example, Aceh, the Democratic Republic of the Congo and Kosovo. In these cases, and others, the CFSP contribution cannot be considered in isolation from the other Community efforts to establish peace and stability. The CFSP/ESDP elements were essential, but contributory aspects of a wider EU peacebuilding effort. This observation, in turn, means that emphasis should be placed on how to weave together the different aspects of peacebuilding into a seamless whole. This is no easy task when considering the modest size of the CFSP budget in relation to the overall

EU external relations budget. It is also no easy task given the political differences that still exist over the extent to which security, and notably the military and some of the police elements, should be *communitarised.*

### 3.4 Peacebuilding and the Lisbon Treaty

The Lisbon Treaty's impact on peacebuilding may well be positive since more attention will be paid to linking up the different facets of peacebuilding and the actors involved, most notably through the emergence of the European External Action Service (EEAS). The objectives of the EU on the international stage are elaborated upon and these include promoting 'peace, security and progress in Europe and the world,' contributing to 'peace, security and the sustainable development of the Earth,' to 'preserve peace, prevent conflict and to strengthen international security.' The Petersberg tasks are expanded slightly to incorporate 'joint disarmament operations, humanitarian and rescue tasks, military advice and assistance tasks, conflict prevention and peace-keeping tasks, tasks of combat forces in crisis management, including peace-making and post-conflict stabilisation.' As in the current Treaty, the word peacemaking is used which is ambiguous in terms of its meaning (but, historically, was a device to avoid mentioning peace enforcement). The addition of explicit mention of 'post-conflict stabilisation' is also of significance for the EU peacebuilding efforts. Nothing explicitly refers to peacebuilding though and, following from the above discussion, it must again be assumed that any peacebuilding mandate is subsumed in other terms, goals and objectives.

The main contribution to peacebuilding in the Lisbon Treaty is through the potential for greater efficiency. The sections above have dwelt on the question of competences and some of the barriers to effective peacebuilding due to the division of the instruments and players across the Pillars. The European Peacebuilding Liaison Office (EPLO) has produced a basic but helpful overview of the main modifications of the Lisbon Treaty and the implications for peacebuilding.[87] The Lisbon Treaty should not, though, be regarded as a panacea since, although the potential is there for greater consistency between and within the Pillars, there remain many questions about how the new or adapted actors will interact. This point applies particularly to the President of the European Council and the High Representative of the Union for Foreign Affairs and Security Policy, who shall also be a Vice-President of the Commission (HR/VP). But, it also applies to the High Representative and the President of the Commission. A host of other issues also surface, including how the attribution of legal personality to the EU will change the Union's representation in international organisations and at international conferences, as well as the precise shape and structure of the Union delegations (based, presumably, on those of the Commission's External Service but including staff from the Council Secretariat and the Member States).

---

[87] See EPLO, *Peacebuilding and the Lisbon Treaty*, available at: <http://www.eplo.org/documents/Peacebuilding%20and%20the%20Lisbon%20Treaty%20final.pdf>.

Of particular interest is the emergence of the European External Action Service (EEAS), which is a type of quasi-European *corps diplomatique*, drawing upon the relevant departments of the Commission and the Council Secretariat, and also involving the Member States. There is a good deal of speculation about the potential shape of any such service, as well as about its precise role and function. In the peacebuilding context, EPLO advocated that:

> 'A specific PB Directorate/Department should be established within the EEAS with the prime responsibility of coordinating all aspects of conflict prevention activities, PB, and crisis management missions, in order to ensure coherence and consistency in this field between the Council and the Commission. Such a coordinating cell should have as its main tasks: co-ordination of internal EU instruments; planning mission support and evaluation for crisis management missions; cooperation with external organisations and non-governmental organisations; training and recruitment of civilian personnel; and research and evaluation. Building on this Cell's coordination work, an EEAS structure should allow for flexibility needed to build up standing civilian capacity for EU crisis prevention and conflict management in third countries without the necessity of further Council decisions.'

The appointment of a dual-hatted HR/VP holds the potential for more coherence in EU external relations since, assisted by the EEAS, it will link more closely the CFSP with the former communautaire aspects. The EEAS will represent all geographical regions and countries of the world and will assume responsibility for much of the high-level programming, with implementation for specific areas (such as trade and development) being executed through the relevant directorates-general in the Commission. The linkage of funding instruments, especially the IfS, under the High Representative may also prove to be of immense benefit to the overall coherence of EU external action. The association of both the military and civilian crisis management capacities with the HR/VP, alongside the assumption of direct responsibilities and coordination functions within the Commission, also holds the potential for a more comprehensive approach to peacebuilding through the linkage of the many instruments and tools involved. Whether the potential of the Lisbon treaty will depend very much upon the practical implementation of the spirit of the treaty and how those holding the key senior positions interpret their respective mandates.

## 4. THE EU'S EXTERNAL PARTNERS IN PEACEBUILDING

The EU's peacebuilding efforts need to be considered in connection with those of the wide range of international partners with whom the EU associates. In particular, the EU collaborates with the UN and its agencies. According to the 2007 *Joint Statement on UN-EU Cooperation in Crisis Management* 'the UN and the EU are united by the premise that the primary responsibility for the maintenance of international peace and security rests with the UN Security Council, in accordance with the UN Charter. In this context the UN recognizes the considerable contribution (...) of the EU to crisis management.'[88] The same report recognised that 'significant enhancement of UN-EU cooperation has taken place in the area of civilian and military crisis management since the Joint Declaration on UN-EU cooperation in Crisis Management of 24 September 2003.' The earlier EU Security Strategy used the same formulation whereby 'The United Nations Security Council has the primary responsibility for the maintenance of international peace and security.'[89] It follows from this, as well as the EU's desire to contribute to the creation of a rules-based international order, that the legality and legitimacy of EU crisis management and related efforts are sought through a UN Security Council resolution.

The possibility for the EU to use the Berlin Plus arrangement, covering assured access to NATO's planning facilities, the presumption of availability of other assets and the provision for the exchange of classified information between the two organisations, was designed with crisis management in mind and not peacebuilding specifically.[90] The possibility that combat forces might be required to establish initial stability or even to halt crimes against humanity, so that other stabilisation operations can take over, cannot be ruled out. The handing over of two NATO operations in the Western Balkans to the EU also suggests that the arrangements have general applicability in a peacebuilding context. The challenges of implementing the agreement, given the differences between Cyprus and Turkey, as well as the overstretch of US military personnel and resources in Afghanistan and Iraq, should not be underestimated. The large overlap of membership between the two organisations has to be balanced against the potential sensitivities of the six neutral or non-aligned EU members who may have reservations about closer relations with NATO.[91]

The Organisation for Cooperation and Security in Europe (OSCE) deals with a wide range of security issues including those relating to conflict prevention. In this context, they are mainly addressed by the Office for Democratic Institutions and Human Rights (ODIHR), which provides a broad range of programmes, ranging from election observation and assistance in drafting and implementing election laws and systems, to assistance in establishing democratic institutions, strengthening the rule of law, fostering the establishment and continued existence of NGOs, and the functioning of civil societies. A number of EU staff in monitoring missions are jointly trained with OSCE staff.

The Council of Europe pre-dates the EU, having been founded in 1949, and is now part of the collective European peacebuilding effort to stop the outbreak of violence or its reoccurrence. The Council of Europe's core mission is the protection

---

[88] Council of the EU, Joint Statement on UN-EU Cooperation in Crisis Management, PRESS, 7 June 2007.

[89] *A Secure Europe in a Better World*, European Security Strategy, Brussels, 12 December 2003, at 9.

[90] NATO, *Berlin Plus Agreement*, 17 March 2003.

[91] These are Austria, Cyprus, Finland, Ireland, Malta and Sweden.

of human rights as guaranteed by the 1950 European Convention on Human Rights (ECHR) and the subsequent protocols. The Council of Europe is one of the main platforms for dialogue and cooperation at different levels, ranging from the intergovernmental, to the inter-parliamentary, to local government and civil society levels. The OSCE, the Council of Europe and the EU frequently work together to reinforce the observance of human rights, minority rights and other fundamental freedoms, as well as to prevent conflict or the spread of conflict within the region. Although all are mutually supportive and all have the adage 'Europe' in their titles, the EU is distinct because of the global nature of its peacebuilding efforts which necessitates close collaboration within the region, as well as with a diverse range of international partners.

The African Union (AU) has become an increasingly important player in promoting peacebuilding on the African continent (in the framework of the EU-Africa joint strategy). The AU has been referred to above and the EU's goal is to provide such support and advice as is necessary so that the AU and the members can increasingly assume local ownership for stability and peace amongst the membership.

The EU also works extensively with a variety of NGOs (as has been noted in the context of the PbP above). The role of EPLO is also prominent, as the umbrella for twenty-five or so European NGOs, networks of NGOs and think-tanks in the peacebuilding area. EPLO's mission is as follows:

> 'EPLO aims to influence the EU so it promotes and implements measures that lead to sustainable peace between states and within states and peoples, and that transform and resolve conflicts non-violently. EPLO wants the EU to recognise the crucial connection between peacebuilding, the eradication of poverty, and sustainable development world wide and the crucial role NGOs have to play in sustainable EU efforts for peacebuilding, conflict prevention, and crisis management.'[92]

The Initiative for Peacebuilding (IfP) is one notable activity being promoted by a cluster of NGOs, including EPLO, headed by International Alert and funded by the European Commission. The aim is to bring together complementary geographical and thematic expertise across ten civil society organisations so that all institutions, including the European Commission, can access strong independent analysis 'in order to facilitate better informed and evidence-based policy decisions.'[93]

A number of non-EU countries play a prominent role in EU peacebuilding efforts, most notably Switzerland's Expert Pool for Civilian Peacebuilding which is run through the Federal Department for Foreign Affairs. The 630 expert volunteers, organised as a militia system, have offered services in areas such as election monitoring, police advisers, specialist constitutional affairs, mediation, rule of law, human rights and humanitarian law. The EU has been one of the international

---

92 See EPLO at:<http://www.eplo.org/index.php?id=1>.

93 See: <http://www.initiativeforpeacebuilding.eu/>.

beneficiaries of their experience and advice, including in the current EULEX mission in Kosovo.

## 5. Conclusions

As reflected at the beginning of this volume, the post-war European integration that created the European Community and then the EU itself was a peacebuilding project. Arguably, this fact imbues the EU with a certain authority as regards peacebuilding. This chapter has sketched out the principal players and instruments when it comes to EU peacebuilding. The task is, however, significantly complicated by the generous parameters of what falls under the 'peacebuilding' rubric. Indeed, when referring to the EU, it almost seems simpler to ask what is not indirectly or directly peacebuilding.

The brief examination above shows how the EU has consciously tried to model the understanding and practice of peacebuilding in terms of international norms, notably those of the United Nations. The initial practice of peacebuilding focused on conflict prevention but has been interpreted either as efforts to halt the outbreak of conflict in the first place or, as efforts to halt the restart of conflict. Implicitly, peacebuilding has included post-conflict stabilisation of the type we see in the Western Balkans, but only more recently, with the advent of the Lisbon Treaty, do we see explicit mention of 'post-conflict stabilisation' among the tasks charged to the EU under CFSP.

The question of what is understood by EU 'peacebuilding' is more than semantics since it has bearing on who the players are and what instruments may be employed. If we accept that peacebuilding in this context has both conflict prevention as well as post-conflict stabilisation facets, the players and instruments are extensive. On the Community side, the involvement of different Directorates-General could be wide, ranging from External Relations, Development and Trade, to EuropeAid and ECHO. Others may be added, as need be, to provide specialist advice or functions. In this context, the role of the delegations within the crisis country or region is also critical since they are the eyes and ears of the Community and the Commission staff, along with the local staff who are familiar with the local political, economic and social aspects, and who will be instrumental in guiding the peacebuilding efforts *in situ*.

The instruments are also extensive, depending in part upon the nature of the crisis and the specific needs. Some of the instruments involve using existing funds, like the EDF or the Instrument for Stability, for targeted funding. Other tools are of a more precautionary nature designed to address the root causes of conflict, such as the Community's participation in the Kimberley Process designed to combat the illegal trade in diamonds, that in turn fuel instability. One of the more interesting instruments in development is the Peacebuilding Partnership (PbP), which is a Commission-backed initiative resting upon the specific acknowledgement that effective peacebuilding must involve civil society.

The primary purpose of the Second Pillar (CFSP) in the peacebuilding context is to create the conditions under which longer-term stabilisation efforts can take place. This may involve a military crisis management mission but the current demand for missions suggests that there will continue be more demand for civilian crisis management tools, such as rule of law missions, civil administration missions, border assistance missions, observation missions and police missions. The players in the CFSP case are also diverse and are, for the most part, the crisis management actors adapting their skills and resources to a peacebuilding role.

The challenge for the EU remains how to knit together the players and instruments in the different Pillars into a comprehensive peacebuilding response. Since peacebuilding tends to be a slower, long-term process, the practical lessons for the EU will only emerge gradually. The concept of peacebuilding is itself slowly evolving and being shaped within the EU institutions and the EU members. The EU has formidable potential to link together all of the various facets of its influence, ranging from its trade, development and assistance tools, to the 'harder' aspects of its profile being developed through ESDP. The attainment of this potential will depend very much upon the internal dynamics of the EU institutions but, in particular, upon the political will of the Member States to support the EU's peacebuilding efforts. In fact, the challenge goes beyond the EU to include the efforts of important partners, notably the UN, to the same end.

The implementation of the Lisbon Treaty holds the potential for greater coherence, effectiveness and visibility for the EU on the international scene – all fundamental aims of the treaty. The question of whether that potential is realised depends very much upon how the key senior appointments interpret their respective mandates. It will also depend upon the eventual composition and functioning of the EEAS which, under the guidance of the HR/VP, should tie together strategic thinking and programming, as well as many of the essential instruments for peacebuilding. As this overview of EU peacebuilding has demonstrated to show, the tools and instruments that apply are extensive. In few other areas of the EU's activity are the demands on coherence so high, let alone the need for effectiveness and visibility.

# Chapter 2
# THE EU AS PEACEBUILDER: ACTORNESS, POTENTIAL AND LIMITS

**Nathalie Tocci***

The European Union, collectively, identifies the promotion of peace as a key priority of its nascent foreign policy. The 2003 Security Strategy explicitly states the need for the EU to engage actively in a full range of activities spanning from conflict prevention to crisis management and post-violence rehabilitation.[1] This approach can be summarised as 'peacebuilding'; that is, engagement in a whole array of policy domains, across all moments of the conflict cycle, through a variety of policy instruments. The concept of peacebuilding is embedded within the notion of the 'liberal peace' and can be traced back to former UN Secretary General Boutros Ghali's 1992 Agenda for Peace.[2] The idea is that of engaging in a wide variety of actions, from specific initiatives aimed at securing ceasefires, demobilisation, disarmament, peacekeeping and reconstruction, to broader activities aimed at promoting good governance, security sector reform, judicial reform and transitional justice, democracy, civil society development, human rights protection and socio-economic development. In view of its comprehensive nature, peacebuilding tends to be pursued in the post-violence phase of conflicts[3] in so far as its key building blocks tend to be tailored to the long-term transformation of conflict rather than the short-term management of crises. The objective of 'peacebuilding' is thus that of creating the conditions for a durable peace following the end of violent conflict through policy actions aimed at state-building and political, social and economic development, which branch out beyond the specific items on the crisis management and conflict settlement agendas.[4]

---

* Dr Nathalie Tocci is a Senior Fellow at the Istituto Affari Internazionali, Rome. Research on this chapter was closed before the entry into force of the Lisbon Treaty.

[1] Council of the EU, *A Secure Europe in a Better World. European Security Strategy*, 12 December 2003, available at: <http://ue.eu.int/pressdata/EN/reports/78367.pdf>, 12.

[2] *Agenda for Peace*, Report of the Secretary-General of 17 June 1992, UN Doc. A/47/277 – S/24111.

[3] Defined by the UN Secretary-General as the first two years after the main conflict in a country has ended. See *Report of the Secretary-General on Peacebuilding in the Immediate Aftermath of Conflict* of 11 June 2009, UN Doc. A/63/881–S/2009/304.

[4] This chapter does not provide a normative assessment of liberal peacebuilding, i.e., whether and why the EU *should* engage in such a goal. For a critical view of the notion of liberal peacebuilding, see O. Richmond, *The Transformation of Peace* (London, Palgrave MacMillan 2007), O. Richmond, 'The Romanticisation of the Local', 44 *The International Spectator* (2009), and D. Chandler, *Peace without*

*S. Blockmans, J. Wouters & T. Ruys, eds., The European Union and Peacebuilding*

Inherent in the EU's approach to conflicts is the link drawn between the promotion of human rights, democracy, the rule of law, good governance and socio-economic development and reform on the one hand, and the prevention, resolution and transformation of conflict on the other. The former, while being viewed as ends in themselves, are also considered as instrumental to achieving the latter. As such, EU institutions have explicitly acknowledged that human rights, the rule of law, a vibrant civil society, strong institutions and sound socio-economic management are essential ingredients of conflict prevention and conflict resolution, as opposed to mere crisis management or conflict settlement.[5]

Beyond these stated intentions, through what policy instruments and mechanisms can the EU engage in peacebuilding? And what are the factors that determine the potential as well as the limits of the EU as an actor in peacebuilding?

## 1. Short and long-term policy instruments to promote peacebuilding

EU peacebuilding activities take a variety of forms. Within the realm of the Common Foreign and Security Policy (CFSP) and the Common Security and Defence Policy (CDSP, until the entry into force of the Lisbon Treaty still called ESDP), the EU generally engages in short to medium-term actions in conflict zones. These include diplomatic mediation efforts carried out by the CFSP High Representative and the EU's Special Representatives in conflict regions around the globe (in 2009, these include Afghanistan, the African Great Lakes Region, Bosnia and Herzegovina, Central Asia, Kosovo, the former Yugoslav Republic of Macedonia, the Middle East, Moldova, the South Caucasus and Sudan). Furthermore, within the context of the ESDP, the EU, at the time of writing in 2009, was engaged in military and civilian operations aimed at peacekeeping, security sector reform, judicial reform and border monitoring in regions such as the Balkans (EUFOR-Althea, EUPM, EULEX Kosovo), the South Caucasus (EUMM Georgia), the Middle East (EUPOL COPPS, EUBAM Rafah, EUJUST Lex), Central Asia (EUPOL Afghanistan) and Africa (EU NAVFOR Somalia, EU SSR Guinea-Bissau, EUFOR TCHAD/RCA, EUPOL RD CONGO, EUSEC RD Congo). These ESDP missions have an average duration of one to two years.

Turning to longer-term peacebuilding actions, we find EU aid and technical assistance programmes alongside EU contractual arrangements with third parties, which are primarily grounded upon trade and embedded within the Union's Common Commercial Policy.[6] Assistance and contractual arrangements are intended to

---

*Politics* (London, Routledge 2006). This chapter takes the EU's commitment to peacebuilding at face value and critically analyses how the EU pursues this goal.

[5] Commission of the EC, *The EU's Role in Promoting Human Rights and Democratisation in Third Countries*, COM (2001) 252, Brussels; and V. Kronenberger and J. Wouters, eds., *The EU and Conflict Prevention: Policy and Legal Aspects* (The Hague, Asser Press 2005).

[6] The Common Commercial Policy is an area of exclusive Community responsibility (Article 133 of the TEU) and implies a uniform conduct of trade relations with third countries by means of a com-

foster sustainable structural change both within and between third countries, which in turn induces conflict prevention, resolution and transformation.[7] Development is the first policy area in which EU assistance and contractual arrangements have aimed at inducing the structural transformation of third countries.[8] The European Development Fund (EDF) has increasingly focused on democracy, good governance, human rights and reconciliation projects beyond the more traditional socio-economic development projects in the African-Caribbean-Pacific countries (ACP). In the Fourth Lomé Convention, as amended in 1995,[9] the Union set out the procedures to hold a human rights dialogue in the context of political dialogue with the ACP countries. The ensuing 2000 Cotonou Agreement[10] spelled out that human rights would be 'essential elements' of the Agreement (Article 8) and that negative measures would be considered in the event of persisting non-compliance in the sphere of human rights (Article 96) by third countries. On this basis, the Union ventured in using different forms of negative incentives to ACP states, taking action against Haiti (2001), Côte d'Ivoire (2001), Fiji (2001) and Zimbabwe (2002).[11]

Closer to home, EU peacebuilding policies have been developed mostly in the European neighbourhood. The first instance in which the Union developed its peacebuilding policies was through its accession policy in Eastern Europe. While a *sui generis* case of EU foreign policy, the enlargement policy was significant in so far as it determined many of the peacebuilding templates and mechanisms that the Union then applied beyond the context of enlargement. At the 1993 Copenhagen European Council,[12] the Union set out the political (as well as economic, legal and technical) requirements for a candidate country to be admitted to the EU. These political conditions include the stability of institutions guaranteeing democracy, the rule of law, human rights and the protection of minorities. By and large, these criteria reflect the principles underpinning the EU system, as stipulated in Article 6.1 of the Treaty on European Union (TEU),[13] which calls upon Member States to uphold the principles of liberty, democracy, human rights and fundamental freedoms, and the rule of law. Beyond setting out political obligations which candidate countries

---

mon customs tariff and common import and export regimes. The Commission negotiates and concludes international agreements, such as those discussed in this chapter, on behalf of the Community at bilateral and multilateral levels.

[7] Commission of the EC (2001), *supra* n. 5, at 4.

[8] D. Marantis, 'Human Rights Democracy and Development: The European Community Model', 7 *Harvard Human Rights Journal* (1994) 1-32.

[9] European Commission, *The Lomé Convention*, available at: <http://ec.europa.eu/development/geographical/cotonou/lomegen/lomeitoiv_en.cfm#4>.

[10] European Commission, *The Cotonou Agreement*, available at: <http://ec.europa.eu/development/geographical/cotonouintro_en.cfm>.

[11] C. Portela, 'Where and Why Does the EU Impose Sanctions?', 17 *Politique européenne* (2005) 83-111.

[12] European Council meeting in Copenhagen, 21-22 June 1993, at 13, available at: <http://www.europarl.europa.eu/summits/copenhagen/co_en.pdfReference?>.

[13] European Union, *Consolidated Versions of the Treaty on European Union and of the Treaty Establishing the European Community*, Article 6.1, at 12, available at: <http://Eur-Lex.Europa.Eu/Lexuriserv/Lexuriserv.Do?Uri=Oj:C:2006:321e:0001:0331:En:Pdf>.

have to fulfil, the accession policy also developed instruments to induce and ensure compliance. In the annual 'Progress Reports',[14] the Commission reviews the performance of the candidate countries, taking as a reference point the rights and obligations enshrined in the EU's *acquis communautaire* as well as in other bodies of law such as the European Convention on Human Rights. On the basis of these reports, the EU publishes Accession Partnership documents spelling out the short (1-2 years) and medium-term (3-4 years) priorities that candidate countries have to fulfil in order to move the accession process forward.[15] The successive steps in this process – such as being recognised as a candidate, opening accession negotiations, opening and closing the over thirty chapters of the *acquis*, signing and ratifying the accession treaty, and entering the EU – are in fact conditioned to the aspirant members' fulfilment of the EU's specified recommendations, including in the sphere of peacebuilding. Pre-accession assistance via the Instrument for Pre-Accession (IPA), while primarily tailored to supporting a candidate country's capability to adopt and enforce the *acquis*, also reserves funds for specific human rights, democracy and reconciliation projects.

In the wake of the Balkan wars and particularly after the 1999 Kosovo war, the EU also intensified its relationships with the Western Balkan countries. At a multilateral level, the EU launched the South East European Cooperation Process and actively supported the Stability Pact for South Eastern Europe, both aimed at inducing reconciliation and regional cooperation. Alongside these regional initiatives, the EU intensified its bilateral contractual relationships with the Western Balkan countries, particularly when (at the 2000 Feira European Council, reconfirmed at the 2003 Thessaloniki European Council)[16] the EU declared its intent to eventually integrate the Balkans into its fold. The EU thus launched the Stabilisation and Association Process (SAP) with these countries, intending to give rise to Stabilisation and Association Agreements (SAAs), which would pave the way into the accession process. Like other types of EU contractual arrangements, the SAAs include an essential elements article (Article 2) mentioning democracy, international law and human rights, alongside a non-execution article allowing the EU to adopt proportional negative measures in the event of a material breach of these agreements. Furthermore, in addition to the human rights, democracy and international law requirements, the EU also inserted Balkan-specific conditions related to refugee return, cooperation with the International Criminal Tribunal for the Former Yugoslavia and regional cooperation.[17] Up until 2007, the financial instrument targeted to the Western Balkans was the Community Assistance for Reconstruction, Development

---

[14] Available at: <http://ec.europa.eu/enlargement/how-does-it-work/progress_reports/index_en.htm>.

[15] Available at: <http://ec.europa.eu/enlargement/archives/key_documents/accession_partnerships_2001_en.htm>.

[16] Presidency Conclusions, European Council meeting in Thessaloniki on 19-20 June 2003, available at: <http://www.consilium.europa.eu/ueDocs/cms_Data/docs/pressData/en/ec/76279.pdf>.

[17] For example, the EU has insisted that Serbia's cooperation with the ICTY, including the arrest and transfer of Radovan Karadžić and Ratko Mladić, is a precondition for the entry into force of the Stabilisation and Association Agreement (SAA) between the EU and Serbia.

and Stabilisation (CARDS), which was partly devoted to democratic reform (Article 105).[18] In 2007 and in view of the Western Balkans' gradual inclusion in the accession process, CARDS was replaced by IPA.

Beyond enlargement, in the post-Cold War period, the EU signed Partnership and Cooperation Agreements (PCAs) with most of the Commonwealth of Independent States.[19] In the context of these agreements, the EU provided for cooperation in the spheres of trade, culture and technology, while institutionalising political dialogue and inserting an essential elements (Article 2) and a non-execution article (Article 93). Furthermore, under the Technical Assistance for the Commonwealth of Independent States (TACIS) programme,[20] the EU supported both socio-economic development and projects aimed at strengthening the rule of law, good governance, human rights and democracy.

Turning from east to south, the EU has also formalised its relations with the southern Mediterranean countries since the mid-1990s. At a multilateral level, the 1995 Barcelona Declaration[21] affirmed the EU and southern Mediterranean countries' commitment to the promotion of peace, security and shared prosperity through multilateral dialogue frameworks at foreign ministers, senior officials, parliamentary and civil society levels. Moreover, the bilateral Association Agreements (AAs) signed and ratified by the EU and the southern Mediterranean countries all include essential elements (Article 2) and non-execution (Article 79) clauses.[22] Lastly, in the context of the Euro-Mediterranean Partnership (since 2008 also Union for the Mediterranean), the EU has supported economic development, redressing socio-economic imbalances, good governance and human rights reforms through its financial assistance instrument (MEDA).[23]

Finally, since 2003, the EU has developed a European Neighbourhood Policy (ENP) covering the eastern and southern neighbours, placing a visibly higher emphasis on political questions compared with its predecessor policies.[24] Indeed, the ENP explicitly aims to promote the EU's values as a means to spread peace, stability, security and prosperity in the southern and eastern neighbourhoods. It also aspires to strengthen the EU's contribution to the solution of regional conflicts.[25] The

---

[18] See <http://ec.europa.eu/enlargement/how-does-it-work/financial-assistance/cards/index_en.htm>.

[19] For example, in 1996, Georgia signed an EU Partnership and Cooperation Agreement with the EU, which included an institutionalised forum for political dialogue, as well as provisions on trade, economic cooperation, culture and technology.

[20] See <http://www.euroresources.org/fileadmin/user_upload/PDF_country_and_Programme_profiles/ec4.pdf>.

[21] See <http://ec.europa.eu/external_relations/euromed/barcelona_en.htm>.

[22] L. Bartels, 'A Legal Analysis of Human Rights Clauses in the EU's Euro-Mediterranean Association Agreements', 9 *Mediterranean Politics* (2004) 368-395.

[23] See <http://europa.eu/legislation_summaries/external_relations/relations_with_third_countries/mediterranean_partner_countries/r15006_en.htm>.

[24] N. Tocci, *Can the EU Promote Democracy and Human Rights through the ENP? The Case for Refocusing on the Rule of Law*, EUI Working Papers (Florence 2007), available at: <http://www.iue.it/LAW/Events/ENP/Papers/PaperTocci.pdf>.

[25] Commission of the EC, *European Neighbourhood Policy Strategy Paper*, Brussels, COM (2004) 373, available at: <http://ec.europa.eu/world/enp/pdf/strategy/strategy_paper_en.pdf>, at 6.

ENP's founding documents, alongside the operational Country Strategy Papers and the ensuing Action Plans (AP),[26] agreed bilaterally with five eastern and seven southern neighbours by 2007, highlight the country-specific political, governance as well as conflict-related priorities and actions that should be undertaken in the context of the ENP. This has been truer for some neighbours than for others. In countries such as Georgia, Moldova and the Palestinian Authority, the Action Plans have specified detailed reform priorities in the areas of institutions and governance, elections and electoral laws, human rights and fundamental freedoms, and the development of civil society. In cases such as Azerbaijan or Israel, reform priorities have been set out in brief, vague and open-ended ways.[27] In 2007, the financial instrument of the ENP, the European Neighbourhood and Partnership Instrument (ENPI), became operational, replacing MEDA for the southern Mediterranean and TACIS for the eastern neighbours.

## 2. EU mechanisms to promote peacebuilding

Having set out the short and long-term policy instruments the EU has at its disposal, how can the EU deploy its instruments at the service of peacebuilding? As pointed out by Hill, an EU role in conflicts can be twofold.[28] First, the EU framework of governance, law and policy can offer a conducive context for peacebuilding. Second, the Union can generate incentives for peacebuilding through the policy instruments outlined above. The role of the EU as a framework and as an actor are not unrelated, particularly in the neighbouring regions.[29] Most EU actions in the neighbourhood, such as the SAP, the EMP and the ENP make use of and are embedded in EU institutional, legal and policy frameworks. But more precisely, through what policy mechanisms can the Union contribute to peacebuilding by embedding conflict parties into its institutional, legal, financial and political frameworks through the use of contractual relations?

One reason underpinning the failure of conflict countries to embark on and pursue conflict transformation is their lack of adequate capability. In these cases, conflicts persist and become entrenched and exacerbated because the conflict country(ies) lack the necessary administrative, judicial, security or economic capacities to engage in peaceful change. The assumption here, embedded in the notion and philosophy of peacebuilding, is that the transformation of conflict requires the prior establishment of the rule of law and effective governance structures. In these cases, the EU can thus induce peacebuilding by supporting capacity building

---

26 Available at: <http://ec.europa.eu/world/enp/documents_en.htm#2>.

27 M. Emerson, G. Noutcheva and N. Popescu, *ENP after Two Years: Time Indeed for an ENP Plus*, Working Paper (Brussels, CEPS 2007).

28 C. Hill, 'The EU's Capacity for Conflict Prevention', 6 *European Foreign Affairs Review* (2001) 315-333.

29 N. Tocci, *Conflict Resolution in the European Neighbourhood: The Role of the EU As a Framework and As an Actor,* EUI Working Paper 29 (Florence 2004).

within third countries through targeted financial or technical assistance. A second reason underpinning the existence and persistence of conflicts, which is more frequent yet far more complex to tackle, relates to the absence of the necessary political will within third countries to engage in conflict transformation. In other words, conflicts persist not because of weak capabilities, but rather because the underlying incentive structure and belief system within third countries induces domestic actors to tolerate or actively encourage conflict. In such cases, EU peacebuilding policies must alter the domestic opportunity structure in third countries, changing incentives in favour of conflict transformation.

## 2.1 Enhancing capability

Beginning with capacity building at the service of peacebuilding, the EU can provide financial and technical support to ensure the transformation of conflicts. This often takes place within the framework of trade agreements in order to assist third states in reforming their administrative structures to meet the obligations specified in the agreements. As briefly outlined above, a portion of funds within EU financial instruments (i.e., EDF, IPA and the ENPI) have targeted reconciliation, human rights, governance, democracy and the rule of law. They have covered a variety of issues, including projects aimed at reforming the judiciary, training and reforming police forces, and supporting administrative and institutional development.[30] These funds however, while notable in absolute levels, pale into insignificance when compared to the budgets allocated to economic, infrastructure or energy projects. Furthermore, projects stemming from these instruments require the participation or approval of third-state authorities, which are often key actors in thwarting the peaceful transformation of conflict. Within the ENPI, for example, the EU has attempted to raise the attention paid to democracy and human rights issues through its Governance Facility targeted to states that demonstrate a willingness to engage in political reform. Yet also this instrument is extremely limited in scope, with an allocation of €300m over seven years (€43m per year) for 16 ENP countries plus Russia.

In addition, in 1994, the EU established the European Initiative for Democracy and Human Rights (EIDHR), applied worldwide but thematically focused on democracy and human rights. The EIDHR has spent approximately €100-140m per year and its programmes have aimed at supporting human rights of individuals suffering from poverty and social exclusion; supporting the rights of minorities, ethnic groups and indigenous peoples; supporting the development of civil society and specifically promoting groups working on human rights education, training and awareness raising; justice and the rule of law; and promoting democratic pro-

---

[30] For example, within the context of the MEDA Democracy Programme in 2002-06, a variety of projects were supported, such as for the amelioration of prison conditions in Egypt, for the protection of the human rights of migrants and asylum seekers in Lebanon, and for the promotion of human rights in school textbooks in Turkey. See European Commission, *Euro-Mediterranean Partnership and MEDA Regional Activities, Information Notes*, June 2002, available at: <http://www.emwis.net/overview/fol101997/fol221357/infonotes_200206-en.pdf>, at 26.

cesses.[31] The advantage of the EIDHR is that it does not require the assent of third states and the funds can be used by international and local NGOs and international agencies. However, the EIDHR has been criticised by many because of the limited funds available and its bureaucratic inflexibility which has rendered the instrument hardly accessible to non-EU local civil society actors.[32] Aiming to reform the EIDHR, extensive discussions took place in 2006 between the Commission, the Council and the European Parliament, with the external advice of academics and NGOs. Yet the new EIDHR Regulation, covering the period 2007-2013 and approved in December 2006, made only marginal improvements in terms of bureaucratic flexibility and simplicity, while aiming to raise its annual expenditure to €160m by 2013.[33]

Finally, and more specifically tailored to conflict contexts, the Commission launched, in 2006, its Peacebuilding Partnership (PbP) in the context of the Crisis Preparedness Component of the Instrument for Stability. The aim of this financial instrument is to assist the Union in developing more effective peacebuilding policies by supporting civil society organisations, especially those present on the field, and providing information and expertise to European policy makers. In other words, rather than primarily aiming to support the capacity of local and international civil society organisations present in conflict contexts, the PbP seeks to enhance the Union's own capacity in peacebuilding through the acquisition of timely and policy-relevant information and analysis.[34]

Lastly, in the context of CFSP and ESDP, the EU has also carried out specific missions aimed at strengthening capabilities within particular sectors. To name a few examples, since 2005 (although actively since 2007) the EU has conducted an ESDP police training mission, EUPOL COPPS, in the West Bank.[35] In Gaza, in the context of the US-brokered 2005 Agreement on Movement and Access, the EU engaged in border monitoring at the Rafah crossing, although the mission ground to a halt in June 2007 following the political separation between the Hamas-controlled Gaza Strip and the Fateh-controlled West Bank.[36] In July 2004, under the Rapid Reaction Mechanism, the EU deployed a seven-month rule of law mission (EUJUST

[31] Projects funded under the EIDHR include (in order of priority): election observation, the promotion of human rights and fundamental freedoms, governance, women, strengthening of civil society, the fight against torture and the promotion of the rule of law. See European Commission, *Types of EIDHR Projects 2000-06*, available at: <http://ec.europa.eu/europeaid/where/worldwide/eidhr/documents/eidhr_statistics_en.pdf>.

[32] R. Youngs, *The European Union and the Promotion of Democracy: Europe's Mediterranean and Asian Policies* (Oxford, Oxford University Press 2002).

[33] European Commission, *New External Cooperation Instruments*, 10 March 2007, available at: <http://ec.europa.eu/europeaid/infopoint/documents/presentations/presentation_20_03_2007_en.pdf>, at 18.

[34] See <http://ec.europa.eu/external_relations/ifs/pbp_en.htm>.

[35] Council Joint Action 2005/797/CFSP of 14 November 2005 on the European Union Police Mission for the Palestinian Territories, available at: <http://eur-lex.europa.eu/LexUriServ/LexUriServ.do?uri=OJ:L:2005:300:0065:0069:EN:PDF>.

[36] Council Joint Action 2005/889/CFSP of 12 December 2005 on establishing a European Union Border Assistance Mission for the Rafah Crossing Point (EU BAM Rafah), available at: <http://eur-lex.europa.eu/LexUriServ/LexUriServ.do?uri=OJ:L:2005:327:0028:0032:EN:PDF>.

THEMIS) to Georgia recommending reforms in Georgia's judiciary, particularly in the field of criminal justice.[37] With the end of the mission, a locally-based support team was established within the office of the EU Special Representative for the Caucasus to follow up the work of EUJUST THEMIS and provide assistance to Georgian border guards. In the aftermath of the Russian-Georgian war in August 2008, the EU launched a monitoring mission (EUMM) intended to stabilise Georgia, monitor the return of internally displaced persons and refugees, and facilitate contacts and confidence building between the conflict parties.[38]

Beyond the shortcomings regarding the quantity of funds available and the modalities of disbursement, EU financial and technical assistance in support of peacebuilding is often ineffective. While necessary to assist countries in recovering from phases of active conflict, if and when undertaken on its own and not alongside policies whose aim is that of altering the incentive structure at the basis of the conflict, EU capacity-building policies can simply adjust to the existing conflict configuration, at times even exacerbating its underlying structural features. In most third states, including those with weak capabilities, the primary reason why conflicts exist and persist lies in the absence of the necessary political will to engage in conflict transformation. In these cases, EU efforts at capacity building at best alleviate the most acute manifestations of conflict (i.e., through financial assistance) and at worst exacerbate conflict dynamics, thus reducing the likelihood of peace. In the case of the Israeli-Palestinian conflict, for example, Le More convincingly argues how EU and international assistance poured into the Occupied Palestinian Territories as a substitute for a veritable political engagement aimed at altering the underlying incentive structure at the root of the conflict, not only failed to prevent the progressive deterioration of the conflict, but contributed to it.[39]

When conflicts persist because of a lack of political will and not simply because of deficient capabilities in conflict countries, what EU mechanisms can be put in motion in order to promote peacebuilding? There are three principal mechanisms aimed at altering incentives in conflict countries, which are primarily differentiated by the extent to which they are coercive and binding upon third countries.

## 2.2 Socialisation

Socialisation represents the least binding and coercive mechanism to alter incentives and thence induce peacebuilding. It is the channel which is least likely to have an impact upon third states, yet at the same time, if effective, can guarantee the

---

[37] Council Joint Action 2004/523/CFSP of 28 June 2004 on the European Union Rule of Law Mission in Georgia, EUJUST THEMIS, available at: <http://eur-lex.europa.eu/pri/en/oj/dat/2004/l_228/l_22820040629en00210024.pdf>.

[38] Council Joint Action 2008/759/CFSP of 25 September 2008 amending Joint Action 2008/736/CFSP on the European Union Monitoring Mission in Georgia, EUMM Georgia, available at: <http://eur-lex.europa.eu/LexUriServ/LexUriServ.do?uri=OJ:L:2008:259:0015:0015:EN:PDF>.

[39] A. Le More, *International Assistance to the Palestinians after Oslo. Political Guilt, Wasted Money* (London, Routledge 2008).

most deep-rooted and long-lasting change in conflict situations. It is also the mechanism of influence by far preferred by EU institutions and actors.

Socialisation takes place through institutional, political, economic and wider societal contact and dialogue between the EU and third states on human rights. This channel of influence not simply aims at altering a third state's cost-benefit calculus regarding their behaviour in conflict. It rather aims at inducing a voluntary transformation of its perceived interests and values regarding conduct in conflict, triggering a progressive shift towards peacebuilding.[40] Through participation in or close contact with the EU institutional framework, EU actors engage in dialogue, awareness raising, persuasion, argumentation, as well as shaming and denunciation vis-à-vis third states. The third country in turn alters its substantive beliefs, visions and purposes, as well as its priorities, strategies and tactics in a manner conducive to the peaceful transformation of conflicts.

As conceptualised by Risse, Ropp and Sikkink in the sphere of human rights practice, change through socialisation takes place through different steps.[41] In a first stage, third states may concomitantly deny the existence of violations or make purely tactical concessions at the international level (e.g., at the UN or in dialogue with major international actors) and intensify repression at the domestic level in order to make repression and protest less visible to the outside world. In a second stage, the conflict state, faced with persistent international pressure, engages in strategic bargaining and instrumental adaptation. In other words, it may start 'talking the talk' of human rights and reconciliation in order to alleviate external pressure and maintain good standing in valued international groupings. Yet it remains in essence committed to conflict-exacerbating practices. It does so believing that 'talk is cheap' in so far as it allows the state to regain and retain international sympathy while leaving its substantive domestic practices unchanged. If at this stage international pressure is lifted the process is interrupted and conflict practices remain unchanged. However, if pressure is maintained, then a third state's purely rhetorical action in support of peacebuilding may acquire substantive meaning over time. Third states may find themselves normatively entrapped in their own language, as over time they start believing their own discourse, particularly if pronounced in public. Rhetorical action may thus gradually lead to rule-consistent behaviour, as peaceful norms and practices are 'habitualised' through changes in a third state's domestic laws, institutional workings and discursive practices. Once this takes place, the way is opened for domestic opposition groups to gain traction, by joining forces with international and transnational peacebuilding advocates. Ultimately, as and when conflict transformation practices become the 'norm' (i.e., what is considered normal), compliance occurs irrespective of individual beliefs and preferences. Empirical cases that have been explored in this light include the impact of global human rights campaigns in Kenya (in the mid-1980s) and Uganda (in the 1970s and

---

[40] J. Checkel 'Norms, Institutions and National Identity in Contemporary Europe', 43 *International Studies Quarterly* (1999) 83-114.

[41] T. Risse, S. Ropp and K. Sikkink, eds., *The Power of Human Rights – International Norms and Domestic Change* (Cambridge, Cambridge University Press 1999).

1980s), the impact of domestic opposition groups backed by international state and non-state actors in South Africa's transition to democracy, and the impact of transnational advocacy networks in influencing the human rights discourse in Tunisia and Morocco.[42]

The principal channel through which the EU induces socialisation in the field of peacebuilding is its institutionalised dialogues with third states. These can take the form of political dialogues with states with which the Union has established contractual relations, including the Association Councils, Partnership and Cooperation Councils, and Stabilisation and Association Councils. In addition, in the context of contractual relations, socialisation can also take place at parliamentary level, through inter-parliamentary delegations including Members of the European Parliament and parliamentarians from the third state. In other cases, the EU may launch a specific human rights dialogue with a third state, and in 2001 guidelines were established by the Commission to this end. Specific human rights dialogues are held with China as well as with Angola, Botswana, Burkina Faso, Congo, Gabon, Ghana, Kenya, Mauritania, Mozambique, Nigeria, Senegal, South Africa, Swaziland, Uganda and Zimbabwe in the context of the Cotonou Agreement (known as 'Article 8 dialogues'). In the context of these dialogues, the EU has discussed with third states issues such as the signing and ratification of international covenants, the death penalty, torture and ill-treatment, discrimination, children's and women's rights, the freedoms of expression and association, democratisation and good governance.

Socialisation can also take place through other means. Through technical committees, training programmes, twinning and selective participation in EU programmes a third state may be socialised into accepting the EU's professed norms in the sphere of conflict transformation. In addition, under a strengthened ENP, as suggested by the Commission, socialisation can also happen at non-official levels, through educational and youth exchanges, enhanced mobility for researchers, facilitated contact between NGOs, regional and local authorities, and business in the EU and the ENP countries.[43] Finally, socialisation can take place through less cooperative means such as public denunciations and criticisms. The EU often issues Council or Presidency declarations on conflict situations, condemning particular events and publicly advocating solutions. It also issues démarches to third states in response to specific events and practices. These are delivered to the third state by the Troika (i.e., CFSP High Representative, External Relations Commissioner and Presidency) or by the Presidency.

Socialisation, however, is not guaranteed to work, and its success depends on a set of conditioning factors. First, the potential for success depends on the scope and

[42] See H. Schmitz, 'Transnational Activism and Political Change in Kenya and Uganda', D. Black 'The Long and Winding Road: International Norms and Domestic Political Change in South Africa' and S. Granzer, 'Changing Discourse: Transnational Advocacy Networks in Tunisia and Morocco', in Risse, Ropp and Sikkink (eds.), *supra* n. 41.

[43] Commission of the EC, *Communication from the Commission to the Council and the European Parliament on Strengthening the European Neighbourhood Policy*, COM (2006) 726 final, Brussels, 4 December, available at: <http://ec.europa.eu/world/enp/pdf/com06_726_en.pdf>.

intensity of contact between the EU and the third state. In this respect, the looser the EU's ties with a third state, the less effective socialisation is likely to be. Second, socialisation depends on the degree of pre-existing overlap between EU peacebuilding norms and the norms and practices prevailing in a conflict state, as well as on the identification of that state with Europe and its proclaimed values.[44] If, for example, the situation within a conflict country is highly securitised, then particular forms of repression, acts of violence and human rights violations may be accepted in that state as the inevitable response to an existential threat. In these cases, EU arguments, declarations and shamings are dismissed by the third state as the patronising attitude of an international actor who 'doesn't understand' because it has the luxury of living in a Kantian world, or as Kagan would put it, of living on Venus.[45] A last determinant of the scope for learning is the degree of popular dissatisfaction with the status quo and of openness to argumentation, persuasion and change. If the public in a third state is dissatisfied with its leadership, it is more likely to be receptive to the ideas, proposals and recommendations emanating from the EU. This was the case of Rauf Denktaş in northern Cyprus and partly of Slobodan Milosevič's regime in Serbia.

## 2.3 Conditionality

Moving up the ladder in terms of the binding/coercive character of EU peacebuilding mechanisms brings us to conditionality. 'Political conditionality entails the linking, by a state or international organization, of perceived benefits to another state, to the fulfilment of conditions relating to the protection of human rights and the advancement of democratic principles.'[46] Change within a conflict party in terms of its policies, actions and statements thus occurs because the EU's granting or withdrawing of a benefit or its infliction or otherwise of a punishment alters the cost-benefit calculus facing policy makers in conflict contexts.

Conditionality can be positive or negative. Positive conditionality entails the promise of a benefit in return for the fulfilment of a predetermined condition. The Governance Facility in the context of the ENP is a clear example of positive conditionality, as is the granting of EU trade preferences or social, cultural or technological cooperation in the context of EU contractual relations. Negative conditionality involves the infliction of a punishment in the event of the violation of a specified condition. Diplomatic and economic sanctions imposed on Serbia (1991-2000), Syria (1987-94), Libya (1987-92/1999-03), Belarus (1998-99) and Palestine (2006-) are clear cases of negative conditionality inflicted for conflict or human rights-related

---

[44] T. Risse, M. Cowles and J. Caporaso, 'Europeanization and Domestic Change', in T. Risse, M. Cowles and J. Caporaso, eds., *Transforming Europe: Europeanization and Domestic Change* (Ithaca, Cornell University Press 2001) 1-20.

[45] R. Kagan, *Of Paradise and Power: America and Europe in the New World Order* (New York, Alfred A. Knopf 2003).

[46] K. Smith, 'The Use of Political Conditionality in the EU's Relations with Third Countries: How Effective?', 3 *European Foreign Affairs Review* (1998) 253-274, at 256.

issues.[47] Visa bans for third-state senior officials have also been used, such as the EU visa ban on the Transnistrian leadership in 2003. Other punishments include the alteration of the contents or the deferral/cancellation of cooperation programmes, the postponement of meetings or projects, trade embargoes, flight bans, the suspension of high-level contacts and military cooperation, and the freezing of assets in EU Member States.

The fulfilment of conditions can also be *ex ante* or *ex post*, i.e., either conditions are fulfilled before the benefit is granted, or specified conditions must be respected, otherwise the benefit may be lawfully withdrawn or suspended. In between these two extremes, conditionality can be exerted over time, and not exclusively at the time or after the delivery of specified benefits. The case of the 1993 Copenhagen criteria for membership is an example of *ex ante* conditionality, whereby a candidate country is expected to fulfil the Copenhagen political criteria before it is given the green light to begin accession negotiations. The 'human rights clause' in EU contractual agreements (e.g., Article 2 in the AAs, SAAs and PCAs), on the other hand, is an example of *ex post* conditionality, whereby the benefits specified in the contract (e.g., political dialogue, trade preferences, cultural, technical, and scientific cooperation) are granted on the understanding that the essential elements, including human rights, will be respected. The exercise of *ex post* conditionality will thus entail the withdrawal of EU benefits, such as trade preferences or the agreement itself, on the grounds of that third country's violation of specified conditions. Aid, however, lends itself to a constant exercise of conditionality over time, given the divisible nature of the benefit on offer.

These different forms of conditionality involve different costs and benefits.[48] Positive conditionality may provide advantages to the EU as well as to the third state. This can increase the credibility of the promise, given the greater likelihood of its delivery. However, it may also reduce the credibility of an attached condition, in view of the EU's desire to deliver the promised benefit irrespective of the third state's behaviour and the latter's awareness of this fact. Negative conditionality, such as economic sanctions, can lose its credibility when the recipient finds alternative suppliers. While positive incentives can be effective through unilateral action, sanctions often hinge on multilateral efforts, unless the recipient depends on a single supplier. Negative conditionality can also have counterproductive psychological effects, strengthening the recipient's siege mentality and reducing its flexibility and receptiveness to compromise, as appears to have been the case in Gaza and Belarus, where the Hamas authorities and the Lukashenko regime respectively appear to have hardened their positions in reaction to European sanctions.[49] On the other

---

47 On the EU's sanctions policy, see Portela, *supra* n. 11.

48 D. Cortright, 'Incentives and Cooperation in International Affairs', in D. Cortright, ed., *The Price of Peace: Incentives and International Conflict Prevention* (New York, Carnegie Corporation of New York, Rowman and Littlefield 1997) 3-20; and H. Dorussen, 'Mixing Carrots with Sticks: Evaluating the Effectiveness of Positive Incentives', 38 *Journal of Peace Research* (2001) 251-262.

49 On the impact of EU sanctions on Belarus, see C. Portela, 'Sanctions against Belarus', in N. Tocci, et al., *The European Union As a Normative Foreign Policy Actor,* Working Paper 281 (Brus-

hand, negative conditionality can have an important socialising function, signalling the inadmissibility of a particular action.

Irrespective of these pros and cons, in practice the European Union has demonstrated its reluctance to engage in negative and *ex post* conditionality.[50] Sanctions are used sparingly and often target small and far-away states.[51] They are used against neighbours only in response to major security threats (e.g., Syria and Libya for state-sponsored terrorism, former Yugoslavia for war crimes and regional instability, and Belarus for the bad treatment of EU and OSCE diplomats). The Union has also demonstrated its unwillingness to engage in *ex post* conditionality by unilaterally suspending signed agreements. With a few exceptions (e.g., Belarus since 1997, Croatia in 1995-6 and Russia in 1995) the EU has never suspended, in whole or in part, any of its agreements in response to a state's violations of human rights or democracy or because of its conduct in conflict. The 'human rights clause', defining the respect for human rights as an 'essential element' of EU contractual relations and inserted in over 120 such agreements since 1995, can allow for suspension when taken together with the non-execution article. However, the principal aim of the essential elements clause is to create a legal basis for positive engagement on political issues, such as the establishment of human rights dialogues, sub-committees or working groups. The clause has been used as a means to upgrade political, including conflict-related, questions to acceptable subjects of official dialogue, rather than as a vehicle to exert conditionality on third countries.

The Union's preference for positive and *ex ante* conditionality has several reasons. Politically, EU actors are well aware that conditional engagement represents a milder challenge to a third country's sovereignty and is thus more acceptable and less likely to fuel antagonism and inflict harm on the local population. As such, the EU considers that retaining open political channels is a more effective tool to exert influence. Furthermore, the suspension of one association agreement could set a precedent justifying the suspension of many agreements, given that, particularly when it comes to the EU's east and south, most countries are responsible for serious shortcomings in the field of conflict, democracy and human rights. Yet several Member States would object to the widespread use of suspension on the grounds of commercial, political and security interests.

Legally, EU actors highlight the difficulties involved in exerting negative or *ex post* conditionality. When it comes to embargoes and sanctions, EU approval is difficult to obtain due to internal decision-making rules.[52] Legal constraints also

---

sels, Centre for European Policy Studies 2008). On the impact of EU sanctions against Hamas, see N. Tocci, *What Went Wrong? The Impact of Western Policies towards Hamas and Hizbollah*, Policy Brief 135 (Brussels, Centre for European Policy Studies 2007).

[50] Commission of the EC (2001), *supra* n. 5, 8-9; and Commission of the EC, *Reinvigorating EU Actions on Human Rights and Democratisation with Mediterranean Partners*, COM (2003) 294, Brussels, at 11.

[51] K. Smith, *European Union Foreign Policy in a Changing World* (London, Polity Press 2004) at 119, and Portela, *supra* n. 11.

[52] For example, under Article 228a of the Maastricht Treaty, the approval of an embargo or sanction requires first a unanimous common position under CFSP and then an implementing decision under the Common Commercial Policy adopted by qualified majority voting.

discourage the use of *ex post* conditionality, given the stringent conditions that need to be met to justify the suspension of an agreement.[53] The violation of human rights may justify a partial or total suspension of an agreement only if it constitutes a material breach, as defined in Article 60 of the Vienna Convention on the Law of Treaties, i.e., violation of a provision essential to the accomplishment of the object and purpose of the agreement.[54] But the 'object and purpose' of EU contractual agreements is not the promotion of peace, democracy or human rights *per se*, but rather the promotion of free trade, political dialogue and dialogue between societies. Hence, only if a human rights violation hinders these primary aims may *ex post* conditionality represent an adequate response.[55] In addition, the total or partial suspension of an agreement will only be accepted if it passes the legal tests of 'effectiveness' and 'proportionality'. Suspension is thus legally justified only if it constitutes an effective and proportional remedy to a material breach. Finally, under mixed treaties (such as the AAs, PCAs and SAAs) suspension requires the consent of all EU signatories, either through unanimity (TEU Article 310) or qualified majority voting (TEU Article 181) in the Council, depending on the specific treaty provisions to be suspended.

The impact of conditionality on peacebuilding can be direct and indirect. The delivery of EU benefits can be made directly conditional on peacebuilding efforts. For example, the 1995 Stability Pact promoted by French Prime Minister Balladur was intended to diffuse minority and border tensions in the CEECs. Unless the candidates settled their most salient disputes, they would be prevented from opening accession negotiations. Although the Pact was a political and non-legally binding document, its inbuilt incentives promoted agreements between Slovakia and Hungary (1995) and later between Romania and Hungary (1996).[56] It also entrusted the OSCE with a monitoring role and set the precedent for future initiatives such as the Royaumont Process and the Stability Pact for South Eastern Europe in the Balkans.[57] In Cyprus, direct conditionality on the Greek Cypriot side was lifted prior to their EU accession, but was retained for the Turkish Cypriot side, given the EU's policy of non-recognition of the Turkish Republic of Northern Cyprus. Direct conditionality has also been exerted on Turkey, particularly since 1999.

Conditionality can also have an indirect effect on conflicts by affecting policy fields linked to the peacebuilding agenda, which can influence the bargaining positions of the conflict parties. EU demands on Turkey to extend language rights to its

---

[53] B. Brandter and A. Rosas, 'Trade Preferences and Human Rights', in P. Alston, ed., *The EU and Human Rights* (Oxford, Oxford University Press 1999) 699-722.

[54] E. Riedel and M. Will, 'Human Rights Clauses in External Agreements of the EC', in Alston, ed., *supra* n. 53, 723-754.

[55] Euro-Mediterranean Human Rights Network, *A Human Rights Review on the EU and Israel – Mainstreaming or Selectively Extinguishing Human Rights?* (2006), available at: <http://www.euromedrights.net/75>.

[56] See K. Smith, *The Making of EU Foreign Policy, The Case of Eastern Europe* (London, Macmillan 1999).

[57] Ibid.

non-Turkish population affected the state's stance towards the Kurds.[58] Likewise, demands made on Ankara to normalise relations with the Republic of Cyprus had an effect on the evolution of the Cyprus conflict. Finally, the conditional disbursement of aid to the Palestinian Authority for the reform of the fiscal and judicial sectors shaped positions and developments determining the nature of Palestinian governance.

### 2.4 Passive enforcement

A last peacebuilding mechanism at the disposal of the EU, and the most binding in character, is that of passive enforcement. Rather than highlighting the logic of punishment, which sets in when rules are violated and negative conditionality is imposed, this EU mode of foreign policy making hinges on a system of rule-bound cooperation. Unlike conditionality, passive enforcement does not attempt to alter the incentives of a third party by altering its cost-benefit calculus with respect to actions in conflict. The EU benefits are not delivered as a recompense for a third country's compliance with specified conditions, and punishments are not threatened and imposed in order to disincentivise the violation of a condition. Third-state obligations rather constitute the necessary rules and standards making mutually beneficial cooperation with the EU possible. To be effective, passive enforcement requires that the system of peacebuilding-related rules presented by the EU is considered as a necessary price that comes with EU engagement. In the case of a third party whose policies oppose these standards, these rules will initially be viewed as high costs (i.e., infringement on a state's sovereign capacity to unconditionally pursue its perceived interests). In these situations, the process of change embedded in passive enforcement requires that costs are viewed as obligatory and that the third state agrees to undertake them. In doing so and thus by experiencing the respect of the specified rule, its attributed cost could change over time, and the respect of the rule may come to be seen as a benefit.

For passive enforcement to work, there must be a clear set of legally defined and definable peacebuilding-related rules embedded in EU contracts. Passive enforcement cannot be easily used for conditions that the EU simply considers politically desirable but have no legal standing. Hence, for example, passive enforcement is not really suitable to govern minority rights regimes in third countries, given the scarcity of EU and international law on this matter. Likewise, it is far easier for the EU to use passive enforcement in the context of accession, whereby the candidate countries are called upon to implement the legally-binding *acquis* and to respect the European Convention of Human Rights as well as the EU Charter on Fundamental Rights.

When it comes to external relations beyond the confines of enlargement, passive enforcement relies on the rules of customary public international law. Community

[58] See N. Tocci, 'The Europeanization of Turkey's Kurdish Question', in J. Joseph, ed., *Turkey and the European Union* (London Palgrave 2006) 122-137.

law requires that all Community-based agreements with third states are interpreted and implemented in accordance with international law. As such, the EU has the legal obligation to respect the peremptory rules of general international law including international human rights law and international humanitarian law, applicable and relevant in many conflict contexts. This means that it can neither break the rules itself nor assist others in doing so. The EU cannot therefore, through the measures of cooperation embedded in its contractual agreements, acquiesce to a third state's breaking of the peremptory norms of international law by recognising, aiding or assisting in the third state's violations within the confines of its EU agreement. A clear case in point concerns the violation of international humanitarian law in the Occupied Palestinian Territory (OPT) and the EU's obligation to avoid acquiescing to such violations within the context of EU-Israel agreements. Specific examples include the EU's obligation to avoid granting preferential treatment to products originating from Israeli settlements in the OPT, its obligation to avoid granting funds to entities based in Israeli settlements under the Research Framework Programmes, and its obligation to take precautionary measures to avoid that funds channelled to Israel under the European Neighbourhood and Partnership Instrument are used to finance activities (e.g., infrastructure) in the OPT. Respecting these obligations does not constitute a policy of conditionality. It rather entails respecting the rules inherent in the EU's own legal system that allow mutually beneficial cooperation with third states. Aware of this, the EU acts out of duty rather than out of choice – thus avoiding political discretion, which often entails a selective application of human rights norms. The third party, aware of the EU's lack of choice on these matters, is thus disinclined to try and lure the EU into neglecting those norms, accepting them instead as obligatory and non-negotiable.

## 3. The EU as a peacebuilder: Potential and limits

What factors determine whether these four policy mechanisms are effective in promoting peacebuilding in third states? Two principal conditions can be identified.

### 3.1 The value of the benefit

First, an effective peacebuilding policy depends on the value of the benefits which the EU has on offer, mapped against the costs of compliance with EU peacebuilding standards, conditions, norms and obligations.[59] Only if the potential gains relative to the costs are sufficiently high can the Union meaningfully exert influence in conflict contexts. Value is determined by the objective nature of the contract. Naturally, when full membership is an option, the EU's potential leverage on conflict countries and its ability to exert conditionality on them is higher than in cases where

[59] F. Schimmelfennig, S. Engert and H. Knobel, *Costs, Commitment and Compliance*, EUI Working Paper Series 29 (Florence 2002).

relations are based on association, partnership or financial assistance. This begs the question of whether the EU can significantly influence third states that it cannot or does not wish to fully integrate. Indeed, this is the core dilemma underlying the ENP, which was born precisely to find an alternative to full membership for aspirant EU members.[60]

The carrots on offer also depend on the degree of proximity of the third country to the Union. The closer the EU is to a conflict – and thus the greater the EU's potential interest in it – the more likely it is to engage in peacebuilding; hence, the EU's relative engagement in the Western Balkans since the 1999 Kosovo war, compared with its relative neglect of conflicts in the South Caucasus or Central Asia. Proximity is also more likely to trigger a sense of urgency to act in moments of crisis, given the greater visibility of a conflict and the more likely its spillover effects into the EU. This may induce a greater EU effort to reach consensus on the forms and modalities of intervention.[61]

The value of the benefit and in particular the distinction between membership and non-membership also affects the potential for socialisation. The key question here is whether socialisation can take place beyond the EU borders, where EU institutional, political, economic and social contact is limited and confined almost exclusively to third-country elites. The question becomes all the more pertinent given that as opposed to reaching inter-elite settlements, conflict transformation calls for a deep-rooted change in the public's attitudes and positions, which does not necessarily occur in response to the workings of elite-driven multilateral institutions.

Finally, the objective value of contractual relations affects the prospects for passive enforcement. As mentioned above, passive enforcement requires that rules are legally defined and definable. As such, passive enforcement can more easily be applied to the accession process than to looser forms of association. In the case of accession, EU institutions have at their disposal thousands of pages of legally binding *acquis*, which candidates are called upon to adopt and implement. Some of the rules embedded in the accession process can have a direct or indirect effect on peacebuilding efforts. In the case of looser forms of association, however, the EU has much less 'material' at hand. It can rely on passive enforcement only when these rules either have a basis in international law (such as in the case of Israeli settlements in the OPT) or relate to the existing legal obligations of the third state (derived from its membership of the UN or the Council of Europe; for example, Turkey's obligation to respect the judgments handed down by the European Court of Human Rights regarding, *inter alia*, the Cyprus conflict).

Beyond the objective value of EU benefits, their subjective value, i.e., the value of EU relations as perceived by the third state, is equally important. Whereas member-

---

[60] J. Kelley, 'New Wine in Old Wineskins: Promoting Political Reforms through the ENP', 44 *Journal of Common Market Studies* (2006) 29-58; M. Comelli, E. Greco and N. Tocci, 'From Boundary to Borderland: Transforming the Meaning of Borders in Europe through the European Neighbourhood Policy', 12 *European Foreign Affairs Review* (2007) 203-218.

[61] Hill, *supra* n. 28.

ship may be the most valuable offer the Union can make, it may be of little interest to a nationalist jealously guarding his/her country's sovereignty and seeking international alliances elsewhere. By contrast, the more a third state identifies with 'Europe', or the more it is dependent upon it, the greater the EU's potential to influence its actions in conflict. However, different actors within a third country may value EU benefits differently. Domestic actors have different aims, strategies and tactics, which are driven by different historical, economic and political interests and beliefs. As such, their assessment of the EU differs. Hence, depending on the internal balance of different actors and their interaction, the overall effect of EU peacebuilding mechanisms can be positive, negative or nil.

Another important determinant is timing. In the case of *ex ante* conditionality, reforms are expected and demanded in the short and medium term but the actual delivery of the benefit occurs in the long term. This generates a set of problems. Long-term benefits are valued less than short-term ones. The unpredictability of the long term reduces the value of the benefit and therefore the potential incentive for peacebuilding. The time lag between the demanded conditions and the subsequent delivery of the benefit may also induce policy makers in conflict countries to delay policy changes until the delivery of the benefit is closer and surer. In other situations, however, the opposite problem may arise. When the benefit is delivered in the short term based on the understanding that respect of its essential elements will follow, its value is absorbed by the recipient party, inducing it to avoid or postpone the respect of human rights, counting on the EU's unwillingness to withdraw the delivered carrot. The case of Turkey highlights this double problem of timing. Whereas the long-term and uncertain prospect of Turkey's full membership, pushed back at least until after 2014, has reduced Turkey's incentive to pursue reforms in the short and medium term, the delivery of the interim 'carrot' of the opening of accession negotiations in 2005 also had a disincentivising effect. First, progress of accession negotiations is not directly related to progress in political reforms. While benchmarks are set for the opening and provisional closure of each negotiation chapter, the relevant benchmarks relate to the substance of the chapter in question. With the exception of the chapter on 'judiciary and fundamental rights', the nuts and bolts of negotiations are thus disconnected from issues relating to democracy, human rights and the Kurdish question. Second, with the opening of negotiations, the timeframe for the delivery of the next 'carrot' has been shifted to a long-term and uncertain future. The opening of accession negotiations was a short-term objective, whose immediacy provided reformist forces in Turkey with an important incentive to pursue controversial political reforms in 2001-2005. Now that the delivery of the next carrot, i.e., that of membership itself, has shifted beyond 2014, the external incentives to pursue political change in the short to medium term have significantly reduced.

### 3.2 The credibility of the EU as a peacebuilder

Second, the effectiveness of EU peacebuilding mechanisms hinges on the credibility of the EU and the conditions or obligations it demands. Credibility depends on a third state's perception of the EU's capacity and will to carry out its declared commitments in the sphere of peacebuilding. In the case of *ex ante* conditionality, credibility is thus related to the Union's track record in delivering its promised benefits when and only when the specified conditions are fulfilled; whereas in the case of *ex post* conditionality, credibility is related to the EU's track record in withdrawing benefits in cases of serious consistent violations. Credibility in passive enforcement, however, entails cooperating when and only when the human rights rules governing engagement are respected. Credibility also impinges on the potential for socialisation, given that a particular norm is more likely to be assimilated when all parties, including the EU, are steadfast in their respect of it.

The EU often falls short in terms of credibility, thus losing its effectiveness, when the conduct of its external relations is determined by political imperatives, operating beyond the blueprint of a contract, *and* the third state in question is aware of this. An effective EU peacebuilding policy would necessitate automatic entitlement to rights and benefits when obligations are fulfilled and automatic withdrawal of or non-entitlement to benefits when they are not. Yet there is never such automaticity in practice. Beyond the contract lie the political imperatives of EU actors, which go beyond the promotion of peace, human rights and international law. Both the granting and the withdrawal of a benefit require consensus within the Union. For an association agreement or an accession treaty to come into force, there must be unanimity of the member governments and ratification by national parliaments and the EP. Such consensus depends on the fulfilment of conflict countries' promises and obligations vis-à-vis the EU. But it also depends on other factors that are motivated by underlying political or economic imperatives. Hence, for example, EU policy in the Caucasus and towards Georgia's conflicts in particular is heavily conditioned by the EU's and particular Member States' sensitivities towards Russia based on geopolitical as well as energy security reasons. In the Middle East, on the other hand, several Member States view the protection of Israel and close relations with it as being of the utmost priority, over and above the interests of promoting a resolution of the Israeli-Palestinian conflict. Europe's history of anti-Semitism has generated a deep-felt EU preference – particularly within some Member States – to maintain close relations with Israel irrespective of its conduct. In addition, EU economic interests in Israel make EU actors receptive to Israeli arguments to set aside the conflict in the conduct of bilateral relations. Another EU priority in the Middle East is to seek close, cooperative and complementary relations with the US, which has generated strong EU incentives, felt particularly by Atlanticist Member States, to accommodate American interests, strategies and policies in the conflict.

The credibility of the EU's contractual relations depends critically on the structure of the wider relationship with the third country. When a third country is highly dependent on the EU, the latter is more likely to stick to the formal and specified conditions included in the contract. When, however, the wider relationship is governed by ties of mutual dependence, as is often the case vis-à-vis major powers as well as important neighbours, then the third country can exert leverage on the EU to obtain the promised benefits without fulfilling its obligations.

Some degree of political management in determining when and whether conditions are met and when and whether benefits should be granted is inevitable. However, when blatant violations persist without consequences or when benefits are not granted despite the general fulfilment of specified EU norms and recommendations, the EU's credibility is harmed. In other words, when other conditions unspecified in the EU's policies govern its relations with conflict countries, then its role as a peacebuilder loses clout.

## 4. Conclusions

The EU has a wide array of policy instruments enabling it to act as a peacebuilder in its near and far abroads. Within the remit of the CFSP and CSDP, it can mobilise a set of short to medium-term instruments in the fields of diplomacy, security and the rule of law typically aimed at short to medium-term crisis management actions. Moving beyond the confines of the CFSP/CSDP, the Union can mobilise assistance for and contractual relations with third countries in a set of regions worldwide. The peacebuilding mechanisms embedded in these policy instruments are directed at two root causes of conflict: deficient capabilities and deficient incentives within conflict contexts. EU financial and technical assistance, typically within the remit of the Treaty on the Functioning of the EU (TFEU), and CFSP/CSDP within the TEU, directly tackles conflicts by assisting the socio-economic, political and societal development within conflict countries. By contrast, EU policies of conditionality, socialisation and passive enforcement aim at altering the underlying incentive structures within conflict contexts.

These peacebuilding instruments and mechanisms and the value they entail for conflict parties often grant the Union considerable potential to promote peace. However, this potential is frequently marred by the wavering credibility of the EU and its policies in conflict contexts. Shaky credibility is often caused or influenced by the EU's political management of contractual relations. By contaminating EU peacebuilding policies with political precepts that fall beyond peacebuilding strategies, the EU frequently punches well beneath its weight as a peacebuilder. Political determinants influencing the conduct of EU contractual relations are sometimes explained by the EU's neglect of a particular conflict. This has been the case in Cyprus and the South Caucasus, and is even truer for conflicts further afield. In other cases, political determinants are related to other national or EU-wide interests beyond conflict resolution, as is evident in conflicts such as those in the Middle East. Indeed, whereas in theory the EU's pursuit of normative goals shapes the external environment in a manner conducive to the accomplishment of its strategic goals, in practice, the pursuit of narrow interests often hinders the EU's potential to advance those peacebuilding goals that reflect the values on which the Union is founded.

# Chapter 3
# EU ENLARGEMENT AS A PEACEBUILDING TOOL

**Steven Blockmans***

## 1. Building peace across the continent

Over a period of more than fifty years, the European Communities of the 1950s have gradually and peacefully expanded to cover almost the entire continent and have been granted the powers to form the strongest union of free and prosperous states that Europe has ever seen. The most recent enlargements of the European Union have made a reality of Robert Schuman's vision of a united and peaceful continent. Originally comprising only 6 Western European states, the EU currently has 27 members and provides a common roof not only for a Catholic, Protestant, Orthodox and Islamic population, but also for a Latin, Germanic, Celtic and Slavic Europe. A peacebuilding process *an sich*, EU enlargement has been dubbed the most successful of the Union's foreign policies, one of immense transformative power. The progressive economic integration and peaceful spread of the rule of law and democracy has seen the shattered societies in the aftermath of the Second World War and the defunct police states in the wake of the Cold War transform into open, secure, stable, prosperous and dynamic democracies. The Union's enlargement policy towards South Eastern Europe continues to provide a successful example of peaceful and durable regime change and post-conflict rehabilitation. Today, this is nowhere more visible than in the post-war region of the Western Balkans.

This chapter looks at the EU enlargement process as a peacebuilding tool. More in particular, it pays attention to one of the central tenets in the emerging doctrine of international peacebuilding, i.e., the belief that the key to successful peacebuilding lies within the (best) practice of state building (section 2).[1] In the EU context, this translates into the process of 'Member State building',[2] which has distinct features

* Senior Research Fellow in EU law at T.M.C. Asser Institute (The Hague) and academic coordinator of the Centre for the Law of EU External Relations (<http://www.cleer.eu>).

[1] See, for example, F. Fukuyama, *State-Building: Governance and World Order in the 21st Century* (Ithaca, Cornell University Press 2004); G. Bächler, *Conflict Transformation through State Reform* (Berlin, Berghof Research Centre for Constructive Conflict Management 2004); H. Fischer and N. Quénivet, eds., *Post-Conflict Reconstruction: Nation- and/or State-Building* (Berlin, BWV 2005); C. Call and E. Cousens, *Ending Wars and Building Peace*, Working Paper, 12 March 2007; C. Call and V. Wyeth, eds., *Building States to Build Peace* (New York, IPI 2008).

[2] The term was coined by G. Knaus and M. Cox, 'The "Helsinki Moment" in Southeastern Europe', 14 *Journal of Democracy* (2005) 39-53.

*S. Blockmans, J. Wouters & T. Ruys, eds., The European Union and Peacebuilding*

when compared to the mechanisms deployed by the international community in other parts of the world. The objective of the EU's strategy is not 'simply' to build stable, legitimate states whose own citizens will seek to strengthen and not to destroy, but rather to establish states that the European Union can accept as full members with absolute confidence. It concerns a process of the kind undertaken by the Union prior to its most recent enlargement waves to include the post-communist states of Central and Eastern Europe (2004 and 2007), and one promoted for the integration of the Western Balkans.[3] Like 'Member State building', this chapter rests on the following building blocks: legal approximation (section 3), institution building (section 4) and constituency building (section 5).[4] A few closing remarks will wrap up this contribution (section 6).

## 2. (Member) State building, epitome of (EU) peacebuilding

There are various accounts of the emergence of the state-building agenda. A comprehensive account has been given by Roland Paris in his book *At War's End: Building Peace after Civil Conflict.*[5] According to Paris, state building is an incipient approach to post-conflict reconstruction, with roots in the failures and limits of what he labels the 'liberal peace approach'. The latter has two main pillars: liberalisation (of markets) and democratisation. According to Paris, the liberal peace was the underlying idea driving the expansion of the activities of various international organisations, above all the UN. This expansion took place in the early post-Cold War period, continued throughout the 1990s, and was given the label 'peace-building',[6] so as to differentiate it from the classical peacekeeping operations that were run throughout the Cold War period. From Paris's argument, it is obvious that there are some elements of liberal peacebuilding in current 'state-building' activities.[7] Considering the wide range of activities that today fall under the heading of state building, defined by Fukuyama as the 'creation from whole

---

[3] International Commission on the Balkans, *The Balkans in Europe's Future* (Sofia, CLS 2005).

[4] On the spoils of war, economic revitalisation and 'Europeanisation', suffice it to refer to M. Kaldor, V. Bojièić and I. Vejvoda, 'Reconstruction in the Balkans: A Challenge for Europe?', 2 *EFA Rev.* (1997) 329-350; V. Gligorov, M. Kaldor and L. Tsoukalis, *Balkan Reconstruction and European Integration*, WIIW Policy Paper (October 1999); and DG ECFIN's annual *Western Balkans in Transition* reports in the Enlargement Papers series.

[5] R. Paris, *At War's End: Building Peace after Civil Conflict* (Cambridge, CUP 2004).

[6] See the contribution by Duke and Courtier to this volume. For an explanation about the use (or lack) of the hyphen in the term 'peace-building', see note 3 in the contribution by Gourlay to this volume.

[7] M. Daoudy, 'State-Building', in V. Chetail, ed., *Post-Conflict Peacebuilding: A Lexicon* (Oxford, OUP 2009) 350-358, at 350, gives the following definition: 'State-building falls within the scope of international programmes through which bilateral or multilateral agencies mobilize resources in order to set up or reinforce weakened or non-existent institutions in those states that are considered to be fragile, weak, moving towards failure, or which have already collapsed. The objective is to build peace and promote security through the political, economic, and social development of states either threatened or affected by violent conflicts.'

cloth missing state capabilities and institutions',[8] it is clear that peacebuilding in many ways set the scene for what was to follow. However, Paris's argument goes further. He claims that peacebuilding, driven by the liberal peace ideology, was based upon a mistaken assumption, namely that of the existence of a functioning state:

> 'By taking the existence of a working government for granted, many scholars have effectively "assumed away" one of the most difficult and important problems that peacebuilders confront in their field of operations: namely, how to establish functioning governments and stable nonviolent politics in conditions of virtual anarchy.'[9]

For Paris, the lesson of the liberal tradition is that

> 'successful state-building [calls for] a careful balancing of two competing imperatives: limiting the power of the state in order to preserve individual liberty, and endowing government with sufficient means to uphold the rule of law and protect the constitutional order itself against foreign and domestic threats.'[10]

As a result, the attempt to push through liberalisation and democratisation, without first working out how to get a functioning government in place, has only tended to exacerbate conflicts or to introduce a fragile truce that cannot serve as a basis for an enduring peace. Paris's alternative is what he calls 'IBL' – institutionalisation before liberalisation. This means focusing on institution building before opening up both economic and political institutions to the dynamics of competition – the market, in the case of the economy, and pluralist party politics in the case of the political system. Arguably, this makes it possible to firmly entrench the integrative forces of institutions before exposing a country to the disintegrative forces of the liberal peace agenda.

In his observation of a shift towards the model of IBL, Paris is effectively charting the emergence of state building as defined by Fukuyama above. In his words,

> 'recent missions in Kosovo, East Timor and Sierra Leone suggest that international agencies have begun to embrace longer term, more interventionist forms of post-conflict peacebuilding that place greater emphasis on institutional reconstruction and on more gradual and controlled approaches to liberalisation.'[11]

In essence, this analysis suggests that the emergence of the state-building agenda above all reflects a learning process on the part of international institutions. Experiences in intervention, from Angola and Bosnia and Herzegovina to Guatemala, have taught the United Nations and the myriad of other international organisations and agencies involved the limits of pursuing a liberalisation and democratisation

---

8 Fukuyama, *supra* n. 1, at xii.
9 Paris, *supra* n. 5, at 46-47.
10 Ibid., at 50.
11 Ibid., at 225.

agenda without strengthening domestic state institutions first. Problems include the reinforcement of ethnic divisions in the cases of Bosnia and Croatia.[12]

Arguably, Paris is right to suggest that institutions such as the UN have moved towards state building in part as a result of experiences in the 1990s. However, what intervening states and international organisations wrongly assumed was not the inexistence of a functioning state in the post-conflict country. Rather, they assumed the existence of the combined power and capabilities of the international community itself. In other words, the liberal peace ideology took for granted the willingness of Western states to substitute themselves for the recipient state. This assumption has led to many a disappointment.[13]

A notable exception is the case of EU enlargement. The reunification of Europe, by way of the European integration process and the EU's enlargement policy, is one of the few unambiguously positive achievements of the post-Cold War world, and nothing short of revolutionary.[14] Elsewhere in this volume, Duke and Courtier have been more cautious in extolling the success of EU 'peacebuilding' through enlargement. After all, the Member States' incapacity to adopt a common approach and their subsequent inability to use the accession process to resolve territorial disputes involving candidate countries (e.g., the Cyprus issue and the maritime border demarcation between Slovenia and Croatia) has marred the EU's image as a peacebuilder.[15]

Evaluations aside, the fact remains that the European Union has put state building at the centre of its enlargement policy. In fact, the Union has gradually elevated it to a new form of art: 'Member State building'.[16] In little over a decade, the prospect of EU membership succeeded in consolidating democratic and market reforms and transforming post-Cold War societies throughout Central and Eastern Europe. Former European Commissioner for Enlargement Olli Rehn liked to repeat that the EU could do the same for the Western Balkans.[17] While one may hope this to be true, there are, however, five critical differences compared to previous pre-accession rounds:

(i) post-conflict tensions (e.g., in Bosnia and Herzegovina, Kosovo and Macedonia);

---

[12] Ibid., chapter 6.

[13] As set out later in R. Paris and T. Sisk, eds., *The Dilemmas of Statebuilding: Confronting the Contradictions of Postwar Peace Operations* (London, Routledge 2009).

[14] See S. Everts, *An Asset But Not a Model: Turkey, the EU and the Wider Middle East*, CER Essays (October 2004).

[15] See also S. Blockmans, 'The EU and Conflict Resolution: De Facto States in the Neighbourhood', in F. Laursen ed., *The EU As a Foreign and Security Policy Actor* (Dordrecht, Republic of Letters Publishing 2009) 115-145.

[16] See *supra* n. 2, and ESI, *The Helsinki Moment – European Member State Building in the Balkans* (Berlin, ESI 2005).

[17] See, e.g., 'EU Enlargement 2009: A Balance Sheet and Way Forward', speech by Mr Olli Rehn, EU Commissioner for Enlargement at the Foreign Affairs Committee of the European Parliament, Brussels, 2 September 2009 (SPEECH/09/358); and O. Rehn, 'The Balkans Remains the EU's Litmus Test', *European Voice*, 12 November 2009.

(ii) unresolved questions of sovereignty (e.g., in Bosnia and Herzegovina and in Kosovo, both still international protectorates) and of borders (e.g., those involving Serbia and Kosovo);
(iii) chronically weak and failing states (e.g., Albania and Bosnia and Herzegovina);
(iv) the Union's lack of experience in integrating such states; and
(v) the presence of other – powerful – international actors on the ground.

Enlargement of the Union with most countries of the Western Balkans is therefore not a matter of business as usual: international issues have to be resolved; constitutions have to be revamped; legal orders have to be strengthened; functioning state institutions have to be developed; the quality of political representation has to be improved; and the economy has to be reformed.[18]

## 3. Legal reform

### 3.1 Peace brokering and constitution-making

The design of a constitution and the constitution-making process can play an important role in the political and governance transition of a country in the post-conflict phase. After all, constitution making is an opportunity to create a common vision of the future of a state and to adopt a road map on how to get there. However, it is also a particularly difficult aspect of peacebuilding, both because there is little understanding of the impact of constitutional processes and constitutional designs in post-conflict states and because the corresponding decisions must be made in highly charged, divided and often still violent environments.[19] Moreover, 'the short-term security concerns of the bargaining parties may be at odds with the long-term institution building needs of the society.'[20] The more participatory and inclusive processes tend to broaden the constitutional agenda and prevent the constitution-making process from degenerating into a mere division of spoils between powerful players. At the same time, such constitutions tend to threaten the established power structures. The key dilemma is therefore how to ensure that the powerful players participate in and are committed to the process, yet also guarantee that the process fosters political dialogue and empowers the people. After all, durable forms of constitutional design and executive power sharing are achieved on an inclusive and voluntary basis. In their contribution to this volume, Humphreys and Jelisiæ point to the inherent weaknesses of the Constitution of Bosnia and Herzegovina, as enshrined in the Dayton/Paris Accords, and the lack of progress since its adoption:

---

18 See S. Blockmans, *Tough Love: The European Union's Relations with the Western Balkans* (The Hague, T.M.C. Asser Press 2007), at 330-336; and *supra* n. 4.

19 See K. Samuels, 'Post-Conflict Peace-Building and Constitution-Making', 6 *Chicago Journal of International Law* (2006) 663-681, at 680-681.

20 D. Rothchild, 'Settlement Terms and Postagreement Stability', in S. Stedman, D. Rothchild and E. Cousens, eds., *Ending Civil Wars: The Implementation of Peace Agreements* (Boulder, Lynne Rienner 2002), at 117-118.

> 'The failure of the constitutional reform process in April 2006 is generally seen by both the national and international community as the key factor leading to the freezing of all significant progress for the next three years. As a compromise package it was not ambitious and did not tackle the more fundamental issue of the entity-blocking mechanisms. However, there is no doubt that if the constitutional reform process had succeeded, it would have provided a new and enormously strengthened impetus to the state-building exercise, and its failure paved the way for the return of nationalist confrontational politics in the lead-up to and aftermath of the October 2006 elections.'

An ideal constitution-making process can accomplish several things: it can drive the transformative process from conflict to peace, seek to transform the society from one that resorts to violence to one that uses political means to resolve conflict, and/or shape the governance framework that will regulate access to power and resources – all key reasons for conflict.[21] It can also put in place mechanisms and institutions through which future conflict in society can be managed without a return to violence. The constitution can be partly a peace agreement and partly a framework setting up the rules by which the new democracy will operate. Examples from the Western Balkans include the 1995 Dayton/Paris Accords,[22] United Nations Security Council Resolution 1244 (1999) for Kosovo[23] and the 2001 Ohrid Framework Agreement for Macedonia.[24] The latter came about thanks to an international effort under the leadership of SG/HR Solana, who used the immediate prospect of the conclusion of a Stabilisation and Association Agreement and the future perspective of EU membership as leverage to strike a deal.

### 3.2 Constitutional reform

The EU has proven to wield great indirect – soft – power over constitutional reform processes in the post-(Cold) war, pre-accession states of Central and Eastern Europe. Since much has already been written about this,[25] the discussion here will be restricted to a single point.

The constitutions of the above-mentioned countries set forth complex provisions and safeguards for the protection of sovereignty and independence, and most

---

[21] See Samuels, *supra* n. 19, at 664.

[22] See R. Holbrooke, *To End a War* (New York, Random House 1998).

[23] See M. Weller, *Contested Statehood: Kosovo's Struggle for Independence* (Oxford, OUP 2009) and the contribution by Keukeleire and Thiers to the present volume.

[24] See Blockmans, *supra* n. 18, at 189-199. Strictly speaking, the 2002 Belgrade Agreement, which provided a constitutional settlement to keep Serbia and Montenegro together, did not follow an armed conflict between the composite republics. Rather, it provided a framework for preventing conflict and for peaceful dissolution after a cooling-off period of 3 years. Ibid., at 199-207.

[25] See, e.g., B. de Witte, 'Constitutional Aspects of European Union Membership in the Original Six Member States: Model Solutions for the Applicant Countries?', in A. Kellermann, J. de Zwaan and J. Czuczai, eds., *EU Enlargement: The Constitutional Impact at EU and National Level* (The Hague, T.M.C. Asser Press 2001) 65-79; F. Jacobs, 'The Constitutional Impact of the Forthcoming Enlargement of the EU: What Can Be Learnt from the Experience of the Existing Member States?', ibid., 183-191; and – most comprehensively – A. Albi, *EU Enlargement and the Constitutions of Central and Eastern Europe* (Cambridge, CUP 2005).

of them did not – for understandable reasons – initially contain provisions concerning the delegation of powers to international organisations.[26] Although at the time of their adoption (i.e., one or two years after the fall of the Berlin Wall) they were progressive documents establishing democratic frameworks and protection of fundamental rights, they failed to provide mechanisms that could accommodate European integration. Whereas the constitutions of the early 1990s did contain provisions on the application of international law, these provisions were not considered to be sufficient to authorise membership of the EU. Moreover, the proclaimed supremacy of the constitutions and – in some cases – the procedures for preliminary constitutional review of treaties and international agreements stood in the way of the full application of two 'supra-constitutional' principles of EU law: primacy and direct effect.[27] As the countries of Central and Eastern Europe moved closer to the European Union, constitutional review processes got underway to eliminate the obstacles to EU accession and prepare for the incorporation of EU law into the domestic legal systems. In some cases, this led to minor revisions, in others the process resulted in the adoption of so-called EU, Europe or Euro-Atlantic integration clauses.[28] Similar constitutional redesigning processes have been or will be undertaken in the Western Balkans.

### 3.3 Approximation of laws to the *acquis*

#### 3.3.1 *More than just legal harmonisation*

Reinforcing the institutional and administrative capacity of applicant countries is a key requirement for enlargement if these countries are to be in a position to adopt, implement and comply with the EU *acquis*. The approximation *and* creation of domestic laws that meet EU standards therefore require modernisation of their administrations and judiciaries, taking account of the principles of professionalism and neutrality. Preparing for EU membership requires in-depth changes across a broad range of sectors in many of the institutions and organisations involved in the legislative and enforcement process (see section 4 below).

#### 3.3.2 *Planning documents and institutional mechanisms*

All (potential) candidate countries are engaged in the harmonisation of their national legislation with the *acquis* of the Union. They are implementing EU law on

---

26 The Lithuanian Constitution was a notable exception.

27 For implicit references to the peacebuilding logic behind the ECJ's conception of the principle of supremacy of EC (now EU) law, see E. Stein, 'Toward Supremacy of Treaty-Constitution by Judicial Fiat: On the Margin of the Costa Case', 63 *Michigan Law Review* (1965) 491-518, especially at 516-518; and B. de Witte, 'Direct Effect, Supremacy, and the Nature of the Legal Order', in P. Craig and G. de Búrca, eds., *The Evolution of EU Law* (Oxford, OUP 1999) 177-213, at 200 and 208-210. For a powerful post-war argument for supremacy of international law in its fullest sense, see F. Morgenstern, 'Judicial Practice and the Supremacy of International Law', 27 *British Yearbook of International Law* (1950), at 91.

28 See Albi, *supra* n. 25, Chapter 5.

the basis of the conditions laid down in their respective (Stabilisation and) Association Agreements.[29] In all associate countries guidelines have been developed for the implementation of the reforms that these countries are expected to carry out on their way to membership. Each country must lay down these guidelines in a so-called National Programme for the Adoption of the *Acquis* (NPAA).[30] These programmes are primarily aimed at fulfilling the obligations undertaken under the (Stabilisation and) Association Agreements. At the same time, the NPAA serves as a road map by which the governments can realistically assess their capacities, and those of society as a whole, (i) to implement all measures and actions necessary for accession to the EU, (ii) to meet the political and economic criteria, (iii) to transpose and apply the *acquis*, and (iv) to reform public administration. This road map is backed up by a financial quantification of the efforts towards alignment and integration over a specific period of time. The NPAA sets out assessments, guidelines and tasks, with the intention that all relevant activities will prepare the candidate for full EU membership.

In each of the associate countries, interministerial working groups for the harmonisation of the national legislation with the *acquis* have been (or will be) established pursuant to the (now 35) chapters under negotiation. The work of these working groups greatly contributes to the process of harmonisation of legislation and the adoption of common standpoints to resolve essential issues, and considerably accelerates the legislative procedures at government level. The Ministry of European Integration, or its equivalent (see section 4.1.2 below), is the coordinating body in the process of the harmonisation of laws and, in regular government procedure, assesses the degree of harmonisation of draft legislation with the relevant provisions of the *acquis*. Recognising the importance of the process of harmonising the legislation, the government of Croatia, on the basis of its rules of procedure, introduced a procedural novelty whereby the opinion of the Ministry of Foreign Affairs and European Integration has to be attached to draft laws and pro-

[29] See, e.g., Article 70(1) SAA Albania: 'The Parties recognise the importance of the approximation of Albania's existing legislation to that of the Community and of its effective implementation. Albania shall endeavour to ensure that its existing laws and future legislation shall be gradually made compatible with the Community *acquis*. Albania shall ensure that existing and future legislation shall be properly implemented and enforced.' At the time of writing, the SAAs with FYROM (*OJ* 2004 L 84/13), Croatia (*OJ* 2005 L 26/3) and Albania (*OJ* 2009 L 107/166) had entered into force, while those with Bosnia and Herzegovina, Montenegro and Serbia were awaiting full ratification. See also the Agreement of 12 September 1963 establishing an Association between the European Economic Community and Turkey (*OJ* 1977 L 361/29), in combination with Chapter IV of Decision No. 1/95 of the EC-Turkey Association Council (*OJ* 1996 L 35/1).

[30] The document has different names in several (potential) candidate countries, e.g., 'National Plan for the Implementation of the Stabilisation and Association Agreement' (NPISAA) in Albania. Notwithstanding the fact that 'their' SAAs have not yet entered into force, other countries included in the Stabilisation and Association Process have already taken steps towards approximating domestic legislation to the EU *acquis*. An example is the adoption of a special Action Plan for the Harmonisation of Laws of the Republic of Serbia with EU law, which called for the fast-track adoption or amendment of 50 priority laws in the internal market sphere ahead of the entry into force of the Interim Agreement on trade and trade-related matters.

posals for other regulations. The Committee for European Integration of the Croatian Parliament also plays a key role in the legislative process. In keeping with the Decision on the Measures in the Procedure of Harmonising the Legislation of the Republic of Croatia with the *Acquis*, state administration bodies, in the preparation of legislative documents which harmonise Croatia's legislation with the *acquis* pursuant to Article 69 of the SAA, are obliged to submit, together with the draft act, a completed statement on the degree of harmonisation and a parallel review of the conformity of the provisions of the draft act with those of the relevant legal acts of the EU (compatibility statement). In Albania, the Ministry of Justice closely cooperated with the Ministry of European Integration to revamp the administration's Law Drafting Manual so as to take account of the specificities of the techniques of drafting national legislation that is in line with the EU *acquis*.

In addition to creating a string of planning documents and central bodies for coordination, each of the (potential) candidate countries has witnessed a proliferation of independent or semi-autonomous institutions tasked with ensuring the effective implementation of adopted legislation. In this respect, one can think of national competition authorities, standardisation and certification bodies, data protection agencies, consumer protection councils, etc. However, whether the proliferation of such institutions may serve to reverse the widening gap between the progress achieved in the approximation of laws in most project countries, on the one hand, and the ability of the administrations to implement and enforce the newly adopted legislation on the other, remains to be seen.

The harmonisation process itself first involves legislation on the basic elements of the internal market, trade and trade-related areas (public procurement, competition and state aid, technical legislation, consumer protection and intellectual property, and industrial and commercial property), and later other elements of the *acquis* referred to in the (S)AA.[31] The difficulties which (potential) candidate countries generally face in the translation of the *acquis* into their national legal orders have become apparent in the wake of the EU's big bang enlargement of May 2004.[32]

### 3.3.3 *Technical and financial assistance*

As part of the Stabilisation and Association Process, a technical mechanism has been established to monitor the development of legislative reform (called the 'matrix', which offers an overview of the state of the legislation). Technical assistance is available to the (potential) candidate countries under the so-called Instrument for Pre-Accession Assistance (IPA) for the period covered by the financial perspective

---

[31] Turkey is the only candidate country which started to implement a customs union before actual EU integration.

[32] See M. Bobek, 'The Binding Force of Babel: The Enforcement of EC Law Unpublished in the Languages of the New Member States', 9 *Cambridge Yearbook of European Legal Studies* (2007) 43-80. For a concrete example of what can go wrong, see A. Łazowski and A. Wentkowska, 'Poland: Constitutional Drama and Business As Usual', in A. Łazowski, ed., *The Application of EU Law in the New Member States: Brave New World* (The Hague, T.M.C. Asser Press 2010 forthcoming).

for 2007-2013.[33] Activities focus on the weaknesses identified at the central, regional and local level, particularly in view of the increased emphasis given to economic and social cohesion. Technical assistance concerns two areas of action: transfer of know-how and technical assistance involving investment. The former is defined as the process of helping the partner countries to develop the structures, strategies, human resources and management skills needed to strengthen their economic, social, regulatory and administrative capacity. Significant resources are allocated for this purpose and are mainly deployed and implemented with Member States through the instrument of , and . This assistance is provided specifically to implement the *acquis* and to prepare for participation in EU policies, as well as to fulfil the requirements of the Copenhagen political criterion (i.e., the stability of institutions guaranteeing democracy, the rule of law, human rights and respect for and protection of minorities).

Under the rules of the IPA Regulation, pre-accession assistance is not automatically and fully made available to the potential candidate countries. Section 1 of the Explanatory Memorandum to the IPA Regulation states that the potential candidates are to be offered a continuation of the same kinds of assistance provided previously:

> 'Potential Candidate Countries will continue to receive assistance along the lines currently laid down in the CARDS Regulation: Institution Building and Democratisation, Economic and Social Development, Regional and Cross-Border Co-operation and some alignment with the [*acquis*], in particular where this is in the mutual interest of the EU and the beneficiary country.'

The official candidates, however, will receive the full package of pre-accession assistance in order to prepare them more intensively for EU membership:

> 'Candidate Countries will receive the same kind of assistance [as the potential candidates], and will additionally receive assistance in the preparation for the implementation of Structural and Rural Development Funds after Accession, as well as concerning the full implementation of the [*acquis*].'

Therefore, official candidates *will* and potential candidate countries *may* receive support under three headings: regional development, rural development and human resources development. Regrettably, this qualitative differentiation between the two

---

[33] See Council Regulation (EC) No. 1085/2006 of 17 July 2006 establishing an Instrument for Pre-Accession Assistance (IPA), *OJ* 2006 L 210/82. IPA harmonised (insofar as possible) the pre-accession financial instruments – PHARE, ISPA, SAPARD, the Turkish pre-accession instrument and CARDS – and is part of a wider reorganisation of the European Union's financial framework for relations with third states, which includes a new European Neighbourhood and Partnership Instrument (ENPI), a new development cooperation instrument, the Instrument for Stability (IfS) and a financing instrument for the promotion of democracy and human rights. The IPA Regulation provides a total envelope of €11.5 billion over a period of seven years for the countries with candidate status (currently Croatia, Macedonia and Turkey) and potential candidate status (Albania, Bosnia and Herzegovina, Montenegro, Kosovo and Serbia).

categories of countries is significant and will exacerbate the differences in the Western Balkans if not compensated for in other domains. This means that all those living in rural areas and in declining industrial towns in Albania, Bosnia and Herzegovina, Montenegro, Serbia and Kosovo who are already suffering from inadequate education systems and a seriously deficient infrastructure, will see the development gap separating them from their neighbours across the border in candidate countries – and from the rest of Europe – grow wider up until the moment that their countries are granted candidate status by the EU.[34]

## 4. Institution building[35]

### 4.1 Creation and reorganisation

Most of the changes in the process of institutional reform present themselves as the consequence of the wish of third countries to establish closer relations and meet the conditions to eventually integrate with the EU. Whereas the collapse of mono-political and centrally planned states has forced governments to create and/or adapt the laws, institutions and economies anyway, the soft power and tough love attitude of the EU help (potential) candidate countries to prepare and implement changes more quickly and – it is hoped – more effectively. The aim is to reform public administration and the judiciary into corruption-free service providers for the citizens, a prerequisite for economic progress and the finalisation of the transition into a market economy system. Also, the (potential) candidate countries have to prepare their institutions to get involved, as Member States, in both the legislative process of the European Union and the implementation of EU law at national level. The preparation for attaining these goals usually provokes substantial changes in the role, *modus operandi* and workload of governments, national administrations and judiciaries. In turn, these changes prompt an inevitable reorganisation of the institutions' services and a revision of the (potential) candidate countries' administrative laws.

#### 4.1.1 *Reforming the bureaucracy*

Most of the (potential) candidate countries are still coping with the legacy of a heavy (communist) state administration, with a highly centralised structure composed of a minister at the top to develop policies and a passive state administration to implement the minister's decrees. Administrative capacity building and increas-

---

[34] For a critical view, see ESI, *Breaking out of the Balkan Ghetto: Why IPA Should Be Changed* (Berlin, ESI 2005).

[35] This section builds on the author's chapter 'Impact of EU Accession on the Role of (Potential) Candidate Countries' Executives', in A. Kellermann, J. Czuczai, S. Blockmans, A. Albi and W. Douma, eds., *The Impact of EU Accession on the Legal Orders of New EU Member States and (Pre-)Candidate Countries: Hopes and Fears* (The Hague, T.M.C. Asser Press 2006) 291-300.

ing political independence, efficiency and accountability of the administration are thus key priorities in the pre-accession process. The reform of public administration includes, *inter alia*, the adoption of laws regarding the status of civil servants, the introduction of transparent selection procedures and the organisation of competitive *concours* for the recruitment of civil servants, reform of the salary system, targeted training of civil servants by national institutes for public administration (specifically also in EU affairs) – enabling greater flexibility in managing human resources and a higher level of workforce mobility between public administration bodies –, the adoption of laws on access to information, the removal of administrative barriers, computerisation and the introduction of e-government, the adoption of a code of ethics, the introduction of disciplinary procedures and the creation of the post of ombudsman.

The reorganisation of public administration in view of future accession to the EU leads, in most cases, to a substantial increase in the number of civil servants. Noteworthy in this respect is the Action Plan 2003-2007 of the government of Croatia. This plan envisaged putting the brakes on further expansion of the administration and stimulated efforts to restructure ministries and state administration organisations (including a reduction in their numbers) to avoid the creation of new governmental bodies and the appointment of new civil servants and employees. Also, it encouraged the process of horizontal decentralisation whereby some of the duties of the government administration were transferred to autonomous organisations outside the administration, such as trade unions, employers' associations, universities, etc.[36]

#### 4.1.2 *Coordination within the executive*

Two kinds of institutional mechanisms exist for the preparation and implementation of EU law: coordination mechanisms between and/or within (potential) candidate countries' ministries and coordination mechanisms consisting of representatives of the EU and the (potential) candidate countries. As the institutional mechanisms for bilateral cooperation with the EU have already been exhaustively dealt with elsewhere,[37] attention will only be paid here to the former (see also section 3.3.2 above).

In most (potential) candidates, coordination of the technical adaptations for *rapprochement* has been facilitated by the creation of (i) a high-level Council on European Integration (e.g., Bulgaria), a Secretariat General for European Affairs (e.g., Turkey) under the umbrella of the Prime Minister's Office, or a 'synthesis' Ministry of European Integration (e.g., Romania, Albania);[38] (ii) medium-level state sec-

---

[36] See T. Ćapeta, D. Mihelin and S. Rodin, 'Croatia', in Kellermann, et al., *supra* n. 35, 69-112.

[37] For literature on the composition, tasks and powers of negotiation delegations, association councils, association committees, etc., see, e.g., A. Evans, 'Institutions', in A. Ott and K. Inglis, eds., *Handbook on European Enlargement. A Commentary on the Enlargement Process* (The Hague, T.M.C. Asser Press 2002) 1043-1078.

[38] Both in Bulgaria and Turkey a separate interministerial mechanism was created at this level to monitor the implementation of the reforms in the framework of the harmonisation process (Coordina-

retaries, coordinators and deputy coordinators, directorates or units for European integration in line ministries; and (iii) lower-level interministerial/interinstitutional working groups for the harmonisation of legislation (usually modelled after the negotiation working groups).

Apart from regular meetings of interministerial monitoring and/or working groups and coordination, monitoring and reporting instruments such as evolving planning documents and national integration and approximation programmes, the importance of working with interactive databases and portals on EU affairs to monitor the adoption and application of decisions implementing the *acquis* should be underlined. In Slovenia, the executive's transformation efforts were supported by the 'European portal' for access to relevant documents. The portal was accessible to all those participating in the adoption of decisions on individual matters. For each document, the Government Office for European Affairs (SVEZ), and in particular cases the Ministry of Foreign Affairs, appointed the ministry in charge of formulating a draft position on the relevant material, as well as the authorities that must be notified of the material, and it set the time limit for the adoption of a coordinated position and determined the method of approval of positions (either only by the ministry or working group in question, or also by the Government and/or National Assembly). Croatia followed suit with the creation of an interactive database (Management Reporting Information System – MRIS) at the Ministry of Foreign Affairs and European Integration for the purpose of facilitating the technical monitoring of and reporting on the implementation of the National Programme. The same system is now also used, albeit imperfectly, in Albania. The idea is that, in order to avoid written reporting, each ministry or body of the administration is given access to the MRIS, into which the European Coordinators enter, on a monthly basis, data on the implementation of the National Programme in their area of competence.

Special mention should also be made of a Croatian initiative for the horizontal exchange of knowledge and experiences at the level of state administration bodies, whereby lawyers of the Ministry of Foreign Affairs and European Integration conduct a national twinning initiative with lawyers in other parts of the administration.

As far as decentralisation is concerned, realisation of the autonomy of decentralised authorities and strengthening of their local and regional self-government is more likely to be a success not only when they are enabled to perform a much broader scope of functions, but also when real powers are transferred (not just delegated) from the level of central government and when local authorities' financial capacity is expanded by means such as the redistribution of revenues from national taxes or the use of non-fiscal financing instruments. In most pre-accession

---

tion Council, resp. Monitoring Group for the EU Reforms). In Croatia, like in other countries, the central government also discusses European integration issues at its regular sessions and adopts reports on the realisation of the National Plan (for implementation of the SAA and legal approximation). In Croatia, the originally separate Ministry of European Integration was incorporated into the Ministry of Foreign Affairs. An atypical division of high-level tasks existed in Slovenia, where different ministries were responsible for the coordination of activities related to each of the three (now defunct) Pillars of the EU Treaty.

countries, this process was given shape by the adoption of laws on local self-government and local administration.

### 4.1.3 *Security sector reform*

As the local and international media focus on crime, drugs, corruption, fraud and illegal immigration, internal security is perceived by citizens of (potential) candidate countries as a key government duty. In political terms, these concerns are translated into efforts to strengthen border control, law enforcement and the operation of the judiciary, often supported by EU-provided financial and technical assistance (previously through RRM and TACIS, now through, *inter alia*, ENPI, EDF and IfS) with a view to realising – in a practical way – the crucial links between democratic governance, state security, human security and implementation of relevant reforms. As noted by Spence in his contribution to this volume, such 'security sector reform' (SSR) is conceptually not just related to a country's armed forces but to governance of the security sector *sensu lato*, i.e., 'all state institutions and other entities with a role in ensuring the security of the state *and* its people.'[39] Reform of justice institutions therefore covers interior and justice ministries, prisons, criminal investigation and prosecution services, the judiciary, bailiffs and ushers, other customary and traditional justice systems, human rights commissions and ombudsmen. Legal reforms and capacity building of law enforcement institutions concern police, border management and customs services, as well as relevant executive branches of government and democratic oversight mechanisms, including parliaments and civil society.[40]

SSR has long been an integral part of the EU's enlargement policy. In fact, the bulk of EU SSR assistance has been provided in the enlargement context. The EU continues to oversee large-scale cultural, legal and institutional change in the security sectors of pre-accession countries and offers technical and financial assistance through IPA and EIDHR. Although largely effective thanks to the EU's power of attraction, such change has not always been easy or has, in some cases, remained elusive. In post-Cold War Romania, for instance, the demilitarisation of the police and the fight against corruption have been serious stumbling blocks. They have been addressed by the entry into force of a new law on the statute of the police which explicitly states that policemen are non-military civil servants operating under the rule of law, and by the setting up of a National Anti-Corruption Prosecutor's

[39] See the Communication from the Commission to the Council and the European Parliament, 'A Concept for European Community Support for Security Sector Reform', COM(2006) 253 final. Spence also points out that the EU has started reflecting on 'an internal security strategy for the EU, which is intended to result in a formal strategy to be adopted in 2010. This will doubtless prove a key contextual document in terms of the EU's ongoing SSR policies, for it recognises the interdependence of internal and external security by building a global security focus. SSR is a logical concomitant.'

[40] See, generally, D. Spence and P. Fluri, eds., *The EU and Security Sector Reform* (London, John Harper 2008). With regard to police reform, see G. Collantes Celador, 'Police Reform: Peace-Building through "Democratic Policing"?', 12 *International Peacekeeping* (2005) 364-376; and M. Merlingen and R. Ostrauskaitė, *European Union Peacebuilding and Policing* (London, Routledge 2006).

Office as an autonomous structure within the Ministry of Public Administration.[41] In Bosnia and Herzegovina it was only possible to put pressure on political leaderships to commit to the necessary changes by making police reform a condition for EU integration. However, slow and uncertain implementation of the reform package agreed to in 2007 have since negatively affected the credibility of EU conditionality.[42] In, Turkey, not a post-conflict country, the army continues to play a 'special' role in the constitutional republic.[43]

### 4.2 Democratic legitimacy?

It has been argued above that a feature of state building is the assumption that institution building should take place prior to political development.[44] In EU enlargement, this assumption is reflected in a number of different ways, with varying consequences. Firstly, the pre-accession process strengthens national executives and creates 'islands of excellence' within individual ministries of (potential) candidate countries.[45] The flipside of the empowerment of executives is the weakening of the legislative branches of government.[46] Secondly, the EU pre-accession process reduces the 'Member State-building' agenda to a technical process of (re-)building public administrations and essential regulatory capacities needed for wealth creation, without due attention to the watchwords of 'good governance' (transparency, accountability, etc.). The process is said to constitute a long string of negotiations. However, as Duke and Courtier point out in their contribution to this volume:

> 'Although often presented as a negotiation process, the accession "negotiations" are more one-sided with the onus being on the candidates satisfying the European Commission and the Member States of their ability to accede to the Union. For the candidates the emphasis is on confirming and not on negotiation.'

This practice is reminiscent of the character of the wider contemporary state-building agenda: it has increasingly become an activity driven by governments from the West, undertaken by private enterprises from the West.[47] Indeed, state building is not a science, but rather a lucrative hobby of Westerners.

---

[41] See V. Duculescu and R. Adam, 'Romania', in Kellermann, et al., *supra* n. 35, 113-141.

[42] See T. Muehlmann, 'Police Restructuring in Bosnia-Herzegovina: Problems of Internationally-Led Security Sector Reform', 2 *Journal of Intervention and Statebuilding* (2008) 1-22. In their contribution to this volume, Humphreys and Jelisić point to similar problems in the visa liberalisation process in BiH.

[43] See the second report of the Independent Commission on Turkey, *Turkey in Europe: Breaking the Vicious Circle* (Open Society/British Council, 2009), at 13-15; and International Crisis Group, *Turkey and Europe: The Decisive Year Ahead*, Europe Report No. 197, 15 December 2008.

[44] See *supra*, section 2.

[45] See H. Grabbe, 'Europeanization Goes East: Power and Uncertainty in the EU Accession Process', in K. Featherstone and C. Radaelli, eds., *The Politics of Europeanization* (Oxford, OUP 2003) 303-327.

[46] See *infra*, section 5.

[47] Naomi Klein describes this process as a form of 'sophisticated colonialism', re-branded as reconstruction and amounting to a bounty for a myriad of non-state actors. See N. Klein, 'The Rise of

Insofar as state building undermines the direct relationship between a domestic public and its representative institutions, it perpetuates and in some cases exacerbates state weakness.[48] This is highlighted in a report entitled *In Search of Responsive Government*, in which a group of European scholars make the distinction between 'bureaucracy building' and 'constituency building' as the two key components of successful state building.[49] In their view, state building must include both and cannot be reduced to the former:

> 'Construed as an instrument of democratic governance, a strong state is both an institutional and a social phenomenon. It is characterised by the particular qualities of institutional apparatuses and by recurring relationship patterns between social (large and small) constituencies and state agents.'[50]

As said, the downside of the empowerment of executives, or at least parts thereof, is the weakening of the legislative branches of government, namely national parliaments. The 'over-parliamentarisation' that was a feature of the early post-communist period is seemingly reversed by the pre-accession process.[51] National parliaments are usually isolated by virtue of the close negotiation process between the European Commission and the national executives of candidate countries:

> 'The negotiation process is conducted in a highly non-transparent manner between national governments and the Commission. Parliamentary committees (let alone sub-national actors) are often not engaged in substantive consultations on the technicalities of realigning the huge body of domestic legislation to conform to EU norms.'[52]

Regarding the negative effect of enlargement on public administration, the World Bank described the pressures that are put on government ministries. It pointed out that

> 'because of limited resources, EU talent has largely been siphoned off from core public administration tasks. Continuing demand for EU skills will further deplete professionals from the government administration.'[53]

---

Disaster Capitalism', *The Nation*, 2 May 2005, available at: <http://thenation.com/doc/20050502/klein>. Klein observes that '[f]ew ideologues can resist the allure of a blank slate – that was colonialism's seductive promise: "discovering" wide-open lands where utopia seemed possible.' Klein's 'blank slate' refers to the crisis of the nation-state out of which the state-building agenda is drawn up and implemented.

48 See, generally, R. Paris and T. Sisk, eds., *The Dilemmas of Statebuilding: Confronting the Contradictions of Postwar Peace Operations* (London, Routledge 2009).

49 The report was produced in 2003 by the Bluebird Project, a product of a three-year research project entitled 'Agenda for Civil Society in Southeast Europe', coordinated by the Centre for Policy Studies at the Central European University in Budapest. The *Bluebird Report* is available at: <http://cps.ceu.hu/bluebird.php>.

50 Ibid., at 47.

51 See A. Agh, *The Politics of Central Europe* (London, Sage 1998), at 89.

52 J. Hughes, G. Sassen and C. Gordon, 'Saying "Maybe" to the Return of Europe', 3 *European Union Politics* (2002) 327-355, at 339.

53 World Bank, *Ready for Europe: Public Administration Reform and European Union Accession in Central and Eastern Europe*, World Bank Technical Paper No. 466 (2000), at 21.

The *Bluebird Report* makes a similar point when it warns that those bureaucratic elements made more efficient through international intervention 'will not be in touch with large local constituencies. They will accord priority to their relationship with fellow Eurocrats in Brussels.'[54]

The extent to which EU accession has demanded a concentration of governmental resources is clear in the case of Hungary.[55] In 1996, Hungary created a European Integration Cabinet, headed by the Prime Minister and consisting of five ministers (Foreign Affairs, Interior, Justice, Economy and Finance), a State Secretariat for Integration, a Strategic Task Force on Integration attached to the Prime Minister's Office, and European Integration Departments in all line ministries. Even with such efforts, Hungary was said not to be able to

> 'adequately present and represent its national interests at the negotiations, since on the Hungarian side there is too small an elite team of negotiators, without assistance from the large group of [elected] representatives who could channel the particular interests of social strata into the national interest.'[56]

The effect of such institutional change on parliaments has been to devalue the role and contribution of parliamentarians. Over the course of the accession process, more value has been placed on the competence of civil servants, who are distanced from the contingency of political life, than on the contribution of non-technical parliamentarians.[57]

The best example of this separation of law from politics is to be found in the measures adopted by (potential) candidate countries to meet the deadlines for harmonisation of domestic legislation with the EU *acquis*. Legal approximation is a membership condition which has the effect of taking the legislative process out of the political sphere of (potential) candidate countries. One of the worst examples is 'fast-tracking', i.e., the creation of exceptional mechanisms through which governments hope to meet the legislative demands of accession by limiting the contribution of parliaments. The Romanian government's law-making practice to bring national legislation in line with that of the EU was, until the very end of the pre-accession process, almost entirely based on government emergency ordinances, a feat which was bitterly criticised in the Commission's progress reports. These legislative instruments entered into force immediately and only required subsequent approval by Parliament. Transparency was thus seriously reduced and Parliament's prerogative to subsequently modify or reject the new legislation introduced by way of such decrees might have induced legislative instability.[58] Similarly, civil service reform in the Czech Republic and Bulgaria was passed without the necessary con-

[54] See *Bluebird Report*, *supra* n. 49, at 48.

[55] See T. Takacs, *Participation in EU Decision Making: Implications on the National Level* (The Hague, T.M.C. Asser Press 2008). Takacs takes Hungary as a case study for her research.

[56] A. Agh, 'Europeanisation of Policymaking in East Central Europe: The Hungarian Approach to EU Accession', 6 *Journal of European Public Policy* (1999) 839-854, at 851.

[57] Ibid., at 843-844.

[58] See Duculescu and Adam, *supra* n. 41.

sensus.[59] Fast-tracking undermines the emergence of a 'procedural culture' whereby bargaining between parties and consensus building is seen as the proper basis for law making.[60] As this practice is no longer grounded in the will of the political community which is subject to it, it should evidently be limited to cases of an exceptional nature since otherwise the law will be empty of democratic legitimacy.

A final consequence of the EU pre-accession process is the narrowing of the political sphere itself. The non-negotiable nature of the accession process erases both detailed and ideological debates over many areas of public policy. In this way, EU accession is an example of what has been called 'valence issues', i.e., issues on which all parties agree and share the same objectives.[61] Political parties in candidate countries have only limited room for manoeuvre given the obligations of economic transition and the accession processes to NATO and the EU. These restrictions mean that on key questions political differences are reduced and that parties have no choice but to differentiate themselves on more symbolic issues, such as past conflict, the previous authoritarian regime, the relationship to religion, etc.[62] One consequence of this narrowing of the political sphere is a clear disillusion with regard to the market economy and parliamentary democracy. Evidence thereof can be found in falling participation rates in elections.[63] That this should end with the completion of the enlargement process is unlikely. Recent events suggest that post-enlargement politics in 'New Europe' remain dominated by a desire of new Member States to prove their European credentials.[64]

## 5. Constituency building

### 5.1 Introduction

A state is not only a legal and administrative entity, it is also a social phenomenon. The strength of a state is dependent on the relationship between its institutions and citizens: 'It is the distance, whether real or imagined, between the state and key social constituencies that renders possible the reproduction of the weak state model.'[65]

---

59 See A. Dimitrova, 'Enlargement, Institution-Building and the EU's Administrative Capacity Requirement', 25 *Western European Politics* (2002) 171-190, at 183. Dimitrova argues that this practice leads to uncertainty in implementation and to greater enforcement problems.

60 See D. Malova and T. Haughton, 'Making Institutions in Central and Eastern Europe, and the Impact of Europe', 25 *Western European Politics* (2002) 101-120, at 112.

61 A. Gryzmala-Busse and A. Innes, 'Great Expectations: The EU and Domestic Political Competition in East Central Europe', 17 *East European Politics and Societies* (2003) 64-73, at 64.

62 See J.-M. de Waele, 'L'émergence, l'organisation et les spécificités des partis politiques dans les pays candidats', in G. Andréani, et al., 'Les Nouveaux Etats de l'Union', *Pouvoirs: Revue Française d'Etudes Constitutionnelles et Politiques* (Paris, Seuil 2003), at 97.

63 See the 2009 Gallup Balkan Monitor survey at: <http://www.balkan-monitor.eu/files/BalkanMonitor-2009_Summary_of_Findings.pdf>.

64 See A. Łazowski, 'Introduction', in Łazowski, ed., *supra* n. 32, at 1-2.

65 See *Bluebird Report*, *supra* n. 49, at 51.

The conclusions of the *Bluebird Report* point to the need to revive the political process as the key to strengthening states in the Balkans and elsewhere. The report defines

> 'the growing gap between the state and the key social constituencies as the major risk for reforming the Balkans. Reforming the public administration and positive changes in the economy are not sufficient to bridge this gap.'

As a priority, the report points to a much-needed

> 'shift from the normative approach to democratization that focuses on democratic institutions (elections, courts and media) and which is most often expressed with the idea of "accountable" or "good government" to the idea of "responsive government" that underlies not the state's autonomy from civil society but the influence of major social constituencies over state decisions.'[66]

This approach has much to commend it. Its emphasis on constituency building rests upon a political understanding of the state, which sees it as a product of the political sphere, and of popular participation. Political disengagement, of the sort seen in Bosnia and Herzegovina and in Kosovo, is thus a primary source of state weakness. The difficulty is that strengthening the political sphere presupposes an acceptance of political autonomy and self-rule, which runs against the interventionist logic of state building. The *Bluebird Report*'s emphasis on constituency building poses the right question: how can the political sphere in weak states be strengthened? Put in this way, it is unlikely that outside intervention can be considered a viable solution, severing, as it does, the link between national institutions and domestic constituencies.

Another valuable contribution to the state-building debate is provided by Robert Hayden, in an article on democracy in Bosnia and Herzegovina.[67] Hayden argues that it was the 1995 Dayton Agreement which imposed upon BiH a political framework that presupposed, in theory, unified popular sovereign will that was absent in practice. It was important for the international community at the time to maintain the fiction of Bosnia and Herzegovina as a single state; yet, in practice, this state amounted to little more than a customs union and a foreign ministry. The Dayton Agreement was therefore signed as a compromise between the desire of the international community to successfully negotiate a peace agreement and the reality of the divisions between Croats, Serbs and Muslims. Hayden describes the situation thus:

---

66 Ibid., at 52-53.

67 See R. Hayden, 'Democracy without a Demos? The Bosnian Constitutional Experiment and the Intentional Construction of Non-Functioning States', 19 *East European Politics and Societies* (2005) 226-259. This article was a follow-up to his much-acclaimed book on the demise of the former Yugoslavia as viewed through the prism of constitutional structures and debates about them. See R. Hayden, *Blueprint for a House Divided: The Constitutional Logic of the Yugoslav Conflicts* (Ann Arbor, The University of Michigan Press 2000).

> 'Bosnia was a house divided, a nominal state without an actual nation, with a population whose self-differentiating ethni preclude the formation of a demos. Since two of the three corporate residents of this condominium would have preferred to tear it down to build their own houses (...) the absentee landlordship of the [Peace Implementation Council (PIC)] has been necessary to preserve the property.'[68]

However, rather than seeking to understand the reasons for the divisions between the communities in BiH, the response of the international community has been in line with Fukuyama's view of the 'cultural component' of legitimate institutions.[69] It is no coincidence that due to the frequent use of the Bonn powers, allowing the High Representative to fire and hire domestically elected politicians, block draft laws and push through laws by decree, the Office of the High Representative has been dubbed the 'European Raj'.[70] The institutions of the state are not those where political decisions are made. Rather, the state is a mechanism for the implementation of political decisions taken elsewhere: 'the system is not at fault, but rather the people running it.'[71] This is reflected in the belief that Bosnians are merely victims of the cynical machinations of their political class. This, in turn, justifies the concentration of powers in the hands of the High Representative, who has generally seen national politicians as obstacles blocking the will of the people, in spite of the fact that his own authority is in no way derived from the will of the citizens of BiH, but rather comes from the PIC.[72]

Rather than accepting that a strong and centralised Bosnian state cannot be built without the active consent of the governed and is thus impossible so long as Bosnia and Herzegovina remains an international protectorate, the state-building agenda has been dominated by the attempt to push through a centralisation programme by *diktat*, i.e., by forcing the country's Constitutional Court to rewrite the Dayton Agreement by fiat. The dangers of such an approach are highlighted by Hayden:

> 'Democracy without a demos requires the imposition of "democratic values" on people who have their own ideas on how to live their lives, liberties and property (...) and this seems inherently undemocratic. A dictatorship of virtue, after all, remains a dictatorship, and the failure of dictatorships to be virtuous is the starting point of democratic theory.'[73]

What the *Bluebird Report* and Hayden's article both emphasise is the political component of the state. That this is missing from state-building theory and practice is

---

68 Ibid., at 248.

69 Fukuyama, *supra* n. 1, at 48: 'a moment's reflection should make it obvious that the development of formal institutions is strongly affected by cultural factors.'

70 See G. Knaus and F. Martin, 'Travails of the European Raj', 14 *Journal of Democracy* (2003) 60-74.

71 Hayden, *supra* n. 67, at 256.

72 See the account of former High Representative P. Ashdown, *Swords and Ploughshares: Building Peace in the 21st Century* (London, Phoenix 2008) and the contribution by Humphreys and Jelisić to this volume.

73 Hayden, *supra* n. 67, at 256.

not surprising, as this political component assumes the existence of self-governing political subjects and their collective existence as the constituent political power of a sovereign state. The 'authoritarian' model of outside intervention contained in state-building activities is a direct negation of such an assumption and reflects a deep hostility to the idea and practice of political autonomy and self-governance in designated weak states.

The growing gap between a state's public institutions and its citizens is a critical risk to the success of the European Union's transformative policies. Political mobilisation and participation are essential. In the Western Balkans, the modernisation of the political culture and discourse is also necessary. The emphasis should be on the future, while progress is made by dealing with the past. In this context, three particular challenges stick out: (i) assuring minority rights protection in decentralised systems of governance; (ii) achieving justice and reconciliation on war crimes; and (iii) the fight against organised crime. These will now be discussed in turn.

## 5.2 Assuring minority rights protection

As elaborated elsewhere,[74] war and ethnic cleansing on the territory of the former Yugoslavia have resulted in significant demographic shifts. While all countries of the Western Balkans still contain multi-ethnic areas, most countries are now nation-states with majorities amounting to 80 per cent or more of the population. Albania, Croatia, Serbia and Kosovo have strong majorities, and most minorities live in a relatively compact part of the country and account for 10 to 20 per cent of the population. Only Bosnia and Herzegovina, Macedonia and Montenegro have a more balanced multi-ethnic set-up, with little or no dominance by one community.[75] Decentralisation policies aggravate the ethnic separation in certain parts of the Western Balkans. Albanian areas around Tetovo in northern Macedonia and the predominantly Serb area around Mitrovica in northern Kosovo are cases in point. While the argument for decentralisation (with more competences exercised at local level, minorities are able to govern themselves to a larger degree, which in turn should increase their loyalty to the state) is perfectly acceptable, its reality in the Western Balkans is not. Human rights violations by regional authorities against minority elements (e.g., Roma and residents or returnees of a different ethnicity) largely escape international monitoring.[76] Hence, what is needed is the recognition of minorities at municipal level and international monitoring of their fundamental rights.[77]

---

[74] See Blockmans, *supra* n. 18, at 332.

[75] See F. Bieber, *Minority Rights in Practice in South Eastern Europe*, Discussion Paper (King Baudouin Foundation, 30 September 2004).

[76] Ibid.

[77] See ICB, *supra* n. 3, at 32-33.

## 5.3 Reinterpreting ICTY conditionality

The second challenge to constituency building in the Western Balkan societies concerns transitional justice and reconciliation on war crimes.[78] Since 1993, the ICTY has played a decisive role in bringing war criminals to justice. However, it has failed to take away the distrust of local people regarding its mission to achieve justice and reconciliation in the Western Balkans.[79] The European Union has defined full cooperation with the ICTY as a threshold conditionality when it comes to the process of integration.[80] The challenge facing the Union at present is how to translate the post-war conditionality of the ICTY, which is charged with examining concrete crimes in the cases of Gotovina, Karadžić and Mladić, into one that looks towards the future and concentrates on the strengthening of European values across the region. While the unprecedented decision by the Council to postpone the start of membership talks with Croatia was – incidentally or not – quickly followed by the arrest of General Gotovina and his transfer to The Hague, similar decisions to suspend negotiations on an SAA with Serbia or to delay a decision on the entry into force of the Interim Agreement on trade-related aspects failed to cajole Belgrade into full compliance with ICTY conditionality.[81] Of course, full and unequivocal cooperation with the ICTY should remain mandatory for the opening of accession negotiations with the European Union. However, failure to transfer a single high-profile fugitive to the Tribunal should not hold back the development of entire countries when it comes to negotiating, signing and implementing SAAs. In practice, the strict interpretation of ICTY conditionality – as requiring Serbia to hand over Mladiæ to the ICTY – was swapped by the Council of the EU for one focused on both the level of openness given about efforts to track down indictees and the width and breadth of such efforts, partially in an attempt to lessen the blow of an internationally imposed decision to let Kosovo secede from Serbia.[82] Indeed, ICTY conditionality should be understood more broadly than just the need to transfer one

---

[78] See the contribution by Unger to this volume.

[79] See, P. Hazan, *Justice in a Time of War: The True Story Behind the International Criminal Tribunal for the Former Yugoslavia* (Texas, A&M University Press 2004).

[80] In addition, the European Union regards the success of the ICTY as critical in its struggle to confer legitimacy on the International Criminal Court.

[81] In December 2009, the Netherlands finally dropped its insistence on delaying the entry into force of the Interim Agreement with Serbia, allegedly after a positive report from the Chief Prosecutor of the ICTY to the Council of the EU that the Serbian government was doing everything in its power (the magic words 'full and unequivocal cooperation' were not used…) to track down and arrest the remaining indictees. See Report of Serge Brammertz, Prosecutor of the ICTY, provided to the Security Council under para. 6 of UNSC Res. 1534 (2004), paras. 30-38 of Annex II to the Letter dated 12 November 2009 from the President of the ICTY addressed to the President of the Security Council, UN Doc. S/2009/589, 13 November 2009; and General Affairs Council Conclusions on enlargement and the SAP, 7-8 December 2009, points 40-41.

[82] In February 2007, the Council confirmed the European Union's readiness to resume SAA negotiations with a new government in Belgrade 'provided it shows clear commitment and takes concrete and effective action *for* full co-operation with the ICTY.' See Council Conclusions of 12 February 2007, in Press Release No. 6037/07 (Presse 18), at 13 [emphasis added).

or two suspected war criminals to The Hague.[83] Instead, it should concentrate, of course, on the willingness of Western Balkan governments to fully cooperate with the ICTY but also to examine the causes and consequences of their countries' troubled past. Hence, the European Union should attach more importance than it does now to the readiness and ability of the domestic judicial, religious and educational authorities to deal with war-related crimes of the past and to promote tolerance and reconciliation. In this respect, recent judgments by Bosnian, Croatian and Serbian courts convicting war criminals to long prison sentences should be taken as a positive sign.[84]

## 5.4 Fighting organised crime

A third challenge in the movement towards moderation and modernisation in the Western Balkans is posed by so-called 'politico-criminal syndicates'. In every country of the region, there are people in high places with the motivation and resources to undermine local reformers' efforts to modernise and clean up their governments and economies.[85] Strengthened by the profits from pirate privatisation and bolstered by cross-border illegal connections, the revenue and survival of these syndicates depend on their ability to suppress efforts to introduce transparency and accountability into the political and economic systems of the states in which they operate. Their combination of influence, access, resources and superficially appealing ideology makes it difficult for new and weak governments to mount sustained campaigns against them. In anticipation of the Western Balkan governments' capacity and will to fight these politico-criminal groups, the Office of the High Commissioner, UNMIK and the European Union have launched such campaigns in Bosnia and Herzegovina, Kosovo and Macedonia, that is to say, where the extent and authority of these international institutions are greatest. Arrests of ethnic extremists, seizure of weapons, control of border crossings, enforcement of travel and financial restrictions on key leaders and improved law enforcement and intelligence cooperation have played important roles in reducing ethnic violence in these parts of the Western Balkans.[86] While these efforts have been limited, the underlying lesson is

---

[83] For the counter-arguments, see G. Evans and J. Lyons, 'No Mladic, No Talks', *International Herald Tribune*, 21 March 2007; and S. Freizer and A. Stroehlein, 'The EU's Inexcusable Pardon for Serbia', *European Voice*, 29 March 2007.

[84] See, e.g., 'Croatian Court Charges Glavas, Six Others with 1991 Crimes against Ethnic Serbs', *Southeast European Times*, 11 April 2007; N. Wood, 'Serbian Court Convicts 4 in Srebrenica Murders', *International Herald Tribune*, 10 April 2007; and N. Wood, 'Serbia Praised Over Trials of Alleged War Criminals', *International Herald Tribune*, 3 January 2006.

[85] In the Western Balkans, a prime example concerns the assassination in March 2003 of the pro-reform Prime Minister of Serbia Zoran Djindjić by Milorad Ulemek, former member of the secret police and condemned, together with his superiors, to a forty-year jail term for the kidnapping and murder of Serbia's former President Ivan Stambolić. See 'Serb President's Killers Jailed', *Financial Times*, 18 July 2005.

[86] In Bosnia and Herzegovina, in particular, progress in moving the country toward European standards of governance was only made when the OHR confronted the syndicates' power over industry, government finances, borders and the media. Examples include the 1997 removal of media from

clear: decisive actions aimed at the levers of power controlled by the politico-criminal groupings produce results and help reformers' efforts to modernise the state. The international community should therefore continue seizing criminal institutions and pursuing, prosecuting and removing from office individuals associated with illegal intersections of government and financial power until local institutions acquire the ability and the will to take it upon themselves.

## 6. THE FUTURE OF ENLARGEMENT: PEACEBUILDING BY DEFAULT RATHER THAN DESIGN?

Robert Cooper, Director-General of External and Politico-Military Affairs at the Council of the European Union, has described the EU as a 'voluntary empire' that uses the lure of membership as a massive carrot to inspire voluntary regime change.[87] For this soft power to yield results, however, the offer has to be real and the instruments must be appropriate to the challenge. As noted above, EU conditionality has hitherto been a one-way process: conditions are defined exclusively by the European Union and its Member States and must be accepted unconditionally by the (potential) candidates. This unequal relationship has been aimed at the transposition of policy templates that reflect EU preferences and past practices.[88] However, the templates used for the post-communist CEECs, which followed the 'classic' transition path, are not the most conducive to effecting EU-proof change in all corners of a war-torn region like the Western Balkans, especially there where a state building process is still underway and the moment of accession to the EU thus far away. The European Union seems to assume that its prescriptions have universal applicability and should therefore be adopted and implemented irrespective of the particularities of countries or regions. As Kekiæ has pointed out, there are some indicative areas in which harmonisation with the EU *acquis* and policies can be detrimental to the hoped-for economic growth in the Western Balkans, for example, capital account liberalisation and competition policies.[89] This paradox reflects the shortcomings of the one-way approach in setting policy targets. Moreover, local priorities often prove to be out of sync with those of the European Union. Espe-

---

nationalist control in the Republika Srpska; the seizure in 2001 of a bank controlled by hard-line Croats who had stolen from their own people; the March 2002 decision by the OHR to remove constitutional provisions that helped nationalist parties retain control of public institutions and resources; and the December 2004 sackings of senior Bosnian Serb security officials accused of harbouring war crimes suspects, including Ratko Mladić. See the six-monthly reports of the High Representative on the implementation of the Dayton Peace Agreement to the UN Secretary-General, available on the OHR's website at: <http://www.ohr.int>.

[87] See R. Cooper, *The Breaking of Nations: Order and Chaos in the Twenty-First Century* (New York, Atlantic Books 2003), at 70.

[88] See D. Chandler, 'The European Union and Governance in the Western Balkans: An Unequal Partnership', 1/2 *European Balkan Observer* (2003) 5-9.

[89] See L. Kekić, 'The EU and the Balkans – To Harmonise or Not to Harmonise', *Economist Intelligence Unit* (ViewsWire, 2002).

cially in the international protectorates, to people who see their country dominated, for better or worse, by foreign masters, the European Union's demands often ring hollow. There is little point in the European Union constantly blowing against the wind. Yet, by doing so in the past couple of years, the European Union – as part of the international community – has bred an unsustainable status quo that might drive parts of the region towards a new period of highly dangerous instability.[90]

Regional input into the Union's policies towards the Western Balkans is a *conditio sine qua non* to effectively stabilise the region. There is one big problem though. Regional input not only requires a perceptive and understanding donor that can demonstrate vision and flexibility but also presupposes sovereign governments that are capable of articulating their needs and demands. The reality is that sovereignty is still a scarce resource in some parts of the Western Balkans. When one considers the extensive powers of the High Representative/EUSR in Bosnia and Herzegovina and those of the International Civilian Office in Kosovo, one may question the domestic ability to address needs and priorities. The result is the definition of a form of EU conditionality that does not involve regional input, does not necessarily generate broad domestic consensus for reform, and poisons relations between the populations and the political elites and, by extension, between the countries concerned and the international actors.[91]

While conditionality is inherently asymmetric and the European Union must not step down from its role of promoter of reform, there is much to be done in terms of establishing a viable partnership with the Western Balkans. Beyond any doubt, EU conditionality has to be based on a process of 'adaptive learning' by paying closer attention to signals coming from the region.[92] There is general agreement across the region, verified by opinion polls, that social and economic matters – as opposed to the old ethno-political repertoire – are the real concern.[93] High unemployment, poverty and corruption typically score high on the list of problems that preoccupy people in the Balkans. It is only when its commitment is better linked to addressing those issues that matter to citizens that the European Union will be able to sell its conditionality approach.[94]

Although EU membership conditionality leads, by definition, to bilateralism and competition, the Western Balkans also require a region-wide strategy. While pack-

---

[90] This observation is supported by, *inter alia*, the results of the survey conducted by the ICB, *supra* n. 3, at 10, and the 2009 Gallup Balkan Monitor survey, *supra* n. 63. See also the contribution by Humphreys and Jelisić to this volume.

[91] See I. Krastev, 'The Balkans: Democracy without Choices', 13 *Journal of Democracy* (2002). One move in the right direction has so far been the greater consideration of the recipients' interests in the timing, for example, of the approximation of legislation. See, in this context, the rationale behind the shorter time frame and the absence of stages for the approximation of legislation in the SAA Croatia as compared to the SAAs with FYROM and Albania.

[92] See Chandler, *supra* n. 88.

[93] Based on an extensive survey of public attitudes conducted by the International Institute for Democracy and Electoral Assistance in January and February 2002, available at: <http://www.idea.int>. See also the 2009 Gallup Balkan Monitor survey, *supra* n. 63.

[94] See O. Anastasakis and D. Bechev, *EU Conditionality in South East Europe: Bringing Commitment to the Process* (Oxford, SEESP 2003).

aging the countries into a single region is not viable, the institutionalisation of the dialogue between Brussels and the Western Balkans has been a step in the right direction. It is imperative that the countries in the region should be involved in setting the regional cooperation agenda. For this reason, the EU should continue to support the activities of the regionally-owned Regional Cooperation Council as a way to speed up integration of the countries into the European Union.[95]

With the principle of conditionality firmly and explicitly built into all phases of the SAP,[96] the countries of the Western Balkans have a clearly marked path and timetable to follow and are aware of the consequences of not abiding by the conditions imposed upon them by the European Union: postponement or cancellation of political negotiations and/or suspension or termination of contractual relations. At the same time, the European Union has confirmed time and again the tangible prospect of EU membership, the most powerful instrument for transformation of the Western Balkans, as the SAP's *finalité*. This gives the governments that are still in doubt as to whether or not to take the Union's 'perspective of membership' offer seriously a strong incentive and clear message to convince their electorates of the advantages of ethnic reconciliation and of tightening belts to reform their countries' administrative, legislative and economic structures. Taking away or indefinitely postponing the prospect of EU membership would rob governing coalitions in (potential) candidate countries of their claim that tough reforms are needed to join the EU. This, in turn, could lead to a polarisation of the political landscape in these countries and potentially disrupt a valuable process that is helping to build stable and effective states in one of the poorest and most volatile parts of Europe, with all its possible consequences. In many ways, Croatia stands out as a model for the rest of the region. With the Croatian case serving as a positive example, the rest of the Western Balkan countries should be persuaded that the European Union is serious about settling the legacy of the Yugoslav wars of the 1990s and does not apply a double standard. Consistency is crucial.

The granting of candidate country status to Macedonia and the progress made on the conclusion of SAAs with the other countries of the Western Balkans do not allow the conclusion that any of these countries is likely to join the European Union as a full member any time soon. However, these developments do provide the European Union's overall approach towards the Western Balkans with a strong strategic objective: further expansion of the European Union south-eastwards. This strategic

---

[95] The RCC took over the responsibilities of the Stability Pact in February 2008. Its Secretariat is in Sarajevo. The RCC (<http://www.rcc.int>) provides the SEECP, for a long time the only regionally-owned initiative, with operational capabilities as well as a framework for the continued involvement of the international donor community in the region. Priority areas for cooperation in the framework of the RCC are economic and social development, infrastructure, justice and home affairs, security cooperation, building human capital and parliamentary cooperation. Social cohesion and gender mainstreaming will also be given due attention. As such, these activities complement and build on achievements within CEFTA, the ECAA and the Energy Community, and should be welcomed.

[96] See S. Blockmans, 'Raising the Threshold for Further EU Enlargement: Process, Problems and Prospects', in A. Ott and E. Vos, eds., *Fifty Years of European Integration: Foundations and Perspectives* (The Hague, T.M.C. Asser Press 2009) 203-220.

reorientation should prompt the Union to vigorously reinforce a guiding principle that has characterised its relations with third countries in general: that of conditionality. At the same time it is important that the EU should not give the impression that membership is too distant, as this might still lead to rapid domestic deterioration in some of the weakest states. A balanced application of the conditionality principle is central to the successful use of EU enlargement as a peacebuilding tool.

# Part II
# *Working with partners*

# Chapter 4
# EU-UN COOPERATION IN PEACEBUILDING: NATURAL PARTNERS?

**Catriona Gourlay***

'The EU is committed to reinforcing its cooperation with the UN to assist countries emerging from conflict, and to enhancing its support for the UN in short-term crisis management situations.'

*European Security Strategy* (European Council, 2003)

'Our commitment to the United Nations is based on shared values and strongly convergent objectives in many areas and translates into an active partnership with the UN in operational, normative, and policy work, backed up by strong financial support.'

Benita Ferrero-Waldner,
*Commissioner for External Relations and European Neighbourhood Policy*

Louis Michel,
*Commissioner for Development and Humanitarian Aid*

*Improving Lives* (United Nations Office in Brussels, 2007)

## 1. Introduction

Given their shared values, their strongly convergent objectives and the EU's stated interest in promoting 'effective multilateralism', the European Union and the United Nations are often considered to be natural partners in peacebuilding. This chapter explores this assumption.

As demonstrated in the contribution by Simon Duke and Aurélie Courtier to this volume, the EU is a hybrid organisation with a supranational dimension characterised by the external action undertaken in the context of the first Pillar and an intergovernmental dimension characterised by its actions carried out in the framework of its

* Catriona Gourlay is a Research Fellow and Project Manager at the United Nations Institute for Disarmament Research (UNIDIR) in Geneva. Previously, she was a Marie Curie Fellow at UNIDIR, funded by the Directorate-General for Research of the European Commission to work on a research project and a doctoral thesis on EU-UN cooperation in crisis management and peacebuilding. This chapter draws on part of this research. The author would like to thank the officials from the EU and UN interviewed in the course of the research. Research on this chapter was closed before the entry into force of the Lisbon Treaty.

*S. Blockmans, J. Wouters & T. Ruys, eds., The European Union and Peacebuilding*

Common Foreign and Security Policy (CFSP) and European Security and Defence Policy (ESDP). The *sui generic* institutional structure of the EU coupled with the fact that peacebuilding straddles different EU institutions and policy areas complicates the form of the EU-UN relationship. One of the principal characteristics of the EU-UN relationship in peacebuilding is therefore that it is multi-layered and multifaceted. Tardy distinguishes between three layers of the EU-UN relationship in crisis management that correspond to three sets of relationships between different actors, each with their own form or 'facets'. He notes, 'What the European Commission is doing with the UN Development Programme (UNDP) is one level of relation; what the Secretariat of the Council is doing with the UN Department of Peacekeeping Operations (DPKO) is another; and what the EU member states do within the UN Security Council is a third.'[1] This is also true for peacebuilding, which is widely acknowledged to include development, political and security dimensions.

This chapter briefly explores two of these dimensions, focusing on the relationship between EU and UN development and security actors. It begins, in section 2, by addressing: whether EU and UN peacebuilding policies are coherent; why different organisational actors within the EU and UN have different conceptions of what peacebuilding involves; and the implications for operational cooperation. Section 3 explores the relationship between the EU and UN development actors. Based on the assumption that the funding relationship is an important dimension of their operational partnership, it uses a mix of quantitative and qualitative analysis to highlight trends in the European Commission's funding relationship with the UN and to identify operational challenges. Section 4 explores the EU-UN peacebuilding relationship in the context of peace operations. Although, for some, peacebuilding comprises military stabilisation missions, this chapter adopts a definition that is consistent with an increasing EU and UN focus on state building. This includes efforts carried out in the context of civilian ESDP missions or UN multidimensional peace operations undertaken by the UN DPKO. In other words, this section examines the record of EU-UN operational cooperation in relation to the civilian aspects of peace operations. It asks whether civilian ESDP helps share the UN peacebuilding burden and whether both organisations work well together in practice. Based on this brief analysis of two dimensions of the EU-UN peacebuilding relationship, section 5 draws conclusions in relation to the chapter's central question: are the EU and UN natural partners in peacebuilding?

## 2. Are EU and UN peacebuilding policies coherent?[2]

The term 'peacebuilding' remains subject to many different interpretations. The EU and UN do not subscribe to a common definition of the term. In the UN, peace-

[1] T. Tardy, *United Nations-European Union Relations in Crisis Management*, Background Paper (International Forum for the Challenges of Peace Operations 2008), at 2.

[2] This section draws on previous work by the author, notably Part 1 of the report *EU-UN Cooperation in Peacebuilding: Partners in Practice?* (United Nations Institute for Disarmament Research, New York and Geneva 2009) 3-48.

building tends to be associated with the system-wide effort to consolidate peace, whereas in the EU the term tends to be linked with a wide range of long-term development activities designed to promote structural stability or with short-term actions with direct conflict prevention objectives. The Council of the EU does not use the term to describe its interventions in the framework of ESDP. Instead, EU support for international missions is rationalised on the basis that they are in line with EU crisis management ambitions and address the threat posed by fragile states to international peace. Nor is there a common understanding of the term within EU and UN member states. While some states frame their post-conflict activities around the term peacebuilding, others use alternative terms such as *stabilisation and reconstruction, state building or nation building*. Thus, although the use of the term peacebuilding[3] has become more common outside the UN since it was first introduced in the 1992 Agenda for Peace,[4] the EU has only partially adopted it and there is still considerable confusion about its conceptual boundaries and policy implications.

A number of factors may account for this. At the most fundamental level conceptual confusion persists because there is no agreement about how to institutionalise peace after war.[5] Peacebuilding has, therefore, become an umbrella term associated with an aspiration rather than a specific procedure, policy, doctrine or operational programme. It is defined by its signal aim of preventing relapse into war. As one UN official put it, 'peacebuilding is not a set of activities, but a reason we are choosing to do them.' In the absence of consensus over what works, the evolution of the term has been shaped by how institutions have chosen to conceptualise their engagement in post-conflict contexts as peacebuilding. This, in turn, reflects their normative rationale as well as organisational interests. One review of how 24 governmental and intergovernmental bodies that are active in peacebuilding have used the term concluded that 'an organization's core mandate will heavily influence its reception to, and definition and revision of, the concept of peacebuilding.'[6]

---

[3] The term 'peace-building' was hyphenated in all UN documents until the 2000 Report of the High-Level Panel on United Nations Peace Operations, the so-called Brahimi Report (United Nations 2000). By this stage, its use had become so widespread, approaching that of the more established terms 'peacekeeping' and 'peacemaking', that the hyphenation was no longer considered necessary. Peacebuilding is not typically hyphenated in European Commission documents, but it is in Council documents.

[4] United Nations, *An Agenda for Peace: Preventive Diplomacy, Peacemaking, and Peace-keeping*, Report of the Secretary-General, UN Document A/47/277-S/24111, 17 June 1992.

[5] For a discussion of the peacebuilding record and a literature review of peacebuilding policy development, see Gourlay, *supra* n. 2, at 5-12.

[6] M. Barnett, H. Kim, M. O'Donnell and L. Sitea, 'Peacebuilding: What's in a Name?', 13 *Global Governance* (2007) 37. The authors observe that there are even more significant differences in how organisations operationalise peacebuilding. They adopt strategies and programmes that 'more often than not, reflect unexamined assumptions and deeply rooted organizational mandates rather than "best practices" born from empirical analysis' (at 53). If, as their review concludes, bureaucratic interests have been a critical factor in framing the concept of peacebuilding and in determining its practice, then one can expect greater conceptual and policy convergence between organisations with similar man-

Elsewhere the author has argued that EU and UN policy discourse has, indeed, been framed in line with institutional mandates and operational approaches. However, this has not resulted in a consensus definition. On the contrary, the dynamics of interinstitutional competition have resulted in a diversity of peacebuilding-relevant concepts and practices.[7] Reflecting on the process of consultation that informed the UN Secretary-General's 2009 report *Peacebuilding in the Immediate Aftermath of Conflict*,[8] one official from the UN Peacebuilding Support Office (PBSO) noted that

> 'we didn't attempt to resolve definitional issues relating to peacebuilding or state building because this would have led us into a black hole. We found that humanitarian, development, political and security actors all had distinct visions of what peacebuilding was and all thought that their view was the mainstream one.'[9]

Despite or perhaps because of the diverse views of what peacebuilding involves in operational terms, peacebuilding discourse within the UN is closely associated with improving systemic efforts to consolidate peace. This is supported by the fact that the principal innovations associated with peacebuilding in the UN system have evolved in response to perceived weaknesses, gaps and incoherence of the collective international response at the systemic level. The UN's principal institutional response to these concerns was the establishment of the Peacebuilding Commission (see chapter 8 of this volume). It was designed to bring together the most significant external actors in an effort to secure their sustained support for peace consolidation around a common strategic approach. More recently, the UN has turned its attention to the collective peacebuilding effort in the immediate aftermath of war, arguing for strengthened in-country capacity to promote strategic coordination and for efforts to bring forward the development response.

Like the UN, the EU is a fragmented institutional actor, in which the principal line of cleavage is between the development and security 'Pillars'.[10] Within these Pillars, different actors are engaged in a variety of activities that can be said to contribute to peacebuilding, using a range of different instruments. Their conceptions of what peacebuilding involves vary accordingly. For example, interviews reveal that for European Commission officials involved in implementing the Instrument for Stability (IfS), peacebuilding is often associated with a subset of activities that are designed to address specific risk factors and promote dialogue and

---

dates and practices. Indeed, Barnett et al. also note that 'organizations do not exist in isolation but instead are nested in structured relationships and exchange of resources and information; those that are linked have tended to converge on a consensus definition' (at 37).

[7] Gourlay, *supra* n. 2, at 12-42.

[8] United Nations, *Peacebuilding in the Immediate Aftermath of Conflict*, Report of the Secretary-General, UN Document A/63/881 – S/2009/304, 11 June 2009.

[9] Interview with PBSO official, New York, May 2009.

[10] This is likely to be the case even after the entry into force of the Treaty of Lisbon.

mediation.[11] Officials working in DG Development and EuropeAid (First Pillar) associate peacebuilding with efforts to promote conflict sensitivity in development assistance and address root causes by supporting long-term processes of democratisation, improving governance and promoting development. Within the Council of Ministers (Second Pillar), officials do not typically define their work in terms of peacebuilding, but rather argue that short-term crisis management interventions, including interventions designed for post-conflict state building, are essential prerequisites for consolidating peace.

Although it is widely recognised in the EU that post-conflict stabilisation, recovery and peacebuilding require a comprehensive approach, combining security, development and governance activities, the EU Member States have not demanded institutional coherence in the same way that they have in the UN context. Rather, to date, the politics of EU integration have served to entrench the security and development divide, with security actors emphasising decision-making autonomy, and development actors privileging conceptual and policy linkage with the broader donor community and national development ministries over internal cross-Pillar alliances. This helps explain why, in the EU, the peacebuilding challenge is primarily viewed at the activity level – designing, supporting or implementing specific actions that are considered to have an impact on the root causes of conflict and the consolidation of peace. Given that the EU tends to view peacebuilding at the programming level, the main focus for the European Commission has been on strengthening operational partnerships to address specific threats to peace. In the UN, the principal interest has been on maintaining EU support for the nascent peacebuilding architecture in New York and for UN-led coordination efforts and programmes in-country.[12] However, although the EU and UN privilege different levels of the peacebuilding challenge and this contributes to conceptual confusion, in practice both organisations combine similar approaches to peacebuilding albeit using different conceptual terms. Their organisational approach to peacebuilding is therefore arguably more similar than it appears from an analysis of terminology.

For instance, the European Commission approach to peacebuilding is similar to that of UNDP in many ways. Both organisations support a conflict transformation approach to peacebuilding, working to transform violent conflict from the bottom up through various actions designed to promote social and political reconciliation. While their engagement with national governments is a prerequisite for their operational engagements, their activities are not typically targeted at changing the behaviour of national leaders in the short term. Rather, they are often designed to create enabling conditions for peace in the longer term. The European Commission and UNDP thus share ambitions to tackle the root causes through long-term pro-

---

[11] This is in line with the original rationale for establishing the Instrument for Stability as set out in the Regulation establishing an Instrument for Stability, initiated by the European Commission and agreed by the European Parliament and the Council of the EU in 2006. See Regulation (EC) No 1717/2006 of the European Parliament and of the Council of 15 November 2006 establishing an Instrument for Stability, *OJ* 2006 L 327/1.

[12] See the contribution by Tomat and Onestini to this volume.

gramming in areas such as justice, rule of law, democratisation, state building at national and local levels and poverty reduction. Their engagement in post-conflict recovery is also increasingly guided by common needs assessments, and the European Commission supports UN efforts to speed up the delivery of peace dividends through better humanitarian-development coordination and funding innovations. In these cases, the approach to conflict transformation is necessarily a soft one based on long-term partnerships with national governments and efforts to build local capacity. Although the European Commission and UN might compete for influence in-country, they tend to share a long-term preventative approach to peace consolidation.

In contrast, the use of political and security instruments for peacebuilding follows a distinct 'crisis management approach' in the EU and UN. Although both organisations stress the imperative of national ownership, priority actions are decided from the top down in line with (military) planning protocol. External actors implement actions and form part of a package of incentives (positive and negative) designed to maintain the support of political elites for the implementation of peace agreements or mutually agreed reforms.

This difference in approach also has implications for how the different actors perceive the imperative of external coherence and coordination. In line with the logic of crisis management, efforts to promote coherence of the external peacebuilding effort are primarily important for strategic political reasons since 'unity of effort' increases the leverage or power of the external actors vis-à-vis key domestic political elites. The same is not, however, necessarily true for efforts that aim to improve structural stability or promote change from the bottom up. In these cases, the external actors require consent from national elites but not in return for short-term concessions. Indeed, the development community has long been cognisant of the negative consequences of strict conditionality. From the perspective of many development actors, then, external coherence is (only) desirable for reasons of efficiency or administrative accountability. Operational partnerships can enable or strengthen interventions, and aid harmonisation is considered important for achieving 'critical mass' without burdening limited state capacity with the administration of external aid. They are not, therefore, principally important for strategic reasons associated with ongoing negotiation processes designed to promote political reform.

Thus, while both long-term conflict transformation and short-term crisis management approaches to peacebuilding can be complementary, they are organised in fundamentally different ways, with different objectives, theories of change, timelines and coordination 'requirements'. In theory, local EU and UN leadership helps synchronise different approaches and ensure that they are complementary. However, in both cases the EU and UN often lack the authority and capacity to do so. Similarly, while the EU and UN have created dedicated peacebuilding funding instruments – the Instrument for Stability of the EU and the Peacebuilding Fund (PBF) of the UN – to fill strategic gaps, or address imminent risks, these are no substitute for agreeing strategic external priorities in line with peace consolidation objectives.

And while both the EU and UN support the ambition of the PBC to guide 'strategic' international engagement, in practice, the PBC has limited geographical scope and has not guided EU operational decisions.[13]

## 3. Operational cooperation in peacebuilding: The development dimension[14]

This section identifies quantitative trends in European Commission (abbreviated in this section as 'EC') funding for peacebuilding and traces the proportion of EC funding for peacebuilding channelled through the UN, drawing on published data. The narrative analysis offers explanations for the key trends observed and is complemented by a discussion of the main organisational obstacles to effective aid delivery, including through the UN, in fragile situations.

### 3.1 Trends in EC policy and funding for state building in fragile states

Since 2000, there has been a concerted effort within the EU to promote good governance and state building in EU development policy.[15] This has been reflected in an increasingly elaborate policy framework and dedicated financial commitments. The policy developments can be traced through a number of European Commission and joint Commission-Council policy documents. These include the joint statement on EC development policy,[16] which identifies institutional strengthening as one of the six priority areas, and the Commission Communication on governance and development,[17] which evolved into the EC Communication on governance.[18] Governance issues also feature prominently in the European Consensus on Development,[19] the EU strategy for Africa[20] and the 2006 Communication on governance.[21]

---

[13] For a review of the UN Peacebuilding Commission and its negligible impact on EC programming, see Gourlay, *supra* n. 2, at 82-86 and 124-131.

[14] This section draws on previous work by the author, notably Part 2 of the report *EU-UN Cooperation in Peacebuilding: Partners in Practice?*, *supra* n. 2, at 49-106.

[15] See the contribution by Darmuzey to this volume.

[16] European Commission, *Joint Statement of the Council and Commission on EC Development Policy* (2000).

[17] Communication from the European Commission, 'Governance and Development', COM(2003) 615 def., 20 October 2003.

[18] Communication from the European Commission, 'Governance in the European Consensus on Development: Towards a Harmonised Approach within the European Union', COM(2006) 621 def., 30 August 2006.

[19] Joint declaration by the Council and the representatives of the governments of the Member States meeting within the Council, the European Parliament and the Commission on the development policy of the European Union entitled 'The European Consensus', *OJ* 2006 C 46.

[20] European Council, Presidency Conclusions, 'The EU and Africa: Towards a Strategic Partnership', Doc. 15702/1/05, 15-16 December 2005.

[21] Communication from the European Commission, 'Governance in the European Consensus on Development: Towards a Harmonised Approach within the European Union', *supra* n. 18.

In line with its elevated policy profile, financial commitments to the good governance agenda have been increasingly significant, although difficult to quantify. The lack of appropriate classification codes has meant that attempts to identify the volume of aid allocated to good governance have been tentative. A 2003 review of country and regional strategy papers conducted by DG DEV nevertheless estimated that €2 billion out of a total programmable envelope of €10 billion for 2002-2007 was allocated to governance-related support.[22] Another estimate of financial volumes (by region) over the period 1995-2004 showed an increase in good governance-related commitments, representing 27% of total EU commitments. But it also revealed a widening gap between commitments and payments, with only one third of the commitments disbursed over the period.[23] The European Commission has also earmarked €2.7 billion to good governance from the 10th European Development Fund (EDF) for 2008-2013, out of a total programmable envelope of €13.5 billion for ACP countries. While 80% of the EDF is allocated through Country Strategy Papers (CSPs), which may also include governance support, the remaining 20% (€2.7 billion) is set aside as an additional 'incentive tranche'. These funds are allocated on the basis of partner countries' commitments to governance plans of action. The European Commission insists that this system does not constitute a form of conditionality since it offers a more collaborative approach to implementation, with joint responsibility for attaining targets.[24] Nevertheless, as one OECD DAC review observed, democratic governance is increasingly seen as a precondition for budget support and it remains unclear how the incentive tranche system will work in fragile states where state capacity is weak.[25] Thus, although aid allocations for good governance are significant and increasing, the fact that recipients must meet minimum governance standards to receive budget support or 'additional' governance assistance suggests that there are significant challenges to aid disbursement on 'governance' in fragile states.

As with global ODA trends, it appears that funding for governance is higher in 'normal' development contexts and in relatively few high-profile fragile states, the so-called 'aid darlings'. The Commission Communication on governance acknowledged that the majority of good governance assistance is delivered in stable political contexts.[26] Likewise, the European Commission report on peacebuilding activities[27] provides relatively few concrete examples of EC support for state building in fragile contexts, with some notable post-conflict exceptions, including Af-

---

[22] European Commission, *Country Strategy Paper (CSP) Assessment of Governance Conclusions*, Directorate-General for Development, January 2003.

[23] European Commission, *Thematic Evaluation of the EC Support to Good Governance*, Evaluation for the European Commission by PARTICIP, Final Report (2006), at 38.

[24] Interview with EuropeAid officials, Brussels, June 2009.

[25] OECD (Organisation for Economic Co-operation and Development), *European Community Development Assistance Committee (DAC) Peer Review*, OECD DAC, 2007, at 64 and 68.

[26] See European Commission Communications on Governance of 2003 and 2006, *supra* nn. 17 and 18.

[27] European Commission, *Support to Peacebuilding: Examples of EU Action*, Memo/05/313, 12 September 2005.

ghanistan, the Democratic Republic of Congo, Iraq and countries of the Western Balkans. EuropeAid's annual reports also show that top recipients of EC aid are often conflict-affected countries. Since 2003, Afghanistan, the Democratic Republic of Congo, Iraq, Sudan and the West Bank and Gaza have featured among the top five recipients.

### 3.2 Operational challenges for EC engagement in fragile states

Although there has been little quantitative analysis of the breakdown of EC assistance in fragile states, there have been a number of qualitative studies in this area. The EC commissioned two of these, the 2006 thematic evaluation of EC support to good governance[28] and the 2008 mapping study on situations of fragility.[29] In addition, in 2007, the Portuguese Presidency of the EU commissioned a study intended to inform EU strategy in response to situations of fragility.[30] These reviews of EC assistance documented the increasing prominence given to the governance dimension in EC development policy, but also identified a gap between policy and practice. As with global reviews of assistance in fragile states, the studies highlighted disbursement pressures combined with an emphasis on financial accountability as factors that served as disincentives for risky and administratively 'heavy' governance programming. Similarly, they noted the difficulty of prioritising governance issues in CSPs where partner governments are not in agreement. All stressed that European Commission in-country capacity was often not sufficient for providing and overseeing governance assistance in many post-conflict contexts.

In addition, the author has argued elsewhere that the European Commission reform agenda launched in the late 1990s with the aim of developing the institutional competence of the EC as an administratively accountable aid disbursement agency, has in practice exacerbated some of these challenges.[31] While neither Member States nor DG RELEX commissioners who orchestrated the reforms foresaw that privileging aid disbursement efficiency might adversely affect aid effectiveness, in practice, it has undermined efforts to build substantive capacity and procedures that promote politically sensitive and transformative funding strategies in fragile states. Rather, EC reforms have reduced institutional incentives and capacity to engage in politically sensitive project-based programming and to allocate relatively scarce staff resources to developing in-house specialist competence. Moreover, the combination of institutional restructuring in Brussels with devolution to the field has

---

[28] European Commission, *Thematic Evaluation of the EC Support to Good Governance*, *supra* n. 23.

[29] European Commission, *Mapping of Donors, Actors, Financial Instruments and Assessment Tools in Situations of Fragility*, Support Study in View of the Follow-Up to the 2007 Commission Communication, Council Conclusions and EP Resolutions on Situations of Fragility, 2008.

[30] F. Faria and P. Ferreira, *An Adequate EU Response Strategy to Address Situations of Fragility and Difficult Environments* (European Centre for Development Policy Management and the Institute for Strategic and International Studies 2007).

[31] Gourlay, *supra* n. 2, at 57-61.

led to the fragmentation of substantive expertise across three Directorates-General in Brussels (DG RELEX, DG DEV and EuropeAid) and between headquarters and the field. It has thereby complicated efforts in Brussels to integrate conflict analysis into the development of CSPs and country programming documents and has led to a wide degree of variation in the capacity and approach to implementing politically sensitive governance programming in EC delegations. This helps explain why, in the absence of substantive capacity and buy-in from geographical desks and delegations, EC governance programming remains scattered, *ad hoc*, projectised and relatively rare in some fragile states.

By the same token, disbursement pressures combined with capacity shortfalls have increased operational imperatives to channel funds through administratively efficient instruments, such as budget support. The European Commission has used budget support for debt relief in fragile states (e.g., in Burundi, Central African Republic, Haiti, Liberia, Sierra Leone and Togo) and is working, together with other donors, on the development of guidance to increase the use of budget support for state building and governance development in fragile states. However, given the limited capacity or 'eligibility' of national government counterparts and the risk aversion of Member States and the European Parliament, the use of budget support in fragile states is not yet widespread, and would, in any case, likely need to be combined with technical assistance programmes in the area of financial administration.

EC capacity shortfalls and risk aversion arguably also contribute to an operational interest in partnering with other donors and other international organisations in the implementation of assistance in fragile states. They help explain the increase in the use of Multi-Donor Trust Funds (MDTFs) in such states, administered by the UN or the World Bank, and the use of the UN as an implementing partner for projects and programmes. Distributing aid through the UN is administratively straightforward for the European Commission, especially since the 2003 Financial and Administrative Framework Agreement (FAFA).[32] It also makes sense in so far as the UN has a comparative capacity advantage and established relationship with the authorities in many fragile states. In short, although the EU may have ambitions to use its political influence and financial clout directly in fragile situations, this has not in many cases been easy to reconcile with its role as an efficient donor. In so far as the UN has a comparative political and capacity advantage in fragile states, one might therefore expect the UN to be a natural implementing partner for the European Commission. The following sub-section explores whether this is borne out by recent funding trends and evaluations of EC assistance.

### 3.3 Trends in EC funding for the UN

*Has the EC increased the proportion of assistance channelled through the UN?*
There have been a number of efforts to track European funding that is channelled

[32] FAFA operationalised Article 53 of the Financial Regulation agreed in 2002, which provided the legal parameters and procedures for all EC assistance. It allowed UN bodies to work within their own procedures, specified mutual obligations and made substantial pre-financing possible.

through the UN. Within the European Commission, EuropeAid has produced an annual report of EuropeAid financial contributions to the UN since 2001,[33] providing statistics on the external aid that EuropeAid disburses. This includes aid from the European Community Budget and EDF, but not humanitarian aid disbursed through the European Commission Humanitarian Aid Office (ECHO). Since 2005, the Brussels Office of UNDP has also produced annual reports highlighting the results of the EC-UN operational partnership.[34] In addition, the European Commission launched an evaluation of external EC cooperation with partner countries through the organisations of the UN family.[35] Most recently, the EC has commissioned an evaluation of its peacebuilding programmes.[36] This section draws on the data published in these reports and aims to provide an overview of the main trends in the EC-UN funding relationship.

*Figure 1.* Financial contributions from the European Commission to the United Nations

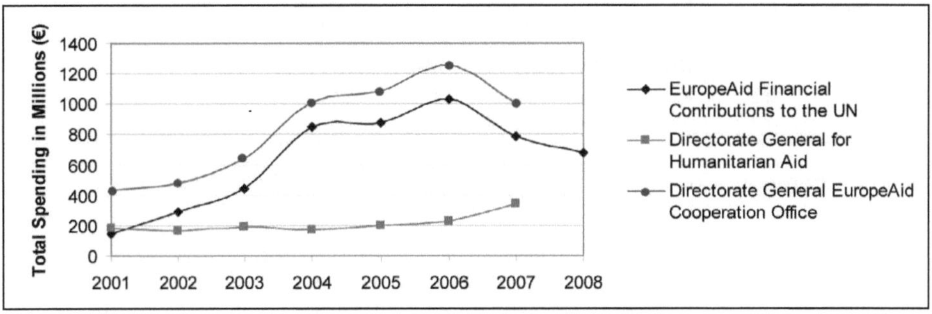


*Source*: EuropeAid financial contributions to the UN, 2001-2008.[37]

Figures 1 and 2 show that since 2001 there has been both an absolute and proportional increase in funding channelled from the European Commission through the UN. From 2002 to 2006, the volume of aid channelled through EuropeAid to the UN quadrupled from some €257 million to over €1 billion in 2006, although from

[33] These annual reports are available on the EuropeAid website <http://ec.europa.eu/europeaid/who/partners/international-organisations/index_en.htm>.

[34] These annual reports are available on the web site of the UNDP Brussels office <http://www.undp.org/eu/>.

[35] European Commission, *Evaluation of the Commission's External Cooperation with Partner Countries through the Organisations of the UN Family*, implemented by Aide à la Décision Economique S.A. (ADE), April 2008.

[36] European Commission, *Thematic Evaluation of the European Commission Support to Conflict Prevention and Peace Building. Preliminary Study: Scoping and Mapping* (EuropeAid Cooperation Office 2009).

[37] These EuropeAid statistics are prepared using data from the Common RELEX Information System (CRIS), which contains information on projects funded from the general EC budget (about €4 billion per year), and the OLAS database, which covers the ACP and includes projects funded by EDF (about €3 billion per year). Since 15 February 2009, however, CRIS also includes data previously included in OLAS. The 2008 data are taken from the report *Improving Lives* (United Nations Office in Brussels 2008), at 20.

2006 to 2007 this declined to around €719 million. The decline since 2006 can be explained by an accounting change[38] as well as the reduction in aid to some of the countries that received a high proportion of EC assistance (demonstrated in Figure 4). Nevertheless, the figures confirm that the European Commission has increased the proportion of the assistance that is channelled through the UN since 2001.

*Figure 2.* Total EC aid and percentage channelled through the UN system (2002-2007)

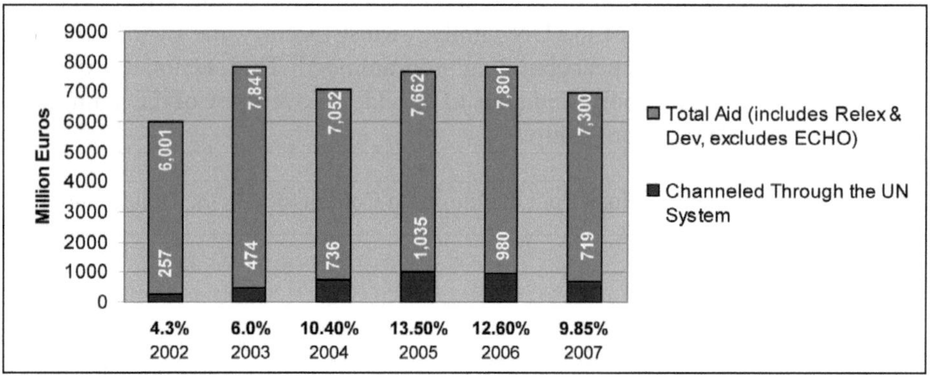


*Sources*: European Commission 2008 Evaluation[39] for 2002-2006 data; EuropeAid[40] for 2007 data.

*Is the UN a key operational partner for the EU in peacebuilding?*

Figure 3 reveals that a large proportion of EC funding for the UN is allocated to situations of fragility. It shows that more than half (55%) of the total funds contracted by the European Commission (DG RELEX, DG DEV, AIDCO) to the UN bodies over the period 1999-2006 was destined for interventions in clear situations of political crisis. Likewise, the annual reviews of the EC-UN partnership conducted by UNDP consistently reveal that most of the UN country programmes that receive high levels of funding from the European Commission (over €15 million per year) have been affected by political crisis.[41]

---

[38] In 2007, all food aid programmes, with a total budget of €220 million, were transferred to the Directorate-General for ECHO and therefore most contracts concluded with the World Food Programme (WFP) do not appear in 2007 figures.

[39] See *supra* n. 35.

[40] European Commission, *Financial Contributions of EuropeAid to the UN Funds, Programmes and Specialized Agencies in 2007* (EuropeAid Cooperation Office 2008).

[41] See the following publications of the United Nations Office in Brussels: *The Partnership between the UN and the EU* (2006); *Improving Lives, Results from the Partnership of the United Nations and the European Commission in 2006* (2007); and *Improving Lives, Results from the Partnership of the United Nations and the European Commission in 2007* (2008). For instance, in 2007, the following UN country programmes received funds (in order of volume) for over €15 million from the EC: Sudan, West Bank and Gaza, Bangladesh, Afghanistan, Iraq, Thailand, Ukraine, Occupied Palestinian Territory, Ethiopia, Democratic Republic of Congo, United Republic of Tanzania, South Africa, Togo, Indonesia and Chad (*Improving Lives*, United Nations Office in Brussels 2008, at 20).

*Figure 3*. EC aid to countries in political crisis 1999-2006 channelled through the UN

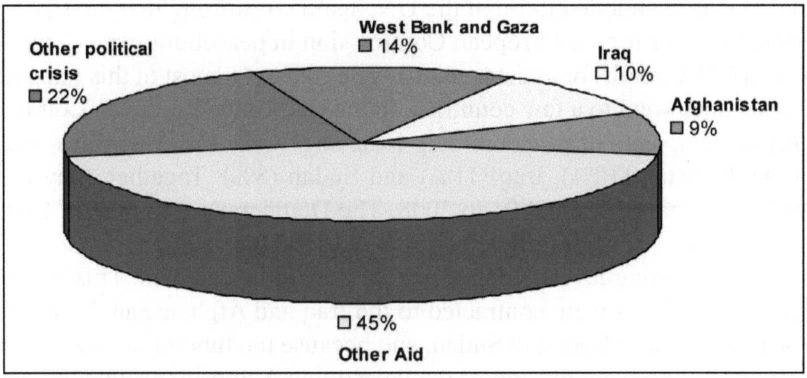


*Note*: Includes DG RELEX and DG DEV aid, excludes ECHO aid.
*Source*: European Commission 2008 Evaluation.[42]

Similarly, the 2009 scoping study of EC assistance for peacebuilding, which includes non-ODA funding (e.g., for African Union peace operations), confirms that: there has been a steep rise in assistance in fragile states; that a high proportion of this assistance is concentrated in a few fragile countries;[43] and that the UN is a key implementing partner in fragile contexts.[44] This is reflected in Figures 4 and 5.

*Figure 4*. Total EC spending on peacebuilding in top five major recepient countries

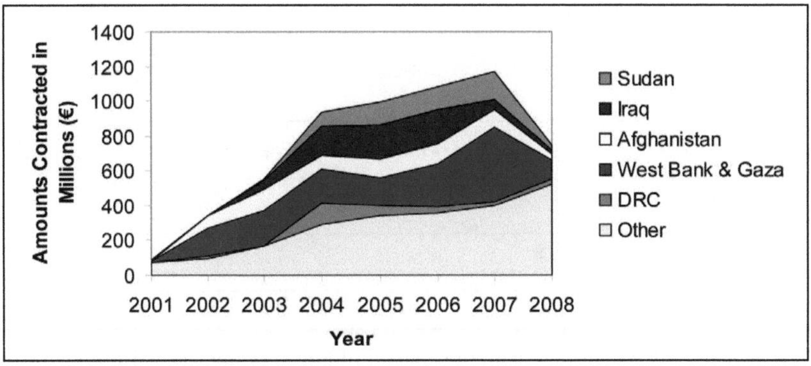


*Note*: DRC = Democratic Republic of Congo.
*Source*: CRIS and OLAS, drawn from the peacebuilding scoping study, European Commission 2009.[45]

More specifically, the study reveals that total spending for peacebuilding increased dramatically from €86 million in 2001 to over €1 billion in 2007, totalling some

[42] See *supra* n. 35.

[43] This chapter uses EC aid categorisation. In some cases, such as the West Bank and Gaza, categories do not refer to a country.

[44] European Commission, peacebuilding scoping study, 2009, *supra* n. 36.

[45] See *supra* n. 36.

€5.9 billion from 2001 to 2008. Of this total spending on peacebuilding, €2.2 billion (37%) was channelled through the UN, again confirming that the UN is a key operational partner for the European Commission in peacebuilding.

As with ODA trends for assistance to fragile states, for most of this time the bulk of EC assistance went to a few countries. In the case of the European Commission, the top four recipients of peacebuilding assistance were the West Bank and Gaza (26%), Afghanistan (12%), Iraq (11%) and Sudan (8%). Together, they received 57% of EC assistance from 2001 to 2008. The Democratic Republic of Congo received a further 5% and 11 other countries received between 1% and 2%.[46] However, in 2008, funding levels for the top four recipients declined. This was largely because no new funds were contracted to the Iraq and Afghanistan Trust Funds or to the African Union Mission in Sudan, and because the funding for the Temporary International Mechanism to support the Palestinian Authority declined. Given that in Afghanistan and Iraq, in particular, much of the EC funding was channelled through the UN-managed trust funds, this largely explains the drop in the EC funding for the UN in 2007 and 2008 as shown in Figure 5.

*Figure 5.* Total EC spending on peacebuilding

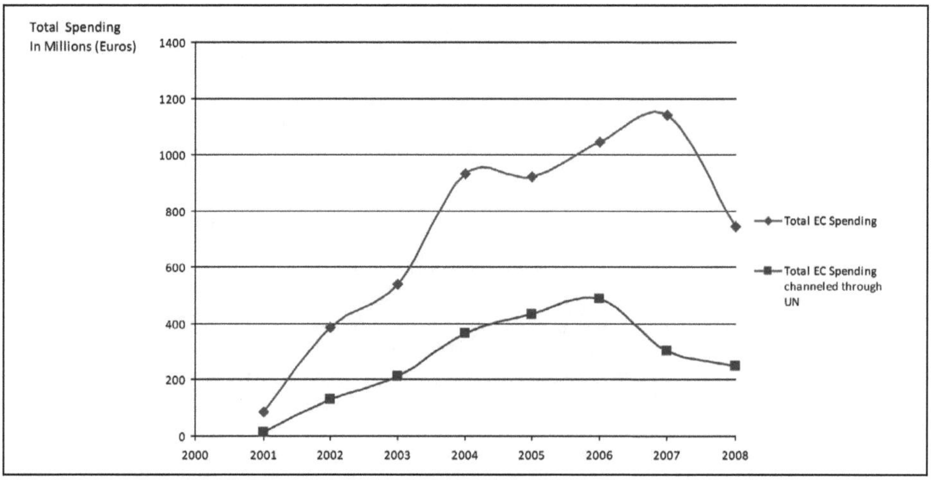


*Source*: CRIS and OLAS, drawn from the peacebuilding scoping study, European Commission, 2009.[47]

*Where in the UN does EC funding go?*

EC assistance is channelled through a wide range of UN agencies and programmes. EuropeAid annual reports routinely report on no fewer than 38 UN bodies that receive EC assistance.[48] However, given that a high proportion of assistance is chan-

---

[46] These countries include: Angola, Bangladesh, Central African Republic, Columbia, Côte d'Ivoire, Haiti, Indonesia, Liberia, Somalia, Timor-Leste and Ukraine.

[47] See *supra* n. 36.

[48] EuropeAid Cooperation Office, 2008, *supra* n. 40.

nelled to countries in situations of crisis, the UN agencies or programmes that are present and have a mandate to deliver recovery assistance receive a relatively large proportion of EC assistance. As shown in Figure 6, which excludes EC humanitarian funding, a large proportion of EC funds were granted to a limited number of UN bodies between 1999 and 2006. UNDP was the main recipient with €1.5 billion, representing 40% of total EC contributions.

*Figure 6.* Distribution of the amount contracted from the EC by UN bodies (% of value, 1999-2006)

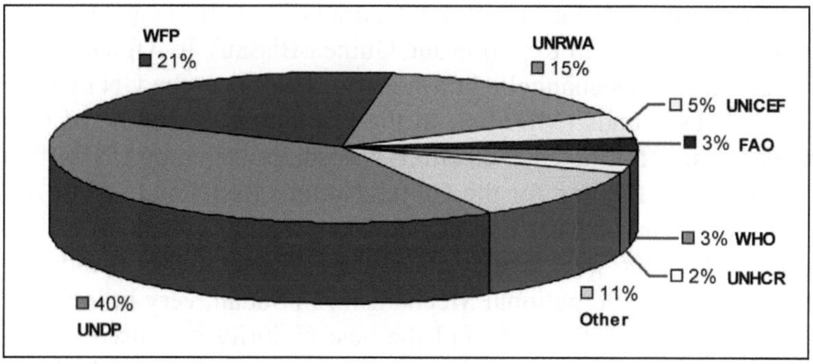


*Source*: European Commission 2008 Evaluation.[49]

Given that EC assistance for the UN is concentrated in a relatively small number of countries and UN agencies, as indicated in Figure 5, it is likely that large fluctuations in country assistance will be reflected in the volume of funding received by the main UN agencies that operate in those countries. This appears to be borne out by the trend in UNDP funding from the European Commission, shown in Figure 7.

*Figure 7.* EuropeAid financial contributions to the United Nations Development Programme (2001-2008).

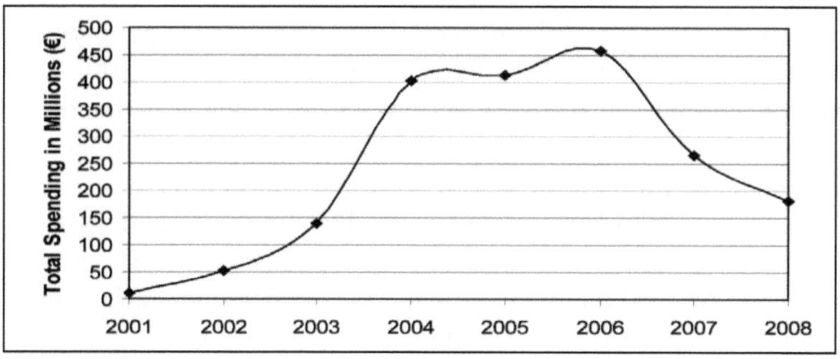


*Source*: EuropeAid Cooperation Office.[50]

---

[49] See *supra* n. 35.

[50] European Commission, *EuropeAid Financial Contributions to the United Nations 2001-2008* (EuropeAid Cooperation Office 2009).

In 2004, 2005 and 2006, when UNDP was conducting large elections and reconstruction projects in the Democratic Republic of Congo, Iraq and Sudan, it received over €400 million per year from the European Commission. In comparison, previous and subsequent levels of funding have been less than half that amount.

*Is the EU-UN funding partnership consistently strong in fragile states?*
In earlier work[51] the author examined the EC-UN funding partnership in relation to nine countries: the top five recipients of peacebuilding assistance (West Bank and Gaza, Afghanistan, Iraq, Sudan and the Democratic Republic of Congo) and the four countries on the UN Peacebuilding Commission (PBC) agenda (Burundi, Sierra Leone, Central African Republic and Guinea-Bissau). In Afghanistan and Iraq, most EC assistance was channelled through the UN due to the UN management of Multi-Donor Trust Funds (MDTFs). In the Democratic Republic of Congo, too, most EC assistance (for the 2006 election) was administered by UNDP. In the West Bank and Gaza, EC funding for the United Nations Relief and Works Agency for Palestine Refugees in the Near East (UNRWA) remained constant, while increases in assistance after 2006 were largely channelled directly to the Palestinian Authority or the Temporary International Mechanism. In Sudan, very little EC assistance was channelled through the UN, and the vast majority was used to support the African Union Mission in Sudan directly. In the four countries on the PBC agenda, the volume of EC aid identified as peacebuilding assistance was far lower and a relatively small proportion of it was channelled through the UN. This was mostly linked to election support implemented by UNDP. In short, in early recovery phases where the use of MDTFs is common or where the UN has been asked by the host country to play a central role, the UN has been a natural implementing partner for the European Commission. But in other cases, the EC-UN partnership is context and sector-specific. The strength of the operational partnership in these cases depends on the relative operational capacity of the UN compared with other implementing partners, and on the political standing of the UN in the country.

*Has the EC Instrument for Stability been used to support UN peacebuilding?*
The Instrument for Stability (IfS) is the principal EC funding instrument for short-term crisis prevention and recovery actions. By EC standards, this is a relatively small instrument with a budget of around €120 million per year. But over 40% of it has been channelled through the UN in 2007 and 2008 for a range of post-conflict actions, often intended to complement EU and UN missions with assistance aimed at helping establish rule of law and security sector reform (SSR) in post-conflict situations.[52] The IfS also includes a small crisis preparedness component (€7 million per year), the so-called Peacebuilding Partnership, which is explicitly intended to build peacebuilding capacity in other international, regional and non-governmental organisations (NGOs). Given its small size, it is perhaps unsurprising that it

[51] Gourlay, *supra* n. 2, at 76-87.
[52] Ibid., at 94-98.

has been spread thinly in an *ad hoc* manner across a range of actors. In the case of the UN, for instance, it has been used to support projects of the Peacebuilding Support Office (PBSO) and UNDP that aim to improve donor coordination. Thus, while a significant proportion of the crisis response component of the IfS is used to support flanking measures for ESDP *and* UN operations, the Peacebuilding Partnership component of the IfS, that aims to promote learning and build capacity through partnerships with key peacebuilding actors, remains relatively insignificant.

### 3.4 Analysis of funding trends

EuropeAid does not offer any evaluation of the funding trends documented in its annual reports, but it has commissioned studies to evaluate the 'added value' of channelling EC funding through international organisations. For instance, in 2006, it commissioned a study to provide an overview of implementation by international organisations, which concluded that the principal reasons for EC cooperation with these organisations were: (i) their ability to mobilise expertise and aid toward emerging global concerns; (ii) their potential for aid coordination; and (iii) their emphasis on capacity building and on a strong policy agenda. It argued that one of the benefits of collaboration with international organisations is that it *increases* EC policy influence at a broader level and contributes to inter-organisational learning.[53] Similarly, the UN 2006 review of its programmatic portfolio with the European Commission noted the importance of UN specialist thematic expertise and its coordination role as important reasons for channelling EC assistance through the UN. In addition, it noted that the European Commission partnered with the UN 'on sensitive issues that require the legitimacy and impartiality of the UN and in fragile country situations where consistent field presence and combined UN mandates facilitate transition out of crises.'[54] This suggested that the strong operational EC partnership with the UN in fragile situations flows from the UN capacity and legitimacy in these contexts. The 2008 evaluation of EC assistance through the UN reinforced this suggestion, concluding that the added value of channelling EC aid through the UN was simply that it was the *only* option for intervention in many cases. It concluded that:

> 'a number of interventions would not have been possible if they had not been conducted through UN bodies. In various cases, the Commission benefited from the unique specific characteristics of the UN system and bodies, which were required for being able to intervene and which no other organisation could offer.'[55]

Of particular importance in this context is the use of multilateral response mechanisms for major events, such as MDTFs, which are administered through the UN.

---

[53] European Commission, *Overview of Implementation by International Organizations* (EuropeAid Cooperation Office, August 2006).

[54] United Nations Office in Brussels, 2006, *supra* n. 41, at 12.

[55] European Commission 2008 Evaluation, *supra* n. 35, at v.

The UN thereby 'made delivery of aid possible in cases where this would otherwise have been difficult, particularly in politically sensitive situations.' The study found that when the UN has a clear mandate to administer multi-donor interventions in the absence of government capacity, notably in crisis or post-conflict situations, 'the organisation becomes a natural partner for the Commission.'[56] This, for example, includes the Iraq Trust Fund (UNDP), the elections in the Democratic Republic of Congo (UNDP) and the mandate of UNRWA in the Occupied Palestinian Territories. In many crisis situations, the evaluation studies found that channelling aid through the UN also 'had impact in terms of policy dialogue with partner countries.'[57] This is because the UN had an established presence and relationship with national authorities. Channelling aid through the UN offered the European Commission access to national authorities and a platform for discussion, which was seen to be particularly valuable in fragile states.[58] Also, in cases where the UN administered multi-donor interventions, European Commission participation enhanced EC influence through the governance structures of MDTFs. This was, for instance, the case in the elections in the Democratic Republic of Congo, where the European Commission actively participated in the technical committee responsible for the elections. There is, therefore, a broad consensus arising out of the evaluations of the EC funding partnership with the UN that in fragile situations the partnership is strong and natural because it is necessary; it enables the European Commission to disburse aid in these difficult contexts and *enhances* EC influence with local partner countries.

While none of the evaluations of EC assistance channelled through the UN set out to explain the funding trends, they nevertheless identify a range of factors that help account for the rise in volume and proportion of EC assistance channelled through the UN between 2001 and 2006. According to European Commission staff interviewed in Brussels and in some delegations, this trend was 'significantly influenced' by the clear EC policy preference for supporting effective multilateralism by working with the UN and a crucial administrative agreement that made it easier to disburse funds to the UN in practice.[59] More specifically, the 2001 Communication *Building an Effective Partnership with the United Nations in the Fields of Development and Humanitarian Affairs*[60] and the 2003 Communication *The European Union and the United Nations: The Choice of Multilateralism*[61] provided a supportive policy framework, which was further strengthened by the emphasis of the Paris Declaration[62] on donor cooperation and harmonisation of external aid. In 2003,

---

56 Ibid., at 22.

57 Ibid., at vi.

58 Ibid., at 25.

59 Interviews conducted for the 2008 European Commission Evaluation, *supra* n. 35.

60 European Commission, *Building an Effective Partnership with the United Nations in the Fields of Development and Humanitarian Affairs* (2001).

61 European Commission, Communication from the Commission, 'The EU and the UN: The Choice of Multilateralism', 2003.

62 Paris High-Level Forum, *The Paris Declaration on Aid Effectiveness, Aid Harmonization and Alignment*, 2005.

however, FAFA was a critical enabling factor. The 2008 European Commission evaluation noted that it 'allowed UN bodies to work within their own procedures, it specified mutual obligations and it made possible substantial pre-financing.'[63] From the European Commission perspective, it reduced the time needed for partner selection compared with calls for proposals. However, it did not necessarily reduce delivery time given that it effectively transferred the administrative burden to the UN. The UNDP report on EC-UN cooperation in 2006 argued that, in addition to FAFA, which lowered the transaction costs of cooperation for the European Commission, assistance channelled through the UN has been aided by the devolution process within the EC that has increased the country-level entry points for cooperation and helped the European Commission assess local UN capacities more accurately.[64] Finally, while the Commission evaluation noted that the increase in volume of funding until 2006 is a general phenomenon and not only applies to countries with high public awareness and donor mobilisation (e.g., Afghanistan, Democratic Republic of Congo, Iraq), the subsequent decline in funding since 2006 can be largely explained by a reduction in funding for some of the major recipient countries, most of which are in political crisis. Thus, while there has been a general rise in the volume of assistance channelled through the UN, this is likely to fluctuate along with trends in funding high-profile crises that precipitate large volumes of aid.

Despite the consensus that the EC and UN are natural operational partners in fragile states where the UN has the capacity, legitimacy and mandate to lead international responses, interviews with European Commission staff[65] and evaluations of the EC-UN partnership reveal persistent frictions that stem from different perceptions of the nature of the partnership and different operational practices. For example, the European Commission has unusually high financial accountability standards linked to the financial regulations relating to ODA, which are required of the European Commission by the European Parliament. They have, however, led to the widespread perception within the UN that the EC is an 'overly' demanding donor when compared with others. Reporting conditions that stipulate that annual interim reports and financial reports be in euros often require distinct management of EC funds within UN interventions, which, in turn, creates problems for the pooling of resources. From the European Commission perspective, however, the UN is often seen as an unreliable implementing partner precisely because of insufficient and delayed narrative and financial reporting, which creates accountability problems for European Commission officials. For example, the EC was forced to take abnormal financial risks in contravention of procedures when funding the elections in the Democratic Republic of Congo through UNDP, although both sides agree with hindsight that a proactive attitude to taking risks was required for the sake of the project's (successful) outcome.

---

63 European Commission, 2008 Evaluation, *supra* n. 35, at vi.

64 United Nations Office in Brussels, 2006, *supra* n. 41.

65 These include interviews for the 2008 European Commission Evaluation, *supra* n. 35, and interviews by the author with officials from EuropeAid and UNDP in May 2008 and June 2009.

At the operational level, the EC-UN relationship is also strained by different interpretations of what partnership means in practice. From the EC point of view, co-management as defined in FAFA requires that the UN provide the European Commission with full information and involve the EC in strategic decision-making relating to project implementation. From the UN perspective, however, the European Commission is viewed as a demanding donor that wants to interfere in UN project management where it has no responsibility for the implementation of the project and does not deserve a 'privileged' status vis-à-vis other donors. While both partners argue that the partnership should be based on mutual respect between 'equals', both often feel disrespected. EC evaluations have concluded that these organisational frictions can be overcome through greater clarification of mutual obligations, including through further guidance on the precise interpretation of FAFA as well as staff training. However, further organisational adaptation may be necessary. There is a strong case for adapting EC financial regulations, making them more risk tolerant in fragile states where the UN has a leading role in early post-conflict recovery, and for the increased use of MDTFs that reduce transaction costs for the European Commission and the recipient country while ensuring that the donors are involved in the governance of the funds. Greater flexibility in the use of EC funding in fragile situations, will, in turn, require empowering local EC leadership. Post-Lisbon Treaty reforms, notably the creation of a European External Action Service, present an obvious opportunity to do so. However, if the European Commission 'principals' – EU Member States and the European Parliament – are to sanction greater flexibility in the use of EC funds in fragile situations, they will likely require greater political accountability in exchange for a relative loss of financial control. In sum, the trick to improving the Commission's ability to support the peacebuilding and state-building agenda in fragile states and to strengthen EU-UN in-country partnerships will be to strengthen the capacity and autonomy of the EU delegations, while also enhancing their political accountability.

## 4. Operational cooperation in peacebuilding: The (civilian) security dimension[66]

This section explores whether the EU-UN peacebuilding relationship in the context of crisis management operations is a 'natural fit' in which the EU supports the objectives of the UN. Although both organisations have made policy declarations underlining their strategic interest in greater cooperation based on a rationale of burden sharing, it shows that this is sometimes undermined by inter-organisational competition. Section 4.1 explores whether civilian ESDP does indeed contribute to burden sharing through the quantitative analysis of international civilian deployments. It aims to address whether ESDP brings 'added value' to the UN through the following research questions: *are the EU and UN in competition over civilian hu-*

---

[66] This section draws on the author's doctoral thesis research, which includes case studies of EU-UN operational cooperation.

*man resources?; and, has ESDP increased the total number of civilians that international operations can draw on?*

Section 4.2 explores the assumption that operational cooperation is complementary and is predicated on common objectives and policy alignment. It briefly examines EU-UN operational cooperation in the two countries in which civilian ESDP missions have been deployed alongside UN missions, the Democratic Republic of Congo (DRC) and Kosovo. *Can the UN rely on the operational support of the EU? Was EU-UN operational cooperation based on common strategic positions and policies? Did they share the same tactical approach? And do they work well together?*

## 4.1 Trends in European civilian deployments

Highlighting the benefits of burden sharing, the UN Secretary-General formally welcomed greater regional engagement in peace operations in the 1992 *Agenda for Peace*. Yet, in practice, this was not easily reconciled with the widely held view that ESDP was a direct competitor for Member State resources. However, the surge in UN peacekeeping since 2000 changed the UN's perception of this competition and increased UN acceptance of the need and inevitability of a greater role for other regional actors in peace operations. To the extent that ESDP has been able to harness human resources through Member State secondments to EU missions that would not otherwise have been available to the UN, the UN clearly welcomes its development. However, an element of competition remains, which is reflected in public discourse. For instance, at a conference on the EU-UN partnership in peace operations in 2008, the representative of the Council General Secretariat to the UN, Pedro Serrano de Haro, emphasised the 'natural partnership' between the EU and UN.[67] He argued that the EU strengthens the UN directly through assessed financial contributions to UN peacekeeping and indirectly through ESDP missions which serve to fill gaps (rapid deployment) in UN capabilities and which shoulder the peace operation burden where the EU has a political advantage. In response, the UN DPKO representative responsible for institutional partnerships, Renata Dwan, argued that the EU-UN partnership was not natural but rather had to be worked at, and noted that ESDP also risked undermining UN capabilities if it led to further European disengagement from UN peace operations. Hence, from the UN perspective, the development of ESDP is in the interest of the UN in so far as it contributes to both ESDP and UN civilian capacities. It is not a question of either/or.[68]

Similarly, in a 2004 study on the emerging civilian ESDP capacity, Peter Viggo Jakobsen concludes that:

---

[67] This position was presented at the International Forum for the Challenges of Peace Operations, 'Partnerships – the United Nations, the European Union and the Regional Dimensions of Peace Operations', Paris, 20-22 October 2008.

[68] Ibid.

> 'the EU civilian rapid reaction capacity is not a 'real added value' for the UN yet. (…) On the contrary, the number of personnel provided by EU member states to UN commanded operations is likely to decline further should the EU decide to launch new civilian operations in the years ahead. The first casualty of such operations would be the EU-UN relationship.'[69]

The empirical record provides a mixed picture in relation to the impact of ESDP on deployments of civilians from EU countries to UN missions. As Figure 8 indicates, there appears to be little correlation between the rise of ESDP missions and the number of EU civilians deployed as international staff in UN missions. This has slowly increased since 2003. In contrast, the number of EU police deployed in UN missions declined dramatically in 2008 as a result of the drawdown of the UN mission in Kosovo and the transition to the ESDP rule of law operation (EULEX) in Kosovo.

*Figure 8*. Civilians from EU countries deployed in UN peace operations

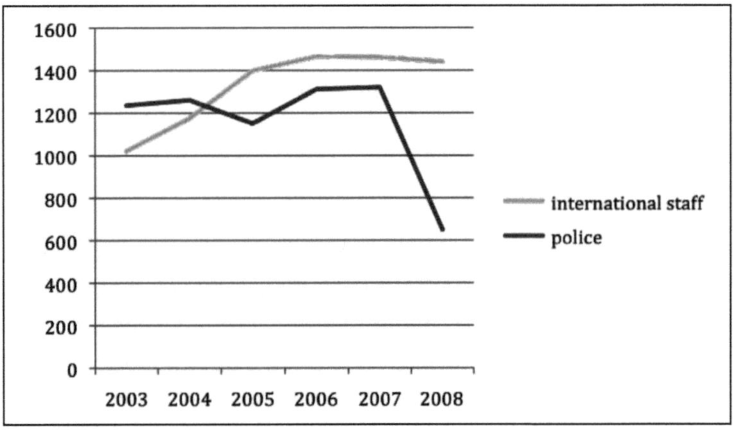


*Source*: UN DPKO, Peacekeeping Public Affairs Unit, 28 August 2008 (international staff) and DPKO website (police).

Nevertheless, ESDP appears to have led to an increase in the total number of European civilians deployed to peace operations. Figure 9 shows that despite the relative decline in EU civilian (police) deployments in UN missions, the development of ESDP operations has led to an increase in the total number of EU civilians deployed in EU and UN operations. However, given that this account does not track civilian deployments to other international organisations such as the OSCE or NATO, it is not possible to conclude that ESDP has increased the total number of European civilians deployed in international peace operations (Figure 9).

---

[69] P. Jakobsen, *The Emerging EU Civilian Crisis Management Capacity: A "real added value" for the UN?*, Background Paper for the Copenhagen Seminar on Civilian Crisis Management, 2004, at 1.

*Figure 9*. Total civilian deployments (police and international staff) from EU countries to UN and EU missions

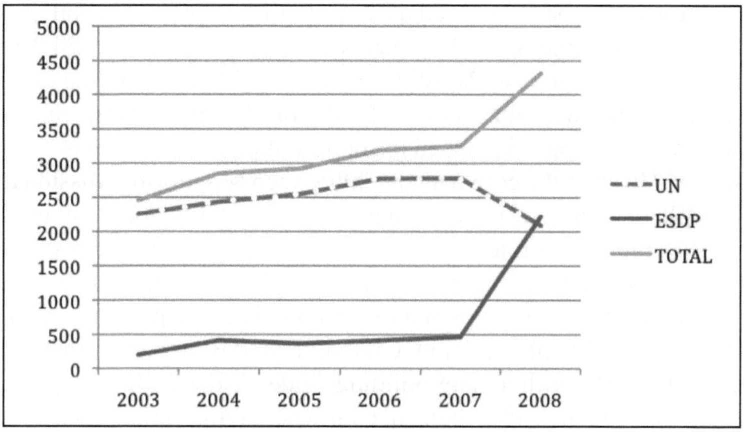


*Sources*: UN DPKO website and Peacekeeping Public Affairs Unit, EU Council General Secretariat (CPCC) and website (figures for ESDP civilian deployments for 2003 and 2004 are based on figures of deployments to EUPM, Proxima and EUJUST THEMIS provided on the Council website).

In summary, although the above quantitative overview is not comprehensive,[70] it does suggest that ESDP *indirectly* benefits the UN in so far as it has captured new European capacities for international civilian deployments.[71] The rise of ESDP has not, however, *directly* contributed to strengthening the civilian dimensions of UN peace operations and there is still the potential for EU-UN relations to sour over competition for civilian resources. Moreover, this competition looks set to intensify. As the EU struggles to meet its civilian capability targets, it plans to squeeze additional capacity from those states that are traditionally strong contributors to UN operations, including non-EU 'third states'.[72] These already make up around 10% of ESDP civilian mission deployments. If, as this plan suggests, the composition of future ESDP missions will be increasingly 'global', the EU is increasingly likely to be in direct competition with the UN, including for non-EU civilian resources.

## 4.2 Civilian ESDP-UN operational cooperation

### 4.2.1 *Operational trends*

The majority of ESDP missions launched since 2005 have been civilian missions, and the majority of these have had state-building objectives. These superficial com-

[70] It does not include figures for civilian deployments from EU countries to OSCE and NATO missions.

[71] It does not, however, address whether ESDP has captured the right kind of experts.

[72] Interview with EU Council official, Brussels, February 2009.

monalities, however, belie great diversity in the geographical and political context of operations as well as the internal political drivers of these missions. ESDP civilian interventions have been justified as contributing to political solutions both before and after peace agreements. For instance, the EU argues that ESDP police and border monitoring missions in Palestine are key confidence-building measures that help create the conditions for a political solution. In other cases, 'rapid reaction' civilian missions have been launched in support of peace agreements which the EU helped broker. This was the case with the 2005 Aceh Monitoring Mission that monitored the implementation of the disarmament aspects of the peace agreement. It is also the case of the EU Monitoring Mission in Georgia that monitors observance of the six-point ceasefire agreement. Similarly, the 2004 EUJUST THEMIS mission in Georgia signified support for an internal political reform process to consolidate a (largely peaceful) political transition. Civilian ESDP is, however, most commonly associated with post-conflict state building. Indeed, the 2003 European Security Strategy states simply that, after regional conflicts, 'civilian crisis management helps restore civil government.'[73] In some cases, notably in the Western Balkans, ESDP engagement in post-conflict state building is also linked to the EU enlargement agenda and underpinned by the view that such actions directly contribute to European security.[74] Similarly, post-conflict interventions in the Democratic Republic of Congo and Afghanistan have been justified as a means to promoting human security and to protecting Europeans from crime. More specifically, the 2008 review of the European Security Strategy added that 'SSR and DDR are a key part of post-conflict stabilisation and reconstruction, and have been a focus of our missions in Guinea-Bissau or Congo.'[75]

The UN has been present and active in all the countries to which the EU has sent a civilian ESDP mission, and UN political missions, country teams and implementing agencies often serve as an important partner to the ESDP missions in a range of roles. For instance, in Guinea Bissau, the UN country office, which had established relationships with key national actors, played a critical role in providing entry points for the ESDP mission. The EU SSR mission had been met with distrust and scepticism by the military elite and it was only six months after it arrived, after the UN country team arranged for an SSR seminar, that it made headway in building working relationships with the host government.[76] Similarly, as has been demonstrated above, the UN is often an ally of the EC in developing and implementing country-specific recovery and development programmes. In the case of Aceh, for instance, the EU Aceh Monitoring Mission was followed by a range of EC-supported actions

---

[73] European Council, *A Secure Europe in a Better World, European Security Strategy*, 12 December 2003, at 7.

[74] See the contribution by Blockmans to this volume.

[75] High Representative's *Report on the Implementation of the European Security Strategy – Providing Security in a Changing World*, Doc. 17104/08 (S407/08), 11 December 2008, as endorsed by the European Council, Presidency Conclusions, Doc. 17271/08 (CONCL 5), 12 December 2008, point 30.

[76] Interviews with in-country UN staff, and European Commission and European Council officials in Brussels, 2008.

to promote DDR and economic recovery. These were jointly designed with and implemented by UN agencies (International Labour Organisation, the International Organisation for Migration and the United Nations Development Programme). It is nevertheless beyond the scope of this chapter to document operational cooperation between all civilian ESDP missions and the broader UN family. Rather, this section will highlight two country cases where civilian ESDP missions have taken place in support of or to follow up UN peace operations. The first country is the Democratic Republic of Congo (DRC) where, in addition to two military missions (Artemis in 2003 and EUFOR in 2006), the EU has deployed a police and security sector reform mission (EUPOL Kinshasa and EUSEC DRC).[77] The second case is Kosovo, where, as of 2009, the EULEX mission had reached full operational capability after a long and complicated 'transition' from UNMIK.

### 4.2.2 *Operational cooperation in the DRC and the EU Police Mission (EUPOL Kinshasa)*

The genesis of the EU police mission in the DRC resulted from a 'model' process of EU-UN cooperation. The EU and UN shared the strategic priority of securing the transition to democracy and the mission was conceived in cooperation with the UN and the transitional government. This involved a pragmatic, joint assessment of how the EU could best help address some of the most strategic gaps in security. More precisely, in 2003, the objectives of the international community in the DRC were aligned with the goal of successfully implementing the 'Sun City' power-sharing peace deal – the Global and Inclusive Agreement signed in Pretoria on 17 December 2002 – and the March 2003 Memorandum on Security and the Army. In relation to the police, MONUC was indirectly engaged at the operational level of the *Police Nationale Congolaise* (PNC) and took the lead in efforts to build its capacity, including through a number of 'train the trainers' and specialised training programmes.[78] In 2003, MONUC was not, however, in a position to provide the training, equipment and monitoring required for the specialist Integrated Police Units foreseen in the Sun City Agreement. Training and equipment of specialised, 'elite' police units clearly required support from other actors. Hence, the UN had previously welcomed the bilateral interventions of Angola and France in training Rapid Reaction Police in Kinshasa and encouraged the EU to play a complementary role in training the Integrated Police Unit that was to be dedicated to securing state institutions. The idea for this EU mission was first raised in 2003 in a meeting of the *Comité International d'Accompagnement de la Transition* (CIAT). This was a mechanism agreed at Sun City that comprised the transition government and in-

---

[77] Although this was formally a civilian mission, it was led by a French General (Joana) and employed personnel with military backgrounds. See also the contribution by Martinelli to this volume.

[78] From January 2005, the focus of the MONUC police training effort was on securing the 2006 election. To this end, it provided basic training to 50,000 territorial officers, in conjunction with efforts supported by a UNDP-managed $48 million fund to provide the equipment and training to secure the election process.

ternational actors and effectively enabled the key international donors 'to steer the domestic political process in the DRC.'[79] The proposal resulted from discussions between the UN SRSG, the EC Head of Delegation and the representative of the EU Presidency. Therefore, as with the EU's first military operation in the DRC, Artemis, the EU's first ESDP mission in Africa was generated in response to a request from the UN, although in this case the request was informal and first discussed at field level rather than between capitals. Formally, the EU mission was launched in response to an invitation from the Congolese authorities, and this also served as its legal base.

Although there were a number of international actors engaged in police training in 2005 with the goal of implementing the peace agreement and securing the 2006 election, there was no commonly agreed plan for police restructuring. Recognising the need for a more coordinated approach, in February 2006, the DRC Ministry of the Interior invited the organisations and states already active in the area, in cooperation with the PNC, to form a *Groupe de Réflexion pour la reforme de la police.* Those invited included MONUC, the EU (European Commission and EUPOL), South Africa, Angola, France and the UK. This led to the creation of an implementation body, *Comité de suivi,* chaired by the DRC with the financial and technical support of donors, including the EC.[80] In this way, EUPOL became gradually more engaged in matters of police reform, but unlike the EUSEC mission described below, this was never the mission's principal mandate. Rather, while EUPOL has been involved in stock-taking initiatives, for instançe, assisting in the census of the PNC (an operation led by South Africa), its actions, in line with its mandate, have focused on building capacity rather than promoting reform. Not only was EUPOL's mandate less politically contentious, it was also relatively clear that the EU did not play a leading role in the area of police reform. In conclusion, EUPOL is a positive example of how an EU capacity-building mission can provide a significant, specialised role in police capacity building, complementary to that of MONUC and other international actors. It is consistently described by UN officials as a targeted and effective operation. It was not, however, designed to contribute to the reform of the PNC and, unsurprisingly, has had little impact on efforts to promote broader police reform in the PNC beyond Kinshasa.

### 4.2.3 *Operational cooperation in the DRC and the EU security sector reform mission (EUSEC RDC)*

Unlike EUPOL Kinshasa, the mandate of the EUSEC RDC mission was broader and more politically intrusive. Its objective was to assist in the reform of the defence sector by providing assistance for the creation of the new integrated Congo-

[79] R. Keane, 'Security System Reform in the Democratic Republic of Congo: The Role Played by the European Union', in D. Spence and P. Fluri, eds., *The European Union and Security Sector Reform* (John Harper Publishing 2008) 220.

[80] The European Commission provided €10 million for the support of the national police census and human resource management in 2007-2008.

lese army, the *Forces Armées de la République Démocratique du Congo* (FARDC). Also, unlike EUPOL, the idea for the mission did not originate in-theatre and in close cooperation with the UN, but rather was the product of a French-Belgian initiative, in the form of a joint non-paper transmitted to the Political and Security Committee in late 2004.

At the time, support for efforts to build army capacity in the DRC was limited. One of the few efforts that existed in 2004 was the Belgian initiative to train the first integrated brigade in Kisangani, 'Operation Avenir', with the support of France and Luxembourg. Frustrated by the slow progress, the Belgians persuaded the French to support the EU SEC idea on the assumption that it would generate greater EU assistance and enhance EU political leverage on issues related to SSR. The mission, as it was originally conceived, was small in terms of human resources – an advisory mission with a team of eight experts, but its scope and political ambition was large. The authorising Joint Action mentioned that the mission should provide 'technical expertise' on command and control, budgetary and financial management, training, accountancy and dealing with contracts and tenders.[81]

One of the tasks that EUSEC undertook early in its operation was an audit of the army's chain of payments system. This found evidence of corruption and embezzlement of funds allocated for 'ghost' soldiers' salaries. Based on this audit, EUSEC developed the so-called 'chain of payments' project. The project separated the chain of payments from the chain of command. It ensured that soldiers based in the new integrated brigades were paid regularly and thereby helped generate confidence for donors willing to support the army reform. This project began in December 2005 under the code-name EUSEC FIN and EUSEC's mandate was revised accordingly. It involved the deployment of a number of international advisors at each level of the chain of payments down to the brigade level.

Although neither EUSEC's first nor second EUSEC FIN mandate were developed in close association with the UN or MONUC in the field, MONUC welcomed the chain of payments initiative and a number of UN officers saw this as the main purpose of the mission.[82] However, the EUSEC also had ambitions to assist with broader reforms in the area of SSR, and, in practice, during the run-up to the 2006 elections, the EU and UN competed over who should lead or coordinate the SSR process. From MONUC's point of view, MONUC should act as the principal coordinator since it was the largest international actor with 17,000 troops and enjoyed greater legitimacy. MONUC also had a track record in efforts to coordinate SSR. In 2004, it had established an SSR planning and coordination structure consisting of a steering committee of donors, a technical advisory group and a secretariat. However, this first coordination architecture failed in early 2005 because of lack of acceptance by either the government or the donors. Indeed, the EU had warned that

---

[81] Council Joint Action 2005/355/CFSP of 2 May 2005 on the European Union mission to provide advice and assistance for security sector reform in the Democratic Republic of the Congo (DRC), *OJ* 2005 L 112/20.

[82] Interviews with UN DPKO officials, New York, December 2008.

the structure was too driven by MONUC and not consultative enough.[83] In the context of MONUC's mixed track record in coordinating issues of SSR, and given that the EU had two missions dedicated to security sector capacity building, the EU argued that it was in a better position and more able to take on the external SSR coordination role. In the spring of 2006, EUSEC developed a framework document for SSR in which it proposed an EU-led cooperation strategy at the multinational level to improve donor coordination. This was not, however, taken up by MONUC or the DRC authorities. On 15 September 2006, the GAERC reaffirmed the EU's ambition to lead international efforts in SSR. It stated that

> 'in view of the need for a comprehensive approach combining the different initiatives underway, the EU would be ready to assume a coordinating role in international efforts in the security sector, in close association with the United Nations, to support the Congolese authorities in this field.'[84]

The EU's ambition to lead SSR efforts was subsequently welcomed in the UN Security Council (UNSC).[85] However, although the EU cited this Resolution extensively as evidence of its leading role, in practice its function had been contested during the transition and, even with UNSC support, it was unable to execute a coordinating role in the post-election context where neither the government nor the donors had an interest in a concerted approach to SSR.

Although in 2005 MONUC was primarily dedicated to the DDR process and to securing the election, when it did engage in SSR during 2006 its work on army reform followed a separate process and took a different form. In June 2006, a DDR/SSR unit was created in MONUC and a military Deputy Chief of Staff was appointed to it. This was subsequently divided and the SSR section began work on a consultation process, which resulted in the 'Strategy to Support the Government of the DRC in SSR 2007-2010'.[86] As with the EU's ambitions, the strategy aimed to support the new government in drafting a National Security Strategy or White Paper on SSR and developing plans for the army, police and justice sector, while providing continued operational support to the *brassage* process. Thus, before the 2006 elections, both the EU and the UN had positioned themselves as the 'key' international counterparts for the new government, ready and able to provide policy and operational advice. Unsurprisingly, therefore, both EU and UN officials have characterised the EU-UN relationship on SSR in the run-up to the 2006 elections as competitive.[87] Dahrendorf's review of SSR in the DRC similarly identifies com-

---

[83] R. Onana and H. Taylor, 'MONUC and SSR in the Democratic Republic of Congo', 15 *International Peacekeeping*, Special Edition on Integrated UN Missions (2008) 507.

[84] Council Conclusions on the Democratic Republic of Congo, Press Release 12555/06, 15 September 2006.

[85] In Security Council Resolution 1756 (2007).

[86] Agreed on 7 February 2007.

[87] Interviews with Council General Secretariat and European Commission officials, Brussels, May and June 2008, and UN DPKO official, New York, December 2008. EU-UN competition over roles was also exacerbated by the different visions for DDR. The EUSEC Head of Mission, General Joana of France, was highly critical of the UN-led DDR process, which he viewed as ill-conceived and

petition within MONUC and between MONUC and the EU as obstacles to the pursuit of a coordinated approach to SSR. She writes that 'The establishment of a more coherent viable SSR coordination mechanism for the DRC was often debated, but fell foul of internal politics and other priorities, such as security and elections.'[88] The review concludes that 'there was no real *locus* for conceiving and coordinating SSR activities. A certain degree of infighting, within the [MONUC] mission itself and between the UN and the EU, posed obstacles.'[89]

In practice, no external actor has played a leading role in coordinating SSR efforts since the 2006 elections. Rather, President Kabila has favoured a bilateral approach to securing assistance. Arguably South Africa has maintained the best relationship with the DRC authorities regarding the issue of SSR. It has, for instance, continued to engage the government in a dialogue process through a series of seminars in relation to army reform. Strikingly, the EUSEC was not even initially invited to one such event in 2007. This reflected the extent to which the relationship between the EUSEC mission and the government had deteriorated. While some argue that the breakdown in EUSEC-DRC government relations was an inevitable consequence of the EUSEC's role in clamping down on corruption within the army through the chain of payments project, others argue that it might have been avoided if EUSEC had been more receptive to alternative models of army reorganisation.[90] In any case, in a context in which EU Ambassadors had publicly condemned Kabila's government after the violent clashes of March 2007 and in which relations between the EUSEC Head of Mission and the Minister of Defence had 'reached a point of no return', there was no option but for the PSC to wind down the EUSEC mission.[91] By mid 2007, the EU had lost all leverage and influence with the government of the DRC in relation to SSR.[92] One perverse consequence of the relative decline in the EU's role and ambitions in SSR in the DRC since 2007 is that, out of necessity, EU and UN informal cooperation has much improved. Since neither the EU (EUSR, EC Head of Delegation and Head of Police Mission) nor the UN (SRSG and MONUC) now plays a coordinating role in relation to SSR, they tend to be better at informally exchanging information.[93]

---

destabilising. In particular, he argued that a DDR process should have been based on a high-level process of power sharing and integration rather than on incentives given to individual soldiers to demobilise. This was reflected in an interview and in the unpublished paper by P.-M. Joana, *Réforme du secteur de la sécurité en RDC: pourquoi aussi peu de progrès?* (2008, on file with the author).

[88] N. Dahrendorf, 'MONUC and the Relevance of Coherent Mandates: The Case of the DRC', in H. Hänggi and V. Scherrer, eds., *Security Sector Reform and UN Integrated Missions* (Geneva Centre for the Democratic Control of the Armed Forces, LIT, 2008) 94.

[89] Ibid., at 96.

[90] Interviews with UN DPKO officials, New York, December 2008.

[91] Interviews with Council General Secretariat and UN DPKO officials, May and December 2008.

[92] The deterioration of relations between the EUSEC HoM and the DRC authorities resulted in the PSC discussing whether the mission should be discontinued before the end of its mandate in June 2007, but the Dutch and Belgians argued in favour of its continuation.

[93] Interviews with EU Council General Secretariat officials and UN DPKO official, May and December 2008.

In conclusion, the DRC case reveals that while the EU and UN shared the priority objective of securing the transition process, they did not share a common approach to the second-order priority of SSR. This resulted, in the lead-up to the 2006 elections, in a more competitive relationship. In addition to underlining that EU and UN approaches (to SSR) are not necessarily aligned, this case also highlights the fundamental challenge to the objective of improving donor coherence, namely that in some cases this is neither in the interest of the host government or nor in that of the principal external stakeholders. Thus, just as EU and UN interests in cooperation cannot be assumed, nor is the OECD-backed Paris agenda of promoting donor coherence and aid effectiveness one that is universally shared in practice. Rather, the DRC case illustrates that in the absence of a commonly agreed strategy, it is rational for the government and key external actors to pursue their interests through bilateral relationships.

### 4.2.4 *Operational cooperation in Kosovo*[94]

It is in Kosovo that civilian ESDP faced its biggest challenge with the largest and most ambitious civilian ESDP operation, EULEX Kosovo,[95] which conducts a mix of executive and supportive tasks in the area of police, justice and customs. It is also the mission with the longest lead time and biggest planning team. Although pre-planning for this mission dates back to 2005 and a robust planning team, the EU Planning Team (EUPT), was deployed to Priština in April 2006 to help design the EU mission that was intended to follow on from the UN,[96] the EU only took over the majority of UNMIK's mandate in late 2008. Moreover, while EULEX is operational, there has been no formal transition in so far that EULEX still operates under the legal 'umbrella' of UNMIK. The Kosovo case therefore also represents the lengthiest, most complicated and most incomplete 'transition' from a UN to an EU mission.

The Kosovo case reveals the adverse operational consequences of EU and UN planning assumptions predicated on EU and UN policy alignment. Specifically, the EULEX mission was planned on the assumption that the transition from UNMIK to EULEX would be authorised by a new Security Council resolution, providing a clear legal framework for an EU operation which was designed to support state building rather than execute the functions of a state, as UNMIK had been authorised to by UNSC Resolution 1244 (1999).[97] Not only did these negotiations take longer than initially envisaged but they were inconclusive in so far as they did not result in an agreement. Rather, they led to a UN Special Envoy 'recommendation' for condi-

---

94 See the contribution by Keukeleire and Thiers to this volume.

95 Council Joint Action 2008/124/CFSP of 4 February 2008 on the European Union Rule of Law Mission in Kosovo, EULEX KOSOVO, *OJ* 2008 L 42/92.

96 Council Joint Action 2006/304/CFSP of 10 April 2006 on the establishment of an EU Planning Team (EUPT Kosovo) regarding a possible EU crisis management operation in the field of rule of law and possible other areas in Kosovo, *OJ* 2006 L 112/19.

97 SC Res. 1244 (1999) of 10 June 1999.

tional independence for Kosovo and a 'Comprehensive Proposal for the Kosovo Status Settlement' (the Ahtisaari Plan).[98] Since neither of these options was acceptable to Serbia and its ally Russia, they did not form the basis for a new Security Council resolution that would have paved the way for the transition to EULEX. Neither did Kosovo's subsequent unilateral Declaration of Independence in February 2008[99] clarify the situation. Rather, it divided the international community, including the EU, and increased tensions over whether and on what basis the EU could take over UNMIK's operational functions. Indeed, from the UN perspective, transition was effectively on hold while the UN negotiated a plan to 'reconfigure' UNMIK's role and provide a new legal framework for EULEX. Consequently, cooperation over the technical details of transition, including the transfer of material assets and human resources, was 'almost impossible'[100] before Ban Ki Moon's 'reconfiguration' plan had been transmitted to UNMIK on 25 July. UNMIK's reconfiguration enabled an overarching agreement on technical arrangements to be reached in August 2008. Reflecting on the transition in 2009, another EU official concluded simply that 'the transition was only difficult when there were no clear instructions.'[101]

However, since the EU's role in Kosovo had been planned on the basis of the Ahtisaari Plan for conditional independence, it was not considered 'status neutral'. Where Belgrade wanted EULEX out and Priština wanted EULEX in, no matter how the mission defined itself, it was not perceived as status neutral. In other words, the EULEX mission was jeopardised in so far as it was seen as a party to the conflict over Kosovo's status. This fuelled fears that EULEX would not be able to deploy in the North of Kosovo – the region of Kosovo where Serbs are the majority ethnic group. Yet operationalisation, including in the North, went more smoothly than many had feared. Similarly, the configuration of the mission under the 'umbrella' of the UN has not been problematic in practice. EULEX reports to the EU Political and Security Committee, which in turn links with New York. Given that the EU 'umbrella' is extended at such a high level, as of mid 2009, it had had little operational impact.

Thus, the Kosovo case reveals that the model of EU-UN operational cooperation in which an ESDP mission is deployed in the framework of a UN one can be made to work. Nevertheless, it also indicates that, with hindsight, EU and UN planning assumptions were nave. It demonstrates that, given their distinct memberships, the EU and UN do not necessarily share a common purpose and strategy upon which effective operational partnerships depend.

---

[98] Report of the UN Special Envoy, *Comprehensive Proposal for the Kosovo Status Settlement*, 2 February 2007. This version of the Comprehensive Proposal was only briefly available at: <http://www.unosek.org>, the website of the UN Office of the Special Envoy for Kosovo. A slightly amended version of the proposal was included in the addendum to the Letter dated 26 March 2007 from the Secretary-General addressed to the President of the Security Council, UN Doc. S/2007/168/Add.1.

[99] Declaration by the Kosovo Assembly, 17 February 2008.

[100] Interview with EU Council General Secretariat official, May 2008.

[101] Ibid.

## 5. Conclusions

Peacebuilding has become something of an 'all and nothing' concept; it is associated with an expansive 'root causes' agenda, yet not appropriated by many EU or UN actors to describe their operations or policies. It is explicitly not limited to multidimensional peace operations, early recovery or conflict prevention, but instead aims to build on all of these operational experiences. Despite or perhaps because of the diverse views of what peacebuilding involves in operational terms, peacebuilding discourse within the UN is associated with improving *systemic* efforts to consolidate peace. It evolved to address incoherence or weaknesses of the collective international response. In contrast, within the EU, peacebuilding is more typically associated with European Commission efforts to address risk factors and promote structural stability through development aid. These efforts are focused on the objectives of state building and economic recovery. Within the Council of the EU, policy debates are couched in terms of post-conflict stabilisation and reconstruction and focus on how to adapt (military) planning for a more comprehensive approach. They are also framed around issues that are subsets of peacebuilding, such as DDR, SSR, and police or justice reform.

Although the EU and UN employ different conceptual frameworks for peacebuilding, both organisations seek to combine bottom-up support for peacebuilding processes with top-down pressure for reform. This creates opportunities for interinstitutional cooperation within sector-specific communities of practice. However, there is no consensus among practitioners or scholars on how to combine these approaches to deliver whole-of-system strategic guidance. This suggests that, in practice, peacebuilding will remain characterised by conceptual and operational competition, both within and between the EU and UN.

The analysis of the EC-UN funding relationship confirms that the European Commission and UN development actors are natural partners in peacebuilding: the UN is often the principal 'implementing partner' for EC assistance, with over a third of all EC peacebuilding assistance being channelled through the UN. More specifically, the greatest volume of EC peacebuilding assistance is channelled through UNDP on the grounds that it is often the only actor with the mandate, legitimacy and capacity to act in many fragile contexts. This is especially true in a few high-profile cases in which large volumes and proportions of EC funding have been channelled through the UN (notably in Afghanistan, the Democratic Republic of Congo, Iraq and the West Bank and Gaza). In these cases the UNDP has had a role in administering MDTFs or has a specific mandate to lead international efforts (e.g., to provide assistance to Palestinians or support the 2006 election in the DRC). However, in most other cases, the strength of the operational and policy partnership is case specific and largely determined at the field level. It depends on UN in-country capacity and comparative advantage as well as the administrative 'fit' between the organisations.

Given that operational partnerships are forged at the field level, it follows that efforts to strengthen EC-UN operational partnerships should be focused in-country.

Although the European Commission has formally championed efforts to promote alignment from the bottom up through joint (EC-UNDP-World Bank) analysis and recovery planning, including through the Post-Conflict Needs Assessment (PCNA) methodology, these have yet to be widely implemented in practice. Developing strong in-country operational partnerships will therefore require that the capacity and autonomy of the EU delegations be strengthened. Post-Lisbon Treaty restructuring provides an ideal opportunity to empower EU delegations in this way.

In the context of (the civilian aspects of) peace operations, however, the EU and UN are not always natural partners. Although the EU employs a similar crisis management approach to that of the UN in this context, the relationship is more competitive. Rather than directly contributing to UN operational capacity, security actors compete over resources and roles. The analysis of civilian deployments for EU and UN missions (in section 4.1) confirms that EU Member States have effectively redeployed many of their police to ESDP missions. Consequently, ESDP has not *directly* contributed to strengthening the civilian dimension of UN operations. There is, however, evidence that ESDP *indirectly* benefits the UN in so far as it has captured new European capacities for international civilian deployments. This suggests that ESDP provides 'added value' to the UN in so far as it helps share the burden without necessarily drawing on the same pool of civilian human resources.

Similarly, the record of operational cooperation is mixed. While operational cooperation can be mutually beneficial and smooth (as in the EU police mission in the DRC), it can also be characterised by interinstitutional competition (EU SSR mission in the DRC) or controversy (transition from UNMIK to EULEX in Kosovo). Once again, these cases suggest that the best approach to achieving operational coherence is to move the assessment, priority setting and planning in-country: where ESDP missions were elaborated in the field following UN requests for assistance (i.e., EUPOL in the DRC) the operational relationship was relatively smooth. In contrast, where the initiative was driven by EU Member States at headquarters level, policies and approaches were not necessarily aligned. Moreover, in Kosovo, where the EU and UN planners assumed EU and UN agreement over the status question, the lack of an agreement had a debilitating effect on the transition from UNMIK to EULEX. This suggests that multilateral security cooperation is not only a matter of burden sharing. As Gowan has put it in a blog posting:

> '[There is] a growing conceptual problem for fans of multilateral security cooperation. This is a nave belief that all international security institutions have, or could have, shared goals and that we simply need to link them up better to meet those goals. This is a hangover from the happy days of the 1990s, when the West still had a grip on pretty much every organization from the UN to Boy Scouts, but it's not sustainable in a more competitive world.'[102]

Indeed, the evidence from EU-UN operational cooperation in relation to (civilian) crisis management suggests that the liberal concept that underpins EU and UN

---

[102] R. Gowan, at: <http://www.globaldashboard.org>, 11 October 2008.

policies of effective multilateralism and UN cooperation with regional organisations is nave on a number of levels. At the political-strategic level, it is nave to assume that international security institutions will always share common objectives and policies, just as it is more often than not the case that there is no common vision or policy within multilateral international security institutions. Even where operational approaches and policies are aligned, the logic of interinstitutional burden sharing is often trumped by interinstitutional competition. And at the technical level, the fact that organisations work differently creates a number of practical challenges to linking up. This is not to say that the EU and UN cannot be effective crisis management partners, but rather that policy and operational compatibility cannot be assumed, especially, as Gowan observes, in a world in which the influence of the West is in relative decline.

# Chapter 5
# THE EU AND THE UN PEACEBUILDING COMMISSION: A SHORT ACCOUNT OF HOW THE EU PRESENCE HAS INFLUENCED THE NEWEST UN BODY

**Stefano Tomat* and Cesare Onestini****

## 1. Introduction

The transition from peacekeeping to political stability, sustainable development and growth is the key challenge confronting the international community in post-conflict situations. While peacekeeping efforts are traditionally short-term and focus on stabilising the immediate post-conflict situation, development policies take a more long-term perspective. In the past, the perceived 'missing link' in the continuum from peace to development was partially addressed by extending mandates, roles and responsibilities of the three traditional instruments of international intervention: peacekeeping operations, humanitarian relief and development aid. However, such ad hoc solutions could only partially address the specific problems of moving from conflict to development.

Since its introduction in UN Secretary-General Boutros-Ghali's 1992 Agenda for Peace,[1] the concept of peacebuilding has become a key focus of attention of the international community, fuelled by the realisation that many countries emerging from conflict relapse into violence soon after the departure of peacekeepers. The new UN peacebuilding architecture that has been developed over the past few years aims specifically at helping post-conflict countries to create conditions for lasting peace and sustainable development.

The UN Peacebuilding Commission (PBC) started in 2006 as the institutional arena mandated to create, at the level of the United Nations, a forum for actors concerned with peacebuilding to compare existing approaches and improve coordination. Its establishment represents an attempt to bring together the 'North' and 'South' of the international community to discuss how best to consolidate peace,

---

* First Secretary, Delegation of the European Union to the United Nations, New York. The views expressed in this contribution are the personal opinion of the author and do not engage the responsibility of his institution. Reasearch on this chapter was closed before the entry into force of the Lisbon Treaty

** First Counsellor, Political Affairs, Delegation of the European Union to the United Nations, New York. The same disclaimer applies.

[1] *Agenda for Peace*, Report of the Secretary-General of 17 June 1992, UN Doc. A/47/277 – S/24111.

*S. Blockmans, J. Wouters & T. Ruys, eds., The European Union and Peacebuilding*

moving beyond the traditional divisions whereby developed countries stress the importance of addressing security issues while developing countries focus on aid and development as the main instrument to break the cycle of violence/conflict. Both are needed and the Peacebuilding Commission strives to define the best possible strategies for the countries on its agenda.

In this contribution, we will describe the origin and establishment of the Peacebuilding Commission within the United Nations, explaining its structures and instruments. We will then turn our attention to the role played by the European Union in the creation of the PBC and to how the EU is represented within the Commission. The final part of this contribution will attempt to present an initial assessment of the PBC's activity since its inception.

## 2. Origins and setting up of the Peacebuilding Commission within the United Nations

### 2.1 Preparatory work

Following the exponential increase in peacekeeping operations around the world, the United Nations started, in the 90s, an internal process of re-thinking the instrument of peacekeeping. The recurrence of conflicts in the same areas, with several countries sliding back to conflict as soon as the blue helmets had left, pushed the United Nations and the international community to reconsider the appropriateness of using a single instrument, military intervention, to bring peace. In the late 90s, a general understanding emerged on the need for a multi-faceted approach in order to break the cycle of violence and create the basis for sustainable development. In 1998, the Security Council expressed its support for measures taken within the United Nations system to strengthen post-conflict peacebuilding efforts[2] and in 2000, the Brahimi report recommended creating a focal point for peacebuilding within the UN Secretariat.[3]

In November 2003, UN Secretary-General Annan announced to the President of the UN General Assembly the creation of a 16-member Panel tasked with identifying new ideas for the reform of the UN system in a post 9/11 world, and chaired by Mr Panyarachun, former Prime Minister of Thailand. In its final report, entitled 'A More Secure World: Our Shared Responsibilities',[4] the so-called High-level Panel on Threats, Challenges and Change made a series of recommendations addressing the main security challenges of the future multilateral system. Noting that there was no body or institution within the UN system clearly designed to avoid a state's slide to war or to assist countries in their transition from war to peace,[5] the High-Level Panel recommended the creation of a Peacebuilding Commission, as a subsidiary

[2] See S/PRST/1198/29.
[3] Report of the Panel on UN Peace Operations (A/55/305 – S/2000/809).
[4] *A More Secure World: Our Shared Responsibilities* (A/59/565).
[5] Ibid., paragraph 261.

body of the Security Council, and of a Peacebuilding Fund, in order to fill this institutional gap. The new body was conceived as reasonably small, capable of addressing both general policy issues and country-specific situations, and involving all the main relevant actors. The creation of a Peacebuilding Support Office within the UN Secretariat was also envisaged. These suggestions were subsequently taken up by the UNSG report – 'In Larger Freedom'[6] –, which conceded that no part of the UN system could properly address the transition from war to lasting peace and re-stated the proposal for the creation of an intergovernmental Peacebuilding Commission as well as a Peacebuilding Support Office, capable of promoting integrated peacebuilding strategies (paragraph 114).

## 2.2 The position of the EU

These proposals were very well received by the European Union, which had been amongst the early supporters of the establishment of the Peacebuilding Commission. Based on the EU's worldwide and sustained efforts and experience in the field of peacebuilding (making use of its development programmes and recent instruments for crisis management, including civilian and military rapid intervention capabilities), the EU saw a clear need for greater focus on and coordination of efforts in the crucial transition from a post-crisis environment to durable peace and return to the conditions for development, and for making sure the international community did not lose sight of fragile post-conflict situations once a conflict was over. A body dedicated to peacebuilding at the UN was therefore seen as a very welcome development that could provide real added value.

In preparation for the 2005 UN Summit, the EU argued consistently in favour of laying the institutional foundations of the Peacebuilding Commission in the final agreement, including all essential elements for its composition and mandate, as well as setting a date by which the PBC would have to become operational.

In particular, the European Commission took active part in the formulation of the EU position on the Peacebuilding Commission, including in its June 2005 Communication on the UN Summit.[7] In the latter communication, it stressed that

> 'consensus on establishing a Peacebuilding Commission [was] essential. Such a body would fill a gap in the UN system. The EU should support a broad mandate entailing a holistic approach to peacebuilding, i.e. covering the whole continuum from peacekeeping to longer-term development issues.'

The European Commission went on to say that

---

[6] United Nations, *In Larger Freedom: Towards Development, Security and Human Rights for All*, Report of the Secretary-General, A/59/2005.

[7] European Commission, Communication from the European Commission to the Council and the European Parliament, 'The 2005 Summit – Addressing the global challenges and making a success of the reformed UN', Brussels, 15.06.2005, COM (2005) 259 final.

> 'the EU will certainly contribute actively to the future work of the PBC, using European Commission and CFSP instruments, in line with the European Security Strategy (...) The EC is well placed to address post-conflict challenges given the financial amounts at its disposal and its all-embracing geographical coverage.'

It concluded by advocating that

> '[g]iven these experiences and its contributions to peacebuilding efforts around the globe, the European Community should fully participate in all meetings of the Peacebuilding Commission.'

Following this preparatory work, the UN General Assembly in its Outcome Document of the 2005 World Summit approved the creation of a UN Peacebuilding Commission as a subsidiary body of both the Security Council and the General Assembly.[8] The Outcome Document prepared by the President of the General Assembly, Jean Ping, met many of the preoccupations expressed by the EU: in the Document, the decision to set up the PBC is explicitly rooted in the need for coordinated, coherent and integrated action in post-conflict situations. The Document also refers to the contribution of regional institutions as well as institutional donors, laying the ground for EC participation. And lastly, the Outcome Document set a clear deadline (end 2005) for the start of the work of this new body.

### 2.3 Creation of the Peacebuilding Commission

The UN Peacebuilding Commission[9] came into being with the adoption of Security Council Resolution 1645 (2005)[10] in concurrence with an analogue act of the General Assembly. The double 'birth certificate' of the Commission as a subsidiary body of both the General Assembly and the Security Council (in accordance with Articles 7, 22 and 29 of the UN Charter) situates it in a unique position within the wider architecture of the United Nations.

The founding resolutions provide a conclusive definition of the concept of peacebuilding, which can be derived from the broad mandate given to the Commission (operative paragraph 2):

- To bring together all relevant actors to marshal resources and to advise on and propose integrated strategies for post-conflict peacebuilding and recovery;
- To focus attention on the reconstruction and institution-building efforts necessary for recovery from conflict and to support the development of integrated strategies in order to lay the foundation for sustainable development;

---

[8] A/Res/60/1.

[9] United Nations, Resolution adopted by the General Assembly on 30 December 2005, A/Res/60/180.

[10] United Nations, Resolution 1645 (2005) adopted by the Security Council at its 5335th meeting on 20 December 2005.

- To provide recommendations and information to improve the coordination of all relevant actors within and outside the United Nations, to develop best practices, to help to ensure predictable financing for early recovery activities and to extend the period of attention given by the international community to post-conflict recovery.

In short, after almost a decade of conceptualisation, peacebuilding was recognised as a coordinated effort, bringing together a wide variety of actors, with the aim of making available predictable funding for integrated strategies encompassing security, recovery and development.

The UN and the international community had finally established a dedicated institutional mechanism to deal with the special needs of post-conflict countries. The inauguration session of the PBC took place on 23 June 2006.

## 3. Structures and instruments of the UN Peacebuilding Commission

### 3.1 Structures

The PBC was established to address both general policy-related issues and country-based problems. As a result, the Commission was conceived to meet in a variety of configurations.

*Organisational Committee*

First, the founding resolutions established a standing Organisational Committee responsible for developing its own rules of procedure and working methods.

The membership of the Organisational Committee is relatively small but still capable of providing adequate representation of all the different relevant actors. It comprises:

- Seven members of the UN Security Council, including its permanent members;
- Seven members of the Economic and Social Council, elected from regional groups;
- Five top providers of assessed contributions to the UN Budgets and of voluntary contributions to UN funds;
- Five top providers of military and police personnel to UN missions;
- Seven members elected by the General Assembly, in order to take into account appropriate representation from all regional groups.

The selected members serve for a renewable period of two years. According to Operative Paragraph 12 of the founding resolutions, the Organisational Committee is responsible for establishing the agenda of the PBC, taking into consideration the requests of the Security Council, the Secretary-General and, in exceptional circumstances, of the ECOSOC, the General Assembly and the members on the verge of lapsing or relapsing into conflict.

The Organisational Committee has played an important role in further defining the role of the Peacebuilding Commission, *inter alia*, by adopting the provisional rules of procedure of the Commission.[11] It continues to be the main driving force in the UN peacebuilding architecture as it defines the framework for the operations of the respective country-specific configurations of the Commission.

*Country-Specific Meetings (CSMs)*

In order to address the specificity of each post-conflict situation, the founding resolutions provide that the Commission should meet in country-specific configurations. The purpose of such configurations is evident: by creating a specific forum addressing solely the post-conflict difficulties of one country and bringing together a pre-established membership, the PBC should be capable of focusing on its tasks and guarantee a constant follow-up of the implementation of the policies decided within the PBC framework.

In order to involve the local government and the main players on the ground, the membership of the CSMs is open and includes, in addition to the members of the Organisational Committee, representatives of the national authorities of the country on the agenda, representatives of the countries in the region, major financial and troop contributors involved in the specific recovery effort and other regional and international institutions as relevant.

The CSMs are the most interesting element of the UN peacebuilding architecture as they establish the bridge between delegations in New York and the actors on the ground. CSMs aim at maintaining international attention on the specific countries on the PBC agenda and to act as an informal tool to put pressure on the national authorities to implement the agreed frameworks. To achieve this, the CSMs have made extensive use of field missions and videoconferencing with in-country key stakeholders.

*Working Group on Lessons Learned (WGLL)*

Part of the mandate of the Peacebuilding Commission is 'to develop best practices', and to this end a Working Group on Lessons Learned was established in January 2007. The WGLL should serve as an informal platform for sharing lessons learned and good practice related to peacebuilding. It meets on an ad hoc basis to discuss thematic issues, which are mainly chosen in light of their relevance to the PBC's Country-Specific Meetings.

In the course of its first years of activity, the Working Group has become an open forum where academics and experts from different backgrounds can meet with UN

[11] United Nations, *Provisional rules of procedure of the Peacebuilding Commission*, as adopted by the Organisational Committee at its first meeting on 23 June 2006 (PBC/1/OC/3).

diplomats to address all aspects of peacebuilding and influence the future debates taking place at the Country-Specific Meetings.

In fact, the CSMs are expected to be the primary beneficiaries of the best practices discussed in the Working Group on Lessons Learned. In theory, the topics discussed in the WGLL should have a direct link with the issues debated in the Country-Specific Meetings and be of relevance to the CSM delegations. The WGLL has tried to address both cross-cutting issues linked to peacebuilding (such as reintegration of former combatants; coordination with regional and sub-regional organisations; national capacity building; and rule of law in post-conflict countries) and regional aspects (such as drug trafficking in West Africa and DDR in the Great Lakes Region). The discussions are usually based on presentations by countries and experts with direct experience of post-conflict transitions and offer examples and experience that can be of direct relevance to the countries on the agenda of the PBC. The regional discussions in particular have been helpful in focusing the attention of the PBC members on the complexity of some of the issues on the agenda of the country-specific configurations.

## 3.2 **Instruments**

### *Peacebuilding strategic frameworks*

At the basis of the Peacebuilding Commission is the need for a coherent and coordinated approach to peacebuilding when dealing with a post-conflict situation. As stated in the founding resolutions, one of the main tasks of the PBC is 'to bring together all relevant actors to marshal resources and to advise on and propose integrated strategies for post-conflict peacebuilding recovery':[12] the Strategic Frameworks are the instruments to achieve these goals.

The origins of the Strategic Frameworks go back to the early 90s when the United Nations started to develop instruments aimed at coordinating the political, humanitarian and development activities of the different actors which were active in the large multi-dimensional operations typical of those days. The problem identified at the time was not the lack of peacebuilding efforts but rather the lack of a common vision and the need to bring together all these unrelated activities of the international community in a comprehensive framework.

The Peacebuilding Strategic Frameworks can be defined as

> 'mutually accountable and time-bound agreements, between a government and international partners, for directing scarce foreign and public technical, financial, and political resources towards building national capacities to address the root causes of violent conflict.'[13]

[12] Operative Paragraph 2, General Assembly Resolution A/60/180 and UN Security Council Resolution 1645 (2005).

[13] United Nations, *Lessons Learned from Peacebuilding Strategic Frameworks Since the Late 1990s*, Briefing Paper of the Peacebuilding Support Office (September 2007).

The Strategic Frameworks were conceptually designed to serve two purposes: on the one hand, to help weak local authorities emerging from a conflict situation to define their priorities, to clarify their needs and to agree on an implementation process; on the other, to bring together the international community in its various forms, to facilitate the understanding of local priorities by the international actors and to avoid the traditional donor-led approach to post-conflict crisis solutions. Thanks to this two-pronged approach, the frameworks have helped to create shared responsibilities and a genuine sense of partnership between the different parties involved: the United Nations, the international community and local authorities.

The Peacebuilding Commission has built on these valuable premises to develop its integrated peacebuilding strategies (IPBS). Acting as an advisory body to the UN General Assembly and the UN Security Council, the PBC has provided additional elements to the basic Strategic Frameworks. The IPBS, in fact, increase the relevance of the political support and oversight. Having a New York-based UN body entrusted with the development and monitoring of these strategies puts some pressure on local leaders and on the donors community to implement the respective commitments identified in the strategies; the regular reporting also ensures that attention does not wane and commitments are updated and closely monitored. Thanks to the PBC, 'forgotten' countries such as Guinea-Bissau and the Central African Republic have received unprecedented attention at the UN headquarters.

In addition, the Peacebuilding Commission has been able to guarantee additional substantial disbursements of 'catalytic' resources thanks to the Peacebuilding Fund, which plays a role in the elaboration of the integrated strategies. The Peacebuilding Commission has also managed to involve a larger number of international actors, not only increasing the number of potential donors but also involving non-state actors such as the media, the private sector and NGOs in the preparation of the Strategic Frameworks.

*Peacebuilding Support Office (PBSO)*

As foreseen in the founding resolutions, the United Nations established, 'within existing resources, a small peacebuilding support office staffed by qualified experts to assist and support the Commission (...).'[14]

The main function of the PBSO is to prepare the substantive inputs for the meetings of the PBC, including the gathering and analysing of information. At the same time, the Peacebuilding Support Office is expected to liaise with UN in-country representatives and to provide inputs to the planning process for peacebuilding operations working together with UN lead departments. Thanks to an increasing expertise, the PBSO is also developing adequate capacity to conduct mapping exercises and best practice analyses and to develop policy guidance.

Since its establishment, the PBSO had to struggle to obtain adequate resources. As stated in the founding resolutions, the UN Secretariat had to find, 'within exist-

---

[14] Operative Paragraph 23, General Assembly Resolution A/60/180 and UN Security Council Resolution 1645 (2005).

ing resources', the staff needed to create the new structure. The PBSO's staff was also expected to have specific peacebuilding expertise, which was spread over various units and could not be found in a single UN department. This implied some difficulties in the identification and transfer of UN staff and had an impact on the PBSO's initial capability to meet the expectations of the UN delegations. However, thanks to the commitment of several senior officials, including the first Head of the PBSO, Carolyn McAskie, Assistant Secretary-General for Peacebuilding Support, the PBSO has constantly increased its staff and expertise and, within a few years, has become a reliable force behind the activities of the Peacebuilding Commission.[15]

*The Peacebuilding Fund (PBF)*

An original and particularly relevant element of the peacebuilding architecture has certainly been the establishment of a

> 'multi-year standing peacebuilding fund for post-conflict peacebuilding, funded by voluntary contributions and taking due account of existing instruments, with the objective of ensuring immediate release of resources needed to launch peacebuilding activities and the availability of appropriate financing for recovery.'[16]

Together with the Peacebuilding Commission and the Peacebuilding Support Office, the PBF is one of the three strategically linked yet functionally different pillars that constitute the United Nations peacebuilding architecture.

The Fund was launched on 11 October 2006 as a global multi-donor fund capable of providing immediate and short-term support to countries in the early stages of a peace process or at risk of relapsing into conflict. The Fund's interventions are based on a distinct 'three-window architecture':

- Window I comprises those countries that are on the PBC agenda. In this case, the Peacebuilding Commission provides advice and guidance on the strategic focus of the PBF.
- Window II addresses the needs of countries designated by the UN Secretary-General. Since the creation of the UN Secretariat, it has used this prerogative to add countries that are at risk of lapsing or relapsing into conflict. The criteria used to decide if a country is eligible are based on an analysis by the PBSO supported by other relevant departments within the UN Secretariat. At present, the following countries receive funds through the Peacebuilding Fund: Comoros, Ivory Coast, Guinea, Liberia and Nepal.
- Window III deals with specific post-conflict needs and can be considered as a sort of 'emergency facility'. It supports projects in eight countries (Ivory Coast,

---

[15] There were only 4 PBSO officials when the PBC was launched, but, drawn from other departments, staff had increased to 12 by December 2006. Today, the PBSO consists of 35 UN officials.

[16] Operative Paragraph 24, General Assembly Resolution A/60/180 and UN Security Council Resolution 1645 (2005).

Central African Republic, Guinea, Liberia, Burundi, Haiti, Kenya and Timor-Leste), financing initiatives dealing with political dialogue, national reconciliation, security and support for peace agreements. The main advantage of this instrument is the possibility for the UN Secretary-General to quickly respond without bureaucratic impediments. Despite some initial delays and thanks to more attention to advance planning, the management of this window has somewhat improved and it might be expected to have more impact in the future.

The PBSO provides the overall direction and guidance regarding programme management and monitoring but, at a same time, the Multi-Donor Trust Fund Office of the United Nations Development Programme serves as Administrative Agent responsible for the Peacebuilding Fund's fiduciary management.[17]

## 4. Activities of the UN Peacebuilding Commission

In its first year of activity, the Peacebuilding Commission focused on Burundi and Sierra Leone, which were placed on the Commission's agenda pursuant to Paragraph 12 of the founding resolutions. The two governments had sent letters to the Presidents of the Security Council and the General Assembly, and the Security Council had referred Burundi and Sierra Leone to the PBC for its consideration.[18] In the subsequent year, the PBC was asked to add Guinea-Bissau[19] and the Central African Republic[20] to its agenda, following a similar procedure.[21]

---

[17] The PBF website (<http://www.unpbf.org/index.shtml>) contains all the details on the funding. The EU/EC does not contribute to the PBF directly, but a number of EU Member States do so in their bilateral capacity. For a list of pledges, see: <http://www.unpbf.org/pledges.shtml>.

[18] See PBC/1/OC/2.

[19] The UN's decision to place Guinea-Bissau on the PBC agenda coincided with the EU's decision to launch an ESDP operation in Guinea-Bissau aimed at providing advice and assistance regarding security sector reform to the local authorities in order to contribute to creating the conditions for the implementation of the National Security Sector Reform Strategy. Thanks to this qualified presence and to the presence of an EC delegation in Bissau, the European Union has become a privileged partner within the PBC configuration on Guinea-Bissau. EU representatives have briefed the PBC on several occasions and members of the ESDP operation are always present at the videoconference from Bissau.

[20] The European Union conducted a military bridging operation – EUFOR Tchad/RCA – from 28 January 2008 to 15 March 2009, under the mandate provided by United Nations Security Council Resolution 1778 (of 25 September 2007). Despite its strong military presence in the northern part of the Central African Republic, EUFOR established limited contacts with the PBC. The EUFOR mandate was limited to the specific area of operation (near the border with Sudan) while the PBC focused on the reforms at central level in Bangui, fully supported by the European Commission, which is the main donor present in the country. The PBC configuration took into account the significant role played by the European Commission in the CAR, including in SSR. Cooperation has been extremely effective and EC officials in Bangui are constantly involved in the work of the PBC.

[21] Upon receiving a formal request from the UNSC (A/62/736 – S/2007/744), the Organisational Committee convened formal meetings and decided to place Guinea-Bissau on the PBC agenda (19 December 2007). Following a similar procedure (A/62/864 – S/2008/383), the Central African Republic was added to the PBC agenda (12 June 2008).

The work of the four country-specific configurations of the PBC has followed broadly similar patterns, and a number of stages in the way the Commission structures its interaction with the individual countries can be identified:

- *Setting up of the Country-Specific Mechanism.* The first step is the establishment of the CSM. The election of a Chair (always with the consensual endorsement of a candidate expressing interest in the task and that of the country under consideration) and the membership of the country-specific configuration are defined by the Organisational Committee. The Chair is then responsible for convening and steering the CSM's work.
- *Identification of priorities for peacebuilding / mapping of existing initiatives.* At the outset, the CSM focuses on an assessment of the situation in the country and a first identification of the needs to consolidate the peace process, including briefings from the country, visits by the Chair of the CSM to the country, visits by authorities from the country to New York and a visit by the PBC to the country (usually with just a few members taking part, but involving the missions and embassies of PBC members in the field). As a result of this process, in the case of Burundi, for example, the PBC and the Government of Burundi, together with other stakeholders, civil society and the private sector, agreed on four critical priority areas for peacebuilding consolidation: promoting good governance, strengthening the rule of law, reforming the security sector and ensuring community recovery. In the case of Sierra Leone, very similar areas of concern were identified; however, it is interesting to note that, following a series of meetings and visits to the country, the PBC decided to add the energy sector as a priority to the previously agreed list, showing that the general approach could be adapted to take into account specific national contexts. This change in the priorities for Sierra Leone has been presented as a good example of the PBC's flexible approach. In the case of the Central African Republic, three main areas of concern were identified: security sector reform, rule of law/good governance and the promotion of development hubs. This last priority had already been one of the pillars identified by the government of the CAR for EC support and was taken up by the PBC as one of its core areas of concern in supporting peacebuilding in this country, taking into account the need to devise a support strategy for creating basic administrative structures in the territory beyond the capital.
- *Development of an Integrated Peacebuilding Strategy / Adoption of a Strategic Framework.* On the basis of the shared assessment, the PBC adopts a Strategic Framework for peacebuilding that becomes the reference document specifying the commitments of the country as well as the areas on which the international community will focus its attention and support. An interesting element in the Sierra Leone CSM was the presence of existing frameworks such as the Poverty Reduction Paper and the Peace Consolidation Strategy. In this case, it was agreed that the Integrated Peacebuilding Strategy (IPBS) would build on these existing frameworks by identifying key peacebuilding priorities and strengthening national and international commitments for their implementation. In parallel, the Peacebuilding Fund can decide to allocate funding to a series of projects.

- *Review of the Strategic Frameworks*. Regarding the Strategic Frameworks, the PBC decided that they would be subject to regular biannual reviews in order to take stock of the progress made and to adjust the priorities identified, taking into account developments on the ground. Twice a year, the PBC therefore assesses the progress made on the Strategic Frameworks: the assessment is made in close cooperation with the government of and actors in the country, including civil society. In the case of Burundi, for example, the biannual review, which was concluded in February 2009, outlined progress in the peace process but indicated that more efforts should be made towards the implementation of the ceasefire agreement and towards the DDR process. The preparation for the biannual review had been thorough and inclusive, involving many meetings in New York and Bujumbura and participation of numerous stakeholders. Similarly, the second biannual review for Sierra Leone, which took place in December 2008, outlined the main challenges to implementation and focused on the need to revive donors' coordination, anti-corruption measures and the launch of strategies by sectors.[22]
- *Monitoring and implementation*. In the case of the first country on the agenda, Burundi, it was immediately evident that the Strategic Framework[23] could not offer sufficient detail to monitor progress. The Framework was therefore accompanied by discussions and the adoption, in December 2007, of a joint monitoring and tracking mechanism for the Strategic Framework[24] which defined benchmarks and indicators for the periodic assessment of progress in consolidating peace in the country. The government of Burundi and its partners agreed to conduct the joint monitoring to assess their respective contributions to the Strategic Framework. The model developed for Burundi has been replicated for all other countries. However, the tendency has been towards simplifying and reducing the number of indicators and objectives in order to avoid an over-bureaucratic monitoring process. Moreover, for Burundi, in order to facilitate the continuing monitoring of the implementation of the Strategic Framework, the PBSO launched an additional exercise consisting in a detailed mapping of resources and contributions of various stakeholders to the peacebuilding process. This mapping prepared the ground for the first biannual review of the implementation of the Strategic Framework, which was held on 23 June 2008, and led to the adoption of recommendations for the future implementation of the Strategic Framework.[25]

At all of these stages, the EU/EC plays a major role in the definition and adoption of priorities. The fact that the European Commission is one of very few members of

[22] United Nations, *Conclusions and recommendations of the second biannual review of the implementation of the Sierra Leone Peacebuilding Cooperation Framework* (PBC/3/SLE/2).

[23] United Nations, *Strategic Framework for Peacebuilding in Burundi (*PBC/1/BDI/4).

[24] United Nations, *Joint monitoring and tracking mechanism for the Strategic Framework for Peacebuilding in Burundi* (PBC/2/BDI/4).

[25] United Nations, *Recommendations of the biannual review of the implementation of the Strategic Framework for Peacebuilding in Burundi* (PBC/2/BDI/9).

the PBC with delegations and major aid budgets in all four countries on the PBC agenda makes it an essential partner in all country-related discussions. Moreover, the multi-annual and long-term commitment of the European Commission provides continuity that allows for the identification of medium-term as well as short-term priorities. In the case of Guinea-Bissau, the presence of an ESDP mission in security sector reform has heightened the profile of the EU and has put emphasis on the need to enhance coordination with other actors, notably the UN (see n. 24 above).

## 5. The presence and the role of the European Union in the UN Peacebuilding Commission

During the long discussions on the composition and membership of the PBC, the participation of the European institutions was far from a foregone conclusion and involved negotiations on two tables: (i) with the wider UN membership which was grappling with the institutional balance of this new body, and (ii) with the EU Member States as to who should be mandated to represent the European Union in the PBC.

### 5.1 Negotiations with the UN on the participation of the EU

The 2005 World Summit Outcome Document stated that 'other institutional donors should be invited to participate in all meetings of the PBC in a manner suitable to their governing arrangements.'[26] The WB and IMF were explicitly identified as 'institutional donors' in this Document as well as in the PBC founding resolutions adopted in December 2005.[27] It was thus generally understood that 'other' referred mainly if not exclusively to the EU.

The EC's involvement as an 'other institutional donor', evidenced by several communications to PBC members, was contested by no one, but was held back by the Organisation of the Islamic Conference's (OIC) request to be granted similar status, regarding which many Western members of the PBC had queries. This issue became a subject of West/Non-Aligned Movement (NAM) polarisation and, as such, a sensitive element of the PBC's institutional set-up, which the PBC did not succeed in formally discussing before the meeting of the Organisational Committee on 16 May 2007 which finally settled the matter. With a letter of 30 May 2007, the PBC Chair formally confirmed the arrangement whereby the European Community would be invited to all meetings of the PBC as an 'institutional donor'.

The decision taken on 16 May 2007 to issue standing invitations to the four candidates (IMF, WB, OIC and EC) therefore came unexpectedly and was made on a 'non-objection basis' rather than through positive endorsement by the PBC members. These issues of membership and structure (including access for civil society) had generated considerable discussions in the course of 2006. The President of the

---

[26] A/Res/60/1, paragraph 102.

[27] General Assembly Resolution A/60/180 and UN Security Council Resolution 1645 (2005).

European Commission had written to the UN Secretary-General in June 2006, asking for participation of the EC. The acceptance of the standing invitation to the four observers to become full members of the PBC should be seen as a pragmatic compromise helped along by the positive role played by the PBC's Angolan Chair, Ambassador Martins.

## 5.2 Negotiations within the EU on its representation in the PBC

The full participation of the European Community in the Peacebuilding Commission had also generated intense discussions in Brussels as to who should represent the EU/EC within this new UN body. These discussions focused on the respective roles and competences of the European Commission and of CFSP in the areas of peacebuilding, post-conflict and recovery as provided for in the mandate of the PBC.

From the outset, the European Commission stressed the role it played in reconstruction and development and the affinity of many of its actions with the goals set out for the PBC. The Commission also stressed that participation in the PBC was linked to the role of 'institutional donor', an essentially First-Pillar competence managed by the European Commission. The internal EU debate also turned to the terminology to be used on the nameplate of the EU delegation in the PBC. This discussion was eventually resolved by the UN's refusal to have a delegation for the 'European Union' as the current arrangements only recognise the observer status of the 'European Community' within the UN.

In the end, a solution on the EU/EC representation at PBC Country-Specific Meetings was agreed between the PBC Chair, the PBSO, the UN Office of Legal Affairs and the EU Troika, based on one nameplate (European Community), two invitations and two seats (one for the Presidency and one for the Commission). This initial solution became the norm and was confirmed by the Organisational Committee in May 2007 (see above).[28]

## 5.3 The role of the EU/EC in the PBC

The de facto common delegation is in some ways a first for the representation of the EU, and there were concerns that the 'two chairs / one delegation' approach could create tensions, notably with Presidencies that are not members of the PBC in their national capacity. The first such case concerned the Portuguese Presidency in the second half of 2007 and confirmed that the arrangement worked out well, in full respect of everybody's interests.

In practice, the EU/EC delegation intervenes as one, via the Presidency, the Commission or both, depending on the issue under discussion, avoiding all unnecessary repetition. The Presidency normally intervenes on the basis of pre-agreed statements and acts as a conduit to keep the EU-27 fully informed of developments in

---

28 United Nations, PBC/1/OC/SR.3.

the PBC. The Presidency organises EU coordination meetings on the PBC on an ad hoc basis. In this task, the Presidency is supported by the Council Secretariat Office. The Council Working Group on the UN – CONUN – holds regular discussions in Brussels on PBC coordination.

The European Commission intervenes on all matters relating to its competence; it coordinates closely with its delegations in the countries on the agenda of the PBC for all the Country-Specific Meetings, as well as with the Commission's headquarters in Brussels for all cross-cutting and thematic discussions.

## 6. The EU and the PBC: Converging institutional interests?

### 6.1 A coherent and active member

The EU plays an active and constructive role in the work of the Peacebuilding Commission. It is in a unique position compared with other members of the PBC, as it has an extensive presence in the countries via the EC delegations and programmes and can mobilise a full range of instruments, from development projects to political dialogue and from security and defence measures under ESDP to mediation action and financial support.

The presence of a number of EU Member States as well as of the European Commission and EU Presidency ensures that all EU areas are represented and dealt with. In turn, this implies a coordination effort on the part of the EU actors to avoid contradictions and duplications; in this regard, the coordination work in the Council working group at the Brussels headquarters as well as the in-country coordination between the EU heads of mission provide the backbone of the EU and EC positions within the PBC in New York.

### 6.2 The role of the Presidency

In general terms, the EU Presidency, supported by the Council Secretariat, takes the floor to address all issues on which there is an agreed EU position and to make political statements and declarations on behalf of the EU-27. This is important in particular for the Member States that are not members of the PBC and, through the Presidency, have an avenue to be closely involved in the work of the PBC. On the other hand, it can be noted that the Member States that are present in the different configurations of the Peacebuilding Commission have less of an interest in coordinating EU positions since they already have direct access to the PBC's work in their national capacity.

EU statements are generally prepared by the Presidency, with the help of the Council Secretariat, and shared with the EU partners for comments. They may also be discussed at coordination meetings. The European Commission takes active part in preparing EU statements and the interventions by the Presidency. Whenever necessary, the European Commission complements the Presidency statement with its own statements focusing on Community instruments and projects.

On the basis of experience so far, the Presidency tends to call formal EU coordination meetings only in the case of major issues or to facilitate exchanges of views regarding major PBC-related reports or when negotiating Strategic Frameworks. In addition, the PBC makes limited use of negotiations as it focuses more on reaching consensus between its members and the national authorities; this, in turn, means that there is less need for frequent EU coordination than is the case for most other UN committees.

### 6.3 Coordination in Brussels

Besides the above-mentioned regional working groups in Brussels where substantive positions vis-à-vis the countries are discussed, an additional element of coordination amongst the EU members is provided by the monthly CONUN meetings in Brussels. In this Committee, the heads of the UN departments within the national ministries discuss the main lines of EU coordination at the UN, including issues relating to the Peacebuilding Commission.

### 6.4 Expert participation

Another recent development is the intervention by the EU as a provider of expertise in panel discussions in the Organisational Committee and on recent developments and EU operations in Country-Specific Meetings. The possibility for EU experts to brief the Peacebuilding Commission from the podium has also increased the EU presence and has provided the EU with a further opportunity to share its assessments and messages with the wider UN membership.

### 6.5 Visits by the PBC Chair to Brussels

As part of the enhancement of UN-EU cooperation, the PBC Chair has, since the PBC's creation, included visits to Brussels in his/her endeavours to present the PBC's activities and to build up direct contacts with relevant counterparts in the EU.

## 7. The Effectiveness of the Peacebuilding Commission: An Initial Assessment from an EU Perspective

Measuring the effectiveness of the PBC is a hard task. However, after three full years of activity, a preliminary assessment can be made of how well the PBC has measured up to the goals set out in the mandate of this new body.

The PBC is mandated to focus the attention of the international community on countries in post-conflict situations, to support their recovery process and to guide the transition towards sustainable development. In order to achieve these goals, the PBC has few 'levers': it can convene a number of actors, call attention to specific needs, improve coordination through recommendations and information exchange, and issue statements.

Its strengths and limitations are linked to its intergovernmental nature: the PBC works on the basis of consensus, and its action is rooted in the concept of 'national ownership' starting with the request from governments to be put on its agenda. The same concept of national ownership guides all PBC actions, and all documents agreed by the PBC are issued with the full support of the government concerned.

With these 'powers' and 'constraints' in mind, we can ask how well the PBC has performed so far.

*The PBC has increased the attention for the countries on its agenda...*

For all the countries on its agenda, the PBC has first and foremost provided increased attention from the international community. Being on the agenda of the PBC implies regular and high-level meetings in New York; it mobilises the country in the chair of the country-specific configuration as the 'champion' within the international community to guide and monitor the peacebuilding process; and it requires the formulation of commitments by the government as well as by the members of the PBC. These commitments are regularly appraised and reviewed and constitute the 'contract' between the international community and the country.

For the pressure of the international community to be effective, a long-term commitment is clearly needed. The PBC therefore needs to adapt its support to the various phases of the peacebuilding process and to articulate its priorities accordingly.

However, the extent to which the attention of the international community can be sustained remains to be tested in two critical respects: firstly in terms of how many countries can simultaneously be on the PBC agenda (stretching the resources available within the UN system and in the delegations in New York); and secondly in terms of how and when a country is taken 'off the agenda' of the PBC. The latter question is one that has not yet been addressed, and discussions on what strategies should be considered to 'disengage', 'phase' or 'graduate' a country are under way.

*...it has brought together security and development considerations...*

In post-conflict situations there is a stronger need for security than for sustainable development interventions. The PBC manages to bring together the different concerns of the national authorities, the traditional donors and civil society in order to focus on what is needed in the short term and in the medium/long term. In the best scenario, this prioritisation (which has been more effective for some countries on the PBC agenda than for others) helps to ensure that the traditional tensions between security and development concerns are eased and sequenced.

*...it has identified mutual commitments and tracking mechanisms...*

Through its country-specific configurations the PBC has identified Strategic Frameworks for peacebuilding for each of the countries on its agenda; these Frameworks have been agreed with the government and adopted by consensus by the PBC and are regularly reviewed and assessed, usually on a biannual basis.

The tracking and monitoring mechanisms put in place are a further guarantee that the Framework remains a 'living document' and partners have to show what they have been able to do to meet the goals agreed in the Frameworks. However, these monitoring mechanisms suffer from a lack of baselines and indicators that can effectively quantify progress towards the more political goals.

Moreover, the quality of the tracking mechanisms varies greatly across the four countries, in terms of both level of detail and of mobilisation of national and international actors in their regular updating. In some cases, the exercise tends to turn into a bureaucratic box-ticking but time-consuming process, overlapping rather than complementing other pre-existing strategies such as the World Bank's Poverty Reduction Strategies.

*... but lacks structural impact...*

Whilst the PBC has managed to focus attention on the few countries on its agenda, its wider mandate of proposing strategies and supporting peacebuilding processes in a more horizontal manner has not yet been fulfilled. Clearly, the country-specific approach is a unique feature of the PBC that should not be lost; however, the intensive nature of the consultations for countries on its agenda implies that the PBC will never be able to handle more than a few countries at any one time.

The Working Group on Lessons Learned has not managed to move beyond academic discussions and is not equipped to tease out operational lessons that can be endorsed by the PBC and applied in other countries.

*... provides a limited regional dimension...*

Many causes of instability have a regional dimension and require solutions at that level. The PBC has tried to mobilise the regional dimension, but this remains a difficult challenge, which is partly due to its intergovernmental and consensual nature.

*...has only slightly broadened the donors base...*

Bringing in new non-traditional donors is one of the goals of the PBC as part of its resource mobilisation goal. These resources need not be financial but can also take the form of technical assistance, training and transfer of know-how. However, the examples of non-traditional donors mobilising in support of countries on the PBC agenda are still far too few.

*...requires new and innovative working methods...*

The question of whether a country situation can only be discussed in a country-specific configuration should be considered. There is already, as would be expected, a difference in pace and intensity of work between the countries that have been on the agenda since the beginning and those with which the PBC became involved more recently.

Moreover, it may be explored whether the PBC needs, in all cases, to engage in a fully- fledged process aimed at defining strategies. Some countries may require advice on a more limited set of issues, not necessarily covered in a formally approved strategy, and could benefit from a more targeted process in that respect.

A more strategic use of recommendations as a tool to strengthen coordination could be considered. This should apply to coordination between UN bodies, other international actors and bilateral donors.

The PBC should also strive to enhance its visibility at the country level. The risk of the PBC becoming a NY phenomenon with little impact on developments in the countries requires renewed efforts to replicate international coordination in the countries on its agenda.

*...and needs to raise its profile.*

Lastly, the PBC suffers from a lack of visibility outside as well as inside the UN system. Raising its profile seems to be a necessary precondition to ensure that its actions are recognised and its recommendations heeded.

The review of the Peacebuilding Commission envisaged for 2010 will be a first opportunity to assess the work of this new body.

# Chapter 6
# COOPERATION BETWEEN THE EU AND THE AU IN THE FIELD OF PEACEBUILDING

**Koen Vervaeke***

## 1. INTRODUCTION: A NEW CONTEXT

In December 2007, the relationship between the African Union and the European Union saw a major boost. The adoption of the Joint Africa-EU Strategy (JAES) in Lisbon set a jointly agreed framework and clear priorities, opening avenues of cooperation, notably in the field of peace and security.[1] The African Union (AU) is the natural interlocutor for the EU in this partnership, but not the exclusive one. Some of the African regional economic communities (RECs) have become important partners for the EU due to their crucial role in the build-up of the African Peace and Security Architecture (APSA). More than ever, peace and security are at the centre of the relations between the EU and Africa. This could only be achieved with two evolutions coinciding, one on the African side, the other on the European side.

Since the late nineties and especially since the first years of the new millennium, there appears to be a growing resolve on the African side to tackle conflicts and find African solutions to African problems. This was clearly demonstrated by the démarches of African lead nations such as South Africa in the Democratic Republic of Congo, and Nigeria in West Africa, by subregional organisations, and, above all, by the transformation of the Organisation of African Unity (OAU) into the African Union. The OAU, intricately involved with the decolonisation movement and the fight against apartheid, had clearly neither the political focus nor the instruments to challenge the threats of conflict still faced by the continent. In addition, the end of the Cold War period and the growing globalisation supported the call for stronger African integration.

Created in 2002, its first Commission taking office in 2004, the AU has a strong peace and security focus. Article 3 of the AU's Constitutive Act sets the promotion

---

* Koen Vervaeke is a Belgian diplomat and since 6 December 2007 the first EU Special Representative and Head of the European Union Delegation to the African Union in Addis Abeba (Ethiopia). The views expressed in this chapter are the author's own and do not necessarily represent the official position of any organisation or institution.

[1] Council of the European Union, *The Africa-EU Strategic Partnership: A Joint Africa-EU Partnership*, doc. 16344/07 (Presse 291), Lisbon, 9 December 2007.

of peace, security and stability on the continent as an objective of the Union.[2] This represented a marked change from the original ambitions of the OAU: the founding fathers of the AU refused indifference with regard to (internal) conflicts and rejected the logic of non-interference followed until then by the OAU. Hence, in Article 4(h), the new AU recognised the right of the Union to intervene in a Member State in case of war crimes, genocide and crimes against humanity. With the African Peace and Security Architecture, structures and procedures were designed to enable the AU to carry out the new tasks, in coordination with the RECs.

On the European side, the self-perception of the EU's role in Africa, traditionally very much focused on development cooperation, has also undergone profound changes to the benefit of a more political approach. The first ever appointment of an EU Special Envoy for the Great Lakes Region in 1996,[3] followed by others in the years to come, in particular for Sudan and for the AU,[4] the first EU-Africa Summit in Cairo in 2000, the revision of the contractual relationship with Africa (and Caribbean and Pacific States) with the more political and comprehensive governance provisions in the Cotonou Agreements of 2000 – in particular as regards human rights –,[5] the adoption of a new EU Strategy for Africa in 2005[6] and the creation of an innovative instrument to fund AU-led peace operations (the Africa Peace Facility)[7] have all been visible steps on the road to such increased political engagement with Africa. They have established a strong link between development, democracy and security. Above all, they are based on the recognition that stability and prosperity on the African continent are of strategic interest to the EU.

This new way for the EU to look at its role in Africa should be seen in the context of the overall development of the EU – often labelled an economic giant but a political dwarf – towards becoming a more global player. The Common Foreign and Security Policy (CFSP) was to be instrumental in that development. The EU, itself called into question for not being able to prevent the war in the Balkans, took

---

[2] The Constitutive Act of the African Union (2000) is available at: <http://www.africa-union.org/About_AU/AbConstitutive_Act.htm>.

[3] Joint Action 96/250/CFSP of 25 March 1996 adopted by the Council on the basis of Article J.3 of the Treaty on European Union, in relation to the nomination of a Special Envoy for the African Great Lakes Region, *OJ* 1996 L 87/1.

[4] Council Joint Action 2005/556/CFSP of 18 July 2005 appointing a Special Representative of the European Union for Sudan, *OJ* 2005 L 188/43; and Council Joint Action 2007/805/CFSP of 6 December 2007 appointing a European Union Special Representative to the African Union, *OJ* 2007 L 323/45.

[5] Partnership Agreement APC-EC, signed in Cotonou on 23 June 2000, *OJ* 2000 L 317/3 (revised in Luxembourg on 25 June 2005).

[6] Communication from the Commission to the Council, the European Parliament and the European Economic and Social Committee of 12 October 2005, 'EU Strategy for Europe: Towards a Euro-African pact to accelerate Africa's development', COM(2005) 489 final.

[7] See Council Regulation (EC) No 617/2007 of 14 May 2007 on the implementation of the 10th European Development Fund under the ACP-EC Partnership Agreement, *OJ* 2007 L 152/1, and Decision No 2/2007 of the ACP-EC Council of Ministers of 25 May 2007 allowing additional bilateral contributions, to be managed by the Commission, in support of the objectives of the African Peace Facility, *OJ* 2007 L 175/35.

decisive steps in the 1990s to strengthen its external action through different new instruments, notably the European Security and Defence Policy (ESDP). In its efforts to bring peace and prosperity beyond its own borders, it seemed then only logical and opportune to deploy these instruments also in Africa.

*European Security and Defence Policy (ESDP)*

The development of ESDP and its early applications in Africa have added a very important new instrument to the EU's toolbox to support African efforts and have proven to be an essential element in making the EU's contribution to peace and stability on the African continent more credible and effective. The role of High Representative Javier Solana in translating this new policy into operations would be a determining factor.

No one could have predicted that Africa, starting with the Democratic Republic of Congo, would become the scene of strong ESDP engagement. The military operation Artemis in 2003 was the EU's first military operation outside Europe.[8] At the point when the peace process was about to collapse, Artemis stabilised the security conditions and improved the humanitarian situation in the north-eastern town of Bunia, strengthening the UN peacekeeping mission MONUC so that after a bridging period it could again take over responsibility. Three years later, again at a critical juncture of Congo's transition, EUFOR RD Congo was deployed in Kinshasa in support of MONUC during the electoral process.[9] In 2008/09, EUFOR Chad/RCA contributed to protecting civilians in danger in eastern Chad and the north of the Central African Republic.[10] Its presence prevented further spill-over into the region of the Darfur conflict.

Besides these autonomous military operations in close cooperation with the UN, the EU used its ESDP capabilities also in a more diversified way. In Darfur, European military and police, in an advisory function, worked side by side with African counterparts in the AU-led peacekeeping mission AMIS. Currently, the EU has three independent ESDP missions deployed on the continent in the field of security sector reform: EUSEC RD Congo's key task is to provide advice and assistance for the reform of the Congolese army.[11] EUPOL RD Congo supports and assists the Congolese authorities in security sector reform in the crucial area of police and its interaction with the justice sector.[12] In

[8] Council Joint Action 2003/423/CFSP of 5 June 2003 on the European Union military operation in the Democratic Republic of Congo, *OJ* 2003 L 143/50.

[9] Council Decision 2006/412/CFSP of 12 June 2006 on the launching of the European Union military operation in support of the United Nations Organisation Mission in the Democratic Republic of the Congo (MONUC) during the election process (Operation EUFOR RD Congo), *OJ* 2006 L 163/16.

[10] Council Joint Action 2007/677/CFSP of 15 October 2007 on the European Union military operation in the Republic of Chad and in the Central African Republic, *OJ* 2007 L 279/21.

[11] Council Joint Action 2007/406/CFSP of 12 June 2007 on the European Union mission to provide advice and assistance for security sector reform in the Democratic Republic of the Congo (EUSEC RD Congo), *OJ* 2007 L 151/52.

[12] Council Joint Action 2007/405/CFSP of 12 June 2007 on the European Union police mission undertaken in the framework of reform of the security sector (SSR) and its interface with the system of justice in the Democratic Republic of the Congo (EUPOL RD Congo), *OJ* 2007 L 151/46.

Guinea-Bissau, a dedicated SSR mission provides advice and assistance in the reform of the security sector in Guinea Bissau in order to contribute to creating the conditions for implementation of the National Security Sector Reform Strategy.[13] Finally, EUNAVFOR Atalanta is the first ever ESDP maritime operation, which aims to help deter, prevent and repress acts of piracy and armed robbery off the coast of Somalia.[14]

Short-term substitution of African efforts with ESDP missions on the continent might also be needed in the future. However, the EU has no intention of becoming the 'gendarme' of Africa. Capabilities are stretched and it would not be the right approach. Each (potential) ESDP contribution should be judged upon its merits and contribution to the overall policy. Therefore, capacity building, direct support to African peace support operations (financially and by giving advice) and contributions to security sector reform will continue to be the priority. We might also reflect on what contribution ESDP can bring to the new security challenges which Africa is facing: terrorism, the impact of climate change, organised crime and drugs trafficking.

The adoption by the EU of its first European Security Strategy (ESS) in 2003 was also crucial for Africa.[15] Generally too much associated with the EU's own security, in particular with the threat of terrorism or the proliferation of weapons of mass destruction, the ESS is however more than relevant also for the EU's relations with Africa. It has added a security dimension to the existing humanitarian and development responsibility of the EU. It not only presupposes that security threats do not stop at borders, not least as a result of globalisation, but also stresses the need to address these threats beyond the territory of the EU. Joint challenges, such as climate change, migration, terrorism and energy, can only be effectively taken up if the Union does so also *in* and *with* Africa. Hence the need to work together more with partners such as the AU. It also acknowledges security as a precondition to development as well as the need for the EU to mobilise all its instruments in a comprehensive approach if it is to be successful: governance and stability are as important as aid and trade.

## 2. The three pillars of the peace and security partnership

The new Joint Africa-EU Strategy was adopted in Lisbon on 9 December 2007 at the second EU-Africa Summit.[16] Based on the principles of ownership and shared responsibility, it offers an overarching political vision of Heads of State and Gov-

[13] Council Joint Action 2008/112/CFSP of 12 February 2008 on the European Union mission in support of security sector reform in the Republic of Guinea-Bissau (EU SSR GUINEA-BISSAU), *OJ* 2008 L 40/11.

[14] Council Joint Action 2008/851/CFSP of 10 November 2008 on a European Union military operation to contribute to the deterrence, prevention and repression of acts of piracy and armed robbery off the Somali coast, *OJ* 2008 L 301/33.

[15] *European Security Strategy*, 12 December 2003, available on the Council's website at: <http://ue.eu.int/uedocs/cmsUpload/78367.pdf>.

[16] See *supra* n. 1.

ernment of both sides on what should guide the mutual partnership in the future. Significantly, the first of the eight partnerships identified in the first action plan deals with peace and security.[17]

The JAES put the EU's relationship with Africa on a new basis. While, as stated earlier, the EU had previously adopted a number of strategies intending to address African issues, this was the first *joint* strategy based on principles of partnership and African ownership. Africa and the EU agreed on a number of key political challenges to be addressed jointly and on common fundamental objectives in four areas of interest: peace and security, governance and human rights, trade and regional integration, and key development issues.

Peace and security are jointly recognised preconditions for political, economic and social development. On this basis the two partners agreed to 'promote holistic approaches to security, encompassing conflict prevention and long-term peace-building, conflict resolution and post-conflict reconstruction, linked to governance and sustainable development, with a view to addressing the root causes of conflicts.'

The Joint Africa-EU Strategy was accompanied by a first three-year Action Plan in order to help implement its commitments. In the area of peace and security, three priority actions were agreed:

- Enhanced dialogue on challenges to peace and security;
- Full operationalisation of the African Peace and Security Architecture (APSA); and
- Predictable funding and support for African-led Peace Support Operations (PSOs).

These priority actions will be discussed in turn below.

## 2.1 Enhanced dialogue on issues related to peace and security

Strengthening institutional ties is essential to reach common positions and implement common approaches on challenges to peace and security in Africa, Europe and around the globe. Although perhaps less visible or spectacular than some other actions, it constitutes without doubt the basis of the joint engagement. Establishing common understanding of threats to stability and security is a first step towards the goal of joint action. The strategic partners might not always reach full agreement on the course of action to be taken, but the bottom line is that both sides no longer aim to take any position or decision on issues of (African) peace and security without having consulted each other and having listened to each other's views.

This dialogue is conducted at several levels, ranging from the three-yearly Africa-EU summits, the six-monthly ministerial troika meetings, the annual College-to-College meeting between the European Commission and the African Union Commission (AUC), to regular contacts between Commissioners on both sides and with the High Representative. On a daily basis, the work of the Delegation of the EU to the AU, led by a double-hatted EUSR for the AU and Head of the EC Delega-

[17] The first action plan is attached to the 2007 Strategy.

tion, and of its AU counterpart in Brussels, has been crucial to build better understanding. The intensification of the political relations is also illustrated by first meetings between the EU Political and Security Committee and the AU Peace and Security Council.

Both sides have also strengthened their dialogue on specific situations and dossiers. Against the background of the resurgence of unconstitutional changes of government in Africa, the AU and the EU have been working together in country-specific International Contact Groups, comprising, in general, the AU's five international partner organisations (UN, EU, the League of Arab States, the *Organisation internationale de la Francophonie* and the Organisation of the Islamic Conference), the EU Member States with a permanent seat on the UN Security Council and the African members of the UNSC. The importance of effective coordination at the international level made the AU call on its bilateral and multilateral partners to lend their support to decisions taken by the AU and to refrain from any action which could undermine AU efforts and send conflicting signals to the perpetrators of unconstitutional change. In particular as regards sanctions, there is recognition that without support from relevant partners, African sanctions would only have a symbolic impact.

Another example was the creation of an AU-EU expert group working on the principle of universal jurisdiction in relation to judiciary action taken by EU Member States against African leaders. It showed that even when the issue was controversial and divisive, the AU and EU could maintain and even deepen their dialogue. Both sides agreed to continue the debate, first in the Sixth Committee before discussion at the next UN General Assembly.

## 2.2 Capacitating Africa to deal with its security challenges

Effective crisis management requires procedures, structures and capacities. Africa has a clear strategy and vision on how it intends to tackle the challenges of conflicts. This is captured in the so-called African Peace and Security Architecture (APSA) that should become fully operational in 2010. At its centre is the 15-member Peace and Security Council, a standing decision-making organ for the prevention, management and resolution of conflicts and for collective security and early warning arrangements to facilitate timely and efficient response to conflict and crisis situations in Africa. It also includes a panel of the wise, a continental early warning system, as well as African standby forces in case troops need to be deployed. Hence the framework is there, the real challenge is to make it operational.

The establishment and functioning of the APSA heavily depends on the interaction between the AU and the different regional organisations and mechanisms. Therefore, the Memorandum of Understanding between the AU and the eight regional mechanisms for the prevention, management and resolution of conflicts is an integral part of the set-up.[18]

---

[18] Memorandum of Understanding on Cooperation in the Area of Peace and Security between the African Union, the Regional Economic Communities and the Coordinating Mechanisms of the Re-

In the framework of the African Standby Force (ASF), Africa has been divided into five regions responsible for generating, among others, five sets of both operational organic and command structures and military, police and civilian human resources, while the AU Commission will build the capacity for preparing and implementing political and strategic decisions. Three Regional Economic Communities (RECs) – ECCAS in central Africa, ECOWAS in the west and SADC in the south – and two Regional Mechanisms – EASBRIG in eastern Africa and NARC in northern Africa – have become essential elements in the ASF operationalisation process and therefore have to be taken into account by the EU and all other AU partners in their support to APSA.

The EU is committed to supporting the AU and the RECs, its regional partners, in this endeavour, reinforcing the link between the two levels. Exchanges of experience as well as expert advice on the development of the relevant conceptual documents, instruments and capacities are one part of the task. Innovative funding mechanisms, mainly through the African Peace Facility but also through regional programmes for the RECs, also ensure the financial means necessary to establish and sustain these needed structures, instruments and capacities. Funds are made available to cover, among others, staff salaries as well as training, office equipment and running costs.

## 2.3 Predictable funding and support to African PSOs

The single most important European instrument for the support of AU-led operations is arguably the African Peace Facility. Established in 2004, it provided for the first time a reliable, predictable and sustainable funding source for such operations.[19] Only recently, a new contract was signed for the second African Peace Facility, providing another €300 million to the African Union over the coming three years, whereby most funds will again go to PSOs.

*African Peace Facility (APF)*

The African Peace Facility was established in 2004 in response to a request of African leaders gathered at the AU Summit in Maputo (2003). As an EU response to the resolve of the African Union to take responsibility for its own peace and security, the APF is based on the recognition that peace and security are preconditions for sustainable development. With its legal basis in the Cotonou Agreement, the APF has brought together security and development, providing an initial amount of €250 million from the European Development Fund (9th EDF). This allocation has increased over time to €740 million available until 2010. An additional €300 million is in reserve.

gional Standby Brigades of Eastern Africa and Northern Africa, available at: <http://www.africa-union.org/root/AU/AUC/Departments/PSC/ps/PSC%20Publications/MOU_AU_RECs_E.pdf>.

[19] See *supra* n. 7.

The APF is built on three core principles: African ownership, solidarity, and partnership between Africa and Europe. Its general objective is to contribute to peace, stability and security in Africa through targeted support to African efforts at the continental and regional level in the areas of conflict prevention, management and resolution, and peacebuilding.

Through the Facility, the EU has been at the forefront of international support to the African peace and security agenda, notably through backing provided to African peace support operations, such as: AMIS (African Union Mission in Sudan, over €305 million), AMISOM (AU Mission in Somalia, €35 million + €60 million in the pipeline), the FOMUC/MICOPAX operation in the Central African Republic (€53.2 million) and two subsequent AU Missions in the Comoros (overall €8.5 million).[20]

The Facility has also significantly contributed to the building up of the APSA, in particular the Continental Early Warning System, the African Standby Force and other relevant continental and subregional structures (e.g., liaison offices of subregional organisations to the AU).

In order to allow for immediate financial support at critical moments, e.g., for the preparation of a peace support operation or initial steps of a mediation process, when urgent funding is essential, an Early Response Mechanism (€15 million) is now part of the Facility.[21]

The APF has been an example of the strengthening of the coordination and coherence of support provided by the EU to the AU. With an innovative mechanism that consists in pooling additional contributions from EU Member States with APF funds, the EU has channelled its support through a single framework, enabling a reduction of transaction costs and of the administrative burden for African partners. This approach, it being the first case of co-financing under the 9th European Development Fund, has now become a permanent feature of the APF and one that remains open to voluntary contributions from both EU and non-EU donors.

Overall, the African Peace Facility has been a successful instrument and the main substantial source of funding for African peace and security and for the implementation of the Peace and Security Partnership. It has enabled the deployment of a number of African-led peace support operations, and the strengthening of APSA. Furthermore, it has helped enhance cooperation between the African Union Commission and Regional Economic Communities/Regional Mechanisms in the area of peace and security. The APF has also contributed to the strengthening of the role of the African Union as a key player in the area of peace and security.

At the same time, innovative ways of supporting PSOs also personnel-wise were found: in the case of AMIS in Sudan/Darfur, the EU, through its ESDP, strengthened the management with police and military advisors. It was the first time ever that the EU decided to deploy personnel to another organisation's operation. On both sides, this experience was seen as part of a learning process. Although the EU

---

[20] Information provided by the European Commission, available at: <http://ec.europa.eu/europeaid/where/acp/regional-cooperation/peace/peace-support-operations/index_en.htm>.

[21] Information provided by the European Commission, available at: <http://ec.europa.eu/europeaid/where/acp/regional-cooperation/peace/early-response-mechanism_en.htm>.

side felt that its advice could have had more impact, it certainly contributed to strengthening the chain of command and was considered valuable by the AU.

In the case of AMISOM in Somalia, the European Commission, through its Instrument for Stability, decided to support the AU Strategic Planning and Management Unit in finding staff necessary for the strategic planning of the operation.[22] As recruitment proved very difficult because of mainly procedural issues, the EU provided 5 EU planners for this Unit.

On a more long-term note, discussions are ongoing in the framework of the United Nations on how best to ensure predicable and sustainable funding for AU-led operations. A high-ranking panel under the chairmanship of former Italian Prime Minister Prodi presented its first conclusions.[23] At the request of the UN Security Council, the UN Secretary-General thereafter produced a report on the support to African Union peacekeeping operations authorised by the United Nations.[24] In its deliberations on 26 October 2009, the UNSC noted the report with appreciation and welcomed 'the intention of the United Nations Secretariat and the African Union Commission to set up a joint task force on peace and security to review immediate and long-term strategic and operational issues.'[25] The EU will continue to engage intensively with its African partners to ensure a best possible outcome enabling the AU and the RECs to conduct PSOs.

## 3. Key challenges

### 3.1 Building a stronger AU capacity

Africa and the EU are in the early stages of the partnership process. The AU is still, in essence, an intergovernmental organisation with a Commission that functions as the Secretariat of the African Union (Art. 20 of the 2000 Constitutive Act). It has no supranational competences. Compared with the EU, it is an organisation with limited mandate and structure. However, over the past years, it has aimed to play a more active role and has proven to bring added value to the African integration and development process, in particular in the area of peace and security. On balance, the achievements are remarkable. The possibility for the AU to sustain the progress achieved and to offer lasting solutions to the challenges will depend on the political will of its Member States and on its own capacity, both of which are interlinked.

There is a need for more overall support for African integration. To a certain extent, the history and dynamics of Africa's integration process are different from

---

22 See: <http://ec.europa.eu/europeaid/where/acp/regional-cooperation/peace/peace-support-operations/amisom_en.htm>.

23 See UN. Doc S/2008/813 of 31 December 2008, available at: <http://www.un.org/ga/search/view_doc.asp?symbol=S/2008/813&Lang=E>.

24 See UN Doc. S/2009/470 of 18 September 2009, available at: <http://daccess-dds-ny.un.org/doc/UNDOC/GEN/N09/510/12/PDF/N0951012.pdf?OpenElement>.

25 See UN Doc. S/PRST/2009/26 of 26 October 2009, available at: <http://daccess-dds-ny.un.org/doc/UNDOC/GEN/N09/577/10/PDF/N0957710.pdf?OpenElement>.

those that have driven and are still driving European integration. Africa should therefore not copy the EU and will have to find its own way. However, it will have to mobilise the necessary political will without which no collective action can succeed. The fact that – and rightly so – one of the AU's first ambitions is to ensure stability on the continent, i.e., impinging on the internal politics of its own Member States, does not make circumstances any easier. The Member States will have to provide stronger support to the values and political instruments underpinning the AU and to decisions taken at summit level or by the AU PSC. Respect for human rights, governance, democratisation, good neighbourliness and the fight against impunity and corruption will all considerably reduce the risk of conflict and consolidate the important progress made in many countries.

Furthermore, there is a need to build capacity to deliver on the high ambitions. Currently, the AUC is still working with the structure agreed in 2003, which provided for a total of 53 staff for the peace and security department. Challenges in recent years, not least resulting from the deployment of AMIS and AMISOM, but also the political willingness to rapidly build up the ASPA have expanded the AUC structures and procedures to their limits. As a result, more and more positions and structures were created outside those authorised and financed by partners. To remedy the shortcomings, the AUC is working on restructuring plans involving a substantial increase of staff (the assumption regarding the staff size is that the AUC should be able to conduct one major and one smaller PSO simultaneously). For the Peace Support Operations Division (PSOD), a staff of around 207 is suggested (compared to the current 49). The political Crisis Management Division (CMD) should increase its staff from currently 28 positions (but actually about 40 posts) to some 65. These reinforcements are urgently needed, yet discussion with Member States on cost implications is still ongoing. These plans also include strengthening of the financial management capacity. Important progress made under the current Commission in terms of strengthening (financial) management still needs consolidation.

### 3.2 Ensuring coherence between the continental and regional level

Efforts to consolidate peace in Africa obviously have an important regional dimension. Proper articulation between the continental and regional level is therefore crucial. It is sometimes difficult to find the right division of labour on the basis of principles such as coordination, complementarity, subsidiarity and comparative advantage. Regional organisations have vested interests, but proximity also opens up the door to partiality. Certainly in conflicts with a dimension that affects the whole continent (like Sudan) or where AU doctrines and principles are at stake (such as unconstitutional changes of government) the African Union has a clear role to play. It also offers the strongest link with the UN and the UNSC, as well as other international partners. The establishment of RECs liaison offices to the AU in Addis, soon to be coupled with AU representations to the RECs, with the EU's support, contribute to a better understanding of each other's role and added value.

As there are considerable disparities among the said eight regional mechanisms and RECs/RMs and in their capacity to contribute to shaping the APSA, differentiated support according to the specific needs of each is essential. Given the considerable overlap in membership and mandate, continued efforts are needed towards further harmonisation and well-coordinated burden sharing and streamlining of efforts.

Partners also bear responsibility in this respect, in particular the EU, which in the coming years will reserve more than €1 billion support for the continental and regional peace and security agenda. Any support should be used as a catalyst for the promotion of coherence and political ownership on the African side.

### 3.3 Developing a productive UN-AU-EU relationship

The relations between the EU and the AU in crisis management and peacebuilding cannot be seen outside the UN dimension. The importance of the triangular relationship is regularly underlined, as both the EU and the UN have the ambition to support the AU in similar fields. A *ménage à trois* is never easy, but in this case indispensable.

Seen from the UN perspective, greater cooperation with regional organisations such as the AU in dealing with conflicts has been a persistent theme in the Security Council since the mid-1990s. This is consistent with the spirit of Chapter VIII of the UN Charter, which envisages that regional organisations should attempt to address regional security issues before putting them to the Security Council. Sometimes cooperation with regional organisations is also the result of the Council's unwillingness or impossibility to take on such tasks. This was the case in the early days of the AU's engagement in Darfur and still is the case for Somalia. But innovative ways have been explored in an attempt to bridge the gap. For instance, the AMIS operation in Darfur already benefitted from a UN support package; in a unique approach it was then decided to even deploy the hybrid operation UNAMID under the leadership of both organisations. The support to AMISOM, partially in the form of assessed contributions (and through a trust fund), was a further step towards a stronger UN engagement with the AU and raised hopes within Africa that this could become a model for the future.

This relationship is not always an easy one. While the hybrid formulas may offer pragmatic solutions, they are not without friction. The issue of the role and responsibilities of regional organisations in peacekeeping compared to those of the UN is an issue of debate in Addis and seen in light of these experiences, in particular in relation to the UN's unwillingness to engage in Somalia. With the UNSC eager to stress its primary role, the overall New York-Addis relation sometimes suffers from a 'hierarchical' dimension, a reality which is not always recognised on both sides.

On a more strategic level, the report on sustainable and predictable funding for AU-led operations, issued by the so-called Prodi Panel in December 2008, garnered a cautiously positive response from African states. Although many would have liked it to go further (in particular in the context of assessed contributions), it was appreciated that the need to fund African peace support operations was, for the first time, officially recognised by the UN. The subsequent Report on Support to African Union Peacekeeping Operations authorised by the United Nations itself, issued in September 2009, acknowledges the need for strengthened coordination and consultation mechanisms to ensure coherence in decision making.[26] With regard to capacity building, it suggests developing a plan and road map, which should then also provide a framework through which other partners and donors could focus their programmes.

Given the EU's more ambitious political role in Africa, the triangular relationship AU-UN-EU will become increasingly important. Besides support to African peace support operations, the UN, like the EU, has developed a very similar agenda on cooperation in the field of capacity building. In 2006, both sides signed the Joint Declaration 'Enhancing UN-AU Cooperation: Framework for the Ten-Year Capacity-Building Programme for the African Union'.[27] It offers avenues for cooperation and division of labour between the EU and the UN within the framework of ongoing UN-EU cooperation in crisis management.

### 3.4 Deepening EU coherence after Lisbon

The EU's approach to the AU is a multi-faceted one. Several instruments are at its disposal. Different EU institutions are working hand in glove to ensure the best possible support to the African Union in both areas mentioned, i.e., immediate crisis management as well as build-up of long-term capacities. Support through the African Peace Facility is combined with support by other Community instruments, notably the Instrument for Stability and EDF programmes, and activities in the CFSP/CSDP remit, combined with individual Member States' contributions. For a coherent use of all these instruments, deepening of EU integration is just as important as further integration on the AU side. The implementation of the Lisbon Treaty and the role of the new High Representative of the Union for Foreign Affairs and Security Policy, Catherine Ashton, with one foot in the Council and one in the Commission, as well as the establishment of a European External Action Service, offer enormous opportunities for increased political and operational coherence. The experience of the integrated Delegation of the EU to the AU in Addis already shows that this approach contributes to deepening relations and to ensuring more coherence by pooling together existing instruments. Finally, work should continue on adapting our support mechanisms to the needs of the African partners, both to overcome the limitations to their use, in particular the restriction on the use of official development aid for military purposes, and to limit the transaction costs for the AU and other recipients.

---

[26] See UN Doc. S/2009/470 of 18 September 2009, available at: <http://daccess-dds-ny.un.org/doc/UNDOC/GEN/N09/510/12/PDF/N0951012.pdf?OpenElement>.

[27] The Joint Declaration is available at: <http://www.uneca.org/nepad/RCM10/UN-AU-CooperationFramework.pdf>.

## 4. Conclusion

As the African Union, together with the regional organisations and its Member States, increases efforts to bring peace and stability to the continent, possible areas for EU support will widen rather than diminish in the coming years. Two factors will remain fundamental. First, the need and, at the same time, respect for the ownership and leadership of the AU. This fundamental principle of the new Joint EU-Africa Strategy should continue to guide the partners; it constitutes the basis for the sense of shared responsibility that inspires them. Second, the EU's contribution to peace and stability in Africa should continue to be based on the widest possible security definition, mobilising a comprehensive approach while not favouring one area of support over the other, or one instrument over another. Within the European Union, the search continues for the best possible coordination and coherence of the different instruments at the EU's disposal – both financial and political, of both the Commission and the Council.

Key to the principle of African ownership is the ability to deliver. Therefore, capacity building for African organisations will continue to be a priority. In this context, partners need to make sure that the AU and the regional organisations are well interlinked. They also need to establish mutually reinforcing relations to ensure that the vision of the African Peace and Security Architecture will be fully implemented as soon as possible.

The EU has developed a unique relationship with the AU based on the conviction that a globalised multipolar world will need strong regional institutions both to support development internally and to defend collective interests in global fora. Building on a shared history and geographic and cultural proximity, it is in this field that the EU can be Africa's privileged partner by sharing its specific integration experience.

# Chapter 7
# CONVERGENCE WITHOUT COOPERATION? THE EU AND OSCE IN THE FIELD OF PEACEBUILDING

**David Galbreath***

## 1. Introduction

The development of the European Union's (EU) relationship with the Organisation for Security and Cooperation in Europe (OSCE) represents the changing nature of cooperation and security in Europe. Cooperation between the two organisations is both a pragmatic and normative result. Pragmatically, there is significant convergence between the two organisations, with all 27 Member States of the EU being participating states of the OSCE. Normatively, both organisations have sought to direct their attention to overlapping interests largely to do with regional stability, democracy promotion and human rights protection. Especially since the end of the Cold War, the relationship between the EU and the OSCE has developed in terms of converging agendas and functions. Such cooperation and overlap is not only a product of the changing geopolitical landscape of Central and Eastern Europe, but has developed since the Helsinki Final Act[1] was signed in 1975, creating the Conference on Security and Cooperation in Europe (CSCE), the forerunner of the OSCE. At the same time, increased cooperation between the EU and OSCE stresses the function and fitness of either organisation to perform their responsibilities in Europe in that it calls into question why the OSCE is still relevant today. As we shall see, as the EU expands its agenda to converge more with the OSCE, the OSCE's niche role in Europe is increasingly under threat from those who would most benefit from its continuing existence.

The focus of this chapter is on the development of the relationship between the EU and the OSCE, with the acknowledgement that this relationship has gone from niche separation to functional convergence.[2] Within this context, the chapter looks at several questions. Firstly, what is the basis for cooperation between the EU and

* Dr. David J. Galbreath is Senior Lecturer in International Relations at the Department of Politics and International Relations, University of Aberdeen.

[1] The CSCE Helsinki Final Act (1975) is available at: <http://at www.osce.org/item/4046.html>.

[2] See also V. De Graaf and A. Verstichel, 'OSCE Crisis Management and OSCE-EU Relations', in S. Blockmans, ed., *The European Union and Crisis Management: Policy and Legal Aspects* (The Hague, T.M.C. Asser Press 2008).

*S. Blockmans, J. Wouters & T. Ruys, eds., The European Union and Peacebuilding*

OSCE in the area of peacebuilding? Secondly, under what conditions have the EU and OSCE increased their cooperation and practical overlap in the area of peacebuilding? In answering these questions, we uncover the nature of converging agendas and functions in the field of peacebuilding.

The structure of the chapter follows in this fashion. Section 2 examines the EU's and OSCE's institutional development since the end of the Cold War and their increased relationship and overlap in the area of peacebuilding. We highlight the converging agendas and functions of the two organisations. Section 3 looks at this relationship in context. We focus on three interlinked areas of mutual interest and cooperation in three areas of peacebuilding: peacekeeping, democracy promotion and human rights protection. Finally, section 4 looks at how the organisations themselves reflect on their relationship in the field of peacebuilding, based on interviews performed in Brussels and Vienna.[3]

## 2. Converging agendas and functions

Given the differences between the EU's and the OSCE's original mandates during the Cold War, it is of little surprise that cooperation between the two organisations was limited. Furthermore, where the EC was a regular organisation consisting of permanent institutions in Brussels, Strasbourg and Luxembourg, the CSCE was simply a series of summits and ministerial meetings without any permanent institutions. Thus, the EC and CSCE were not similar institutions in substance or structure. In general, the EU attitude towards the CSCE was as an organisation with a Cold War function. Where the latter organisation included the US and the Soviet Union, the former only included the countries of Western Europe. Where the EC had an explicitly economic function, the CSCE provided predominantly a geopolitical function. However, the EC began to change in the 1980s, culminating in the Single European Act in 1986 which created an explicitly political dimension to the organisation, under the heading of 'European Political Cooperation', from which CFSP would spring.

Changes in the Cold War likewise changed the CSCE. The effective end of the Cold War with Soviet reform and the collapse of the Berlin Wall and of several communist regimes in Central and Eastern Europe meant that the primary function (or niche) of the CSCE, 'common and comprehensive' security, was no longer needed, or at least not in the same way. With these changes, the CSCE set out a 'new agenda'.[4] In 1989, the CSCE conducted a series of meetings on the 'human dimension'. 'The role of the OSCE following the collapse of the Berlin Wall was to

---

[3] The author would like to thank the Leverhulme Trust for financial support for interviews carried out on the project 'The European Minority Rights Regime: Power, Interests and Knowledge'. Also, the author would like to thank the post-doctoral researcher on the project, Joanne McEvoy, for her fieldwork assistance in Brussels and Vienna.

[4] D. Galbreath, *The Organization for Security and Cooperation in Europe* (London, Routledge 2007), at 41-43.

help transitioning states remain on the path to democracy and market reforms (…) the democratisation agenda of the CSCE was directed at "locking-in" institutions and actors that would further transition.'[5] At the same time, the EC was developing its relationship with transitioning Central and Eastern Europe with the establishment of the PHARE (Poland and Hungary: Assistance for Restructuring their Economies) programme. While there was a great deal of attention on integration and support for public institutions, the PHARE programme did not explicitly deal with democratisation. Overall, both organisations were renegotiating their relationship with Central and Eastern Europe, which is where their agendas and functions began to converge in the post-Cold War period.

As the EC was increasingly institutionalising its political agenda, such as a result of the Maastricht Treaty in 1992, the CSCE was likewise institutionalising an organisation that had otherwise had no institutions. The first institutions to be created in the 'OSCE' were a Secretariat, the Council of Senior Officials (later to become the Permanent Council), the Conflict Prevention Centre (CPC) and the Office for Free Elections (later to become the Office for Democratic Institutions and Human Rights or ODIHR). These institutions were created in the 1990 'Charter of Paris for a New Europe'.[6] In 1992, the Helsinki Document established several additional institutions, including the Forum for Security Cooperation (FSC) and the High Commissioner on National Minorities (HCNM). The earlier created CPC is an institution within the OSCE Secretariat headed by an OSCE ambassador, where the FSC is a regular committee staffed by participating-state delegations that meets once a week. ODIHR and the HCNM are semi-autonomous institutions under the OSCE remit charged with conflict prevention. Incidentally, the HCNM was the first institution created in any European organisation dealing specifically with national minorities, although the Council of Europe's Advisory Committee for the Framework Convention for the Protection of National Minorities now plays a similar role.[7] While the EC was going through a major re-haul with the development of the Pillar system in the Maastricht Treaty, the OSCE was improving its capacity and competence in peacebuilding by creating a myriad of institutions.

Nowadays, the OSCE makes four contributions to the European security architecture and it is in these niches that the EU engages with the OSCE in terms of peacebuilding.[8] Firstly, the OSCE has a substantial epistemic component or input in the European security architecture. This knowledge-based approach to peacebuilding is clear in the Secretariat, ODIHR, the HCNM, as well as other institutions

---

[5] Ibid., at 41.

[6] The Charter of Paris for a New Europe (1990) is available at: <http://www.osce.org/item/4047.html>.

[7] R. Zaagman, *Conflict Prevention in the Baltic States: The OSCE High Commissioner on National Minorities in Estonia, Latvia, and Lithuania* (Flensburg, Germany, European Centre for Minority Issues 1999); W. Zellner, *On the Effectiveness of the OSCE Minority Regime: Comparative Case Studies on Implementation of the Recommendations of the High Commissioner on National Minorities of the OSCE* (Hamburg, Hamburger Beiträge zur Friedensforschung und Sicherheitspolitik, Heft, 1999).

[8] Galbreath, *supra* n. 4, at 122.

such as the Representative on Freedom of the Media. The European Commission relied on this epistemic component during the accession negotiations and monitoring that led to the 2004 and 2007 enlargements. Secondly, the OSCE has concentrated on a 'quiet diplomacy' approach to conflict prevention. Such a 'quiet' approach is part of the organisation's 'political' (rather than legal) nature, but also addresses a central observation in diplomacy more generally: regardless of regime type (i.e., more or less democratic), governments generally do not want to be seen as 'bad'.[9] Thus, the OSCE might often work behind closed doors as a way to preserve a government's or group's appearance in the region. 'Quiet diplomacy' insinuates engagement over confrontation. Thirdly, as stated before, the OSCE was the first to establish an institution solely focusing on national minorities. The EU itself only had a vague reference to the status of national minorities in the Copenhagen criteria[10] and even today lacks a legal or institutional framework with which to engage national minorities in terms of groups rather than as individuals.[11] As stated earlier, the Council of Europe has established an institution that focuses on the rights of national minorities. However, the OSCE HCNM is the only institution within an international organisation in the world that focuses on national minorities as a source of potential conflict. Again, the European Commission referred to the HCNM when making its annual reports on accession states.[12]

Finally, the OSCE has had a substantial presence in the field before and after conflict situations. The Stockholm Summit of 1992[13] set out the mandate for the OSCE to establish field missions in the OSCE area. All of these have been 'East of Vienna', focusing on the Former Yugoslavia and Soviet Union. The first mission to be established in August 1992 was the 'OSCE Missions of Long Duration in Kosovo, Sandjak and Vojvodina'. The OSCE presence in the field ranges from missions with strong mandates, to offices and centres that simply maintain a presence. Missions have ordinarily been established in areas of potential or post conflict, where centres and offices are primarily focused on stressing basic international commitments around such issues as competitive elections and human rights. The current Mission to Kosovo is the largest OSCE field presence thus far, with activity in all 30 municipalities. In addition to exacting mandates, which may include coordinating elections or monitoring inter-ethnic policing, the OSCE presence in the field is

---

[9] K. Abbott, 'Hard and Soft Law in International Governance', 54 *International Organization* (2003) 421-456.

[10] See *Bull. EU* 6-1993, point 13.

[11] D. Galbreath and J. McEvoy, *The European Minority Rights Regime: International Organizations, Impact and Influence* (Basingstoke, Palgrave 2010).

[12] J. Dorodnova, *Challenging Ethnic Democracy: Implementation of the Recommendations of the OSCE High Commissioner on National Minorities to Latvia, 1993-2001*, CORE Working Papers 10 (2002); E. Jurado, 'Complying with European Standards of Minority Education: Estonia's Relations with the European Union, OSCE and Council of Europe', 24 *Journal of Baltic Studies* (2003) 399-431; D. Galbreath, *Nation-Building and Minority Politics in Post-Socialist States: Interests, Influence and Identities in Estonia and Latvia* (Stuttgart, Ibidem Verlag 2005).

[13] *Summary of Conclusions, Decision on Peaceful Settlement of Disputes*, Stockholm, Third Meeting of the Council (1992), available at: <http://www.osce.org/documents/mcs/1992/12/4156_en.pdf>.

also a source of information for other European organisations. A recent example of this information transfer was the OSCE Mission to Georgia's report to the EU concerning the events that led to and occurred during the Russian invasion of the breakaway region of South Ossetia.[14] As we shall see, the OSCE's presence in the field may be a stabilising force but in and of itself is rarely the single key institution for conflict prevention or peacebuilding.

Today, cooperation between the EU and OSCE covers soft security issues, such as border management, as well as democratisation and marketisation efforts, such as judicial reform and entrepreneurial development. The 'framework for cooperation' between the OSCE and EU consists of several contacts. For instance, the OSCE Troika meets with the heads of the European Commission, Council and Parliament. As discussed, the EU Presidency addresses the OSCE PC during weekly sessions. The European Commission also maintains a delegation in Vienna. Finally, the OSCE and EU often invite respective representatives for informal meetings and working groups on common objectives.

Competition between the EU and OSCE has come about as the former institution has developed an interest in activities ordinarily associated with the OSCE. An example is election observation.[15] In the Ukraine elections at the end of 2004, election observers were present from the OSCE, the EU and the Council of Europe, which begs the question why three regional organisations were required to do the same job. Perhaps the OSCE's position has been compromised since some of its key participating states, such as the Russian Federation, have heavily criticised the work of ODIHR and the Parliamentary Assembly in monitoring elections in the post-Soviet area. Moscow has charged the OSCE of being regionally biased against the East. The last few years have seen the OSCE monitor elections in Western OSCE participating states, such as the Canadian elections in 2006. Furthermore, the Russian Federation, distrusting ODIHR in the post-Soviet region, has taken to submitting election observers of their own, beginning in 2002, in order to balance the Western bias in ODIHR's conclusions.[16] While ordinarily states would be restricted as to how many observers they could send, Russia sent hundreds more than the quota to the Belarusian elections in 2006. Unfortunately for Moscow, the positive observations of the elections did not make it into the final ODIHR conclusions. Furthermore, perhaps the EU can employ a revolutionary foreign policy towards transitioning states more so than can the OSCE. Brussels is only restricted by its own Member States, the majority favouring a constructive engagement for change in states whose transition has stalled. The EU's European Neighbourhood Policy (ENP) seeks a stable and democratic border in both the East and South. In the end though, do two organisations doing the same job mean duplication, inefficiency and a waste of resources? From the OSCE perspective, increased collaboration in overlapping areas is vital for the continued relevance of the OSCE.

---

[14] 'The Russia-Georgia War: The Blame Game', *The Economist*, 1 October 2009.

[15] D. Galbreath, 'Putting the Colour into Revolutions? The OSCE and Civil Society in the Post-Soviet Region', 25 *Journal of Communist Studies and Transition Politics* (2009) 161-180.

[16] Interview at the OSCE Secretariat in Vienna, 17-19 May 2006.

## 3. Peacebuilding cooperation in context

Cooperation between the EU and OSCE is primarily a post-Cold War phenomenon. Such a relationship between the two organisations is a basis of converging agendas and thus functions. Of these, peacebuilding, democracy promotion and human rights protection are the most important. Secondly, cooperation between the EU and the OSCE is a product of the EU's enlargement eastward and geopolitical expansion in its 'neighbourhood'. In relation to the first instance, as we have seen already, the EU often relied on the OSCE as a source of information for the process leading to the 2004 and 2007 enlargements. In the second instance, the EU has become increasingly interested in the areas of the former Soviet Union which do not have a direct path to membership. Of these, Ukraine, Georgia and Moldova are most easily identified. At the same time, the international community's high representation, initially in Bosnia (OHR) and then in Kosovo (UNMIK), allowed a structure under which the EU and OSCE could each provide their different level of services to the two post-conflict societies in terms of peacebuilding, democracy promotion and human rights protection. The three policy areas are inherently connected in that democracy and human rights are in themselves paths to peacebuilding.

We progress with this 'common and comprehensive' approach to security laid out in the OSCE Helsinki Final Act, not to mention contemporary security studies. Furthermore, as is clearly evident in EU actions in the former Yugoslavia (Bosnia, Kosovo and FYR Macedonia), the EU itself places great importance on democracy and human rights promotion as being an essential part of a successful peacebuilding exercise. This comprehensive view of security is seen on the ground, in project planning and in the EU's European Security Strategy.[17] Peacebuilding, democracy promotion and human rights protection are considered by both organisations as interconnected strategies to break the cycle of conflict, and it is at these points that the EU and OSCE exhibit their clearest cooperation.

### 3.1 Conflict prevention and resolution

Conflict in Europe was evident in both the former Soviet Union and former Yugoslavia. In the first instance, ceasefire agreements in Moldova (over Transdniestria), Georgia (over South Ossetia and Abkhazia) and Azerbaijan (over Nagorno-Karabakh) were dictated from Moscow. In each of these cases, the Russian Federation made itself an active part of the conflict, whether as peacekeeper (in Azerbaijan) or colluder (in Moldova and Georgia).[18] In the latter cases, peace agreements in the earlier 1990s were commonly characterised as three-party talks between Russia, the state and the breakaway region. With Russia's overbearing role in the ceasefire agreements and a general unwillingness to see an end to potential conflict, it is little

[17] European Security Strategy, Brussels, 2003.

[18] See, for example, C. Neukirch, 'Russia and the OSCE: The Influence of Interested Third and Disinterested Fourth Parties on the Conflicts in Estonia and Moldova', 2 *Journal of Ethnopolitics and Minority Issues in Europe* (2001) 1-18.

wonder that these four cases were commonly referred to as 'frozen conflicts', or at least until Russia invaded South Ossetia and thus Georgia in August 2008. While the OSCE has had an active presence in these 'frozen conflicts' since the ceasefire agreements were first arranged in the early 1990s, the EU has traditionally shown little interest as an organisation.[19]

The most recent conflict in South Ossetia illustrates however how the EU has grown in terms of geopolitical presence (for what little it helped Georgia). At the same time, the conflict also illustrated the difficulty in the OSCE to bring about peace independently of other organisations. More recently, the EU has become increasingly interested, and in some cases involved, in the western former Soviet Union, as seen in the 2003 European Neighbourhood Policy and the 2009 Eastern Partnership.[20] With increasing unease over what the Kremlin sees as intrusion into its own 'neighbourhood', Moscow has made it clear that increased political conditionality in the former Soviet Union is of great concern.[21] Up until the ENP, the OSCE had been the primary international organisation in the former Soviet Union. The question remains over whether the Eastern Partnership programme can provide a basis for stronger links of countries like Ukraine, Georgia and Belarus with the EU. Furthermore, will greater EU involvement be to the detriment of the OSCE?

Peacebuilding in the former Yugoslavia perhaps gives us a clearer idea as to the degree of cooperation and collaboration between the EU and OSCE. Following NATO bombing in Bosnia (1995) and Kosovo (1999), both organisations have entered into the post-conflict societies as peacebuilders.[22] Each organisation has had its own role to play in the peacebuilding process. As seen elsewhere in this volume, the EU has contributed a great deal of resources to the political and economic transition in the two countries. Furthermore, the EU has played an important advisory role through European integration and eventual EU accession for Bosnia and Kosovo. Finally, the EU largely replaced the United Nations as the primary governing organisation of Bosnia and Herzegovina (2004) and Kosovo (2008). The EU has established peacebuilding missions in both countries, focusing on governing and the rule of law. Within this EU-dominated framework, the OSCE has played a specific role in peacebuilding.

The OSCE has missions in both Bosnia and Kosovo with representations in nearly every major urban municipality. With the UN and then EU dominating events at the national level, the OSCE has played a greater role at the local level.[23] In Bosnia, the OSCE was named as one of the main organisations in the Dayton Peace

---

[19] See F. Sabahi and D. Warner, eds., *The OSCE and the Multiple Challenges of Transition* (Aldershot, Ashgate 2004).

[20] Prague Eastern Partnership Summit (2009), available at: <http://www.consilium.europa.eu/uedocs/cms_data/docs/pressdata/en/er/107589.pdf>.

[21] *Kommersant*, 22 May 2009.

[22] A. Heinemann-Grader and I. Grebenschikov, 'Security Governance by Internationals: The Case of Kosovo', 13 *International Peacekeeping* (2006) 43-59.

[23] See M. Huber, et al., *The Effectiveness of OSCE Missions: The Cases of Uzbekistan, Ukraine and Bosnia and Herzegovina* (The Hague, Netherlands Institute of International Relations 'Clingendael' 2003).

Accords.[24] The OSCE Mission to Bosnia and Herzegovina, created in 1998, has four mission aims, one of which is security cooperation.[25] The OSCE's main objective in this area is to assist Bosnia in completing its commitments to the organisation's 'Code of Conduct on Politico-Military Aspects of Security'.[26] The Code states that '[w]ith a view to enhancing security and stability in the OSCE area, the participating States reaffirm their commitment to pursue arms control, disarmament and confidence- and security-building measures.'[27] The Department of Security Cooperation (established within the OSCE mission) has three sections: Arms Control, Institutions Building and Parliamentary Section. The primary aim of the Department, as set in the 'Code of Conduct', is democratic control over the country's armed forces and destruction of arms in excess of its needs. In both areas, the OSCE has been in close cooperation with the EU's military force in Bosnia, EUFOR. The OSCE's primary focus in Bosnia in this regard has been the excess small and light weapons, including man-portable surface to air missiles (known as 'man-pads'), which are remnants of the conflict which ended in 1995.

There is little evidence to suggest that the hand-over from NATO (SFOR) to the EU (EUFOR) in 2005 caused many problems for the OSCE Mission to BiH. At a press conference in 2004, the Head of Mission, Ambassador Douglas Davidson, responded to a question about the OSCE's response to this hand-over, saying:

> '[t]he OSCE is still in this picture. According to [the] Dayton Peace Accord, we have, what is generally known as regional military stabilisation. Some tasks, pertaining the weapons control, are finalised. In the last two years, [the] Mission has been focused on providing the support for the defence reform. That will shift towards the new NATO Headquarters. We closely co-operated with SFOR regarding the military stabilisation and I believe that co-operation will continue with EUFOR as well.'[28]

In fact, the cooperation between the OSCE and SFOR continued between the OSCE and EUFOR. Clear examples can be seen in the area of 'disarmament, demobilisation and reintegration' (DDR). For instance, in 2006, the OSCE cooperated with EUFOR to identify the best storage sites for medium to light weapons and ammunition as well as to close down those deemed the worst.[29]

Overall, there is a clear indication that the OSCE Mission to Bosnia is devoted to ensuring two things. Firstly, the OSCE aims at ensuring that ethnic conflict does not reoccur. The organisation has done this through arms control and institution

---

[24] The General Framework Agreement for Peace in Bosnia and Herzegovina (1995) is available at: <http://www.ohr.int/dpa/default.asp?content_id=380>.

[25] Huber, et al., *supra* n. 23.

[26] Code of Conduct on Politico-Military Aspects of Security. Budapest: Conference on Security and Cooperation in Europe (1994).

[27] Sub-section 16, ibid.

[28] 'We want to create efficient local administration in Bosnia and Herzegovina', Head of the OSCE Mission to BiH, 3 December 2004, see: <http://www.oscebih.org/public/print_news.asp?id=890)>.

[29] Statement of the Head of Mission to the Permanent Council, 1 December 2006, available at: <http://www.oscebih.org/public/print_news.asp?id=1960)>.

building in the military and government. But the OSCE has also used education as a method of peacebuilding. Nelles illustrates how the OSCE has used education as a way to improve relations between Bosniaks, Croats and Serbs in Bosnia.[30] Most importantly, the OSCE Mission to Bosnia shows how the OSCE has become a leading organisation in using education as a method of conflict prevention. Secondly, the OSCE mission has an explicit aim to help Bosnia become a member of the EU and NATO. Such an aim can be seen as the result of internal policies within the Bosnia government, but is nevertheless amazing considering that the OSCE includes 56 participating states, many of which are not in either the EU or NATO. Bosnia illustrates how the EU and OSCE have worked together in terms of peacebuilding, although each in their own way. Where the EU has an established military and police force in Bosnia, the OSCE has focused on arms control, institution building and socialisation through education. This focus makes sense since, as Hopmann explains, 'it is clear that [the] OSCE's comparative advantage lies in the diplomatic, political, and humanitarian dimensions of security rather than in the military domain.'[31] As we shall see, the OSCE's presence in Kosovo is similar, but we focus on democracy promotion as a way to see further convergence between the EU and OSCE.

### 3.2 Democracy promotion

While the EU has always acted as a club of democracies, the OSCE has never been such. Granted, the fifth enlargement process forced the EU to look closer at what was desirable or, in other words, to ask the question, 'How democratic should the new Member States be?'. While the OSCE is not an organisation composed solely of democracies and the Helsinki Final Act did not include any reference to 'democracy', the OSCE has still worked considerably towards insuring that the principles of democracy are established and maintained in the region. Within the OSCE, there are several institutions that deal with democracy promotion or at least individual democratic principles. ODIHR is the clearest example of an institution working towards democratic promotion in the OSCE region. In fact, ODIHR has become a leading actor in ensuring free and fair elections, as evidenced in the Georgian, Ukrainian and Kyrgyz 'coloured revolutions'.[32] Likewise, the Representative on Freedom of the Media aims to insure the role of the media as an important part of democratic societies and governance. Nevertheless, the role of the OSCE and its institutions is focused on conflict prevention. The degree to which the OSCE has moved away from its original role of ensuring 'common and comprehensive security' is an issue much derided by the Russian government, which claims that the

[30] W. Nelles, 'Bosnian Education for Security and Peacebuilding?', 13 *International Peacekeeping* (2006) 229-241.

[31] P. Hopmann, 'Managing Conflict in Post-Cold War Eurasia: The Role of the OSCE in Europe's Security Architecture', 40 *International Politics* (2003) 75-100, at 77.

[32] Galbreath, *supra* n. 15.

OSCE has moved away from its original purposes.[33] Where the OSCE is working with other international organisations that promote liberal democracy, it is only natural for OSCE institutions which focus on democratic promotion to flourish. This is the case where the OSCE works with the EU.

As discussed earlier in relation to Bosnia, the OSCE has played an important role in the former Yugoslavia. The case of Kosovo illustrates how the EU and the OSCE operate together in the field. Like Bosnia, Kosovo illustrates the different levels at which the EU and the OSCE work. The OSCE had a presence in Kosovo from 1992-1993 (OSCE Missions of Long Duration in Kosovo, Sandjak and Vojvodina) as well as 1998-1999 (OSCE Kosovo Verification Mission).[34] The current OSCE Mission to Kosovo was established following the NATO bombing raids and the subsequent establishment of the UN Administration for Kosovo (UNMIK) in July 1999. Under UNMIK Pillar III, the OSCE is tasked specifically with institution and democracy building as well as human rights protection.

While originally the OSCE took the lead in these matters, events have moved on in Kosovo since 1999 and with them the EU has taken on a greater role in institution and democracy promotion. Originally, the EU's role in Kosovo was designated under UNMIK as Pillars II and IV (civic administration and economic reconstruction, respectively).[35] What focus there was on democracy promotion was represented under these headings. The EU's approach to democracy promotion previous to Kosovo had largely been through the tool of conditionality, deployed for acceding states. As Dimitrova and Pridham argue, there is a problem in that the EU cannot offer Kosovo the same deal of 'sooner rather than later' membership for the pain of conditionality simply because the problem is not only democracy building but, more importantly, state capacity building.[36] The EU's focus on Kosovo is driven by its (pre-)accession programme. In other words, there is no specific democracy promotion institution of the EU, but rather the support it receives from the EU through the EU Special Representative, EULEX (EU Rule of Law Mission in Kosovo) and the European Commission is devoted to meeting the selection criteria set out in Copenhagen in 1993 and in Madrid in 1995. Within these criteria, there is an underlying theme of democracy promotion, as there is support for state capacity and market transition, but the EU lacks an 'in-the-field' institution to support democratic institutions.

Prior to the establishment of EULEX in 2008, the EU was directed towards economic redevelopment. As an ESDP (European Security and Defence Policy) mission, EULEX goes beyond economic restructuring towards the OSCE's mandate of 'institution building', though with a larger remit to support the police ser-

---

33 On the crisis, see P. Dunay, *The OSCE in Crisis*, Chaillot Paper 88 (Paris, Institute for Security Studies 2006).

34 A. Bellamy and S. Griffin, 'OSCE Peacekeeping: Lessons from the Kosovo Verification Mission', 11 *European Security* (2002) 1-26.

35 UNSC Res. 1244 (1999).

36 A. Dimitrova and G. Pridham, 'International Actors and Democracy Promotion in Central and Eastern Europe: The Integration Model and Its Limits', 11 *Democratisation* (2004) 91-112, at 98.

vice, justice system and customs agency. This remit was originally the responsibility of the UN, while the EU took over the role of Pillar 1, 'police and justice' in 2008. The EULEX 'Programme Strategy'[37] sets out the mission's mandate to support the institutions of the rule of law in Kosovo through 'monitoring, mentoring, and advising'. For instance, EULEX supports the rule of law through the EULEX Programme of Judges who 'monitor, mentor and advise the Kosovo judges, in the respect of the principle of independence of the judiciary and according to the modalities as established by the present law and by the EULEX Kosovo.'[38]

Nevertheless, previous to the establishment of EULEX, the OSCE was working closely with the justice system. For instance, the OSCE has been monitoring the civil and criminal justice systems since 1999 with the OSCE Mission to Kosovo's Legal System Monitoring Section (LSMS).[39] The differences between the two organisational missions in Kosovo come down to technical rather than substantive matters. For example, in April 2009, the OSCE mission in Kosovo stated that the fundamental difference between the two missions was

> 'that EULEX works closely with the police, the judiciary and the customs, and has deployed almost 1,400 of its own officers to work together with the Kosovo police. The OSCE, meanwhile, continues to monitor the functioning of the courts, report on possible shortcomings and suggest improvements, as well as checking that the Kosovo police comply with human rights standards.'[40]

In terms of democracy promotion, the EU and OSCE have converging aims and functions, but continue to work as parallel institutions, as can be seen in the Kosovo case. This relationship is partly the result of how the UN allocated roles in 1999, tasking the EU with administration and economic recovery and the OSCE with institution and democracy building. However, the more that the EU allows Kosovo down the path of accession, the more it has to become involved in the OSCE remit. Overall, Kosovo illustrates a case of organisational convergence without substantial cooperative engagement, as prescribed by the UNMIK Pillar structure.

### 3.3 Human rights protection

Unlike democracy or democratisation, fundamental human rights were a part of the Helsinki Final Act and the early CSCE. The Helsinki Final Act speaks of the 'human dimension' of 'common and comprehensive' security. These rights were akin to what we today attribute to organisations like the International Red Cross, such as

---

37 See: <http://www.eulex-kosovo.eu/strategy/EULEX%20Programmatic%20Approach.pdf>.

38 *Guidelines on Monitoring, Mentoring and Advising (MMA) of EULEX Judges* (2008), available at: <http://www.eulex-kosovo.eu/justice/docs/MA-guidelines-for-EULEX-Judges%20_2_.pdf>.

39 See the OSCE Department of Human Rights and Rule of Law document *Kosovo: First Review of the Civil Justice System* (2006), available at: <http://www.eulex-kosovo.eu/training/material/docs/KR/KR_Material/osce19407_en.pdf>.

40 'OSCE Mission in Kosovo Steers Steady Course in Changing Environment', OSCE Mission in Kosovo, 7 April 2009, see: <http://www.osce.org/item/37167.html>.

communication between distant family members and basic provisions for livelihood. A broader conception of human rights in the OSCE, as seen in the Council of Europe's European Convention on Human Rights, was introduced at the series of meetings on the human dimension in the late 1980s.[41] Human rights became institutionalised in the CSCE when the Office for Free Elections became ODIHR in 1992. Also, the HCNM was created focusing specifically on minority rights, or at least minorities with a geopolitical dimension. Subsequent OSCE field missions have also often had mandates around improving the conditions of human rights in a country. Most importantly, which brings us back to the subject of peacebuilding, is that human rights in the OSCE are viewed through the lens of regional stability, or more specifically conflict prevention.

Cooperation between the EU and OSCE on human rights has primarily been limited to minority rights. After all, the Council of Europe is the primary defender of human rights in Europe. As the next section will illustrate, both the EU and OSCE cooperate extensively with the Council of Europe in the area of human and minority rights. In the EU, the recently established Fundamental Rights Agency has further developed the organisation's ability to set standards on human rights. At the same time, where the OSCE has the HCNM and the Council of Europe has the Advisory Committee for the Framework Convention for the Protection of National Minorities, the EU lacks an institution entrusted with examining the status of minorities in the EU area. An extensive examination of sections within the European Commission illustrates how minority rights slip between remits, for example, between DG Enlargement and DG Freedom, Security and Justice.[42] Such a gap in the EU's policy range is where the OSCE becomes an important actor for the EU.

National minorities are important for all organisations concerned. After all, it is the reason why these same organisations are in the former Yugoslavia and why Russia's neighbours with large Russian minorities eyed the South Ossetian conflict nervously. During the accession process, the OSCE HCNM investigated areas where conflict could erupt between majorities and minorities who were sponsored by their external national homelands. The HCNM made investigations across Central and Eastern Europe, including Slovakia and Romania with their Hungarian minorities and Estonia, Latvia, Ukraine and Kazakhstan with their Russian minorities.[43] Under the first High Commissioner, Max van der Stoel, the HCNM used a combination of 'quiet diplomacy' and 'naming and shaming' as a means of influencing contested actors or groups.[44] However, later High Commissioners have opted for the 'quiet diplomacy' technique as a way of influencing state behaviour. This change in behaviour by the HCNM is less surprising if seen in the context of different areas

---

[41] A. Warkotsch, 'The OSCE As an Agent of Socialisation? International Norm Dynamics and Political Change in Central Asia', 59 *Europe-Asia Studies* (2007) 829-846.

[42] Based on interviews at the European Commission in Brussels, held from 28 January to 23 February 2009.

[43] Notably, the HCNM has not openly investigated the status of the Turkish minority in Bulgaria.

[44] See W. Kemp and S. Wolff, 'Quiet Diplomacy in Action: The OSCE High Commissioner on National Minorities', 31 *Nationalities Papers* (2003) 358-359.

of interest. When the states of Central and Eastern Europe were keen to enter the EU, they were more susceptible to 'naming and shaming' techniques. However, as the attention of the HCNM has moved further eastward, open critiques are more likely to entrench state behaviour rather than change it.[45]

Returning to the four niches of the OSCE as laid out in section 2, cooperation between the EU and OSCE in the field of human rights protection can be found in the epistemic contribution of the expert agencies in the OSCE.[46] Again, these institutions are ODIHR and the HCNM, which have an ongoing cooperative relationship with the EU's related institutions, such as DG Enlargement, DG Employment, DG External Relations and the recently established EU Fundamental Rights Agency. As indicated earlier, while there is substantial cooperation between experts at the European level, it is difficult to talk about cooperation between the EU and OSCE in the area of human rights protection without taking into consideration the role of the Council of Europe. In particular, the above highlighted institutions of the EU and OSCE also work with the Council of Europe's Office of the Commissioner for Human Rights, the Advisory Committee for the Framework Convention for the Protection of National Minorities, the European Commission for Democracy through Law (better known as the Venice Commission), the European Commission against Racism and Intolerance (ECRI) and the Committee of Experts Relating to the Protection of National Minorities. Together, this cooperation constitutes what Moravcsik has described as a 'human rights regime'.[47]

## 4. Conflict or cooperation?

Now that we have had a contextualised view of the relationship between the EU and OSCE, let us look at how the organisations reflect upon this convergence and cooperation in the field of peacebuilding. Author interviews at the EU in Brussels and the OSCE in Vienna focused specifically on the relationship between the two organisations, while officials commented on a range of issues and how they viewed the role of the two organisations in the field of peacebuilding. Firstly, the defining feature is that the two organisations occupy different areas within European governance, as highlighted in an earlier section. For instance, the OSCE Secretary General, Ambassador Marc Perrin de Brichambaut, argued that the OSCE and EU might have different members, processes and practices but had the 'same or similar goals and objectives'.[48] Perhaps most importantly, the organisations share a common vision of 'comprehensive' security that ties peacebuilding together with a wide range of institutional and rights-based agendas.

---

[45] F. Schimmelfennig, S. Engert, and H. Knobel, *International Socialization in Europe: European Organizations, Political Conditionality and Democratic Change* (Basingstoke, Palgrave 2005).

[46] See also Galbreath, *supra* n. 4, at 121-122.

[47] A. Moravcsik, 'The Origins of Human Rights Regimes: Democratic Delegation in Postwar Europe', 52 *International Organization* (2000) 729-752.

[48] Interview on 6 November 2008 at the OSCE Secretariat in Vienna.

Second, the organisations represent different things to different actors. With the OSCE's role in peacebuilding built upon the 'troubles' of the former Yugoslavia and Soviet Union, many states see the organisation as representing a 'badge of dishonour'.[49] One official at the European Commission Delegation to International Organisations in Vienna compared the cases of Albania and Croatia. For Albania, beginning from a level of relative poverty and years of isolation, the OSCE was welcomed as a peacebuilder. On the other hand, Croatia saw the OSCE as presenting the country to the 'West' as problematic and thus less likely to be admitted to the EU in future rounds of enlargement. The official stated that 'there are very few countries, such as Bosnia and Herzegovina, and Georgia, who want [the OSCE] there'.[50] Yet, perhaps this says something about the use of the OSCE in contemporary European security. Namely, the OSCE can often be used as 'bad cop' to the EU's 'good cop', allowing for the OSCE to apply political pressure through the principle of reputation.

Thirdly, the increasing convergence of the OSCE and EU has a historical explanation in that as the nature of regional stability and the needs of peacebuilding changed, the OSCE and EU both developed in this area as organisations politically willing to enter, sometimes potential, conflict zones. At the same time, we can also see the relationship between the two organisations as strategic. Several interviews at the OSCE pointed towards this explanation. The OSCE has traditionally stressed how it goes about peacebuilding, through such procedures as CSBMs and 'quiet diplomacy', while the EU has used both political leverage and, more recently, military deployment as a means to build peace. Thus, a strategic level of coordination allows both organisations to have access to the full range of approaches to peacebuilding while at the same time preventing certain governments from forum shopping between organisations. Another OSCE official stated that a strategic relationship also resulted in efficiency and burden sharing.[51] Yet, as we saw in the case of Kosovo, the relationship between the OSCE and EU can also become an issue of overlap, raising the question of the position of the OSCE in future peacebuilding.

Can there be cooperation and convergence without overlap? The OSCE Secretary General suggested that while the OSCE and EU are doing the same work, they go about it with different 'logics'.[52] The logic of the OSCE since the time of its inception in 1975 has been focused on 'common and comprehensive' security in the Euro-Atlantic area. The EU's peacekeeping logic is more complex. Firstly, the ESDP as an initiative has a legacy from even before the end of the Cold War, though at the time not within the auspices of the European Communities themselves. As the political character of the EU began to develop, it was a logical extension of that character to develop instruments to ensure regional stability and thus peacebuilding. Secondly, the EU's engagement with Central and Eastern Europe has until recently

[49] Interview on 8 November 2008 at the European Commission Delegation to International Organisations in Vienna.

[50] Ibid.

[51] Interview on 4 November 2008 at the OSCE Secretariat Section for External Relations in Vienna.

[52] Interview on 6 November 2008 at the OSCE Secretariat in Vienna.

been focused on enlargement. Any future enlargement requires that the EU should have the ability to engage in peacebuilding operations in and outside the common market. Thus, from the organisations' perspectives, both the OSCE and EU may be engaged in peacebuilding, but for different reasons. Contrarily, the more the EU becomes enmeshed in state building in the Balkans and further afield, the less different the EU's logic will be from that of the OSCE.

At the same time, the OSCE provides some things that the EU cannot, and in some cases will not, offer. An EU official in Vienna stated that while there is overlap between the OSCE and the EU, this overlap recedes the further you move away from the EU area.[53] The official stated that 'while the OSCE has a smaller budget it plays a major role in countries in Central Asia, the South Caucasus and the Balkans so these countries can claim ownership of activities.' And thus, because the EU does not, and arguably cannot, engage with the entire OSCE area as a power broker, there may be overlap but not duplication.

The sensitivity to overlap is understood from the OSCE perspective. Overlap for the OSCE confirms what some see as the growing futility of the organisation, as discussed earlier. Likewise, the EU's willingness to acknowledge overlap illustrates the organisation's place in European governance. The EU's ability to shunt aside the OSCE over the Russia-Georgia conflict in August 2008 is a good example. Reflecting on the OSCE's relationship with the EU, the OSCE Secretary General created an image summing up the power relationship: 'The EU is the elephant in the room. But we can think of the EU as the elephant, the Council of Europe as the dog and the OSCE as the flea. And of course, the flea can bite the dog that bites the elephant.'

Finally, perhaps the OSCE has a role to play in enhancing the geopolitical power of the EU. Specifically, there is knowledge transfer between the organisations, such as the DDR programmes in Bosnia and the justice and judiciary monitoring in Kosovo. One official in the OSCE Secretariat[54] suggested that the OSCE was becoming increasingly important in terms of relaying EU dynamics further afield, such as in the Central Asia Strategy.[55] More controversially, the EU has arguably outsourced certain policies to the OSCE. For instance, one official at the Council of the EU stated that 'the whole question of minority rights was functionally outsourced to the OSCE and Max van der Stoel who was the authority from which the European Union asked whether this country was up to par on minorities or not.'[56] This reflection illustrates the power dynamics between the OSCE and EU, which is unsurprising but worth highlighting here. An increasing role for the EU does not necessarily mean an end to the OSCE in peacebuilding, but it may push the OSCE

[53] Interview on 8 November 2008 at the European Commission Delegation to International Organisations in Vienna.

[54] Interview on 4 November 2008 at the OSCE Secretariat Section for External Relations in Vienna.

[55] 'The EU and Central Asia: Strategy for a New Partnership', The Permanent Representatives Committee (2007), available at: <http://register.consilium.europa.eu/pdf/en/07/st10/st10113.en07.pdf>.

[56] Interview on 5 February 2009 at the Council of the European Union, Human Rights Unit, in Brussels.

ever onwards in searching for a new mandate. An official at the European Commission Delegation to Vienna put it in a more 'matter-of-fact' way:

> 'What we do and the nature of the cooperation will always be reinvented. The management positions at the OSCE are seconded, there will be fresh faces, there will be different staff members reinventing continuously the wheel. The Ministerial Council will give new tasks to the Secretariat, someone will point to new problems and say they could be done by the OSCE and so there will be a lot of trading, agreement on budgets, people will be watching out for issues such as refugee returns, there will be draft codes of conduct.'[57]

An understanding of cooperation between the OSCE and EU should be based on what we have identified in this chapter. The two organisations offer particular niche functions in the region. We begin to see convergence in areas of political transition, such as the former Yugoslavia and Soviet Union, as exhibited earlier. Secondly, where cooperation does exist, we should expect the EU and OSCE to have strategic reasons as to why they cooperate. At the same time, their cooperation is predated by a change in the political needs of the region. As these needs have changed, naturally so have the organisations. Finally, OSCE offers an epistemic input to the European security architecture. The official interviews have shown how this expert, in-the-field knowledge has helped to shape EU policies. These characteristics will continue to represent the relationship between the EU and OSCE.

## 5. Conclusion

This chapter has illustrated the growing convergence and cooperation between the EU and the OSCE in the area of peacebuilding. From the beginning of the Helsinki negotiations, the EU had an important impact on the initial foundations of 'common and comprehensive' security in Europe. Changes in the Cold War reshaped both organisations giving them a greater political character. As Central and Eastern Europe went through a massive triple (political, social and economic) transition, both the EU and OSCE developed new ways to engage in and stabilise this region. For the EU, many states strived to bear the brunt of accession for the sake of membership, while for the OSCE, the institutions and field missions were deployed to prevent and resolve conflict. The post-Cold War European security architecture naturally drew all regional organisations together, but the 'common and comprehensive' approach to security of the OSCE meant that it would have an important role to play with all other European organisations. As the EU became a greater political force in the former Yugoslavia, the rest of Central and Eastern Europe and the western part of the former Soviet Union in the ENP, naturally (and strategically) the EU and OSCE would begin to cooperate more. From our case studies, we can

[57] Interview on 8 November 2008 at the European Commission Delegation to International Organisations in Vienna.

see how this cooperation around peacebuilding is working on the ground in Bosnia and Kosovo. Finally, we saw how officials within the EU and OSCE see their own organisations in relationship to each other. At least at the organisational level, there is little to indicate the growing futility of the OSCE, although some participating states may have other views. The true test will be when Kazakhstan takes the Chairman-in-Office post in 2010. This will be the first time that a non-EU Member State or at least aspiring EU accession state will be taking over the CiO position since it was created in 1991.

# Part III
# *Peace and security*

# Chapter 8
# THE EUROPEAN UNION AND SECURITY SECTOR GOVERNANCE*

**David Spence****

## 1. Introduction: Discovering the concept of SSR

Just as Molière's Monsieur Jourdain was delighted to hear that he had been speaking 'prose' throughout his life, so the European Commission was in a sense content when the term security sector reform (SSR) became popular in the early 2000s. The Commission found it had been unwittingly promoting SSR for years through its long-standing efforts abroad to foster democracy, human rights and good governance, of which good security sector governance was a fundamental component. So, if 'SSR' was a relatively new way of defining aspects of the Commission's work in the governance field,[1] it was not a new area of engagement, but had long been an integral part, near to home, of EU enlargement and the EU's stabilisation policy in the Western Balkans and, further afield, development policies in regions across the world. It was already enshrined in the European Community's '*acquis*', but the link between security, development and governance was now formally recognised as crucial in several policy papers; not least the Commission's Communication on Governance and Development of 2003, which argued 'there is no development in chronically insecure environments (...) security systems reform is an

* As of 1 December 2009, the Lisbon Treaty was formally in legal existence. This means that the 'European Community' disappears, that the Commission Delegations abroad become Union Delegations and that previous interinstitutional conflicts should also disappear, as do the EU's '3 Pillars' introduced by the Maastricht Treaty. There is thus potential confusion in historical accounts of EC and EU policy making, for some of the terms used have no meaning in the post-Lisbon framework; e.g., EC often means the European Community and often the European Commission; likewise, ESDP for European Security and Defence Policy, as opposed to the new term CSDP, Common Security and Defence Policy. In this chapter, when it is relevant to do so, I use terms legally valid at the time of their usage. For a discussion of the issues, see P. Stancarelli, 'La Commission et le Traité de Lisbonne', *European Affairs Review* (2010, forthcoming) and G. Avery, 'Europe's Foreign Service: From Design to Delivery', EPC, Brussels, December 2009.

** First Counsellor, Delegation of the European Union to the United Nations in Geneva. The views expressed in this article are those of the author and do not reflect the position of the European Commission.

[1] Claire Short, UK Minister for Development in the late 1990s, is credited with its first use.

*S. Blockmans, J. Wouters & T. Ruys, eds., The European Union and Peacebuilding*

integral component of good governance.'[2] This explicit mention of the link between security and development presaged a later communication on SSR in 2006, which forms the basis of EU policy today.[3]

There were several contemporaneous realisations. First, recipient governments consider the Commission as a neutral rather than a self-interested partner, and this has facilitated the trust necessary for effective cooperation on the sensitive issues raised by SSR. Second, the Commission's global reach and its long-term presence on the ground in over 130 countries outside the EU through its network of Delegations has been a prime facilitator of efforts to build this trust in individual countries. Its insistence on local ownership of the development process and related projects is a feature of aid and technical assistance and is viewed by the Commission and other donors as key to successful development – and SSR support. Third, SSR had often been conceived as a post-conflict necessity, as a crisis-induced policy within a context of early recovery, and related mainly to a country's armed forces. Viewing it as an integral part of development meant it became part of a long-term process of peacebuilding and reconstruction, requiring cultural, legal, institutional and organisational change. Fourth, the European Community's external assistance instruments, most of which focus on long-term developmental processes, were actually well adapted to respond to SSR needs. They were less suitable for the previous, more exclusive (and today outmoded) focus on reform of military structures alone, which had been the more traditional usage of the term SSR by armies, ministries of defence and, indeed, NATO, but where the Commission had been left out of the picture by dint of its competence, restricted to civilian rather than military action.

This chapter reviews the evolution of the EU's conception of security sector reform, describing its policies with regard to SSR implementation in its partner states. The chapter discusses EC and EU funding of SSR operations worldwide and describes the background and content of the Commission's and Council Secretariat's perception of the issue area.[4] An important feature in the development of the EU's approach to SSR has in fact been the conflict of interpretations of the term between the Council Secretariat and the Commission's Directorates General, arising largely from competence issues whether SSR involved policy with regard to military and security services alone, or whether it should cover a larger agenda, including democratic governance issues. Related competence, inter-Pillar and interinstitutional disagreements in fact hindered the emergence of coherent policy making. The chapter also reflects on whether the Lisbon Treaty, in particular the establishment of a European External Action Service, is likely to end these inter-Pillar and interinstitu-

---

[2] Commission Communication on Governance and Development, COM(2003) 615 Final, 20 October 2003.

[3] It is important to note that developments in EU thinking were paralleled by developments in policy at the United Nations, in particular by UNDP and DPKO. For a review of the concepts used by the UN, see UNDP, *Strengthening the Rule of Law in Conflict- and Post-Conflict Situations: A Global UNDP Programme for Justice and Security, 2008-2011* (2008).

[4] A comprehensive account of the EU's perspective on SSR, including case studies, can be found in D. Spence and P. Fluri, *The EU and Security Sector Reform* (London, John Harper 2008).

tional disputes, thereby allowing an efficient, comprehensive and coherent approach to SSR to emerge in the post-Lisbon setting.[5]

## 2. Issues of security in international context

Why would the Western world wish to become involved in security sector reform outside its own borders? There was indeed an important international context to the emergence of the EU's 'holistic' approach to SSR. It is perfectly acceptable and indeed customary for Western militaries to cooperate with the military staff of developing countries, a fact underlined by long-standing training agreements for officers from developing countries in St Cyr or Sandhurst. But there were also political, strategic and developmental reasons to do so. Unlike NATO and EU Member States (with a few notable exceptions) non-European countries have very real military threats to contend with in their own region, both from within their own states and from each other. They, and other countries closer to the EU, such as Georgia, Moldova and Azerbaijan, are painfully aware, through their own experience, of the need for modern and efficient security forces, whether for territorial defence or simply as a guarantee of state security. Western ministries of defence are keen to support this, and NATO's conditions for membership have required it. Security perceptions and threat perceptions in aid-recipient countries may be different from Europe's. The absence of clear military threat in Western countries, both from outside and from within, is recognised by governments and publics alike, though there is also consensus that military threats from outside and revolutionary threat from within have ceded place to threats from new forms of radicalism of a nebulous, non-governmental, usually terrorist kind. The events of 9/11 and after have thus been a fillip to continued reflection on the complex nature of internal and external security, between international security strategy and the quest for good governance worldwide. Indeed, in early 2010, the EU began reflections on an internal security strategy for the EU, which is intended to result in a formal strategy to be adopted in 2010. This will doubtless prove a key contextual document in terms of the EU's ongoing SSR policies, for it recognises the interdependence of internal and external security by building a global security focus. SSR is a logical concomitant.

Separate from the interests of Western ministries of defence, development ministries and international organisations have advocated assisting developing states to achieve democratic control of their security sectors. The case for military efficiency and cost-effectiveness heard in ministries of defence[6] has been drawn *volens no-*

---

[5] Turf battles characterised the relations between the Commission and the Council Secretariat after Amsterdam. The Lisbon Treaty was designed to end inter-Pillar rivalry, both by ending the 'three-Pillar' EU and melding Commission and Council Secretariat staffs into a European External Action Service. See D. Spence, 'Days of Dogs and Roses: The European Commission between External Relations and Foreign Policy', 15 *European Foreign Affairs Review* (2010, forthcoming).

[6] Awareness of the need for 'security issues' to be integrated into development policies was reinforced by the World Bank-commissioned study *Voices of the Poor*, which demonstrated that the main

*lens* into reflections on the place of SSR in the relationship between successful economic development, successful transition from state fragility to liberal democracy and overall security – both for the developing countries concerned and, by extension, for the interests of the donor countries themselves. Arguably, encouraging security sector reform is as much in the strategic interest of the donor countries as it is in that of the recipient countries. Thus, while a main Western aim has clearly been to win international friends and influence the military systems of developing nations along Western lines for traditional reasons of national prestige, cooperation with former colonies, and, not least, securing of defence-industry related markets, for the EU and its Member States a normative position has also been involved. Political and economic stability and regional security are obvious key interests, but simultaneously efforts have been made to ensure that security arrangements in fragile states are based on sound governance. Security enhancement has often been a shorthand term for maintenance in power of often disputable governments, corrupt leaders and fragile elites. Importantly, therefore, 'good governance' has become an integral part of formal military assistance and security sector reform in general. It provides an acceptable face to military cooperation between Western states and the developing world.

Modernisation and increased efficiency at home have thus been coupled with awareness by defence and development ministries and NGOs of the strategic importance of SSR in post-conflict or fragile states abroad. NATO states have needed to reform their own military structures to take into account fundamental military and security developments and to create efficient defence structures based on cooperation, policy on human resources and technical interoperability. NATO's partnership agreements have made reform of military structures a condition of membership of countries formerly part of the Soviet Union or the Warsaw Pact, and the EU's emphasis on democratic governance as a *sine qua non* of EU membership has unwittingly, but helpfully, flanked this exercise by including the aspiration of democratic control of armed forces.

Threats and attacks, if and when they do arise, are likely on the one hand to require an international response and on the other, increasingly, to come under democratic scrutiny from parliaments and specialised non-governmental organisations. The desire to provide guidance and support to other countries therefore arises from a threefold commitment: for their own good in terms of enhanced security and security sector governance, because creating sound security in fragile and turbulent environments is in the EU's self-interest, and because SSR epitomises a general commitment to good governance.

Self-interest is nonetheless evident. The European Security Strategy has the aim of 'promoting a ring of well governed countries' with which the EU can 'enjoy close and cooperative relations.'[7] Self-interest in preventing instability in the Euro-

---

priority for people living in impoverished areas was security and that crime and violence were prime concerns of the poor, as was abuse by government forces, such as the police. See D. Narayan, et al., *Voices of the Poor* (2000), available at: <http://www.worldbank.org/poverty/voices/reports.htm>.

[7] *European Security Strategy*, 12 December 2003, available on the Council's website at: <http://ue.eu.int/uedocs/cmsUpload/78367.pdf>, at 10.

pean neighbourhood goes without saying. There are obvious dangers not from traditional military attack, but from the spread of organised crime and terrorism and too much of the 'wrong kind' of immigration to European countries. The EU also has an economic interest in general stability worldwide, but the conscious motives of the actors involved within the EU have probably more to do with the export of the EU's norms than with making the world safe for EU exports.

## 3. Two concepts of SSR: Armed services-specific and holistic-societal

### 3.1 Reforming the armed services

Whether the main objective is sound security sector governance as part of overall good governance or self-interested long-term security, OECD states engage in an agreed approach to advocacy, project financing and extensive intergovernmental cooperation on security sector governance; and they are no longer restricted to policy making merely for the West's own security and defence on the assumption of a military attack. Designing, training and equipping military forces to take part in multilateral military interventions abroad are also now crucial. Western governments engage in this, either alone in the case of France and the UK, or in cooperation within the UN or the EU, where links between the military, the police and civilian actors as potential partners in crisis-relief scenarios, and mediation, peacekeeping, peacebuilding and assistance in natural disasters become part of what the UN terms 'integrated missions'.[8]

But as to the recipient states themselves, many have frozen conflicts and serious internal insurgencies affecting their territory daily. Others are recovering from conflict, for instance, in regions such as Africa, where Europe supports SSR in several countries as part of an overall attempt at peacebuilding. Their defence priorities alter as they enter the process of change from fragile to strong statehood. Strong territorial defence policies go hand in hand with cost effectiveness and the maintenance of internal order, and newly democratised states naturally seek sound models for the organisation of their security forces. Western states are perhaps alone in having the luxury of assessing how their own security structures can be a model for others. They are able to concert their efforts in the attempt to analyse comprehensively the role of the military in Western liberal democracy and to combine this with assistance to other states not yet far along the path to practical realisation of the crucial links between democratic governance, state security, human security and implementation of relevant reforms. As to the issue of whose interest is promoted by SSR, third world governments may be forgiven for assuming that it is in the strategic interest of their individual Western partners to provide such assistance. Yet when the UN or the EU offers help, at least *national* interests seem absent. The

[8] See the contribution by Gourlay to this volume.

norms of the EU, like those of the UN, are perceived as standing above sordid national interests.

### 3.2 A holistic-societal approach to SSR

SSR has largely been promoted by overall changes in thinking on development itself, adding development aims to specific security concerns. Over the last decades, the focus of European development cooperation, whether that of individual EU Member States or the European Commission, has shifted from purely economic growth and poverty reduction to include aspects of human rights and good governance, including security sector governance. Policy makers have come to realise that successful development requires effective security and that a traditional approach to reform of the security sector, in short the military and police sectors, may not be sufficient to fulfil Western governments' overall objectives of sound governance and development within an overall sound security framework. These objectives, it is now believed, are only achievable with 'whole of government' or 'holistic' approaches to SSR. Thus, the restriction in use of the SSR concept to reform of military and police structures has become outmoded; necessary, of course, but not sufficient.

Of course, military and police institutions in donor countries continue to focus on what they are good at and thus to maintain relations with their equivalent institutions abroad. But there is general recognition that reforming the security sector should not focus solely on these security institutions but include reform of social and political mechanisms designed to provide democratic control. In short, the traditional view of SSR, primarily focused on reform of defence forces and civilian institutions with a right to use force (i.e., the police), has ceded place to a holistic concept of SSR, reaching beyond security institutions to the legal and political institutions of the state. This is an important change from a concept with exclusively military and police relevance to a comprehensive and system-wide approach to security sector reform, based on a broad liberal-democratic governance perspective. The objective is now not only security sector *reform*, i.e., changes to arrangements within the existing security sector, but the achievement of further-reaching sound security sector *governance*.

EC support to SSR-related programmes and projects over the previous 5 years were compiled and summarised in 2006 in a Commission 'Staff Working Document', which formed one of the annexes to the Commission's SSR Communication.[9] The EC has been engaged in over 70 countries around the world in support of SSR.[10] The 2006 Communication on SSR defined the security system as

---

[9] Commission Staff Working Document, Brussels, 24.5.2006, SEC(2006) 658, and Annexes to the Communication from the Commission to the Council and the European Parliament, 'A Concept for European Community Support for Security Sector Reform', COM(2006) 253 final.

[10] See Annex for a list of current projects.

'(…) all state institutions and other entities with a role in ensuring the security of the state *and* its people (…) *Justice institutions*: justice ministries; prisons; criminal investigation and prosecution services; the judiciary (courts and tribunals), implementation justice services (bailiffs and ushers), other customary and traditional justice systems; human rights commissions and ombudsmen; etc. (…).' [emphasis added]

This large spectrum of activities was in a sense redefined as SSR once the Commission became apprised of the need for a holistic SSR concept as work with partners within the OECD-DAC proceeded. In the area of justice reform alone, it included legal reforms and capacity building of interior or justice ministries, judicial and prosecution institutions, prison services, judicial and law faculties, legal aid, human rights commissions and ombudsman functions. Reforms of law enforcement institutions included police, border management and customs services as well as support to relevant executive branches of government and democratic oversight mechanisms, including parliaments and civil society capacity building. Border management, training of border guards and reform of customs institutions were also included, as was police reform (for example, in the Western Balkans, Central America, Afghanistan, South Africa and the DRC).

This European Commission support for reform of armed forces was limited to human rights and humanitarian law training and support to army integration centres and army families, not only because defence reform strictly falls outside formal eligibility for development cooperation assistance, but also because EU Member States consider military aspects to be Second Pillar rather than Community competence. Yet, while there might have been a Second Pillar will, there was no financial way for CFSP and ESDP to envisage major involvement until recently. Now, however, more flexible and rapid support under the Instrument for Stability has allowed the Commission to kick-start Community support even for action under the European Security and Defence Policy (ESDP). This was the case of rule of law and institutional reform of the judiciary in Georgia and police reform and army integration in the DRC, and Second Pillar ESDP action in crisis management missions, such as the EU border management mission for Moldova-Ukraine. The latter was a First Pillar mission funded first under the now defunct Rapid Reaction Mechanism introduced by Commissioner Patten, later under the TACIS programme and now under the European Neighbourhood Policy Instrument. By contrast, the EU border management mission in Rafah is an ESDP mission.[11] How management of the Instrument for Stability develops after implementation of the Lisbon Treaty will be crucial, as previously delineated areas are grouped together under the management of the new European External Action Service.

[11] See F. Hoffmeister, 'Inter-Pillar Coherence in the EU's Civilian Crisis Management', in S. Blockmans, ed., *The European Union and Crisis Management: Policy and Legal Aspects* (The Hague, T.M.C. Asser Press 2008) 157-180, at 166

## 4. The origins and precepts of the EU's holistic approach to security sector reform

While SSR was traditionally envisaged in relation to reform and restructuring of armed forces, particularly in the framework of NATO's conditions for its own enlargement, the EU, the European Commission, the OECD[12] and the OSCE[13] have gradually become wedded to the more holistic approach to the concept, covering the whole security *system* of a given state. This is precisely where the EU's 'First Pillar', i.e., European Community policies, was the most relevant within the gamut of EU policies. The mix of development and security concerns has meant that European foreign, defence, development and security policies are now all seen as vital components of advice and assistance abroad. Adopting the holistic view of SSR, particularly in Africa and Asia, has been crucial to admitting SSR to the cluster of policies agreed by the OECD as capable of formal categorisation as development assistance – in brief 'OECD Dac-able'.

Borrowing from the OECD-DAC, the EU notion of SSR includes all state institutions formally committed to the security of the state and its people, not only those with purely military or police implications:

> 'The "security system" is defined by the OECD as encompassing: a) the state institutions, which have a formal mandate to ensure the safety of the state and its citizens against acts of violence and coercion (e.g. the armed forces, the police, paramilitary forces, the intelligence services and similar bodies); and b) the elected and/or duly appointed civil authorities responsible for control and oversight of the institutions (the Parliament, the Executive, defence ministries, and judicial and penal systems), [where] reform [is] of fundamental importance to create safe security environments and to keep the security sector permanently subject to the same governance norms as other parts of the security sector and military forces under the political control of a civilian authority. These institutions are part of a broader security picture and dependent on the existence of effective justice and law enforcement institutions.'[14]

The Commission analyses and funds SSR within this framework, now also inspired by notions of peacebuilding and the quest for good governance, to be found, *inter*

[12] The OECD's Development Assistance Committee, known as the OECD-DAC, on which the Commission sits, agreed in 2003 that assistance to SSR could be considered development assistance. It was, in the jargon, 'Dac-able'. The OECD Development Assistance Committee's (DAC) work in the area of security sector reform was carried out primarily through its subsidiary body, the International Network on Conflict and Fragility (INCAF), in which the European Commission participates. The Commission uses the DAC Guidelines on Security System Reform and Governance, referred to in the EC Communication on Security Sector Reform. DAC work on security systems started with a 1997 review of DAC members' approaches to military issues, which linked diverse issues relevant to security. The DAC then developed a conceptual framework for security assistance: 'Security Issues and Development Co-operation: A Conceptual Framework for Enhancing Policy Coherence', which subsequently led to the Guidelines. See also OECD DAC, Development Co-operation Directorate, *DAC Statistical Reporting Directives: Addendum*, DCD/DAC(2000)10/ADD1/REV1.

[13] See the contribution by Galbreath to this volume.

[14] Commission Communication on Governance and Development, para. 24. See *supra* n. 2.

*alia*, in the rules of the European Development Fund and in the governance sections of the Lomé and Cotonou Agreements and other financial instruments discussed below. Its holistic conception of SSR relies on a political (even moral) commitment to democratic governance and legitimacy.[15] So, its use of the term 'security' in SSR is not restricted to a conception based on territorial security or the security of a particular regime. In expanding the concept to cover human security,[16] and thus covering freedom from want, freedom from fear and individuals' freedom, the EU clearly puts the security of citizens at the heart of its policy preoccupations, rather than restricting its policy framework and funding mechanisms to an approach focused exclusively on state security and military/police institutional parameters. The EU point of departure is the hypothesis that citizens rightfully expect the state to maintain peace and to guarantee the strategic security interests of the country, yet at the same time to provide a secure environment for human lives and property, on the one hand, and political, economic and social rights and development, on the other; in short, the state is expected to ensure overall security, sound security governance *and* development.

## 5. Human security

Parallel to the development of the European Union as a global security actor has been the evolution of the concept of security itself, namely from the concept of 'state security' to this broader notion of 'human security'. Human security, which 'takes the individual and his community as point of reference, rather than the state' and which maintains that state security is not an end in itself but rather 'a means of – and necessary precondition for – providing security for people', sits well with the aims of SSR.[17] SSR, which strives for the civilian, democratic *and* liberal governance of the security sector in its broadest sense, appears indispensable to ensuring human and civil rights, the fundaments of human security.[18] The emphasis on security sector governance thus includes the notion that internal security provided by paramilitary forces, police and intelligence services, which in many states are infamous for causing human *in*security and fear, is of particular relevance to the human

---

[15] See D. Spence, 'EU Governance and Global Governance: New Roles for EU Diplomats', in A. Cooper, B. Hocking and W. Maley, eds., *Worlds Apart? Exploring the Interface between Governance and Diplomacy* (New York, Palgrave 2008) and D. Spence, 'Deconstructing EU Governance: How the European Commission Constructed EU Governance Policy and How It Attempts to Export It', in J.-U. Wunderlich and D. Bailey, eds., *The EU and Global Governance: A Handbook* (London, Routledge 2010, forthcoming).

[16] See *A Human Security Doctrine for Europe*, also known as the Barcelona Report of the Study Group on European Security Capabilities, presented to Javier Solana on 15 September 2004, available at: <http://www.lse.ac.uk/depts/global/studygroup.htm>.

[17] S. Biscop, *The European Security Strategy: Implementing a Distinctive Approach to Security*, Sécurité & Stratégie, Paper No. 82 (March 2004), at 11.

[18] J. Chanaa, *Security Sector Reform: Issues, Challenges and Prospects*, Adelphi Paper 344 (London, IISS 2002), at 28.

security agenda. Germany's foremost development institution in the field, the *Deutsche Gesellschaft für Technische Zusammenarbeit* (GTZ), has argued that SSR 'embraces not only security from external threat, but also material, physical and social security as well as protection from bodily harm (...) *Above all* security sector reform means guaranteeing human security' [emphasis added].[19] In sum, just as the Cold War period was characterised by bilateral security and military assistance agreements, used mainly to promote state security, in turn to serve key strategic interests, SSR in the post-Cold War period promotes human security and serves humanitarian aims, while nonetheless leaving the strategic interests of global security and development as part of the security equation.

The concept of human security thus gained prominence after the Cold War. Clearly, capitalism seemed to have outlived communism, but its triumph had not ended human suffering. The 'first non-academic attempt to define human security was probably the United Nations Development Programme (UNDP) initiative in 1994 to design a Human Development Index', which served to inspire further UN work.[20] At the 2000 UN Millennium Summit, Secretary-General Kofi Annan called for a world 'free of fear' and 'free of want', and as a response, in January 2001, through an initiative of the Government of Japan, the Commission on Human Security was established.[21] It focused its attention on problems linked to conflict and poverty. Human security was conceptualised as the protection of people's vital freedoms from severe threats, in ways that empower people to fulfil their strengths and aspirations. In addition to this work carried out by the UN, Canada, Japan, the UK, Switzerland and the EU became active in advocating the concept of human security and have integrated variations of it into their foreign policies.

The aim of the *Human Security Doctrine for Europe*, a report drafted by a Study Group and presented to Javier Solana, was to 'examine the possibility of formulating an EU human security policy and draw up plans to implement the European Security Strategy (ESS).'[22] The report was a response to the mention in the European Security Strategy that the EU should be 'more capable' by specifically elaborating the capabilities the EU needs to make a credible contribution to global security, on which the security of Europe itself depends. It posited seven ethical principles for human security, each of which relativised a purely military conception of SSR: the primacy of human rights, clear political authority, multilateralism, a bottom-up approach, regional focus, use of legal instruments and the 'appropriate' use of force. It then posited the capabilities needed for the EU to increase human security worldwide, calling for the establishment of a 15,000 soldier-strong 'Human Security

---

[19] Deutsche Gesellschaft für Technische Zusammenarbeit, Division 43, *Security Sector Reform in Developing Countries* (Eschborn 2000), at 21.

[20] J. Kotsopoulos, *A Human Security Agenda for the EU?,* EPC Issue Paper No. 48 (June 2006), at 8.

[21] F. Fouinat, 'A Comprehensive Framework for Human Security', 4 *Conflict, Security & Development* (2004), at 289-290.

[22] *A Human Security Doctrine for Europe*, the Barcelona Report of the Study Group on Europe's Security Capabilities", 2004, *supra* n. 16.

Response Force', of which at least a third would be civilian, and for a new legal framework to govern both the decision to intervene and operations in the field.

The EC Communication on Security Sector Reform[23] outlined how the human security concept was useful not only in defining the relationship between citizens' needs and the state's responsibilities (including the state's ability to maintain peace and guarantee security of life, property, political, economic and social rights), but in understanding the interlinkage between external and internal security needs. It underlined the separation of tasks between the different institutions and bodies constituting a security system. The European Commission held that SSR encompasses the responsibilities of other law enforcement institutions than the military and police, such as border guards and customs authorities. Its approach to SSR therefore involves the security system, but also covers the wider justice system (the judiciary, prisons, prosecution services, human rights commissions and ombudsman functions) as well as security management and oversight bodies (the legislature, the executive, traditional authorities and civil society). Democratic oversight is deemed vital. The Commission thus defines its SSR concept to cover 'those aspects which are designed to contribute to peace, the protection of life and limb, and to ensure the upholding of the law and oversight through the justice system and democratic institutions of the relevant executive bodies.'[24]

The state, on the 'human security' hypothesis, has a duty to establish and continually reform its security institutions, with the aim of protecting citizens from the threats of social insecurity, violent conflict and terrorism, while simultaneously protecting rights and institutions from being undermined by these threats. Arising from this, the EU concept of SSR covers both reform of those state institutions which provide security to citizens, reform of traditional military structures to create greater efficiency, and reform of the institutions responsible for management and democratic oversight.[25] The EU conception of SSR thus came to incorporate the basic idea that SSR was more than reforming the effectiveness of individual services such as the military, the police and the legal system *per se;* it was also an attempt to focus on the overall functioning of the security system as part of democratic governance. Strengthening security for citizens and addressing governance deficits were thus brought into line with the EU's self-image as a liberal-democratic polity, as a donor and as a normative actor.

But there is also a pragmatic angle to this normative approach. Sustainable development is clearly unlikely to be achieved in countries that spend too much on the military or where the military and other security actors have excessive rights and

---

[23] European Commission, 'A Concept for European Community Support for Security Sector Reform', Brussels, 24 May 2006, COM(2006) 253F, available at: <http://eur-lex.europa.eu/LexUriServ/site/en/com/2006/com2006_0253en01.pdf>.

[24] Ibid., at 4-5.

[25] The work of DCAF (Geneva Centre for the Democratic Control of Armed Forces), the leading Swiss research and training organisation, has been instrumental in the growth of the Commission's conceptualisation. See: <http://www.dcaf.ch> and H. Hänggi and F. Tanner, *Promoting Security Sector Governance in the EU's Neighbourhood*, Chaillot Paper No. 80 (July 2005).

advantages. Thus, lasting external and internal security for a fragile state is more likely to be successful if external aid contains conditions designed to avoid such potentially perverse effects. It was this mix of development and security preoccupations, plus the notion of human security – a fusion of the visions of the 2003 European Security Strategy and the 2005 European Consensus on Development[26] – which thus formed the formal basis for the Commission's view that peace and security are concomitants of sustainable development, and vice versa. This conscious link between security and development, formally recognising the dangers since the end of the Cold War of state failure, fragile states and humanitarian emergencies, has become a prime policy concern for the EU.

The conflicts in Bosnia, Somalia, Iraq and Afghanistan underlined and justified such a refined EU approach to assistance. But there was one further constitutive element. The Cold War had seen an emphasis on crisis management tools and a fundamental evolution of the UN as the main peacekeeper. The emergence of regional actors, among which the European Union, prompted the idea that the relationship between regional organisations and the UN could be formally based on cooperation between them as security actors. A debate on strengthening the relationship between the UN and regional organisations in the maintenance of international peace and security was held in the UN Security Council (UNSC) in April 2008. It largely focused on Africa but also discussed the relationship between the UN and the AU, and other regional organisations. In 2009, the UN Institute for Disarmament Research then published a report on EU-UN relations in the field of conflict prevention and peacebuilding,[27] which made a series of recommendations for enhancement of EU-UN relations in the peace and security field. Some of these recommendations appeared in a UN Security Council report on these issues in January 2010.[28] One of the UNSC recommendations concerned the role that regional and sub-regional organisations might play in post-conflict peacebuilding, recovery, reconstruction and development, and the value of better interaction between these organisations and the Security Council and its subsidiary bodies. SSR is clearly an area of considerable relevance in this wider security sphere, a lesson which has not been lost on the UN's Peacebuilding Commission.[29]

## 6. The evolution of the EU policy framework for SSR

In July 2006, the Council of the EU provided an overall EU Policy Framework for Security Sector Reform. This brought together the (Council Secretariat-authored)

---

[26] Commission Communication on 'Policy Coherence for Development – Accelerating Progress towards Attaining the Millennium Development Goals', COM(2005) 134 final, 12 April 2005.

[27] C. Gourlay, *EU-UN Cooperation in Peacebuilding: Partners in Practice*? (UNIDIR 2009).

[28] *UN Cooperation with Regional and Subregional Organisations in the Maintenance of International Peace and Security*, to be made available at: <http://www.securitycouncilreport.org/site/c.glKWLeMTIsG/b.2400825/k.8D8/Publications_on_Cooperation_w_Regional_Organisations.htm>.

[29] Recommendations were made in each country reported on in the Report of the Peacebuilding Commission, 8 September 2009 General Assembly Sixty-Fourth Session, UN Doc. A/64/341-S/2009/444-0950441.

Concept for ESDP Support to Security Sector Reform (October 2005) and the (European Commission) Concept for European Community Support for Security Sector Reform (June 2005).[30] The three 'Pillars'[31] of the EU thereby became involved in a holistic, multi-sector and long-term process. Importantly, EU action on SSR, whichever the concerned Pillar, was based on principles drawn from the OECD-DAC definition of SSR:[32]

a) nationally/regionally owned participatory reform processes designed to strengthen good governance, democratic norms, the rule of law and the respect and promotion of human rights;
b) focusing on the core requirements of a well-functioning security system;
c) addressing diverse security challenges facing states and their populations;
d) based on a gender-sensitive, multi-sector approach to the provision of security and access to justice; and
e) targeting reform needs in different key sectors.

Lessons learned first in the DRC had led to the development of this joint Commission-Council SSR concept and to consequent steps taken to implement the related policy commitments. Joint EU assessment missions in SSR conducted after June 2006 included staff from the Commission, the Council Secretariat and Member States. Discussions between the Commission and Member States on common profiles and training standards for staff deployed to the field have professionalised the approach, and training courses for Commission headquarters and field staff have strengthened support functions in thematic departments responsible for SSR within the Commission and the Council.

In his contribution to this volume, Blockmans reviews EU support provided to candidate and potential candidate countries, but its impact in terms of peacebuilding is perhaps more obvious in transitional and developing countries, both through EC external assistance instruments and CFSP/ESDP activities.[33] More than 70 countries have received some form of EC SSR support since 2004,[34] and there have been SSR-related ESDP operations in more than a dozen countries.[35] In several

[30] Council Conclusions on a Policy Framework for Security Sector Reform (2736th General Affairs Council meeting, Luxembourg, 12 June 2006).

[31] The European Communities (EC), the European Common Foreign and Security Policy (CFSP) –including the European Security and Defence Policy (ESDP) – and Police and Judicial Cooperation in Criminal Matters (PJCCM).

[32] 'Is it ODA?', OECD DAC Factsheet, October 2006, available at: <http://www.oecd.org/dataoecd/21/21/34086975.pdf>; see also Canada's Coalition to End Global Poverty (CCIC), 'Should the Criteria Be Expanded? Frequently Asked Questions on ODA Criteria and Security Expenditures', May 2006, available at: <http://www.ccic.ca/e/docs/002_aid_2006-05_oda_security_criteria.pdf>.

[33] In addition, there is bilateral support provided by EU Member States, which is not the subject of this chapter.

[34] Ukraine, Albania, Bosnia and Herzegovina, Serbia, Montenegro, Georgia, South Africa, DRC, Colombia, Guatemala, Afghanistan and Indonesia are some of the countries that have received the most substantive multi-sector SSR support from the EC. For a list of examples of EU projects under various SSR-related headings, see Annex.

[35] For a comprehensive survey of EU-assisted SSR projects, see Spence and Fluri, *supra* n. 4.

cases, such as Afghanistan, Kosovo,[36] Democratic Republic of Congo, Guinea-Bissau and the Occupied Palestinian Territory, there are parallel EC projects and ESDP missions supporting SSR. A distinction is necessary. EU activities in support of SSR are predominantly 'civilian', with a few exceptions, such as the European Development Fund's (EDF) 'African Peace Facility', which supports military peace-keeping operations of the African Union (AU), and ESDP military missions in countries such as Bosnia and Herzegovina and Chad/Central African Republic.

## 7. Learning on the job: Cross-Pillar approaches to SSR

There have been many divergences of view on where overall responsibility in the EU for SSR should lie.[37] This has depended on the particular aspects of SSR that actors have wished to pursue and the Pillar within which action is envisaged. The rapid development since the late 1990s, and especially after 2001, of strengthened EU capacity and objectives in the areas of conflict prevention and crisis management had a significant impact on the way the Union came to approach SSR, both in policy and operational terms. But in practical terms, the Commission's DGs RELEX, DEV and JLS each found legal justification for action within their own Pillar framework, Pillars One and Three, while the Council Secretariat argued strongly that the word 'security' implied that European Security and Defence Policy supplied the relevant legal framework. Notwithstanding the fact that ESDP, the EU's Second Pillar, was bereft of sufficient funding to have more than a token impact, the Council Secretariat argued the case for SSR to remain part of its Second Pillar tool bag.

In the EU's First Pillar, SSR could be covered by specific projects financed under country programmes (as part of the European Development Fund (EDF) or the Development Cooperation Instrument (DCI)) or specific financing facilities. Of the latter, between 2002 and 2006, the Rapid Reaction Mechanism allowed the Commission to respond urgently to the needs of countries threatened by serious political instability or suffering from the effects of an industrial or natural disaster. As to the 'Third Pillar' – justice, home affairs and security, known by its French acronym 'JLS' – Monar has argued that it is perfectly logical to view the EU's external attempts to encourage SSR as a reflection of its internal security perceptions and objectives.[38]

On 1 January 2007, the Instrument for Stability (IfS) replaced the Rapid Reaction Mechanism and several other funding instruments in the fields of drugs, mines, displaced people, crisis management, rehabilitation and reconstruction.[39] The new

---

[36] Under UNSCR 1244 (1999), Kosovo is not recognised as an independent state by several EU Member States.

[37] See S. Duke, 'Areas of Grey: Tensions in EU External Relations Competences', 1 *EIPASCOPE* (2006).

[38] J. Monar, 'Justice and Home Affairs: Security Sector Reform Measures As Instruments of EU Internal Security Objectives', in Spence and Fluri, *supra* n. 4.

[39] *OJ* 2006 L 327/1.

'Stability Instrument' allowed, for example, support to the United Nations Interim Mission in Kosovo and the Office of the High Representative in Bosnia and Herzegovina. In general, SSR-related activities are usually integrated into country strategies within the framework of wider development and external cooperation under the EDF and the DCI, but ESDP missions, the Community's Rapid Reaction Mechanism, and now the Instrument for Stability have covered a number of SSR-related activities, especially in post-conflict settings. Here, they have been decoupled from individual country strategies, where they are already mainstreamed but where extra forms of funding can reflect the urgency of EU preoccupations. They complement SSR support under long-term Community instruments and include both civilian aspects of SSR and more recently even defence reform such as that of EUSEC Congo (2005).[40] The DRC was the test case for the EU in SSR, following the adoption in 2006 of the overarching EU policy framework. Civil-military coordination, cross-Pillar coordination, sequencing of short and long-term instruments and EU coordination and cooperation with national and international actors have been carefully honed. EUSEC Congo was the first time the EU engaged in defence reform, though undertaking police and justice reform at the same time. Whether there will be another case on the same scale and level of political commitment for some years is a moot point. In most geographical locations the main focus of EU support is likely to continue to be on civilian aspects of SSR.

To enhance cross-Pillar cooperation, as the EC Communication advocated and as practice showed, there was a clear need to establish better coordination between EC and ESDP activities, including joint needs assessments and improved complementarity in implementation. To enhance the professionalism of staff involved, ongoing work now includes internal training of desks and delegations on how to conduct security sector analyses and how to prepare support programmes, select implementing agencies and supervise implementation.[41] Member States and EU institutions have also begun joint work on common training standards for personnel to be sent on international missions and on the establishment of pools of experts. This includes Commission support to a network of Member States' training institutions and the European Training Group, which provides training for experts to be deployed in the field. Member States' experts are being deployed in twinning or other types of security sector reform programmes or ESDP missions.

Steps have also been taken to establish crisis response teams in the framework of ESDP and Commission assessment teams, as well as a pool of EU SSR experts, accessible to both Council and Commission, and henceforth to the European External Action Service. A number of joint assessment missions have taken place since 2006, for example, in Guinea Bissau, demonstrating that common analyses, better coordination and sequencing of support are possible. Mechanisms are also being set up at field level to enhance coordination. The DRC and Kosovo are again prime

---

40 See the contributions by Martinelli, Vervaeke and Gourlay to this volume.

41 At the beginning of 2010, the Commission's DG AIDCO began a major evaluation of all SSR projects to date.

cases.[42] The EC Communication also recommended improvements to planning and implementation tools, including comprehensive SSR analyses and operational guidelines. The Commission assessed and evaluated existing guidelines for Integrated Border Management (IBM) for the Western Balkans and developed IBM Guidelines for Central Asia, as well as general IBM guidelines and a Guidance Framework for EU SSR Assessments, developed later by the Swedish Presidency in 2009 in consultation with the Council Secretariat and the Commission. Collaboration with other donors in the OECD-DAC has also been important. The DAC SSR Handbook, launched in the spring of 2007, provides donors with tools for analysis and operational guidance and offers a framework for coordination at field level.[43] The Commission is also working closely with the SSR and DDR units at the UN and with the Swiss-funded international foundation Geneva Centre for the Democratic Control of Armed Forces (DCAF) and its International Security Sector Advisory Team (ISSAT).

Competence debates between Commission and Council were frequent until a European Court of Justice (ECJ) ruling in 2008, which held that support in certain security-related areas such as SSR, small arms and light weapons (SALW) control, border management and rule of law, may be legally pursued both either under EC external assistance instruments or through CFSP/ESDP missions.[44] The Court decision made clear that if an action can be adopted legally under the Community Pillar, it cannot be adopted in the framework of CFSP/ESDP. It thereby confirmed the Commission's view on the primacy of the First (EC) Pillar as the legal basis for EU support in these areas. The ECJ ruling clarified that the 'aim and content' of action should determine the framework for EU intervention and that if goals pertaining to development, rule of law or good governance were the objectives pursued, an EC legal basis would be necessary. By contrast, it made clear that if a purely security goal were pursued, such as creating institutions from 'scratch' or within a context of military intervention, then a CFSP/ESDP legal basis would be required. Importantly, if the thrust of an action could be considered as pursuing both objectives, according to the Court, an EC legal basis should be used, and CFSP could not 'trump' EC procedures. How the Lisbon Treaty might change the institutional interaction involved remains to be seen. Whereas the creation of the EEAS obviates the interinstitutional turf battles previously involved, the same issues may still arise, this time between Member States and the EEAS. After all, several Member States have been involved in SSR missions on a purely bilateral basis – France in Côte d'Ivoire, the UK in Sierra Leone and the Netherlands in Rwanda to name just three.

---

[42] See the contributions by Martinelli, resp. Keukeleire and Thiers to this volume.

[43] OECD, *OECD-DAC Handbook on Security Sector Reform: Supporting Security and Justice* (2006).

[44] ECJ, Case C-91/05 *Commission* v. *Council* (SALW/ECOWAS) [2008] *ECR* I-03651. For a brief overview of the issues, see D. Spence, 'The Commission and CFSP', in D. Spence, ed., *The European Commission* (London, John Harper 2006).

Other security-related issues, such as disarmament, demobilisation and reintegration of former combatants (DDR),[45] small arms and light weapons control (SALW) or mine clearance, are similarly crucial flanking areas of a holistic SSR concept. Significantly, however, it was generally accepted before the Lisbon Treaty came into force that EC SSR actions could not have defence or military implications, since these areas were deemed to remain Member State competence. This restriction did not prevent the Commission from working with the military on DDR, SALW or mine clearance, which in many countries are considered defence issues. There is also the odd exception of the African Peace Facility (under the EDF), which mainly supports military peacekeeping operations of the African Union (AU) yet is nevertheless managed by the European Commission. It includes support to the development of an African Union SSR policy and capacity.[46] Again, the implications of the Lisbon Treaty are not yet tested. Will the new EEAS be able to work with both military and civilian sectors, since the previously interinstitutional split has ended? It remains to be seen.

## 8. The Commission's external assistance instruments in support of SSR

Former RELEX Commissioner, Chris Patten, was aghast at the myriad financial instruments usable in crisis management and peacebuilding and pushed for a simplification of the financial instruments at the disposal of policy makers. The situation became simpler with the new instruments created for the 2007-2013 financial period. Commission support to SSR is currently possible through several development, non-development and mixed external assistance instruments. SSR is covered in the 10th European Development Fund (EDF), which covers the African, Caribbean and Pacific states and the Development Cooperation Instrument's (DCI) thematic Programme on Asylum and Migration.[47] Some SSR-related actions are funded under the European Instrument for Democracy and Human Rights (EIDHR), in particular in the area of democratic control and the enhancement of the watchdog role of civil society. Then there are 'mixed instruments', which provide for support for SSR in Eastern European and Southern Mediterranean countries, funded under the European Neighbourhood and Partnership Instrument (ENPI). The Instrument for Stability covers the highest number of SSR-related projects, particularly in the form of exceptional assistance measures in response to crisis and decoupled from

[45] EU Concept for Support to Disarmament, Demobilisation and Reintegration (DDR), approved by the European Commission on 14 December 2006 and by the Council of the European Union on 11 December 2006.

[46] Eligibility for funding nevertheless excludes ammunition, arms and military equipment (as well as their spare parts), soldiers' salaries and military training, but all other costs of a military peacekeeping operation such as soldiers' per diems, rations, medical consumables and facilities, transport, fuel, troop allowances, communication equipment, etc., are eligible.

[47] Eligibility under the DCI Asylum and Migration Programme is also open to non-DCI countries.

any form of geographical limitation. Finally, there are non-development instruments, which cover support for a relatively large number of SSR-related projects in Turkey and the Western Balkans through the Instrument for Pre-Accession Assistance (IPA).

## 9. The Commission's international role: donorship and coordination

As mentioned above, the OECD's Development Assistance Committee produced the DAC Guidelines on Security System Reform and Governance.[48] Efforts within the DAC reflect the role development cooperation has come to play in support of the civilian aspects of SSR, not only because of the financial resources it can bring to bear, but because of its direct link to overall development objectives, which include governance, human rights, democratisation and conflict prevention, as we have seen. SSR is not only, or even primarily, linked to crisis. It requires long-term engagement and a comprehensive approach. Of the some 70 countries that received support between 2000 and 2005, more than half were not in a crisis or post-crisis phase.[49] The bulk of EC support went to countries in transition, in particular as part of the EU enlargement and stabilisation and association processes.[50] Comprehensive reform processes generally require a more stable environment for the development of democratic institutions and culture.

The DAC work not only provided an important basis for Community policy developments to take this into account, but affected efforts within the Second Pillar of the EU (CFSP/ESDP). Both the Commission's Communication and the ESDP concept paper drew on definitions and principles established in the DAC guidelines, recognising that the essence of the impact of the new SSR concept was less the efficiency of individual services and more the system-wide effects, where reforms in one sector must necessarily be linked to reforms in others, based on their specific functions and their distinct tasks within the overall system. By taking a whole-of-government approach, cutting across the EU Pillars, the DAC work provided EU Member States and the EU institutions with a policy basis and a useful implementation framework for operational coordination with other major actors.

SSR-related projects are most frequently implemented in partnership with UN agencies (UNODC, UNDP, UNOPS, UNHCR, UNICEF, etc.) or other international organisations, such as the World Bank and the International Organisation for Migration (IOM), which have the necessary experience and expertise and are keen to promote SSR together with the EU in the framework of regular dialogue and cooperation with the UN family. This requires sharing information on best practice, developing jointly shared concepts, doctrines and training curricula, and coordinating planning and implementation in the field, where countries are undergoing transition towards a greater degree of democracy.

---

[48] *Security System Reform and Governance, Policy and Practice*, DAC Guidelines and Reference Series (Paris, OECD 2004)

[49] Ibid.

[50] See the contribution by Blockmans to this volume.

As is the case for other multilateral and bilateral donors, the focus of EU development cooperation (both European Community and Member States) has gradually shifted from growth-related aspects to poverty reduction, including human rights and democratic governance. This was reflected in the European Consensus on Development adopted in December 2005[51] and in the 'Governance and Development' Communication of 2003,[52] which argued that a country's ability to eradicate poverty and promote sustainable development hinges on the quality of its governance, with SSR being an integral component of good governance.

As a major provider of external assistance, the Commission thus works closely with other donors. The UN system and especially UNDP and IOM are important implementers of EU support to security sector reform and DDR, and EU-UN cooperation in crisis management constitutes an important element of ESDP.[53] The Joint Declaration on EU-UN Cooperation in Crisis Management (2003) included planning, training, communication and sharing of best practice, and the Joint Statement on EU-UN Cooperation in Crisis Management in 2007 stressed the importance of enhancement of EU-UN coordination and cooperation mechanisms for crisis situations, building on the UN Secretary-General's report, *In Larger Freedom*,[54] which argued for a coherent approach by all parties concerned with conflict management, and the *Delivering As One* report on UN system-wide coherence.[55] The message was not lost on the Commission. It had already committed to policy coherence in the European Consensus on Development of 2005 and published a first assessment of its endeavours in 2007. In November 2009, it followed this up with a second progress report and a new communication on policy coherence for development.[56]

Progress is regularly evaluated in twice-yearly Progress Reports on Recommendations for the Implementation of the Joint Statement on EU-UN Cooperation in Crisis Management, and in the EU-UN Steering Committee. These meetings are co-chaired on the EU side by the Commission and the Council Secretariat and on the UN side by DPKO – lately together with UNDP. They have led to innovations, such as a UN roster of deployable SSR experts, paralleling deployable EU expert teams (a French initiative endorsed by the PSC in November 2008[57]), itself an initiative proposed in a report of the UN Secretary-General on UN approaches to

---

[51] 'The European Consensus on Development' was adopted by the Council on 22 November 2005.

[52] The Commission Communication on Governance and Development, 2003, *supra* n. 2.

[53] T. Tardy, 'UN-EU Relations in Crisis Management. Taking Stock and Looking Ahead', *International Forum for the Challenges of Peace Operations*, Folke Bernadotte Academy, 2009. See also the contribution by Gourlay to this volume.

[54] Report of the UN Secretary-General, *In Larger Freedom: Towards Development, Security and Human Rights for All*, 21 March 2005, UN Doc. A/59/2005.

[55] UN Secretary-General's High-Level Panel on UN System-Wide Coherence in the Areas of Development, Humanitarian Assistance, and the Environment, *Delivering as One* (United Nations, 9 November 2006).

[56] Communication from the Commission to the Council: Policy Coherence for Development – Establishing the policy framework for a whole-of-the-Union approach, COM(2009) 458 final. The previous report was the EU Report on Policy Coherence for Development, COM(2007) 545 final.

[57] Document 14576/1/08 REV 1, adopted by the PSC on 20 November 2008.

SSR in January 2008, entitled *Securing Peace and Development: The Role of the UN in Supporting SSR*. Similarly, in 2009, the EU Council argued for a single focal point for the SSR in the framework of ESDP to be established in the Council Secretariat. The point was to reflect the development on the UN side, where a core expert capacity for SSR was created in the newly established Office for Rule of Law and Security Institutions in DPKO in 2008. Shortly after, there was a further proposal to establish a coordination mechanism involving all the EU actors responsible for the SSR-related agenda in different EU Pillars. In addition, DPKO appointed a permanent high-level liaison officer in Brussels to enhance practical EU-UN cooperation and related institutional arrangements.[58] The relevance and importance of coordination and common approaches with other donors in addition to training and tools for implementation is underlined by the fact that many partner countries lack comprehensive SSR analyses and there is a need to prioritise a limited number of areas, with most strategies focusing on one or two sub-sectors.

But there is a wider context to these issues. Security governance in Europe is part of overall governance in liberal-democratic societies. It may be superior to that on any other continent of similar size, yet national practices and philosophies continue to differ. They are not consistent in terms of democratic process and control, any more than the defence forces of NATO states share the same national defence philosophy and force profiles. Divergent national views in Europe on principles such as the legitimate use of force and the acceptability of pre-emption became clear after the engagement in Iraq, which demonstrated how far countries' constitutions vary in terms of parliamentary control of declaring a war, running a war, financing a war and withdrawing from a war, including democratic control of the security sector as a whole, not least the sensitive area of intelligence gathering. Even the nature of police forces themselves varies in practice and concept. Whereas the UK starts from the assumption that a permanently armed police force would be unacceptable, France's CRS and its Gendarmerie and Italy's armed Carabinieri clearly contradict this philosophical premise. Yet, they do not arouse the kind of opposition in those countries which mere mention of arming police in the UK immediately produces.[59] So, underlying these differences lies the question of which ground rules EU SSR policy can actually espouse without disagreement between Member States, or between Member States and the new EEAS. Whether the new High Representative/Vice-President of the Commission should or could resolve such philosophical conundrums remains to be seen, but it is clear that a line to take on them would not go amiss.

---

[58] In early 2010, the appointed UN official had still not left New York to take up his post in Brussels.

[59] All EU Member States, except the UK, have permanently armed police services, all of them civilian with the exception of the so-called gendarmerie-like police forces. Yet, there is an important distinction between the French Gendarmerie and the Spanish Guardia Civil, on the one hand, and the Italian Carabinieri, on the other. In the French and Spanish cases, these are internal 'military' organisations, but work under the authority of the Ministry of the Interior (as do their National Police Forces). By contrast, the Italian Carabinieri are a military body, reporting to the Ministry of Defence. As to the proposed European gendarmerie, see: <http://www.eurogendfor.org/>.

## 10. Conclusion: SSR and the EU's normative role

What, finally, are the lessons that have been learned from this transition from the realisation that much EU aid had already contributed to SSR, but under another name, to the current situation where the EU's stance on SSR is the basis not only for its own work but increasingly for that of other international organisations, not least the UN?

Irrespective of specific SSR programmes, EU capacity depends on the preparedness of its institutions, its staff and its Member States to redefine traditional barriers between development, security, justice support and foreign policy *per se*. Earlier EU aid showed that it was essential for SSR to be carried out on the basis of partnership and local ownership. The EU concluded that it should always infuse its post-modern philosophy of national SSR achievements into regional perspectives, not only in fragile post-conflict situations but wherever the UN and regional organisations responsible for individual cases might deem it appropriate.

The normative role of the EU is rapidly coming the most heartening feature of EU policy on SSR. Its normative aspirations are considered an enormous asset and source of legitimacy for the EU in its endeavour to count in world affairs, as the many citations in this chapter amply demonstrate. On the one hand, the EU has encouraged regional communities when shaping specific country-based EU policies and linking SSR into the wider liberal-democratic normative context. On the other hand, by embedding its own SSR concept in practice, along with its liberal-democratic precepts in general, the EU believes it provides clear benefits to countries it deems worthy of development assistance. This simultaneously 'constitutes a crucial test for the Union's ability to shape trans-boundary security in an innovative and strategic manner.'[60] Nonetheless, a series of questions arise concerning both the legitimacy of EU policies, when the EU itself is arguably not so legitimate as formal declarations state, and its right, anyway, to set itself up as a model.

Lack of transparency and parliamentary oversight have meant that 'parliamentary scrutiny of European security policy is extremely weak' and

> '(...) effective oversight is difficult to realise due to weak and uneven scrutiny practices and control rights in the different Member States. Furthermore, national parliaments still rely on the information provided by their own executives. There are no formal mechanisms in European security policy for informing national parliaments about other Member States' positions or to receive reports directly from the European Union.'[61]

Was the EU, while an active promoter of SSR abroad, potentially guilty of not heeding its own message? This rhetorical question was never answered.

Today, after the implementation of the Lisbon Treaty, there may remain reasons why the EU cannot simply externalise its internal security success story to the rest

---

[60] A. Bailes, 'Introduction', in Spence and Fluri, eds., *supra* n. 4.

[61] Barcelona Report, *supra* n. 16, at 26.

of the world and thereby be deemed to have fulfilled the normative role it has set itself. In Africa or Asia, for example, as noted above, the need for the kind of SSR Europe went through in the 1990s at NATO instigation may quite simply not be relevant, since traditional territorial military threats, which the European continent has put behind it, will likely continue in those countries. Reform of the institutions for Europe's particular brand of post-Westphalian international relations and international humanitarian missions may not be what other countries need or want, but the normative lesson on good governance will doubtless remain useful in countries wedded to public decency and be accepted reluctantly but incontrovertibly by the governments of states where corruption and egoistic leadership have not yet met a suitable Don Giovanni-like end.

After Lisbon, the need to coordinate EU Member States' efforts and EU projects will continue, but their management is likely to be faced with a new series of challenges, which can only be surmised at the beginning of 2010. As Blockmans points out in his chapter, a structural feature of SSR policy where it has been the most successful has been the incentive of membership of NATO or the EU. This 'soft power' tool with which the Union pursued SSR in Europe will patently not be available in Africa or Asia. But if it was such a major contribution to the success of EU efforts in Europe, what, in these countries, will be its structural replacement? If there is no ready replacement, the incontrovertible fact remains that it may take considerable time for acceptable security sector governance to emerge. Conceivably, in the African case, membership of the African Union might have been the carrot of successful SSR implementation, but this pass has already been sold by the blanket geographical arrangements for AU membership. The EU does need to preserve the image stemming from its internal commitment to good governance and democracy as a prerequisite for support of SSR in any country/region of the world. In Africa, the focus of EU advocacy of SSR will doubtless continue to be the goals of democracy and good governance, and this will most likely continue to be linked to a reward structure based precisely on good governance, as is already the case in the Cotonou arrangements. Yet, one problem is that exhortations to good governance may in the end be no more than a rhetorical comfort to the donor community. Economic incentives may prove more effective to the success of any SSR effort, particularly in post-conflict environments where economic development is crucial for peacebuilding and peaceful development. Indeed, the crucial difference between European targets for SSR at home and targets for concerted international efforts in aid-recipient countries is that SSR in *post-conflict* states, with often newly formed democratic governments deserving EU assistance and SSR help, runs a gauntlet between violent opposition, on the one hand, and arms-backed corruption, on the other; important examples are SSR efforts in Afghanistan and Iraq, Colombia or, nearer to EU home, Georgia and Moldova.

In the end, however, SSR *is* a tool of 'good governance', and the EU will lose its distinctness and credibility if it breaks the link with such fundamental goals and values as pluralistic democracy and democratic control. The World Bank's authoritative definition (and the OECD-DAC's and the EU's espousal of it) of what constitutes 'good governance' in general refers to a voice for the people and accountability for the government: political stability and non-violence; government effectiveness, regulatory quality and the rule of law; and last but not least, control of corruption. 'Good governance' in all these senses can actually coincide with sensible defence and security precautions, so supporting SSR while also promoting defence and internal security modernisation and efficiency is not the contradiction that some well-meaning observers may argue.

There is a final related argument of consequence. The interaction between a holistic EU SSR programme, related assumptions about CSDP policy for the purposes of purely military cooperation (bases, logistics, etc.) and what individual EU states may propose as part of their security-related assistance agreements (even with the same countries) may end up in contradiction with each other unless there is adequate EU-level monitoring, supervision and control. This will require authoritative coordination, rather than mere information exchange. This arguably forms an important task for Catherine Ashton, the new High Representative for Foreign Affairs and Security Policy, and her European External Action Service. The EU has been successful at SSR precisely because it is not (yet) playing its own military strategic game in most parts of the world and its policy makers seem genuinely to want to see states at peace and democratic. The hope must be that this basic set of parameters continues to hold, notwithstanding subsequent 'coordination' efforts. Yet, there is an important caveat. This chapter has argued that EU support for the governance of others may be considered, so far, as evidence of the disinterested nature of EU assistance *per se*. But it would be naive to assume that this will always be the case. The EU's normative role is very likely contingent on unstated interests of one kind or another. The EU's SSR policies and its development policies thus stand at a crossroads after implementation of the Lisbon Treaty. Can a newly galvanised (yet still essentially contested) EU meet the challenge of SSR in countries where one political leader makes all the security and defence decisions and even considers the army, the judiciary and the police as his extended personal staff? And could the EU's governance incentives provide the sticks and carrots to induce change? This, again, remains to be seen.

## Annex

## EC/EU Support to SSR
## Selected Ongoing and Planned Actions 2010[62]

| PROGRAMME/COUNTRY | FINANCE |
|---|---|
| **Strategic support to SSR** | |
| Guinea Bissau SSR Support Team | €0.7 million (Instrument for Stability) |
| Central African Republic SSR Technical Support | €1.5 million (Instrument for Stability) |
| **Police reform** | |
| EC Police Assistance Mission to Albania (PAMECA III) | €4.5 million (CARDS) |
| Support for Police Reform in DR Congo | €5 million (Instrument for Stability) |
| Honduras Security Sector Support Programme (PASS) | €43 million (Development Cooperation Instrument) |
| Mozambique Police Reform Programme | €7 million (European Development Fund) |
| European Police Training Support to Yemen | €3 million (Development Cooperation Instrument) |
| **Justice, including criminal justice** | |
| European Justice Assistance Mission to Albania (EURALIUS II) | €5.5 million (Instrument for Pre-Accession Assistance) |
| Support to the Strengthening of the Judiciary in the Republic of Kazakhstan | €3.5 million (Development Cooperation Instrument) |
| Afghanistan Justice Sector Reform | €2.3 million (Instrument for Stability) |
| Justice Support Programme in Chad (PRAJUST) | €25 million (European Development Fund) |
| European Criminal Justice Support to Jordan | €3.5 million (European Neighbourhood Policy Instrument) |
| **Transitional justice** | |
| Support to the Special Court for Sierra Leone | €2.5 million (Instrument for Stability) |
| Justice Assistance Mission to the Philippines (on extrajudicial killings) | €3.9 million (Instrument for Stability) |

[62] Commission internal document – Cases valid as of January 2010.

| | |
|---|---|
| Strengthening the Justice Sector in Colombia to Reduce Impunity | €10.5 million (ALA) |
| Support to the Special Tribunal for Lebanon | €1.5 million (Instrument for Stability) |
| Support to the Truth and Reconciliation Commission in the Solomon Islands | €1.8 million (Instrument for Stability) |
| **Prison management and juvenile justice** | |
| Kyrgyzstan: Support to Prison Reform | €3 million (Development Cooperation Instrument) |
| Human Rights and Penitentiary Reform in Jordan | €1 million (European Neighbourhood Policy Instrument) |
| Prisons and Penal Reform in Moldova | €0.95 million (European Neighbourhood Policy Instrument) |
| Support to Good Governance and Rule of Law in Madagascar | €9 million (European Development Fund) |
| Establishing a Juvenile Justice System in Yemen | €3 million (Development Cooperation Instrument) |
| **Disarmament, demobilisation and reintegration (DDR)** | |
| Support to the Defence and Security Reform in Guinea Bissau (RSDS) | €7.7 million (European Development Fund) |
| Support to the Banda-Aceh Reintegration Agency (BRA) and Peacebuilding in Indonesia | €3 million (Rehabilitation and Reintegration Programme) |
| Assistance to Demobilised Child Soldiers, Victims of the Armed Conflict in Colombia | €1.9 million (Rehabilitation and Reintegration Programme) |
| Support to Demobilisation and Reintegration in Liberia | €9.1 million (European Development Fund) |
| Support to the Demobilisation and Transitional Reintegration Process in Burundi | €4 million (Instrument for Stability) |
| **Border management** | |
| EU Border Assistance Mission to Ukraine and the Republic of Moldova (EU BAM VI) | €12 million (European Neighbourhood Policy Instrument) |
| Border Management and Fight against Illegal Migration in Morocco | €67 million (MEDA) |

| | |
|---|---|
| Border Management in the Philippines (2005-2008) | €5 million (ALA) |
| Border Management in Central Asia (BOMCA VII) | €6 million (Development Cooperation Instrument) |
| **Asylum, migration and trafficking in human beings** | |
| Asylum and Refugees Protection System in Tanzania | €1.5 million (ÆNEAS) |
| Border and Migration Management in Central America | €1 million (Thematic Programme for Migration and Asylum) |
| Fight against Human Trafficking in Cambodia | €2 million (ÆNEAS) |
| Centre for Migration Management in Mali (CIGEM) | €10 million (European Development Fund) |
| Management of Labour Migration in Moldova | €3 million (Thematic Programme for Migration and Asylum) |
| Yemen: Addressing the Mixed Migration Flow from the Horn of Africa | €2 million (Instrument for Stability) |

# Chapter 9
# STRENGTHENING SECURITY, BUILDING PEACE: THE EU IN THE DEMOCRATIC REPUBLIC OF CONGO

**Marta Martinelli***

## 1. Introduction

Conflict prevention and reduction have become central tenets in EU external policies, based on the understanding that no development is possible unless conditions are established that favour peace and stability. The principles of peace and security, development and good governance are enshrined in various official documents and notably the EU Security Strategy, which states that the EU is a global actor and as such must be prepared to take responsibility for international security and for a better world.[1] The link between the dimensions of peace/security/development and governance has also become an operational concept in the EU's instruments for external action such as development, trade, environmental policies, as well as Common Foreign and Security Policy (CFSP) and, increasingly, European Security and Defence Policy (ESDP).[2] In the process, Member States have increasingly come to recognise that security implies more than force and coercion and they are striving to improve coordination and coherence between the hard and soft tools at their disposal. The capacity to use such tools in the pre-, during and post-conflict phases, as well as the capacity to handle structural, cultural and direct aspects of violence and of intervening at all levels of the societal pyramid (grass roots, middle leadership and top leadership level) contributes to the development of a European strategic culture for dealing with conflicts. This means that beyond a pragmatic approach

* Dr. Marta Martinelli is Research Fellow at the Pôle Bernheim for Peace and Citizenship, Institute of European Studies, Université Libre de Bruxelles. The author would like to thank the *Groupe de Recherche en Appui aux Politiques de Paix* (GRAPAX) and the *Recherche et Enseignement en Politique Internationale* (REPI/ULB) for their financial support during the research leading to the present publication.

[1] *A Secure Europe in a Better Wold. European Security Strategy* (Brussels, 12 December 2003), available at: <http://eu.eu.int/uedocs/cmsUpload/78367.pdf>. For critical reviews of the ESS, see G. Quille, 'The European Security Strategy (ESS): A Framework for European Union Security Interests?', 11 *Journal of International Peacekeeping* (2004) 1-16, and G. Quille, 'Making Multilateralism Matter: The EU Security Strategy', 18 *European Security Review* (2003), available at: <http://www.isis-europe.org>.

[2] See, German Development Institute, *Development Policy – A Core Element of European Security Policy*, Briefing Paper No. 3 (Bonn, Deutsches Institut für Entwicklungspolitik (DIE) 2004).

to resolving conflicts, focused on deploying all the tools and resources at its disposal, the EU has also been developing a global discourse which can become the embryo of a doctrinal culture. In other words, we are witnessing the emergence of a strategic culture, meaning a complex of beliefs, values, attitudes and frameworks that come to define the European approach to conflict management and post-conflict peacebuilding beyond the plurality of approaches adopted by its Member States.[3]

Further to this and consistent with the Paris Principles on Aid Effectiveness,[4] the development of such an EU strategic culture must be 'negotiated' within the context in which the EU intervenes. In the DRC, this context is one of security volatility caused, amongst other things, by a lack of state control over its territory; a lack of monopoly of the use of violence on the part of the state; and undisciplined, untrained and inefficient security forces which are very much part of the problems of the country. With this as the starting point of its analysis of the situation in the DRC, the EU has identified the reform of the Congolese security forces as a key area where EU intervention could provide some added value to the ongoing peacebuilding effort.

Against this background, this chapter will focus on the EU's contribution to peacebuilding in the DRC, particularly through initiatives aimed at increasing security and stability in the country. Following an introduction on the historical determinants of the security environment in the DRC today, the specificity of the EU's approach will be presented and critically reviewed in order to highlight the strengths and weaknesses of the EU's intervention in support of security sector reform. Finally, some considerations will be raised with the aim to reflect on a 'way forward' that can be truly transformative for the Congolese people.

Part of the information presented has been gathered through access to confidential and classified EU and diplomatic documents as well as through interviews. Referencing that may obviously point to any of these sources will be avoided in order to respect the necessary confidentiality.

## 2. Background to the security situation in the DRC[5]

Since its independence from Belgium in 1960, the DRC has known political instability, massacres, proliferation of security actors and sustained involvement of ex-

[3] M. Aligisakis, ed., *Europe et sortie des conflits* (Geneva, Institut européen de l'Université de Genève 2005).

[4] Paris Declaration on Aid Effectiveness. Ownership, Harmonisation, Alignment, Results and Mutual Accountability, High Level Forum (Paris 28 February – 2 March 2005) paragraph 13, at 3.

[5] Part of the information in this paragraph has been published in previous publications by Marta Martinelli. See, for example, 'Implementing the ESDP in Africa: The Case of the Democratic Republic of Congo', in R. Ostrauskaitė and M. Merlingen, eds., *European Security and Defence Policy. An Implementation Perspective* (London, Routledge 2008) 111-127. For a very interesting and informative analysis of the conflicts in the Great Lakes Region, including the DRC, see J. Ewald, et al., *A Strategic Conflict Analysis for the Great Lakes Region* (Stockholm, SIDA – Division for Eastern and Western Africa 2004).

ternal actors. By the end of the 1960s, the government was firmly run by Joseph-Desiré Mobutu. His policies led to ethnic conflicts and a series of coup attempts in the 1970s as well as to serious economic decline in the 1980s. As the distinction between business, state administration and security forces became increasingly blurred, the state gradually lost its monopoly on the use of force and its capacity to control unrest.

In these circumstances, the 1994 Rwanda genocide worsened the situation when almost one million (mostly) Hutu Rwandese fled to the Kivus, in the eastern part of the DRC. Among them were Hutu militias who almost immediately began to organise and to attack Rwanda from Congolese soil, leading to increased tensions between the two countries. Refugee flows upset the precarious social balance between the different ethnic groups in the area. Hutu militants from Rwanda exploited the resentment of the Banyarwanda towards other ethnic groups in the region in order to recruit them for their militias. Massive recruitment campaigns were also organised in the Hutu refugee camps set up in the wake of the exodus from Rwanda. The inability of the Congolese forces to respond to this situation was interpreted by the Tutsi government of Rwanda as a deliberate policy of Hutu forces and the Congolese state to undermine it. In response, Kigali, joined by the Tutsi government of Burundi, formed an anti-Mobuto alliance with Uganda and the Banyamulenge elite in the DRC, headed by Laurent Kabila.

The resulting 1996/1997 conflict led a victorious Kabila to establish a new government. However, concerned about the country's instability and the military presence of foreign troops from Rwanda and Uganda, Kabila decided to reinforce his domestic political and social base by forging an alliance with Hutu forces. The result of this strategic turn-around was that Uganda was denied control over the economic resources that had motivated its support for Kabila whilst Rwanda's security concerns remained unaddressed. Kabila's decision to expel Rwanda and Uganda prompted a second generalised war involving the whole region.[6] The 1999 Lusaka ceasefire agreement[7] largely failed and violence continued on a large scale until Kabila's assassination in January 2001 brought to power his son, Joseph, whose government resumed peace negotiations and ended the ban on political parties. The signature, in December 2002, of the Global and All-Inclusive Agreement,[8] facilitated by South Africa and other international players including the EU, opened the way for a transitional period during which a new constitution had to be approved; armed groups had to be dismantled and reunified into an integrated, reformed Congolese army; and general elections had to be organised.

---

[6] Zimbabwe, Angola and Namibia supported the government, whilst Rwanda, Uganda and Zambia backed various rebel groups.

[7] 'Secretary-General Welcomes RDC Signing of Lusaka Ceasefire Agreement on Democratic Republic of Congo', *UNIS/SG/2351*, 1 September 1999, available at: <http://www.unis.unvienna.org/unis/pressrels/1999/sg2351.html>. For the text of the agreement see: <http://www.reliefweb.int/rw/RWB.NSF/db900SID/MHII-65HB37?OpenDocument>.

[8] Global and Inclusive Agreement on the Transition in the Democratic Republic of the Congo: Inter-Congolese Dialogue – Political Negotiations on the Peace Process and Transition in the DRC, available at: <http://www.reliefweb.int/rw/rwb.nsf/db900sid/MHII-65G8B8?OpenDocument>.

A power-sharing transitional government led by President Kabila and an interim parliament, came to office in June 2003. The peace process, however, was complicated by political leaders' refusal to integrate their troops into the new Congolese national army – 'a deliberate strategy on the part of the leaders who fought the 1998-2002 war to preserve their ability to respond with force if elections do not turn out to their satisfaction.'[9] In spite of these difficulties and renewed bouts of violence between splintering rebel groups, especially in Katanga and in Ituri, voters approved the new constitution in December,[10] paving the way for the election of a new government. The first round of presidential elections was held in July 2006 and the second three months later. The winner was Kabila.

## 2.1 The security context today

The security situation continues to be characterised by both internal and external/regional dynamics. Internally, since the elections, fighting in the North Kivu, where various militia groups have been operating for over a decade, has been exacerbated by the presence of the CNDP (*Congrès national pour la défense du peuple*) led by Laurent Nkunda whose purported agenda was one of uniting and protecting the Tutsi population in the area. Governmental attempts at bringing him to reason by force led to a series of humiliating defeats for the Congolese army (FARDC). Eventually, all belligerents, including various Mayi Mayi groups, met in Goma in January 2008 where they signed an *Acte d'engagement* facilitated by the UN, the EU and the US.[11] Unfortunately, the Goma Agreement failed to make any difference on the ground. Fighting continued unabated in the area, exposing civilians to massive human rights violations by all armed groups, including government forces. Nkunda's arrest in January 2009 was saluted with a major sigh of relief by the region and led to his replacement with Bosco Ntaganda, now an ally to the Congolese government in exchange for fighting the FDLR and accepting the demobilisation of his group as well as the integration of his forces into the Congolese national army. However, the demobilisation of the CNDP has proved rather chaotic. Its assimilation into the FARDC leaves its combatants in the same areas where they have been fighting for years prior to the group's dismantlement. They are still loyal to Ntaganda, which has obvious risks for the unity of the Congolese forces, and, moreover, the creation of new army units sharing command posts with the ex-rebels has upset the army's operational structures.[12] Soldiers are not paid and resort to harassing the population

---

[9] International Crisis Group, *Africa Report No. 104* (Brussels, 13 February 2006), at i. See also, H. Boshoff, *Situation Report. Update on the Status of the Army Integration in the DRC* (Pretoria, Institute of Security Studies, 2 September 2005), at 2-3.

[10] 'Congo-Kinshasa: DRC Voters Give Constitution Overwhelming Support', *AllAfrica*, 16 January 2006, available at: <http://www.allafrica.com/stories/200601120003.html>.

[11] 'Congo-Kinshasa. Acte d'engagement de Goma: après l'espoir, l'inquiétude', *Le Potentiel*, 30 January 2008.

[12] Interview with Congolese Senator, Brussels, 3 September 2009. See also Institute of Security Studies, 'The Security Situation in the DRC Since the Arrest of Laurent Nkunda', 23 June 2009, available at: <http://reliefweb.int/rw/rwb.nsf/db900SID/ASAZ-7TAJ9Y?OpenDocument>.

with the consequence that elements in the new units desert to go back to defend those villages that were under their previous influence.[13] Thus, even today, the success of Congo's reconstruction depends largely on events in the Kivus.

Other internal dimensions affect the chances of effective peacebuilding. Political space in the country is getting narrower with opposition virtually being excluded from participation in government despite its performance in the 2006 elections; political pluralism is restricted, the media are either intimidated or corrupted and opposition leaders as well as human rights activists are the target of intimidation and even murder.[14] Substantial challenges include the fragility or non-existence of state institutions; the creation or recreation of accountable governance structures; and the development of an integrated and professional security apparatus that protects civilians rather than abusing them.

At the regional level, the threat posed by the continued presence and operability of foreign troops on Congolese soil and reciprocal accusations of support between Congo and Rwanda led to a common approach to peace and stability in the region through the adoption of the Nairobi Declaration on 9 November 2007.[15] Commitments made in Nairobi included: 1) full cooperation to implement a joint approach to dismantling the ex-FAR Interahamwe as well as suspension of any direct or indirect support – political, material or human – to any national or foreign armed group operating in the DRC; 2) the setting up of a Joint Verification Mechanism and the sharing of information through the Tripartite Plus; and 3) the preparation and submission to Rwanda of a detailed Congolese Plan to disarm and deal with the Interahamwe threat by 1 December 2007. Following Nairobi, an important Tripartite Plus[16] meeting in Addis Abeba in December 2007 sponsored by the US resulted in the decision to normalise diplomatic relations between the members of the Tripartite Plus and to work jointly to eliminate the threats posed by foreign armed groups in the region.[17] A joint verification commission between Rwanda and the DRC and including the US was set up to this effect.

In January 2008, the government convened a large conference in Goma to discuss peace, security and development issues in the Kivus. The conference recommendations[18] together with the Nairobi communiqué and the Goma ceasefire

---

13 EUSEC confidential document, July 2009.

14 Human Rights Watch, 'Letter to the Prime Minister of DR Congo Regarding Public Attacks on Human Rights Organisations', 31 July 2009, available at: <http://www.hrw.org/en/news/2009/07/31/letter-prime-minister-dr-congo-regarding-public-attacks-human-rights-organizations>.

15 Communiqué conjoint du Gouvernement de la République Démocratique du Congo et du Gouvernement du Rwanda sur une approche commune pour mettre fin à la menace pour la paix et la stabilité des deux pays et de la Région des Grands Lacs, available at: <http://www.iss.co.za/dynamic/administration/file_manager/file_links/GLCOM9NOV07FR.PDF?link_id=29&slink_id=5117&link_type=12&slink_type=13&tmpl_id=3>.

16 Gathering representatives from Rwanda, the DRC, Burundi and Uganda.

17 Communiqué conjoint du Gouvernement de la République Démocratique du Congo et de la République du Rwanda sur une approche commune pour mettre fin à la menace pour la paix et la stabilité des deux pays et de la Région des Grands Lacs, *supra* n. 15.

18 'Acte d'engagement de Goma, après l'espoir, l'inquiétude', *Le Potentiel*, 30 January 2008, *supra* n. 11.

agreement form the so-called Amani (Peace) Programme which aims at restoring peace in east DRC through demobilisation of all the armed groups and their reintegration into either the national army or community reintegration programmes supported by UNDP.[19]

The Goma conference was saluted as a major success and an opportunity for all stakeholders in the DRC peacebuilding process. Nevertheless, enthusiasm for the process has probably blinded international and perhaps local actors to the seeds of further fighting in Nkunda's lack of confidence about Kinshasa's real intentions to keep its commitments as well as to the CNDP's lack of willingness to take responsibility for human rights violations or the recruitment of child soldiers.[20]

The role of the EU Special Representative (EUSR) for the Great Lakes Region was particularly instrumental in developing the context leading to these arrangements. EUSR Roeland van de Geer was in fact convinced that elimination of the FDLR would progressively weaken Nkunda's position as a protector of Tutsis' rights in the region and contribute to the elimination of his CNDP movement. The EU's position, combined with fears of Rwandan intervention on Congolese soil as a response to Kabila's threats against Nkunda's movement and a certain fatigue on the part of South Africa in facilitating the resolution of conflicts in the area, was gradually accepted by the US, leading to the progressive configuration of an international consensus on how to deal with the regional implications of the situation in the DRC. In Van de Geer's mind, this was to be done mostly through military pressure rather than action, possibly combined with small surgical attacks intended to capture FDLR leaders and demoralise their troops whilst the 'Nkunda problem' was to be dealt with through dialogue and mediation by the US. The ensuing international division of labour to deal with rebel groups' threats was confirmed (informally) at Goma. Here, Van de Geer also outlined the EU contribution to SSR in the country, consisting of: 1) an EC approach, through implementation of Community projects; 2) an ESDP approach, through the deployment of ESDP missions; and 3) coordinated EU Member States' bilateral initiatives in the DRC. He also recommended establishing an interministerial coordinating mechanism capable of bringing together the different facets of the SSR process and facilitating in particular the interface between police and national defence as well as police and judiciary.[21]

Regional agreements took an uncharacteristic turn at the end of 2008 when bilateral arrangements between the DRC and Rwanda allowed for the deployment of joint operations to fight CNDP/Nkunda and the FDLR (*Forces Démocratiques pour la Libération du Rwanda*, including ex-*genocidaires* in their senior ranks). Similarly, agreements between Uganda and the DRC have resulted in a joint military operation in the western district of Haut Huelé called 'Thunderstorm' (*coup de*

---

[19] Interview with Lt. Col. J. Defabribeckers, Belgian Ministry of Foreign Affairs, 30 March 2009.

[20] Diplomatic document summarising the CNDP's analysis of the Goma conference at a meeting with international facilitators. Unpublished and confidential, 28 January 2008.

[21] Intervention de l'Ambassadeur Roland van de Geer, Représentant Spécial de l'Union Européenne pour la Région des Grands Lacs Africains, Kinshasa, Table Ronde sur la Réforme des Secteur de la Sécurité, 26 February 2008.

*tonnerre*) intended to curb the LRA's presence in the DRC. This cooperation can be saluted as a step forward in the development of good neighbourly relations between the two countries, particularly considering the rise in tensions over the oil exploitation in Lake Albert since 2007. Nevertheless, it has sparked controversy as the terms of the operations have never been made clear, and nor have the number of troops involved or the exit strategies envisaged. Furthermore, in concrete terms, the involvement of Ugandan troops in the DRC has resulted in a recrudescence of rebels' attacks and brutality against local villagers. In a similar vein, FARDC/Rwandese joint operations have resulted in decreased security for local populations as the FDLR has splintered into very small groups across the whole of the Kivu region, penetrating deeper into the forest (as opposed to operating especially in the south and particularly at the border with Rwanda), and is now a more difficult threat to tackle.[22] Besides, decisions over these operations have been taken exclusively by the Congolese executive, without prior consultation with the government, leading to a serious institutional crisis when the president of the National Assembly resigned in protest over the lack of transparency and accountability in the agreements and operations.[23]

## 2.2 Security providers?

Apart from the internal and external dynamics outlined, human and state security in the DRC is consistently undermined by the state of the security forces themselves. Serious weaknesses affect all areas of the security sector.

Central political control of the various branches of the security sector remains weak, partially as a legacy of the transitional period when the president and the four vice-presidents retained control over parallel military groups and, most importantly, as a consequence of badly managed DDR processes. The structural problems of the Congolese security sector were made abundantly clear by the 2007 armed confrontations between Kabila's troops and elements loyal to Jean-Pierre Bemba.[24] They were confirmed and even reinforced throughout 2008 when fighting in the eastern part of Congo highlighted the weakness of the Congolese army and the 'glaring absence of state authority'.[25] Today, EU actors involved in SSR in the DRC admit that the chain of command is malfunctioning, leading everyone to just fight for their own interests. In addition, due to the accelerated integration process, commanders are no longer sure about the structures they preside, which weakens the

---

[22] Interview with Lt.-Colonel J. de Fabribeckers, Belgian Ministry of Foreign Affairs, 30 March 2009.

[23] 'RDC: vers une défenestration annoncée du président de l'Assemblée Nationale', *Documentation et information pour l'Afrique*, 5 March 2009, available at: <http://www.dia-afrique.org/suite.php?newsid=11354>.

[24] H. Hoebeke, 'The EU and "Conflict Peacebuilding" in the DRC', LX *Studia Diplomatica* (2007) 43, at 50.

[25] H. Hoebeke, H. Boshoff and K. Vlassenroot, *Assessing Security Sector Reform and Its Impact on the Kivu Provinces,* Situation Report (Pretoria, Institute of Security Studies, 26 November 2008).

operational capacity of the army, and, vice versa, soldiers are unable to identify their chain of command.[26]

Congolese security forces, particularly the *Forces Armées de la RDC* (FARDC) and the National Police (PN), constitute a major threat to human security in the DRC and a source of destabilisation for the country. Human rights violations on a massive scale continue unabated, as testified repeatedly by the MONUC Human Rights Section. Massacres have occurred most recently in the region of the Bas-Congo, whilst torture, disappearance, rape and ill-treatment are all reported by the population and by human rights organisations, and are attributed to the security forces.[27]

This situation is the result of essentially two factors: on the one hand, the 'working conditions' of the security forces, both the army and the police; and on the other, the widespread, politically sustained and historically rooted culture of impunity. Salaries are very low and irregularly paid, and there are virtually no social security provisions (such as health care, housing and pension schemes) for the soldiers or their families. Training for the police or the army is very basic, except when provided in the framework of small and *ad hoc* bilateral defence agreements, such as in the cases of defence engagements between Belgium or France and the DRC (which nevertheless have a relatively limited impact considering the number of security forces that need to be trained). These poor working conditions result in security forces abusing the local population in order to increase their revenues by pillaging, robbing or bribery.

Corruption is 'institutionalised' in the DRC, resulting in a seemingly never-ending governance crisis driven by predatory dynamics that have marked the DRC's history. Military involvement in the lucrative predation of Congo's resources is well documented and has generated socio-economic networks that are strictly linked to political violence, particularly in the eastern provinces. Moreover, such corruption is not only limited to extractive activities related to mining, but has also taken on a somewhat administrative character in the form of invented and arbitrary fees and taxes imposed by the administration and unpaid security forces with the bless-

---

[26] EUSEC confidential report, July 2009. Telephone interview with former EUSEC member, Brussels, 16 September 2009.

[27] L. Clifford, et al., *Sexual Violence in the Democratic Republic of Congo*, Special Report (Institute for War and Peace Reporting, October 2008). MONUC, *Enquête spéciale sur les événements de mars 2007 à Kinshasa, Résultats préliminaires*, Rapport Spécial (Bureau des Nations Unies pour les Droits de l'Homme en République Démocratique du Congo, January 2008). UN Security Council, *Twenty-Sixth Report of the Secretary-General of the United Nations Organisation Mission in the Democratic Republic of Congo,* S/2008/433, 3 July 2008, available at: <http://daccessdds.un.org/doc/UNDOC/GEN/N08/403/27/IMG/N0840327.pdf?OpenElement>; Division des Droits de l'Homme de la MONUC, *Enquête spéciale sur les événements de février et mars 2008 au Bas Congo*, May 2008, available at: <http://www.reliefweb.int/rw/RWFiles2008.nsf/FilesByRWDocUnidFilename/RMOI-7FLL29-rapport_complet.pdf/$File/rapport_complet.pdf>; Human Rights Watch, ' "On va vous écraser". La restriction de l'espace politique en République Démocratique du Congo', November 2008, available at: <http://www.hrw.org/sites/default/files/reports/drc1108frwebwcover.pdf>.

ing of their political masters who are all too aware of their inability or unwillingness to pay regular salaries.[28]

Abusive behaviour and corruption are compounded by a culture of impunity which is particularly evident at the higher levels of the military chain of command and at the political level. As Davis states: 'Impunity for human rights violations was established as the basis for the new political order as a result of the domination of the political institutions by the belligerents. Concomitantly, impunity was firmly entrenched within the new national army, the FARDC (…).'[29] Even though in principle anyone suspected of crimes against humanity was excluded from the new integrated army, in practice no procedures were put in place to implement sanctions against human rights violators, and civil society organisations have often denounced their 'promotion' to higher ranks in spite of their abusive track record.[30] To top it all up, the justice sector suffers from the same ills and is itself inefficient, understaffed, corrupted and underpaid if paid at all, and completely lacks independence.

## 3. The role of the EU in promoting stability in the DRC

Cooperation between the then Zaire and the European Community was suspended in 1992 as a result of the country's high level of corruption and lack of progress in democratisation. Only humanitarian and emergency aid assistance was provided, until the resumption of full direct cooperation in 2002 when progress of the All-Inclusive Dialogue leading to the Pretoria Agreement was well underway. Since then, the EU has played a very active role in the DRC by participating in the international transitional architecture devised to support it; by contributing to all diplomatic efforts, both internal and external, through the active role of the EU Special Representative for the Great Lakes Region; by financing and supporting the electoral process with election monitors; and by increasing its development cooperation to the point that it is often cited as the largest donor in the DRC.[31] Justice, good governance and institution building, poverty reduction and macro-economic sup-

---

[28] E. Rackley, 'Democratic Republic of the Congo: Undoing Government by Predation', 30 *Disasters* (2006) 417-432; L. Ndikumana and K. Emizet, 'The Economics of Civil War. The Case of the Democratic Republic of Congo', in P. Collier and N. Sambanis, eds., *Understanding Civil War. Evidence and Analysis* (Washington, World Bank 2005) 63-87.

[29] L. Davis, *Justice-Sensitive Security System Reform in the Democratic Republic of Congo* (International Alert and International Center for Transitional Justice 2009), at 16.

[30] Telephone interview with a representative from the *Cadre de Concertation des Femmes Congolaises*, 11 September 2008, and with a representative from Human Rights Watch, DRC Division, 16 September 2008.

[31] The interaction between the tools deployed by the EU to support the transitional period in the DRC has been presented more extensively in M. Martinelli, 'Les opérations EUPOL et EUSEC au Congo: l'UE entre engagement et apprentissage', in B. Delcourt, E. Klimis and M. Martinelli, eds., *L'Union Européenne et la gestion des crises* (Brussels ULB, Presse Universitaire 2008) 85-101. Martinelli, *supra* n. 5; M. Martinelli 'Helping Transition. The European Union Police Mission in DRC (EUPOL KINSHASA) in the Context of EU's Policies in the Great Lakes', 11 *European Foreign Affairs Review* (2006) 379-399. In this chapter, the emphasis is on EU support for SSR.

port represent as many priorities and particular foci of attention for EU intervention in the country. However, alongside these dimensions, great emphasis has been placed on the necessity to stabilise the country and provide the population with the necessary security and predictability. Thus, a great deal of the EU's involvement in the DRC focuses on security matters, and the complexity of the resulting task is reflected by the launch of two military (terminated) and two civilian missions (ongoing).

### 3.1 Military intervention: from Artemis to EUFOR RD Congo

The military intervention in the DRC in 2003 was the first ESDP initiative in Africa. Code-named Artemis,[32] it was a 1,500 strong operation deployed in the capital of Ituri at the request of the UN Secretary-General when Uganda's withdrawal from the province precipitated a crisis that MONUC was unable to control.[33] With France as the 'framework nation' responsible for the operational command, the mandate for the operation was limited to the town of Bunia. Artemis was tasked to, among other things, stabilise security conditions and ensure the protection of internally displaced people and UN and humanitarian personnel. It had a 'Chapter VII' mandate and proved willing to use force. Although of short duration – lasting from June to September 2003 – the operation secured the town and thus prepared the ground for a reinforced MONUC to take over.

Artemis was a case of successful UN-EU cooperation, representing in concrete terms what the European Security Strategy would term, later that same year, 'effective multilateralism'. It demonstrated the EU's operational readiness and proved a good indicator of its ability to act outside its neighbourhood without the use of NATO assets.[34] Finally, it confirmed that ESDP could be put at the service of the wider objectives of other organisations when such objectives are shared by the EU. Far from being a 'one-off' operation,[35] Artemis provided a precedent for subsequent operations, as demonstrated by the UN request to assist MONUC in maintaining peace and stability during the upcoming presidential elections.[36]

With the endorsement of the Congolese authorities, on 30 July 2006,[37] the EU deployed about 400 troops to Kinshasa flanked by a stand-by, battalion-size force stationed in Gabon, bringing the total EU force (plus Turkey and Switzerland as third states) to about 1,800 troops under the command of EU Force Commander Major-General Christian Damay from France. The latter reported to the Operation

---

[32] See Council Joint Action 2003/319/CFSP of 8 May 2003.

[33] C. Mace, 'Operation ARTEMIS: Mission Improbable?', 18 *European Security Review* (Brussels, July 2003).

[34] S. Ulriksen, C. Gourlay and C. Mace, 'Operation ARTEMIS: The Shape of Things to Come?', 1 *International Peacekeeping* (2004) 508-525.

[35] C. Gegout, 'Causes and Consequences of the EU's Military Intervention in the Democratic Republic of Congo: A Realist Explanation', 10 *European Foreign Affairs Review* (2005) 429.

[36] Interview with Mr Aldo Ajello, former EU Special Representative for the Great Lakes Region, 19 January 2006.

[37] Council Joint Action 2006/319/CFSP of 27 April 2006.

Commander, the German Lieutenant-General Karlheinz Viereck, whose headquarters were in Potsdam (with overall command of all elements and logistics of both the force in Kinshasa and the 'stand-by force' in Gabon). EUFOR's objective was to add a rapid reaction capability to MONUC by providing a back-up should the UN troops face serious difficulties in fulfilling their mandate, and to assist them in providing security in the run-up to, during and after the presidential elections. EUFOR was tasked to contribute to the protection of civilians in its areas of deployment; to secure the airport in Kinshasa; and to extract individuals in danger. Twenty-one EU countries contributed troops. However, not least because of Berlin's insistence, the mandate of the mission was limited to a maximum of four months after the first round of elections.[38] In line with this schedule, EUFOR RD Congo was terminated on 30 November 2006.

Although EUFOR was an element of the EU's broader commitment to transition in the DRC, its international political context was different from that of Artemis. If the latter can be cast in terms of crisis management, EUFOR was not characterised by the same urgency and can rather be seen as an example of muscular EU conflict prevention to prevent disruptions of the electoral process. Coordination with the UN in New York and at field level was a clear requirement. In the field, meetings between the two actors were quite frequent and constructive: Major-General Damay, together with the EUSR, established close contacts with MONUC as well as with local authorities. In addition, Lieutenant-General Karlheinz Viereck liaised with the UN Department of Peacekeeping Operations. At the political level, CFSP High Representative Solana, assisted by the EUSR and in coordination with the EU Presidency, acted as the primary point of contact with New York. Cooperation between the two institutions was good, although there were some problems with the exchange of intelligence – linked to the military nature of the operation and the sensitivities that go with it – both in the field and between Brussels and New York.

The Council's Political and Security Committee exercised political control over, and provided strategic direction to, the operation via a chain of command that linked the Operation Commander in Potsdam to the headquarters of the stand-by force in Libreville and, finally, the Force Commander in Kinshasa. In short, communications between Kinshasa and Brussels went via Gabon and Germany. Not surprisingly, this set-up made decision making on the ground rather cumbersome. Unlike Artemis, EUFOR was charged with protecting decision makers and institutions as well as expatriates, but not the ordinary population. The duration of the mandate itself, coinciding with the electoral schedule, meant that EUFOR effectively left the country even before the new president was officially installed, giving the impression of a hasty departure.[39] Moreover, the fact that EUFOR could act in support of MONUC only at the explicit request of the UN force meant that during unrest in

[38] Before the deployment of the mission, the German Defence Minister promised that German troops would be back home before Christmas, mirroring the general unwillingness of Germans to get involved militarily in areas that do not appear to be of strategic importance to their country.

[39] M. Martin, 'A Force for Good? The European Union and Human Security in the Democratic Republic of Congo', 16 *African Security Review* (2007) 71.

Kinshasa following the results of the first round of elections in August 2006, EUFOR's reaction was delayed. In a similar vein, when the building of the Supreme Court of Justice was set on fire, MONUC did not ask for EUFOR's help. This resulted in confusion amongst the local population as to why and when EUFOR was supposed to intervene. Last but not least, the operation highlighted gaps in interoperability among national contingents making up EUFOR, particularly in terms of secure communications capabilities. All these aspects contributed to EUFOR being met with scepticism, if not ridicule, both in and outside Congo, at least initially.

In spite of this, important strong points should also be mentioned in relation to EUFOR because they highlight the specificity of the EU's approach to crisis management, including through forceful stabilisation. Efforts by the mission and its personnel to become accepted by the local population have been favourably remarked upon. The EU's resolve to use force and deter attacks on civilians and the state institutions has been welcomed with appreciation by the Congolese population, highlighting differences with the local perception of MONUC's approach. The EU has been appreciated for clearly and unequivocally communicating to the population the objectives of its presence as well as its 'working methods'; its troops have been noted for befriending the population, including (importantly) women, and not avoiding but rather encouraging contacts with the locals during their functions. An important part of this strategy was an emphasis on supplying clear information to the public and to promote positive perceptions of the operation, through news publications and media broadcasts as well as focus groups and public opinion polling in order to give a voice to local perceptions of the mission. EUFOR RD Congo was appreciated for its visibility, professional behaviour and appearance, its equipment and most of all for its display of resolve making people *feel* protected.[40] This was possible thanks to a clear mandate, good equipment and good logistics that allowed for effective operational support. Furthermore, EUFOR was characterised by the practice of zero tolerance against sexual exploitation and violence by EU forces, and although the troops themselves were not mandated to respond directly to rape episodes, they were trained to direct civilians in need to appropriate contact points.[41] Finally, the way EUFOR handled the attacks on Bemba's headquarters in August 2006 erased the population's initial perception of a biased force deployed in support of Kabila.[42]

---

[40] Author's interview with various representatives from the Congolese National Assembly and the diplomatic community, Kinshasa, June 2007.

[41] See *Final Report on Gender Work inside EUFOR RD Congo* by the Operation Commander of EUFOR RD Congo and the first ESDP mission gender adviser, available at: <http://www.honvedelem.hu/files/9/8008/eu_operation_headquarters_final_gender_report_eufor_rd_con.pdf>.

[42] Although when later on, in November, supporters of Bemba's camp attacked the Supreme Court, MONUC failed to call for EUFOR support, leaving the Europeans frustrated and the locals puzzled as to their role. See Martin, *supra* n. 39, at 73.

## 4. THE EU AND SECURITY SECTOR REFORM IN THE DRC

### 4.1 A country-specific approach

With the Pretoria Agreement,[43] signed on 17 December 2002, participants in the inter-Congolese dialogue abandoned hostilities and embarked on a transition period leading to the adoption of a new constitution and the creation of a government of national unity. Problems persisted however, relating to, for instance, the creation of a unified army and of an efficient and accountable police force. These two aspects represented an essential condition for the restoration of order and of the government's monopoly of the use of force, as well as for the state's capacity to control its territory and its resources and, above all, for allowing citizens to rebuild their confidence in the state as a security and justice provider.

Amongst the priorities identified in the Pretoria Agreement, Article 2 engages all parties to create a restructured and integrated army. Article 3 mentions the retreat of all foreign troops from Congolese soil and the disarmament of all armed groups and militias. Article 5 mentions all measures relating to citizens' safety as well as the security of Congolese institutions and political decision makers. Further to this, the 2003 Memorandum on the Army and Security[44] outlines the mechanisms necessary for the establishment of an integrated Congolese army. Thus, reform of the security sector (SSR) and the disarmament, demobilisation and reintegration of former combatants are at the heart of the Agreement and represent a crucial element of the post-conflict reconstruction effort in the DRC. Similarly, the setting up of an efficient, transparent and accountable police force capable of supporting an efficient judiciary also counts among the priorities identified by the government. As a consequence, comprehensive security sector reform focusing on the armed forces, the police and the judicial sectors has become a sort of 'building site' that sees a plethora of actors, both local and international, working together to ensure its successful completion. For the EU it is an important part of the implementation of its Common Foreign and Security Policy and European Security and Defence Policy in the DRC.

The EU's approach to SSR has been outlined in the previous chapter.[45] However, as regards the DRC, the EU has gone as far as outlining a country-specific approach to SSR. This was finalised by the Council and Commission services in November 2006,[46] following an October 2006 joint Commission/Council evaluation mission to the DRC which underlined the interest of pursuing a comprehensive SSR approach based on a broad definition of the security sector in line with OECD/

---

[43] *Global and Inclusive Agreement on Transition in the Democratic Republic of the Congo: Inter-Congolese Dialogue – Political Negotiations on the Peace Process and on Transition in the DRC*, available at: <http://www.reliefweb.int/rw/rwb.nsf/db900SID/MHII-65G8B8?OpenDocument>.

[44] Memorandum sur l'armée et la sécurité pendant la transition II, Pretoria (6 March 2003), available at: <http://www.congolite.com/doc13.htm>.

[45] See the contribution by Spence to this volume.

[46] *A Comprehensive EU Approach to SSR in the Democratic Republic of Congo*, Document 2473/06 (Brussels, 10 November 2006).

DAC criteria.[47] The document was integrated a few days later with the advice of the EU Military Committee (EUMC), which insisted on the necessity to enhance coordination between ESDP missions, Community activities and Member States' initiatives, as well as with all relevant non-EU actors. The EUMC also insisted on establishing an accountable, effective and efficient security service that 'should ensure *self-sustaining* stability'.[48] Thus identified, there were essentially four principles of a comprehensive Community/ESDP approach to SSR in the country:

- A nationally owned SSR concept: the EU's overall SSR should be developed with the DRC authorities through a process of 'local ownership in partnership';
- The focus of the EU's involvement in SSR is premised on strengthening governance of the security institutions and enhancing service delivery in the security sector;
- SSR is to be treated as a mainstreaming governance and security issue that cuts across Member States' bilateral activities and the EU's external policy instruments (including ESDP and Community programmes);
- The SSR framework must be consistent with a coordination and support mechanism.

From these principles the idea was launched that the two civilian missions (EUPOL and EUSEC) should be established as a single integrated ESDP mission in order to enhance coherence of actions between the EU, the Member States and other actors in the field. However, resistance among Member States to this project has left the composition of the mission untouched.[49] The paper went on to outline EU activities concerning:

A) *The defence sector*, particularly in the field of army integration and the development of a broad strategic defence planning process through preparation of a defence white paper; the provision of flanking measures (such as socio-humanitarian support for the dependents of soldiers of the integrated brigades); and support to the National Assembly in order to enhance civilian oversight of the security forces.

B) *The justice sector*: Following a 2003 organisational audit supported by the European Commission and other partners,[50] the EU's response in the justice sector

---

[47] In 2005, the Development Assistance Committee (DAC) of the OECD approved a series of guidelines establishing the general principles of donors' engagement with SSR. Two years later, it published a Handbook on SSR providing guidance for the implementation of the guidelines. The two documents currently provide the background for the development of national and multilateral SSR strategies for virtually all donors participating in the DAC. See DAC Guidelines and Reference Series, *Security System Reform and Governance* (Paris, 2005) and *OECD DAC Handbook on Security Sector Reform: Supporting Security and Justice* (Paris, 2007).

[48] *Military Advice on a 'Comprehensive EU Approach to SSE in the Democratic Republic of Congo (DRC)'*, Document No. 15862/06, European Union Military Committee (Brussels, 27 November 2006). Emphasis added.

[49] Telephone interview with EU Council representative, Brussels, 11 September 2008.

[50] *Mission Multi-Bailleurs de l'Audit du Système Judiciaire en République Démocratique du Congo. Rapport final des ateliers et du séminaire pour un programme cadre de la Justice en République Démocratique du Congo* (Kinshasa 10-12 November 2004 and 15 November 2004).

has been articulated around the following priorities: the fight against impunity and the application of international human rights standards; human recourse development through the provision of training and equipment; attention to the prison system and to access to justice; regulation of and support to the status of magistrates and the High Council of Magistrates; pay structure reforms; constitutional judiciary institutions; case management and legal information system; and strengthening of the *Commission permanente de réforme du droit congolais* (CPRDC). The ESDP contribution to justice reform in the DRC also envisaged a possible rule of law element with the aim of strengthening coherence with European Commission and Member States' initiatives by providing political and technical support as well as mentoring in the area of military justice.

Further to this, the Commission has been running a justice reform project in the east of the DRC, called REJUSCO,[51] which mainly focuses on capacity building for all personnel working in the judicial sector and on institutional support. Launched in Bunia as a very successful pilot project which included regular payment of judicial personnel salaries, it was extended to Goma and Bukavu in 2007. However, the salary dimension of the initiative was dropped on the understanding that the government should take charge of this. The result is a return to unpaid justice personnel and a drop in the cases brought before court during the second phase of the REJUSCO programme.[52] Similarly, in 2007, the Commission started a Governance Support Programme including a strong institutional justice reform component.

C) *Police*: In line with contributions from South Africa, Belgium, France, Angola and, last but not least, MONUC, the EU context-specific approach to SSR in the DRC has focused on the training and development of an integrated police unit in Kinshasa (described below) through ESDP operations. Besides, following a request from the DRC Ministry of the Interior, the European Commission and MONUC have actively supported the establishment of a *Groupe Mixte de Réflexion de la Police Nationale Congolaise* (GMRRR) gathering together the National Congolese Police (referred to as PNC, in its French abbreviation) and representatives and key international actors working in this policy area. The *Groupe* identified as areas of priority the implementation of a proper police census, the development of policing curricula and the adoption of an organic law on policing. Subsequently, a *Comité Mixte de Suivi* was set up chaired by the Ministry of the Interior which is responsible for police reform implementation in the DRC.

On the basis of these priorities, the Council and the Commission have proceeded to share their tasks on the ground with an ESDP mission to mentor and monitor the setting up and working methods of an integrated police unit and EC efforts to establish clear criteria for recruitment, training and qualifications of the PNC as well as

---

[51] For more information on this programme as well as partner donors and activities, see: <http://www.rejusco.org>.

[52] Telephone interview with Human Rights Watch representative, Kinshasa, 16 September 2008.

for the development of a nationwide qualitative and quantitative census of the police.

## 4.2 EUPOL Kinshasa[53]

The EU has shown a clear commitment to supporting the Congolese government in virtually all of these areas.[54] In 2003, the government of the DRC requested the EU High Representative to provide assistance in setting up an Integrated Police Unit (IPU) to ensure the protection of the state institutions and reinforce the internal security apparatus. In December of the same year, the Political and Security Committee (PSC) agreed on the establishment of the IPU following a three-strand approach: 1) technical assistance and rehabilitation of a training centre and provision of basic equipment for the IPU (with the exception of arms and anti-riot equipment); 2) provision of adequate training; and 3) follow-up, monitoring and mentoring of the concrete implementation of IPU's mandate after the initial training phase.[55]

The three phases required the collaboration of the EU Council and Commission to ensure their implementation. Thus, the Commission proceeded to finance, through EDF funds, the basic training of police officers recruited to form an IPU of 1,008 men in charge of protecting the institutions and political leaders of the transition government. It has also been involved in the restoration of a training centre and the provision of basic equipment. The 'Community aspect' of the mission was terminated on 30 April 2005 and was followed up by an ESDP mission – EUPOL Kinshasa – deployed to guide and supervise the IPU in carrying out its policing tasks.[56]

Whilst creating some synergies between the Council and the Commission, the IPU project also highlighted some institutional rivalry and different institutional cultures. Reflecting its long-standing experience in development-oriented work based on local capacity and institution building, the Commission favoured deploying a small team of no more than 15 subcontracted independent experts, equipped with a precise mandate and terms of reference. Conversely, the Council preferred a crisis management approach focused on a rapid response to a well-identified situation requiring the coordination of multiple tasks by a centrally located actor; the rapid deployment of an adequate number of personnel and equipment; and a well-defined, hierarchically organised chain of command through which Brussels could

---

53 Council Joint Action 2004/847/CFSP of 9 December 2004; Council Joint Action 2005/822/CFSP of 21 November 2005; and Council Joint Action 2006/300/CFSP of 21 April 2006

54 Statement by H.E. Mr Dirk Jan van den Berg, Permanent Representative of the Netherlands to the United Nations on behalf of the European Union, on the report of the Security Council mission to Central Africa, 21-25 November 2004.

55 Council Joint Action 2004/494/CFSP of 17 May 2004 on European Union support to the establishment of the Integrated Police Unit in the Democratic Republic of the Congo (DRC). See also N. Pauwels, 'EUPOL Kinshasa: Testing EU Coordination, Coherence and Commitment to Africa', 25 *European Security Review* (2005), available at: <http://www.isis-europe.org/pdf/esr_26.pdf>.

56 Ibid.

exercise control over the mission. A clear division of labour between the two institutions reconciled these opposing views.

Launched in April 2005, EUPOL Kinshasa was mandated 'to monitor, mentor, and advise the setting up and initial running of the IPU in order to ensure that the IPU acts (...) according to international best practices.' Concretely, it assisted the IPU in establishing an effective chain of command and in developing the leadership capacities of its senior officers. Also, EUPOL advisers accompanied the IPU on patrols of areas where official buildings were located, helped in the identification of operational shortcomings and offered recommendations on how to overcome them. Finally, the mission verified that the military equipment distributed to the IPU was used in strict accordance with European standards.[57]

### 4.3 EUPOL RD Congo[58]

If EUPOL Kinshasa fitted the logic of international support during the transitional period, EUPOL RD Congo is an expression of continued EU engagement in the country with a view to reforming its security sector focusing particularly on the police and its interaction with the judiciary. This is not an easy task considering that the Congolese police suffer from logistics and equipment shortages, lack of capacity and adequate training, as well as poor working conditions, and are well known for abuses of power, corruption and ill-practices, contributing with its behaviour to undermining human security in the country and to a lack of confidence among the population in the Congolese authorities and the agents of order.[59]

Reflecting its wider mandate, EUPOL RD Congo personnel has increased and diversified. Launched on 1 July 2007, it currently counts fifty-three international agents (contributed by nine Member States as well as Switzerland and Angola), including police officers, criminal justice experts and experts in the cross-cutting aspects of security sector reform. In particular, it has joint expertise with EUSEC RD Congo in the fields of human rights, children associated with armed forces or armed groups, and gender equality.[60]

The mandate of the mission is to provide advice and assistance for security sector reform with the aim of contributing to Congolese efforts to reform and restructure the National Congolese Police (PNC) in its interaction with the judicial system.

---

57 For a detailed account of EUPOL Kinshasa, see Martinelli, *supra* n. 31.

58 Council Joint Action 2007/405/CFSP of 12 June 2007, Council Joint Action 2008/38/CFSP of 20 December 2007; Council Joint Action 2008/485/CFSP of 23 June 2008; and Council Joint Action 2009/466/CFSP of 15 June 2009.

59 See, for instance, MONUC, Human Rights Division, *Enquête spéciale sur les événements de février et mars 2008 au Bas Congo*, Special Report (May 2008), at 11-18. Human Rights Watch, *World Report 2009* (New York, January 2009), at 61-65.

60 European Union Factsheet, 'EU Police Mission for the DRC – EUPOL RD Congo' (November 2008), available at: <http://consilium.europa.eu/uedocs/cmsUpload/081117-Factsheet_EUPOL_RD_Congo-version4_EN.pdf>.

Such assistance is provided directly to the relevant Congolese authorities and through the Police Reform Monitoring Committee[61] and the Joint Committee on Justice.[62]

Consistent with the EU's overall objective of supporting the rule of law, EUPOL RD Congo has also contributed its expertise to the Auditing Inspectorate which, under the responsibility of the Ministry of the Interior, is currently being developed to handle any criminal, administrative or financial offences committed by the police. Further initiatives intended to build capacity of the PNC include assistance to the development and training of a Police Research and Intervention (PRI) unit to strengthen the Congolese Criminal Police and support in the establishment of a Coordination, Command and Control Centre (C3C) with a national and provincial dimension.

### 4.4 **EUSEC RD Congo**[63]

Disarmament and demobilisation, on the one side, and the integration of former combatants into the military, on the other, have been central features of the Congolese peacebuilding process. Another ESDP mission – EUSEC – is an important player in this area. Following a request by the DRC government, it offers technical assistance and practical support for the creation of leaner, professional and accountable armed forces. EUSEC, which was launched in June 2005, is thus conceptually and operationally different from EUPOL as it focuses on the army rather than the police. Currently comprising some 46 people, it has given support to projects such as the payment of soldiers' wages ('chain of payments project' or CHOPA) and the drawing up of a military statute and administrative and financial regulations, and has provided technical and logistical support for the biometric census of all DRC troops.

The mandate of EUSEC is:

> 'to provide advice and assistance for security sector reform in the DRC with the aim of contributing to a successful integration of the army (...) while taking care to promote policies compatible with human rights and international humanitarian law, democratic standards and the principles of good governance, transparency and respect for the rule of law.'

---

[61] The CSRP provides a coordinating mechanism bringing together all ministers concerned by the reform of the national police and international partners engaged in supporting it, for consultation and exchange of views. Its main priority is the development of a Global Action Plan for the Reform of the Police.

[62] Council Joint Action 2007/405/CFSP of 12 June 2007 on the European Union police mission undertaken in the framework of reform of the security sector (SSR) and its interface with the system of justice in the Democratic Republic of Congo (EUPOL RD Congo), *OJ* 2007 L 151/46, at 48.

[63] Council Joint Action 2005/355/CFSP of 2 May 2005; Council Joint Action 2007/192/CFSP of 27 March 2007; Council Joint Action 2008/491/CFSP of 26 June 2008 amending and extending Council Joint Action 2007/406/CFSP on the European Union mission to provide advice and assistance for security sector reform in the Democratic Republic of the Congo (EUSEC RD Congo).

The mission, headed by the French General Jean-Paul Michel since June 2008, has an office in Kinshasa and cells in Kisangani, Goma, Bukavu and Bunia. In Kinshasa, mission staff are assigned to key posts in the Congolese administration, such as the private office of the Defence Minister, the army general staff and the National Committee for Disarmament, Demobilisation and Reintegration. As in all civilian ESDP operations, the head of mission is responsible for the day-to-day management. Mission members are seconded by Member States or EU institutions and remain under the control of the sending authority which covers all costs relating to the secondment and deals with any complaints of or about seconded personnel. The chain of command linking EUSEC to Brussels is the same as in the case of EUPOL Kinshasa, as is its funding source, the CFSP budget.

In line with its mandate, EUSEC supports and mentors the disarmament, demobilisation and reintegration processes, and continues to work on reforming the chain of payment of the armed forces. The latter was identified as a major problem by the EU fact-finding mission preparing the launch of EUSEC. It concluded that there was a complete assimilation between the chain of command and the chain of payment. This created an ideal breeding ground for corruption. Money and food for the troops that was to be distributed through the military hierarchy disappeared as it was 'privatised' by senior officers. The rank and file, in turn, resorted to extorting money and food from the population. Furthermore, the number of troops, estimated at 120,000 by EU experts and at three times that level by local sources, was inflated to maximise the illicit gains. All this reinforced the mistrust between the population and the military, further widening the gap between the 'rulers' and the 'ruled' in the DRC. To address this problem, EUSEC has worked (since 2005) on decoupling the system of payment from the chain of command by transferring the former to the Defence Ministry and developing the Ministry's institutional capacity to manage the additional task. Besides tackling corruption, a regularly paid and professional army is more appealing to those ex-combatants who have been opposed to their integration into it. The identification of 130,000 military personnel[64] through the biometric census mentioned above is meant to increase transparency in the administration, thus avoiding overinflated budgets for the payment of 'ghost' soldiers, as well as to increase control over personnel intakes, providing the basis for the development of a human resources policy in the armed forces.

Although formally EUSEC has been a response to a request for assistance by Congolese authorities, its rationale lies in the strategic interests of two Member States, France and Belgium, which have been deeply involved in defence programmes in the DRC. There was some reluctance on the part of other EU capitals to get involved in and financially support a Congolese security sector reform mission. This was partly due to the suspicion that France wanted to use the European platform to finance its activities in the area. While these doubts translated into a rather small mission, EUSEC has had some success: it is grounded in locally identified

---

64 EU Factsheet on EUSEC (March 2009), available at: <http://www.consilium.europa.eu/uedocs/cmsUpload/090327%20Factsheet%20EUSEC%20RD%20Congo%20-%20version%204_EN.pdf>.

needs and an awareness of local constraints. It attempts to tackle issues such as corruption, which may lead to a redefinition by Congolese officials of acceptable and unacceptable behaviour on the part of locals and donors alike. The potential impact of the mission thus goes beyond the security sector as such and addresses issues of governance in the DRC with the aim of promoting transparency and accountability. It is also a response to the need for donors' coordination on SSR initiatives, albeit Congolese and international actors' attitudes towards coordination mitigate its success in this area. The inclusion of an adviser in charge of civil-military relations and of supporting Congolese authorities by suggesting measures to build confidence between civil society and the defence sector (including through involvement of parliament) is one step towards increasing the mission's role in security governance[65] and creates synergies with the human rights and gender dimensions.

## 5. The contribution of ESDP to peace and stability in the DRC: Some preliminary reflections

### 5.1 Strengths

ESDP missions in the DRC have been innovative from many points of view. These have partly been discussed above, but it is worth noting them more explicitly with reference to their impact on peacebuilding and moving from an institutional and technical perspective to reflect on how 'Community working methods' and the approach developed by the European Commission in crisis management have effectively informed ESDP work on the ground.

Amongst the most innovative aspects, EUFOR has benefited for the first time from the inclusion of a gender focal point to 'guide' and coordinate the gender dimension of the mission. EUFOR instigated several activities to integrate a gender dimension, such as creating a structure of gender focal points throughout the mission units to further raise gender awareness and promote gender training; and taking female personnel on foot patrols to engage with the population. EUFOR experience has been followed up by the decisions to include a gender dimension and to appoint a gender adviser for EUSEC and EUPOL.[66] Since then, the Council has worked with a checklist to ensure gender mainstreaming and implementation of UN Security Council Resolution 1325[67] in the planning and conduct of ESDP operations.[68] Whilst this is partly motivated by a need to make operations more efficient on the ground, in the DRC it is also a reflection of the particular human security

---

65 From October 2009.

66 See in particular J. Valenius, *Gender Mainstreaming in ESDP Missions,* Chaillot Paper No. 101 (Paris, EU-ISS, May 2007).

67 UN Security Council Resolution 1325 (2000) adopted by the Security Council at its 4213th Meeting (31 October 2000), S/RES/1325 2000, available at: <http://www.un.org/events/res_1325e.pdf>.

68 EU Council Document 12068/06, Brussels, 12 July 2006.

condition suffered by women and an attempt to signal the attention of the EU to the gender dimension of the conflict, including through increased women's participation in the security forces. With reference to DDR, the EUSEC gender adviser highlighted that female combatants were not registered correctly – the consequence being that married women and their children did not receive the same benefits as their male colleagues – thus allowing Congolese authorities to address this anomaly.

Countering gender-based violence, a phenomenon which has taken on catastrophic dimensions in the DRC, is also part of the work of EUPOL and EUSEC. The missions form part of the UN Task Force on sexual violence, coordinated by the UN special adviser for sexual violence, and in this framework they participate in the development of action plans on impunity and SSR. Further to this, they offer advice to the DRC authorities on legal structures (particularly regarding access to justice for women) and on reform of the police and army through gender-sensitive training.

Originally limited in their financial capacity to effectively support local women's needs, the EUPOL and EUSEC gender advisers have been able to benefit from a small grant set aside by the UK Department for International Development (DfID) to help them implement initiatives for leaders of women's groups in the military camps and for alphabetisation and teaching of income-generating skills.[69] In doing so, the ESDP missions have collaborated with local NGOs, thus ensuring cross-fertilisation of Community and intergovernmental working methods. Obviously, a lot of work remains to be done, but it is an important signal to civil society and decision makers alike of the values that underpin an EU approach to peacebuilding through ESDP. Attention to local actors, although not formally made explicit in policy reflection and of limited impact, is part of the important effect that ESDP missions can have on local culture and in building bridges between decision makers and the population, thus contributing to confidence building between these actors.

Similarly, in the framework of army reform, EUSEC conducted a feasibility study for the setting up of an *Ecole d'administration*, designed to train army officers in administration as part of the modernisation of the Congolese administration; it has contributed to the elaboration of military statutes and administrative and financial regulations for the army. In the same framework, EUSEC has also supported the IT training of 150 military and civilian personnel of the FARDC.

Best practices of the missions also include informal communication processes and regular meetings with the European Commission Delegation on the ground, particularly in the framework of the European Working Group on SSR, as well as with civil society organisations. Finally, EUSEC has also been successful in retaining a strategic position within the different actors involved in the reform of the Congolese security sector. This has allowed the mission to react quickly to local blockages and to exploit opportunities for action, as well as to gain in credibility

---

[69] For a fuller overview of gender and ESDP operations in the DRC see G. Gya, C. Isaksson and M. Martinelli, 'Report on ESDP Missions in the DR Congo', background study for the conference *From Commitment to Action: The EU Delivering to Women in Conflict and Post-Conflict*, Brussels, UNIFEM, December 2008.

with international partners. Immediate results include the relationship established with the United States as an important non-EU actor; the appointment, in late February 2009, of a US liaison officer working closely with EUSEC; and the signing of a technical agreement between MONUC and EUSEC allowing for the implementation of MONUC's revised mandate which explicitly states MONUC's need to work in close coordination with EUSEC.[70]

## 5.2 Weaknesses

Evaluating the ESDP contribution to peacebuilding in the DRC is not an easy task. Tangible results directly attributable to EU intervention are difficult to identify and often interplay with several actors, at several locations (DRC, Brussels, New York, etc.) and with several initiatives. The 2002 peace accord left a number of problems unresolved, including the establishment of a unified army and of an effective and accountable police. Whilst the EU is supporting the DRC in this area, the transitional period has been marked by persisting mistrust between rival political groups which have kept a grip on their own armed militias. The state, in turn, has not been a neutral provider of public security but an interested party in the local power game. This situation has made many local actors reluctant to move forward with security sector reform and unwilling to rely on the public police and the armed forces for the maintenance of peace and security.[71] Things have not improved greatly since SSR has been defined as the central component of the national and international policy toolkit in the DRC's post-conflict stabilisation, including through the improvement of human security and the firm establishment of state authority.[72] Not only do Congolese authorities show a marked preference for playing donors off against one another and maximising their gains through bilateral rather than multilateral relations, but donors themselves are entangled in a complex set of motivations that do not allow for easy coordination. These include the need for visibility of own initiatives, which is best achieved through bilateral approaches to SSR (thus French and Belgian defence programmes do not always promote coherence of EU efforts)[73] and the ambition to occupy a privileged position at the SSR table with resulting access to very sensitive issues of national sovereignty, thus encouraging competition. International leadership on SSR issues in the DRC has recently been clearly defined through the setting up of an SSR Cell within MONUC in charge of providing coordination of all international partners involved in SSR activities, with EUSEC's support. The Cell arranges regular meetings with all partners in the *Group de Travail RSS.*

Sustainability of the reforms encouraged by donors is another major issue and partially refers to coordination and harmonisation issues. For instance, the EUPOL

---

70 EU Council Document 7081/09, *Rapport trimestriel de la mission EUSEC RD Congo*, Brussels, 2 March 2009.

71 International Crisis Group, *Africa Policy Briefing No. 34* (Brussels, 2005).

72 Hoebeke, et al., *supra* n. 25, at 1.

73 K. Berwouts, 'La contribution contre-productive de la Belgique à l'armée congolaise', *La Libre Belgique*, 22 July 2008, 32.

mission has had positive results, at least as regards the Integrated Police Unit and other specialised units, such as the Rapid Intervention Police (French acronym: PIR), set up in the framework of bilateral cooperation projects (in this instance between Angola and France). These units have been noted for working professionally and have a deterrent function on the ground, partially owing to the supervision and training provided by EUPOL and to the bilateral cooperation projects. A non-negligible element of this professional ethos has to do with the extra payment provided together with the ongoing training organised for the police, but it remains questionable whether without the assistance provided by Europe and the international community, such police units would not disintegrate or become divided among the different political factions and ethnic groups and revert to sub-optimal standards of behaviour. Linked to this is the problem of harmonisation of training methods and equipment. To date, there is no unified approach to the training of the Congolese forces and police, and contributing donors each tend to refer to their national training programmes.[74]

Also important is the soaring issue of evaluation, lessons learned and collection of evidence reflecting on the link between EU and international actors' intervention to train and equip local security forces and improved standards of behaviour. Even if preliminary accounts seem to indicate that more appropriate equipment, regular payment of salaries and proper training do result in badly needed changes in professional behaviour, this is strictly limited to the few police and army units that are the object of targeted and *ad hoc* international support. These elements are missing from the EU's approach to SSR in the DRC. Officials in the European Commission point to the need for increased rigour in collecting lessons learned; greater transparency in sharing lessons learned across EU Pillars and institutions; and more readiness to integrate them into improved terms of engagement and mission operational plans.[75] Accounts of abuses and human rights violations by security forces are so widespread that it remains questionable whether these initiatives are effectively impacting the human security of the ultimate beneficiaries of such interventions, i.e., the Congolese population.

This also links to the already cited endemic impunity. Even when notions of human rights and professional behaviour are included in international training programmes, without strong internal controls in security institutions and in the absence of an effective justice system it remains very difficult to combat the widespread abuse of power. It is all very well for the ESDP missions to include a rule of law expert, but the fight against impunity must go beyond technical assistance and include action at the legislative, justice and diplomatic level, adding political leverage to the relations between donors and security and political actors in the DRC. As

---

[74] Assembly of the WEU, *European Union Operations in the Democratic Republic of Congo (DRC) – Reply to the Council*, Doc. A/1954 (20 December 2006), available at: <http://www.assembly-weu.org/en/documents/sessions_ordinaires/rpt/2006/1954.php#P201_44933>.

[75] Interview with EU official from DG RELEX, European Commission, Brussels, 6 April 2009, and with Council representative from DG 8, Defence Issues of Crisis Management, Council General Secretariat, Brussels, 10 September 2008.

documented by Davis, impunity relates to, amongst other things, the link between disarmament, demobilisation and reintegration (DDR) initiatives and SSR, which is all the more relevant in the follow-up to the Amani process. She states: 'Because using stricter selection criteria – including on human rights grounds – has not been part of the DDR processes in the DRC to date, the risk is that the armed groups would not accept it now, when there is no accompanying scrutiny of the current FARDC.'[76]

Moving on to problems created by EU structures and processes, the different institutional cultures informing Council and Commission interventions in crisis areas have been troubling the EU's peacebuilding efforts. This was especially evident in the case of EUPOL Kinshasa, but the point can be applied more generally. The EU Council squarely frames security sector reform as a tool that may play an important role in serving the EU's strategic objectives as outlined in the European Security Strategy. Conversely, the European Commission's institution-building agenda views security sector reform in terms of both state and human security and regards the military only as one instrument for providing security for the population. For the Commission, security sector reform is part and parcel of its objective to strengthen good governance, democracy, the rule of law and protection of human rights and to efficiently use public resources. As such, the Commission's assistance in SSR goes beyond the state and its institutions to include civil society but may also, as a result, become less focused. These interinstitutional differences and rivalries have been partially remedied by the agreement between the Commission and the Council on a comprehensive EU approach to security sector reform in the DRC which effectively provides a road-map for bridging short and long-term aspects of SSR; favouring a nationally owned reform concept developed in partnership with the international community and framed by a good governance agenda;[77] increasing EU-UN cooperation on reforms in this issue area; and meeting the need for coordination among international stakeholders and between them and the host government.

Finally and as importantly, there is the issue of national ownership of the SSR process and, by implication, of peacebuilding. Much of SSR in the DRC is 'done to them' rather than 'by them'. One cannot avoid the impression that it is something heavily pushed, shaped and determined by external actors. In spite of positive signals, such as the organisation of annual round tables and the adoption of a master plan for reforming the army, international actors point to the lack of sustained participation by Congolese representatives in the local coordination mechanisms[78] that are intended to bring together donors and local authorities on issues of SSR. The plan itself is always presented as if in draft form and waiting for further adjustments, and a committee for its implementation has never been set up. This is tantamount to effective feet-dragging and results in the process being slowed down, thus

---

76 Davis, *supra* n. 29, at 17.

77 Even if one must realistically admit that such local ownership is slow to materialise.

78 Such as the various *Comités de suivi* for the defence, police and justice sector.

not reflecting any sense of urgency on the part of Congolese decision makers to address human security concerns as a matter of priority

Lack of political will only partially explains this attitude which is reinforced by different cultural understandings of SSR. Security actors in the DRC see themselves as serving the state's and not the population's security. This 'hard' security attitude is reflected in the militarisation of the reformed police through the appointment of high-ranking military officers to police command positions and in the tendency to flank police operations to control crowds and unrest by military involvement. As long as the Congolese themselves do not develop a clearer and broader understanding of what 'security' means to them and how best to achieve it, any international effort designed to reform the DRC security forces is bound to be unsustainable and irrelevant to the local context.

## 6. Conclusion: Promoting peacebuilding through SSR

An evaluation of how ESDP missions focusing on reform of the security sector in the DRC contribute(d) to peacebuilding in the country must start from the basic understanding that SSR is a very long process. As such, it may not be smooth and may be marked by successes and failures alike, and encompasses cultural, political and technical aspects. Clear-cut judgments are therefore very difficult to make. The capacities of post-conflict and fragile states such as the DRC cannot bear the weight of, or meet the demands placed on them by, SSR programmes. These in turn tend to focus on short-term objectives to strengthen capacities of security and justice providers; do not consider whether public revenues can sustain SSR programming past the expiration of the donors' assistance; and may not reflect on the local cultural value systems and historical legacies and on whether SSR efforts are sustainable. The international approach to SSR, including the EU's approach, seems particularly focused on increasing efficiency of the army and of the police, but addressing abusive behaviour, particularly of the former, has yet to alleviate the population's security concerns in any meaningful way. With regard to the latter, international attention for the prison system counts amongst the many 'Cinderellas' of SSR in the DRC, and the need to reform the police and detention facilities remains a key concern of the population across the country.[79] In the DRC, as elsewhere, donors have not been able to enlarge this technical understanding of SSR. Too little attention is paid to issues of impunity and democratic control and oversight of the security forces, the result being a very limited impact on human security.

SSR can be understood as effective service delivery in the security sector, but at its core are also considerations of governance and accountability. Thus, any SSR policy should focus on supporting the development of effective and efficient security institutions that serve the security interests of citizens, society and the state alike. For the moment, this is not really happening. However, the experience in the

---

[79] Davis, *supra* n. 29, at 20.

DRC highlights some of the potentials and limits of the EU's ambition to be an effective international peacebuilder. Arguably, the key structural limit is that 'internationals' find it hard, if not impossible, to promote such reforms if the locals do not cooperate. In the case of the DRC, many local stakeholders show little interest in having accountable and professional police services and armed forces. Beyond structural weaknesses, the events in 2007 and 2008 have brought to light three points. On the one hand, all the limits of international engagement in support of security sector reform call for a critical evaluation indicating urgent measures of redress to increase the chances of successful SSR. On the other hand, it appears quite obvious that SSR in the DRC cannot take place without sustained international involvement in terms of resources, expertise and political mobilisation. Finally, it is an absolute necessity to develop Congolese ownership of the process without which international efforts are bound to prove unsuccessful and wasteful. Unfortunately, Congolese authorities seem to have mistaken ownership for intolerance of external intervention in sensitive areas such as security and fight against corruption. Whilst this is understandable, it is also unsustainable as it is not compensated by the political will to mobilise Congolese political resources to carry the project forward. Interministerial coordination at the level of the Congolese authorities is not materialising either. SSR is at the crossroads of several ministries and their competences and requires a high level of integration. This is extremely difficult to realise as ministries are run as personal fiefdoms of political personalities. The nomination of a new team within the Defence Ministry in February 2009 raised hopes of renewed relations and increased participation of key Congolese stakeholders in the reform process. However, this is slow in materialising and contingent on the setting up of a *Comité de Suivi pour la Reforme de l'Armée* which would provide the forum for structured international/local engagement in army reform.

With regard to the EU, one must also realistically consider the enormity of the challenge ahead compared with very ambitious objectives and the relatively small resources deployed. This helps not to set standards too high but sadly also encourages a 'poor' notion of success and a compromised understanding of peacebuilding.

Effective security sector reforms require a combination of short and longer-term measures. The EU is well positioned in this regard as it can act through flexible modules, including quick-impact interventions carried out under the CFSP/ESDP and longer-term European Community programmes. Flexibility is slowly being incorporated into ESDP missions through concrete steps such as the creation of a project cell within EUPOL RC Congo to finance small projects in support of and within the mission's mandate through the CFSP budget.[80] Also, the variety of tasks and coordination groups in which EUSEC/EUPOL representatives are involved, dealing with such policy areas as rule of law, gender, human rights and justice issues, are all important components of a comprehensive approach to peacebuilding. The challenge is to stay engaged in the long term. The case of the DRC illustrates

[80] EU Council Document 7088/09, *Implementation of a Project Cell within EUPOL RD Congo*, Brussels, 2 March 2009.

the synergies that can be generated by joining diplomacy, military force and development aid. Furthermore, the progressive blurring of Commission and Council initiatives holds the potential for a cross-fertilisation of methods, which may improve on the overall coherence of ESDP operations in crisis areas and the effectiveness of the EU's approach to peacebuilding.

# Chapter 10
# THE EUROPEAN UNION AND PEACEBUILDING: THE CASE OF CHAD

**Cees Wittebrood* and Christophe Gadrey****

## 1. Introduction

In 2007, the European Union (EU) took the initiative to help promote peace and security in the African region covered by western Sudan, eastern Chad and north eastern Central African Republic (CAR). For a considerable length of time this region had been affected by various internal and cross-border conflicts, most notably in the Darfur region of Sudan. Convinced that only a truly comprehensive approach could effectively address the various conflicts in this region, the EU decided to contribute to international efforts aimed at the stabilisation of the region by deploying a wide range of tools and instruments to tackle the political, security, development and humanitarian challenges. This included the deployment of a military mission to Chad and CAR from 15 March 2008 to 15 March 2009, called EUFOR TChad/RCA (hereafter EUFOR). It was the first EU autonomous military operation of such a scale.[1]

EUFOR was established on the initiative of France, which initially pleaded in favour of the creation of humanitarian corridors to ensure security and access. When it became clear that this would be neither feasible nor desirable, the French changed tack. Since the Chadian authorities were not ready to accept the immediate deployment of a UN military operation, France encouraged the EU to set up its own military mission and develop a crisis management concept within the framework of the European Security and Defence Policy (ESDP).

From the outset, EUFOR was conceived as a temporary bridging operation with a view to providing security and protection while allowing for the full deployment of a more long-term United Nations Mission in CAR and Chad (MINURCAT). EUFOR was conducted on the basis of UN Security Council Resolution 1778 (2007)[2]

* Head of Unit for Humanitarian Operations in Africa, Directorate-General for Humanitarian Aid (DG ECHO), European Commission. The views expressed in the chapter are the author's own and do not represent the official position of any organisation or institution.

** Desk Officer for Chad, DG ECHO, European Commission. The same disclaimer applies.

[1] In comparison with EUFOR's 3,700 troops, Operation Artemis accounted for 2,000 troops from 14 Member States as well as Brazil, Canada and South Africa.

[2] Security Council Resolution 1778 of 25 September 2007.

*S. Blockmans, J. Wouters & T. Ruys, eds., The European Union and Peacebuilding*

with the agreement of the Chadian and Central African Republic governments. It lasted until 15 March 2009, when the United Nations took over in accordance with Security Council Resolution 1861 (2009).[3]

The deployment of EUFOR should be understood in the context of the broader crisis in the region, notably in Darfur, in neighbouring Sudan. It was precisely because the crisis in Darfur was figuring so high on the international agenda that France wanted the EU to be fully involved. Without the crisis in Darfur the EU would most likely not have launched such a military operation in Chad. In conducting this operation, the EU aimed at complementing its action in support of other efforts to tackle the crisis in Darfur as part of a wider regional approach.

The central question is whether the EU has been able to achieve its objective of developing and implementing a comprehensive, complementary and coordinated approach so as to effectively address the issue of peace, security and stability in this part of Africa, notably in Chad. A subsidiary question is whether EUFOR has been an effective tool in that regard. With a view to answering these questions, the regional context and different drivers of the conflict situation will be described (section 2), after which the multi-faceted nature of the EU response will be explained in more detail (section 3). The lessons learned from this response will be examined in section 4, with finally some concluding remarks at the end (section 5).

## 2. Regional context

Sudan, Chad and CAR form a region in the heart of Africa where the Horn meets Central and West Africa. The borders of these countries have been defined by the whims of history, drawn by former colonial powers, with no relation to the ethnic demography of the region. The countries are made up of large territories endowed with natural resources and opportunities but also full of risks and tensions. Chad and CAR are among the poorest countries in the world.[4] State authorities have few means and little capacity to effectively rule and govern. This has not been without major consequences. Demographic factors coupled with an intense competition for access to and use of agricultural land, food and water have led to widespread conflicts between local tribes. There has always been a struggle for survival in an extremely harsh environment. Localised low-intensity conflicts existed alongside politically inspired rebellions. The regimes of Presidents Omar al-Bashir (Sudan), Idriss Déby (Chad) and François Bozizé (CAR) all faced a multitude of rebel insurgencies. Historically, insurgency came close to being a permanent feature of politics in the region. Although these insurgencies were often portrayed as a simple confrontation between the Christian-African agricultural south and the Muslim-Arabic nomadic north, their origin lay more in the socio-economic and political

---

[3] Security Council Resolution 1861 of 14 January 2009.

[4] In the Human Development Index, Chad ranks 175$^{th}$ and CAR 179$^{th}$ on a total of 182 countries, *Human Development Report 2009*, UNDP.

marginalisation of the peripheral regions of the countries. Furthermore, the limited ability of the state authorities to provide effective governance over the entire territory, especially the lack of an effective police and legal system and the conflict between traditional and modern justice, provided an ideal breeding ground for armed opposition groups or rebel movements dissatisfied with the status quo.

The problems in Chad and CAR should be seen in a regional context. Contrary to a widely existing misconception that the situation in the two countries is no more than a simple spill-over from the war in Darfur, the conflict context underlying the insecurity, instability and corresponding population movements is much more complicated.

The region encompassing Sudan, Chad and CAR is tightly linked by ethnic, social, economic and political ties and in many instances by common historical experiences.[5] Partly because of this, the crisis in Darfur has fuelled instability in neighbouring Chad and CAR, having internal political and security problems themselves. Armed opposition and rebel movements easily move across borders and constitute a major cause of destabilisation in the region. Armed groups in Chad are reportedly supported by the Sudanese government in Khartoum, while similar groups in Darfur get support from the Chadian government in N'Djamena. The overall security situation in the region has been compounded by the issuance by the International Criminal Court in March 2009 of an arrest warrant against Sudanese President Al-Bashir.[6]

The conflicts have been fuelled by various factors, including the abundance of revenues from oil production,[7] the influx of arms and the demographic changes putting increasing pressure on dwindling natural resources. Weak state control, corruption and impunity have enabled widespread trafficking and banditry, including killings, kidnapping and hijacking. These developments have translated into a deeply entrenched humanitarian crisis. The needs of the vulnerable groups of the population have increased while overall security and access have decreased. In essence, the conflict in Chad is driven by three interlinked and volatile trends:

1) the crisis in Darfur, with the government of Sudan's support to Chadian armed opposition groups, on the one hand, and close Chadian ties to Darfur militias, on the other – in accordance with the traditional war logic of 'the enemy of my enemy is my friend';
2) the political crisis inside Chad, in particular the impediments to the democratisation process and to the promotion of good governance and the rule of law; and
3) an increase in local conflicts in eastern Chad, mainly based on clan and ethnic allegiances and on common crime.

---

[5] See J. Giroux, D. Lanz and D. Sguaitamatti, *The Tormented Triangle: The Regionalisation of Conflict in Sudan, Chad and the Central African Republic*, Working Paper No. 47 (Crisis State Research Centre, April 2009).

[6] See ICC Press Release No ICC-CPI-20090304-PR394, 4 March 2009.

[7] See *Tchad: sortir du piège pétrolier*, ICG Policy Briefing, 26 August 2009.

These trends have had an impact on Chad's southern neighbour CAR. Itself a fragile post-conflict country, CAR has been affected by a multiplicity of internal and external security threats involving irregular armed groups, rebel factions, road bandits, criminal gangs and poachers. State authority is almost absent in the north of the country. Meanwhile, CAR's security and armed forces are unable to protect the civilian population and are often themselves a source of insecurity for civilians. Finally, due to CAR's inability to secure its borders, its national territory has frequently been used as a basis for foreign armed militias from neighbouring countries such as Sudan, Uganda, Chad and the Democratic Republic of Congo.

## 3. EU RESPONSE

Faced with the continuing conflict in Sudan/Darfur and the risk of a spill-over to neighbouring Chad and CAR further complicating the political and security situation in this part of Africa, the EU agreed to step up its efforts to contribute to reducing the level of insecurity and to promoting peace and stability in eastern Chad and northeastern CAR.[8] It decided to develop a comprehensive approach combining different EU instruments and tools in order to achieve this goal. In doing so, the EU wanted first of all to increase its support for ongoing African Union (AU) and UN efforts to revitalise the process of conflict resolution in Darfur.[9] It intended to provide support to speeding up the full and effective deployment of the AU/UN hybrid operation (UNAMID) in Darfur[10] and the full and effective implementation of the Comprehensive Peace Agreement[11] between North and South Sudan. The EU also wanted to help stabilise eastern Chad and north eastern CAR through the deployment of a military force. It wished to create a basis for the deployment of a UN mission in eastern Chad –starting with EUFOR as a 'bridging operation'. The EU aimed at securing humanitarian operations in the region, in particular through improved access and enhanced security, and at maintaining funding and improving coordination of humanitarian assistance. As part of an exit strategy, it committed itself to providing long-term support through rehabilitation, recovery and sustainable development.

Various EU instruments and tools – political and diplomatic engagement, security support, development cooperation and humanitarian assistance – have been mobilised to carry out this multi-faceted approach (see Diagram 1).

---

[8] See European Commission, 'Commission to Boost Support for Refugees and Displaced People in Chad and the Central African Republic', Press Release IP/07/1425, 1 October 2007.

[9] Council Joint Action 2007/677/CFSP of 15 October 2007 on the European Union military operation in the Republic of Chad and in the Central African Republic, *OJ* 2007 L 279/21.

[10] Security Council Resolution 1769 of 31 July 2007.

[11] See: <http://www.aec-sudan.org/docs/cpa/cpa-en.pdf>.

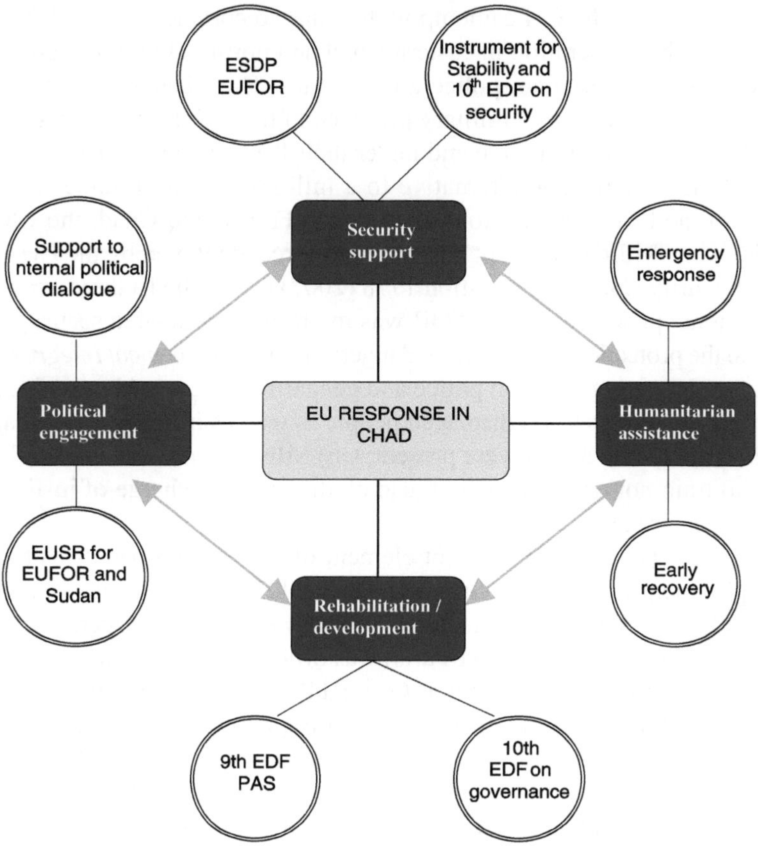


*Diagram 1*

### 3.1 Security support

International involvement to address the issue of security and stability in the region started in the aftermath of the outbreak of the war in Darfur in 2003 and has taken many different shapes since then. The African Union undertook the first peace-keeping efforts in Darfur with the AU Mission in Sudan (AMIS). As this relatively small operation rapidly acquired a reputation of ineffectiveness, the UN Security Council decided by Resolution 1769 (2007)[12] to transform AMIS into UNAMID. The authorised troop strength was raised from 7,700 to 26,000 (military and police forces combined).

Already in 2006, when the UN first contemplated taking over AMIS, the establishment of a multidimensional presence in Chad and CAR was brought up notably at the request of some humanitarian organisations. From a military perspective, it made little sense to try and stabilise a given area when a proxy war could continue

[12] Security Council Resolution 1769 of 31 July 2007.

across the border. The UN came up with a plan to complement the UNAMID deployment with an operation in eastern Chad and northeastern CAR encompassing three components: civilian, police and military. The Chadian government, however, was not in favour of a military presence of the UN. It was in this context that EUFOR, on a French initiative and under their lead, eventually came to serve as a politically more palatable alternative to a military operation under the UN flag. Thanks to the historical relationship between France and Chad, the Chadian authorities were willing to accept a French-led force, deployed by the EU.

UN Security Council Resolution 1778 (2007) established a three-pronged 'multidimensional presence': (i) EUFOR was to provide 'wide-area security' and contribute to the protection of civilians in danger; (ii) the *Détachement Integré de Sécurité* (DIS), an 850-strong Chadian police and gendarme unit, would provide security in the camps for refugees and displaced people as well as in some of the major towns where humanitarian actors were present; (iii) MINURCAT was intended to deploy efforts to train not only police, but also civilian staff in charge of justice, law and human rights issues.

The most visible and prominent element of the EU approach was the creation and deployment of EUFOR. On 15 October 2007, the EU Council adopted Joint Action 2007/677/CFSP as the legal act formally establishing Operation EUFOR.[13] In doing so, Mont Valérien (near Paris) was officially designated as the EU Operational Headquarters, and Lieutenant-General Patrick Nash (Ireland) and Brigadier-General Jean-Philippe Ganascia (France) were appointed as Operation Commander and Force Commander, respectively. In terms of mandate, EUFOR was labelled a 'military bridging operation', a concept developed earlier in the context of EU-UN cooperation in crisis management.[14] From the start, it was the EU's clear intention to conduct a mission for one year, after which the UN would take over with a mission of its own.

Upon the adoption of the Joint Action, the EU Military Staff was tasked with the preparation of the military directive to translate this into military guidance. The strategic objective was to contribute to a safe and secure environment by: (i) contributing to protecting civilians in danger, particularly refugees and displaced persons; (ii) facilitating the delivery of humanitarian aid and the free movement of humanitarian personnel by helping to improve security in the area of operations; and (iii) contributing to protecting UN personnel, facilities, installations and equipment and to ensuring the security and freedom of movement of its staff and associated personnel. The military directive also imposed constraints as well as restraints: EUFOR was to maintain an impartial and neutral posture and not become involved in the ongoing confrontations between the National Army and the armed groups.

The deployment of EUFOR presented considerable planning and logistic challenges. It was a demanding operation because of its location some 5,000 km away

---

[13] Council Joint Action 2007/677/CFSP of 15 October 2007, *supra* n. 9.

[14] See, more generally, J. Wouters and T. Ruys, 'UN-EU Cooperation in Crisis Management: Partnership or Rhetoric?', in S. Blockmans, ed., *The European Union and Crisis Management: Policy and Legal Aspects* (The Hague, T.M.C. Asser Press 2007) 215-232.

from Brussels and 2,000 km from the nearest sea port, with little or no infrastructure in a vast area with difficult climatic conditions. Overcoming the logistic challenges to provide the necessary infrastructure was essential in establishing an early EUFOR presence and visibility in theatre. The availability of a logistic lead nation, i.e., France, was central to sustaining the operation throughout its duration. Six military bases were constructed *ex nihilo* in addition to enhanced facilities at the two major airports in N'Djamena and Abéché. The early deployment of the force, self-sustaining and with medical support, was critical to the success of the operation. To this end, the French *Epervier* forces, already deployed in Chad on the basis of an agreement between France and Chad, provided essential support to EUFOR, enabling it to reach initial operating capability.

Total force capacity was set at 3,700 troops. Initial operating capability was declared on 15 March 2008 and the deployed elements reached Full Operating Capability (FOC) on 17 September 2008. For over a year, EUFOR deployed more than 10,000 militaries on the ground, coming from 23 Member States and three non-EU countries (Russia, Croatia and Albania). In total, over 2,500 short-range patrols and 260 long-range patrols were carried out after the deployed elements had reached FOC. Despite difficulties in assessing the costs of the operation, including common and bilateral costs, it is estimated that EUFOR cost amounted to around €1 billion.[15] Alongside and in support of the EUFOR mission, the UN trust fund for the DIS was supported by the European Commission through the Instrument for Stability (IfS). The IfS provided €10 million for the MINURCAT police programme and €5 million for the demographic census in Chad which constituted the first phase leading to an electoral census and the elections themselves. €6.5 million were also dedicated to security system reform in CAR.[16] EUFOR's deployment indeed lasted one year. Since 15 March 2009, following UN Security Council Resolution 1834 (2009), MINURCAT has taken over the role of EUFOR in securing the area of operation.

## 3.2 Political engagement

Apart from supporting security initiatives led by the UN and AU, the EU had also taken various steps to underpin the diplomatic process aimed at ensuring peace and stability in the region. One way of doing so was through the EU Special Representative (EUSR) for Sudan, Mr Torben Brylle, whose mandate had been extended to cover EUFOR Chad. His task, as defined by Council Joint Action 2009/134/CFSP,[17] was to:

---

[15] G. Grevi, D. Helly and D. Keohane, eds., *European Security and Defence Policy: The First 10 Years (1999-2009)* (Paris, European Union Institute for Security Studies, October 2009).

[16] See: <http://ec.europa.eu/development/geographical/regionscountries/countries/country_profile.cfm?cid=cf&type=short&lng=en>.

[17] *OJ* 2009 L 46/57 of 17 February 2009.

- liaise with the Presidency, the Secretary-General/High Representative (SG/HR), the EU Operation Commander and the EU Force Commander of Operation in order to ensure close coordination of their respective activities (close coordination also had to be ensured with the local Commission Delegations);
- assist the SG/HR in relation to his contacts with the United Nations, the Chadian authorities, the authorities of CAR and neighbouring countries as well as with other relevant actors;
- without prejudice to the military chain of command, provide the EU Force Commander of Operation with political guidance, in particular on issues with a regional political dimension;
- with respect to his tasks related to Operation EUFOR, consult with the EU Force Commander on political issues with a security dimension.

The EUSR had a role of observer in the Contact Group created to monitor the implementation of the Dakar Agreement signed in March 2008 between the Chadian and Sudanese governments.[18] After some initial progress in the implementation of the Dakar Agreement, in particular the revival of diplomatic relationships between the two countries in October 2008, new tensions arose between Chad and Sudan in the first semester of 2009. A new agreement between the two countries, signed in Doha on 3 May 2009,[19] had been quickly overshadowed by a major attack by the Chadian armed opposition hosted in Sudan.[20]

With the exception of the leaders of armed groups, almost all political leaders in Chad concluded a Political Agreement on 13 August 2007 with a view to revitalising the national democratic process and setting out a road map to legislative elections in 2010.[21] This political dialogue has been supported and followed closely by the EC and the EU as a whole. Through funding from the 9th European Development Fund – on top of its support to the demographic census under the IfS – the European Union provided €5 million to support the electoral process.[22] The aim was to contribute to the consolidation of political parties' capacity to support the functioning of the *Commission Electorale Nationale Indépendante* (CENI) and the implementation of the electoral census.

## 3.3 Humanitarian assistance

The conflicts have provoked widespread internal and external displacement of vulnerable groups of people. Within Darfur it is estimated that some 2.7 million people

18 Dakar Agreement between Sudan and Chad signed in Dakar, Republic of Senegal, on 13 March 2008 (see MINURCAT website: <http://minurcat.unmissions.org/Portals/MINURCAT/Dakar%20Agreement.pdf>).

19 As reported on: <http://english.mofa.gov.qa/newsPage.cfm?newsid=6265>.

20 'Intenses batailles dans l'est du Tchad', *Le Monde*, 8 May 2009.

21 Electoral reform agreement between the Government of Chad and the political parties (commonly referred to as the 'August 13th Agreement', 13 August 2007.

22 See: <http://ec.europa.eu/delegations/deltcd/fr/eu_and_country/fiches_projets/FP10_IFS-RRM_147-346%20_DIS.htm>.

have fled their homes. Around 260,000 refugees have fled from Sudan to Chad and CAR. In Chad, some 170,000 internally displaced persons have flocked together in camps in the eastern part of the country after having been uprooted by violence, insecurity, crime and deprivation. The humanitarian picture has been further complicated by the presence of some 45,000 Chadian refugees in Darfur and 74,000 CAR refugees in Chad and by the impact of their presence on the local host population who find themselves faced with a suddenly increased competitive claim on scarce natural resources and the risk of discriminatory treatment in terms of support and assistance compared to refugees and displaced people.

The humanitarian community has faced two major challenges in Chad. First, there is the challenge of a protracted crisis. The worrying outlook for the Darfur crisis and the risk of a never-ending insecurity in the sub-region means that the question of sustainability of humanitarian assistance in an unstable, uncertain environment has to be seriously considered.[23] It has been necessary to step up the transition from emergency responses to early recovery programmes designed to encourage the beneficiaries of humanitarian aid to take more responsibility in the provision of basic needs.[24] Nevertheless, this strategy has remained mostly hypothetical due to the difficulty faced by the Chadian administration to restore its authority and resume the provision of basic services such as health, education and water and sanitation and the land scarcity and harsh environment in some areas of operations. Since 2007, movements of Chadian displaced persons returning to their villages of origin have been recorded in a few regions, such as Assoungha and Dar Sila. Massive voluntary returns cannot be expected without lasting and durable security conditions in the areas of return.

A second challenge has consisted in the restriction of humanitarian space and access. The humanitarian community has never been directly targeted by the parties to the conflict in eastern Chad, i.e., the National Chadian Army (NCA) and the Chadian dissident movements. The humanitarian delivery routes have been, however, exposed to random security threats from banditry and to collateral damage from clashes between NCA soldiers and dissident movements. With widespread impunity and criminality, humanitarian workers have been victims of security incidents, armed robbery and physical intimidation. Their possessions are often coveted, particularly vehicles and communication equipment. For those reasons, the humanitarian 'space' has often been reduced to the refugee camps and the IDP sites located close to urban areas.

Since 2003, the humanitarian operations supported by the European Commission have targeted the most vulnerable population in Chad. EC support to the crisis in Chad amounted to a total of €163 million over the period 2003-2009, covering all the traditional humanitarian aid sectors – health and nutrition, water and sanitation, shelter and non-food items, protection of the community, common services, in

---

[23] See ICG, 'Chad: Powder Keg in the East', *Africa Report* No. 149, 15 April 2009.

[24] Commission Decision of 26 January 2009 on the approval and financing of a Global Plan for humanitarian actions in the Republic of Chad from the general budget of the European Communities.

particular coordination and humanitarian air services, and food aid and food security.[25]

### 3.4 Development cooperation

While humanitarian assistance has aimed at alleviating urgent needs in the short term, development support has tried to achieve long-term goals of poverty reduction, sustainable growth, good governance and political stability. The EU has elaborated a development strategy aimed at contributing to poverty reduction in Chad and CAR.[26] Unlike humanitarian assistance, which is provided – in line with the principles of independence, neutrality and impartiality – on the basis of needs, this development strategy has been agreed between the partners on the basis of political priorities and equal partnership. In close cooperation with the Chadian authorities, the European Commission provides support to local administrations and populations in eastern Chad through the so-called *Programme d'Accompagnement à la Stabilisation* (PAS), designed to have an impact on the political dynamics, especially in the areas of local governance and grass-root conflict resolution. A key objective of the PAS programme is to link humanitarian assistance, rehabilitation, reconstruction and development with a view to ensuring a voluntary and sustainable return of displaced people to a secure environment where security is to be provided by local civil law enforcement systems, under the umbrella of EUFOR.

More widely, the National Indicative Programme (NIP) for 2008-2013 for Chad[27] gives priority to governance issues in the area of justice and security, public finance, local governance and decentralisation and provides support to democratic processes. One third of the available development funding (32% of the $10^{th}$ European Development Fund, amounting to €311 million) is earmarked for this priority. This involvement in a longer-term approach can be seen as part of a coherent 'policy mix' between short-term security and humanitarian actions and long-term reform. In CAR, the European Commission is involved in the disarmament, demobilisation and reintegration (DDR) process, security sector reform (SSR) and the preparation of elections in 2010.

## 4. Lessons learned

As stated in the introduction, the central question is whether the approach of the EU in Chad and CAR has been sufficiently comprehensive, complementary and coordinated to effectively address the issue of security and stability in this part of Africa. A subsidiary question is whether the European Union's military operation has been an appropriate and effective tool in that regard.

---

25 Ibid.

26 Document de stratégie pays et Programme Indicatif National (PIN) 10ème FED pour la période 2008-2013, available at: <http://ec.europa.eu/delegations/deltcd/fr/eu_and_country/td_pin10_fr.pdf>.

27 Ibid.

### 4.1 Has the EU approach really been comprehensive?

It has been the EU's more or less explicit ambition to develop a comprehensive approach to addressing the issues of security, protection and access in the region. One of the key elements has been the planning and deployment of the EUFOR operation in Chad and CAR, thus enhancing the overall impact of EU actions in the region. This approach included various instruments and tools, such as political engagement, security support, diplomatic involvement, stabilisation programming, development cooperation, alongside humanitarian assistance. In practice, the main focus has been on the deployment of EUFOR. This has not been matched by an equivalent focus on the other areas, in particular political and diplomatic engagement and development cooperation. More resources have been devoted to the military operation than to the other tools, thus reducing the very comprehensive nature of the approach.

The limited achievement in terms of comprehensiveness of the EU response in Chad is related to various constraints:

- The differences in mandates and responsibilities between the various stakeholders (humanitarians, diplomats, militaries) made it difficult to define common objectives structuring a comprehensive approach;
- The organisational differences in this multi-layered operation complicated the picture. As far as security was concerned, throughout the lifetime of the operation it was difficult to 'synchronise' the constraints of the UN, the EU and the Chadian government. This situation resulted in the absence of one of the main components of the security scheme, the DIS, its police component;
- Even though at EU level there were various attempts to include the European Commission services at the planning stage of the EUFOR operation, the process of defining the objectives of the operation was largely driven by the European Council.

### 4.2 What about complementarity?

Neither the relatively short duration of the EUFOR deployment nor the different mandates, procedures and timelines were conducive to ensuring effective complementarities between the different instruments and tools. For instance, it was not easy to match the deployment of EUFOR with the political and diplomatic engagement in the process of dialogue between Sudan and Chad or the national reconciliation process within Chad. Nor was it easy to ensure complementarity between the security activities of EUFOR/MINURCAT and the humanitarian operations and between the short-term humanitarian activities and the mid-term recovery and rehabilitation projects.

EUFOR played a crucial role in this context. Since it was sufficiently credible in terms of military capability and political intent, it could have provided an effective response strategy if it had been able to tackle criminality and impunity. The effect of such a strategy has only been limited and temporary, as it was not accompanied by appropriate steps and measures in other relevant areas of intervention. In other words, EUFOR alone has not been able to change the internal dynamics of conflict in so far as the extra time bought by its deterrent effects has not been put to use in the political and diplomatic domain. Without due complementarity, such an operation was bound not to have a lasting effect.

The case of EUFOR raises the question of how a military operation can produce political effects. At least two scenarios can be identified. Either a political conflict is addressed directly through military means by entering the conflict itself and choosing sides. This was clearly not the case in Chad. Or, the military operation tries to keep the political conflict at bay and at arm's length from the civilian population and the vulnerable groups of refugees and displaced persons by deterrence, as was the case in Chad. Consequently, there is less impact on the conflict. EUFOR was useful in mitigating security threats arising from combats between government forces and rebel troops, but had no mandate to address impunity and provide an effective answer to the lack of security, rule of law and governance. In the end, local people felt more insecure on account of the prevalence of crime and banditry than because of threats from irregular armed groups.

A year into implementation of the PAS no results have been achieved on the grass-root conflict resolution. This is due notably to the very cautious involvement of the Chadian authorities in the matter. Post-emergency operations covering health and infrastructure (such as roads and water points) have been implemented in areas of return in eastern Chad, mainly through humanitarian organisations in the absence of any development actors. The link between humanitarian assistance and early recovery programmes has remained mostly hypothetical for lack of a genuine security stabilisation in eastern Chad.

The process of implementing the Political Agreement of 13 August 2007 has been slowed down by recurrent attempts by Chadian armed groups to topple the regime (2007, 2008 and, to a lesser extent, 2009) and by tensions between the regime and the legal opposition in N'Djamena regarding various issues, such as the creation of the CENI and the Electoral Code. Moreover, the implementation of Chapter 4 of the Agreement – on demilitarisation and de-politicisation of the administration and reform of the judiciary and armed forces – has not made significant progress. However, the legal electoral framework was eventually modified and finally complied with the terms laid down in the Political Agreement. The Electoral Commission was created in July 2009. These efforts should stimulate the political process and lead to legislative elections in 2010.

The latest report of the Secretary-General on MINURCAT was very cautious:

> 'regional peace efforts remain stalled as a result of continued tensions between Chad and the Sudan. The Dakar Contact Group has not met since November 2008, while the Doha commitment of 3 May has not been realized. The perpetuation of the hostility between Chad and the Sudan continues to frustrate solutions to the conflicts in Darfur and eastern Chad, exacerbating the plight of civilians in both regions.'[28]

---

[28] Report of the Secretary-General on the United Nations Mission in the Central African Republic and Chad, S/2009/535, 14 October 2009.

It is important to note that the promotion of complex approaches to crisis management should integrate different 'tempos' or 'time limits' for the different actors. Quick short-term security is achieved differently from mid or longer-term security, just as early recovery and development efforts are conducted differently from humanitarian actions. The establishment of such a 'multi-tempo' strategy in Chad has encountered many constraints and limitations.

### 4.3 Has EUFOR been an appropriate and effective tool?

Generally speaking, EUFOR is said to have contributed to improving the overall security in the region.[29] It has, however, not been able to reduce the frequent threats from criminal groups, armed gangs, bandits and localised violence and to address the individual protection and security needs of the vulnerable refugees, displaced and local people as well as humanitarian agencies. One of the reasons invoked by some analysts is that the concept of operation was mainly drafted with a specific focus on cross-border insecurity rather than on internal banditry.[30] The absence of the police component (DIS) and the increase in criminal acts[31] in EUFOR's area of operation compelled the EUFOR Commanders to adapt their initial concept of operation to the realities on the ground.[32]

In this respect, the operation has probably created a better understanding of what is really at stake on the ground: not only regional security, but also local protection against crime, banditry and violence. The extent to which this common understanding may result in better policy design depends on the readiness to keep Chad and CAR on the political agenda after the departure of EUFOR. The concept of operation mandated EUFOR to create a Safe and Secure Environment (SASE), but the question is whether this was realistic and feasible. In the words of Mattelaer:

---

[29] See A. Mattelaer, *The Strategic Planning of EU Military Operations – The Case of EUFOR Chad / RCA*, IES Working Paper 5/2008: 'Improving the security situation was felt to be as much a matter of perception as well as of the number of security incidents. In any event, the security situation would be hard to measure in quantitative terms. For example, there were no statistics available about the security situation prior to EUFOR deployment. Even if there had been, one planner remarked, the number of reported incidents might very well have risen because the presence of EUFOR meant that now there was at least always someone to report to.'

[30] R. Marchal, 'Understanding French Policy towards Chad/Sudan? A Difficult Task': 'While in the early weeks of the planning, the focus was on communal conflicts, banditry and land issues, in summer 2007 the French Military Intelligence reframed the concept: the problem was created by the rebels' columns and Janjaweed. It took months to EUFOR to accept that most of the violence and insecurity in Eastern Chad was coming from Chad, not Darfur and that the Chadian officials and military had their good share of responsibility in the predicament of the population', available at: <http://blogs.ssrc.org/darfur/2009/06/04/understanding-french-policy-toward-chadsudan-a-difficult-task-1/>.

[31] OCHA reported 135 security incidents between January 2008 and January 2009 involving humanitarian actors. See *Est Tchad: récapitulatif des incidents sécuritaire (janvier 2008 – janvier 2009)*, OCHA, March 2009

[32] General Ganascia in *Le Figaro* of 16 June 2008: 'There is a discrepancy between what contributed to the initial set-up of the forces deployed here and the actual reality. The background situation has changed enormously (…) It is therefore essential that we adapt our methods of action in order to counteract the *coupeurs de route* (highwaymen) whilst still remaining within the framework we were given. We need to review the EUFOR missions in Chad.'

> 'What does SASE mean? It presupposes the rule of law, relying on police, judiciary and border control mechanisms. It presupposes economical perspectives to make it sustainable. In essence it presupposes a functioning state. But which of these elements can be achieved militarily?'[33]

The delay in the deployment of the DIS has moreover complicated the ability of the joint operation to tackle banditry and common crime.[34] The reason for this delay has been two-fold: the slow process of deployment of the UN machinery and the administrative impediments created by the Chadian authorities, in particular against the UN Department for Peacekeeping Operations (DPKO).

Despite its participative character, including various stakeholders from inside and outside the EU institutions, the EUFOR planning process did not result in the design of a realistic operation. The risk inherent in this multi-pronged operation and the high dependence on MINURCAT/DIS deployment as well as the temptation to measure its success by counting the number of IDPs returning to their homes generally fuelled criticism of EUFOR's ability to provide protection to the civilian population and humanitarian organisations.

In general, for missions such as EUFOR, it is necessary for humanitarian actors to insist on the need to focus the mandate of these operations on clear security objectives. Objectives such as 'the establishment of conditions allowing the voluntary return of displaced people' or 'the establishment of conditions allowing the rehabilitation of the areas of origin of displaced persons' can easily lead to tendentious interpretations following the deployment of the force. It is therefore essential to clearly define the expected results in order to avoid attempts to set benchmarks that could threaten humanitarian principles such as the voluntary nature of any return movement. The return of displaced people to their places of origin depends on various factors, many of which are beyond the control of a military mission and can therefore not be used as a benchmark for its success.

The negative response from humanitarian organisations to the attempts by EUFOR to evaluate its results based on the number of returnees should prompt a reflection on: (i) the risks associated with the assumption of a causal link between the security services provided by EUFOR and the return of populations to their areas of origin, as well as the problems associated with the quantification of these movements, which tends to overlook complex local realities; and (ii) the risks of too simplistic an interpretation of population movements in eastern Chad (the definition of return itself is problematic in a context where the mobility of populations is a fundamental aspect of their adaptation to an extremely inhospitable environment). In Chad, the

---

33 Mattelaer, *supra* n. 29

34 OXFAM, 'Mission Incomplete: Why Civilians Remain at Risk in Eastern Chad', September 2008, available at: <http://www.oxfam.org/en/policy/bp119-chad-mission-incomplete>: 'The threats facing civilians – banditry, criminality, and forced recruitment, all exacerbated by an underlying culture of impunity – are threats for which MINURCAT and the DIS were designed. However, their deplorable lack of deployment has meant that civilians are not benefitting from any of this protection. As of August 2008, only around 300 of a planned total of 850 Chadian police/gendarmes had completed training, and none had been sent to the camps or sites.'

implications and consequences of inter-community conflicts are complex, localised and necessitate a reflection that goes beyond instant security (real or declared) to consider, *inter alia*, reconciliation mechanisms, resource-sharing schemes and the application of the rule of law.

### 4.4 Has coordination been adequate?

An essential element of the EU's comprehensive approach has been the realisation that there is an urgent need for close coordination between Member States within the context of the European Security and Defence Policy. The experience with EUFOR has shown that the ESDP (now CDSP) encompasses an intricate set of planning procedures largely drawn from the NATO model complemented by a limited civil-military approach. This planning system has important merits: it is geared towards ensuring continuous political oversight; it structures the planning discussions; and it allows for the incorporation of a wide range of relevant factors. However, difficulties in the force generation process delayed the launch of the operation until 28 January 2008. Five force generation conferences were necessary to reach a workable size. The main difficulties arose with regard to the usual critical capacities such as fixed-wing (planes) and rotary-wing assets (helicopters) as well as medical facilities.[35]

From a military perspective, this operation was highly challenging but manageable. From a political perspective, it was far more problematic. It was not easy to define the common European interest in addressing the conflict, but consensus emerged on the need to protect civilians in danger. In the political planning process of EUFOR the EU did not act in a unified and resolute way. Rather than a problem of procedures, this is a fundamental consequence of the diverging political priorities of the 27 Member States and underlines the structural weakness in the political credibility of the CSDP.

According to the EUSR, for some participating Member States with no particularly deep knowledge of African operations the experience gathered on EUFOR will be 'useful, as, in the future, there will most likely be discussions of other possible European contributions on the African continent.'[36]

At the start, the bridging[37] nature of the operation was far from obvious. The unwillingness of the Chadian government to host a UN force as well as UNDPKO's reluctance were mentioned at an early stage of the EUFOR planning process.[38] The

---

[35] See Mattelear, *supra* n. 29.

[36] ESDP Newsletter No. 8, Summer 2009.

[37] On the qualification of EUFOR as a bridging operation the ICG argues: 'Faced with the Chad government's determined opposition to the deployment of an integrated peacekeeping force, EUFOR was thus never designed as a proper «bridging mission» like Europe's Operation Artemis in Congo in 2003, whose role was to stabilise the security situation, in order to give the United Nations time to deploy into the theatre of operations. Indeed, right up to the end of 2008, it remained unclear whether MINURCAT was going to be mandated to take over from EUFOR.' See ICG, *supra* n. 23.

[38] Grevi, Helly and Keohane, eds., *supra* n. 15: 'From the start, some in the UN Department of Peacekeeping Operations (UN DPKO) had expressed resistance to the very idea of a peacekeeping

decision to make EUFOR a bridging operation was finally adopted very late in the process in January 2009, through UN Security Council Resolution 1861. Despite this reluctance, EUFOR helped MINURCAT to become more operational in the whole area of action. It enabled MINURCAT to use the infrastructure built during EUFOR's deployment, to re-hat some troops formerly under EUFOR's flag and to share the intelligence data gathered during its deployment. Despite these various arrangements, the UN would have preferred a longer presence of EUFOR on the ground in order to allow for a smoother transition. Despite numerous disagreements between the two organisations during the implementation of this operation, the EUFOR experience has probably, through mutual learning, paved the way for better UN-EU coordination mechanisms in future joint operations. Yet, MINURCAT continued facing capacity problems after six months of deployment.[39]

At HQ level in Brussels, coordination between the EU institutions (particularly between the Council and the Commission) has been facilitated by the Crisis Response Coordination Team (CRCT).[40] For most CRCT participants, this coordination mechanism has allowed a frank and smooth relationship between Council and Commission services. The CRCT proved to be an effective platform to facilitate a common understanding between the military and civilian parts of the EU response in Chad on various subjects, such as the benchmarking of voluntary returns of IDPs, the limited use of quick-impact projects (QIPs) and, more broadly, the preservation of humanitarian space.

The coordination in the field between EUFOR and the EC Delegation in N'Djamena was, however, considered by some observers as less effective:

> 'Despite efforts by Brussels staff in the planning phase, the cooperation between ESDP and the European Commission has been disappointingly sub-optimal because of a combination of unfortunate factors. The Delegation of the Commission partly shared some of the humanitarian community's concerns regarding the role of EUFOR and, while in charge of supporting internal political dialogue, viewed the military operation

---

operation in Eastern Chad on the grounds that conditions identified by the Brahimi Report (a peace to keep, firm commitments of troops, clarity of mandate and instructions) were not met.'

[39] 51% of its military staff deployed in September 2009. Furthermore, the report of the UNSG of 14 October 2009, *supra* n. 28, mentioned that 'the Secretariat has still not received pledges for 11 of the 18 military utility helicopters detailed in the force requirements.'

[40] The *ad hoc* crisis response coordinating team (CRCT) is a vehicle for inter-service coordination in response to a given crisis. It consists of officials from the relevant services in the Council Secretariat and the Commission. It is not a standing body but will be convened when a particular crisis occurs. The *ad hoc* team is a practical and effective way of ensuring at working level that the Council and the Commission are in the position to ensure consistency in the external activities of the Union, in accordance with Article 3, second subparagraph TEU. The relevant coordination takes place between services and is without prejudice to the prerogatives and obligations of the institutions themselves. The team thus helps to ensure close two-way coordination in the planning of military and civilian measures. The team is not a Council working group. *A fortiori*, it does not take decisions. The SG can draw on its work so that the draft crisis management concept presented to the PSC is both coherent and comprehensive and encompasses all relevant civilian and military instruments. Council of the European Union, 'Crisis Management Procedures: Suggestions for Procedures for Coherent, Comprehensive EU Crisis Management', 3 July 2003.

with some mistrust. (…) Expected synergies between the PAS and EUFOR have thus developed slowly but the programme started to be implemented late 2008 and went on after the re-hatting of EUFOR.'[41]

*Civil-military coordination*

With regard to civil-military coordination, the experience with EUFOR has shown that there are two distinct phases in the relationship between the civilian actors, in particular the humanitarian organisations, on the one hand, and the military, on the other.

First, the deployment of EUFOR in Chad and the inadequate communication regarding its mandate created a lot of scepticism and mistrust within the humanitarian community. Reinforcing communication and coordination at an early stage is vital for better interaction in the future. Civil-military coordination officers should be considered essential in this process and be deployed in the early phase of the operation. More communication in the planning phase regarding the mandate and its interpretation may also help avoid misunderstanding about the mandate and enhance fine-tuning of its interpretation on the ground. The implementation of quick-impact projects by national contingents within EUFOR was questioned as not being in line with the principles of neutrality and the provisions of the EU Consensus on Humanitarian Aid. It has to be acknowledged that thanks to the involvement of humanitarian actors at Brussels and Chad level, the scope of the QIPs implemented by EUFOR was very limited. Nevertheless, it remains important to circumscribe the use of QIPs by a force's contributing nation from the outset of a military operation and, in so doing, to prevent that the lines between humanitarian and military activities become blurred, causing potential damage to the former.

Later on, after a couple of months, civil-military coordination between EUFOR and the humanitarian organisations became, in the eyes of many humanitarian stakeholders, much better and even exemplary when finally the humanitarian mandate became well respected and well understood by EUFOR. It was remarkable to see how in the context of civil-military coordination EUFOR's central command showed an increasing readiness to understand and apply the rules and principles of international humanitarian law (IHL).[42] The return of displaced people to their place of origin is a good example in this regard. Where initially it was proposed to use this return as a benchmark of EUFOR's success, it was later accepted that such return is subject to autonomous factors beyond EUFOR's control. According to humanitarian principles, the decision of displaced people to return should be autonomous and voluntary and be anticipated through efforts to secure and rehabilitate areas of return.

---

[41] See Grevi, Helly and Keohane, eds., *supra* n. 15.

[42] International humanitarian law (IHL) is a set of rules which seek, for humanitarian reasons, *to limit the effects of armed conflict.* It protects persons who are not or are no longer participating in the hostilities and restricts the means and methods of warfare. International humanitarian law is also known as the law of war or the law of armed conflict. See ICRC, 'What Is International Humanitarian Law?', available at: <http://www.icrc.org/Web/eng/siteeng0.nsf/htmlall/humanitarian-law-factsheet/$File/What_is_IHL.pdf>.

The European Commission has reinforced the civil-military coordination mechanism in Chad through its humanitarian funds by supporting both OCHA and the NGO community in Chad. Concretely, the European Commission has financed the civ-mil coordination officer in OCHA and a policy advisor in the NGO Coordination Committee, seconded by OXFAM. Their work has been useful in promoting and advocating the preservation of humanitarian space by attending and organising coordination fora and joint training on civil-military relationships.

## 5. Conclusion

The EUFOR operation and the overall response of the EU in Chad have been assessed in terms of comprehensiveness, complementarity and coordination. Where the comprehensive nature of the EU response remained very limited mainly because of the inability of the various stakeholders to agree on common objectives, more progress has been achieved in terms of complementarity and coordination. In spite of this, many challenges still lie ahead in terms of complementing the security response by longer-term development efforts and political stability and reconciliation, particularly due to the very different time limits within which military forces, on the one hand, and political and development actors, on the other, have to operate. The main positive lesson learnt from EUFOR relates to the continuous improvement of coordination between the various actors involved in the process of promoting peace, stability and security in Chad and CAR, such as between humanitarian actors and military forces, between UN and EU, among EU institutions and between humanitarian organisations themselves. The new institutional set-up following the entry into force of the Lisbon Treaty may provide new opportunities in this respect.

Since the end of EUFOR's mandate, the EU has stated that it wants to continue its commitment to Chad and CAR. A number of Member States and third countries have indeed remained on the ground after the termination of EUFOR, in the framework of MINURCAT (France, Ireland, Austria, Finland, Poland, but also Albania, Croatia and Russia). Around 2,000 men serving under EUFOR have come under the MINURCAT banner. Moreover, the EU has also expressed its ambition to remain active at the political and diplomatic level in Chad, CAR and especially Sudan, where the implementation of the Comprehensive Peace Agreement and the Darfur peace process is considered to be crucial for the stabilisation of the whole region. The EU has stressed its intention to continue to support a political solution to the Darfur conflict as well as the improvement of relations between Chad and Sudan. However, it has not gone unnoticed that since the termination of EUFOR, Chad and CAR have not kept the same place on the EU foreign policy agenda as before.

The root causes of violence and insecurity in Darfur, Chad and CAR need to be urgently and fully addressed in order to foster a genuine dynamic of reconciliation and stabilisation. What is needed is a strong and lasting effort to support sustainable development and the establishment of the rule of law, independent justice and good governance. Only an overall approach that is truly comprehensive, complementary and well coordinated can create the necessary conditions for a peaceful, stable and secure development of the countries in the region. The deployment of EUFOR was a new, challenging and useful step in this process of peacebuilding, but definitely not sufficient.

# Chapter 11
# EU PEACEBUILDING IN GEORGIA: LIMITS AND ACHIEVEMENTS

**Michael Merlingen* and Rasa Ostrauskaitė****

## 1. Introduction

Since the separatist wars of the early 1990s, the ethnic conflicts in Georgia have gone through a number of phases: post-violence, endurance, escalation, return to war, de-escalation and post-violence. Using variegated tools, the EU has been active in each phase. The Union has assisted in reforming governmental institutions in Georgia and the break-away territories to promote democracy and the rule of law; provided humanitarian assistance to internally displaced persons to alleviate suffering; supported rehabilitation programmes to provide hope for a better future; funded confidence-building measures to tackle mutual mistrust; encouraged multi-track diplomacy to involve civil society in peacemaking; supported mediation and negotiations efforts to de-escalate the tensions and address the underlying disagreements; deployed civilian peacekeepers to monitor the post-war ceasefire; and led international negotiations to manage and possibly resolve the ethnic conflicts.

Our purpose in this chapter is to describe and analyse all peace-related activities of the EU regarding Georgia. The term 'peacebuilding' is employed to refer to a range of political, economic and humanitarian activities designed to entrench peace in post-conflict societies. It covers structural policies aimed at what liberal peacebuilders consider to be the root causes of intra-state wars such as faulty institutions, enemy perceptions and underdeveloped civil societies. It also covers shorter-term policies aimed at the reconstruction and rehabilitation of damaged physical and social infrastructure such as power plants and the housing stock. Peacebuilding has been the central element of EU activities in Georgia. However, the EU has also carried out actions falling under the heading of peacekeeping, conflict management and conflict resolution. Through these latter activities the Union has sought to in-

* Michael Merlingen is Associate Professor at Central European University, Budapest. He has published two books on the ESDP with his co-author Rasa Ostrauskaitė. His third book – *European Security and Defense Policy: What It Is, How It Works, Why It Matters* – will be published by Lynne Rienner.

** Until recently, Rasa Ostrauskaitė was a member of the Policy Unit of the EU Council General Secretariat. In this capacity she worked as, among other things, political advisor to the EUSR for the Southern Caucasus and as chief political advisor to the EUSR for the Crisis in Georgia.

*S. Blockmans, J. Wouters & T. Ruys, eds., The European Union and Peacebuilding*

fluence the political context within which peacebuilding takes place. Our main argument is that the peace process in Georgia has failed because third-party interveners such as the EU have allowed a huge gap to open up between their role as 'apolitical' peacebuilders and their role as politically engaged peacebrokers.

If the large literature on how to build sustainable peace after ethnic violence teaches anything, it is that conflict transformation is demanding. In most cases it requires a committed international actor ready to mobilise resources and power to broker a mutually acceptable agreement and to guarantee its implementation, including through assisting the country in putting in place the structural conditions for sustainable peace. Neither of the third-party interveners in Georgia rose to the occasion. Arguably, the upshot of this failure has been a demonstration of what critics of liberal peacebuilding have called the 'peacemaking potential of war'.[1] Though no one in the wider West is yet ready to acknowledge it, the war between Georgia and Russia may have solved Georgia's territorial conflicts once and for all.

The chapter proceeds as follows. We first provide an overview of two decades of conflict in Georgia and of the role of the principal third-party interveners in conflict management and conflict resolution prior to the 2008 war. Next, we turn to the EU. We show that after a slow start, the Union upgraded its peace activities in the country in the first half of the new millennium. Since the 2008 war, the EU has taken the lead in conflict settlement. We explain the reasons for the growing assertiveness of the Union's Georgia policy in the new millennium. Moving from the general to the concrete, we then disaggregate the EU into its distinct foreign policy components and discuss and critically assess how each of them has tried to advance the peace process.

## 2. Two decades of conflicts and tensions in Georgia

In April 1991, Georgia declared its independence. Two ethnicities, which had lived in autonomous territories within Georgia when the latter was part of the Soviet Union, refused to be incorporated into the newly sovereign country.[2] Both were backed by Moscow. Separate armed conflicts between Georgia and Abkhazia and Georgia and South Ossetia ensued.

The war over control of South Ossetia started at the end of 1991. It led to about 1,000 casualties and 60,000 to 100,000 internally displaced persons (IDPs) and refugees fleeing to Georgia and North Ossetia in Russia. In 1992, Georgia accepted a ceasefire to avoid confrontation with Russia – the so-called Sochi Agreement.[3] It

[1] E. Luttwak, 'Give War a Chance', 78 *Foreign Affairs* (1999), at 38.

[2] Abkhazia was an autonomous republic and South Ossetia an autonomous oblast (district) within the Soviet Socialist Republic of Georgia. For an historical background on the conflicts, see S. Cornell, *Small Nations and Great Powers: A Study of Ethnopolitical Conflict in the Caucasus* (London, Routledge 2001).

[3] The text of the Sochi Agreement is available at: <http://www.rrc.ge/law/xels_1992_06_24_e.htm?lawid=368&lng_3=en>.

established a 1,500 strong Joint Peacekeeping Force consisting of Russians, North Ossetians (of the Russian Federation) and Georgians, each contributing 500 troops.[4] In December 1992, the Conference for Security and Cooperation in Europe (CSCE) deployed a mission to Georgia with a mandate to promote a negotiated settlement of the conflict.[5] About a year later, the mandate was enlarged to incorporate new tasks such as democratisation, human rights and the rule of law.[6] Moreover, the mission was charged with monitoring the Joint Peacekeeping Forces to check whether they complied with CSCE principles. As part of this task, military observers monitored the ceasefire by, among other things, carrying out independent patrols and investigations of alleged violations. In addition, the mission facilitated the operation of the conflict resolution mechanism established by the Sochi Agreement – the Joint Control Commission (JCC) comprising representatives of North and South Ossetia, Russia and Georgia. The EU supported the JCC financially[7] and the European Commission participated as an observer in its meetings. In the second half of the 1990s, the JCC made some progress in advancing the demilitarisation of the conflict zone and in contributing to building confidence. Also, the OSCE mission initiated Experts' Group meetings in 1997, which, in 1999, led to a preliminary agreement on an 'intermediary document' that spelled out four principles guiding the political settlement process, including Georgia's territorial integrity.[8] However, with the election of hard-liner Eduard Kokoity as South Ossetia's President, the negotiations on what became known as the Baden document came to an end.

Abkhazia declared independence from Georgia in July 1992. In response, Tbilisi dispatched troops and heavy fighting ensued. While Georgia took control of most of Abkhazia, its victory was short-lived as Chechen and other North Caucasian volunteers joined Abkhaz fighters in mounting a counter-offensive against Georgian forces. Several ceasefire agreements were reached and broken. The agreement of July 1993 gave rise to the establishment of the United Nations Observer Mission in Georgia (UNOMIG), mandated to monitor the cessation of hostilities.[9] However, while the mission was deployed, fighting resumed. In September 1993, the capital of Abkhazia, Sukhumi, fell to the insurgents. The UN mission received an interim mandate to continue monitoring the situation. On 14 May 1994, the Georgian government and the Abkhaz secessionist leadership signed an Agreement on a Ceasefire and Separation of Forces in Moscow.[10] It put an end to a conflict that had cost the lives of tens of thousands of people and had forced about 250,000 people from their

---

[4] South Ossetian troops were part of the North Ossetian battalion.

[5] 17th CSO Meeting, 6 November 1992, Journal No. 2, Annex 2.

[6] 14th Permanent Committee Meeting, 29 March 1994, Journal 14/Revised, Annex 1.

[7] Council Joint Action 2001/759/CFSP of 29 October 2001 regarding a contribution from the European Union to the conflict settlement process in South Ossetia, *OJ* 2001 L 264/8.

[8] M. König, 'The Georgian-South Ossetian Conflict', in Institute for Peace Research and Security Policy at the University of Hamburg, ed., *OSCE Yearbook 2004: Yearbook on the Organization for Security and Co-Operation in Europe (OSCE)* (Baden-Baden, Nomos 2005).

[9] UNSC Resolution 858 (1993) of 24 August 1993.

[10] The text of the Moscow agreement is available at: <http://www.c-r.org/our-work/accord/georgia-abkhazia/keytext3.php>.

homes. The agreement included the establishment of a peacekeeping force under the auspices of the Commonwealth of Independent States (CIS). UNOMIG subsequently received a new and expanded mandate to verify compliance with the agreement.[11] Its unarmed military observers monitored the operation of the CIS peacekeepers and patrolled disputed areas, including the strategic Kodori valley. In 1996, a separate office was set up within the mission to promote respect for human rights in Abkhazia. In 2003, a small, non-executive police element was added to UNOMIG to facilitate conditions for the return of IDPs. As to the political settlement process, in 1994, the UN initiated what came to be known as the 'Geneva process'. After languishing for some years, it was revived in 1997. A new Coordinating Council composed of Georgia, Abkhazia, Russia and the UN was set up to serve as the main forum for negotiations. The 'Group of Friends of the UN Secretary-General for Georgia' (America, Britain, France, Germany and Russia) and the OSCE participated as observers. However, little progress was made as the talks were bogged down in 'negotiations about negotiations'.[12] The 2001 Boden plan – a settlement proposal elaborated by the UN Secretary-General's Representative for Georgia and the Group of Friends – was rejected by Sukhumi.[13]

Prior to 2003, Georgia was a post-Soviet backwater, characterised by an incomplete transition to democracy and capitalism, high levels of corruption and widespread poverty. President Eduard Shevardnadze, who together with Mikhail Gorbachev had been one of the architects of the Soviet Union's rapprochement with the West, managed to maintain equidistance between Moscow and Washington. In the wake of rigged parliamentary elections, mass demonstrations forced Shevardnadze out of office at the end of 2003. The 'Rose Revolution', named after the roses held by demonstrators who stormed the parliament in protest against the fraudulent elections, led to new presidential and parliamentary elections in 2004. They brought into power a pro-American and nationalist President – Mikhail Saakashvili.

Tensions between, on the one hand, Georgia and, on the other hand, the break-away territories and Russia, began to rise in the wake of the Rose Revolution. Emboldened by his success in reasserting central control of the region of Adjara within a few months of his Presidency, Saakashvili began to pursue a pronounced nationalist agenda of building up the country's armed forces and of pushing for the reintegration of the break-away territories. This policy led to a flare-up of violent clashes between Georgia and South Ossetian forces, destroying the inter-ethnic confidence at grass roots level that had been built up since the mid-1990s.[14] The

---

[11] UNSC Resolution 937 (1994) of 21 July 1994.

[12] B. Coppieters, 'Introduction', in B. Coppieters, D. Darchiashvili and N. Akaba, eds., *Federal Practice* (Brussels, VUB Press 2000), at 16.

[13] For more on the Boden plan, see N. Tocci, *The EU and Conflict Resolution: Promoting Peace in the Backyard* (London, Routledge 2007), at 129 and 134.

[14] International Crisis Group, *Georgia: Avoiding War in South Ossetia*, Europe Report No. 159 (Tbilisi/Brussels 2004); International Crisis Group, *Georgia's South Ossetia Conflict: Make Haste Slowly*, Europe Report No. 183 (Tbilisi/Brussels 2007).

government subsequently sought to isolate the self-declared political authorities in the two entities and to 'Westernise' efforts to resolve the conflicts. It identified Russia as the main culprit in keeping the conflicts frozen. Moscow could not be, at the same time, a neutral broker and a party to the conflicts, supporting the secessionist leaders and refusing to assist in the return of refugees and IDPs.[15] To raise the salience of the conflicts, the Georgian government tabled unilateral conflict resolution plans at the UN, the Organisation for Security and Cooperation in Europe (OSCE) and the Council of Europe. These measures reinforced the siege mentality of the de facto authorities in the break-away territories and angered Russia. Political dialogue between the parties stalled. In response to the deteriorating political situation, further aggravated by Georgia's reinvigorated push for membership of the North Atlantic Treaty Organisation (NATO), all conflict parties began to build up their military positions in and around the conflict zones. Hostage takings, shootings and explosions on both sides of the boundary lines separating Georgia from the secessionist entities increased. Georgia refused to commit itself unambiguously to the non-use of force. In the fall of 2006, it arrested four alleged Russian spies. Moscow retaliated with a partial economic blockade, the expulsion of Georgians from Russia, the closure of the only land border and the suspension of air travel and postal communication between the two countries. In addition, it reinforced its political ties with the break-away regions. Following the Western-backed unilateral declaration of independence of Kosovo in February 2008, Russian-Georgian relations deteriorated further. Moscow unilaterally withdrew from CIS sanctions against Abkhazia, which had been imposed back in 1996.[16] Russian ministries began to establish official links with their counterparts in the two break-away republics. Furthermore, a number of Georgian unmanned reconnaissance drones were shot down over Abkhazia. An investigation into one of the incidents carried out by UNOMIG determined that it was downed by a Russian fighter plane.[17] This was denied by Moscow, which subsequently reinforced its peacekeeping troops in the region.[18] These and other steps were denounced by Georgia as de facto annexation of the break-away territories.

---

[15] Russia supported Abkhazia and South Ossetia by, among other things, seconding the political demands of secessionist leaders, providing free energy to the entities and granting Russian citizenship to the concerned populations.

[16] Interestingly, Tbilisi's stance on the Kosovo issue has been closer to that of Moscow than to that of its main Western backers. As stated by Deputy Foreign Minister Giga Bokeria, Tbilisi has 'no plans to recognize Kosovo's independence', cited in D. Smith, 'The Saakashvili Administration's Reaction to Russian Policies before the 2008 War', in S. Cornell and S. Starr, eds., *The Guns of August 2008: Russia's War in Georgia* (Armonk, NY, M.E. Sharpe 2009), at 128. As to the CIS sanctions against Abkhazia, Russia had not enforced them since 1999. See A. Akçakoca, T. Vanhauwaert, R. Whitman and S. Wolff, *After Georgia: Conflict Resolution in the EU's Eastern Neighbourhood*, EPC Issue Paper No. 57 (Brussels, European Policy Centre 2009), at 12.

[17] Report of UNOMIG of 26 May 2008 on the incident of 20 April involving the downing of a Georgian UAV over the zone of conflict.

[18] Subsequent (alleged) downings of Georgian drones were publicised by both Moscow and Sukhumi but denied by Tbilisi.

On the domestic front, Saakashvili's reform agenda ran into problems and the democratic transition began to stall as conflicts among the political forces which had been behind the Rose Revolution began to intensify. In November 2007, the government violently repressed social unrest. A state of emergency was declared. Media freedom took a turn for the worse as the government sought to weaken the political opposition. In 2008, Freedom House downgraded Georgia to a 'partly free' democracy.[19] The snap presidential and parliamentary elections in the first half of 2008 did not do anything to calm the situation. On the contrary, they contributed to the polarisation of the country's political elite. It was in this domestic and international context that Georgia tried to reintegrate South Ossetia by force.

On 7 August 2008, Georgian troops entered South Ossetia, shelling its capital Tskhinvali.[20] About 30,000 persons fled to Russia. Moscow responded quickly and with massive military action. It pushed the Georgian armed forces out of the break-away region and then expanded the war into Georgia proper in an effort to systematically destroy the country's military hardware and infrastructure and, possibly, to send a signal to the West that Tbilisi's aspirations to join NATO were unacceptable to Moscow. At the same time, Abkhaz and Russian troops drove out Georgian forces from the eastern part of their statelet. As the war on Georgian territory continued, the French Presidency of the EU brokered a ceasefire on 12 August.[21] However, despite the agreement signed by Presidents Sarkozy, Medvedev and Saakashvili, Russian troops remained deep within Georgia in a self-declared security zone around Abkhazia and South Ossetia. Moreover, on 26 August, Moscow officially recognised the self-declared sovereignty of the two territories.[22] The European Council unanimously condemned the move.[23] At the beginning of September, the EU and Russia agreed that Russian forces withdraw from the areas adjacent to the break-away republics within 10 days of the deployment of an EU Monitoring Mission (EUMM) to the conflict area.[24] The agreement de facto designated the EU as guarantor of peace in Georgia. Yet this breakthrough did not prevent Russia from establishing formal bilateral military ties with Tskhinvali and Sukhumi later in the same month.[25]

---

[19] Freedom House, *Country Report: Georgia (2009)*, available at: <http://www.freedomhouse.org/template.cfm?page=22&country=7612&year=2009>.

[20] For a chronology of the crisis see 'A Chronology of the Crisis', 14 *Strategic Comments* (2008), available at: <http://www.iiss.org/publications/strategic-comments/past-issues/volume-14-2008/volume-14-issue-7/a-chronology-of-the-crisis/>. For the report of the Independent International Fact-Finding Mission on the Conflict in Georgia (Tagliavini Report), see A. Lobjakas, 'EU Report on 2008 War Tilts against Georgia', *Radio Free Europe*, 30 September 2009.

[21] The text of the agreement is available at: <http://ambafrance-us.org/spip.php?article1101>.

[22] Statement by President of Russia Dmitry Medvedev of 26 August 2008, available at: <http://www.kremlin.ru/eng/speeches/2008/08/26/1543_type82912_205752.shtml>.

[23] Presidency Conclusions, Extraordinary European Council, 1 September 2008, 12594/08.

[24] For the text of the 8 September 2008 agreement, detailing the implementation of the 12 August 2008 six-point plan, see: <http://ambafrance-us.org/IMG/pdf/mise_en_oeuvre_plan_12_aout_2008.pdf>.

[25] Statement by President of Russia Dmitry Medvedev of 17 September 2008, available at: <http://www.kremlin.ru/eng/speeches/2008/09/17/1948_type82912type82914type82915_206565.shtml>.

The bilateral accords have provided the legal basis for Russia's continuing military presence in the entities, albeit no longer as peacekeepers but as allied forces. Moscow deployed some 3,700 troops in each republic and announced that it would permanently station naval vessels in Abkhazia.[26] In April 2009, Russia went one step further and signed agreements with Sukhumi and Tskhinvali on the joint protection of their 'state borders'.[27]

In the aftermath of the war, Georgia severed diplomatic relations with Russia and revoked its assent to the 1994 Moscow ceasefire agreement with Abkhazia and the 1992 Sochi agreement. Tbilisi has since considered Russian troops on its territory as illegal occupation forces. It has been particularly concerned about the Akhalgori, which, prior to the war, was 85 per cent Georgian and administered by Tbilisi.[28] Since then, it has been occupied by South Ossetian and Russian forces. Not least because the town is only about 40 kilometres from Tbilisi, Georgia has regarded the situation as a threat to its security. Also, the war with Russia has strengthened Georgia's determination to join NATO. This is seen as the best guarantee against future Russian aggression. While there is widespread consensus on this issue within the country, the lost war has further polarised the domestic political scene and has weakened the domestic legitimacy and international reputation of President Saakashvili. Last but not least, the human costs of the war have been heavy for Georgia. Several hundred Georgians and South Ossetians were killed.[29] About 137,000 people were displaced within Georgia. Most have returned to their homes but about 30,000 remain in long-term displacement, with no immediate prospect of going back. The new IDPs join an estimated 200,000 people who had not been able to return to their homes after the conflicts in the early 1990s.[30] With hindsight, the Georgian assault on Tskhinvali can only be described as a serious misjudgment on the part of the country's political and military leadership. They and the country as a whole have paid a high price for this miscalculation.[31]

## 3. EU peace activities in Georgia: From hands-off to hands-on engagement

Prior to the 2008 summer war, the main third-party interveners in Georgia's territorial conflicts were UNOMIG and the OSCE. The EU played a secondary role, though

---

[26] Georgia has challenged the accuracy of these numbers, believing there are up to 10,000 Russian troops in the entities.

[27] Statement by President of Russia Dmitry Medvedev of 30 April 2009, available at: <http://www.kremlin.ru/eng/speeches/2009/04/30/2000_type82912type82914_215748.shtml>.

[28] International Crisis Group, *Georgia-Russia: Still Insecure and Dangerous*, Europe Briefing No. 53 (Tbilisi/Brussels 2009), at 7.

[29] There is no consensus on precise casualty numbers. See O. Antonenko, 'A War with No Winners', 50 *Survival* (2008), at 25; P. Felgenhauer, 'After August 7: The Escalation of the Russia-Georgia War', in Cornell and Starr, eds., *supra* n. 16, at 178.

[30] International Crisis Group, *supra* n. 28, at 1.

[31] Antonenko (2008), *supra* n. 29; V. Cheterian, 'The August 2008 War in Georgia: From Ethnic Conflict to Border Wars', 28 *Central Asian Survey* (2009) 155-170.

it began to increase its contribution to the peace process in the first half of the new millennium. This policy upgrade notwithstanding, Brussels neither had an operational role with regard to peacekeeping forces in the two break-away republics nor was it a member of the principal multilateral negotiation formats dealing with the management and resolution of the conflicts – the JCC and the Geneva process.

After the 2008 war, OSCE monitors were prevented from returning to South Ossetia, with the authorities of the break-away republic accusing the mission of having failed to give prior warnings of the Georgian attack.[32] In mid-June 2009, UNOMIG ceased operations as Russia vetoed a Security Council resolution to renew its mandate.[33] The same fate befell the OSCE mission to Georgia at the end of the month.[34] While the UN and the OSCE thus have to be counted among the losers of the Russia-Georgia conflict, the EU, somewhat unexpectedly, was able to impose itself as peacemaker. Due to the policy entrepreneurship of the French Presidency, the EU played the key role in bringing the short war to an end, in monitoring the ceasefire and in leading the international talks that were convened to deal with the fall-out from the conflict. Since then, Georgia has been the theatre with the most EU institutional actors on the ground.[35]

The EU's limited, albeit evolving role in Georgia prior to the summer of 2008 was shaped by both intra-EU politics and geopolitics. Just as in post-Soviet space more generally, EU involvement in Georgia throughout the 1990s was characterised by timidity. Virtually all Member States regarded it as a no-go area for the Common Foreign and Security Policy (CFSP). They considered it self-evident that Russia's shadow loomed too large over the region. Prudence and lack of interest also characterised the European Commission's activities. Its peacebuilding role in Georgia was limited compared to the role it has played in the Western Balkans. The Southern Caucasus was initially not included in the plans for the European Neighbourhood Policy (ENP). 2003/04 marked a turning point of sorts in the EU's *Ostpolitik*.[36] Policy was gradually firmed up and the visibility of the Union's presence in the region was enhanced.[37]

A milestone in this development was Georgia's inclusion in the ENP.[38] This has had the effect of drawing it closer into the EU orbit both in terms of Tbilisi's legisla-

---

[32] The de facto authorities would have let the monitors back into South Ossetia provided the OSCE established an independent presence in Tskhinvali, which would have bestowed a degree of legitimacy on their self-declared statelet.

[33] UNSC Press Release SC/9681 of 15 June 2009.

[34] OSCE Press Release of 22 December 2008, available at: <http://www.osce.org/georgia/item_1_35781.html>.

[35] The members of the EU family in Georgia comprise the EUSR for the South Caucasus, the EUSR for the Crisis in Georgia, the EUMM, the Border Support Team and the EC (now EU) Delegation.

[36] See S. Blockmans, 'La Nouvelle Vague: The Introduction of a More Significant Ost-politik in the EU's Security Policies', in A. Łazowski, ed., *The Application of EU Law in the New Member States: Brave New World* (The Hague, T.M.C. Asser Press 2010, forthcoming).

[37] See A. Łabędzka, 'The Southern Caucasus (Armenia, Azerbaijan and Georgia)', in S. Blockmans and A. Łazowski, eds., *The European Union and Its Neighbours: A Legal Appraisal of the EU's Policies of Stabilisation, Partnership and Integration* (The Hague, T.M.C. Asser Press 2006) 575-612.

[38] Communication from the Commission, of 12 May 2004, 'European Neighbourhood Policy: Strategy Paper', COM (2004) 373.

tive and regulatory alignment with the EU *acquis* and in terms of its foreign policy alignment with the CFSP. As to the CFSP, the EU appointed an EU Special Representative (EUSR) for the South Caucasus in 2003.[39] In 2004, the first mission run under the European Security and Defence Policy (ESDP) in post-Soviet space was deployed to Georgia – EUJUST THEMIS.[40] All these policies sought to contribute, in one way or another, to ongoing efforts to entrench peace in Georgia and to resolve its conflicts. The Union's growing activeness in the country (and post-Soviet space more generally) from 2003/04 onwards was due to the increasing geopolitical importance of the region as well as to changes in the balance of preferences within the EU.

The eastern enlargement of the EU has redistributed power among existing camps within the Union.[41] Although they were, at the time, only accession countries, the eight Central and Eastern European states poised to join the EU at the beginning of 2004 played a crucial role as policy advocates for Georgia. They successfully made the case for including the country in the ENP and initiated the deployment of EUJUST THEMIS.[42] Ever since, they have been tireless advocates of a more pro-active collective policy towards Georgia and of a tougher line on Russia. They have been motivated primarily by geopolitically and historically mediated security concerns about Russia, and Russian influence in Eastern Europe. Moreover, their geographical location makes them particularly vulnerable to negative externalities such as organised crime and human trafficking originating in or transiting through Georgia.[43]

The advocacy of the ex-communist EU states took place against the backdrop of broader geopolitical developments that prompted the EU to reinforce its involvement in the Eastern neighbourhood. First, and most obviously, the eastward enlargement of the EU brought the problems and conflicts of Eastern Europe right up to the borders of the EU.[44] Most importantly, there has been the growing salience of energy security. Russia accounts for about 50 per cent of the total gas imports of the EU and for over 30 per cent of its oil imports.[45] With world energy markets

[39] Council Joint Action 2003/496/CFSP of 7 July 2003 concerning the appointment of an EU Special Representative for the South Caucasus, *OJ* 2003 L 169/74.

[40] Council Joint Action 2004/523/CFSP of 28 June 2004 on the European Union Rule of Law Mission in Georgia, EUJUST THEMIS, *OJ* 2004 L 228/21.

[41] G. Müller-Brandeck-Bocquet, ed., *The Future of the European Foreign, Security and Defence Policy after Enlargement* (Baden-Baden, Nomos 2006); T. Valášek, 'New EU Members in Europe's Security Policy', 18 *Cambridge Review of International Affairs* (2005) 217-228.

[42] The ex-communist countries used their observer status in CFSP decision-shaping and decision-making bodies to vigorously lobby for greater Union involvement in Georgia.

[43] For detailed analyses, see D. Lynch, *Why Georgia Matters*, Chaillot Paper No. 86 (Paris, EU Institute for Security Studies 2006); M. Merlingen, *European Security and Defense Policy: What It Is, How It Works, Why It Matters* (Boulder, CO, Lynne Rienner, forthcoming).

[44] See R. Aliboni, 'The Geopolitical Implications of the European Neighbourhood Policy', 10 *European Foreign Affairs Review* (2005) 1-16.

[45] By 2020, the numbers are expected to rise to 70 per cent and 50 per cent, respectively. See F. Proedrou, 'The EU-Russia Energy Approach under the Prism of Interdependence', 16 *European Security* (2007), at 334.

predicted to become tighter in the next decades – a development which will increase the power of resource holders – European decision-makers have become increasingly uneasy about their energy relationship with Moscow. The EU has been reminded of its dependency on Russia's oil and gas spigot by recent supply disruptions. For instance, at the beginning of 2009, a gas row between Russia and Ukraine led to major gas shortages in Eastern and South-Eastern Europe.[46] The knock-on effects were felt in Western Europe. Many European capitals have interpreted incidents of this sort as a worrisome manifestation of what the former head of the European Commission delegation in Moscow called 'Gazprom politics'.[47] In this view, the Russian state is not a reliable energy supplier. It is ready to violate contractual obligations and use energy as 'a currency of power in the international system' to gain political leverage in target countries.[48] These concerns, in turn, have increased the geo-economic salience of Georgia as an energy corridor linking the EU to Caspian oil and gas while bypassing Russia.

Second, the escalating tensions between Tbilisi and Moscow and between the former and the break-away authorities in Sukhumi and Tskhinvali persuaded the EU of the need to do more to build peace among the parties. The European Commission and the EUSR for the South Caucasus organised a joint fact-finding mission in early 2007 to explore what concrete steps the EU could take. The upshot of the visit was a joint paper in which the Commission and the EUSR elaborated a set of new peacebuilding measures with a view to creating conditions conducive to finding a political settlement. It was given the green light by the EU states in September 2007. Among the envisaged activities were economic projects such as the reconstruction of infrastructure connecting Georgia and the break-away republics, for instance, the rehabilitation of the Black Sea Railway through Abkhazia; people-to-people contacts; education and information projects, including the opening of EU information centres in Abkhazia and South Ossetia; and cooperation in the field of law enforcement.[49] Most of these planned measures had not gone beyond the preparatory phase when the Russia-Georgia war erupted in August 2008.

A third factor conducive to the EU's reinforced engagement in Georgia was Russia's drift towards illiberal policies at home, carried out under the banner of 'sovereign democracy',[50] and its reinvigorated insistence on a sphere of special

---

[46] Commission Staff Working Document, 'The January 2009 Gas Supply Disruption to the EU: An Assessment', COM (2009) 363.

[47] Cited in G. Edwards, 'The New Member States and the Making of EU Foreign Policy', 11 *European Foreign Affairs Review* (2006), at 159.

[48] Enno Harks, cited in D. Triantaphyllou, 'Energy Security and Common Foreign and Security Policy (CFSP): The Wider Black Sea Area Context', 7 *Southeast European and Black Sea Studies* (2007), at 290.

[49] In June 2008, the European Commission and the EUSR for the South Caucasus put together a 'Non-Paper on way forwards for Georgia', which proposed to further intensify and enlarge the scope of EU peacebuilding measures. The proposal included the deployment of EU advisors to the break-away territories and the introduction of 'political' peacebuilding measures, such as pushing the parties to make commitments to the non-use of force and to the right of refugees and IDPs to return to their homes.

[50] D. Averre, '"Sovereign Democracy" and Russia's Relations with the European Union', 15 *Demokratizatsiya* (2007) 173-190.

interests in Eastern and South-Eastern Europe. Russia's resurgence on the international stage led to clashes with the EU, not only over Georgia but also over Ukraine, Moldova and Kosovo. This made the EU more willing to harden its *Ostpolitik*.[51]

## 4. Building peace through political dialogue

Political dialogue is one of the main foreign policy instruments of the EU. It used it to insert itself into the management and resolution of the territorial conflicts in Georgia. It sought to moderate the conflictual behaviour of the parties and to change their attitudes and negotiation positions. In relations with Russia, the EU discussed the frozen conflicts at the highest level – the EU-Russia summits, established under the Partnership and Cooperation Agreement (PCA).[52] Consultations on the issue also took place in, amongst others, the Permanent Partnership Council and during monthly talks between the Troika of the EU Political and Security Committee (PSC) and the Russian ambassador to the EU. Last but not least, local EU Troikas carried out démarches in both Moscow and Tbilisi to defuse escalating tensions.[53] In relations with Georgia, the EU discussed the frozen conflicts at senior political level, including in the Cooperation Council after the entry into force of the PCA between the EU and Georgia in 1999.[54] After EU ministerial and PSC Troikas became part of the institutionalised channels of communication between Brussels and Tbilisi, the secessionist conflicts were also discussed at these venues.[55] EU consultations with representatives of the de facto authorities of Abkhazia and South Ossetia were less frequent. They were primarily conducted by the EUSR for the South Caucasus.

The overall impact of political dialogue on the peace process was marginal. This had to do with the fact that the EU failed to create sufficient leverage over the conflict parties that would have enabled it to broker peace. In particular, it proved incapable of using policies of conditionality. In the case of Abkhazia and South Ossetia, such polices were excluded because the EU did not have official relations

---

[51] See M. Merlingen, M. Mireanu and E. Stavrevska, 'The Current State of European Security', in Institute for Peace Research and Security Policy at the University of Hamburg, ed., *OSCE Yearbook 2008: Yearbook on the Organization for Security and Co-Operation in Europe (OSCE)* (Baden-Baden, Nomos 2009) 91-117.

[52] The full text of the PCA between the EU and the Russian Federation is available at: <http://eur-lex.europa.eu/LexUriServ/LexUriServ.do?uri=CELEX:21997A1128(01):EN:HTML>.

[53] The PSC Troika for Russia comprises the PSC ambassador from the country holding the EU Presidency, the Director of the Policy Planning and Early Warning Unit of the Council General Secretariat, the Deputy Political Director of the European Commission and the PSC ambassador of the incoming Presidency. Local EU Troikas comprise the ambassadors of the current and future holders of the Presidency, the head of the Commission delegation and, in the case of Georgia, the EUSR for the South Caucasus, if he happens to be in the country at the time of the démarche.

[54] The full text of the PCA between the EU and Georgia is available at: <http://eur-lex.europa.eu/LexUriServ/LexUriServ.do?uri=CELEX:21999A0804(01):EN:NOT>.

[55] EU ministerial Troikas comprise the Foreign Minister of the country holding the Presidency, the High Representative for the CFSP, a member of the European Commission, often, though not always, the Commissioner for External Relations, and the Foreign Minister of the incoming Presidency.

with them. Divisions among Member States made it impossible for the EU to make its relations with Russia conditional on Moscow's willingness to settle the frozen conflicts. Finally, EU relations with Georgia were too limited to allow for strong conditionality policies.[56] This said, on occasion political dialogue did play a role in containing tensions among the parties. For instance, the EU persuaded Tbilisi not to declare the Russian-only CIS peacekeepers in Abkhazia illegal, a measure that would have further poisoned relations between Georgia and Russia and between Tbilisi and Sukhumi at a time when all possibilities for a peaceful conflict settlement had not yet been exhausted.

Third-party mediation for the secessionist conflicts was provided by the Group of Friends of the UN Secretary-General for Georgia. While the Group, which has been defunct since the 2008 summer war, was not an EU body, EU states played a prominent role in it.[57] In 2005, the EU states Estonia, Latvia, Lithuania and Poland and the soon-to-be EU members Romania and Bulgaria formed an informal group – the New Friends of Georgia.[58] They acted not as mediators but as policy advocates, making the case for, among other things, a greater EU role in negotiations to resolve the frozen conflicts and in the internationalisation of peacekeeping forces in Abkhazia and South Ossetia. Over the years, members of the Group put forth a number of proposals. For instance, they called for closer EU relations with Tbilisi, including a visa facilitation agreement, and the deployment of an ESDP rule of law mission or an incident verification mission to Abkhazia. Also, they advocated putting pressure on Moscow to constrain it to reduce its military posture in the two break-away territories and, after 2006, to lift its economic blockade against Georgia.

As tensions between Georgia, on the one hand, and the secessionist entities and Russia, on the other, increased in the first half of 2008, the EU, the UN Group of Friends and the US engaged in high-level, hectic diplomacy to prevent further escalation. Georgia topped the agenda of all EU-Russia political dialogue meetings at the time. In addition to being discussed at meetings between the PSC Troika and Russia, it featured prominently on the EU-Russia summit agenda. At the beginning of June 2008, the High Representative for the CFSP Javier Solana visited Georgia and Abkhazia in order to signal the Union's resolve to inject new momentum into the resolution of the conflicts. The Georgian President, in turn, toured the key EU capitals, including Brussels, Berlin and Paris, at the end of the same month in an attempt to persuade the EU to put pressure on Moscow to stop undermining Georgia's territorial integrity. At the beginning of July, Secretary of State Condoleezza Rice visited Georgia to assure Saakashvili of American support while urging restraint.[59]

---

56 For an analysis of EU conditionality in Georgia, see Tocci (2007), *supra* n. 13, at 146-147.

57 The Group of Friends continues to function in a reduced format – the Western Group of Friends, which excludes Russia.

58 Other countries, such as Sweden and Britain, have subsequently joined the group, or regularly attend its meetings.

59 H. Cooper and T. Shanker, 'After Mixed U.S. Messages, a War Erupted in Georgia', *New York Times,* 13 August 2008.

About a week later, it was German Foreign Minister Steinmeier, acting as coordinator of the Group of Friends, who sought to calm the situation. He flew into Tbilisi and Sukhumi to present a peace plan to Georgia and Abkhazia. The plan had previously been discussed with Moscow. Yet the summer of 2008 was a time of war, not peace in Georgia.

## 5. The peacebuilder: The European Commission in Georgia (including Abkhazia and South Ossetia)

European Commission peace activities in Georgia have squarely focused on peacebuilding. The Commission has sought to address what it considers the underlying causes of the enduring conflicts – bad governance, economic underdevelopment, human misery and images of the 'other'. It has done so through the ENP and project funding in the conflict zones.

In the pre-ENP period (1992-2005), the European Commission allocated to Georgia €505 million in technical assistance, with a focus on democracy and reforms of the judicial system, notably the penitentiary system and the prosecution service.[60] Also, it provided technical assistance to local consultants of the Georgian Ministry of Conflict Resolution and financed the JCC.[61] In 2006, the ENP Action Plan for Georgia was adopted.[62] It lays out the strategic objectives of EU-Georgia relations, identifying eight priority areas. They cover, amongst others, the strengthening of the judicial system, economic development and trade-related issues, cooperation in justice and home affairs, and energy security. Priority 6 concerns the peaceful resolution of internal conflicts. Compared to the other chapters, this priority is less developed. It has little to say about how the conflict settlement process could be pushed forward, besides the mantra about the importance of political dialogue and confidence-building measures. The funding mechanism for the ENP – the European Neighbourhood and Partnership Instrument (ENPI) – provides €120 million between 2007 and 2010.[63] The funds are spread over four priority areas (democracy, rule of law, good governance; economic development and the implementation of the ENP Action Plan; poverty reduction; and support for the peaceful settlement of territorial conflicts). The latter is funded by only €19 million, which is significantly less than the money allocated to the other priorities. As part of the package of peacebuilding measures agreed in 2007, the Commission also provided technical assistance to the Georgian Ministry of Conflict Resolution and an EU external advisor on minority issues to the Ministry of Civic Integration.

With the ENP, the EU has only half-heartedly translated its structural power into bargaining leverage to push forward the resolution of Georgia's territorial conflicts.

---

[60] European Neighbourhood and Partnership Instrument: Georgia: Country Strategy Paper 2007-2013, at 16, available at: <http://www.delgeo.ec.europa.eu>.

[61] *Supra* n. 6.

[62] EU/Georgia Action Plan, available at: <http://ec.europa.eu/world/enp/documents_en.htm#3>.

[63] European Neighbourhood and Partnership Instrument: Georgia, *supra* n. 60.

This has to do with the fact that the EU does not have a coherent strategy in post-Soviet space. Its attempts to pursue milieu goals in the region are timid, sometimes even contradictory. Another, albeit related reason for the Union's limited structural power in Georgia is that the ENP does not include the juiciest carrot available to the EU to influence third countries – EU accession. This is without doubt a major reason for the limited 'bite' of Brussels' conditionality policy vis-à-vis Tbilisi. In the wake of the Russia-Georgia summer war, Tbilisi asked to reinforce the conflict-related chapter of the ENP Action Plan. The politically cautious Commission refused on the grounds that the plan is about the country's long-term needs and reform priorities, not about short-term fixes. The Eastern Partnership (EaP), which was launched in May 2009,[64] is an upgrade of the ENP for Eastern European countries. However, it does little to reinforce the structural power of the EU in relation to the conflict between Georgia and the break-away entities. Conflict resolution is dealt with under the EaP's thematic platform on 'democracy, good governance and stability', but the envisaged measures do not really go beyond what is already included in the ENP Action Plan for Georgia.

Commission projects in the conflict zones have been aimed at improving the living conditions of IDPs, rebuilding infrastructure, alleviating the economic consequences of the conflict as well as strengthening civil society and NGOs.[65] In 2007, the ENPI provided €4 million in support of projects in Abkhazia and South Ossetia. In 2008, prior to the war, €6 million was allocated. In Abkhazia, UNOMIG and the UN Development Programme (UNDP) were the main implementation partners of Commission-funded projects, though NGOs (local and international) also played a role. Projects focused on public health, electricity, agricultural development and police aid. The Commission also supplied funding for the de-mining activities of the HALO trust and provided €420,000 from the Instrument for Stability to promote multi-track dialogue on the human and economic dimensions of the Georgian-Abkhaz conflict. A flagship programme, which was financed together with the European Bank for Reconstruction and Development (EBRD), was the rehabilitation of the Enguri hydro-power plant, which provides electricity to both Georgia and Abkhazia.[66] As to South Ossetia, in 2006 an Economic Rehabilitation Programme was launched by an international donor conference co-organised by the Commission and the OSCE. Commission-funded projects included the rehabilitation of electricity and gas networks and schools.[67] The OSCE coordinated the implementation of these and other international programmes. The intended rehabilitation of the outdated irrigation and water supply system that covers both South Ossetia and adjacent parts of Georgia was derailed by the war. The associated problems of insufficient water supplies and poor sanitary conditions thus remain.

---

64 Joint Declaration of the Prague Eastern Partnership Summit of 7 May 2009 (8435/09).

65 The conflict zones cover the adjacent territory on both sides of the administrative boundary lines. A detailed overview of EC projects in the conflict zones is available at: <http://www.delgeo.ec.europa.eu/en/programmes/rehabilitation.html>.

66 The dam is located on the Georgian side, the power station on the Abkhaz side.

67 Further information on EC projects in South Ossetia/Georgia is available at: <http://www.delgeo.ec.europa.eu/en/index.html>.

The Commission hoped that its peacebuilding projects would change enemy perceptions, encourage institutional change and empower civil society to hold local political elites to account. Moreover, project implementation required cross-border interaction and thus offered the conflict parties opportunity to discuss, in a depoliticised setting, the operational aspects of political hot potatoes such as the return of IDPs and cross-border law enforcement cooperation. Yet this form of bottom-up peacebuilding by stealth failed to bear fruits. Although the Commission was the largest international donor in Abkhazia and South Ossetia, the impact of its projects on the peace processes was at best marginal. This strongly suggests that small-scale projects cannot substitute for a lack of political will and strategic vision to act as a committed peace broker.

The 2008 Russia-Georgia summer war severely disrupted European Commission activities in the conflict zones. Moreover, it shifted the focus of the interventions from long-term peacebuilding to the short-term alleviation of human suffering. The unilateral declaration of independence by the de facto authorities, Russia's recognition thereof and Georgia's post-war 'negative agenda' of further isolating them economically and politically have made it impossible for the Commission to deliver urgently needed humanitarian aid to the entities. Georgia's new Law on Occupied Territories[68] strictly limits and controls any international aid and reconstruction activities in the areas. International activities in the territories need permission from the government in Tbilisi and have to be coordinated by it. The break-away regions consider this as unacceptable meddling in their own 'sovereign' affairs. This political deadlock has severely limited the Commission's ability to continue its rehabilitation projects in Abkhazia and South Ossetia.[69] The termination of the mandates of its major implementation partners – the UN and the OSCE – has made a bad situation even worse.

In October 2008, the Commission and the World Bank organised an international donor conference for Georgia.[70] The participants pledged about 4.5 billion dollars in assistance. The Commission promised to provide up to €500 million to the country in the period 2008-2010. This figure includes previously committed funds from the ENPI and new funds disbursed through ECHO and the Instrument for Stability as well as the costs of the EUMM. ECHO has funded humanitarian assistance such as food aid, firewood distribution, psycho-social support for children and the provision of shelter.[71] The Instrument for Stability has paid for, among other things, the winterisation of the shelters of IDPs; small infrastructure rehabili-

---

68 Law on Occupied Territories of Georgia of 23 October 2008, available at: <http://www.venice.coe.int/docs/2009/CDL(2009)004-e.asp>.

69 Incidentally, the law also creates disincentives for IDPs to return to their homes as it undermines the living conditions in the territories and limits economic and financial transactions across the boundary line.

70 Georgia Donors Conference, 22 October 2008, available at: <http://ec.europa.eu/external_relations/georgia/conference/index_en.htm>.

71 A detailed breakdown of ECHO assistance is available at: <http://www.delgeo.ec.europa.eu/en/programmes/echo.html>.

tation; the reintegration of IDPs, including the construction of new housing; confidence-building measures; and civil society capacity building.[72] By the end of 2008, the Commission had provided about €120 million in extra funding for Georgia. Its total aid for the country in 2008 amounted to about €182 million.

## 6. The EU Special Representative for the South Caucasus: Security sector reform and confidence building

EUSRs are an important CFSP instrument through which the EU seeks to 'play an active role in efforts to consolidate peace, stability and the rule of law' in troubled regions.[73] In 2003, the EU appointed the first EUSR for the South Caucasus.[74] Since 2006, Peter Semneby has held this post.[75] He has managed to raise the profile of the position considerably, notably through his hands-on engagement in Georgia. EUSR Semneby has been a more visible EU actor in the country than the Commission delegation, even though he has been a roving diplomat who is not permanently stationed in the country. One of the principal objectives of his mandate has been to 'prevent conflicts in the region' and to 'contribute to the peaceful settlement of conflicts'. However, he has been given few means to achieve these objectives. He has not been authorised to act as mediator between the conflict parties, nor has he been given any strong material leverage to exert influence on them. His main role has been to act as the local relay of EU messages designed to moderate the conflictual behaviour of the parties and to persuade them to reinvigorate their search for a negotiated settlement. He has held political dialogue with the parties to the conflict and other interested actors such as the UN, the OSCE and the UN Group of Friends. In close cooperation with the European Commission, which has the funds he does not have, he has developed numerous small-scale peacebuilding projects, including the promotion of multi-track diplomacy. For instance, together with the EU Institute for Security Studies, EUSR Semneby launched a series of seminars/round tables on conflict resolution in Georgia, with participation of independent experts and civil society actors from Georgia, Abkhazia and South Ossetia. The appointment of the EUSR for the Crisis in Georgia in the wake of the war in August 2008 has cut into Semneby's conflict-related responsibilities.[76] Conversely, the deployment of the EUMM in October 2008 has given him the additional task of providing local political guidance to the head of the ESDP mission.[77] After the war, the EUSR

[72] For further details on EC assistance, see <http://www.delgeo.ec.europa.eu/en/programmes/rehabilitation.html>.

[73] General Secretariat of the Council of the EU, 'EUSR Factsheet', 2007.

[74] Council Joint Action 2003/496/CFSP of 7 July 2003 concerning the appointment of an EU Special Representative for the South Caucasus, *OJ* 2003 L 169/74.

[75] Council Joint Action 2006/121/CFSP of 20 February 2006 appointing the EU Special Representative for the South Caucasus, *OJ* 2006 L 49/14.

[76] Council Joint Action 2008/760/CFSP of 25 September 2008 appointing the EU Special Representative for the Crisis in Georgia, *OJ* 2008 L 259/16.

[77] Council Joint Action 2008/796/CFSP of 13 October 2008 amending the mandate of the EU Special Representative for the South Caucasus, *OJ* 2008 L 272/19.

office in Tbilisi was temporarily reinforced by seven Crisis Response Team (CRT) personnel. They joined up with existing EUSR staff to form temporary field teams, providing daily reporting on the security and humanitarian situation on the ground. Moreover, they played an important role in preparing the launch of the EUMM.

One of the main practical peacebuilding contributions of the EUSR has been the small Border Support Team (BST), which is part of his Tbilisi office.[78] The BST followed on the heels of the OSCE Border Monitoring Operation in Georgia, which was forced to close down because of Russia's refusal to agree to prolong its mandate. The OSCE mission had been deployed because of mutual allegations by Tbilisi and Moscow about border violations by the other side in relation to Moscow's military campaign in Chechnya. The deployment of observers was designed to calm the situation, to provide unbiased information about the actual situation along Georgia's border with Chechnya, Ingushetia and Daghestan, and, most importantly, to prevent the escalation of the Russian-Chechen war into armed clashes between Russia and Georgia. At its peak, the mission had 148 observers. The EU BST is considerably smaller. Its staff of nine internationals has been active at all levels of the chain of command of the Georgian Border Police. Unlike their OSCE colleagues, they have not been mandated to monitor the border, but to contribute to security sector reform related to border management. The team has advised Georgian political authorities involved in border and customs issues, notably the Ministries of the Interior and Finance. Also, it has provided hands-on advice to border police units in the field. At the political level, the BST assisted Georgian authorities in devising a border management strategy. The strategy was endorsed by the President in February 2008. Subsequently, the BST has focused on providing input into the elaboration of the implementation action plan; the drafting of the required secondary legislation, including on inter-agency cooperation between the border police and the customs administration; and the development of standard operating procedures (SOPs) for the border police. In the field, the BST has assisted the Border Police in implementing EU best practice, including the new SOPs. An important limitation of the BST has been that, for political reasons, its mandate excludes any operational activities in the break-away territories. This has made it impossible for the team to contribute to building confidence across the administrative boundary lines.

## 7. EUJUST THEMIS: Building peace through reinforcing the rule of law?

In the wake of the Rose Revolution, the EU upgraded its involvement in Georgia. The European Commission increased its aid package and the Council agreed to

[78] For a discussion on the legal basis of this 'invisible' ESDP mission, see F. Hoffmeister, 'Inter-Pillar Coherence in the EU's Civilian Crisis Management', in S. Blockmans, ed.. *The European Union and Crisis Management: Policy and Legal Aspects* (The Hague, T.M.C. Asser Press 2008) 157-180, at 166.

deploy its first-ever ESDP mission in post-Soviet space.[79] While the rule of law mission EUJUST THEMIS had no official peacebuilding role, a generous reading of its mandate may conclude that it assisted in creating the preconditions for the peaceful reintegration of the break-away republics. By promoting the rule of law, it sought to create an environment in which Abkhaz and South Ossetians could enjoy effective self-determination within Georgia's internationally recognised borders. While in principle right, this assessment has to be qualified by emphasising the extremely limited impact of the mission on the ground. THEMIS had a very limited mandate, very few resources and very little time to carry out its mission. In July 2004, eight European rule of law experts were co-located with Georgian authorities. They were given a one-year mandate to assist their local counterparts in evaluating the justice system, in drafting a criminal justice reform strategy and in elaborating an implementation plan. The mission members had to accomplish their assignment in an institutionally difficult environment. The new Saakashvili administration launched a massive purge of personnel associated with the old regime, including ministry staff, judges and prosecutors. At the same time, American and European experts vied for influence on how to restructure the justice system. Given their divergent legal cultures and philosophies, it frequently happened that they gave conflicting advice to their Georgian interlocutors.[80] In view of the internal and external challenges it faced, THEMIS did not manage to complete its mandate tasks. The elaboration of an implementation strategy was left to a follow-on team of rule of law experts who were placed at the Tbilisi office of the EUSR for the South Caucasus. As to the inevitably lengthy process of implementing the strategy, and getting down to actually reforming the justice system, this task was left to the Commission-run ENP.

## 8. The EU Monitoring Mission in Georgia

At the beginning of September 2008, a few weeks after the conclusion of the 12 August ceasefire agreement that ended the Russia-Georgia war, Brussels and Moscow agreed a follow-up deal.[81] Russian forces would withdraw from the areas that they occupied outside the break-away republics within 10 days of the deployment of an EU Monitoring Mission to the conflict area. With this agreement the EU considerably expanded its role repertoire in Georgia. It took on a civilian peacekeeping role. First, reminiscent of a classical UN interposition force, the EUMM has facilitated the separation of Georgian and Russian forces and the creation of

---

[79] See X. Kurowska, 'More Than a Balkan Crisis Manager: The EUJUST Themis in Georgia', in M. Merlingen and R. Ostrauskaitė, eds., *European Security and Defence Policy: An Implementation Perspective* (London, Routledge 2008) 97-110.

[80] D. Helly, 'EUJUST Themis in Georgia: An Ambitious Bet on Rule of Law', in A. Nowak, ed., *Civilian Crisis Management: The EU Way*, Chaillot Paper No. 90 (Paris, EU Institute for Security Studies 2006) 87-102.

[81] *Supra* n. 24.

what amounts to a buffer zone around the administrative boundary lines. It has monitored the ceasefire in this zone. Second, the EUMM has sought to contribute to conditions on the ground that are conducive to the resumption of the interrupted peacebuilding and conflict resolution processes. Just as in the case of UN peacekeeping, these two functions have proven difficult to reconcile. One is about separating the conflict parties, the other about bringing them together in a joint quest for peace. While the EUMM has been largely successful in its first role, it has little to show when it comes to its second role.

The EUMM, which is a civilian, unarmed operation run under the ESDP, became operational in early October.[82] It has been headed by a German diplomat. Military expertise has been provided by the Deputy Head of Mission, a French general. The mission's initial mandate of 12 months was prolonged for one more year.[83] In the fall of 2009, the mission had about 340 people, including over 200 unarmed monitors hailing from 26 EU states. Initially, the Concept of Operations (CONOPS) foresaw a smaller deployment. However, Member State demands for participation were overwhelming; hence, the increase.[84] Most of the monitors have a policing or military background, though the mission does include monitors with expertise in human rights, gender and so forth.[85] The speedy start-up of the EUMM was made possible by the bending of EU crisis management procedures and the deployment of pre-equipped national teams which had their own vehicles, communications equipment, etc.

The mission initially focused on monitoring the implementation of the agreed withdrawal of Russian forces to their positions prior to the outbreak of the conflict.[86] Once the pull-back had by and large been completed, the focus shifted towards promoting the stabilisation and normalisation of the conflict zones and towards contributing to building confidence among the parties across the administrative boundary lines. Like other EU actors in Georgia, the mission has had limited means to achieve its goals. It has been able to do little besides monitoring developments on the ground, reporting back to Brussels on what it has observed and establishing communication channels with all actors on the ground. Thus, through its 24/7 day and night-time patrols it has monitored the resettlement and treatment of IDPs; the freedom and security of movement of civilians to and from Abkhazia and South Ossetia; law enforcement; de-mining; and the humanitarian situation in the conflict area. Other tasks have included the identification of farmland ownership in the conflict zone, which has become inaccessible as a result of the war, and the engage-

---

[82] Council Joint Action 2008/736/CFSP of 15 September 2008 on the European Union Monitoring Mission in Georgia, *OJ* 2008 L 248/26.

[83] Council Joint Action 2009/572/CFSP of 27 July 2009 amending and extending Council Joint Action 2008/736/CFSP on the European Union Monitoring Mission in Georgia, *OJ* 2009 L 197/110.

[84] No third party was invited to participate in the EUMM.

[85] See the chapter by Hazelzet in this volume.

[86] Disagreement between the EU and Russia remains over whether Moscow is in full compliance with the peace agreement. For instance, the town of Akhalgori has been a flashpoint, with the EU criticising Russia and South Ossetia for continuing to occupy it 'illegally'.

ment of civil society. The mission has worked on developing a mechanism to allow IDPs to visit their homes and cemeteries in an organised and secure manner. Among its more high-profile activities have been investigations of shooting incidents and kidnappings in its area of operation. Its contacts with all sides have facilitated the peaceful management of these and other localised problems, tensions and conflicts. Furthermore, it has participated in the Incident Prevention and Response Mechanisms set up to deal with the most serious security problems (for details, see next section). Through all these activities, the EUMM has doubtlessly contributed to containing hostilities in the post-conflict area.[87] However, it has not been able to move beyond this 'negative' task to the positive task of contributing to conditions on the ground that are conducive to reinvigorating the peace process. Notably, it has not succeeded in rebuilding confidence among the actors across the boundary lines; there are no signs that this is about to change any time soon.

Mission successes have been small-scale. It has succeeded in getting Georgian police to mark their uniforms and vehicles with clearly visible police badges and signs in order to ensure that Abkhaz and South Ossetian militias would not mistake them for members of the Georgian armed forces. In a similar vein, it successfully intervened to prevent the Georgian police from using armoured vehicles in the areas adjacent to the break-away republics as this might have been seen as inflammatory or threatening by the militias. The most tangible impact of the mission's negative task of containing tensions has been to help create a situation on the ground that has enabled more than 30,000 IDPs to return to their homes. Since the termination of the mandates of UNOMIG and the OSCE mission in Georgia in June 2009, the EUMM has been the sole international monitoring presence in the country. Moreover, the agreement it has with Tbilisi – the Memorandum of Understanding between the Ministry of Defence and the EUMM[88] – is the only remaining legal constraint on Georgia's military activities in the buffer zones. Access, however, has remained a challenge. The mission has not been allowed into Abkhazia and South Ossetia by their authorities. This has prevented it from monitoring the situation on their side of the administrative boundary line. This limit on the implementation of the mission's mandate is closely related to the continuing political stalemate regarding the resolution of the territorial conflict. Georgia and the West remain at loggerheads with Russia and the self-declared states of Abkhazia and South Ossetia.

## 9. The Geneva talks

The Sarkozy-Medvedev settlement plan of 12 August 2008 called for international talks on South Ossetia and Abkhazia.[89] With this agreement, the EU for the first

---

[87] By mid-July 2009, the EUMM had carried out 4,600 patrols; each week about 100 patrols are added. For the latest updates, see the EUMM website at: <http://www.eumm.eu/>.

[88] EUMM Press Release of 26 January 2009, available at: <http://www.eumm.eu/en/press_and_public_information/press_releases/796/>.

[89] *Supra* n. 21. Point 6 of the agreement stipulates: 'the opening of international discussions on the modalities of security and stability in Abkhazia and South Ossetia.'

time started to act as an official mediator between Tbilisi, Moscow, Tskhinvali and Sukhumi. Still in the preparatory phase, the EU decided to limit its meditation to issues related to conflict management, as opposed to conflict resolution. This was the result of a realistic assessment on the part of the EU of the dim prospects of a genuine peace conference along the lines of the Dayton negotiations on Bosnia.[90] The discrepancy between, on the one hand, the divergent preferences of the parties to the conflict and, on the other hand, the limited leverage that the EU was willing and/or able to bring to bear on them was simply too large to allow for a successful peace conference. The unspoken implication of the Union's limited negotiation posture is that the time for status negotiations between Georgia, Abkhazia and South Ossetia has passed. The two territories are, and are likely to remain, de facto independent, protected by Russia.

To prepare and facilitate the international talks, the EU appointed an EUSR for the Crisis in Georgia. From the very beginning, this has been a challenging task as the job description requires the postholder, Pierre Morel, both to represent the EU position at the talks and to act as mediator, driving the negotiation process forward. For instance, as an agent of the EU, the EUSR is bound by its non-recognition policy towards the separatist entities. Conversely, his success as a mediator is shaped by his ability to act with impartiality. This structural tension has not been the only challenge. In the preparation for the Geneva talks, the EUSR team considered how to strengthen the legitimacy of the talks and how to tap into the more than a decade-long field experience of the UN and the OSCE with the conflict dynamics and the politics of the region. These deliberations led the EUSR to propose to the UN Special Representative of the Secretary-General for Georgia and the Special Envoy of the OSCE Chairman-in-Office to join him as co-chairs of the Geneva talks. They agreed. Incidentally, at the time the talks were launched in October 2008, the mandates of the three international institutions covered the whole of Georgia, thus symbolically reaffirming the country's territorial integrity.

The first few rounds of the Geneva talks were bedevilled by procedural and status issues related to the divergent policy preferences of the parties. Tbilisi considers Abkhazia and South Ossetia to be Georgian territory. This position is supported by virtually the whole international community. The Georgian government has regarded the Geneva talks as a vehicle for internationalising the territorial conflicts and for reaffirming the country's territorial integrity and sovereignty. It has pressed the international community to establish new security arrangements to cover Abkhazia and South Ossetia and to monitor Russian conduct in the regions. Responding to Russian demands, it has declared its readiness to sign up to a binding non-use of force agreement with Moscow, provided it is part of a broader security regime that includes international executive policing on both sides of the conflict lines. Last but not least, Tbilisi has expressed its preference to see the talks evolve into a fully fledged international peace mechanism leading to the reintegration of

---

[90] Tbilisi initially called for the talks to be called 'International Peace Conference on the Russian-Georgian conflict'.

the territories into Georgia. Conversely, the two secessionist territories, backed by Russia, consider themselves sovereign states. Tskhinvali, Sukhumi and Moscow have sought to instrumentalise the talks to legitimise the 'sovereign' status of the two break-away republics. Moreover, Russia has called for legal and operational guarantees that Georgia will not attempt to retake Abkhazia and South Ossetia by force. It has insisted on the asymmetric demilitarisation of Georgia in its zone along the (administrative) border with the two break-away territories. Also, it has advocated imposing a weapons import ban on the country. To this toxic mix of divergent interests has to be added a pronounced lack of trust among the conflict parties. As to the EU, it has gone into the talks with four key objectives: getting the parties to commit to the Geneva process, and thus to working together; de-escalating tensions in the conflict zones and in bilateral relations between Russia and Georgia and the latter and the break-away territories; preventing further conflict; and gradually building confidence among the parties on the ground. To this end, the EUSR proposed to set up two working groups (WGs) – WG 1 deals with security issues and WG 2 with IDPs and refugees – and to negotiate an incident settlement mechanism to defuse the tense situation along the boundary lines separating Georgia from the entities.

The first few rounds of the Geneva discussions proved very difficult. It was only during round four of the talks in February 2009 that the co-chairs managed to persuade the parties to agree to the first tangible outcome of the meetings – an agreement in WG 1 on the establishment of two parallel Incident Prevention and Response Mechanisms for the boundary lines between Georgia and Abkhazia and Georgia and South Ossetia.

The Mechanisms are a classic instrument in the peacebuilder's toolbox, namely confidence-building measures. Abkhaz and South Ossetian representatives take part in their respective Mechanisms; the EUMM participates in both. They are joined by Georgian law enforcement representatives and Russian military representatives. The Mechanisms are designed to identify and review potential risks; share information; facilitate access of humanitarian aid to the break-away territories and free movement across the boundary lines; ascertain the facts about incidents; and provide recommendations on how to prevent future ones. Each Mechanism has its own 'hotline' through which the participants can contact each other in case of serious incidents.

WG 2 has been devoted to the return of IDPs and refugees. Discussions have covered technical and financial assistance for the rehabilitation of housing and infrastructure; the rehabilitation of the water supply linking villages north and south of the South Ossetian administrative boundary line; the non-discriminatory registration and profiling (sex, age, vulnerability criteria) of IDPs by local authorities (important to provide targeted and effective assistance to them); the restitution of or compensation for property of IDPs; and their return and reintegration. During the fifth round of the Geneva talks, agreement was reached on the formation of a joint assessment team to investigate disruptions of the water supply across the boundary line from South Ossetia to Georgian villages. Over winter, the parties, acting outside WG 2, had agreed on a similar mission looking into the disruption of gas supplies from Georgia into South Ossetia. It had resulted in the resumption of gas deliveries across the boundary line. More far-reaching measures have so far escaped the negotiators in WG 2 as even the most technical discussions inevitably have had political ramifications. For instance, even though all parties quickly reached a consensus that humanitarian assistance to South Ossetia was urgently required, one year into the Geneva talks no implementing decision had been taken. Georgia insisted that aid be delivered from the South (through Georgia), and South Ossetia argued that it would only accept aid if it was delivered from the North (through Russia). To find a way out of the conundrum, the co-chairs proposed 'double access' – convoys entering South Ossetia from the South and the North at the same time. Even this compromise formula did not lead to a breakthrough. In short, the Geneva discussions have proved difficult. Progress has been slow. This said, after some initial hesitation, all parties to the conflicts seem to have realised the importance of maintaining the viability of the only political forum in which they all participate. This recognition has gradually led to a more cooperative atmosphere in which agreements on limited peacebuilding measures and localised dispute settlement have become feasible.

## 10. Conclusion

The EU has imposed itself as peacemaker and mediator during and after the 2008 war between Russia and Georgia. Its role in bringing the conflict to an end, ensuring the withdrawal of Russian forces from Georgia and leading the Geneva talks has justifiably been celebrated by many in Brussels as a major diplomatic success, in particular when compared to the virtual absence of effective American diplomacy during the events in August and September. Yet the EU's involvement in peacebuilding, conflict management and conflict resolution in Georgia since the 1990s also shows the limitations of its capacity to act as a force for peace. These limitations can largely be attributed to two interrelated factors: the structural shortcomings of 'apolitical' peacebuilding and of the EU foreign policy system. Beginning with the former, for more than a decade the European Commission's checkbook diplomacy in Georgia has focused on funding peacebuilding projects aimed at reforming the socio-economic, institutional and cognitive conditions of the frozen conflicts. The purpose was to sow the seeds for a peaceful settlement and sustainable peace in the long run. Yet in the short term, an eminently political event – war – disrupted these efforts. While proponents of micro-level conflict transformation may argue that the failure of the Commission's long-term and bottom-up approach in Georgia was due to 'insufficient "quantity" rather than "quality" of input',[91] a

[91] Tocci (2007), *supra* n. 13, at 143; N. Tocci, *The European Union, Civil Society and Conflict Transformation: A Conceptual Framework*, MICROCON Policy Working Paper No. 1 (Brighton, MICROCON 2008).

more realistic assessment may be that the Commission's peacebuilding projects failed because they did not address the political dimension of the territorial conflicts. The Commission's structural peace policy towards Georgia and the secessionist entities has been constrained by 'an emerging contest between the EU and Russia over the political rules that are to govern the neighbourhood.'[92] The Commission's soft power to transform the conflicts was further undermined by the fact that the rivalry between Brussels and Moscow has been embedded in a new great game with both geopolitical and geo-economic stakes. It centres on hydrocarbon resources and energy transit routes and geopolitical bridgeheads for the war against terrorism and counter-proliferation. The players are not just Russia and the EU but all the regional states in Central Asia, the Southern Caucasus and the Black Sea region as well as extra-regional actors, especially the US.[93] On a more practical level, the limits of EU peacebuilding have been related to the fact that the small-scale projects that have been promoted by the Commission and the EUSR for the South Caucasus do not work (well) when they are most needed. They only work if there are limited tensions and good will on all sides. In tense situations such as those prevailing prior to the outbreak of the 2008 war, peacebuilding projects fall victim to the worsening political atmospherics. Apolitical projects aimed at transforming conflicts bottom-up are no substitute for tackling conflicts head-on at the highest political level.

Turning to the EU's foreign policy system, it is not about enforcing a common policy when Member State interests diverge but about facilitating a collective policy when national interests converge. On some important issues, national differences outweigh commonalities and, consequently, European foreign policy remains to a significant extent virtual.[94] The Union's relations with Russia and its policies in post-Soviet space are a case in point. As Grant puts it, 'Russia presents a test case for the EU's ambition to run a coherent and effective foreign policy, and it is a test that the EU is currently failing.'[95] The upshot of this political limit on collective foreign policy is a consensus-expectations gap. The EU 'is unable to deliver the foreign and security policies expected' due to 'a lack of decision making procedures capable of overcoming dissent.'[96] Such consensus-expectations gaps have clearly been present in the Union's policy on the territorial conflicts in Georgia.

---

[92] N. Popescu and A. Wilson, *The Limits of Enlargement-Lite: European and Russian Power in the Troubled Neighbourhood* (London, European Council on Foreign Relations 2009), at 1. See also T. German, 'Visibly Invisible: EU Engagement in Conflict Resolution in the South Caucasus', 16 *European Security* (2007) 357-374.

[93] For instance, since the early 1990s, Georgia has been a major recipient of US aid. In the new millennium, America has also provided significant military aid. See Tocci (2007) *supra* n. 13, at 140-141.

[94] J. Bitterlich, 'How to Get Europe's Common Foreign Policy out of the Doldrums', *Europe's World* (summer 2007) 15-19.

[95] C. Grant, *Is Europe Doomed to Fail As a Power?* (London, Centre for European Reform 2009), at 12.

[96] A. Toje, 'The Consensus-Expectations Gap: Explaining Europe's Ineffective Foreign Policy', 39 *Security Dialogue* (2008) 121-141.

They have prevented it from acting as a more forceful conflict resolver and peace-builder.

This assessment is not contradicted by the fact that it was the EU that brokered the 12 August ceasefire and that it has since made a crucial contribution to the stabilisation and normalisation of the former war zone. The EU's take-charge attitude was by and large determined by the French Presidency and notably President Sarkozy himself. EU policy during these crucial weeks was not so much the product of a collective foreign policy as the result of the real-time Europeanisation of French initiatives. What this suggests is that foreign policy leadership on 'high politics' issues is more likely to come from the most powerful Member States, acting unilaterally or in small groups, than to emerge from the collective deliberations of all Member States. This said, the increased visibility and political weight of the EU in Georgia, Abkhazia, South Ossetia and beyond since the summer of 2008 benefit the Member States collectively. The war has added to the Union's foreign policy stature. Incidentally, the guns of August 2008 have also set in motion a learning process in Brussels. With the Geneva talks the EU has for the first time been thrust into the role of mediator. It was caught off guard but has been quick to reflect on the implications. The report on the Implementation of the European Security Strategy, which was presented by foreign policy supremo Solana in December 2008,[97] referred to the need for expanding the Union's 'mediation capacities'. Since then, in-house deliberations have been initiated to develop such capacities.

---

[97] *Report on the Implementation of the European Security Strategy: Providing Security in a Changing World*, S407/08, 11 December 2008.

# Chapter 12
# THE EU IN AFGHANISTAN: PEACEBUILDING IN A CONFLICT SETTING

**Eva Gross***

## 1. Introduction

Recent international engagement in Afghanistan holds a number of lessons for individual actors involved in the country's reconstruction, but also in peacebuilding more broadly defined. Among these are a wider engagement with the challenges of civil-military coordination and the sequencing, or simultaneous provision, of security and development in a deteriorating security environment. In this context, governance has emerged as one of the central challenges to the success but also the sustainability of collective international efforts. Given its crisis management as well as its broader political and developmental toolkit, the EU is in principle in an advantageous position to deliver in the areas of development, governance and the rule of law – all of which constitute aspects of peacebuilding.

This chapter provides an overview of the EU's engagement in Afghanistan to date. It analyses peacebuilding activities undertaken by the EU and shows that the European efforts at reconstruction have become progressively more coherent and better coordinated. It also highlights the way in which the case of Afghanistan and the political as well as developmental aspects of the country's reconstruction continue to illustrate the complexities facing the EU's and the wider international community's peacebuilding efforts. The chapter is structured in three parts: it first analyses the trajectory of international reconstruction efforts as well as the military, political and developmental starting points in Afghanistan on the basis of which these efforts operate (section 2). Against this background, the chapter analyses EU activities in the country in the areas of development, governance and the rule of law. It puts particular emphasis on the internal coordination of EU instruments but also on their cooperation with other international efforts (section 3). The chapter concludes by placing current European engagement in Afghanistan in the context of a renewed focus on the country as well as the broader region, and by considering the role of governance and development in light of the outcome of the 2009 presidential and provincial elections (section 4).

* Dr. Eva Gross is Senior Research Fellow at the Institute for European Studies, Vrije Universiteit Brussel. Research on this contribution was closed in November 2009.

*S. Blockmans, J. Wouters & Tom Ruys, eds., The European Union and Peacebuilding*

This contribution argues that while EU but also broader international efforts in the provision of security and development have become more coherent and targeted, good governance and issues of legitimacy, transparency and accountability have not always received the necessary attention. To date, emphasis has tended to focus on a 'top-down' approach where the international community, including the EU, has worked on setting up institutional structures as well as providing security. Without a 'bottom-up' approach that focuses not just on the broader population's acceptance of international efforts but also on its ability and readiness to invest and thus legitimise formal institutional structures, sustainability of these efforts will be difficult to achieve.

## 2. Contextualising EU engagement in Afghanistan

### 2.1 The international post-conflict reconstruction framework

EU policies in Afghanistan have to be assessed in the framework of both the overall international involvement in the country and the political, economic and social conditions in which it takes place. The picture that emerges is one of complexity and fragmentation, with an enduring disconnect between political, military and developmental spheres of engagement. Since the fall of the Taliban in 2001, international engagement has centred on establishing central state structures and institutions – but increasingly also on defeating a growing insurgency. The Bonn Conference in December 2001 established a transitional process that was to lead to the election of a 'broad-based, gender-sensitive, multi-ethnic and fully representative government.'[1] It set up the Afghan Interim Authority (AIA) under the leadership of Hamid Karzai, who became the first democratically elected president of the Islamic Republic of Afghanistan in 2004. Following on from the Bonn process, a new partnership was established at the London Conference in 2006. The so-called Afghanistan Compact identified security, governance, rule of law and human rights as well as social and economic development as key pillars of activity. Consequently, the Compact seeks 'to continue in the spirit of the Bonn, Tokyo and Berlin conferences, to work toward a stable and prosperous Afghanistan, with good governance and human rights protection for all under the rule of law.'[2] Afghan ownership of the reconstruction process and reliance on domestic governance and security institutions were intended to follow on from this agreement.

Beyond efforts at establishing central state structures by means of the Bonn Process and the Afghanistan Compact, the 'light footprint approach' adopted by the

---

[1] United Nations, *Agreement on Provisional Arrangements in Afghanistan Pending the Re-establishment of Permanent Government Institutions* (S/2001/1154), Bonn, 5 December 2001, available at: <http://www.un.org/News/dh/latest/afghan/afghan-agree.htm>.

[2] 'Building on Success: The London Conference on Afghanistan. The Afghanistan Compact', London, 31 January – 1 February 2006. See: <http://www.nato.int/isaf/docu/epub/pdf/afghanistan_compact.pdf>.

UN in the overall reconstruction tasks emphasised a quick turnover of responsibility to the Afghans at the start of international engagement in the country.[3] An effort to also include a broad range of stakeholders, albeit under a UN lead, reinforced the fragmentation of international engagement, even if it was to signal a broad-based international consensus on the reconstruction of Afghanistan. Following the 2002 Geneva Conference, individual lead nations assumed responsibilities for central tasks in security sector reform (SSR), including the areas of disarmament, demobilisation and reintegration (DDR) (Japan), army (USA), police (Germany), justice (Italy) and narcotics (UK).

Military contributions to reconstruction in turn were delivered through Provincial Reconstruction Teams (PRTs), headed by individual lead nations as part of the International Security Assistance Force (ISAF). ISAF's main role is to assist in the establishment of a secure and stable environment, through the conduct of security and stability operations and involvement in the development of the Afghan National Army (ANA) through mentoring, training and equipping.[4] NATO was not initially involved in ISAF, but the combination of organisational requirements in running a multilateral peacekeeping operation and a deteriorating security situation led to NATO assuming ISAF command in August 2003. ISAF has since gradually expanded its geographical and functional reach, in particular in the area of training of Afghan Security Forces with the establishment of a NATO Training Mission Afghanistan (NTM-A) at the NATO Summit in Strasbourg-Kehl in April 2009.[5]

Increasing demands made on ISAF both in terms of its geographical reach, mission strength but also operational tasks have shifted the focus to questions of burden sharing and a transatlantic division of labour. Attention thus moved from an emphasis on broad-based and political contributions to the reconstruction of Afghanistan, to debates centred on security. In operational terms, NATO's experience in Afghanistan has also led to the emergence of the notion of 'comprehensive approach' in which military, political and developmental instruments and actors engage in a coordinated fashion. Lessons from fighting the Taliban point in a similar direction: focusing on security without a concurrent emphasis on good governance and economic development will not yield sustainable results.[6] While the international community has increasingly come to realise the detrimental effects of frag-

---

[3] The light footprint approach emphasised Afghan involvement and a speedy devolution to Afghan ownership rather than a heavy-handed international presence and a large number of troops in pursuit of post-conflict reconstruction. See also United Nations, *The Situation in Afghanistan and Its Implications for International Peace and Security*, UN Doc. A/56/875-S/2002/278, New York, 18 March 2002.

[4] *International Security Assistance Force (ISAF): Facts and Figures*, available at: <http://www.nato.int/ISAF/docu/epub/pdf/isaf_placemat.pdf>.

[5] 'NATO Training Mission – Afghanistan', NATO, 4 April 2009, available at: <http://www.nato.int/cps/en/natolive/news_52802.htm>.

[6] See Council of the European Union, Council Conclusions, 'Strengthening EU Action in Afghanistan and Pakistan', 2971st External Relations Council Meeting, Luxembourg, 27 October 2009; Headquarters International Security Assistance Force Kabul, Afghanistan, *Commander's Initial Assessment*, 30 August 2009, available at: <http://media.washingtonpost.com/wp-srv/politics/documents/Assessment_Redacted_092109.pdf>.

mentation and has worked towards creating more coherence and synergies between international efforts, the deteriorating security and political situation in Afghanistan has led to a convergence of a number of negative trends that put the success of peacebuilding efforts at risk.

Indeed, the growing insurgency and the deteriorating security situation have several implications, and none too positive, for international engagement in Afghanistan. On a practical level, the growing insurgency makes it difficult to administer development programmes across the country. Many agencies have ceased to operate in those areas of the country that are considered unsafe. There is a political consensus on the part of key international actors – the US as well as the EU – that a change in strategy towards Afghanistan is needed.[7] The Obama administration has refocused its engagement in Afghanistan on increased civilian efforts (the so-called 'civilian surge' or 'uplift') to train Afghan army and police as well as to increase troop levels to fight the Taliban and to train national security forces. At the same time, it has emphasised the importance of governance and is placing greater focus on Afghanistan's regional dimension, particularly Pakistan. Current US strategy focuses on a more narrow set of interests that include both the fight against terrorism and the build-up of Afghan capacities and capabilities so as to hand over security responsibility to the Afghan government within a reasonable time period. However, in the US as well as in Europe, strategic readjustments and considerations over a short-term increase in troop numbers also coincide with growing domestic calls for the withdrawal of troops. European publics in particular increasingly withdraw support for continuous military engagement. Recent public opinion survey results accordingly show that more than half of Europeans support either reducing or withdrawing troops from Afghanistan; and disapprove of sending more combat troops to the country.[8] Communicating the need for further engagement is made difficult also in light of a deteriorating security situation and the lack of positive political or economic developments in the country.

On the political level, the 2009 presidential elections did not add the positive momentum the international community had hoped for. Rather, the allegation of fraud highlighted corruption, tribal linkages and a system based on personal affiliations rather than transparency and accountability. The conduct of the 2009 elections emphasised once more the importance of governance but also the essentially political nature of Afghanistan's challenges. Together with growing instability and the lack of public support for increasing troop numbers, this reinforced international calls for a renewed emphasis on Afghan-led political and military processes so as to hand over responsibility for security to the Afghan government at the earliest possible time. The starting point of an analysis of international engagement, therefore, is a deteriorating security situation at a time of waning public support for increased or sustained engagement in Afghanistan, coupled with weak local governance structures that are unable to support a self-sustaining political process. Across the board, be it in security, political or economic terms, international engagement in

---

[7] Ibid.

[8] See 'Transatlantic Trends: Key Findings 2009', available at: <http://www.transatlantictrends.org>.

the past 8 years has not resulted in a stable or economically prosperous country. This has clear implications for the conditions in which peacebuilding activities take place: rather than in a post-conflict setting, peacebuilding actors operate in an increasingly insecure environment and under an overall military lead.

### 2.2 Local starting points, Afghan realities

The analysis of EU peacebuilding efforts in Afghanistan, as well as conclusions over their effectiveness, have to be mindful of the political, economic and societal starting points of reconstruction after three decades of violent conflict. Some of these factors have moreover been exacerbated by broader regional dynamics, the fragmentation of international efforts and the deteriorating security situation mentioned above. In purely developmental terms, Afghanistan remains one of the poorest countries in the world: despite having received close to USD 36 billion in development contributions over the past 8 years, Afghanistan ranks second to last on the UN Human Development Index.[9] Apart from poverty and lack of development, a high rate of illiteracy coupled with issues of geography and demography (e.g., a large rural population[10] that can be difficult to reach) poses a dual challenge to development and reconstruction tasks. Beyond the need for security in light of a growing insurgency and the difficult task of training military and civilian personnel in the ANA and ANP, these indicators starkly illustrate the low starting point for international development and peacebuilding efforts.

The international military presence has been too small but also insufficiently embedded in and accepted by the local population to contain the Taliban and to either protect the population or offer a credible alternative to joining forces with them. While the Afghan population recognises the continued need for international support in training Afghan security forces,[11] incidents of accidental targeting of civilians as well as the lack of overall security provided to the population have resulted in a lack of confidence in the international community's (let alone the Afghan security forces') efforts to provide security.[12] Nevertheless, uncertainty as to the long-term commitment of the international presence as well as the government's inability to contain the insurgency have permitted the Taliban not only to re-emerge but also to create a culture of fear among the general population.

The legacy of decades of conflict and large-scale human rights violations, coupled with a lack of trust in the political system, has negatively affected local acceptance

---

[9] This is reflected in several key human development indicators: 2007 data show life expectancy at birth at 43.6 years, an adult literacy rate of 28% and fertility rates of 7.5, United Nations, *Human Development Report – Afghanistan*, 2009, available at: <http://hdrstats.undp.org/en/countries/country_fact_sheets/cty_fs_AFG.html>.

[10] Of a total population of 25.1 million, only 22% live in urban areas. See European Commission, Country Strategy Paper (CSP), 'Islamic Republic of Afghanistan 2003-2006', 11 February 2003.

[11] The Asia Foundation, 'Afghanistan in 2009: A Survey of the Afghan People', Kabul, October 2009, available at: <http:// www.asiafoundation.org>.

[12] 'Afghan People "Losing Confidence"', *BBC News*, 9 February 2009.

of government structures. Beyond the government's lack of delivery of basic services to the population, the decision to include local militia leaders – many of whom have been involved in past conflict and in human rights violations – in the 2005 parliamentary elections has further alienated parts of the population. In addition to the tensions inherent in formal centralised state structures in what is essentially a decentralised social, political and economic Afghan reality, the appointment system of regional government officials reinforces the control by the centre and the President. Accountability and transparency are made more difficult on account of a centralised political system. Governors are appointed by the President rather than through popular elections.

The drug trade – and its connection to government – has proven particularly corrosive. In addition to a pervasive culture of corruption, which is endemic to many branches of government, criminal structures have increasingly permeated government and are often reinforced by close personal connections between holders of government offices and those involved in the drug trade. The fact that these individuals can often also rely on private security companies that are outside the reach of government further exacerbates the problem.[13] The re-emergence of the Taliban and the very real security threat this poses have led to a mix of a government preoccupied with staying in power and alternately unable or unwilling to root out corruption, and insurgent forces that prey on the population and prevent governmental, non-governmental and international actors from implementing development and reconstruction programmes.

Regional variations in violence and levels of development make a uniform approach to reconstruction in the country difficult. Taliban activity has been strongest in the Pashtun-dominated south. However, even the north with its Tajik/Uzbek majority has not been immune to rising levels of violence, as the deteriorating security situation in Kunduz illustrates. The same holds for the northwest of the country. Central Afghanistan by comparison is relatively stable but faces significant challenges as far as its economic development is concerned. Regional variations in the level of security and economic development mirror the ability of central government structures to reach beyond the capital, Kabul. Regional, provincial and local levels of government often have weak ties with the central government in Kabul. This constrains the delivery of government services, thereby further alienating the population from the government. However, the overall increase in violence over the past years has led to a securitisation of international efforts in Afghanistan at the expense of a focus on good governance.

Finally, the broader regional context in which Afghanistan is placed has contributed to instability, both on account of contested borders and due to broader political forces, including India/Pakistan relations as well as Iranian influence in the country. Afghanistan is not only situated in an unstable region, but has also been further destabilised by proxy wars fought on its ground by its more powerful neighbours.

---

[13] See J. Sherman and V. DiDomenico, *The Public Cost of Private Security in Afghanistan*, Briefing Paper (New York University Center on International Cooperation, New York, September 2009), available at: <http://www.cic.nyu.edu/afghanistan/pubcost_sherman_vididom.pdf>.

Contested or porous borders with Pakistan in particular but also with Iran, Tajikistan and Uzbekistan in the north, have facilitated narcotics trafficking. A legacy of external interference, most importantly the support of Pakistan's intelligence agency, the Inter-Service Intelligence (ISI), for the Taliban,[14] not only challenges reconstruction efforts. Divergent regional interests and security dynamics also interfere with the pursuit of a comprehensive regional solution. Given the complex domestic and regional setting, coupled with a trajectory of international activities in Afghanistan that have increasingly focused on military efforts to counter growing insurgency, EU efforts have not always gained the visibility that should correspond to the resources made available. Rather than engaging in military reconstruction, the EU's main contribution consists of its expertise in civilian crisis management as well as in the area of economic development.

## 3. The EU in Afghanistan

### 3.1 Activities since 2001: An overview of the broader EU presence

The EU has been engaged in Afghanistan, as have individual EU Member States, through their contributions to the International Security Assistance Force (ISAF) since the fall of the Taliban. For the EU, its engagement in Afghanistan represents a steep learning curve in light of the magnitude of the reconstruction task. However, it also signals the external recognition of its increasing role as an international security provider: EUPOL Afghanistan, the ESDP police mission launched in 2007,[15] came into being in no small part on account of Member State discussions over an ESDP mission but also US demands for the EU to make use of its civilian crisis management instruments. In this sense, Afghanistan represents a coming of age for ESDP and the EU's ability to deliver a comprehensive approach in international crisis management. EU engagement has been negatively affected both by the broader fragmentation of international efforts and by the insufficient political and financial commitments on the part of Member States, particularly as far as EUPOL is concerned. However, it is also an illustration of how far the EU has come in its ability to deliver in peacebuilding and post-conflict reconstruction as well as in its growing international reach.

Since the fall of the Taliban, the EU has been a key actor in Afghanistan: for the period of 2002-2010, the EU together with its Member States has committed around EUR 8 million to Afghanistan.[16] Beyond EUPOL Afghanistan, the EU deploys a range of political and economic instruments and is represented by two main institu-

---

[14] See A. Rashid, *Taliban: Militant Islam, Oil and Fundamentalism in Central Asia* (Yale University Press 2000).

[15] Council Joint Action 2007/369/CFSP of 30 May 2007 on establishment of the European Union Police Mission in Afghanistan (EUPOL AFGHANISTAN), *OJ* 2007 L 139/33.

[16] EU Council, Factsheet, 'EU Engagement in Afghanistan', March 2009, available at: <http://www.consilium.europa.eu/uedocs/cmsUpload/090330-EU_engagement_Afghanistan.pdf>.

tions. The European Commission oversees programmes that focus on economic development, governance and the rule of law. The EU Special Representative (EUSR), on the other hand, fulfils a more explicitly political role.[17] By conveying the EU's view on the political process and establishing and maintaining contact with key Afghan institutions and stakeholders, the EUSR fulfils an important function in coordinating and shaping the EU's political position and increases the EU's political visibility on the ground.[18] Formal EU-Afghanistan relations are governed by the 2005 EU-Afghanistan Joint Declaration, which was concluded following the completion of the Bonn process. The Declaration commits the EU to formalised bilateral cooperation and annual meetings at the ministerial level. Key priorities include 'consolidating a democratic political system, establishing responsible and accountable government institutions, strengthening the rule of law, and safeguarding human rights (including the rights of women) and the development of civil society.'[19]

### 3.2 Europeanising EU efforts: Development, governance and the rule of law

While the EU had been active in Afghanistan since the fall of the Taliban in financial and political terms, the 2006 London Conference marked a turning point. It entrusted the EU with additional areas of engagement: justice reform was turned over to the Commission, thereby relieving Italy from its national lead in this area. In order to increase efforts in police reform overall, but also to coordinate various other national activities in this area, the Council launched EUPOL Afghanistan in June 2007. This growing role for the EU in civilian reconstruction and governance resulted from considerations of moving beyond the fragmentation of international efforts and lending EU weight to previously bilateral efforts in police and justice reform. It also resulted from the realisation that more would have to be done in the area of police and justice than Germany and Italy had provided in their respective functions as 'lead nations'. Engagement thus became 'Europeanised' in an effort to increase the EU's political profile in Afghanistan but also to better coordinate European contributions to the country's reconstruction. Since the launch of EUPOL Afghanistan, EU commitments currently span the full range of peacebuilding activities and include development assistance and support for (good) governance and the rule of law. Support for the 2009 presidential election emerged as an additional field for the EU to engage in through the launch of an Election Observation Mission (EOM).[20]

---

[17] Council Joint Action 2008/612/CFSP of 24 July 2008 concerning the appointment of the European Union Special Representative for Afghanistan, *OJ* 2008 L 197/60.

[18] See also G. Grevi, *Pioneering Foreign Policy: The EU Special Representatives*, Chaillot Paper No. 106 (Paris, EU Institute for Security Studies, October 2007), at 71-78.

[19] European Council, *EU-Afghanistan Joint Declaration: Committing to a New EU-Afghan Partnership*, 14519/05 (Presse 299), Strasbourg, 16 November 2005, available at: <http://register.consilium.europa.eu/pdf/en/05/st14/st14519.en05.pdf>.

[20] European Union Election Observation Mission to Afghanistan: Presidential and Provincial Council Elections 2009, Fact Sheet, available at: <http://www.eueom-afghanistan.org/EN/PDF/Press/Afghanistan_fact_sheet.pdf>.

EU activities in Afghanistan thus fairly comprehensively cover relevant areas in peacebuilding and reflect the EU's range of abilities in the delivery of a comprehensive approach. On the downside, the number of largely independent actors and financial instruments that make up the collective EU engagement affect the EU's performance in terms of its coherence and its overall political leverage in the country. An inherent function of the EU's institutional structure, it nevertheless diminishes the EU's overall political influence: the EU does not present a coherent external image to its interlocutors.

### 3.2.1 *Health and rural development*

Among the priority sectors identified by the European Commission for the 2007-2013 period are rural development, governance and health.[21] In these activities, the Commission's assistance has increasingly shifted from humanitarian assistance immediately after the fall of the Taliban, towards post-conflict reconstruction. Given the large percentage of the population that lives in rural areas, rural development represents a key challenge. Together with the provision of primary health care, the two areas serve as important measures that underpin political and institutional reconstruction. In development terms, the EU has contributed significantly to infrastructure, technical assistance and capacity building. In the area of health, in addition to the provision of basic health services, EU funds have been used to support infrastructure – the building or repairing of health centres – and the delivery of equipment and medicines. EU support has enabled some 80% of the population to have access to primary health service.[22] Similarly, rural development programmes have focused on infrastructure development, including building roads to enable farmers to bring their crops to the market and drilling wells. This also includes the improvement of water management systems along the Kunduz River to prevent drought and environmental degradation. Additional EU aid has centred on social protection, with a focus on vulnerable groups, and financial and technical assistance for demining, as well as aid to uprooted people (AUP).[23] Beyond these developmental efforts, the EU also engages in areas more directly associated with peacebuilding: good governance and the rule of law.

### 3.2.2 *Governance and the rule of law*

The EU's engagement in the area of governance and the rule of law most directly contributes to peacebuilding and post-conflict reconstruction. EU activities in this

[21] European Commission, Country Strategy Paper , 'Islamic Republic of Afghanistan 2007-13'.

[22] European Union, European Commission Delegation to Afghanistan, *Overview of EU Assistance to Afghanistan*, June 2007, available at: <http://www.delafg.ec.europa.eu/Pa/downloadable_documents/report/Overview_of_EU_Assistance_to_Afghanistan_English.pdf>.

[23] European Commission, 'State of Play: January 2009. Major Milestones towards Reconstruction and Peace Building in Afghanistan', available at: <http://ec.europa.eu/europeaid/where/asia/documents/afgh_state_of_play_january_09_en.pdf>.

area are channeled through financial contributions by the European Commission, political engagement through the EUSR, but also EUPOL Afghanistan. The European Commission makes substantial financial contributions to the Afghanistan Reconstruction Trust Fund (ARTF) as well as to the Law and Order Trust Fund (LOTFA) that was established in 2002. LOTFA supports police reform through the payment of police salaries as well as the provision of equipment, facilities and broader institutional development. Since annual costs cannot be covered by budget revenues, LOTFA will continue to finance salaries. According to estimates, 93% of Afghan public expenditure is paid by foreign aid,[24] and weak Afghan state structures remain largely dependent on foreign support. Still, this does not give the international community leverage over government authorities: conditionality is difficult to enforce in light of the essential nature of various expenditures.

Contributions to LOTFA are closely related to the work undertaken by EUPOL Afghanistan. Beyond the challenge of building transparent government structures, the state of the Afghan police at the beginning of the international efforts once more illustrates the difficulty of building public institutions in a deteriorating security environment and following decades of violent conflict. Prior to the creation of EUPOL, Germany had been the key partner in police reform through the German Police Project Office (GPPO). Germany contributed EUR 12 million per year for the reconstruction of the police force, including training and equipment.[25] Germany also built the Police Academy in Kabul that was declared operational as of August 2002 and generally focused on long-term training. In view of the state of the Afghan police, which required not just the establishment of structures and training procedures but also the quick training of a large number of police officers, the German approach was considered too thorough and not appropriate for training large numbers of police staff.[26] Considering the recognised need to focus on the ANP, the US got involved in police training as of 2003 as well, focusing on rapid training, with a view to equipping police with essential skills to take part in counterinsurgency efforts. The increasing focus on police reform, together with the EU's emerging profile in civilian crisis management – including the reform of police and the wider rule of law –, led to increasing discussion over a potential EU mission that was eventually decided upon under the German EU Presidency in the first half of 2007. A Joint EU Assessment Mission report presented to the Political and Security Committee (PSC) in October 2006 recommended to 'consider contributing further to support the police sector through a police mission.'[27] The Council approved the Crisis Management Concept for a EU police mission on 12 February 2007.[28] The mission was launched in June 2007.

---

24 C. Maas, *Afghanistan: Staatsaufbau ohne Staat*, SWP Studie (Berlin, February 2007).

25 'Funding for Police Assistance in Afghanistan Tripled', Federal Foreign Office, Berlin, 18 November 2007.

26 International Crisis Group, *Reforming Afghanistan's Police*, Asia Report No. 138 (August 2007).

27 Council Joint Action 2007/369/CFSP of 30 May 2007 on establishment of the European Union Police Mission in Afghanistan (EUPOL AFGHANISTAN), *supra* n. 15.

28 Ibid.

The main tasks of EUPOL Afghanistan are to

> 'significantly contribute to the establishment under Afghan ownership of suitable and effective civilian policing arrangements, which will ensure appropriate interaction with the wider criminal justice system (…). The mission will support the reform process towards a trusted and efficient police service, which works in accordance with international standards, within the framework of the rule of law and respects human rights.'[29]

Rather than being conceived as a training mission, it aims at contributing to the formulation of an overall strategy and at mentoring staff of the Ministry of the Interior (MoI), police commanders and upper ranking officials. EUPOL's added value lies in its merging of Member and third states' police efforts and its potential to improve coordination among the various actors engaged in police reform.

At the time of writing, EUPOL's authorised mission strength is 400, and the mission is headed by Police Commissioner Kai Vittrup. EUPOL staff is deployed in Kabul, the regional commands and the provinces. Deployments through PRTs were slowed down by the need to draw up bilateral technical agreements with individual lead nations. In the absence of a formalised EU-NATO agreement, this means that EUPOL is currently not deployed in Turkish and US-led PRTs.

EUPOL admittedly got off to a slow start, not just on account of interinstitutional issues between NATO and the EU. Frequent changes of heads of mission as well as Member State reluctance to staff EUPOL as promised meant that EUPOL could not perform the functions it had set out for itself. In particular, the objective of coordinating existing police reform activities proved unrealistic, especially in light of a financial and political US lead. As a result, both EUPOL's visibility and the value of its contributions to police reform were diminished. In this respect, two sets of challenges facing EUPOL are the internal and external coordination of reform efforts and the cooperation of Afghan stakeholders in the pursuit of institutional reform. Despite EUPOL's growing pains, there are positive signs on both counts, and EUPOL could effectively fine-tune its objectives to support and complement efforts undertaken by the US through the Combined Security Transition Command Afghanistan (CSTC-A) and soon also the NATO training mission.[30]

The Afghan Minister of the Interior, Hanif Atmar, has explicitly requested EUPOL to take on a number of reform functions, including the formulation and implementation of an anti-corruption strategy.[31] While the ANP continues to suffer from corruption, a less than transparent hiring process and low police salaries that make recruitment difficult,[32] the Minister of the Interior is credible in the eyes of the

[29] Ibid.

[30] Derived from an interview with EUPOL official, Kabul, October 2009.

[31] See L. Peral, 'The EU Police Mission in Afghanistan (EUPOL Afghanistan)', in G. Grevi, D. Helly and D. Keohane, eds., *European Security and Defence Policy: The First Ten Years (1999-2009)* (Paris, EU Institute for Security Studies, October 2009).

[32] For analyses of the state of the ANP, see A. Wilder, *Cops or Robbers? The Struggle to Reform the Afghan National Police*, Issue Paper Series (Afghanistan Research and Evaluation Unit (AREU), July 2007); International Crisis Group, *supra* n. 26.

international community. EUPOL also had to readjust its objectives not just in view of Atmar's requests but also on account of US training efforts through CSTC-A and of the preparations for the NATO training mission. More fundamentally, EUPOL's policing philosophy is also different from that of the US. Whereas US training efforts focus overwhelmingly on the establishment of security, EUPOL concentrates on the build-up of a professional civilian police force. In pursuit of this goal, EUPOL has consolidated its objectives into 6 areas: 3 regarding the rule of law and 3 relating to police. With respect to the rule of law, EUPOL's objectives include the formulation and implementation (together with other international actors involved, including CSTC-A, UNDP and UNAMA) of an anti-corruption strategy under EUPOL lead; establishing links with prosecutors; and a focus on human rights and gender.[33] As regards policing, objectives include 'PC3' (command, control and communication), intelligence-led policing based on a UK approach, and the continuation and geographic expansion of the city police project in Kabul. In addition, based on an agreement with the UN, EUPOL is also to train officers in preparation of the 2010 elections. Despite the differing approaches when it comes to police reform, cooperation with CSTC-A on an institutional level is good and 5 EUPOL officers in CSTC-A work in training to ensure an interlocking operation.

Over the past two years, therefore, EUPOL has fine-tuned its approach from assuming a coordination function to supporting an Afghan-led anti-corruption initiative and working in support of CSTC-A. This was also done in recognition of the security environment in which the ANP operates. In light of deteriorating security and the need 'to put boots on the ground', long-term objectives of civilian policing had to be subordinated to immediate security concerns. While the external coordination in the field thus seems to have been worked out satisfactorily, Member States' lack of flexibility in deployment and delays in staffing the mission threaten to undermine the EU's credibility. The remaining challenge for EUPOL is to reach the 400 personnel authorised and to deploy throughout the various provinces.

Beyond police reform, the EU, through the European Commission, also contributes to justice reform. The decision in 2006 to push for greater EU involvement stems from the realisation that the justice sector had so far not received the attention it deserved. It was also assumed that the institutional link-up within the EU institutions was likely to improve coordination between the two sectors. An additional challenge in this context is that reform of the justice sector has been neglected in the overall focus on training and reform of the ANA and ANP. There are significant gaps in outreach to parts of the population; low salaries; and inadequate training of personnel. There is also a contradiction inherent in the Afghan legal system, which is based on a mixture of civil and sharia law.[34] The EU assuming the overall coordination, together with former lead nation Italy, has given it a coordinating function and has moved justice reform higher up the political agenda. EC contributions con-

---

[33] Derived from an interview with EUPOL official, Kabul, October 2009.

[34] See J. Thier, *Reestablishing the Judicial System in Afghanistan*, CDDRL Working Papers No. 19 (Stanford University, September 2004).

sequently focus on support for the 'Access to Justice at District Level' project and the provision of technical assistance in the drafting of the National Justice Strategy and National Justice Programme. Finally, a new justice programme that is implemented as of 2009 includes support to the ARTF justice project, payment of salaries of uniformed prison personnel through LOTFA, continued support for the Access to Justice project and provision of technical assistance. The overall financial commitment to the rule of law in the 2007-13 period is EUR 200 million.[35] Within this remit, the Commission also supports customs and border management, public administration and reform programmes.

A final component of institution building in which the EU has engaged in Afghanistan is support for the presidential and provincial council elections in 2009 and the National Assembly and district elections in 2010, respectively. In light of the country's history of conflict and lack of central governing institutions, the deteriorating security situation and the fractured political scene in the country, elections undeniably constitute a test of the strength of the country's institutions. As the first Afghan-led elections since the first post-Taliban elections in 2004/05 that were a joint UN-Afghan effort, the 2009 elections were conducted under the stewardship of the Afghan Independent Election Commission (IEC), with the UN acting in support. The EU was active in supporting the 2009 presidential elections through the launch of the EU Election Observation Mission (EOM) on the part of the European Commission. Deployed on 13 July 2009 (under the lead of Philippe Morillon), this was one of the most challenging EOMs ever undertaken.[36] The European Commission assisted the election process also financially through a contribution of €35 million to the UN fund for electoral support (ELECT), which will moreover be directed towards long-term institution building, voter education and civic outreach, also in preparation of Afghanistan's parliamentary elections scheduled for 2010.

## 4. Peacebuilding along the security-development nexus: Strategic and implementation challenges

EU peacebuilding activities take place in a war-like environment and under an overwhelming US political and military lead. This has implications for the EU's ability to contribute to determining or impacting the strategic direction of the overall international engagement in Afghanistan. It also affects the implementation of EU policies and activities. They have also been made difficult on account of low starting points where the state of the institutions was concerned: a national police force did not exist upon the commencement of international involvement. Rather, the estimated 50,000 men working as police were untrained, ill-equipped and often served local military commanders rather than the central government.[37] Low police sala-

[35] European Commission, 'Multiannual Indicative Programme 2007-10: Islamic Republic of Afghanistan', Brussels, October 2007.

[36] *Supra* n. 20.

[37] International Crisis Group, *supra* n. 26.

ries in part also fuelled the spread of a culture of corruption. Training efforts on the part of international actors, including the EU, were significantly expanded, particularly since the US identified this as a priority area. However, police reform remains bedevilled by the twin problem of high casualties and low attractiveness of police services, as well as by a culture of corruption endemic to the police in particular. As a result, public trust in the police is generally low. The lack of progress in reforming the justice system concurrently to the reform of the ANA and ANP has further impeded progress in improving the rule of law in Afghanistan.

The focus on security also affected approaches to institution building and training in the rule of law sector, specifically the police. Whereas initially police reform was conducted – admittedly with insufficient resources for the task at hand – with the construction of a civilian police force in mind, over the past four years police training under US lead has increasingly focused on the police fulfilling security functions rather than civilian policing tasks. This means that, for the time being, aspects of institution and state building have become securitised, with less emphasis being paid to civilian aspects of policing, including a focus on outreach to civil society in general or vulnerable groups of the population in particular.[38] Here lies a contradiction between the short-term measures that focus on training and on 'putting boots on the ground' and the aim of establishing a civilian police force, i.e., one that enjoys the trust of the population. EUPOL, though focusing on longer-term civilian policing, currently does not prioritise gender and human rights concerns in its programming. Given the increasingly in-conflict rather than post-conflict environment in Afghanistan, prioritisation of security aspects in training is understandable. However, in the long run, institution-building measures are unlikely to succeed without fostering public acceptance and trust in the Afghan security forces.

A broader challenge for European peacebuilding, but also for international engagement in Afghanistan more broadly, goes beyond training Afghan security forces or reforming central institutions. The centralised structures that most international efforts are working to sustain neither reach nor resonate with the broader population, which remains largely excluded from government processes. A presidential system where governors are appointed rather than elected further removes the government from its population. The 2009 presidential elections and the degree of fraud reported amply illustrate the legitimacy gap between the population and the formal government institutions.

## 5. Conclusion

The difficult environment in which the EU operates – in both security, economic and political terms – easily obscures the range of EU commitments to Afghanistan. It also obscures the programmatic and institutional improvements made since the

[38] Derived from an interview with a EUPOL official, Kabul, December 2008. See also Peral, *supra* n. 31.

launch of EUPOL Afghanistan in particular. Although the EU's commitment to security sector reform pales in comparison to that of the US as far as quantity is concerned,[39] the tasks of EUPOL Afghanistan have been fine-tuned so as to be able to make a specific contribution to police reform in Afghanistan and one that builds on the EU's strength in civilian policing, mentoring and advising. Together with the office of the EUSR's and the European Commission's contributions to the rule of law, the EU is able to deliver a comprehensive set of political, economic and civilian crisis management tools in Afghanistan. On the whole, this represents a positive balance for the EU's peacebuilding activities in Afghanistan, even if the inter-institutional divide makes coordination between the EUSR and the European Commission challenging. The EU has recognised the lack of coordination as a liability and has pledged to 'work towards one single EU representation in Kabul.'[40] The difficult environment in which the EU's but also broader international activities take place require continued emphasis not just on reforming and building institutions, but also on countering corruption. To succeed at these tasks, the EU, as part of the broader international community, has to deliver a comprehensive and coordinated set of policies. The extent to which the EU is able to do so will determine the effectiveness of its peacebuilding activities in Afghanistan.

---

[39] The annual US budget for police training through CSTC-A is USD 2 billion. See D. Korski, *Afghanistan: Europe's Forgotten War*, European Council of Foreign Relations, 21 January 2008.

[40] Council Conclusions, *supra* n. 6.

# Part IV
# *Rule of law, democracy and human rights*

# Chapter 13
# THE EUROPEAN UNION AND ELECTORAL SUPPORT

**Patrick Dupont, Francesco Torcoli and Fabio Bargiacchi***

## 1. Introduction

Elections play a vital role in democratic and democratisation processes. They represent a crucial opportunity for political participation and representation as well as for holding elected officials to account. Moreover, elections provide important entry points for the enjoyment of a wide range of human rights, such as freedom of expression, assembly and association. They aim to bring about legitimate governments that are able to protect and respond to the needs of citizens, including sustainable peace and development.

Confirming its external policy objectives in the area of democracy and human rights, notably since the early 1990s, the EU has evolved into an active player in the promotion of sustainable, transparent and genuinely democratic elections. This article will illustrate the increased activity, both quantitatively and qualitatively, of the EU in election support in particular over the past ten years, often within a broader governance enhancement strategy and complementing other, civil society support and institution-building actions.

---

* Patrick Dupont started working for the European Commission (DG External Relations) in 2003, initially in the area of crisis response, and, since 2006, has worked on election observation issues. Prior to joining the Commission, Mr Dupont served as a peacebuilding expert for the Belgian Federal Ministry of Foreign Affairs and the Universities of Antwerp and Leuven, focusing on the political economy of violent conflicts and post-conflict democratic governance. Francesco Torcoli, Ph.D. in International Relations (University of Pisa), has fifteen years of experience in the field of electoral assistance, electoral observation and human rights, acquired in 25 countries throughout the world. Mr Torcoli currently works as an Election Specialist/Quality Management Officer at the DG EuropeAid Cooperation Office of the European Commission. Fabio Bargiacchi has, since 2007, worked as Senior Electoral Assistance Advisor at the UN/UNDP Brussels Office, his main task being to coordinate the activities of the EC-UNDP Joint Task Force on Electoral Assistance. From 2004 to 2006, he worked as an Election Specialist for the European Commission (DG EuropeAid). Mr Bargiacchi has extensive experience in election observation and electoral assistance for the EU, the UN and the OSCE. The views expressed in this contribution are entirely personal and cannot be attributed to the organisations to which the authors are affiliated.

*S. Blockmans, J. Wouters & T. Ruys, eds., The European Union and Peacebuilding*

## 2. Election assistance and election observation

EU electoral support mainly includes two activities: election observation and electoral assistance. Election observation is generally defined as 'the purposeful gathering of information regarding an electoral process, and the making of informed judgements on the conduct of such a process on the basis of the information collected, by persons who are not inherently authorised to intervene in the process.'[1] A further distinction can be made between short-term observation (focusing mainly on election day observation) and long-term observation (including pre-and post-electoral aspects). The EU is involved in the latter type of election observation.

Electoral assistance, on the other hand, can be defined as the technical or material support given to the electoral process. It may comprise a broad range of activities, the most common being advice and support provided to the national election authorities, including for the actual organisation of the elections. Election assistance can be provided in the short term, directed at the specific election event taking place, and, for instance, take the form of material or logistic support.

While short-term assistance is crucial in many cases, there is a clear tendency today among donors such as the EU to develop governance reform-oriented, longer-term support programmes. This has occurred in parallel with the development of an 'electoral cycle approach', which covers the electoral process over time and aims to engage different stakeholders and entry points throughout the three main periods of an electoral cycle, i.e., the pre-electoral, electoral and post-electoral period (see *infra*).

Longer-term assistance activities may include: support to the establishment of a legal framework for the elections; capacity building of electoral management bodies; targeted assistance to the national electoral body in accomplishing its mandate, for instance, with respect to the establishment of voter and candidate lists; the development of an operational plan for election day or the tabulation and transmission of election results; support to civil society in areas such as voter and civic education or training of domestic observers; support for media monitoring and training of journalists; and advice to political parties regarding campaign regulations or complaints mechanisms.

While electoral observation focuses on the process surrounding the electoral event,[2] electoral assistance may thus be provided throughout the electoral cycle.[3] Also, while election observation is based on the principle of independent and impartial assessment of an election process, with respect for the laws of the country,

---

[1] International IDEA, *Code of Conduct for the Ethical and Professional Observation of Elections* (Stockholm 1997), at 10. See for a more extensive description, *Declaration of Principles for International Election Observation and Code of Conduct for International Observers*, available at: <http://ec.europa.eu/external_relations/human_rights/election_observation/docs/code_conduct_en.pdf>.

[2] For instance, so-called long-term observers, in spite of what their title may suggest, are typically in country for a maximum period of two to three months around election day.

[3] C. Binder, 'Two Decades of International Electoral Support: Challenges and Added Value', 13 *Max Planck Yearbook of United Nations Law* (2009) 213-246.

electoral assistance directly supports national authorities and other stakeholders but will not include publically commenting on the quality of the electoral process.

Both activities, when embedded in a broader institution-building and democracy support strategy, serve a broader, political purpose. Obviously, election observation, with dozens of observers deployed throughout a country around election day, is the most visible action. However, its longer-term impact will depend on accompanying programmes such as assistance to electoral processes.

## 3. EU ELECTION OBSERVATION AND ASSISTANCE

EU support to elections combines election observation and assistance. Reflecting the complementary, mutually reinforcing objectives of both activities, they are funded through separate financial instruments: the centrally managed European Instrument for Democracy and Human Rights (EIDHR) programme for the funding of observation missions[4] and, in most cases, geographical funds[5] for electoral assistance. As a consequence, the decision-making process regarding the actual financing decision also differs, with national authorities often to an important extent being involved in the decision making on and implementation of electoral assistance. For instance, the EU Delegation and the national authorities in a given country are responsible for the identification, formulation and implementation of assistance programmes and projects.

While EU Election Observation Missions (EOMs) are conducted with the consent of the national authorities concerned, they operate and report independently of them. Their funding under the EIDHR symbolises this independence as well. Given the political implications as well as the high level of visibility attached to the European Union Electoral Observation Missions, this aspect of EU support to elections generally attracts most of the attention. In financial terms, however, it draws less from the budget. For instance, in the period 2007-2009, election assistance absorbed almost three times as many funds as election observation.[6]

This article will address both sectors, drawing a broad picture of EU support for elections while placing it in its historical and conceptual perspective.

---

[4] Under the EIDHR budget for 2007-13, an average amount of around €32 million can be allocated to EU Election Observation Missions on a yearly basis.

[5] Funding can take place under three geographical financing instruments: 1) European Neighbourhood and Partnership Instrument; 2) European Development Fund (EDF); and 3) Development Cooperation Instrument (DCI); but also under non-geographical instruments such as: 4) European Instrument for Democracy and Human Rights (EIDHR); and 5) Instrument for Stability (IfS).

[6] In his 2006 paper on the EU experience of election observation, Michael Meyer-Resende gives as an example the EU's financial support to the electoral process in the Democratic Republic of Congo, which represented, on its own, the equivalent of 10 years of the election observation budget. M. Meyer-Resende, *Exporting Legitimacy: The Record of EU Election Observation in the Context of EU Democracy Support*, CEPS Working Document No. 241 (Center of European Policy Studies, March 2006).

## 4. EU ELECTORAL ASSISTANCE

Larger-scale EU electoral assistance projects kicked off in 1994, with technical and financial support to the legislative and presidential elections in Mozambique and, two years later, with support to the elections in the Occupied Palestinian Territory.[7] EU electoral assistance has since grown considerably in number and scope. To date, more than 100 electoral assistance projects have been developed and implemented, contributing to electoral processes in over 60 countries worldwide.

The EU's position as a key international donor in the field of electoral assistance has strengthened over the past five years. In particular, the complexity of electoral assistance in post-conflict contexts, such as the DRC and Haiti – both for elections which eventually took place in 2006 but which were prepared long in advance – has triggered further investments – in coordination with partner organisations – as well as the development of capacity-building tools. In this context, an election assistance focal point for quality operations support was established within the European Commission.[8]

Since then, the EU has seen a steep increase in the volume of funding and in the number of electoral assistance operations. It has moreover been increasingly involved in the development of knowledge products and training tools for partner country institutions and development agency officials, in association with other electoral assistance providers.

## 5. EC-UNDP PARTNERSHIP IN ELECTION ASSISTANCE

EU electoral assistance has mostly, but not exclusively, been provided through and with the UN Development Programme (UNDP). Over the past ten years, the EU and the United Nations have been increasingly working together in the conceptualisation and implementation of electoral assistance.[9]

To facilitate programmatic cooperation, a Financial and Administrative Framework Agreement (FAFA) was established in 2003, providing for a single shared legal, financial and administrative framework for all programmatic cooperation between the EU and UN. Since its entry into force, the FAFA has made cooperation more efficient, ensuring faster start-up of activities and providing administrative consistency across operations.

On 28 June 2004, UNDP and the European Commission (EC) entered into a Strategic Partnership Agreement (SPA), with a Memorandum of Understanding (MoU) setting out and defining the relational focus between both organisations. The aim of the SPA was to facilitate policy dialogue and specific cooperation at

---

7 For these elections EU Election Observation Missions were deployed as well.

8 Directorate-General EuropeAid.

9 As stated in the Commission Communication of 2001 'Building an Effective Partnership with the UN', reinforced in 2003 by another Communication, entitled 'EU-UN Relations: The Choice of Multilateralism', the EU has established itself as a major partner of the UN.

global, regional and country level, notably in the area of governance (including support to electoral processes), conflict prevention and post-conflict reconstruction.

While the European Commission and UNDP have been working together in the field of electoral assistance since 1995, their partnership has intensified with and since the support for the electoral process in the Democratic Republic of Congo, which culminated in a constitutional referendum in December 2005 and presidential, parliamentary and provincial elections in July and October 2006. Further to lessons learned from this partnership, Operational Guidelines for the Implementation of Electoral Assistance Programmes and Projects were agreed upon, reviewed and updated in December 2008.

The EC-UNDP partnership in electoral assistance has relied on solid cooperation between services at headquarters level for quality support. Activities have included, through a dedicated Joint Task Force:[10] formulation and monitoring missions, advice on the selection of experts and procurement of election material, joint training, development of guidelines, gathering of lessons learned and participation in specialised electoral networks.

With their partnership, the Commission and UNDP have sought to facilitate cooperation with and among the different actors involved in electoral assistance programmes, such as the respective Commission and UNDP services, electoral management bodies, other multilateral and bilateral development agencies, partner country governments, civil society organisations, political parties, media, and service providers.

The Council Conclusions of 17 November 2009 on Democracy Support in the EU's External Relations[11] highlight the value of cooperation with regional and international organisations, mentioning specifically the United Nations. In the area of electoral assistance, over the three-year period from 2007 to 2009, the EU has channelled a total amount of €178 million through UNDP-managed basket funds (see Annex 1).

While UNDP remains the main partner of the EU in the field of electoral assistance, the Commission has been working with other partners as well.[12] The Council Conclusions of 17 November 2009 also call for further strengthening of the relationship between the EU and regional and sub-regional organisations. In the field of electoral assistance the EU is currently developing partnerships with the Southern African Development Community's (SADC) Electoral Commission Forum, the Economic Community of West African States (ECOWAS), the Economic

---

[10] A Joint EC-UNDP Task Force (JTF) on Electoral Assistance was established. The role and mandate of the JTF is to support all EC-UNDP electoral assistance projects as regards identification, formulation and implementation upon request by EU Delegations and UNDP Country offices. It has also an important task in encouraging inter-service cooperation, consolidating operational experience into best practices and developing training and supporting material.

[11] 2947th External Relations Council Meeting, Brussels, 17 November 2009.

[12] See, for instance, the West Bank/Gaza case study in the EC Methodological Guide on Electoral Assistance, at 179-185, available at: <http://ec.europa.eu/europeaid/what/human-rights/election_observation_missions/documents/election-assistance-methodological-guide_en.pdf>.

Community of Central African States (ECCAS) and the African Union (AU)[13] with a view to facilitating peer-to-peer networking and capacity building adapted to regional contexts and strategies. In addition, relationships have been built with electoral management bodies in key regional countries such as South Africa and Brazil.

## 6. EU ELECTION OBSERVATION

With 78 EU Election Observation Missions deployed in 44 countries over the past ten years,[14] the EU has made ample use of the observation instrument. In terms of missions, its engagement doubled in the last five years as compared to the first half of this decennium (see Annex 2). Different from other organisations involved in election observation,[15] the European Union has been exclusively observing elections in non-Member States. This results from a *de facto* division of labour between the European Commission and the Office for Democratic Institutions and Human Rights of the Organisation for Security and Cooperation in Europe (OSCE/ODIHR). Historically, the OSCE/ODIHR was at the origin of comprehensive election observation and election assessment in OSCE participating states, including EU countries. Hence, given that the OSCE/ODIHR and EU observation missions are based on a similar observation methodology, the EU has not been observing in countries such as Moldova, Ukraine and Georgia, which belong to its so-called Eastern Neighbourhood.[16] The EU has however made ample use of the OSCE/ODIHR reports in its political dialogue with these countries and in formulating assistance programmes.

The EU can deploy EU EOMs when invited by the political and electoral authorities of the country concerned. Since 2000, when the Commission issued a Communication on Election Observation and Assistance,[17] EU EOMs have been consistently focusing on politically independent, comprehensive and impartial observation. In that context, every EU EOM deployment is preceded by the conclusion of a formal agreement with the partner country (usually a Memorandum of Understanding – MoU). These MoUs typically confirm the freedom of movement of the observers throughout the country and freedom of access to all relevant sources of information on the electoral process. The guarantees in the MoU given by the authorities in regard to the work of the observers are linked to the latter's obligation

---

[13] Also in the area of election observation, cooperation was agreed between the European Commission and the African Union Commission in October 2008. This has led to: EU financial support to AU election observation capacity development, through the Instrument for Stability; increased cooperation between EU and AU Election Observation Missions; and a training/observation activity for election experts from AU countries in Brussels in June 2009, against the background of the European Parliament elections.

[14] Source: European Commission.

[15] For instance, the Organisation of American States (OAS), the Organisation for Security and Cooperation in Europe (OSCE), the African Union (AU) and the Commonwealth.

[16] See: <http://ec.europa.eu/world/enp/index_en.htm>.

[17] Communication on EU Election Assistance and Observation, COM(2000) 191 of 11 April 2000.

to strictly abide by a code of conduct, including the principles of impartiality and full respect of the laws of the country.

EU EOMs have consisted of 60 to 300 observers on election day, the size depending on the complexity of the electoral process, the geographical and demographical characteristics of the country concerned as well as budgetary, logistic and security constraints. For instance, over 250 observers were deployed for the elections in Indonesia in 2004 and the DR Congo in 2006, in contrast to 60 in Liberia in 2005 and in El Salvador in 2009. Noteworthy were the over 200 observers deployed for the parliamentary elections in the Occupied Palestinian Territory of 2006, including one of the largest EP observation delegations ever sent in the context of election observation.

EU EOMs have been increasingly deployed to unstable countries or countries in a conflict or post-conflict situation (e.g., DR Congo, Yemen and Haiti in 2006, Nigeria and Timor Leste in 2002 and 2007, Bangladesh and Pakistan in 2008, and Afghanistan in 2009). Such missions are deployed for the same reasons as other missions, i.e., to enhance transparency of and public confidence in the election process, deter fraud and manipulation and contribute to preventing election-related conflicts. However, at times they have involved serious methodological challenges in addition to security and logistic constraints. Some missions have been working under challenging circumstances due to security and safety reasons and have therefore been unable to meet the political expectations triggered by conflict or post-conflict elections. Despite the number of observers deployed (Afghanistan and Pakistan), also in the post-election process (Haiti 2006 and Kenya 2007), it has proved difficult to cover aspects of the election process comprehensively.

While for reasons of mandate, visibility and methodology EU EOMs have continued to operate independently, experience has highlighted the benefit of regular cooperation among other longer-term, domestic and international observation missions.[18]

## 7. Composition of EU Election Observation Missions

EU EOMs are usually in a country for a period of two to three months around election day. They consist of a long-term (core team and long-term observers) and a short-term component (short-term observers, frequently including observers from the European Parliament) and are led by a Chief Observer, who has been nominated by the Commissioner for External Relations[19] and in almost all cases has been a Member of the European Parliament.

This leadership has proven largely advantageous for the political visibility of the EU EOM in the country concerned and for the integration of short-term European Parliament observers into the longer-term EU Election Observation Missions. In

[18] Reference is made to a network established among international observer organisations which are signatory to the 2005 Declaration of Principles for International Election Observation (see *infra*).

[19] Pre-Treaty of Lisbon.

the past years, in over half of the countries where EU EOMs were deployed, the European Parliament had a short-term Observation Delegation present around election day, closely associated to the EU EOMs. Chief Observers have been instrumental in making the EU observers speak with one voice and in supporting the missions' independence in judging and reporting on an election process. They are the sole spokesperson of an EU EOM.[20]

In terms of reporting, EU EOMs issue interim reports on a 7 to 10-day basis, which are EU internal reports as well as two public reports:[21] the politically most watched preliminary statement of findings issued within 48 hours of election day and a final report issued within two months of election day. The final report contains a detailed assessment of the election process, including a list of recommendations for further electoral reform and development.

The Chief Observer and the other members of the so-called core team of analysts and experts,[22] are based in the country's capital and typically deployed to the country six to eight weeks before election day; they are joined by a larger group of long-term observers covering, in country, the campaign period, election day events as well as post-electoral aspects. Short-term observers, mandated to assess polling and counting over the immediate election day period, are usually in the country for a period of 7 to 10 days around election day.

All observers, i.e., core team members and long and short-term observers, are selected by the European Commission. Given the independent nature of EU EOMs, EU EOM observers cannot be staff of EU institutions.

Core team members, with the exception of the Chief Observer, are recruited following an open call for experts, published for every mission on the Europa website.[23] They are independent experts, contracted in the same manner as other consultants recruited by the European Commission. Long and short-term observers are selected by the Commission services involved in election observation following a proposal by the EU Member States[24,25] further to a call by the Commission services concerned. The European Commission strives to achieve a fair nationality and gender balance among the observers and to respect the ranking order of the candidates as proposed by the EU Member States, provided the requirements as

---

20 Unless tasks are delegated to the Deputy Chief Observer in the Chief Observer's absence from the country.

21 EU EOM reports can be retrieved at: <http://ec.europa.eu/external_relations/human_rights/eu_election_ass_observ/index.htm>.

22 Besides the Chief Observer, core teams typically include a Deputy Chief Observer, an electoral analyst, a legal analyst, a media expert, a press and public outreach officer, an observer coordinator and at times also a political and/or human rights expert. Core teams are further assisted by security and operational experts.

23 See: <http://ec.europa.eu/europeaid/what/human-rights/election_observation_missions/index_en.htm>.

24 Through so-called election focal points, based at the respective Ministries of Foreign Affairs. See: <http://ec.europa.eu/europeaid/applications/eom/index.cfm?fuseaction=c.show_focal_point_list>.

25 Norway and Switzerland are also invited to propose names for LTO and STO positions whenever elections are of interest to them.

regards experience, language, training[26] and mission-specific skills and aptitudes[27] are met.

While for long-term observers experience in previous observation missions is required, the Commission aims, in every mission, to include a number of short-term observers with no previous observation experience. This gives 'newcomers' the possibility to participate in the system. Finally, the selection process has been harmonised through a uniform CV system, the so-called observer roster introduced in 2004.[28] Only candidates registered in this easily accessible roster can be considered for participation in EU EOMs.

The roster has also been effective as a communication tool between the Commission services involved in election observation, the Member State election focal points as well as the EU EOMs on the ground. For instance, the roster includes information about the participation and respective assessment of observers in EU EOMs and trainees in the NEEDS training programme. Also, Member States can only propose candidates for EU EOMs who are registered in the roster; they are informed on-line of the outcome of selection processes for EU EOMs.

## 8. Towards an integrated strategy

The longer-term presence of EU EOMs in a given country has enabled them to assess in detail the strengths and weaknesses of an election process and, to some extent, the state of democracy. The EU, through its observation missions, is one of the few international observer organisations, with the OSCE/ODIHR, that evaluates the legal framework for elections, the degree of plurality of the media covering the election process as well as post-electoral complaints and appeals issues. Such assessments have proven very useful for formulating recommendations for electoral reform which can be included in follow-on electoral assistance programmes, media and civil society support projects, as well as in political dialogue with the authorities concerned.

As a result of an integrated strategy set up in 2000, EU EOMs and electoral assistance projects are increasingly synchronised. For instance, in all but three countries that benefitted from electoral assistance from 2007 to 2009, the EU was engaged or was planning to involve itself in election observation.[29] While further efforts may be required to enhance synergy and complementarity of actions, this

---

26 For instance, in the context of training programmes conducted in Member States or the EU-funded NEEDS project 'Network for Enhanced Electoral and Democratic Support', see: <http://www.needsproject.eu/>.

27 Including the ability to work in physically difficult (e.g., Bolivia and Mauritania) and conflict environments (e.g., Afghanistan, Pakistan, Yemen, Timor Leste, DR Congo and Nigeria).

28 The observer roster can be retrieved at: <http://ec.europa.eu/europeaid/what/human-rights/election_observation_missions/index_en.htm>.

29 Moreover, two of these three countries are Georgia and Moldova, where the EU has been politically supportive of election observation conducted by OSCE/ODIHR.

indicates the potential for a comprehensive election support strategy within a context of good governance and peacebuilding.

## 9. Historical perspective – learning by doing

Electoral support is a relatively new field of external assistance. Leaving aside experiences prior to the 1980s,[30] electoral support really started to structurally figure on the international community's agenda in the late 1980s/early 1990s,[31] supported by the wave of optimism that followed the fall of the Soviet Union. Subsequently, the OSCE, through ODIHR, its specialised branch, was instrumental in developing the methodological tools underlying international election observation. Further to this, EU EOM methodology was developed and updated, notably through the establishment of an analytical approach based on international standards deriving from universal[32] and regional instruments[33] and best practices in the electoral field. In parallel, the UN Development Programme and other international agencies played an important role in raising fundamental strategic issues in the field of electoral assistance.

In the early 1990s, Eastern European countries and the former Soviet Union absorbed most of the efforts.[34] While the fall of the Soviet Union represented a powerful stimulus for the development of the sector, similar needs also emerged in other parts of the world, such as Africa and Asia, in contexts where political transition processes and post-conflict stabilisation were increasingly attracting EU political attention, also in the domain of electoral support.

Whereas the first EU election observation experience was in Russia, in 1993, in 1994 European observers were deployed to South Africa and Mozambique. From 1993 to 1999, the EU carried out thirteen election observation missions,[35] in most

---

[30] Capacity-building support granted by US agencies and European political foundations to political party organisations in the 60s/70s in southern Europe and Latin America can be considered as the first form of electoral support. The UN engaged in election observation in the 1960s with the observation or supervision of some 30 post-colonial plebiscites, referenda or elections in various regions of the world, whereas UNDP started to engage in technical assistance projects, including setting up the infrastructure required for conducting elections.

[31] In the late 1980s/early 1990s, the UN started to become involved in major electoral operations in the framework of conflict resolution and peacebuilding processes (e.g., Namibia in 1989, Cambodia in 1993 and El Salvador in 1994). General Assembly Resolution 46/137 'Enhancing the Effectiveness of the Principle of Periodic and Genuine Elections' of 1991 was adopted in this context of massive direct UN involvement.

[32] Starting with Article 21 of the Universal Declaration of Human Rights and Article 25 of the International Covenant on Civil and Political Rights, establishing the right to take part in government directly or through freely chosen representatives.

[33] For instance, in 1990, the OSCE developed specific commitments, known as the Copenhagen Declaration.

[34] This was mainly linked to the crisis in the Balkans, leading to the massive and direct involvement of the international community in organising and/or supervising elections, through the OSCE.

[35] See the annexed table.

cases in relation to electoral assistance. While they were valuable experiences, these missions took place outside a structured methodological, institutional, managerial and financial framework, following a case-by-case approach.

In the absence of a uniform legal basis, these missions were decided using a variety of legal instruments.[36] A turning point was the adoption, on 29 April 1999, of Council Regulations (EC) No 975/1999 and No 976/1999[37] placing electoral support under Community competence,[38] followed by the 2000 Commission Communication on EU electoral assistance and observation.[39] These documents marked a significant step towards the conceptualisation of electoral assistance and observation as complementary activities and towards the harmonisation of electoral support interventions.

Based on an analysis of the experience since the early 1990s and integrating the elements of previously adopted Council Decisions,[40] the 2000 Communication proposed a consistent and global approach to EU electoral support. In addition to methodological and political aspects, it also addressed several practical points, such as the need to: set up a clear framework for the decision-making process; build specific European capacity and establish specific structures at EU level; establish a clear budgetary framework; and clarify the legal basis for EU action.

It was further complemented by the Staff Working Paper, adopted by the Commission in 2003, on the Implementation of the Communication on Election Assistance and Observation,[41] reviewing the procedures and practice of EU EOM deployment and developing a strategy for election assistance and observation. Based

---

[36] For instance, the Lomé Convention, partnership and cooperation agreements with the 'New Independent States', regional programmes such as PHARE or TACIS, or specific CFSP Joint Actions on EU election observation in a particular country.

[37] Council Regulation (EC) No. 975/1999 laying down the requirements for the implementation of development cooperation operations and Council Regulation (EC) No. 976/1999 laying down the requirements for the implementation of Community operations, other than those of development cooperation, which, within the framework of Community cooperation policy, contribute to the general objective of developing and consolidating democracy and the rule of law and to that of respecting human rights and fundamental freedoms; these Regulations provided the legal basis. A complementary legal basis was the Lomé Convention. European Union electoral missions were fielded under the auspices of the Common Foreign and Security Policy or under the European Community's development cooperation.

[38] The two Regulations only differed in their geographical scope and legal basis: Article 308 TEC for countries benefitting from TACIS, PHARE, MEDA and OBNOVA, and Article 179 TEC for developing countries, the goal being to 'contribute to the general objective of developing and consolidating democracy and the rule of law and to that of respecting human rights and fundamental freedoms' in third countries. More specifically, it was stated that the European Community shall provide technical and financial aid for operations aimed at supporting the processes of democratisation, in particular 'by supporting independent electoral commissions, granting material, technical and legal assistance in preparing for elections, including electoral censuses, taking measures to promote the participation of specific groups, particularly women, in the electoral process and by training observers.'

[39] Communication on EU Election Assistance and Observation, *supra* n. 17.

[40] Council Decision 9262/98/PESC 157/COHOM 6: Guidelines – EU Policy on Electoral Observation, and Council Decision 8728/99/PESC 165/COHOM 4: EU Guidelines on Common Criteria for the Selection of Electoral Observers.

[41] SEC(2003) 1472 of 19 December 2003.

on the experience acquired since 2000, this document basically confirmed the practice of interinstitutional consultation prior to the Commission Decision on the election observation calendar for a given year; programming criteria; the analytical independence of EU EOMs; and the cooperation with other international observers, consolidated in October 2005 through the Commission's endorsement of the Declaration of Principles for International Election Observation.[42]

Additionally, guidelines and handbooks have been developed and updated as part of a continuous learning process, such as the EU Handbook for EU Election Observation Missions (second edition in 2008),[43] the EC Methodological Guide on Electoral Assistance (2006)[44] and the Compendium of International Standards for Elections (2008).[45] This has enabled the EU to refine the scope of EU election observation and assistance. With respect to observation, the guidelines and handbook have helped clarify the definition and mandate of EU EOMs. In that context, a number of expert meetings as well as two Commission-European Parliament seminars on EU election observation in 2007 and 2009 have been a useful reflection forum as well. Finally, through the funding, under the EIDHR since 2001, of training programmes for candidates for core team positions and long-term observers and through briefings and debriefings for EU EOMs, the Commission has integrated updated methodologies and lessons learned into mission practice.

## 10. INTERNATIONAL AND LEGAL FRAMEWORK: STANDARDS AND GOOD PRACTICES

Initially, EU initiatives in electoral support took place in the absence of a consistent, methodological framework. The various documents adopted within the Council and the Commission in 1999 and 2000 acknowledged the need for a structured and well-grounded approach. Still, while these documents represented a turning point, they were also, in many ways, just a starting point.[46] For instance, election observation reports produced prior to 2006 vary widely in format, structure and content. EU EOM methodology developed gradually, inspired initially by the OSCE/ODIHR's experience and subsequently by the EU's own experience.

A similar learning path was followed in the case of electoral assistance, largely benefitting from the UN and UNDP experience, in order to build a systematic method-

---

[42] This Declaration has also been subscribed to by the European Parliament (2008) and the Council (2009). The Declaration has served as a benchmark for impartial, consistent and credible international election observation; its normative significance has been confirmed by the adoption by the UN General Assembly in December 2009 of a Resolution on strengthening the role of the UN in enhancing the effectiveness of the principle of periodic and genuine elections and the promotion of democratisation.

[43] EU Handbook for EU Election Observation Missions (2nd edition in 2008).

[44] See Methodological Guide on Electoral Assistance (2006), *supra* n. 12.

[45] Compendium of International Standards for Elections (2008), see: <http://ec.europa.eu/external_relations/human_rights/election_observation/docs/compendium_en.pdf>.

[46] R. Chambers, 'The European Experience: EU Election Observation Missions, Strengths, Weaknesses and Opportunities', European Commission-European Parliament Seminar *Perspective on EU Election Observation: Successes and Challenges since 2004*, Brussels, 17 March 2009.

ological approach to technical assistance, which in 2006 was translated into the European Commission Methodological Guidebook on Electoral Assistance.

The development of EU EOM methodology implied the definition and application of specific benchmarks, i.e., international standards for democratic elections, going beyond arbitrary indicators such as 'free and fair' elections.

International standards refer to international treaty standards, international political commitments[47] and best practices.[48] The first category includes legally binding standards agreed upon in the UN framework, such as the 1948 Universal Declaration of Human Rights (UDHR), which, though as a General Assembly Resolution in principle not legally binding, is generally held to codify customary international law, and the widely ratified 1966 International Covenant on Civil and Political Rights (ICCPR).[49]

Of central importance to the work of election observers are Article 21 of the UDHR and Article 25 of the ICCPR:

**'Article 21 Universal Declaration of Human Rights**

(1) Everyone has the right to take part in the government of his country, directly or through freely chosen representatives.
(2) Everyone has the right of equal access to public service in his country.
(3) The will of the people shall be the basis of the authority of government; this will shall be expressed in periodic and genuine elections which shall be by universal and equal suffrage and shall be held by secret vote or by equivalent free voting procedures.

**Article 25 International Covenant on Civil and Political Rights**

Every citizen shall have the right and the opportunity, without any of the distinctions mentioned in Article 2 and without unreasonable restrictions:

---

[47] For a systematic review of these sources, see the European Commission's Compendium of International Standards for Elections, 2nd edition, 2008, *supra* n. 45. This Compendium outlines the obligations and commitments as regards human rights related to election processes that each state has entered into by signing international and regional instruments .

[48] Such as transparency of the election process, impartiality in the conduct of the election administration and in the use of state resources, and equitable access to and balanced coverage by any public media.

[49] Further standards are laid down in the 1965 International Convention on the Elimination of Racial Discrimination (ICERD), the 1979 Convention on the Elimination of All Forms of Discrimination against Women (CEDAW), the 1952 International Convention on the Protection of the Rights of Women (CPRW) and the 2006 Convention on the Rights of Persons with Disabilities. The relevant standards have been given concrete shape by the respective human rights monitoring bodies: see, e.g., General Comment No. 25 of 1996, which was adopted by the Human Rights Committee (for details, see below) or General Recommendation No. 23 of 1997 on Political and Public Life, which was adopted by the CEDAW Committee. Further relevant (non-binding) standards are contained in the Declaration on the Elimination of All Forms of Intolerance and of Discrimination Based on Religion or Belief (1981), the Declaration on the Rights of Persons Belonging to National or Ethnic, Religious and Linguistic Minorities (1992), General Assembly Resolution (2001) A/RES/55/96 on Promoting and Consolidating Democracy, General Assembly Resolution A/RES/56/154 (2002) on Respect for the Principles of National Sovereignty and Non-Interference in the Internal Affairs of States in Electoral Processes As an Important Element for the Promotion and Protection of Human Rights, etc.

(a) to take part in the conduct of public affairs, directly or through freely chosen representatives;
(b) to vote and to be elected at genuine periodic elections which shall be by universal and equal suffrage and shall be held by secret ballot, guaranteeing the free expression of the will of the electors;
(c) to have access, on general terms of equality, to public service in his country.'

Additionally, also in the context of regional organisations, the basis has been laid for norms and standards in the electoral field.[50]

The second category of international standards includes political commitments, such as the 1990 OSCE (at the time CSCE) Copenhagen Meeting Document.[51]

Furthermore, the basic features of elections have been detailed by the Human Rights Committee in its General Comment on Article 25 of the ICCPR.[52] While the General Comment is not legally binding on the states that have ratified the ICCPR, it serves as a powerful guideline for the realisation of the right to political participation and as a useful tool for election observers. It sets out fundamental issues related to the periodicity of elections, the oversight of election processes by an independent authority, a person's right to vote and stand for election (with the obligation for state authorities to enact necessary measures in that respect, e.g., an inclusive and accurate voter register), the importance of the freedom of expression, assembly and association as essential preconditions for the effective exercise of the right to vote, as well as the importance of the secrecy of the vote, non-interference by state authorities in the election process and the exercise of the right to vote free from intimidation or fear.

Finally, guidelines issued by expert bodies such as the Council of Europe's 'Venice Commission'[53] have provided additional appropriate benchmarks.

## 11. The conceptual framework: A cyclical approach towards elections

The above sources represent a rich corpus of texts establishing a yardstick for participation in public affairs. They have enabled EU Election Observation Missions

---

[50] See, e.g., Art. 24 of the 1969 American Convention on Human Rights, Art. 3 of the First Protocol to the European Convention on Human Rights (ECHR), and Art. 13 of the 1981 African Charter on Human and Peoples' Rights (ACHPR), as well as the 2003 Protocol on the Rights of Women in Africa and the 2007 African Charter on Democracy, Elections and Governance (not yet in force). Non-binding regional instruments include moreover the 2002 Declaration on the Principles Governing Democratic Elections in Africa, the 1994 Arab Charter on Human Rights, the 1990 Cairo Declaration on Human Rights in Islam, the 1994 Inter-Parliamentary Union (IPU) Declaration on Criteria for Free and Fair Elections, etc.

[51] See: <http://www.osce.org/documents/odihr/1990/06/13992_en.pdf>.

[52] Human Rights Committee, General Comment No. 25/57, 12 July 1996, UN Doc CCPR/C/21/Rev.1/Add.7

[53] Official name: European Commission for Democracy through Law; e.g., its Code of Good Practices in Electoral Matters of 2002.

to systematically assess a variety of aspects of an election process[54] and to formulate recommendations for electoral reform which subsequently can be of use to electoral assistance programmes. The next EU EOM can then assess the extent of the follow-up to be given to the preceding EU EOM. As mentioned earlier, increasing attention has been paid to an electoral cycle approach whereby electoral assistance is firmly established as an entry point for promoting democracy, rule of law and good governance.

The electoral cycle approach is based on the idea that elections are made up of a sum of interacting elements where a wide range of legal, technical and organisational aspects have to be considered simultaneously and addressed within a rolling methodological framework, as shown in Figure 1.

*Figure 1.* Electoral cycle

*Source*: European Commission and International IDEA; see: EC Methodological Guide on Electoral Assistance (2006), at 84, available at: http://ec.europa.eu/europeaid/multimedia/publications/documents/thematic/ec_methodological_guide_on_electoral_assistance_en.pdf.

[54] For instance, the legal framework, election administration, voter and candidate registration, campaign environment, plurality of the media, secrecy and transparency of the vote, transparency of the counting process and tabulation of results, and appeal provisions. EU EOM reporting guidelines can be found at: <http://ec.europa.eu/external_relations/human_rights/election_observation/docs/2007_eu_eom_reporting_guidelines_en.pdf>.

The electoral cycle contains eight interrelated segments:

1. Legal framework: constitution; legislation; electoral systems and boundaries; electoral bodies; codes of conduct;
2. Planning and implementation: budgeting, funding and financing; procurement and recruitment; logistics and security;
3. Training and education: operational training for election officials; civic education; voter information;
4. Voter registration: registration of voters, registration of parties and candidates; accreditation of domestic and international observers;
5. Electoral campaign: media access, rules and regulations; campaign coordination; party financing; breaches and penalties; code of conduct;
6. Voting operations and election day activities: voting; counting; special and out-of-country voting;
7. Verification and results: tabulation of results; compilation and announcement of official results; complaints and appeals;
8. Post-electoral period: update of voter lists; audits and evaluation; archiving and research; legal reform; voter lists update; institutional strengthening and professional development.

Each segment allows for specific interventions in support of an election, either integrated within a comprehensive programme or limited to more targeted projects.[55] Each segment also provides for interaction with a wide scope of governmental and civil society actors, for instance, electoral management bodies, other national administrations or agencies, civil society organisations, political parties, etc.

In a long-term holistic perspective, the electoral cycle aims to achieve, apart from technical improvement, *sustainability* of electoral assistance efforts by building capacity that will last until and beyond the next election event and by consolidating technical assistance within a broader democratic governance and development support framework, i.e., increased participation in the democratic process, development of democratic values, enhancement of accountable and responsive institutions, promotion of sound electoral practices and efficient use of public resources.

This cyclical approach was conceived by the European Commission and the International Institute for Democracy and Electoral Assistance (International IDEA), initially for training purposes. It was further developed and formalised in documents such as the EC Methodological Guide on Electoral Assistance (2006),[56] the

[55] For instance, support to the development of technical, managerial and administrative capacities of the electoral management body; technical and financial assistance to civil society, particularly as regards the development of public awareness campaigns; assistance to domestic observer groups; financial and logistic support as well as training of the media sector; training of candidates, particularly female candidates as part of a strategy to promote gender equality in political processes; training of police and other security agencies, etc. Notably, cross-cutting issues such as gender, youth and disabled persons are mainstreamed throughout projects with the overall objective of increasing participation of marginalised groups in political processes.

[56] See Methodological Guide on Electoral Assistance (2006), *supra* n. 12.

International IDEA Handbook on Electoral Management Design (2006)[57] and the UNDP Electoral Assistance Implementation Guide (2007).[58]

The cyclical approach to elections was further recognised in the Council Conclusions of 17 November 2009 on Democracy Support in the EU's External Relations, which highlighted that 'the EU support should take into account the full electoral cycle and not focus on ad hoc electoral support only.' With the electoral cycle approach the EU has recognised the opportunity for a continuous process of review, analysis, codification of lessons learned and strategic planning and the importance of a longer-term approach.[59]

## 12. Election observation and assistance – complementary activities

As mentioned, the EU views election observation and assistance to electoral processes as complementary activities. This view was established in the Commission Staff Working Paper 'Implementation of the Communication on Election Assistance and Observation' of 2003, which states that:

> 'Observation, while contributing potentially to better elections, involves the assessment of the strengths and weaknesses of an electoral process and the presentation of recommendations. This provides an important basis for deciding on further assistance after elections. Assistance on the other hand, can improve an electoral process before elections. Assistance is best programmed with sufficient time before the next elections are held. Assistance efforts can inform the political process vis-à-vis a country, as election reform issues often have a political component.'

With different internal and external stakeholders involved in EU election support, the Commission has sought to maximise the synergy between EU election observation and assistance through different modalities:

- Enhanced inter-service cooperation within the Commission with a view to improving consistency and coherence in the EU approach to elections;
- The recommendations provided by the EU EOMs are increasingly drafted in such a way as to be effectively fed into specific follow-up assistance activities;
- The use of the electoral cycle approach in the formulation and implementation of new projects opens the opportunity to take on board EU EOM recommendations beyond those relating to the technical organisation of the electoral process;

---

57 See: <http://www.idea.int/publications/emd/ar.cfm>.

58 See: <http://www.undp.org/governance/docs/Elections-Pub-EAGuide.pdf>.

59 Electoral assistance projects designed under this framework were conducted in, for instance, the Democratic Republic of Congo, East Timor, Sierra Leone and Togo. The case of the Democratic Republic of Congo, where in the context of the 2006 elections the EU (including Member States) provided 80% of the electoral assistance budget, was particularly relevant as it contributed to triggering an institutional learning curve towards more in-depth, integrated cooperation between the European Commission and UNDP in the field of electoral assistance (see *supra*).

- The production of capacity-building tools, including knowledge products.[60] The efforts undertaken to maximise the synergy between EU observation and assistance fit into a broader rule of law and democratic governance strategy.

In the following sections the strategic framework for EU electoral support is further addressed.

## 13. The strategic framework (1): Whether to engage?

In its 2000 Communication, the European Commission proposed to seek to achieve the following goals through electoral support to third countries:

- Partnership with state institutions[61] and civil society organisations (with specific attention paid to domestic observation);
- Strategic use of resources (assistance only where it is really needed);
- Flexibility (case-by-case decision on the basis of established criteria and adaptation to changing situations);
- Complementarity between assistance and observation;
- Sustainability (development of national capacity of national election commissions and civil society and long-term commitment to technical assistance);
- Promotion of political and societal pluralism;
- Promotion of self-regulation mechanisms.

These principles implicitly contain some guidance for defining where and when to engage. As regards election observation, further orientation is provided by the three assessment benchmarks included in the Commission Communication of 2000 which provide the evaluation criteria for the exploratory missions sent in advance of a political decision on whether or not to deploy an EU EOM.

**The 3 considerations for sending EU observation missions (extract of the 2000 Communication on electoral assistance and observation)**

1) *Is EU participation advisable?*
*To avoid the EU being drawn into a situation where its presence might give credibility to a flawed election process, full account should be taken of the relevant political and legal factors in situ. Minimally acceptable conditions should normally include:*

---

[60] For instance, the EC Methodological Guide on Electoral Assistance and the Handbook for EU Election Observation, as well as training programmes (such as the EC-UNDP-IDEA Joint Training on Effective Electoral Assistance and observer training through the so-called NEEDS project, see *supra*).

[61] See Communication on EU Election Assistance and Observation, *supra* n. 17: 'The Community should help the host government to create and sustain an independent national capacity for the holding of elections based upon democracy, the rule of law and respect for human rights and fundamental freedoms.'

- *a universal franchise;*
- *freedom for individuals and political parties to participate in the elections;*
- *freedom of expression to criticise the government;*
- *the right to free movement;*
- *the right of assembly;*
- *reasonable access to the media for all contesting parties and candidates.*

*Other important factors should also be weighed up carefully and form a part of the EU's judgment and decision, e.g., is the election the first following a period of conflict or oppression? Do the elections accompany a peace process or the possible return of refugees?*

2) *Is EU participation viable?*
Even where a situation exists for free and fair elections the EU should still seek to establish certain conditions for its participation:

- *a request to observe the election by the government of the host country. A formal request from the government should be sought but in some circumstances, a clear indication of the government's willingness to have EU observers, even when not formally expressed, may be acceptable;*
- *a host government responsive to EU requests for specific amendments or improvements to the electoral preparations;*
- *the support by all the main contesting political parties or candidates for the involvement of EU observers;*
- *the existence of previous EU monitoring of political developments in the host country;*
- *a time-scale which permits any EU monitoring team to be in place sufficiently in advance.*

3) *Is EU participation useful?*
*An observation exercise normally provides some degree of legitimisation, contributes something to confidence building and always acts as a deterrent to fraud. However observation is a costly business. Priorities need to be established, and usefulness must partially be defined in terms of cost/benefit ratio. This concept of 'usefulness' is largely technical and must be balanced by an EU assessment of whether its global relations with the country concerned and EU general objectives make an EU electoral presence 'politically useful'.*

*Normally all EU electoral missions should have written Terms of Reference (TOR) agreed with the government and the electoral authorities of the country being observed. The TOR should include the objectives and the requirements of the observation activity such as a guarantee for observers of freedom of movement and freedom of access to all political parties, candidates and election officials as well as to all polling and counting stations. In addition, observers should be entitled to receive all necessary information about the electoral process. The safety of the observers should also be guaranteed.*

*Source*: COM(2000) 191 of 11 April 2000.

In the meantime, the 'viability' criterion has been broadened to include 'feasibility' considerations related to the operational and security conditions for deploying EU election observers, with a view to ensuring a credible EU EOM. As for the 'usefulness' of deploying a mission, increasing attention is focused on the extent to which recommendations for electoral reform formulated by previous EU EOMs have been followed up by the host country, as well on the possibility to integrate election observation into a broader electoral and political support approach to a given country.

Given the context in which EU election observation takes place, political priorities, in addition to budgetary and operational constraints, have been guiding final decisions on observer deployment. These have included the EU's overall strategy towards a given country and the added value expected of an EU EOM and other support activities. Increasingly, EU EOMs have been sent to fragile, (post-)conflict countries hosting ESDP and/or UN peace support missions. Examples include Timor Leste (2002), DR Congo (2006), Aceh/Indonesia (2006-07) and Afghanistan (2009). Given the political, security and logistic context of some of the countries observed, the challenge has at times been the reconciliation of the political importance of the presence of election observers within a broader political strategy with the requirement to uphold EU EOM methodology.

With regard to electoral assistance, the criteria are less clear-cut in the 2000 Communication:[62]

- A request from the host government for EU election assistance;
- The general agreement of the main political parties and the other potential partners (e.g., NGOs, civil society organisations, women's groups, journalists' associations, etc.) to a programme of EU election assistance;
- The existence of previous EU political monitoring or of EU development programmes in the host country;
- An adequate time-frame for preparation;
- A guarantee of freedom of movement and freedom of access to relevant government ministries and other, non-governmental, partners for members of the EU Election Assistance Team;
- A guarantee of access to all information relevant to the EU Election Assistance Team's activities; and
- A guarantee on the safety of the EU Election Assistance Team members, as far as possible.

In line with the 2003 Commission Staff Working Paper, additional criteria have been applied. Taking into account that organising an election is a state obligation, EU assistance is only provided as complementary to the host country's investments. When it comes to conflict-affected environments where authorities are not always fully functional, this criterion has not been applied to the same extent. Another criterion is the potential impact of electoral assistance on reducing or preventing

---

62 See Communication on EU Election Assistance and Observation, *supra* n. 17, at 18-19.

election-related conflict. 'Electoral assistance can play a role in preventing violent conflicts since genuine elections create legitimacy, strengthen inclusion and help for tension and conflicts to be managed in democratic ways.'[63] Finally, two other criteria have affected EU involvement. Assistance efforts need to be result-oriented and politically advisable, i.e., minimum democratic space and political will must exist to allow for the organisation of genuine elections

## 14. The strategic framework (2): Where to engage?

Over the past years, the EU has been increasingly involved in electoral support. Where from 2000 to 2004, 28 EU Election Observation Missions were deployed, this number almost doubled to 50 between 2005 and 2009,[64] across Latin America, Asia and sub-Saharan Africa. EU funding for electoral assistance tripled in 2005-2009 as compared to 2000-2004.

Elections in the EU's Eastern Neighbourhood,[65] Russia and Central Asia have been systematically monitored by OSCE/ODIHR missions. Their conclusions and recommendations have been used in EU strategies and programmes regarding those countries. In contrast, it should be noted that elections have not been followed (mostly for lack of invitation) in a similar comprehensive manner in the EU's so-called Southern Neighbourhood,[66,67] where, in principle, the EU could play a pioneering role in the future. Instead, alternative, lower-profile election support activities have been developed.[68]

EU EOMs have been increasingly deployed in post-conflict contexts, including countries with a particular international peacebuilding agenda, which also illustrates the political importance attached to EU election observation. However, due to the nature of these environments, the consistent application of a comprehensive observation methodology has proven to be challenging. For instance, the mission deployed in Afghanistan, in the second half of 2009, faced complex security, logistic and political challenges.

Not every election provides the framework for an EU EOM. The appropriateness of deploying an EU EOM is assessed on a case-by-case basis, taking into consideration not only the methodological aspects, but also longer-term political

63 2003 Commission Staff Working Paper, *supra* n. 41, at 13.

64 An overview of EU EOMs in 2005-2009 can be found at: <http://ec.europa.eu/external_relations/human_rights/election_observation/index_en.htm>.

65 Referring to the EU Eastern Neighbourhood Policy (see: <http://ec.europa.eu/world/enp/index_en.htm>), these countries are: Ukraine, Belarus, Moldova, Georgia, Armenia and Azerbaijan

66 These countries fall outside the OSCE area; there are ten in total: Morocco, Tunisia, Algeria, Libya, Egypt, Lebanon, Israel, Occupied Palestinian Territory, Jordan and Syria.

67 Except in Lebanon in 2005 and 2009 and the Occupied Palestinian Territory in 1996, 2005 and 2006.

68 For instance, support to domestic observers in Morocco in 2007 and a capacity-building seminar for Arab League Secretariat staff in 2009.

strategies, budgetary constraints and certain geographical considerations.[69] Further to the yearly definition – for planning and programming purposes – of a list of EU EOM priority countries for a given year,[70] the political decision[71] on mission deployment is taken on a country-by-country basis. Prior to the political decision, exploratory missions are deployed to the country concerned in order to assess the advisability, usefulness and feasibility of EU EOM deployment (see *supra*).

One of the reasons for deploying an EU Election Observation Mission is the added value it can bring to an election process in terms of transparency and public confidence. Observation missions can operate most effectively when and where their observers can move freely around the country and where they have full access to all appropriate aspects and actors in an electoral process and are unhindered in their work. Such conditions are subject to a formal agreement with the authorities of the country to be observed; this agreement, which often takes the form of a Memorandum of Understanding, also details the observers' obligations, including abidance by the law of the country and impartiality during observation. In general, these agreements have provided the basis for a good working relationship between the EU (EOMs) and the authorities.

The added value criterion also relates to the potential long-term impact of an observation mission, in terms of both political partnership between the EU and the country observed and the potential for electoral and governance reform in that country. More specifically, to what extent can EU EOM recommendations be conducive to reform, for instance, through electoral assistance? The answer to this question will also determine the scope of possible follow-on to electoral support in a given country.

## 15. The strategic framework (3): How to engage?

As far as election observation is concerned, EU EOMs offer an appropriate tool for a comprehensive, systematic and human rights-related assessment of an election process, provided there is scope and political willingness in the country to engage in electoral reform further to the recommendations of the observers.

EU EOMs are deployed in the context of a positive partnership between the EU and the country concerned, with a view to strengthening the latter's democratic process. Hence, in a number of situations an EU EOM might not be advisable, for instance, where the EU EOM might be seen as rubber-stamping a flawed election

[69] This analysis is conducted by the Commission, in regular consultation with Member States in the Council and with the European Parliament Election Coordination Group. This consultation has taken place both in the context of the yearly definition of EU EOM priority countries for a given year, and when mission deployment was considered in the context of a specific mission.

[70] These lists are adapted during the year, taking into account volatile election calendars, budgetary possibilities, elections not foreseen in the yearly planning, or no invitation for an EU EOM.

[71] Until the entry into force of the Lisbon Treaty on 1 December 2009, these decisions were taken by the Commissioner for External Relations.

process or where it might have a destabilising effect through the use made by some of criticisms formulated by the EOM. Also, this implies that EU EOMs are not the appropriate tool in situations where the minimum conditions for genuine, democratic elections do not exist and where an EU EOM might end up providing only negative reports.

In light of a sustainable partnership between the EU and the country concerned, including the EU's efforts to promote the rule of law, human rights and democratic values and norms, alternative and less visible tools would have a more prominent role to play.[72]

EU EOMs have not always been possible, even if desirable, for instance, in situations where elections were called at short notice (such as Zambia in 2008, following the death of the President), because of security (Iraq 2009) or logistic constraints (Maldives 2008 and 2009), or in situations where an EU EOM was not politically appropriate (Honduras 2009).

For such scenarios, where there was a EU political interest to obtain some analytical information on the election process, small-scale, low-visibility and technical election expert teams were deployed. These missions cannot be assimilated to EU EOMs, notably for lack of an observation aspect during the polling, counting and tabulation process, and due to their focus on the normative aspects of an election. Still, they have provided useful election-specific input into political reporting.

Useful work has also been done by an independent expert team assessing the crucial and politically sensitive pre-election voter identification process in Côte d'Ivoire since 2008. This important aspect of an election process easily takes place six months or more before the election, hence does not fit in most observation missions' agendas. The same applies to post-electoral judicial disputes over an election process, which can go beyond the time span of an observation mission and regarding which, in terms of reporting, diplomatic correspondence is the main information instrument.

## 16. Further orientations

Over the past ten years, the EU has significantly stepped up its activities in the domain of election support. This epitomises the EU's increased attention to democratic governance and human rights promotion in its external assistance programmes as well as in its political dialogue with partner countries. Along with this quantitative expansion, continuous efforts have been made to improve the quality and complementarity of the actions undertaken. Today, the EU is considered as one of the most credible actors in international election observation and electoral assistance. Election support has become one of the success elements of the EU's 'soft

---

[72] Support to domestic observers and electoral assistance, such as capacity-building programmes for independent election commissions and the judiciary, as well as training initiatives enhancing pluralistic, professional media.

power' in international relations, largely because efforts have been made to promote consistent methodological approaches and coordinate various sectors of intervention.

While progress has been made with the development of an election cycle approach, more can be done to increase the impact of EU Election Observation Missions, notably in terms of support to governmental, parliamentary and civil society stakeholders involved in electoral and governance reform, through electoral and other assistance, as also highlighted in the European Parliament Resolution on EU Election Observation Missions.[73] The Council Conclusions on Democracy Support in EU External Relations of 17 November 2009 underline the same need for a comprehensive approach.[74]

Election observation and assistance serve a political purpose, i.e., to enhance transparent and genuine elections with a view to consolidating the rule of law and sustainable democracy. This underlines the relevance of embedding election support into a broader democracy support approach and prioritising a programmatic over a project approach.

The European Union has the 'soft power' political and development tools to develop such an approach. With the creation of an External Action Service under the Treaty of Lisbon there is scope for further increasing the consistency, coherence and complementarity of EU action, also in the area of election support, with a continued focus on long-term investment.

---

[73] European Parliament Resolution of 8 May 2008 on EU Election Observation Missions: objectives, practices and future challenges (2007/2217(INI)). The European Parliament also advised, amongst other things, to set aside, within the budgetary framework, funds for preparatory activities in anticipation of upcoming elections with a view to the longer-term sustainability of free and fair elections.

[74] Council Conclusions on Democracy Support in EU External Relations of 17 November 2009, available at: <http://www.consilium.europa.eu/uedocs/cms_data/docs/pressdata/en/gena/111250.pdf>, including an EU Agenda for Action on Democracy Support in EU External Relations in all regions. 'The Agenda for Actions aims to enhance the overall effectiveness of EU action in support of democracy without introducing new conditionality for EU development aid', see: <http://www.se2009.eu/polopoly_fs/1.24070.1258489534!menu/standard/file/111287.pdf>. Article 8 of the Council Conclusions is noteworthy: 'The Council invites the responsible EU institutions, in cooperation with Member States, to implement the (…) EU Agenda for Action on Democracy Support in EU External Relations in all regions, and to report back to the Council in 2010 on the progress achieved in its implementation. It also invites the responsible EU institutions to include in their progress report a proposed list of pilot countries for more specific follow-up. Once such a list and the proposed follow-up are agreed, a course of action and a timetable for implementation should be drawn up in partnership with the countries concerned.'

## Annex 1

## EC contributions to UNDP-managed basket funds in the field of electoral assistance, 2007-2009

| YEAR | COUNTRY | PROJECT TITLE |
|---|---|---|
| 2009 | Afghanistan | Enhancing Legal and Electoral Capacity for Tomorrow |
| 2009 | Benin | Projet d'Appui pour la Liste Electorale Permanente et Informatisée (LEPI) au Bénin |
| 2009 | Comoros | n/a |
| 2009 | Global | Global Training Platform 2009 |
| 2009 | Haiti | Appui au processus électoral en Haïti – Elections sénatoriales 2009 |
| 2009 | Moldova | Electoral Support to Moldova Project |
| 2009 | Nigeria | EC-UNDP Partnership with Nigeria for support to the electoral cycle, phase II, 2009-2011 |
| 2009 | Guinea-Bissau | Projet d'appui aux élections législatives en République de Guinée Bissau 2008 (PACE) – Addendum 3 |
| 2009 | Guinea Conakry | Appui aux élections législatives 2007, phase 1 – Addendum 3 |
| 2009 | Sudan | Support to elections and democratic processes |
| 2009 | Zambia | Support to the 2009-2012 Zambian electoral cycle |
| 2008 | Global | Preparation and delivery of training programmes on effective electoral assistance |
| 2008 | Zambia | Support to the 2008 presidential by-election in Zambia |
| 2008 | Côte d'Ivoire | Programme d'appui au processus électoral en Côte d'Ivoire |
| 2008 | DRC | Appui à la CENI dans le cadre du PACE (Projet d'Appui au Cycle Electoral) |
| 2008 | Georgia | Developing Capacities of Democratic Institutions for Fair Electoral Processes and Active Civil Participation |
| 2008 | Guinea Bissau | Projet d'appui aux élections législatives en République de Guinée Bissau 2008 – PACE phase 1 |
| 2008 | Malawi | Support to electoral reform and elections in Malawi |
| 2008 | Sierra Leone | Support to electoral management bodies in Sierra Leone – Phase II |
| 2008 | Tanzania | Deepening Democracy in Tanzania |
| 2008 | Yemen | EC-UNDP Joint Electoral Assistance Project in Yemen |
| 2007 | Bangladesh | Preparation of Electoral Roll with Photographs |
| 2007 | Comoros | Appui au Processus Electoral aux Comores (APEC-II) |
| 2007 | Fiji Islands | National Initiative for Civic Education (NICE) |
| 2007 | Guinea Conakry | Appui aux Elections Législatives 2007, phase 1 |
| 2007 | Iraq | Support to the electoral process |

| | | |
|---|---|---|
| 2007 | Kenya | 2007 Election Assistance Programme / Domestic Observation / Kenyan Domestic Observation Forum |
| 2007 | Timor Leste | Support to the Timorese Electoral Cycle |
| 2007 | Togo | Appui aux Processus Electoraux Togolais 2007-2008 |
| 2007 | Zambia | Preparatory Assistance to the Electoral Cycle 2007-2011 in Zambia |
| 2007 | Zimbabwe | Three-Year Rolling Multi-Donor Parliamentary Support Programme |

*Source*: European Commission.

# ANNEX 2

## EU EOMs, 2000-2009

| | | Europe | Middle East | Africa | Asia | Central and South America |
|---|---|---|---|---|---|---|
| Pre- 2000 missions | 1993 | Russia | | | | |
| | 1994 | Ukraine | | Mozambique South Africa | | |
| | 1996 | Russia | Occupied Palestinian Terr. | | | Nicaragua |
| | 1997 | | Yemen | | | |
| | 1998 | | | Togo | Cambodia | |
| | 1999 | | | Nigeria Mozambique | Indonesia | |
| Post- 2000 Communication missions | 2000 | | | Côte d'Ivoire Zimbabwe | Cambodia Sri Lanka | |
| | 2001 | | | Zambia | Bangladesh Timor Leste Sri Lanka | Guyana Nicaragua Peru |
| | 2002 | | | Rep. of Congo Kenya Madagascar Sierra Leone | Cambodia Timor Leste Pakistan | Ecuador |
| | 2003 | | | Mozambique Nigeria Rwanda | Cambodia | Guatemala |
| | 2004 | | | Malawi Mozambique | Indonesia Sri Lanka | |
| | 2005 | | Lebanon Occup. Palestinian Terr. | Burundi DR Congo (referendum) Ethiopia Guinea Bissau Liberia | Afghanistan Sri Lanka | Venezuela |
| | 2006 | | Occup. Palestinian Terr. Yemen | DR Congo Mauritania Uganda Zambia | Province of Aceh (Indonesia) Fiji | Bolivia Haiti Mexico Nicaragua Venezuela |
| | 2007 | | | Kenya Mauritania Nigeria Sierra Leone Togo | Timor Leste | Ecuador Guatemala |
| | 2008 | | | Angola Ghana Guinea Bissau Rwanda | Bangladesh Bhutan Cambodia Nepal Pakistan | Ecuador (referendum) |
| | 2009 | | Lebanon | Malawi Guinea Bissau Mozambique | Afghanistan | Bolivia (referendum) El Salvador Ecuador Bolivia (elections) |

# Chapter 14
# MAINSTREAMING HUMAN RIGHTS AND GENDER INTO THE COMMON SECURITY AND DEFENCE POLICY: THE CASE OF THE EU MONITORING MISSION IN GEORGIA

**Hadewych Hazelzet***

## 1. Introduction

The EU Monitoring Mission (EUMM) in Georgia, which was launched in the wake of the conflict between Russia and Georgia in August 2008,[1] is one of the very few Common Security and Defence Policy (CSDP) Missions with human rights incorporated into its mandate. It is also among the very few missions that do not formally have a human rights or gender advisor among their staff. Have human rights and gender issues been mainstreamed so successfully that special advisors are no longer needed? Or is mainstreaming of these 'soft' issues into the Common Security and Defence Policy still an uphill battle? This chapter gives an overview of six years of mainstreaming human rights and gender issues into the European Security and Defence Policy (ESDP) (2003-2009) (section 2 and Annex I), discussing in particular the case of EUMM Georgia (section 3) and suggesting steps to close the implementation gap (section 4).

## 2. Mainstreaming human rights and gender into ESDP

The EU started to deploy military and civilian staff to Bosnia, the Former Yugoslav Republic of Macedonia (FYROM) and the Democratic Republic of the Congo (DRC) in 2003.[2] Since then, EU civilian and military crisis management has been the growth business of the EU's Common Foreign and Security Policy (CFSP), amounting to eight finished and thirteen ongoing missions. The EU's human rights policy has been part of its foreign policy from the very beginning and was captured in the

* Dr. Hadewych Hazelzet works as an official at the General Secretariat of the Council of the European Union, Directorate General External and Politico-Military Relations, Directorate for Civilian Crisis Management. From 2002-2006, she was the desk officer for human rights in the Council. This contribution is written on a personal basis. The views reflected are those of the author only.

[1] See the contribution by Merlingen and Ostrauskaitė.

[2] See the introduction by the editors for an overview.

*S. Blockmans, J. Wouters & T. Ruys, eds., The European Union and Peacebuilding*

Treaties as well as in the European Security Strategy.[3] However, despite much talk about a 'coherent approach', the link between human rights policy and ESDP has not been easy to establish, neither on paper nor in practice.[4]

Why is it important to mainstream human rights and gender aspects into crisis management efforts? The main reason – which has both an internal and an external dimension – is that effectively integrating human rights and gender concerns into ESDP contributes to the success of the mission. Failing to do so has a price tag both for the success and credibility of ESDP and for the security and stability in host countries. EU efforts in post-conflict situations will not be sustainable if human rights protection and questions relating to transitional justice are not effectively addressed. EU efforts to train, monitor and advise judges, prosecutors, police and military in fragile states will backfire if these forces do not respect human rights or if the judiciary system remains corrupt. The EU's objectives regarding crisis management, such as contributing to security sector reform, building the rule of law, monitoring peace agreements or establishing a safe environment for elections, will not be fully reached if human rights and gender issues are neglected. On the contrary, the EU will be more successful and the governments and security sector in host countries will be trusted more if these aspects are visibly integrated into crisis management efforts.[5]

The internal aspect influencing the credibility of the mission refers first to the behaviour of EU staff abroad and the rules and standards they need to live up to. These missions and their staff are the 'face' of the EU abroad – a good local reputation reflects well on the EU, but, similarly, one scandal and the credibility of the EU as a whole will be at stake. The UN learned this lesson the hard way. Secondly, apart from the code of conduct for staff, so-called 'rules of engagement' define under what circumstances the use of force by military operations is permitted. For instance, one important question regarding one of the first ESDP operations in 2003, i.e., Artemis in the Democratic of Congo (DRC), was whether EU staff could shoot back in self-defence if threatened by a child soldier.[6] For some military operations,

---

3 Art. 11 TEU and Art. 177 TEC (pre-Lisbon Treaty). European Security Strategy (2003), in particular pages 4, 7 and 10, see Council website: <http://ue.eu.int/uedocs/cmsUpload/78367.pdf>.

4 For an earlier analysis of human rights and gender aspects of ESDP, see H. Hazelzet, 'Human Rights Aspects of EU Crisis Management Operations: From Nuisance to Necessity', in 13 *International Peacekeeping* (2006) 564-581; J. Arloth and F. Seidensticker, *The ESDP Crisis Management Operations of the European Union and Human Rights* (Berlin, Deutsches Institut fuer Menschenrechte, 2007); T. Hadden, ed., *A Responsibility to Assist. Human Rights Policy and Practice in European Union Crisis Management Operations*, COST Report (Oxford and Portland, Oregon 2009); J. Valenius, *Gender Mainstreaming in ESDP Missions*, Chaillot Paper 101 (Paris, EU Institute for Security Studies, 2007).

5 See H. Hazelzet, 'Six Years of Mainstreaming Human Rights into ESDP: A Success Story?', in W. Benedek, M. Kettemann and M. Moestl, eds., *Mainstreaming Human Security: Potentials, Problems, Policies* (London, Routledge, forthcoming). See also S. Kouvo, *State-Building and Rule of Law: Lessons from Afghanistan?*, NDC Forum Paper (Rome, NATO Defense College, Research Division, 2009).

6 Hazelzet (2006), *supra* n. 4, 564.

these rules as well as the code of conduct have been clarified in internal pocket cards for staff.

The external aspect of a mission's success and credibility relates to the EU's engagement with the host country. Host countries are usually emerging from or still involved in a crisis situation, which typically goes hand in hand with human rights violations. The ESDP missions often have as one of their objectives to contribute to the restoration or building of the rule of law or the creation of a secure environment. Most host countries have signed and ratified the main UN human rights instruments. They also often have an active or nascent civil society and national institutions, such as an ombudsperson, promoting respect for human rights.[7] Therefore, their obligations under international law and the support of local actors can be used as building blocks for the missions' work on the ground and can contribute to establishing a sustainable and secure situation. An example is the Aceh Monitoring Mission (AMM) – this was the first ESDP mission to include human rights monitoring in its mandate in 2005, and was based on a Memorandum of Understanding whereby the host country government agreed to ratify the ICCPR and ICESCR and to set up a Truth and Reconciliation Committee as part of the peace deal which the EU would monitor.[8] Other examples include the planning documents for the EU police mission in Afghanistan in 2007 which refer to the national obligations under international human rights law and provide for cooperation with the Afghan Independent Human Rights Commission. The planning documents for the monitoring mission in Georgia in 2008 also refer to national obligations and stipulate cooperation with the national ombudsperson.

From the overview of efforts, provided in Annex I, it becomes clear that the number of EU documents underlining the importance to or giving directions on how to mainstream human rights and gender has steadily grown since the first deployments six years ago. Also, the scope has been expanded, starting with children affected by armed conflict in 2003, standards of behaviour and international humanitarian law in 2005 and transitional justice, gender and cooperation with NGOs in 2006, to efforts to raise awareness and focus on implementation in 2008 and 2009. This reflects a growing interest on the part of Presidencies and delegations to make progress in these areas.

What has been the impact of the growth in the number and types of ESDP missions on the mainstreaming of human rights and gender into these missions? One indicator to measure such impact would be the number of human rights and gender advisors appointed to ESDP missions. Looking at the figures, it appears that with the increasing number of civilian and military ESDP missions, the number of these

[7] See overview of signatures and ratifications in the 'EU Compilation of Relevant Documents on Mainstreaming Human Rights and Gender into ESDP' (2008), at 18, available at: <http://www.consilium.europa.eu/ueDocs/cms_Data/docs/hr/news166.pdf>.

[8] Memorandum of Understanding signed on 15 August 2005 between the Government of Indonesia and the Free Aceh Movement (GAM), para. 2, available at: <http://www.consilium.europa.eu/uedocs/cmsUpload/MoU_Aceh.pdf>.

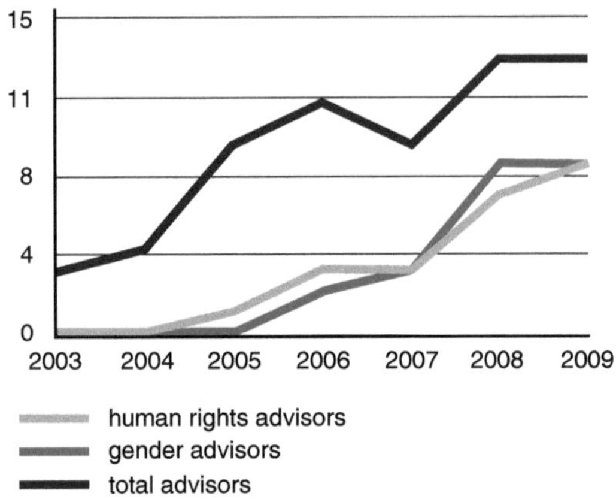


*Figure 1.* Number of human rights and gender advisors in ESDP missions (2003-2009)

special advisors has also steadily risen over time (Figure 1).[9] This is a positive step forward and a real sign of progress towards mainstreaming. It is true that the number remains small in proportion to the overall increase in the number of staff – 16 special advisors in 2009 on a total of 9202 deployed internationally seconded staff (from zero on a total staff of 2376 in 2003) –, yet this is similar for certain other special positions such as political or legal advisors. The number of such advisors need not be proportionate to the total number of staff, yet the tasks should be feasible in relation to the size and mandate of the mission.

For instance, EUSEC and EUPOL RD Congo – both mandated to contribute to the reform of the security sector – currently share one gender and one human rights advisor on a total of 70 staff in a country that is as big as Europe with daunting human rights and gender-related abuses and challenges, not seldom caused by men in uniform. Efforts are currently being undertaken to strengthen the mission's capacity to contribute to combating sexual violence, especially in eastern DRC. The much larger mission in Kosovo has a small human rights and gender unit. Some missions have no human rights or gender advisor, either because of their small size (EUSSR Guinea Bissau) or due to the type of mandate (Operation EUNAVFOR Atalanta in the horn of Africa).

Finally, we see that the number of gender advisors has quickly caught up with the number of human rights advisors. The lobby for the implementation of UN Security Council (UNSC) Resolution 1325 (2000) on women and peace and security has thus been quite successful in this regard. Five years after the adoption of this Resolution – which calls on UN members to involve women in peacemaking and peacekeeping – the EU started to adopt a series of guidelines and checklists to ensure its implementation at EU level, not least in the context of ESDP missions.[10]

---

[9] Data compiled by the author from internal statistics provided by the General Secretariat of the Council of the EU.

[10] See, for instance, EU Council documents 15782/2/08 REV 2, 14779/06, 12068/06 and 11932/2/05.

UNSC Resolution 1325, later followed by UNSC Resolution 1820, offered a very focused target to successfully push for mainstreaming. Some EU Member States have also started to organise specific training. Similarly, UNSC Resolutions 1539 (2004) and 1612 (2005) on children affected by armed conflict spurred EU efforts to adopt guidelines and a checklist on implementation, although no specific child protection advisors have been appointed to ESDP missions, nor has specialised training taken place in an EU context.[11] Human rights issues are much broader with a more dispersed constituency, leading perhaps to less focused efforts as regards mainstreaming.

The question remains whether simply counting the number of human rights and gender advisors per mission is the most telling indicator of progress made in mainstreaming these issues into ESDP. A qualitative case study of EUMM Georgia could provide additional insights into assessing the extent to which the EU has made progress towards mainstreaming.

## 3. Case study: EU Monitoring Mission (EUMM) Georgia

Following the outbreak of hostilities between Georgia and Russia on 8 August 2008, the EU Presidency brokered a ceasefire agreement, the so-called six-point plan,[12] and rapidly deployed a monitoring mission with two hundred EU monitors on the ground to observe and report on compliance.[13] The mandate of the mission, which deployed on 1 October 2008, consists of four components: stabilisation, normalisation, confidence building and informing EU policy (see Table 1 below).[14] The mandate explicitly provides that the mission should monitor and analyse violations of human rights and international humanitarian law (IHL) as well as the situation regarding the return of internally displaced persons (IDPs) and refugees. Although its mandate is country-wide, thus far EU monitors have been denied access to Abkhazia and South Ossetia.

Given the need for rapid deployment, the initial planning phase of the mission took less than a month. Normal procedures regarding calls for contributions of staff to be deployed by Member States were drastically shortened. Participating Member States were requested to deploy teams of monitors, including cars and translators. As a result, initially, the number of monitors with a human rights background as well as other staff with human rights or gender expertise depended completely on the (two or three) Member States that had such experts on their teams. In addition,

[11] References are found in the 'EU Compilation of Relevant Documents on Mainstreaming Human Rights and Gender into ESDP' (2008), *supra* n. 7.

[12] The six-point agreement concluded on 12 August 2008 on the basis of the EU's mediation efforts remains the basis for the stabilisation efforts. See Council Joint Action 2008/736 of 15 September 2008, recital 3.

[13] See the contribution by Merlingen and Ostrauskaitė.

[14] Council Joint Action 2008/736/CFSP of 15 September 2008, *OJ* 2008 L 248/26 of 17 September 2008.

*Table 1.* Mandate of EUMM Georgia

1. *Stabilisation*: monitoring and analysing the situation pertaining to the stabilisation process, centred on full compliance with the six-point agreement, including troop withdrawals, as well as on violations of human rights and international humanitarian law.
2. *Normalisation*: monitoring and analysing the situation as regards governance, rule of law and public order as well as the security of transportation links, energy infrastructures and the return of internally displaced persons and refugees.
3. *Confidence building*: contributing to the reduction of tensions through liaison, facilitation of contacts between parties and other confidence-building measures;
4. *Information provision*: informing EU policy about the situation on the ground.

experts selected from the so-called 'Civilian Response Team', an EU pool of experts trained for short-term assignments, some with human rights expertise, were deployed to assist the EU Special Representative for the Southern Caucasus as well as the mission during the first months following the crisis.[15]

For the first time, the planning documents carefully followed the 'EU Compilation of Relevant Documents on Mainstreaming Human Rights and Gender into ESDP'[16] and a special annex was included in the operations plan on human rights and international humanitarian law as well as gender.[17] This annex gives guidance on, for instance, training requirements, reporting by the monitors on issues pertaining to human rights and international humanitarian law as well as gender, and on how to coordinate the monitors and work with local human rights organisations such as the ombudsperson. It also gives job descriptions of human rights and gender advisors in the mission (based on those developed for EULEX Kosovo).

Also for the first time, the new Head of Mission was briefed by the Secretary General/High Representative (SG/HR) Personal Representative for Human Rights (PR/HR) prior to his departure. The PR/HR was closely involved by the planning team throughout the strategic and operational planning phase of the mission and also visited the mission in 2009 in follow-up to EU human rights consultations with Georgia.[18] Another novelty was that during the planning of the mission, various meetings were organised to specifically discuss issues relating to human rights, IHL, IDPs and refugees with the UN and OSCE, Council of Europe, ICRC, local and international NGOs, the ombudsperson, the Georgian Ministry for Refugees and others. As was later stated in the internal report on lessons identified and rec-

[15] The concept of Civilian Response Teams is set out in Council document 10462/05 of 23 June 2005.

[16] Available at: <http://www.consilium.europa.eu/ueDocs/cms_Data/docs/hr/news166.pdf>.

[17] The Operations Plan (OPLAN) is a restricted document established under the responsibility of the Head of Mission to execute the Concept of Operations (CONOPS) for the mission.

[18] The EU Special Representative for the Southern Caucasus and the EUSR for the conflict in Georgia of course also regularly raise human rights issues with relevant counterparts as part of their mandates.

ommendations on the planning phase, the early inclusion of human rights expertise in the planning team made these advancements possible.

Since the start of the mission, human rights, IHL, IDPs and gender have been included systematically in the reporting by the mission and a number of internal special reports on these topics have been issued.[19] Training was organised together with the Council of Europe to provide in-mission training to the monitors in the field offices as well as at headquarters, and the relevant EU human rights policy documents were distributed.

Although staffing positions were slowly regularised over the course of the months following the rapid deployment in October 2008, the positions of human rights and gender advisors were never formally published. Instead, one of the political advisors was asked to engage with human rights organisations as part of the tasks. Eventually, one of the monitors with human rights expertise was officially appointed as coordinator for the human rights monitors in the field offices. Also, one of the members of staff was asked to take on the role of gender focal point on top of other responsibilities. In early 2009, the monitoring teams were re-organised and focal points were appointed in the field offices, which, *inter alia*, raised the visibility of the human rights and IDP monitors as part of the composite teams. Finally, the position of gender advisor will now be officially created, starting from January 2010, following the extension of the mandate for another year.[20]

Given the mandate, human rights issues were actively and systematically monitored and reported by the mission. Therefore, the case of EUMM Georgia shows that much can be done in this area without official advisors, provided that the mandate stipulates such action.

## 4. Conclusion and way forward

What can we learn from the case of EUMM Georgia compared with general trends in mainstreaming human rights and gender into CSDP?[21]

First, it is essential to include human rights and gender expertise from the very beginning when planning a mission at strategic and operational level. This helps to ensure that EU human rights policy will be mainstreamed in the planning documents, during the induction of the Head of Mission and key staff, in early contacts with relevant partners on the ground and at headquarters. If such expertise is not

[19] General information and press briefings on EUMM can be found at: <http://www.consilium.europa.eu/showPage.aspx?id=1512&lang=EN>.

[20] Council Joint Action 2009/572/CFSP of 27 July 2009. Openings for seconded expert positions in missions are generally advertised by the Council Secretariat through calls for contributions addressed to Member States.

[21] For further analysis of mainstreaming efforts since 2003 as well as additional recommendations on the way forward, see H. Hazelzet, 'Six Years of Mainstreaming Human Rights into ESDP: A Success Story?', in W. Benedek, M. Möstl and M. Kettemann, eds., *Human Security and Human Rights in Peace Operations* (Routledge, forthcoming).

included from the outset and if the relevant references are included neither in the mandate nor in the conceptual and operational planning documents, it is very difficult if not impossible to add such expertise at a later stage. Indeed, even if it has been included from the beginning, it is hard enough to implement it on the ground. Templates from the planning documents of EUMM Georgia as well as the practice of reaching out to relevant experts and organisations can now be used and adapted for the planning of other missions.

Second, Member States are instrumental in ensuring that the appropriate experts are seconded to EU missions. Apart from dedicated human rights and gender experts and monitors, other staff members should be trained and made aware of these issues. This could be included as a requirement in calls for contributions at EU level or, in case of rapid deployment, at national level. To that end, most Member States would need to step up training efforts in the field of human rights and gender. Experience teaches that the openness of staff members to learn about such issues is much higher when trained at home prior to deployment compared with when deployed.[22] Such so-called in-mission training is still important, mainly to clarify the EU context and the expected day-to-day practice.

Third, even if no dedicated experts are appointed, headway can be made in reporting on and monitoring human rights, IHL and gender issues, as long as it is clearly included in the mandate. However, focal points do not usually carry the same weight as advisors, nor do they tend to have the same level of knowledge and expertise. These are not easy issues to work on in CSDP missions, especially since they may not be a central element of the mandate or may not be regarded as important to the success of the mission. Experience, for instance from EUFOR DRC, has shown that in order to make a real impact, human rights and gender advisors should be located at a strategic level with direct access to the Head of Mission.[23] Experience also shows that, at first, gender issues have to be mainstreamed from the top.[24] The same is true for Headquarters in Brussels. Until June 2009, focal points or advisors from the field did not know whom to call in Brussels when they had a question or required conceptual, strategic or practical guidance. The appointment of experienced human rights and gender advisors (rather than adding on the label of focal point to staff in charge of many other issues) at strategic and operational level in Brussels could make a real difference on the ground as well.

Finally, judging from the overview of mainstreaming efforts since the very first ESDP missions in 2003, the link between the EU's human rights policy and its security and defence policy has – at least on paper – been considerably and steadily

---

[22] Monika Larsson, former gender advisor to the Operations Commander of EUFOR Tchad/RCA, pointed this out at a seminar in Graz on 7-8 May 2009.

[23] Charlotte Isaksson, former gender advisor to the Operations Commander of EUFOR DRC, pointed this out at a seminar in Budapest on 6 May 2007.

[24] This was mentioned by various speakers at the gender seminar at the Swedish Permanent Representation in Brussels on 6 July 2009, quoting experience from, for instance, the Dutch and Swedish Ministries of Defence and armed forces.

strengthened. Most CSDP missions now have a human rights and/or a gender advisor. The case of Georgia shows that the wider policy also has an impact on the ground. However, for missions that do not include explicit references to human rights and international humanitarian law in their mandate – that is, most missions – particular attention should continue to be paid to making mainstreaming efforts a reality in practice. Here, the EU can certainly learn from other international organisations, in particular the UN, which has longer experience of training and deploying human rights, gender and child protection advisors at Headquarters and in the field, leading to identification of best practices. The UN also has a pocket card for peacekeepers, and the UN Department of Peacekeeping (DPKO) and the Office of the High Commissioner for Human Rights (OHCHR) have a clear understanding on how to cooperate on cross-cutting issues and effectively ensure mainstreaming including through reporting procedures.

Six years after this uphill battle was initiated, it is high time for all actors involved in CSDP – that is, in EU institutions and Member States – to develop an automatic reflex to follow through on public commitments expressed repeatedly at the top level, namely by the EU Council of Ministers. Mainstreaming human rights and gender into CSDP will indeed ultimately be successful only once dedicated advisors are no longer needed to ensure compliance with and coherence of these two essential components of the EU Common Foreign and Security Policy. There is no security without human rights protection. CSDP missions will be more successful and the situation in host countries more stable when both components are effectively integrated.

## Annex I

## Overview of efforts to mainstream human rights and gender into ESDP (2003 – June 2009)

| YEAR | EFFORTS |
|---|---|
| 2003 | • EU Guidelines on Children Affected by Armed Conflict (CAAC)[a]<br>• PSC working document on protection of civilians[a] |
| 2004 | • Distribution of booklets with EU Human Rights Guidelines (death penalty, torture, children affected by armed conflict, human rights dialogues, human rights defenders)[b]<br>• Questions regarding how to deal with issues relating to children affected by armed conflict are included in an EU military exercise and representatives of UNICEF are invited to take part<br>• Guidelines on human rights defenders[a] |
| 2005 | • Memorandum of Understanding with the Indonesian Government refers to the ratification of the UN human rights instruments (ICCPR and ICESCR)<br>• Appointment of first human rights monitors and advisor in AMM<br>• Human rights advice on the Aceh Monitoring Mission (AMM)[c]<br>• Council document on implementation of UNSCR 1325[a]<br>• Generic standards of behaviour for ESDP operations[a]<br>• Mandates of EU Special Representatives (EUSRs) start to include instructions on the EUSRs' role in promoting respect for human rights and implementing EU human rights policy[d]<br>• Guidelines on promoting compliance with international humanitarian law[a]<br>• The pool of 100 Civilian Response Teams (CRTs) includes human rights experts – the number of human rights experts in the pool is later increased to ca. 10 (Council document 10462/05 of 23 June 2005) |
| 2006 | • Checklist on mainstreaming gender into ESDP, leading, *inter alia*, to the recording of gender statistics in ESDP missions[a]<br>• First gender advisor appointed to EUFOR DRC – a special-lessons identified report on gender aspects is issued following the finalisation of the operation[c]<br>• Pocket card for EUFOR DRC soldiers[c]<br>• Council Conclusions on Gender Mainstreaming[a]<br>• Council document on mainstreaming human rights into ESDP[a]<br>• Gender seminar for Heads of Mission (December)<br>• Checklist on Children Affected by Armed Conflict and implementation of UNSCR 1612[a]<br>• Planning documents for the EU Police Mission in Afghanistan include first clear references to human rights and gender, the need for training, cooperation with local NGOs and the national Human Rights Commission, work on the basis of Afghanistan's obligations under international human rights law as well as EU human rights policy[c]<br>• Some NATO members start concluding agreements with Afghanistan on the transfer of detainees, demanding guarantees of humane treatment<br>• PSC working document on Transitional Justice and ESDP[a] |

- Document on enhancing cooperation with NGOs and CSOs in the framework of EU civilian crisis management and conflict prevention[a]
- Agreement between the International Criminal Court and the EU on cooperation and assistance (*OJ 2006* L 115/50, 28 April 2006)
- Lessons-identified reports of EUFOR DRC and AMM include lessons on mainstreaming human rights and gender[c]
- Human rights and gender issues related to peacekeeping operations are starting to be discussed in the EU-UN Steering Committee (based on the 2003 EU-UN Declaration on Cooperation in Crisis Management)[c]
- Documents and job descriptions related to the EU Civilian Headline Goal and civilian capability planning process begin to include references to human rights and gender
- Human Rights and Gender Focal Points are appointed to the Council Secretariat's Directorates for civilian (DG EIX) and military (DGEVIII) affairs as well as to the EU Military Staff (EUMS)

2007
- Presidency Programmes, ESDP mandates, six-monthly conclusions and the Presidency report on ESDP start to include human rights and gender aspects
- Adoption of compilation of texts to mainstream human rights and gender into ESDP[a]
- Political and Security Committee (PSC) Agreement to develop a manual on how to implement human rights and gender issues on the ground
- First training on mainstreaming gender into ESDP is organised in Budapest, and other national training institutes start organising training on human rights and gender (Sweden, Austria, Germany and the UK) coordinated through the European Group on Training
- The EU-UN Statement on Cooperation in Crisis Management includes explicit references to human rights and gender issues. Similarly, the EU-US Work Plan on Cooperation in Crisis Management also contains such references[b]

2008
- Publication of Compilation of Relevant Documents on Mainstreaming Human Rights and Gender into European Security and Defence Policy (adopted in 2007)[a]
- Pocket card for EUFOR Tchad soldiers[c]
- A special Annex on Human Rights is approved for the operational plan for EULEX KOSOVO[c]
- The legal basis of Operation Atalanta includes a reference to transfer of detainees to countries where they face the risk of death penalty or inhuman treatment, and an agreement with Kenya is concluded on that basis (Council Joint Action 2008/851/CFSP of 10 November 2008, Article 12, *OJ* 2008 L 301/33).
- Updated version of the booklet with EU Human Rights Guidelines is published, including the Guidelines on International Humanitarian Law and Violence Against Women[b]
- Updated version of the Guidelines as well as Checklist on Children Affected by Armed Conflict[a]
- The new Head of Mission (EUMM Georgia) is, for the first time, briefed by the SG/HR Personal Representative for Human Rights on human rights and gender issues
- The planning documents for EUMM Georgia use the new template provided by the compilation of texts on mainstreaming and include an updated and improved annex on human rights and gender[c]

- At least one human rights and/or gender advisor per mission (with a few exceptions: none in the small EU SSR mission in Guinea Bissau or in EU NAVFOR Atalanta, versus an entire unit in Kosovo), two advisors specifically include CAAC in their mandates (Iraq and DRC)
- Inclusion of correct references into virtually all planning documents as well as into the draft guidelines for Joint Actions (2009)[c]
- Paper on the implementation of the European Security Strategy includes references to gender and human rights in the context of ESDP[b]
- Regular inclusion of human rights and gender into some mission reports (for instance, EUMM Georgia and EUPOL RD Congo), ESDP exercises, the six-monthly Council Conclusions on ESDP, Presidency mandates in ESDP and references to ESDP in the annual Human Rights Report as well as EU statements during UN Security Council and General Assembly debates[c]

2009
- Reports on lessons identified and recommendations from the planning phase of EUMM Georgia and EUSSR Guinea Bissau include sections on human rights and gender[c]
- An options paper on combating sexual violence in the DRC is discussed at the request of the PSC and recommendations are included in revised planning documents for EUPOL RD Congo and EUSEC RD Congo, which now also use the template with references based on the compilation of texts on mainstreaming and request more gender and human rights experts for the missions, particularly in the east of the country[c]
- EUPOL Afghanistan increases its rule of law component, including its human rights and gender-related activities
- Human Rights and Gender Focal Points are appointed to the Civilian Conduct and Planning Capability (CPCC)
- The Swedish Presidency of the EU organises a seminar on mainstreaming gender into ESDP in Brussels as well as various training activities on SSR and gender

---

[a] Included in the Compilation of Relevant Documents: Mainstreaming Human Rights and Gender into European Security and Defence Policy, available at <http://www.consilium.europa.eu/ueDocs/cms_Data/docs/hr/news166.pdf>.

[b] Available at the Council's website: <http://www.consilium.europa.eu>.

[c] Restricted.

[d] See mandates of EU Special Representatives at the Council's website ('EU Representatives and Envoys').

# Chapter 15
# EULEX KOSOVO: WALKING A THIN LINE, AIMING FOR THE RULE OF LAW

**Stephan Keukeleire and Robin Thiers***

## 1. Introduction[1]

The European Union Rule of Law Mission in Kosovo (EULEX Kosovo), which has as objective to strengthen the rule of law in Kosovo, is one of the flagships of the Common Security and Defence Policy (CSDP) and, until the entry into force of the Lisbon Treaty in December 2009, of the preceding European Security and Defence Policy (ESDP).[2] It is also one of the best examples of a structural foreign policy conducted by the EU, as it is aimed at influencing and creating structures and rules of the game that will impact upon the behaviour and actions of the actors in that country.[3] EULEX Kosovo, which started late 2008, is the largest civilian mission launched thus far by CSDP (with over 2,500 staff) as well as the most ambitious and challenging one. It not only tries to create or strengthen various dimensions of the rule of law – including police, justice and customs components –

---

* Stephan Keukeleire is a Jean Monnet Professor in European Foreign Policy at the Institute for International and European Policy of the Catholic University Leuven (KU Leuven) and Visiting Professor at the College of Europe in Bruges. He is a member of the Leuven Centre for Global Governance Studies and coordinates the Jean Monnet Centre of Excellence (JMCE) on 'The EU, Foreign Policy and Global Governance'. He wrote various publications on EU foreign policy and is co-author of *The Foreign Policy of the European Union* (Palgrave Macmillan 2008). Robin Thiers holds an MA in Comparative and International Politics from the KU Leuven. In 2008-09, he was the administrative coordinator of the JMCE. His research focuses on EU and OSCE democratisation efforts regarding the Balkans and South Caucasus. Currently, he is working as a policy advisor within the Agriculture Department of the Flemish government in the framework of the Belgian EU Presidency.

[1] The analysis in this article is based on primary and secondary literature as well as on around 60 interviews (in addition to informal talks) conducted in Kosovo in April 2008, April 2009 and July-August 2009, including interviews with Kosovar diplomats, civil servants and staff from various Kosovar ministries and agencies; diplomats and civil servants from the ICO/EUSR, EULEX and ECLO offices; and staff members from the UN, the OSCE and international and local NGOs and think-tanks. It was agreed with most officials that neither their name nor their institutional allegiance would be mentioned in the article.

[2] In this article, only the term CSDP will be used (independently of the time period that is discussed).

[3] See S. Keukeleire and J. MacNaughtan, *The Foreign Policy of the European Union* (Basingstoke, Palgrave Macmillan 2008), at 25-28.

*S. Blockmans, J. Wouters & T. Ruys, eds., The European Union and Peacebuilding*

but has to take up this task in a context of not only peacebuilding but also (contested) state building. The success of the mission is important both for Kosovo and for the credibility of CSDP and for future EU peacekeeping and peacebuilding efforts. The stakes for the EU in terms of regional security and stability, internal development and international credibility are so high that the EU cannot afford to let its CSDP flagship fail. However, despite the EU's heavy lever in its close neighbourhood and the high investment of money and personnel, the sensitive international diplomatic context, internal divergences and daunting challenges on the ground give rise to the question of whether EULEX will manage to fulfil its high ambitions.

This chapter analyses EULEX Kosovo as one specific example of EU involvement in peacebuilding through the promotion of the rule of law in post-conflict societies. It first provides some indispensable insight into the historical background both of the rule of law challenges in Kosovo (section 2) and of the involvement of the international community and EULEX (section 3). Next, it focuses on Council Joint Action 2008/124/CFSP of February 2008, which provided the legal basis for the EULEX mission, and gives an overview of its provisions with regard to the mandate, objectives and methodology (section 4).[4] The fifth section assesses the two EULEX components that were considered as the easiest parts of the mission (EULEX Police and EULEX Customs), followed in the sixth section by a more detailed evaluation of the most problematic part: EULEX Justice. The chapter provides more insight into the set-up of these three components of EULEX and illuminates the difficulties EULEX is facing.

Since, at the time of writing, the CSPD mission has only been fully operational for eight months, it is obvious that our analysis can only lead to tentative conclusions.[5] Drawing hard conclusions about the effectiveness of EULEX as such is not evident either, as it is only one (albeit important) element within the very comprehensive peacebuilding efforts of the EU and the international community at large. This CSDP operation is indeed linked to and embedded within a broader context of multi-Pillar (up to the entry into force of the Lisbon Treaty), multi-level and multi-location foreign policy towards Kosovo and towards the rule of law in this coun-

---

[4] Council of the EU, Council Joint Action 2008/124/CFSP of 4 February 2008 on the European Union Rule of Law Mission in Kosovo, EULEX KOSOVO, *OJ* 2004 L 42/92-98 of 16.2.2008, available at: <http://www.eulex-kosovo.eu/home/docs/JointActionEULEX_EN.pdf> (retrieved on 3.10.2009).

[5] For preliminary conclusions, see EULEX, *EULEX Programme Report* (July 2009), which includes the first EULEX evaluation of the performance of Kosovo's rule of law institutions and makes a number of key recommendations for the reform of Kosovo's judiciary, available at: <http://www.eulex-kosovo.eu/news/docs/programmereport/EULEX-PROGRAMME-REPORT-July-2009-new.pdf> (retrieved on 3.10.2009). See also Commission of the European Communities, *Kosovo under UNSCR 1244/99 2009 Progress Report*, Brussels, 14 October 2009, SEC(2009) 1340, available at: <http://ec.europa.eu/enlargement/pdf/key_documents/2009/ks_rapport_2009_en.pdf> (retrieved on 9.11.2009); Report of the Secretary-General and High Representative for the Common Foreign and Security Policy of the European Union to the Secretary-General of the United Nations on the activities of the European Union Rule of Law Mission in Kosovo, Annex I to the Report of the Secretary-General on the United Nations Interim Administration Mission in Kosovo to the UN Security Council of 10 June 2009 (S/2009/300).

try.[6] This means, firstly, that also the European Commission (and its Liaison Office in Kosovo) plays a major role in Kosovo, particularly as it can rely on a high budget and a wide array of instruments – including in support of strengthening the rule of law sector.[7] Secondly, it means that the EU is only one actor in developing rule of law policies towards Kosovo, in addition to the bilateral initiatives of various of its Member States, other major actors such as the US, other international organisations (e.g., the Organisation for Security and Cooperation in Europe, the World Bank and UNDP) and a wide range of NGOs and consultancies.[8] This chapter though mainly focuses on the EULEX mission as such and not on the interaction and coordination between these actors.

## 2. Setting the stage: The UN's peacebuilding efforts in a post-conflict society

In the winter of 1998-1999, years of ethnic conflict culminated in the violent Kosovo war. While the roots of the conflict went back deep into the twentieth century, it was under the regime of the Serb president Slobodan Milošević in the 1990s that the situation escalated. From 1989 onwards, the Serb authorities conducted a policy of severe de-Albanisation of Kosovo's public life, leading to a situation where government institutions, such as the judiciary and the police force, were dominated by ethnic Serbs. This situation led to resistance from Kosovo Albanians, who installed a parallel informal system and were increasingly longing for independence of the province. In 1998-1999, a part of the resistance movement turned violent, with the Kosovo Liberation Army (KLA) becoming more and more active and gaining popularity among ethnic Albanians. Kosovo increasingly became the scene of a violent ethnic conflict between the majority Albanian population and the Serb security forces. In 1999, after a decade of neglect of the Kosovo situation, the escalation of the Serb oppression and violence against the Albanian Kosovars eventually attracted the international community's attention, with NATO bombardments between March and June 1999 eventually bringing the conflict to an end. The final balance of the conflict was 800,000 internally displaced people and refugees, a death toll of 12,000 and thousands of people reported missing.[9] The end of the war was the start of a

[6] Keukeleire and MacNaughtan, *supra* n. 3, at 28-33.

[7] For a critical analysis of the EU's policy towards Kosovo in general, see S. Keukeleire, A. Kolaja and A. Collaku, 'The European Union's Policy on Kosovo', in P. Koutrakos, ed., *European Foreign Policy: Legal and Political Perspectives* (Cheltenham, Edward Elgar Publishers, forthcoming 2010). For a short overview of the various EC measures in support of the rule of law, see *Overview of the EC Assistance in the Rule of Law Sector in Kosovo*, available at: <http://www.delprn.ec.europa.eu/repository/docs/060809EU%20assistance%20in%20the%20Judiciary%2027%2007%202009%20ENG.doc> (retrieved on 20.10.2009).

[8] See the overview of other international organisations involved in Kosovo, available at: <http://www.ks-gov.net/portal/eng.htm and http://www.delprn.ec.europa.eu/?cid=2,145>.

[9] For a historical overview of the conflict, see N. Malcolm, *Kosovo: A Short History* (New York, New York University Press 1998); T. Judah, *Kosovo. War and Revenge* (New Haven, Yale University

UN-led effort to fill the administrative vacuum that remained on the Kosovo territory. Based on UN Security Council Resolution 1244 (adopted on 10 June 1999) the UN set up its Interim Administration Mission in Kosovo (UNMIK). The UN civilian administration was structured into four Pillars: Pillar I was responsible for refugee return and later also for the judiciary and police; Pillar II for civilian administration; Pillar III for democratisation and institution building (led by the Organisation for Security and Cooperation in Europe); and Pillar IV for economic reconstruction and development (led by the EU).[10]

When UNMIK came in, it found a society torn apart by ethnic conflict, facing huge problems of institution building. The dismantlement of the Serb-dominated government institutions, in combination with the shortage of well-trained and experienced Albanians who could work within government institutions or the judiciary had created a situation in which an entirely new governance and rule of law system had to be created. Additionally, there was a serious risk of a new ethnic bias, this time directed against the formerly dominant Serb minorities in Kosovo. Ten years later, the balance of the international UN presence is mixed. It achieved some results in reconstructing some of the country's infrastructure and economy and in maintaining relative stability throughout the territory. It failed, however, in building a functioning rule of law system.[11] The weakness of the territory's rule of law institutions had made Kosovo an attractive arena for corruption, organised crime and illegal trafficking. Core conditions for the establishment of the rule of law, such as full respect for human rights and unity and independence of the judiciary, were problematic. While international diplomacy failed to reach agreement on a final settlement of the status question of the former province (independence or self-governance within Serbia), the Kosovo Albanian population became increasingly dissatisfied with the functioning of the international presence and the unclear legal status of its 'country'. Riots in March 2004 against both the Kosovar Serbs and the international community illustrated the fragility of the 'stability' as well as the growing frustration among the population.[12]

It was in the context of growing pressure to unilaterally declare independence that UN Special Envoy Martti Ahtisaari – the former Finnish President who had

---

Press 2000); J. Mertus, *Kosovo. How Myths and Truths Started a War* (Berkeley, University of California Press 1999). See also various articles in the Special Issue on Kosovo, 85 *International Relations* (2009) 447-606.

[10] United Nations Resolution 1244 (1999) adopted by the Security Council at its 4011th meeting on 10 June 1999, S/RES/1244 (1999). For an overview of UNMIK, see B. Reka, *UNMIK As International Governance in Post-War Kosovo: NATO's Intervention, UN Administration and Kosovar Aspirations* (Pristina, Logosa 2003).

[11] See, e.g., D. Decker, 'Enforcing Human Rights: The Role of the UN Civilian Police in Kosovo', 13 *International Peacekeeping* (2006) 504. D. Marshall and S. Inglis, 'The Disempowerment of Human Rights-Based Justice in the United Nations Mission in Kosovo', 16 *Harvard Human Rights Journal* (2003) 95-146.

[12] I. King and W. Mason, *Peace at Any Price. How the World Failed Kosovo* (London, Hurst & Co 2006). See also the Special Issue 'Intervention and Statebuilding Ten Years On', 3 *Journal of Intervention and Statebuilding* (2009) 135-275.

been appointed by the UN Secretary-General to lead the Kosovo status negotiations – presented his conclusions in a letter to the UN Security Council in March 2007. As the final negotiations over Kosovo's status did not lead to an agreement, he presented a 'recommendation' on Kosovo's status (indicating that this should be 'supervised independence') and a more technical Comprehensive Proposal for the Kosovo Status Settlement without direct reference to independence but providing the framework for a restructured international presence.[13] The idea was to have a renewed presence that would no longer be the supreme power in the territory (as UNMIK had been) but would supervise the implementation of the Ahtisaari proposal at the invitation of the Kosovo authorities themselves, thus placing more responsibility in the hands of the local authorities. The lead of this international presence would no longer be taken by the UN, but by the EU.[14]

The rationale behind the enhanced role for the EU lay in the idea that the EU had a significant comparative advantage on the Kosovo issue. As both the provisional Kosovo authorities and the Serb authorities have the ambition of becoming EU Member States, the prospect of EU membership and the related accession policies and instruments were perceived by the international community as important levers that would stimulate progress on the Kosovo issue. On the one hand, the EU's power of attraction was assumed to play a serious role in stimulating internal reforms and obedience on the part of the Kosovo authorities. On the other hand, it was also assumed that the prospect of possible accession would provide enough levers to ensure a pragmatic stance by the Serb government in cooperating with the EU and Kosovo authorities. The EU was thus seen as the best placed actor to have a direct impact on both sides. At the same time, the EU, on its side, was very willing to show its growing relevance on the peacebuilding scene in the Balkans by launching a large flagship CSDP mission in its own backyard, where it could fully exploit synergies with other policy instruments in an environment that is relatively stable when it comes to security issues.[15] As early as May 2006 it had a preparatory CSDP

---

[13] United Nations Security Council, Letter dated 26 March 2007 from the Secretary-General addressed to the President of the UN Security Council (S/2007/168, 26 March 2007), available at: <http://www.unosek.org/docref/report-english.pdf> (accessed on 8.11.2009); United Nations Security Council, Letter dated 26 March 2007 from the Secretary-General addressed to the President of the UN Security Council. Addendum, Comprehensive Proposal for Kosovo's Status Settlement (S/2007/168/ Add.1, 26 March 2007), available at: <http://www.unosek.org/docref/Comprehensive_proposal-english.pdf> (accessed on 8.11.2009).

[14] For an overview of the international involvement in the conflict and the negotiations on the final status of Kosovo, see M. Weller, *Contested Statehood. Kosovo's Struggle for Independence* (Oxford, Oxford University Press 2009): M. Weller, *Negotiating the Final Status of Kosovo*, Chaillot Paper No. 114 (Institute for Security Studies of the European Union, December 2008).

[15] International Crisis Group, *Breaking the Kosovo Stalemate: Europe's Responsibility*, Europe Report No. 185 (21 August 2007); A. Shepherd, 'A Milestone in the History of the EU: Kosovo and the EU's International Role', 85 *International Affairs* (2009) 513-530. On the EU's role in stabilising the Balkans in general, see S. Blockmans, 'EU Conflict Prevention in the Western Balkans', in V. Kronenberger and J. Wouters, eds., *The European Union and Conflict Prevention. Policy and Legal Aspects* (The Hague, T.M.C. Asser Press 2004) 293-321; S. Blockmans, *Tough Love: The European Union's Relations with the Western Balkans* (The Hague, T.M.C. Asser Press 2007); M. Emerson and E. Gross, eds., *Evaluating the EU's Crisis Missions in the Balkans* (Brussels, CEPS 2007).

mission on the ground, the EU Planning Team (EUPT),[16] which had to prepare the rule of law mission and make sure that the EU was ready for what in fact was 'uncharted territory' for the EU.[17]

## 3. The bumpy road from UN(MIK) to EU(LEX)

The Ahtisaari proposal provided relatively clear lines along which the enhanced EU engagement would take place in practice. The main international presence in Kosovo would be an internationally appointed International Civilian Representative, who would be double-hatted as EU Special Representative (ICR/EUSR). His task would be to oversee the implementation of the Ahtisaari plan (retaining some executive powers) and to give political guidance to a CSDP rule of law mission that would take over UNMIK responsibilities in the field of police, justice and customs. The CSDP mission would have a mentoring and advisory role which would be different from the UNMIK approach. EULEX would not be an interim administration but rather a 'supporting' mission, leaving room for local ownership so that local capacity could develop for taking up responsibility in managing the new political entity.

However, the Ahtisaari proposal never received approval from the UN Security Council, due mainly to Russian resistance. As a consequence, Resolution 1244, which provided for the interim administration by UNMIK, remained in place. At this point, several EU Member States also became reluctant to continue on the Ahtisaari path. This became overtly clear from the diverging reactions of EU Member States when Kosovo's Provisional Institutions of Self-Government (PISG), which had been installed since 2001, unilaterally (but in close consultation with major international actors such as the EU and particularly the US) declared Kosovo's independence on 17 February 2008. Although earlier that month, on 4 February 2008, the Council had managed to adopt a Joint Action on the deployment of the EULEX mission and on the appointment of an EU Special Representative,[18] no common position could be reached on the issue of independence. While most Member States did recognise Kosovo as an independent state, Spain, Greece, Romania, Slovakia and Cyprus were very clear in their non-recognition, which contributed to the problematic start of the mission.

As a result of the remaining cleavage within both the international community and the EU, the smooth handover, after a transitional period of 120 days, of UNMIK responsibilities to the local institutions, ICR/EUSR and EULEX, as foreseen in the

---

[16] Council Joint Action 2006/304/CFSP of 10 April 2006 on the establishment of an EU Planning Team (EUPT Kosovo) regarding a possible EU crisis management operation in the field of rule of law and possible other areas in Kosovo

[17] E. Pond, 'The EU's Test in Kosovo', 31 *The Washington Quarterly* (2008) 98.

[18] Council Joint Action 2008/123/CFSP of 4 February 2008 appointing a European Union Special Representative in Kosovo, *OJ* 2008 L 42/88-91 of 16.2.2008, available at: <http://eur-lex.europa.eu/LexUriServ/LexUriServ.do?uri=OJ:L:2008:042:0088:0091:EN:PDF> (accessed on 3.10.2009).

Ahtisaari proposal, could not take place. Instead, what was left on the ground were an increasingly unpopular UNMIK, Serb minorities refusing to cooperate with the Kosovar authorities, a Kosovar government aiming to implement the Ahtisaari proposal, an ICR/EUSR that faced difficulties in coming to terms with its own double-hatted role in a context of internal divisions within the EU, and a preparatory EULEX presence that still did not know what its actual mandate would entail as regards its own legal basis and the status question.

UN Secretary-General Ban Ki-Moon (UNSG) got involved himself in order to break the deadlock by presenting a six-point plan to the UNSC in a letter on 12 June 2008.[19] The plan gave the UNSG Special Representative in Kosovo (SRSG), Lamberto Zannier, a mandate to negotiate temporary agreements for Kosovo Serb majority areas in six fields: police, courts, customs, transportation and infrastructure, boundaries and cultural heritage. On 26 November 2008, the Security Council approved this proposal which provided for the deployment of a status-neutral EULEX under a continued 'UN umbrella', with Resolution 1244 staying in force.[20] It was eventually the Ban plan that paved the way for EULEX's deployment, but at the same time it had a direct and severe impact on EULEX's mandate: UNMIK would stay in Kosovo and remain the official counterpart for the Serbs. This had mainly repercussions for Kosovo's Serb-dominated north, where UNMIK would continue to play a leading role, thus increasing the risk of a *de facto* division of the Kosovo territory.

After nearly a year of discussion, EULEX Kosovo could finally deploy on 9 December 2008, with full operational capability only being reached on 6 April 2009 – nearly three years after the EU had sent its preparatory EU Planning Team. By this time, the failure of the EU to adopt a common approach towards the independence of Kosovo had severely undermined its credibility at the international diplomatic level, had hampered the potential lever it had in dealing with the Serb authorities, and the situation on the ground had become even more problematic. In the course of 2008, Serb resilience had further undermined the already fragile rule of law institutions: hundreds of Serb police officers withdrew from the Kosovo Police Service (KPS), the parallel administrative structures were strengthened and in May 2008 Serbia organised local elections in Kosovo. In the north, the situation was becoming even more lawless, as UNMIK was taking up less responsibility and EULEX was not willing to deploy unless it could do this throughout the whole territory at once. Meanwhile, part of the Kosovo Albanian population was seriously questioning the legitimacy and added value of any international presence, be it UNMIK or EULEX. Public confidence in the mission was at a very low point of some 13% in May 2008, but increased to 39% in June 2009, two months after EULEX had become fully operational.[21]

---

[19] Report of the Secretary-General on the United Nations Interim Administration Mission in Kosovo, 12 June 2008 (S/2008/354).

[20] Statement by the President of the UN Security Council on Security Council Resolutions 1160 (1998), 1199 (1998), 1203 (1999) and 1244 (1999), 26 November 2008 (S/PRST/2008/44).

[21] UNDP Kosovo, *Fast Facts – Early Warning Report No. 26*, November 2009, at 1, available at: <http://www.ks.undp.org/repository/docs/Fast_Facts_26_English.pdf>.

The delay in the deployment of EULEX Kosovo was also the result of the particular challenges related to the deployment of a civilian crisis management operation – challenges that became particularly obvious in a mission of the magnitude and complexity of EULEX Kosovo. First, although Ministers of Foreign Affairs can adopt political decisions on civilian crisis management in the Council of Ministers of the EU, they are dependent on others to fulfil their commitments and get these missions implemented in the field, which implies that Ministers of Foreign Affairs and diplomats partially lost control over the operation. And as the EU institutions do not have policemen or judges of their own to send abroad, civilian crisis management requires the involvement of a wide array of services within the Member States and other participating countries. In addition to the Ministries of Foreign Affairs and of Defence, Ministries of the Interior, of Justice, of Finance and of Budget have to be involved – each with their own bureaucracy, procedures and cultures – in order to second the required number of qualified police officers, judges, prosecutors, customs specialists, financial experts and other civilian specialists to Kosovo. Second, establishing and deploying civilian capabilities cannot be treated in the same way as deploying military personnel. The preparation of the EULEX Kosovo mission pointed to major difficulties in extracting a large number of civilian experts from their domestic duties. Whereas participation in foreign missions is part of the normal duties of soldiers, extracting judges or policemen from domestic duties and asking them to leave at short notice is much more complex and expensive. National ministries also proved rather reluctant to contribute with personnel and other resources to the civilian crisis management mission, particularly where these were in relatively short supply at national level and when no clear financial compensation was foreseen at European or national level.[22]

## 4. Council Joint Action 2008/124/CFSP: Mandate, tasks and organisation of EULEX Kosovo

Council Joint Action 2008/124/CFSP of 4 February 2008 on the European Union Rule of Law Mission in Kosovo provides the legal basis of the EULEX mission.[23] Article 2 of the Joint Action outlines the Mission Statement of this CSDP operation and summarises both the objectives and the methodology to be used. Its first paragraph states that

> 'EULEX KOSOVO shall assist the Kosovo institutions, judicial authorities and law enforcement agencies in their progress towards sustainability and accountability and in

[22] Keukeleire and MacNaughtan, *supra* n. 3, at 184-185.

[23] *OJ* 2008 L 42/92-98 of 16.2.2008; Council Joint Action 2009/445/CFSP of 9 June 2009 amending Joint Action 2008/124/CFSP on the European Union Rule of Law Mission in Kosovo, EULEX KOSOVO, *OJ* 2009 L 148/33 of 11.6.2009, available at: <http://www.eulex-kosovo.eu/home/docs/LexUriServ-EULEX-EN.pdf> (retrieved on 3.10.2009). This second Joint Action prolongs the EULEX Kosovo mission by another year (until 14 June 2010) and increases the EULEX budget for its second year (€265,000,000 instead of €205,000,000 for its first year).

> further developing and strengthening an independent multi-ethnic justice system and multi-ethnic police and customs service, ensuring that these institutions are free from political interference and adhering to internationally recognised standards and European best practices.'

The key concepts in this mission statement – sustainability, accountability, multi-ethnicity, freedom from political interference, internationally recognised standards and European best practices – point to the EU's major ambitions. They also show the daunting challenges which the EULEX mission faces, as the lack of accountability, the lack of multi-ethnicity and the presence of political interference have been characterising the Kosovo context for decades. Paradoxically, also the remedy proposed in the Joint Action – adhering to internationally recognised standards and European best practices – is, in practice, causing many troubles to the Kosovars and is sometimes even becoming part of the problem. It has indeed become clear that there is no international consensus whatsoever on what the best standards and practices are. Kosovar politicians and civil servants were confronted with international actors (the US, UN, EU and individual EU Member States) competing with each other in promoting and imposing their own interpretation of best international standards or European best practices – often leading to a cacophony of advice to be borne by the Kosovar counterparts.

The second paragraph of the Mission Statement clarifies the methodology to be followed in the EULEX mission: 'EULEX KOSOVO, in full cooperation with the European Commission Assistance Programmes, shall fulfil its mandate through monitoring, mentoring and advising, while retaining certain executive responsibilities.' It already indicates that the EU's 'assistance' to the Kosovo institutions, judicial authorities and law enforcement agencies can take various forms, including methods that imply a more active and even intrusive role of the EU: it includes not only 'advising', but also 'mentoring', 'monitoring' and even assuming 'executive responsibilities'. The EULEX Programme Strategy gives more information on the nature of these various methods.[24] Whereas 'advising' refers to the provision of expert information and professional counselling to the Kosovo authorities, 'mentoring' indicates that the EU's role is more far-reaching than just giving advice: the EULEX staff actively assist the Kosovo staff in the development of new skills and knowledge by coaching or showing how a task can be carried out, convey their own experience and skills and encourage the Kosovo staff to take action and discuss the consequences of decisions and actions. 'Monitoring' means that the EULEX staff observe and assess how the Kosovo rule of law institutions and staff are performing in relation to the aims of the EULEX mission, which is done through a comprehensive system of measuring performance. Or in less diplomatic terms: EULEX also has the task to control the Kosovo institutions and to evaluate the progress they make. Finally, the mandate indicates that EULEX itself can retain certain 'executive responsibilities', which means that the formal responsibility with

[24] EULEX Programme Strategy, available at: <http://www.eulex-kosovo.eu/strategy/EULEX%20Programmatic%20Approach.pdf>, at 3.

regard to certain issues can remain or be placed in the hands of the EU, which thus, in these cases, partially or in full, substitutes for Kosovo actors.

Article 3 of the Joint Action enumerates the nine tasks of the EULEX mission, thereby further spelling out and reflecting the objectives mentioned in the previous Article. Three of these nine tasks refer to the possibility of EULEX retaining executive responsibilities. EULEX Kosovo shall

> 'ensure the maintenance and promotion of the rule of law, public order and security including, as necessary, in consultation with the relevant international civilian authorities in Kosovo, *through reversing or annulling operational decisions taken by the competent Kosovo authorities*';
>
> 'ensure that cases of war crimes, terrorism, organised crime, corruption, inter-ethnic crimes, financial/economic crimes and other serious crimes are properly investigated, prosecuted, adjudicated and enforced, according to the applicable law, *including, where appropriate, by international investigators, prosecutors and judges jointly with Kosovo investigators, prosecutors and judges or independently* (...)';

and

> '*assume other responsibilities, independently or in support of the competent Kosovo authorities*, to ensure the maintenance and promotion of the rule of law, public order and security, in consultation with the relevant Council agencies.'[25]

As these provisions are quite far-reaching, it is clear that the usual qualification of EULEX Kosovo as an MMA mission (monitoring, mentoring and advising mission) is rather misleading. Qualifying EULEX as an EMMA mission (executing, monitoring, mentoring and advising mission) would indeed be more correct – though also less diplomatic and less politically correct. This possibility of retaining executive responsibilities also somewhat contradicts the principle of 'local ownership' which is strongly emphasised as the key concept on the EULEX website and in EU documents and as the major difference with the 'UNMIK approach', where the internationals were often seen as 'substituting for, rather than bolstering, domestic capacity.'[26] By cooperating with Kosovo counterparts and putting responsibility into their hands (or as the EULEX website puts it: 'the Kosovo authorities are in the driver's seat'[27]), EULEX is supposed to contribute to local capacity building – although it is clear that the EU does not yet consider the local capacities as sufficiently developed to take full responsibility for all tasks.

Articles 6 to 13 of the Joint Action spell out the command and organisational structure of EULEX Kosovo. The Director of the Civilian Planning and Conduct Capability (CPCC), which is part of the Council structures in Brussels, is the Civil-

---

[25] Emphases added.

[26] T. Perriello and M. Wierda, *Lessons from the Deployment of International Judges and Prosecutors in Kosovo*, Prosecution Case Studies Series (International Center for Transitional Justice, March 2006).

[27] See: <http://www.eulex-kosovo.org>.

ian Operation Commander of EULEX Kosovo. He exercises command and control of the mission at the strategic level under the political control and strategic direction of the EU's Political and Security Committee (which consists of Ambassadors from all EU Member States) and under the overall authority of the Secretary General/High Representative for CFSP. He also issues instructions at strategic level to the Head of Mission in Pristina, who bears responsibility and exercises command and control of the EULEX mission in Kosovo itself. Following a Political and Security Committee Decision of February 2008, the French General Yves de Kermabon was appointed Head of Mission of EULEX.[28] Besides its main headquarters in Pristina (and a Brussels support element), EULEX can rely on regional and local offices across Kosovo. In functional terms, the mission is divided into three components: a police component, a justice component and a customs component. In each component, where appropriate, EULEX staff (police officers, judges, prosecutors and customs specialists) are co-located with their Kosovo counterparts in the relevant institutions (such as the Kosovo Police Service, Kosovo ministries, the Kosovo judiciary and the Kosovo Customs Service).

The next two sections of this chapter deal in more detail with the organisation, challenges, first results and remaining obstacles of these three components. These sections also provide insight into the way the objectives of EULEX Kosovo have been translated into more operational goals through the so-called 'Programmatic Approach'. In view of the magnitude of the operation (with 1,900 international and 1,100 local staff), the complexity of this civilian crisis management operation – including staff members with tasks as diverse as patrolling the streets, mentoring policy advisors within a ministry, and being a panel member in cases before the Supreme Court – and the need to reach results in the field, a well-functioning internal management was seen as indispensable, which resulted in the 'EULEX Programme Strategy'.[29] As explained in this Strategy, the aims and strategic objectives of EULEX have been translated into a number of specific activities for the EULEX staff of each rule of law component. For each monitoring activity, quantitative and/or qualitative performance measures were designed to guide EULEX monitors in their assessments, which subsequently have to be reported in a structured way to the EULEX Programme Office in Pristina. This programmatic approach has to allow the mission to adapt or reorient its activities, in accordance with the progress achieved and the barriers revealed by this system.[30] The approach has been presented as a major innovation since it is intended to allow the EU to first draw an elaborate picture of the actual situation, to give clear direction to the mission's priorities, to measure progress and to develop an institutional memory which is generally lacking in international peacebuilding missions.

---

[28] Political and Security Committee Decision EULEX/1/2008 of 7 February 2008 concerning the appointment of the Head of Mission of the European Union Rule of Law Mission in Kosovo, EULEX KOSOVO (2008/125/CFSP), *OJ* 2008 L 42/99 of 16.2.2008.

[29] EULEX Programme Strategy, *supra* n. 24.

[30] Ibid., at 4-5.

Whether this approach will indeed increase the effectiveness of the EU's crisis management operations or – as some EULEX staff have argued – mainly results in bureaucratising what essentially is a foreign policy activity, can only be judged after some time.[31] Nevertheless, a well-organised approach is quite necessary in view of the large number of staff, the staff turnover as well as the different national backgrounds (different administrative, legal and police cultures and legal frameworks). In late 2009, EULEX consisted of a total of approximately 2,600 staff, including 1,015 local and 1,585 international staff (with final staff targets being 3,000, including 1,100 locals and 1,900 internationals). The international staff are provided by all EU Member States (except Cyprus) and 6 non-EU countries: Canada, Norway, Switzerland, Croatia and particularly Turkey (61 staff) and the US (80 staff) – reflecting what a EULEX official called 'ESDP+'.[32] In late 2009, the five countries seconding most staff were Romania (191), Italy (190), France (184), Poland (132) and Germany (88). Moreover, with 523 staff, the Central and Eastern European countries together provide nearly one third of the total number of international staff, which points to the major contribution that the newest Member States make to the EU's civilian crisis management operations. Equally interesting: except for Cyprus, the four other countries that have not recognised Kosovo's independence nevertheless participate in EULEX Kosovo, with Romania even being the main contributing country in what is considered as a 'neutral' ESDP mission.[33]

## 5. Police and customs: The easy job?

Of the three EULEX components, the police component is clearly the largest, with an envisaged strength of approximately 1,400 international police officers. EULEX Police personnel are co-located with their Kosovar counterparts and are supposed to play an MMA role. In the first phase of the mission, this mainly consisted of drawing up a map of current performance and local capabilities of the Kosovo institutions. As such, EULEX has people working as officers in the field, but also within the Kosovo police headquarters and regional headquarters, counter-terrorism units, forensic services, the Ministry of the Interior, etc. Under its executive mandate, EULEX Police also has a right to intervene in cases deemed to be necessary, e.g., violence against minorities or political interference in the work of the Kosovo Police Service. To this end, a three-stage cascade of responsibilities has been created. Following the principle of local ownership, the Kosovo Police Service is always the first responder in case of security incidents. In these instances, EULEX's role is limited to MMA activities. As the second responder, EULEX can take up executive responsibilities in cases deemed necessary (due to the reasons

31 Interview with Mr Zuccarini (Chief of the Programme Office, 9 April 2009) and with several civilian specialists involved in the EULEX mission (Pristina, April 2009).

32 Interview (Pristina, April 2009).

33 EULEX Staff Info, available at: <http://www.eulex-kosovo.eu/?id=36&m=2> (accessed on 20.10. 2009).

mentioned above or to capacity problems of the Kosovo Police Service). The third responder is NATO's Kosovo Force (KFOR), in cases where security incidents are so grave that also EULEX would fall short in maintaining peace and order.

From the start, the police component has been seen as the easiest part of the job, as the overall performance of the Kosovo Police Service is relatively good. This, in turn, has been the result of the long-standing and quite successful involvement of the Organisation for Security and Cooperation in Europe (OSCE) in capacity building in the field of policing. Having trained over 8,000 policemen and women and having coached police officers all over the region, the OSCE, in general, has produced a sense within the Kosovo Police Service that the first task of a policeman is to act as a protector of the community rather than as an enforcer of a powerful ruler or a collector of bribes, as has been the case in the past.[34] This major capacity-building success was also reflected in opinion polls. In early 2009, the Kosovo Police Service ranked first among Kosovo's main institutions, with a satisfaction level of around 80%. Moreover, considering that less than 20% of the population feels that there is large-scale corruption within the Kosovo Police Service, the police score well on the corruption issue.[35]

However, two major obstacles remain for EULEX Police and its counterparts in the Kosovo Police Service. The first relates to the cooperation with the Serb minorities, particularly in the northern area around Mitrovica. Serb police officers throughout Kosovo refused to show up at work after the unilateral declaration of independence, thus undermining the idea of a multi-ethnic Kosovo Police Service. The attempts of EULEX to get these Serb police officers back to work initially had limited success, with only a small minority returning to work. Moreover, the fact that these police officers were receiving double wages (both from the Kosovo authorities, which continued payments so as to avoid a definite secession of Serb police officers, and from the Serb authorities, which supported the police officers in their action) was not encouraging for those police officers (Serb and Albanian) willing to return to service. However, in the course of 2009, EULEX Police managed to gradually upgrade its activities in the north, including steps to improve the integration and cooperation of the Kosovo Serb police in the north – which were lacking because of the growing problems of the Serb government in Belgrado in paying Serb policemen in Kosovo.[36]

The second fundamental problem is related to organised crime, particular when criminal networks can be closely linked to some of the main political leaders. Within the context of ownership, EULEX Police has set itself the goal of involving Kosovar

[34] See also E. Pond, 'Policing Kosovo: The Challenges Awaiting EULEX', *Europe's World*, Summer 2008.

[35] UNDP Kosovo, *Fast Facts – Early Warning Report*, No. 24, April 2009, available at: <http://www.ks.undp.org/ews>.

[36] Interviews (Pristina, April and August 2009). See also Commission of the European Communities, *Kosovo under UNSCR 1244/99 2009 Progress Report*, *supra* n. 5; Report of the Secretary-General and High Representative for the Common Foreign and Security Policy of the European Union to the Secretary-General of the United Nations, 10 June 2009, *supra* n. 5; International Crisis Group, *Serb Integration in Kosovo: Taking the Plunge*, Europe Report No. 200 (12 May 2009).

counterparts as much as possible when dealing with the most important cases of organised crime. It is however mainly in these instances of major organised crime that the Kosovo Police Service's performance is weakest. Dependency networks within Kosovar society make it particularly difficult for local police to tackle this sort of crime, which is further complicated by important linkages between a part of the Kosovar political and economic elite and organised crime networks. This makes it likely that addressing organised crime will require international involvement for many years to come. However, it remains to be seen how well EULEX can hold its ground when confronted with cases involving members of the Kosovar elite. Doubts are indeed raised as to whether EULEX (and the EU in general) is strong enough to use its executive powers in order to tackle the most serious criminal networks and whether it is willing to risk a possible destabilisation of the country by putting pressure on part of the political elites when they are related to these networks.[37] Seen from this angle, it becomes clear that the police component in general can perhaps be seen as the easiest job of the EULEX mission, but that this is not at all true when it comes to dealing with organised crime, the dimension that will be the most important in determining the internal legitimacy and credibility of EULEX.

EULEX Customs forms the second component of the mission. It is the smallest within EULEX, comprising less than 30 international officers, supported by around 20 local staff. The overall goal concerning customs is to further professionalise the existing customs service in line with international standards and European best practices. Also in the field of customs, EULEX officers mainly operate with an MMA mandate. When deemed necessary, the customs component aims to only take up executive responsibilities in mixed teams of international and Kosovar customs services personnel. The main goals here involve improvements of the legal framework, management and avoidance of political interference in appointments, promotion, and operational issues. Deployment of EULEX Customs was pretty straightforward in most of Kosovo, with EULEX Customs mobile teams and monitoring units becoming operational in November 2008. Moreover, in general, the tasks of EULEX Customs were considered not that problematic as the customs services had overall been performing rather well over the last couple of years (contributing, in 2007, over 70% to the income of Kosovo's total consolidated budget).[38] Nevertheless, whereas financially they performed quite well, they were much less effective in countering smuggling and various kinds of illegal trafficking. Millions in revenue were and are lost at the border crossing between Serbia and Kosovo's northern Serb-majority area – which again points to the underlying fundamental problem of the EU's involvement in Kosovo.

The big challenge is to be found at two border crossings (Gates 1 and 31) in the north that were destroyed in the aftermath of the declaration of independence. Subsequently, UNMIK withdrew from the Gates, leaving behind a customs black hole, with no international force being prepared to risk bloodshed over Kosovo's cus-

---

[37] Interviews (Pristina, April 2009).

[38] EULEX Programme Strategy, *supra* n. 24.

toms area. However, EULEX's deployment, also at these two Gates, has been crucial in preventing a practical secession of the north at the start of the mission. Currently, these Gates are the only border crossings where EULEX Customs is actually taking up executive responsibility, with EULEX data collection activities gradually becoming more and more comprehensive.[39] The way forward had been to convince Serbia that re-establishment of customs control would also be beneficial for them, as this customs black hole was equally costly to the Serb state. However, this approach was undermined by the fact that some political leaders in both Serbia and Kosovo itself might gain from maintaining this rule of law black hole between both countries. The discussions over customs control between Serbia and Kosovo, in any case, have remained a sensitive political topic, not making EULEX's 'technical' customs work any easier.[40]

## 6. EULEX JUSTICE – OR WHAT IT ALL COMES DOWN TO IN THE END

The hardest task for EULEX can be found in the justice system. In this area, multiple problems intersect, making it the most difficult field to succeed in. It is the justice component that will eventually determine the success of EULEX in the long term, particularly since the achievements in the EULEX police and customs components can, in the long run, only last if EULEX Justice succeeds too. The most difficult challenge in tackling crime and building the rule of law in Kosovo is indeed the follow-up in Kosovo's courts. A fundamental change in the judicial system is also urgent in view of its extremely negative image among the population, with opinion polls indicating that the satisfaction of the population in Kosovo with the courts is and remains very low, i.e., 25%, which is much lower than the score of most of the other institutions in Kosovo.[41]

In mid-2009, the justice component consisted of some 330 staff, including around 130 locals and 200 internationals (in the future, this number is supposed to grow to 470 people when EULEX is fully staffed).[42] EULEX legal experts are deployed within the Ministry of Justice, within the Kosovo Judicial Council and within other agencies, such as the Kosovo Property Agency. Forensic experts are working within the Office of Missing Persons and Forensic Medicine, which has to deal with 1,900 cases of missing persons and 400 remains still to be identified. 70 EULEX experts

---

[39] See Report of the Secretary-General and High Representative for the Common Foreign and Security Policy of the European Union to the Secretary-General of the United Nations, 10 June 2009, *supra* n. 5.

[40] Interviews (Pristina, April 2009).

[41] UNDP Kosovo, *Fast Facts – Early Warning Report No. 26*, November 2009, available at: <http://www.ks.undp.org/repository/docs/Fast_Facts_26_English.pdf>, at 1-2.

[42] EULEX Programme Strategy, *supra* n. 24, at 20-30; 'Alberto Perduca: "To Heal the Wounds of the Past" ', *EULEX News Archive*, 3 June 2009, available at: <http://www.eulex-kosovo.eu/?id=8&n=105> (retrieved on 20/10/2009); 'EULEX Justice Component – "A Successful Beginning",' *EULEX News Archive*, 6 September 2009, available at: <http://www.eulex-kosovo.eu/?id=8&n=136> (retrieved on 20.10.2009).

have been deployed to Kosovo's penitentiary administration and the various 'correctional service' units (prisons) in Kosovo. The groups of EULEX specialists are all involved in the MMA functions of EULEX.

The situation is different for the approximately 40 EULEX judges in the criminal and civilian field and the 20 EULEX prosecutors (all from EU countries) who are part of the EULEX staff and have been deployed to the various District Courts and District Prosecutors Offices throughout Kosovo and in Pristina at the Supreme Court and the Office of the Special Prosecutor. EULEX judges and prosecutors not only monitor, mentor and advise their local counterparts in all areas related to the rule of law.[43] As stated in Art. 3, Joint Action on EULEX Kosovo, they also retain certain executive responsibilities in order to

> 'ensure that cases of war crimes, terrorism, organised crime, corruption, inter-ethnic crimes, financial/economic crimes and other serious crimes are properly investigated, prosecuted, adjudicated and enforced, according to the applicable law, including, where appropriate, by international investigators, prosecutors and judges jointly with Kosovo investigators, prosecutors and judges or independently (…).'

Three major challenges arise from this description of responsibilities: the nature of the crimes, the relationship between EULEX staff and their Kosovar counterparts, and the problem of applicable law. These are three problems that, at least in the short run, cannot be resolved properly and almost unavoidably lead to disappointment among part of public opinion in Kosovo.

The first major problem is related to both the high number and the nature of crimes that have to be tackled. One of the inheritances of the UNMIK period is the substantial backlog in cases (with often unclear case files) that were handed over from UNMIK and that have increased steadily since 2001. By the end of 2008, the backlog in the Kosovo judiciary amounted to more than 260,000 cases, which was an increase of more than 10% in comparison to 2007.[44] Although the backlog issue can be seen as mainly a workload problem, it is also strongly related to the problems of capacity building, which are analysed below and are more structural in nature. Although quite diverse in nature, the various kinds of crimes are to a major extent interconnected, and therefore tackling them is a sensitive matter. War crimes and inter-ethnic crimes (during and after the war) were often committed by individuals or groups that fought for the liberation of Kosovo. They were often also involved in illegal trafficking, organised crime and financial/economic crimes – in a first stage to finance the anti-Serb struggle, and later because it was considered a lucrative business. The fact that the current political and economic power and leadership structures and elites have largely emerged from this previous liberation movement complicates EULEX's task. Moreover, these crime cases have to be tackled in

[43] Assembly of EULEX Judges, *Guidelines on Monitoring, Mentoring and Advising (MMA) of EULEX Judges – Final Document*, approved on 23 October 2008 in Prizren, Kosovo, available at: <http://www.eulex-kosovo.eu/justice/docs/MA-guidelines-for-EULEX-Judges%20_2_.pdf>.

[44] EULEX, *EULEX Programme Report* (July 2009), *supra* n. 5, at 100-101.

a context where EULEX can obviously only prosecute people in Kosovo itself (and not those who committed or still commit crimes in Serbia) and has no full control of the northern part of Kosovo yet.

Within this context, it is not surprising that some of the first people sentenced for war crimes were Albanian Kosovars, including former members of the Kosovo Liberation Army (KLA), who were found guilty of violence against Serb Kosovars or other Albanian Kosovars.[45] Nor is it surprising that EULEX's commitment to investigate and prosecute war crimes regardless of the ethnicity of those involved in them – in other words, including Kosovo Albanians – resulted in resentment among part of the population, who, as a matter of principle, consider Serbs as offenders and Kosovo Albanians only as victims. This became particularly clear in cases where Serb defendants were acquitted of all charges and released for lack of evidence.[46]

Whereas the above-mentioned resentment flows to a large extent from the unavoidable adaptation pains related to the introduction of a neutral rule of law system, another criticism may be more fundamental. The legitimacy of the EULEX judgments indeed threatens to be further undermined as EULEX is perceived as mainly focusing on the 'small fish' (the less important criminals) and on old war crimes and inter-ethnic crimes, to the detriment of cases involving the 'big fish' (including current political and economic leaders) and those related to current organised crime, financial/economic crime and corruption which presently undermine both the faith of people in the rule of law and their ability to, for instance, start a new business in a safe and pressure-free context. However, depending on the source, this approach can be interpreted as a sign of weakness of EULEX, as an indication that it considers the 'stability paradigm' as more important than the 'rule of law paradigm' (see below), or as a conscious strategy to gradually build up the gravity of its cases (in parallel to the gradual build-up of its capabilities, experience and case law).[47]

A second set of structural problems concerns the relationship between the EULEX staff and their Kosovar counterparts, which, in turn, is related to the problematic human resources situation in the field of justice and the resulting lack of public trust in the local judiciary.[48] First, the exclusion of Kosovo Albanians from public office has led to a real lack of well-trained and experienced Albanians capable of taking serious responsibility in building a new justice system from scratch. Moreover, this is not going to change any time soon in view of, for instance, the limited number of young Kosovars studying law at the University of Pristina. Second, the trauma of

---

[45] See various press releases of the EU, *News Archives*, on the EULEX website (i.e., press releases of 4/3/2009, 29/4/2009 and 13/3/2009), available at: <http://www.eulex-kosovo.eu/?id=8&n=12220> (accessed on 20.10.2009).

[46] Such as in the Nis Express case, see EULEX press release, 'A Decision on the "Nis Express" case', Pristina, 13 March 2009, available at: <http://www.eulex-kosovo.eu/news/docs/pressReleases/EULEX-Press-Release-Nis-Express-case-Eng.pdf> (accessed on 20.10.2009).

[47] Interviews (Pristina, April 2009).

[48] Interviews (Pristina, April 2008 and April 2009).

the war and particularly the inter-ethnic violence of 1999 have made it virtually impossible for judges to pronounce ethnically unbiased judgments in cases of war crimes. Third, as indicated before, the situation in Kosovo is characterised by an important grey zone between war crimes, criminal networks, illegal trafficking and current political and economic leadership, making it very difficult for local judges and prosecutors to objectively uphold the rule of law without taking personal risks. Moreover, some of the local judges or prosecutors have been appointed to these functions precisely because they had close links with or were part of the dominant political, economic and/or criminal networks. From 2000 onwards, this combination of low local capacity and the risk of ethnically biased or politically inspired judgments has led to the gradual deployment of international judges and prosecutors, leading to a parallel judicial system of cases judged by mixed local-international panels.

The need to use international judges and prosecutors is also recognised in the set-up of the EULEX Justice component through the executive tasks given to EULEX and in particular through the use of mixed panels or teams and the possibility for EULEX judges to act on their own. The system of mixed panels implies that court panels (of three or five judges) include both local and EULEX judges. If necessary, a panel can also solely include EU judges. This reflects the provision in the Joint Action on EULEX Kosovo that cases have to be tackled 'where appropriate, by international investigators, prosecutors and judges *jointly with Kosovo investigators, prosecutors and judges* or *independently*' (Art. 3) [emphasis added]. However, it is obvious that particularly this system contradicts the principles of 'local ownership', 'mutual trust' and 'professional respect' so strongly emphasised in the formal documents and on the website of EULEX. These are indeed difficult to reconcile with the reality on the ground where local capacity may be such that actual local ownership would be rather counterproductive to the effort of building the rule of law. From the start of the mission, many EULEX staff have had the feeling that actually implementing the local ownership principle might be one of the hardest tasks the mission is facing. Already after the first months of operation, the perception prevails that the mission has had to take up more executive responsibilities than actually intended, with EULEX judges also being perceived as international watchdogs rather than as equal partners.[49] Both the EULEX Programme Report of July 2009 and the Commission's 2009 Progress Report on Kosovo confirmed that progress in the area of justice was very slow and on some points non-existent and that, overall, the justice system remained 'weak, vulnerable to political interference and inefficient.'[50]

Deploying internationals into the legal system has engendered some new problems as well. A first problem concerns the appointment of judges to specific cases. EULEX judges have been mainly designated to chair in sensitive cases of war crimes,

---

[49] Interviews (Pristina, April 2009).

[50] Commission of the European Communities, *Kosovo under UNSCR 1244/99 2009 Progress Report*, *supra* n. 5 at 11. See also EULEX, *EULEX Programme Report*, *supra* n. 5, at 14-16, 83-119.

organised crime, drug trafficking or corruption: cases that local judges are often reluctant or refusing to try themselves and, in cases of war crimes, where local judges could be susceptible to ethnic bias or external pressure. Problems have indeed arisen with local judges refusing to be appointed to a certain case or proving very willing to pass responsibility on to the internationals, as their low wages do not outweigh the risks, in terms of personal safety, involved in convicting members of powerful criminal networks. In these cases, panels consisted of two EULEX judges and one local judge (or three EULEX judges without a local judge), with the prosecutor also being EULEX.[51] While this system of appointment makes sense in terms of personal safety for local judges and the holding of unbiased trials, it creates at the same time a sort of dual justice system, with some cases being dealt with by predominantly Kosovo judges and others by mainly international judges. Besides the fact that the somewhat *ad hoc* way of assigning cases is questionable in terms of equal conditions of trial, this situation also further undermines the build-up of the necessary confidence in Kosovo's own local judges. By taking responsibility away from local judges in sensitive cases, an implicit sign is given that the local system is not capable of dealing with them in a fair and unbiased way.[52] This also explains why in the course of 2009 the Assembly of the EULEX judges gradually refined and formalised the case selection system and the judicial system in general so as to counter allegations of *ad hockery* and partiality.[53]

Moreover, EULEX itself does not really structurally tackle the problems related to the safety risks, the poor working conditions and particularly the very low salaries – structural problems which make the profession of judge or prosecutor rather unattractive and lead to a large turnover of judicial personnel (in many cases working as an independent lawyer is more profitable). It is in this context that the vetting process of judges and prosecutors in Kosovo, managed by the European Commission Liaison Office since mid-2009, may be at least as important for structurally strengthening and transforming the judicial system as the EULEX mission. Financed through the European Commission's Instrument for Stability (and co-financed by the US Office), this vetting process screens, evaluates and selects candidates for (re-)appointment as judges and prosecutors on the basis of merit in terms of professional qualifications and experience as well as professional and personal integrity. The process will be accompanied by an increase in salaries of judges. It is this combination of a thorough vetting process, an increase in salaries, training in various projects (supported by the Commission and the OSCE), and a systematic monitoring, mentoring and advising process through EULEX that can contribute to the development of an independent and professional judiciary and prosecution service as a prerequisite for building public confidence and trust in the rule of law.[54]

---

[51] Interview (Pristina, April 2009). See also press releases regarding EULEX trials, *EULEX News Archive*, available at: <http://www.eulex-kosovo.eu/?id=8&n=12220>.

[52] Interviews (Pristina, April 2009).

[53] See rules, advice and guidelines adopted by the Assembly of the EULEX Judges, available at: <http://www.eulex-kosovo.eu/?id=10&j=51>.

[54] Interview (Pristina, August 2009); *Overview of the EC Assistance in the Rule of Law Sector in Kosovo*, *supra* n. 7.

However, building public confidence and trust in an independent judiciary will depend not only on the Kosovar judges, but also on EULEX itself. One, if not the main question surrounding EULEX at the moment is what will happen when the first cases involving top elite figures will have to be dealt with – and whether they will be dealt with in the first place. If necessary, will EULEX be prepared to arrest and condemn figures having top positions in or close links with the Kosovo government? If so, this might risk destabilising the still fragile Kosovar society, possibly endangering the work of the international community in the region. While EULEX officially advocates the primacy of the rule of law, thus not letting other interests interfere with the work of the judiciary, it is doubted whether EULEX itself will manage to put this into practice.[55] In other words, mirroring the challenge of the Kosovar judicial system, EULEX too may have problems upholding the rule of law in an unbiased and politically neutral way, unaffected by other considerations and outside pressures.

A third major structural problem is related to the 'applicable law' (mentioned in Article 3 of the Joint Action) and is linked to the wider problem of various parallel and competing judicial systems. This problem not only concerns the unresolved Kosovo status issue, which indeed contains the risk of a parallel Serb justice system as ethnic Serb judges and prosecutors refuse to cooperate within Kosovo's judicial system and Serb-dominated areas and enclaves do not recognise the judicial system operated by the central Kosovar authorities and EULEX. The problem also – and even more importantly – follows from the sequencing of different governing regimes, each announcing its own pieces of legislation. In July 1999, UNMIK Regulation 1999/1 provided that the law applicable in Kosovo would be the law in force prior to the NATO intervention earlier that year. The Kosovo Albanians, however, considered it an offence to reinstate the laws of the Milošević regime, and many judges refused to apply them. In December, UNMIK repealed Regulation 1999/1, reinstating the laws applicable in 1989, before the Milošević regime had revoked Kosovo's autonomous status. However, they could only be applied as far as they were compatible with international human rights standards and if no new UNMIK Regulation on the issue were promulgated. With Kosovo's unilateral independence in February 2008 and the entry into force of its Constitution on 15 June of the same year, the situation has become even more complex – particularly as the new state did not immediately have a fully fledged legal system, which implies that there is often no other choice but to refer to previous legal rules. Possibilities of applicable law now vary between pre-1989 laws, pre-1999 laws, UNMIK regulations and the new Kosovo laws. No clear distinction and criteria exist on what law is applicable in what case. This is clearly not merely a technical legal discussion: in the eyes of many involved, opting for one specific law is essentially a political choice. Choosing to apply Kosovo laws inherently means recognising Kosovo's independence; letting UNMIK regulations overrule Kosovo laws means a continued respect of Resolution 1244 and a denial of Kosovo's new constitutional order; applying Serb

[55] Interview (Pristina, April 2009 and July 2009).

law means recognition of the Serb rights regarding Kosovo. As noted by a senior EULEX official, in the Kosovo context 'everything technical becomes political', thus complicating the role of the mission as it is supposed to act under a mere technical, status-neutral mandate.[56] EULEX's way of dealing with the problem of applicable law has thus far been a pragmatic one. Without making a decision on the overall applicable law, EULEX is now working on a pragmatic, case-by-case basis, trying to determine the law applicable at the place and time an alleged crime was committed.[57] However, also this probably unavoidable (in the current situation) pragmatic approach raises questions concerning legal certainty and therefore not necessarily strengthens people's belief in the rule of law, since it confirms that various rules of law can exist.

## 7. Conclusions

This chapter focused on the EU's largest and most ambitious civilian crisis management operation conducted in the framework of CSDP: the EULEX Kosovo mission, which has as its central aim to assist and support the Kosovo authorities in the rule of law area – specifically in the police, justice and customs areas – by monitoring, mentoring and advising these authorities whilst retaining a number of executive powers for itself. It described a specific case of CSDP's current involvement in peacebuilding, which, however, has to be situated within the broader context of a multi-level and multi-location foreign policy towards Kosovo.

This case study brings to the fore some remarkable paradoxes and dilemmas which characterise the EU's involvement in peacebuilding. A first paradox is that the EU and all its Member States were clearly willing to conduct this 'technical' rule of law mission as part of a UN-inspired roadmap for Kosovo, but were unable to agree on the overarching legal issue: the status of Kosovo – which has clearly undermined the effectiveness of its peacebuilding efforts. This reflects the view of the EU being a foreign policy actor which can contribute to the execution or funding of peacebuilding initiatives if these are devised by other international actors, but which has trouble finding consensus on politically sensitive matters. On the other hand, the Kosovo case can also be seen as a testimony to CSDP's own strength and dynamics: the lack of political consensus on the independence of Kosovo did not lead to a deadlock. It resulted in delays and complications but did not block the launch and implementation of the EU's largest civilian crisis management operation.

Secondly, focusing on the specific context in which the EULEX mission takes place has allowed us to shed light on some dilemmas which the EU and the international community in general are facing in peacebuilding operations – dilemmas that arise not only in Kosovo but also in other countries and regions where the EU is

56 Interview (Pristina, April 2009).
57 Interviews (April 2009).

active. For instance, the EU wants to promote ownership, which is indeed essential to achieving sustainable results, but retains some executive functions in view of the specific post-conflict situation in Kosovo, which, in turn, undermines the principles of ownership as well as the idea of an independent judicial system. Or rather: the rule of law is the overarching paradigm that the EU wants to transplant to the Kosovar judicial system, but its own actions ultimately seem to be inspired in the first place by the stability paradigm – the predominant goal of maintaining stability and peace in Kosovo –, which undermines a straightforward implementation of the rule of law (for instance, the investigation of actions of current political leaders).

Only 8 months after EULEX's full deployment it is far too early to assess whether the EU's approach will indeed prove successful. However, it is clear that the various dilemmas and structural problems analysed in this chapter cannot be easily overcome, which also indicates that success can only be achieved in the long term. The success of the EULEX mission will also depend on the successful realisation of numerous other, interrelated initiatives taken by both the Kosovar authorities and other European and international actors. Most importantly, the question is whether EULEX Kosovo and other international rule of law initiatives will not only be able to establish the institutional and legal frameworks required to uphold the rule of law, but also be successful in changing the mindset of the people concerned. The results of the EULEX Kosovo mission will indeed only be sustainable if the basic principles that are at the basis of the rule of law are internalised by both the elites and the population of Kosovo.

# Chapter 16
# THE ACEH MONITORING MISSION: SECURING PEACE AND DEMOCRACY

**Justin Davies***

## 1. Introduction

Four years after the Memorandum of Understanding (MoU) was signed in Helsinki on 15 August 2005 between the Government of Indonesia (GoI) and the separatist Free Aceh Movement (GAM), peace still reigns in the Indonesian province of Aceh. The signing of the MoU and the events that followed on the ground in Aceh immediately thereafter brought to an end one of the world's longest-running armed conflicts, which had lasted nearly thirty years, claimed over 15,000 lives and displaced tens of thousands more. The ending of the conflict has heralded an unprecedented era of peace in which the rule of law, human rights and democracy can flourish – a far cry from the days when Aceh was in the throes of a separatist war and under martial law.

The Aceh Monitoring Mission (AMM) played an important role in ensuring that the agreement reached in Helsinki was implemented in Aceh and, through proactive monitoring and facilitation, that peace could take hold in a province that had suffered from the trauma of war and large swathes of which had been devastated in the tsunami of 26 December 2004. AMM itself was a unique international endeavour, being the first, and to date only, partnership between the EU and contributing countries from the Association of South East Asian Nations (ASEAN). As a mission, it had a wide-ranging mandate, from the decommissioning and destruction of GAM weapons to monitoring the re-location of non-organic Indonesian police and military forces[1] and the reintegration of active GAM members into society, through to investigating and ruling on complaints and alleged violations of the MoU and establishing and maintaining liaison and good cooperation between the parties. As

* Justin Davies is currently the EU Coordinator/Political Advisor to the European Union Special Representative in Kosovo. He was the Chief of Staff of the Aceh Monitoring Mission, having been the Head of the Technical Assessment Mission that established AMM and the Chief of Staff of its Initial Monitoring Presence. The views expressed in the chapter are his own and do not represent the official position of any organisation or institution.

[1] Non-organic forces were those that did not originate in Aceh but had been drafted into the province to counter the separatist insurgency.

*S. Blockmans, J. Wouters & T. Ruys, eds., The European Union and Peacebuilding*

well as decommissioning, two further elements of its mandate marked a new departure for ESDP missions: monitoring the human rights situation and ruling on disputed amnesty cases. This latter task was the first executive task given to an ESDP mission.

The implementation of the peace process would have broken down at an early stage if AMM had not been successful in achieving its mandate right from the start. In Aceh and indeed wider, the deployment of AMM was met with some scepticism as previous attempts at peace in Aceh had failed, most recently with the collapse of the Cessation of Hostilities Agreement (CoHA) in 2003. AMM operated in a fragile environment and the mission itself was a complex structure, incorporating both civilian and military personnel and a wide variety of experts in areas ranging from explosive ordnance disposal to human rights and reintegration. The fact that the peace process still holds is the ultimate marker that AMM was a success. Many of the important elements that contributed to this success are discussed below and should form a basis for further peace implementation missions of this kind. Some of the weaknesses associated with AMM, such as the lack of readily available logistics for EU rapid deployment, are currently being addressed by the EU, but it is important that they are also noted. It is also useful to consider the benefits and limitations of including a human rights mandate in a mission of this type. In crisis management and peace implementation there is no 'one size fits all', and any further EU missions in this field will need to adapt to their local circumstances accordingly. However, in the wider context of rule of law, democracy and human rights it is correct to state that unless AMM had played its pivotal role in achieving physical peace on the ground, it would not have been possible for others to progress in addressing these areas that are so important for a sustainable peace process.

## 2. AMM in the context of the Memorandum of Understanding

The 2004 tsunami gave fresh impetus to the newly elected government in Jakarta's push for peace in Aceh, and GAM's decision to give up its long-standing demand for the province's independence meant that conditions were ripe for a possible agreement to end, once and for all, the armed conflict that had begun in 1976. It was a vicious conflict and Aceh was closed to the world for much of it. Over 15,000 people were killed, tens of thousands more were displaced and human rights abuses were rampant. For part of the conflict, Aceh was under martial law. Under the auspices of former Finnish President Martti Ahtisaari and his NGO Crisis Management Initiative (CMI), secret negotiations were held between the parties in Helsinki and were partly funded by European Commission instruments.[2] The negotiations progressed fast and well in the early months of 2005 and concluded with the sign-

[2] The costs of the mission were financed from the EU budget (EUR 9.3 million) and by contributions from EU Member States and participating countries (EUR 6 million). See the Council Secretariat's Factsheet on AMM, ACEH/07, 15 December 2006.

ing of the MoU on 15 August 2005 in which 'The Government of Indonesia (GoI) and the Free Aceh Movement (GAM) confirm their commitment to a peaceful, comprehensive and sustainable solution to the conflict in Aceh with dignity for all.'[3] Under the MoU, GAM agreed to end its armed struggle and hand over its weapons in exchange for broad autonomy, including the right to form local political parties, and local control over a portion of the revenues from natural resources in the oil and gas-rich province.

As the negotiations appeared to be leading to a tangible agreement, the parties and President Ahtisaari sought to identify a suitable monitoring body for the eventual agreement. After the experience of East Timor, the GoI did not want the United Nations to oversee the implementation of the peace process and GAM was uncomfortable with a purely ASEAN mission, which, it was felt, would be partial towards the Indonesian authorities. President Ahtisaari suggested that the European Union could play a role. Their discussions resulted in the proposal for an Aceh Monitoring Mission (AMM) to be established by the European Union and ASEAN contributing countries with the mandate to monitor the implementation of the commitments made by the parties in the MoU. This unusual coalition of EU and ASEAN countries was an untried and untested formation in international peacekeeping. In the MoU, both GAM and the GoI agreed to give all their support to the carrying out of the mandate of AMM, committed themselves to providing AMM with secure, safe and stable working conditions and pledged their full cooperation with the mission.[4]

From the side of the European Union, views were mixed amongst the Member States in the Political and Security Committee (PSC) as to the merits of undertaking such a complex mission under ESDP, at such a distance and in such a potentially dangerous environment at such short notice.[5] First intimations of a possible EU engagement emerged in June 2005, while the negotiations were still secret, and on 18 July the General Affairs and External Relations Council (GAERC) took note of an EU assessment mission that had taken place at the end of June. Whilst welcoming the successful conclusions of the last phase of the Helsinki negotiations that had ended on 17 July, the GAERC 'agreed that the EU was prepared, in principle, to provide observers to monitor implementation of the MoU.'[6] The opportunity for peace could not be missed. Contacts between the Government of Indonesia and ASEAN countries resulted in Brunei, Malaysia, the Philippines, Singapore and Thailand being invited to participate in an AMM alongside the EU, which received a similar invitation. At subsequent meetings between the EU Technical Assessment Mission that was despatched towards the end of July 2005 and representatives of

---

[3] Memorandum of Understanding between the Government of the Republic of Indonesia and the Free Aceh Movement, signed in Helsinki, 15 August 2005, available at: <http://www.consilium.europa.eu/uedocs/cmsUpload/MoU_Aceh.pdf> and at <http://www.cmi.fi>.

[4] Ibid., Chapter 5.

[5] For a detailed examination of the establishment of AMM, see P.-A. Brand and G. Grevi, *The EU Mission in Aceh: Implementing Peace*, Occasional Paper No. 61 (Paris, Institute of Security Studies 2005).

[6] Council of the EU, Press Release 10813/05 (Presse 177), 18 July 2005, at 3.

the five ASEAN contributing countries in Jakarta at the beginning of August, it was agreed that the EU would provide the framework and the lead in AMM. However, the planning was a joint endeavour and, to that end, six ASEAN planners joined the Technical Assessment Mission when it flew to Aceh on 2 August 2005.

## 3. Mandate of AMM and immediate challenges

The MoU listed the tasks of AMM as to:

a) monitor the demobilisation of GAM and decommissioning of its armaments;
b) monitor the relocation of non-organic military forces and non-organic police troops;
c) monitor the reintegration of active GAM members;
d) monitor the human rights situation and provide assistance in this field;
e) monitor the process of legislation change;
f) rule on disputed amnesty cases;
g) investigate and rule on complaints and alleged violations of the MoU;
h) establish and maintain liaison and good cooperation with the parties.

This mandate was reflected *verbatim* in the EU Council Joint Action that established the European Union Monitoring Mission in Aceh and provided the framework for AMM, with the exception of the human rights part, which was amended to read 'monitor the human rights situation and provide assistance in this field in the context of the tasks set out in points (a), (b) and (c) above.'[7] There was considerable discussion within the EU bodies as to how exactly to define the human rights monitoring part of the mandate. No previous ESDP mission had featured a human rights role in its mandate and there were no set EU doctrines or procedures for this. Considerable progress has since been made by the EU in mainstreaming human rights, including gender issues,[8] in ESDP, but in mid-2005, there were no guidelines for a mission's planning staff to follow. There was some concern that the human rights mandate as outlined in the MoU might be interpreted so as to include monitoring the *sharia* laws active in Aceh, which was never the intention of the parties to the negotiations. There was also concern that an unlimited human rights mandate might well result in the mission being swamped with hundreds of human rights cases unrelated to the conflict or historical cases related to the conflict that it did not have the capacity to deal with. If this had happened, it would have been detrimental to AMM achieving its main, but unstated, goal, which was to ensure that a peace signed in Helsinki became reality on the ground in Aceh. Given these considerations, human rights monitoring and providing assistance in that field was linked to the first three elements of the mandate – namely, GAM's demobilisation

---

[7] Council Joint Action 2005/643/CFSP of 9 September 2005 on the European Union Monitoring Mission in Aceh (Indonesia) (Aceh Monitoring Mission – AMM), *OJ* 2005 L 234/13.

[8] See the contribution by Hazelzet to this volume.

and reintegration and the withdrawal of non-organic forces. In effect, though, AMM's human rights monitoring went further than the narrow confines listed in the mandate provided for in the Council Joint Action. Important human rights provisions in the MoU were also monitored through the monitoring of the process of legislation change, such as Indonesia's ratification of the United Nations International Covenants on Civil and Political Rights and on Economic, Social and Cultural Rights.

The most immediate operational challenges faced by AMM were due to the cumbersome EU procedures for establishing an ESDP mission. The GAERC of 18 July 2005 asked 'the competent bodies to continue planning for a possible monitoring mission at the request of the parties',[9] but with the parties declaring that the MoU would be signed on 15 August, it became rapidly apparent that it would not be possible to launch an ESDP mission through its legal stages before mid-September at the earliest. In the event, the Technical Assessment Mission that was despatched to Indonesia on 30 July became the set-up vehicle for the Initial Monitoring Presence (IMP) of the Aceh Mission as well as for the planning and writing of the Operations Plan for the mission itself. The concept behind the IMP was that an international presence was needed to fill any possible vacuum between the signing of the MoU and the start of AMM. After 29 years of armed conflict, the first four weeks after the declaration of peace could have proved particularly susceptible to challenges to the process. Therefore, willing EU Member States and the five ASEAN contributing countries provided and funded 80 monitors who would fill the gap, under the leadership-designate of AMM, and provide the core of the subsequent mission. It was a wise and timely decision, at the request of the GoI and GAM. Whilst the peace process did not come under sustained challenge in the early days, the IMP investigated and ruled on two early shooting incidents, resulting in casualties, that might have contributed to derailing the process if they had not been dealt with effectively by the Head of Mission of AMM-designate after thorough investigation.

Establishing the IMP was an idea lifted from the international community's engagement in Kosovo in 1998-9 where Kosovo Diplomatic Observer Missions (KDOMs) had been deployed from embassies in Belgrade prior to the establishment of the OSCE Kosovo Verification Mission (KVM). As with the KDOM deployment in Kosovo, the IMP monitors were temporarily accredited to the embassies of their respective countries with the agreement of the GoI. Another idea lifted from previous Balkans experience was to establish a Commission of Security Arrangements (COSA) that would bring the parties together on a weekly basis in a forum chaired by the Head of Mission of AMM to define the progress of the implementation of the MoU, plan its next stages and address transparently any contentious issues, complaints or violations of the MoU. The COSA comprised the Head of Mission of AMM, his Deputies and senior staff; the representatives of the Government of Indonesia responsible for the peace process; the representatives of GAM; the Governor of Aceh; and the Chief of the Indonesian Army (TNI) in Aceh. Impor-

[9] Council of the EU, Press Release 10813/05, *supra* n. 6, at 3.

tantly, every COSA meeting was followed by a joint press statement by those present, which was disseminated widely across Aceh and Indonesia. The COSA, which was not foreseen in the MoU, became a central facet in the MoU's implementation and was a defining structure for demonstrating the even-handedness of AMM and ensuring its credibility in the eyes of the signatory parties and the public.

## 4. Organisational elements

At its peak, AMM comprised 240 internationals drawn from the Member States of the European Union, the five ASEAN contributing countries, Norway and Switzerland. For its initial phase, it was organised into a Headquarters in Banda Aceh, 11 geographically distributed District Offices (DOs) across Aceh and four Mobile Decommissioning Teams (MDTs). As various phases were completed and implementation accomplished, the mission downsized as it prepared to withdraw and allow local ownership to take effect. AMM finally disbanded on 15 December 2006 after one year and three months in the field.

Two important decisions were taken in the planning phase that contributed to AMM's operational success as a mission. The first was that the HQ, DOs and MDTs would be mixed in terms of nationality, expertise and leadership. Unlike United Nations peacekeeping operations, where each country tends to have responsibility for a particular sector or district, each AMM District Office of 12 monitors contained one from each ASEAN contributing country and the remaining seven from an EU Member State but never two of the same nationality. Each DO contained a mix of expertise in terms of civilian and military monitors and no ranks were used. Six of the DOs were headed by ASEAN monitors with EU deputies and vice versa for the remaining five. At the HQ, there was the same civilian-military mix, with the EU assuming the leading positions with ASEAN deputies. The Head of Mission (Pieter Feith) was a senior diplomat seconded from the EU Council Secretariat, with an ASEAN 3-star General (Nipat Thonglek) as his Principal Deputy who was replaced on rotation by a Malaysian 2-star General (Rosi Baharom).

Groundbreaking as it was, the partnership between the EU and ASEAN was mutually beneficial. ASEAN participation gave regional legitimacy to the mission and the ASEAN monitors had a better understanding of the local culture and customs than the European monitors. A majority of the ASEAN monitors were military personnel, could speak the local language and many were Muslims. The European monitors were mainly civilians with a wider range of expertise and tended to have greater peacekeeping experience. The administration and finance of the mission was almost exclusively provided by the European Union. As with the legislative procedure for establishing AMM, it was not possible to procure equipment for the mission under the then current European Commission rules for procurement in time for a start date of 15 September 2005. This was not only the start date of AMM but also the day on which GAM started the decommissioning of its weapons through public destruction by the AMM MDTs. In the event, Sweden very generously offered to provide the entire logistics set-up through the good services of the Swedish Rescue Services Agency (SRSA) which delivered personnel and equipment. The importance of this cannot be overestimated for without Sweden's timely offer, AMM, and certainly the IMP, would have failed to deploy in time to meet the demands on the ground for an international presence.

## 5. Proactive monitoring – rule of law, human rights and democracy

Thanks to the work of the IMP, AMM was able to hit the ground running on 15 September 2005 when the first batch of GAM weapons was publicly destroyed in the centre of Banda Aceh. At the same time as this most visible of signals that peace might be truly on the way, the GoI began the repatriation process for its non-organic forces. It was the AMM MDTs that travelled across Aceh and destroyed the GAM weapons in public ceremonies in four phases. AMM monitored each withdrawal of non-organic military forces and police troops. Both processes ran smoothly, although there was a slight hiatus between phases three and four when GAM temporarily declared that it had no more weapons to decommission, without having reached the number of 840 stated in the MoU. The decommissioning and withdrawal phases lasted until 31 December 2005 and, combined with a visible outreach campaign by AMM across Aceh, they inspired confidence in the peace process across the population.

AMM took the lead in ensuring the implementation of the MoU and took on an active facilitation rather than a mere monitoring role. As Pieter Feith, the AMM Head of Mission, wrote:

> 'A monitoring mission can sit back and wait for something to happen, or it can lead and try to influence the tempo of the implementation, set priorities, and suggest the agenda to the parties. The AMM opted for a proactive approach that helped move the process forward quickly. This was appreciated by the parties, as they felt included in the process. The mission members were constantly in contact with the parties and civil society representatives, proposing new ideas and running a substantial public information campaign. (...) The public also needed to feel that it had a role in the process and its concerns were taken into account. Thus, the weapons taken from the rebel movement were cut and publicly destroyed for all to see, giving a strong signal that everybody's security was enhanced. Confidence and trust building are probably the most important ingredients in a post-conflict environment for furthering the reconciliation process. By conducting proactive monitoring, a mission can also provide the best possible conditions for the self-sufficiency of the peace process, ensuring that its achievements will not collapse when the mission concludes its work.'[10]

---

[10] P. Feith, *The Aceh Peace Process: Nothing Less Than Success*, United States Institute for Peace Special Report 184 (March 2007).

It is only the creation of such conditions that can allow the thorough development of democracy and widespread promotion of human rights and ensure the rule of law in a peaceful society. In terms of democracy, the MoU contained provisions for a new Law on the Governing of Aceh (LOGA) and for 'political participation'.[11] Under the latter, the GoI agreed to and facilitated the establishment of Aceh-based political parties and gave the people of Aceh the right to nominate candidates for the positions of all elected officials in the Aceh local elections. These elections took place in December 2006, just before the end of AMM's mandate, to which the GoI invited a European Union Elections Observation Mission, led by the European Parliament and funded by the European Commission. After an election campaign that was relatively incident-free and short on violence, a former GAM rebel, Irwandi Yusuf, was elected as the Governor of Aceh. These were the first direct and democratic elections to be held in Aceh. It marked an important turning point in the history of Aceh and a defining moment in the peace process. The conditions for peace had taken hold to such an extent that they enabled an enormous turn-out of electors and that vibrant election campaigns could take place without fear of violence or widespread intimidation. These conditions remain today.

As far as human rights monitoring was concerned, it has been noted in the introduction that there were no EU precedents or procedures to fall back on. At the pre-mission training held in Medan and in directions given to the HQ and DOs, it was made clear to every AMM monitor that human rights monitoring was a core component of the mandate and that every monitor should consider themselves a human rights monitor. Additionally, each DO contained at least one monitor with a specific human rights background. Therefore, human rights monitoring ran through the body of the mission. AMM was able to connect with civil society and the population by socialising the MoU across Aceh, organising meetings, events and concerts whilst providing continuous availability through the DOs for public complaints and concerns. Civil society had been excluded from the negotiations in Helsinki and there was a strong feeling, especially amongst women's groups, that the provisions of the MoU unfairly excluded them. Whereas financial provision was provided for the 3,000 GAM fighters that were reintegrated, no such provision was granted to the thousands of GAM supporters who had provided logistic support and intelligence. By establishing civil society forums and reaching out to those who wished to raise their human rights as an issue, AMM was in a position to action their concerns and monitor steps taken by the GoI to address them. AMM did not act alone in reaching out to civil society. In a show of transparency and faith in the peace process, socialisation events were attended by the police, military and GAM as well as GoI local officials. Others in the international community, such as the World Bank, IOM and UNDP, also provided much valued assistance and resources.

With the conditions for peace being increasingly met, the attitudes of police and military within Aceh changed perceptibly. As they no longer had to fight a counter-insurgency campaign, an atmosphere was created where the rule of law, and human

---

[11] MoU, *supra* n. 3.

rights as a consequence, could begin to flourish in a more benign and normal environment. As Aceh moved from a war to a peace footing, AMM was a reassuring factor for the civil population, the former GAM rebels and, indeed, the military and police themselves as they adapted to the new circumstances. The success of the HQ-level COSA was replicated across the DOs with the establishment of District level COSAs (DiCOSAs) which brought together GAM, police, military and elected civil officials on a local and regular basis.

As far as the rule of law, human rights and democracy are concerned, AMM was an initial facilitator and, as stated, made an invaluable short-term contribution in creating the space for them to develop. Longer-term programmes addressing these areas had already been established by the European Commission, other international partners and contributing Member States by the time AMM left Aceh.[12] After nearly 30 years of armed conflict, full normalisation and development of these areas will take time, as will the reintegration of all citizens affected by the conflict. This includes training for the police in community policing and human rights, assistance to civil society groups in improving their effectiveness and contribution to Aceh's growing democracy as well as capacity building for Aceh's new governor and civil administration.

As noted elsewhere in this book, one of the European Union's great strengths is its ability to deploy multiple tools to support crisis management, conflict resolution and peacebuilding.[13] AMM, therefore, was only one facet in a broader EU engagement in response to the tsunami disaster and the signing of the Memorandum of Understanding. It was the European Commission, for example, which provided the reintegration funding from the Stability Instrument for the GAM fighters through their implementing partner, IOM. The presence and activity of the Commission allowed AMM to leave Aceh when a great majority of the provisions in the MoU had been implemented and longer-term development and peace support programmes could take root. AMM was a peacekeeping operation and the deployment of foreign monitors or missions is always a sensitive issue for a host country. Most of all, a successful peace process needs to be owned by the parties and the population concerned, not by foreign bodies. This concept of local ownership is a guiding principle of ESDP and one of great importance to AMM.

A peace process can only succeed when it is locally owned and supported. Two elements were crucial for its success in Aceh: the political will of the GoI and GAM to see it succeed, whatever challenges to it occurred, and the overwhelming desire for peace that was exhibited by the public as the process continued. The peace process could easily have been derailed without the continual and central role of the President and Vice-President in Jakarta, who engaged comprehensively and continuously throughout the process. The MoU and the Aceh peace process were not universally accepted in Indonesia and certain elements feared that international

---

[12] For example, Denmark and Sweden have addressed police and human rights training, whilst the Commission has provided governance support.

[13] See the introduction by the editors to this volume.

involvement would lead to the independence of Aceh as had happened to East Timor. As it began to deploy in the summer of 2005, over 100 former TNI Generals and Admirals wrote an open letter in which they rejected AMM and the peace process. Eventually, AMM gained the confidence of the TNI by proving that it was a rigidly neutral and professional organisation. The early support of the President and Vice-President was key to winning this confidence. It was also helpful that in the Joint Action launching AMM the EU declared that it fully respected Indonesia's territorial integrity.

So, in the midst of this, AMM had to conduct itself in such a way that it would be a beneficial facilitator for the process and time its departure carefully so that it did not overstay its welcome and become a hindrance. By always promoting local ownership, AMM was effectively able to do itself out of a job – a rare position for a peace operation to find itself in. More often than not, lingering doubts or tensions amongst protagonists make it difficult for the independent peacekeepers, monitors or observers to extricate themselves and let the natural order of things run its course. It is self-evident that the rule of law, democracy and human rights are never going to flourish in normal circumstances whilst foreign bodies remain on the scene. Two excellent examples of local ownership in the implementation of the MoU are the COSAs/DiCOSAs and the way in which AMM handled the part of its mandate relating to the amnesty of jailed GAM fighters.

With regard to the COSAs/DiCOSAs, Pieter Feith explained their rationale:

> 'Throughout the mission, the AMM brought the parties together to discuss and resolve issues through regular meetings of the COSA. Consisting of representatives from both sides and chaired by AMM, COSA meetings were held at both provincial (senior representatives) and local (district) levels. Thus AMM steered and gauged progress on the various steps in the implementation of the agreement and facilitated resolution of any problems along the way. Holding meetings at district level helped disseminate the peace process, gave local leaders on both sides ownership and responsibility, and ensured that local problems were solved at local level rather than being allowed to escalate and grow out of proportion.'[14]

These channels of communication and the mutual responsibility for problem solving have remained open and effective since AMM's departure. It should be noted that the MoU contains a dispute resolution mechanism involving President Ahtisaari and the Head of Mission of AMM that can still be activated if needed. It never has been – a testament to how the continued progress in Aceh is now entirely locally owned, that is, between the Government of Indonesia, GAM and the wider Acehnese public. However, a close eye is kept on developments in Aceh, not least by the European Commission through its Europe House in Banda Aceh, as well as through visits to the province by President Ahtisaari and Pieter Feith.

If it had not been properly handled, the amnesty for former GAM fighters and supporters could possibly have become one of the most contentious issues of the process and, without doubt, one of its most emotive.

---

[14] Feith, *supra* n. 10 .

Enormous executive responsibility was given to the Head of Mission of AMM. The MoU stated that:

> 'GoI will, in accordance with constitutional procedures, grant amnesty to all persons who have participated in GAM activities as soon as possible and not later than within 15 days of the signature of this MoU. (...) Political prisoners and detainees held due to the conflict will be released unconditionally as soon as possible and not later than within 15 days of the signature of this MoU. (...) The Head of the Monitoring Mission will decide on disputed cases based on advice from the legal adviser of the Monitoring Mission.'[15]

Nearly 2,000 GAM fighters or supporters were in prison in August 2005 and the great majority of them were released by the end of the month. There was initial disagreement between the parties as to whether those remaining in jail were eligible for the amnesty or not. For example, it was disputed whether those that had bombed the Jakarta Stock Exchange, with consequent loss of life, could be considered as related to GAM's struggle in Aceh or whether they more correctly classified as terrorists. The Head of Mission encouraged the parties to seek agreement amongst themselves. Not only was local ownership infinitely preferable to judgment being made by outsiders, but there were few subjects more emotive than human freedom. The parties eventually narrowed the numbers of disputed amnesty cases down to double figures. At this stage, AMM sought and was provided with a senior international judge from an EU Member State who reviewed all the outstanding cases and discussed them in detail, but confidentially, with the parties. The result was that all amnesty cases were undisputed, mutually agreed and supported by the parties. It was a triumph for AMM's approach and left the parties in full ownership of the outcome.

## 6. Conclusion and the future

AMM encountered some classic EU mission problems in its set-up phases, notably cumbersome legislative procedures and lack of readily available logistics. Creative planning circumvented all of these and was supported by experienced staff who could rely on previous crisis management experience, notably in the Balkans. The EU will continue to hone its procedures so that CSDP can achieve the rapid deployment of missions, properly resourced and staffed. Whilst resources depend more on procedural than human elements, staff cannot be merely pulled from existing and unrelated jobs, and the EU must gather and grow a core of suitably operationally experienced crisis management personnel who can provide precisely the depth of experience that was so valuable to AMM. It is also to be regretted that little progress has been made in cementing EU-ASEAN crisis management/peacekeeping/con-

[15] MoU, *supra* n. 3, Chapter 3.1.

flict resolution experience and operability after the first and only joint endeavour, which was such an undeniable success.

AMM played a pivotal role in ensuring that a peace agreement signed in Helsinki became reality on the ground in Aceh over 10,000 km away. It set the pace and agenda for the implementation of the MoU and then allowed the parties and the public in Aceh to attain ownership of the peace process, withdrawing itself from the ground and allowing others to continue the process with longer-term initiatives to foster the peace. AMM's proactive monitoring led to local ownership and the appearance of conditions where democracy, the rule of law and human rights could thrive. These aspects of Aceh are naturally in their infancy in many regards and therefore require careful nurturing and sustained international support. Regarding human rights monitoring, it must be noted that the clearer the mandate of the mission, the better. Unless it is going to stay in a post-conflict area for an indefinite amount of time, a peacebuilding mission must have objectives that can be clearly benchmarked. This will facilitate a timely exit and allow local ownership to take hold. Above all, the overwhelming objective of a peace implementation mission must be to ensure that peace becomes as nearly as possible irreversible. This objective must be demonstrably and transparently achieved and communicated to all parties and the wider public in a way that will engender trust and confidence in the mission, the political will of the parties and, most of all, the sustainability of the peace process itself.

# Chapter 17
# THE EUROPEAN UNION AND TRANSITIONAL JUSTICE

**Thomas Unger***

## 1. Introduction

Over the last few years, transitional justice has emerged as a recognised field within the European Union after previously languishing in obscurity. Today, nearly everyone in the EU-related human rights and conflict resolution fields is familiar, at least to some extent, with transitional justice, and several important policies and statements have been issued at the EU level to promote transitional justice as a political as well as financial priority.

However, there remains a need to expand and deepen transitional justice as an EU priority. There is also a need to ensure that transitional justice is understood properly as an issue concerning both the Council and the European Commission, as opposed to a post-conflict issue important only to the Council, or a development-related issue important only to the Commission. The new Lisbon Treaty will assist in this endeavour, especially by creating the post of an 'EU foreign minister' bridging the institutional gap between the Commission and the Council especially in the areas relevant to transitional justice, such as the Common Security and Defence Policy (CSDP). The possible benefits for the EU, and for the transitional justice field, are immense. Indeed, the EU has the potential to become one of the leading transitional justice actors in the world. It is already, alongside the UN, one of the most important actors in the fields of human rights and conflict resolution. It has become the world's largest aid donor: together with its Member States, the EU provides over half of all Official Development Assistance (ODA).[1] In addition, the EU has already committed itself to the same core values which guide transitional

---

* Thomas Unger is currently working within the Human Rights Department of the Austrian Foreign Ministry and previously worked as a Senior Associate at the International Center for Transitional Justice. The author wishes to thank Mark Freeman for providing a first substantive outline for this article and for his great guidance and support in the course of the drafting process. He would also like to thank Alexandra Nerisanu for her outstanding research assistance. The views expressed in the working paper are those of the author and do not represent the official position of any organisation or institution.

[1] See the website of the Organisation for Economic Cooperation and Development: <http://www.oecd.org/>.

*S. Blockmans, J. Wouters & T. Ruys, eds., The European Union and Peacebuilding*

justice, and in practice, to an increased role in transitional contexts and peace-building.[2]

Against this background, this chapter will examine the opportunity for the EU to take its interest in and commitment to transitional justice to a new level by creating a framework document and a related set of operational strategies to add greater coherence and depth to its transitional justice engagements. The EU's current policy and practice in the areas of justice and the fight against impunity are scattered. A framework document, or set of institutional guidelines, will allow for more balanced policy-making across the system and an increase in the EU's impact on the ground.

The chapter is organised into five main sections. Section 2 will define transitional justice. The third section will explain the link between transitional justice and peacebuilding. The fourth section will examine why transitional justice is relevant to the EU, in general terms. Section 5 will describe current EU policy and practice in the area of transitional justice. Last but not least, possible future directions for EU policy and practice in the area of transitional justice will be examined in section 6.

## 2. Defining transitional justice

Transitional justice is a multidisciplinary and victim-centred field of theory and practice that is linked to the fight against impunity and to the broader domains of human rights and conflict resolution. Although its historical roots may be traced back to the end of the Second World War (Nuremberg) and earlier, the term 'transitional justice' did not enter the modern political lexicon until the early post-Cold War period.[3]

The emergence of the field of transitional justice reflects a sea change in the global approach to dealing with legacies of mass abuse. Whereas previously the dominant view was that societies emerging from periods of conflict or mass abuse had to choose between trials and amnesties, today there is recognition of the wide spectrum of tools and mechanisms that exist between those two extremes, as well as of their complementary nature.[4] Indeed, one could say that the international viewpoint today is not to ask *whether* to deal with the past, but rather to ask *how* to deal with it. Transitional justice is a field that purports to offer principled and pragmatic answers to that challenge.

---

[2] See European Council, *Report on the Implementation of the European Security Strategy – Providing Security in a Changing World* (December 2008), S4047/08, at 12.

[3] For a comprehensive overview and analysis of practice on transitional justice, see R. Teitel, *Transitional Justice* (Oxford, Oxford University Press 2000); N. Roht-Arriaza, *Transitional Justice in the Twenty-First Century* (Cambridge, Cambridge University Press 2006); see also the website of the International Center for Transitional Justice: <http://www.ictj.org>.

[4] See *Report of the UN Secretary General, The Rule of Law and Transitional Justice in Conflict and Post-Conflict Societies* (23 August 2004), S/2004/616.

Countries recovering from genocide or similar mass atrocities naturally face a myriad of moral, legal and political dilemmas. Among these dilemmas, the challenge of dealing with the past is among the most urgent. That is because, in such contexts, the demand for justice is typically at or near its apex whereas the possibility of delivering justice is typically at or near its nadir – whether due to insufficient capacity, insufficient political will, or both. In that respect, transitional justice might be described as an exercise in the 'art of the possible'. It is premised on the idea that extraordinary times call for extraordinary measures. More specifically, it holds that in dealing with the past, courts and trials are important but insufficient to handle the multiple and complex prejudices flowing from legacies of mass abuse. Trials need to be accompanied by non-judicial measures which focus on the vindication, *inter alia,* of victims' rights to truth, reparation, and guarantees of non-recurrence.

In this respect, transitional justice is defined by a holistic approach to dealing with the past that encompasses four main mechanisms.

(i) *Criminal prosecutions*: Criminal prosecutions hold a privileged place in the fight against impunity, in particular because of the grave character of the crimes involved. Prosecutions are preferably carried out at the national level, where they have the greatest potential to contribute to deterrence and the restoration of public confidence in the rule of law.[5] The reality, however, is that there are usually tremendous challenges facing domestic criminal justice systems in investigating and prosecuting international crimes. The main challenge is often the lack of political will, but in addition, legal barriers such as amnesties, the lack of an independent judiciary and lack of capacity in terms of technical and professional skills to investigate and prosecute serious widespread or systematic crimes, as well as security and access issues, including a volatile security environment, continued armed conflict and lack of a safe environment for legal actors or victims and witnesses, pose extra challenges at the national level in holding perpetrators to account. Many *ad hoc* international and hybrid criminal tribunals have thus emerged in recent years to deal with those bearing the greatest responsibility for atrocities that were committed in specific countries and regions such as Rwanda, the former Yugoslavia, Sierra Leone, Timor-Leste and Cambodia.[6] Today, there is of course also a permanent International Criminal Court (ICC) in place to try international crimes of genocide, crimes against humanity and war crimes where states are demonstrably unable or unwilling to do so themselves.[7] In recent years, many pros-

---

[5] Rome Statute of the International Criminal Court, Preamble, paragraph 4; see also recent examples of domestic prosecutions in Argentina and Peru.

[6] For more information on hybrid courts and tribunals, see the website of the International Center for Transitional Justice: <http://www.ictj.org>.

[7] For a recent analysis of domestic justice systems and the impact of the ICC, see the recent discussion paper by C. Aptel, Senior Fellow, International Center for Transitional Justice, on domestic systems and the International Criminal Court, prepared for the Consultative Conference on International Criminal Justice, 9-11 September 2009, United Nations Headquarters, New York, available at: <http://www.internationalcriminaljustice.net/prereg2009/>.

ecutions have been pursued in third states too, through reliance on legal principles such as universal jurisdiction.

(ii) *Truth commissions*: Truth commissions are *ad hoc* commissions of inquiry established in, and authorised by, states for the primary purposes of investigating and reporting on key periods of recent past abuse, and of making recommendations to remedy such abuse and prevent its recurrence.[8] There have been scores of truth commissions created around the world during the last few decades in places as different as Chile, Sri Lanka, Canada and Liberia. Of these, the most famous one is still the South African Truth and Reconciliation Commission, with its unique truth-for-amnesty procedure and its internationally televised public hearings. Although no prior or subsequent truth commission has possessed an equivalent power to grant amnesty, most subsequent ones have held public hearings for victims, since such hearings appear to significantly increase public awareness and open public debate about the past.

(iii) *Victim reparation programmes*: Victim reparation programmes are state-sponsored initiatives that aim at contributing to the reparation, on a universal scale, of the material and moral consequences of past abuse experienced by designated classes of victims.[9] Typically, they are established upon the recommendation of a truth commission or at a legislature's initiative, like in Germany in the years and decades after the Holocaust. Contemporary reparation programmes usually provide compensation payments to victims and their families, together with privileged or dedicated access to certain public or private services, such as health care rehabilitation services, pension benefits and educational services.[10] Modern reparation programmes increasingly encompass various symbolic forms of reparation too, including monuments and memorials to preserve and honour the memory of victims. Community or collective reparation measures are also beginning to be recommended and used, as, for example, in Peru and Morocco.

(iv) *Security system reform*: Security system reform (SSR)[11] is a crucial means for helping to reduce the likelihood of renewed conflict or abuse.[12] While there is a wide range of different reform measures that may be needed or applied in any given context, in practice, the field of transitional justice places special emphasis on 'vetting programmes', in particular in the police, army

[8] For a comprehensive analysis of truth commissions, see M. Freeman, *Truth Commissions and Procedural Fairness* (Cambridge, Cambridge University Press 2006); P. Hayner, *Unspeakable Truths: Facing the Challenge of Truth Commissions* (New York, Routledge 2002).

[9] See International Center for Transitional Justice, 'Reparations in Theory and Practice', *Reparative Justice Series* (2007), available at: <http://www.ictj.org>.

[10] OHCHR, *Rule of Law Tools for Post-Conflict States, Reparations Programmes* (2008), at 22.

[11] On SSR more broadly, see *OECD DAC Handbook on Security System Reform: Supporting Security and Justice* (2007).

[12] L. Davis, 'Transitional Justice and Security System Reform' (June 2009), published in the framework of the Initiative for Peacebuilding funded by the EU. A. Mayer-Riekh and P. de Greiff, eds., *Justice As Prevention: Vetting Public Employees in Transitional Societies* (Social Science Research Council 2007).

and judiciary. These are integrity-focused personnel screening procedures which have as their central aim to transform specific public institutions into defenders rather than violators of the public interest.[13] Vetting programmes have been used in places such as El Salvador and Bosnia. They seek to ensure greater procedural fairness than the so-called 'purges' programmes used in recent years in places such as Albania and Iraq.[14] Another emerging tool of security sector reform, known as 'census and identification', is increasingly employed as a first step in establishing good governance.[15] Census and identification encompasses technical audits of dysfunctional public institutions to verify their current state of membership, and ultimately 'closure' of the institutions' formal boundaries so that subsequent reform processes can be more controlled and effective. Currently a census and certification exercise is undertaken by the government of Burundi with the support of the international community.

## 3. The link between transitional justice and peacebuilding

As noted above, transitional justice is a field that lies at the intersection of human rights and conflict resolution. While the field cannot be completely subsumed within a peacebuilding framework, given that transitional justice also encompasses legacies of abuse that have nothing to do with armed conflict (e.g., transitions from periods of dictatorship), there is a clear recognition among peacebuilders of the added value of transitional justice in restoring public security and contributing to long-term reconciliation. Transitional justice is already among the explicit priorities of the UN Peacebuilding Commission (PBC)[16] and is an integral component of the approved activities in its first two client member states, Sierra Leone and Burundi.

Since transitional justice strategies are often crafted in situations where peace is fragile or perpetrators retain real power, they must carefully balance the demands of justice with the realities of what can be achieved in the short term. Bearing this in mind, below is an outline of some of the main links between peacebuilding and the four chief mechanisms of transitional justice.

(i) *Criminal prosecutions and peacebuilding*: Prosecutions may be viewed as a vital part of ending impunity, restoring the rule of law and building a culture of human rights. Especially during the last several years, there have been many important legal developments: the evolution and strengthening of inter-

---

[13] See *Report of the UN Secretary General on The Rule of Law and Transitional Justice in Conflict and Post-Conflict Societies* (23 August 2004), *supra* n. 4, at 17-18.

[14] Purges differ from vetting in that purges target individuals for their membership in or affiliation with a group rather than for their individual responsibility for human rights violations.

[15] See International Center for Transitional Justice, *Census and Identification of Security Personnel after Conflict* (2008), available at: <http://www.ictj.org>.

[16] See Security Council Resolution 1645 (2005) and UN General Assembly Resolution 60/180 (2005) establishing the Peacebuilding Commission.

national law concerning accountability for serious crimes, the creation of the ICC, and a growing global consensus that third-party exile and blanket amnesties should generally be rejected.[17] These developments have had a profound impact on peacemaking, mediation and peacebuilding, creating tensions but also new ideas about the proper balancing of the interests of peace and those of justice.[18]

(ii) *Truth commissions and peacebuilding*: Establishing an official truth about a brutal past can help inoculate future generations against revisionism and can empower citizens to recognise and resist a return to abusive practices. In recent years, truth commissions have been established in an increasing number of countries as part of a broader peacebuilding agenda.[19] Under the right conditions, truth commissions in such contexts can play a number of significant roles: they can serve as repositories of data concerning victims, perpetrators, policies and key institutions that can be used for peacebuilding projects; they can provide a diagnosis of violations, as well as a roadmap for institutional and legal reforms; they can give victims a voice in public discourse, acknowledging their sufferings and hence reducing resentment and anger; and they can help identify structural inequalities that might have been at the root of past conflict.

(iii) *Victim reparation programmes and peacebuilding*: In the context of peacebuilding processes, reparation policies must take into account the obligation to provide reparation for human rights and international humanitarian law violations attributable to the state.[20] Reparation programmes can make an important contribution to poverty reduction, not only because they have the potential to transfer financial resources and institutional support to their recipients, but also because they often target communities at risk for whom these resources might make the difference between continued marginalisation and the beginning of self-sufficiency. Reparation programmes must also interface with disarmament, demobilisation and reintegration (DDR) programmes.[21] If demobilised perpetrators receive financial assistance disproportionate to that for victims, this can create a moral asymmetry between

---

[17] For a comprehensive analysis on the question of amnesties for grave international crimes, see M. Freeman, *Necessary Evils: Amnesties and the Search for Justice* (Cambridge, Cambridge University Press 2009).

[18] P. Hayner, 'Negotiating Peace in Sierra Leone: Confronting the Justice Challenge' (December 2007) and P. Hayner, 'Negotiating Peace in Liberia: Preserving the Possibility for Justice' (November 2007). These reports are part of the Humanitarian Dialogue Centre's project *Negotiating Justice: Strategies for Tackling Justice Issues in Peace Processes*.

[19] E.g., Sierra Leone, East Timor, Kenya, Uganda and Liberia.

[20] Basic Principles and Guidelines on the Right to a Remedy and Reparation for Victims of Gross Violations of International Human Rights Law and Serious Violations of International Humanitarian Law, General Assembly Resolution 60/147 of 16 December 2005

[21] P. de Greiff, 'DDR and Reparations: Establishing Links between Peace and Justice Instruments', in K. Ambos, J. Large and M. Wierda, eds., *Building a Future on Peace and Justice: Studies on Transitional Justice, Peace and Development* (Boulder, Springer 2009) 321.

victim and perpetrator, inflame tensions and undermine the reintegration of former combatants into society.

(iv) *Security system reform and peacebuilding*: In responding to mass atrocity, it is not sufficient to punish perpetrators, establish the truth about violations and provide victims with reparations. It is also necessary to fundamentally change those institutions responsible for systematic human rights abuses. In some contexts it may also be important to integrate former non-state combatants into state security institutions as part of the terms of a broader peace accord, as we currently see in the DRC.[22] By reforming main institutions in the security sector – through a combination of legislation, census and identification, vetting, redeployment and retraining – the prospect of a return to armed conflict can be significantly diminished.

## 4. The relevance of transitional justice for the EU

There are various other stakeholders besides the EU which play an important role in the area of peacebuilding. At the global level, the UN plays the leading role in this respect. At the regional level in Europe, the Council of Europe and the Organisation for Security and Cooperation in Europe (OSCE) are key stakeholders. The EU has to be seen in contrast to these institutions and has to develop its own niche in cooperating closely with them in order to avoid duplications or confusions on the ground. Given the fact that the EU is represented in all these institutions, it has a huge potential to ensure greater coherence in integrating transitional justice in peacekeeping and peacebuilding agendas, and to push for consistent policies in implementation at field level. The Lisbon Treaty gives the EU as an institution even a stronger potential in this respect.

In this regard, it will be important to identify what the EU's role in the area of transitional justice should logically be in broad terms. Key questions have to be asked in this respect. They include the following: what is the opportunity for the EU in the area of transitional justice? How can it play a useful flanking role and not duplicate efforts undertaken in other multilateral institutions?

Broadly speaking, the EU has a chance to play a leading role in transitional justice standard- setting. First, the EU comprises exclusively democratic states committed to an international rule of law. Second, as already mentioned, it is one of the biggest funders of transitional justice initiatives, given its lead in global Official Development Assistance (ODA). Finally, the EU is increasingly moving into situations of high relevance from a transitional justice perspective through the missions established in the framework of the Common Security and Defence Policy (CSDP, previously ESDP) (e.g., DRC and Kosovo).

---

[22] L. Davis, Small Steps, 'Large Hurdles: The EU's Role in Promoting Justice in Peacemaking in the DRC' (May 2009), published in the framework of the Initiative for Peacebuilding funded by the EU, available at: <http://www.initiativeforpeacebuilding.eu/>.

However, transitional justice is not only relevant to EU foreign policy, but also to its internal policies. This is especially true given the number of countries within the EU where legacies of abuse and reconciliation processes remain on domestic political agendas.[23] In this context, transitional justice should not be conceived by the EU as only a matter of foreign policy. Doing so would risk that the EU would be perceived as leading a policy of double standards and not one of promoting the universality of human rights. This might be especially true in the context of the EU's enlargement policy, since transitional justice was not an explicit or implied conditionality for past EU candidates. In this context, it will be important for the EU to promote the idea of transitional justice in Community policy and to also recall the several 'positive examples' and best practices of transitional justice in Europe that have already occurred.[24] Finally, it has to be acknowledged that the term 'transitional justice' is a major challenge in the European context. Few, if any, EU Member States see themselves as still being in 'transition', which makes it hard to put transitional justice on the political agenda without re-labelling it as something else (e.g., 'dealing with the past').

## 5. Current EU policy and practice on transitional justice

Given the overall relevance of transitional justice for the EU, in particular in the area of peacebuilding, it is worth focusing on the role played therein by the different institutions of the EU. This should help in identifying and closing potential policy and operational gaps in order for the EU to further develop and strengthen its role in the area of transitional justice.

### 5.1 General overview

Transitional justice (TJ) as a concept only recently entered the political discourse in Brussels. Up until the end of 2004, there was only a single reference to transitional justice in EU documents: an affirmative statement by the EU Presidency regarding the UN Secretary-General's 2004 Report on transitional justice and the rule of law.[25] 'Transitional justice' has tended to be associated by the EU mainly with the idea of

---

[23] For example: UK/Northern Ireland, Cyprus (internal armed conflicts), Spain (Franco era but also Basque conflict), Baltic and Central/Eastern European Member States (communist past and Soviet occupation legacies), Germany (Holocaust) and Belgium (colonial past). There are many other Member States where legacies *should* be on the domestic agenda but are not, or only partially, such as: Austria and Baltic/Central/Eastern European Member States (Holocaust), Portugal/France/Netherlands/UK/Italy (colonial past) and Romania (communist past).

[24] For example: Germany (reparations for holocaust victims, public education), Greece (torture trials after military dictatorship in the 70s) and Northern Ireland (national dialogue on transitional justice after internal conflict).

[25] EU Presidency Statement – The Rule of Law and Transitional Justice in Conflict and Post-Conflict Societies, 6 October 2004, available at: <http://www.europa-eu-un.org/articles/en/article_3872_en.htm>.

'reconciliation'; 'justice' (or the 'fight against impunity') with the functioning of the International Criminal Court (ICC); and the 'rule of law' with security system reform. Transitional justice should, however, be understood as a holistic and comprehensive concept encompassing justice, reconciliation and the rule of law.[26] Hence, it will be important to change the EU's perception in order for the ICC and SSR to be seen as *part of* a transitional justice framework, as opposed to *external* elements or approaches.

Also, EU institutions have different approaches to the concept of transitional justice. The Council has considered transitional justice as a short-term post-conflict issue. The Commission, on the other hand, has tended to understand TJ as a long-term reconciliation issue. In light of this apparent contradiction, it will be important to get the Council and Commission to understand that they are both right and that transitional justice is an important issue of relevance to both of them, conceptually and operationally.

### 5.2 The Council (the 'voice of Member States')

Transitional justice is already of great relevance to the work of the Council and is explicitly or implicitly mentioned in various documents and policies established by it. The following examples should illustrate the various areas where transitional justice is at the centre of the Council's work and discussions.

- *EU Guidelines and mandates of the EU Special Representatives (EUSRs)*: The EU Guidelines on Children and Armed Conflict refer explicitly to transitional justice as a priority in order to address children's special short and long-term post-conflict needs.[27] There are several EUSR mandates which encompass SSR actions, for example, those pertaining to Bosnia-Herzegovina, Afghanistan and the Great Lakes Region (DRC).[28] The EUSR mandate for Sudan refers explic-

[26] *Report of the UN Secretary General on The Rule of Law and Transitional Justice in Conflict and Post-Conflict Societies*, 23 August 2004, *supra* n. 4.

[27] EU Guidelines on Children and Armed Conflict (5 June 2008), 10019/08, at 1: the EU recognises the particular vulnerability of children in situations of conflict and their particular needs in post-conflict situations, including 'for tracing of family members, redress and social reintegration, psycho-social rehabilitation programmes, participation in disarmament, demobilisation and reintegration programmes as well as within *transitional justice frameworks.*' [emphasis added]. See also European Union Guidelines on Promoting Compliance with International Humanitarian Law (IHL) (2005/C 327/04): 'Individuals bear personal responsibility for war crimes. States must, in accordance with their national law, ensure that alleged perpetrators are brought before their own domestic courts or handed over for trial by the courts of another State or by an international criminal tribunal, such as the International Criminal Court', para. 14.

[28] Council Joint Action 2008/130/CFSP of 18 February 2008 extending the mandate of the EUSR in BiH: the mandate contains provisions related to rule of law, support for police restructuring and cooperation of BiH authorities with the ICTY; Council Joint Action 2008/133/CFSP of 18 February 2008 amending and extending the mandate of the EUSR for the Middle East peace process: the mandate contains a provision on engaging in wider collaboration on SSR; Council Joint Action 2008/612/CFSP of 24 July 2008 concerning the appointment of the EUSR for Afghanistan: mandate to advise on the progress achieved in meeting the objectives of the Afghanistan Compact, in particular in the areas

itly to the fight against impunity.[29] In addition, every existing EUSR mandate involves a country or sub-region where transitional justice issues are extremely relevant.

- *Council Conclusions*: In some country contexts the Council mentioned specific transitional justice mechanisms. In the recent Council Conclusions on the Great Lakes Region the Council referred to the importance of vetting and stated that '[t]he Council calls on the Government of the DRC to ensure without exception that those responsible for violations of international law, including human rights and international humanitarian law, are held accountable. Timely vetting of FARDC commanders and soldiers is of crucial importance in this respect.'[30] Also in recent Council Conclusions on promoting compliance with international humanitarian law the council emphasised 'the importance of dealing effectively with the legacy of serious violations of international humanitarian and human rights law by supporting appropriate accountability mechanisms.'[31]
- *ESDP/CSDP Missions*: There have been several ESDP/CSDP missions with transitional justice elements, such as Georgia (EUJUST THEMIS) encompassing judicial reform,[32] Aceh (AMM)[33] covering amnesty proceedings, and Kosovo (EULEX KOSOVO) and Iraq[34] (EUJUST LEX) involving judicial and police reform. Kosovo is generally designed as a rule of law mission.[35] According to the mandate, the EULEX judges and prosecutors in Kosovo shall assist the judicial authorities in their progress towards sustainability and accountability and in further developing and strengthening an independent multi-ethnic justice system, ensuring that these institutions are free from political interference and adhering to internationally recognised standards. In following a similar model as the previous UN Mission in Kosovo (UNMIK), EULEX judges and prosecutors retain certain executive responsibilities by working together with their local Kosovo counterparts in mixed panels or mixed teams, ensuring that cases of war

of rule of law and SSR. Council Joint Action 2008/108/CFSP of 12 February 2008 amending and extending the mandate of the EUSR for the African Great Lakes Region: mandate to provide advice and assistance for SSR in the DRC.

[29] Council Joint Action 2008/110/CFSP of 12 February 2008 amending and extending the mandate of the EUSR for Sudan: mandate to maintain regular contacts with the OTP of the ICC with regard to human rights and the fight against impunity.

[30] Council Conclusions on the Great Lakes Region, 2971st External Relations Council Meeting, Luxembourg, 27 October 2009, para. 3.

[31] Council Conclusions on promoting compliance with international humanitarian law, 2985th Foreign Affairs Council Meeting, Brussels, 8 December 2009, para. 2.

[32] Council Joint Action 2004/523/CFSP of 28 June 2004. This was the first rule of law mission launched by the EU in the context of the European Security and Defence Policy (ESDP).

[33] Council Joint Action 2005/643/CFSP of 9 September 2005 on the EU Monitoring Mission in Aceh (Indonesia) (Aceh Monitoring Mission – AMM); Memorandum of Understanding between the Government of the Republic of Indonesia and the Free Aceh Movement, Helsinki 2005.

[34] Council Joint Action 2005/190/CFSP of 7 March 2005 on the EU Integrated Rule of Law Mission for Iraq (EUJUST LEX).

[35] Council Joint Action 2008/124/CFSP of 4 February 2008 on the EU Rule of Law Mission in Kosovo (EULEX Kosovo).

crimes, terrorism, organised crime, corruption, inter-ethnic crimes, financial/economic crimes and other serious crimes are properly investigated and prosecuted.[36] The mission has so far not made extensive progress in further investigating war crimes allegedly committed by the Kosovo Albanian side during the conflict at the end of the 90s. How the mission deals with the legacy of past abuses especially by the ruling Kosovo Albanian majority will be an important factor in evaluating its success, but also beyond reflect on the EUs credibility in implementing its clear policies towards fighting impunity for serious human rights violations of the past.

- *Enlargement*: Full cooperation with the ICTY was always a condition of accession for the states comprising the former Yugoslavia. This is perhaps the most 'high profile', but also controversial, example of the EU's transitional justice practice to date. The approach so far is, however, to think of this as an example of 'international' justice and not 'transitional' justice. Transitional justice features as a condition, at least indirectly, of future accession for other official candidate countries.[37]
- *The Political and Security Committee (PSC) and the Committee for Civilian Aspects of Crisis Management (CIVCOM)*: At the Political and Security Committee level, a transitional justice seminar was held in March 2006 under the auspices of the Austrian Presidency. The key document resulting from the seminar was the June 2006 report *Transitional Justice and ESDP*,[38] which mentioned, *inter alia*: the need for planning to include an analysis of the transition process in the host country, the need for transitional justice expertise within EU Member States, the need to include transitional justice in existing and future training for EU crisis management operations, and the need for guidelines on transitional justice that would be inspired by, and be consistent with, UN standards. Apart from various transitional justice briefings in CIVCOM, no real follow-up has been given to this public PSC document. The Council Working Group on Human Rights (COHOM) has so far not addressed the issue. At the Secretariat level, Solana's first Personal Representative on Human Rights (Michael Matthiessen) played a key role in 2006 in putting TJ on the Secretariat's agenda. Since then, however, the debate has not gone further at the level of the Secretariat.
- *Mediation*: The EU, as a global actor committed to the promotion of peace, democracy, human rights and sustainable development, is generally seen as a credible and ethical actor in situations of instability and conflict and is thus well

---

[36] Ibid., Law No. 03/L-053 'On the Jurisdiction, Case Selection and Case Allocation of EULEX Judges and Prosecutors in Kosovo'; Law No. 03/L-052 'On the Special Prosecution Office of the Republic of Kosovo'.

[37] For example: Croatia (ICTY, domestic prosecutions), FYROM (ICTY) and Turkey (SSR, compensation of Kurdish civilian victims, acknowledgment of Armenian events). Potential candidate countries: Albania, BiH (ICTY, domestic prosecutions and police reform), Serbia (ICTY, domestic prosecutions and SSR) and Montenegro (ICTY).

[38] *Transitional Justice and ESDP* (19 June 2006), 10674/06.

placed to mediate, facilitate or support mediation and dialogue processes. The EU is currently seeking to conduct a more coordinated and focused approach in the area of conflict mediation. The Council adopted a Concept on strengthening EU mediation and dialogue capacities.[39] The joint Council and Commission Concept should provide a policy basis for EU engagement in the area of mediation and dialogue, with concrete proposals on how to strengthen the Union's capacity and support to EU and EU-backed mediators. Based on the tasking by the Political and Security Committee of 31 July 2009, the Concept is part of the follow-up and implementation of the European Security Strategy (ESS) of 2003[40] and the SG/HR's 2008 Report on the Implementation of the ESS,[41] both of which refer to EU engagement in the area of mediation and dialogue. The Concept also prominently mentions transitional justice by acknowledging that in many cases mediation efforts take place in highly complex contexts, where one or several parties to the conflict have committed serious violations of international human rights and humanitarian law. Issues such as holding human rights violators accountable before court for their actions, reparations to victims, reintegration of ex-child soldiers, restitution of property and land as well as the return of internally displaced persons (IDPs) and refugees have to be tackled during the peace negotiations and the drafting of peace agreements. The Concept paper also seeks to address the difficult question of 'justice versus peace'. In order to effectively deal with its mediation tasks, the EU will have to take into consideration the international experience and expertise available through the UN, EU Member States and other countries active in mediation, NGOs and research bodies, especially in the area of transitional justice. There is also a need to provide efficient guidance and support to EU-appointed and EU-supported mediators on these issues, including through expert advice.

## 5.3 Commission (the 'driving force of the EU')

At the Commission level, there is a growing awareness that the rule of law and the civic dialogue and reconciliation processes, all ingredients and components of a transitional justice strategy, create a foundation for sustainable development.[42] In the 2007 Communication from the Commission on the EU response to situations of fragility, the fundamental role of nationally owned transitional justice and rule of

---

[39] The Concept Paper is on file with the author.

[40] *A Secure Europe in a Better World, European Security Strategy* (2003).

[41] European Council, *Report on the Implementation of the European Security Strategy – Providing Security in a Changing World* (December 2008), *supra* n. 2.

[42] *The European Consensus on Development* (2006/C 46/01) (the general framework for action on EU development cooperation): one of the common principles of EU development policy is 'addressing state fragility', whereby the EU commits to preventing state fragility through governance reforms, rule of law, anti-corruption measures and the building of viable institutions: 'in a post-crisis situation development will be guided by integrated transition strategies, aiming at rebuilding institutional capacities (…)' (paras. 20-21).

law systems in post-conflict settings was recognised, as was the importance of parallel advancement of justice and reconciliation initiatives in stabilising divided societies after conflict.[43]

The importance of transitional justice is also reflected in the various policies of the European Commission as well as in its financial instruments. Transitional justice and mechanisms are explicitly mentioned in several places in the European Instrument for Democracy and Human Rights (EIDHR) as well as in the Instrument for Stability (IfS).[44] TJ also implicitly figures in other instruments, such as in the Citizenship Programme 2007-2011, which supports a wide range of activities and organisations promoting 'active European citizenship', especially the involvement of citizens and civil society organisations in the process of European integration. Action 4 (Active European Remembrance) provides support to projects aimed at preserving the sites and archives associated with deportations as well as the commemoration of victims of Nazism and Stalinism.[45]

The European Commission (EC) is also directly funding transitional justice initiatives. For example, the EC is providing 80% of the total cost of the reparation scheme recommended by the Moroccan Truth Commission. In Colombia, the EC is financially supporting the Peace and Justice Law, including civil society work on reparation and domestic prosecution efforts. In the area of institutional reform, the EC has a 'Community Concept' on SSR, which is, however, currently not understood as being part of transitional justice.[46]

From a transitional justice perspective, the Directorate-General for External relations (DG RELEX) is the key DG, especially the Human Rights and Democracy Unit and the Conflict Prevention Unit. Their key funding instruments are the European Initiative for Democracy and Human Rights, which provides funding to NGOs, multilateral organisations and international tribunals without the requirement of host government consent, and the European Neighbourhood and Partnership

---

[43] Commission Communication, 'Towards an EU Response to Situations of Fragility' (Brussels, 25 October 2007), COM (2007) 643, at 9.

[44] Article 3 IfS, *OJ* 2006 L 327/1. Also note that a specialised 'TJ Facility' has been established allocating 12 million euros for 2008; Regulation (EC) No 1889/2006 of the EP and the Council of 20 December 2006 on establishing a financing instrument for the promotion of democracy and human rights worldwide (EIDHR Regulation), *OJ* 2006 L 386/1, provides for Community assistance in promoting and strengthening the ICC, *ad hoc* international criminal tribunals and the process of transitional justice and truth and reconciliation mechanisms (Art. 2(1)(a)(iii)); Compendium of projects financed by the EC under the EIDHR, 2000-2006, at 154-164 – projects in the areas of international justice (including funding to the ICC, ICTY and ICTR), truth and reconciliation mechanisms and peaceful conciliation; Document de travail des services de la Commission, *Mise en œuvre de la Politique européenne de voisinage en 2007. Rapport de Suivi Maroc* (Bruxelles, 3 avril 2008), SEC(2008)398: 'En revanche, des recommandations importantes de l'Instance Equité et Réconciliation (l'IER) ne sont pas encore mises en oeuvre, notamment en matière de réforme de la Justice, de révision constitutionnelle, d'adoption des conventions internationales et de leurs protocoles, malgré la mise en place de commissions spécialisées', at 5.

[45] See: <http://eacea.ec.europa.eu/citizenship/programme/action4_en.php>.

[46] 'A Concept for European Community Support for Security Sector Reform', COM(2006) 253: sets out principles and norms for the European Community's engagement in SSR.

Instrument (ENPI), which covers MEDA countries, Southern Caucasus countries and Eastern European countries. DG RELEX is also responsible for the Instrument for Stability, including the new TJ Facility as well as the Peacebuilding Partnership Facility.[47]

Also crucial is the Directorate-General for Enlargement (DG ELARG), in particular in relation to EU candidate and potential candidate countries. The relevant funding instrument is the Instrument for Pre-Accession (IPA), which covers human rights generally, albeit without specifically referring to transitional justice.

The Directorate-General for Development (DG DEV) is also of relevance, especially in terms of the mainstreaming of human rights – and thus indirectly of transitional justice – into development policy. It relies above all on the Development Cooperation Instrument, which deals with African, Caribbean and Pacific (ACP) countries and is based on the Cotonou Agreement.[48] The Directorate-General for Justice, Freedom and Security (DG JLS) is also relevant in terms of transitional justice in the external dimension of its policies, but thus far there are no relevant documents on transitional justice. DG JLS is also the main Directorate-General dealing with the question of universal jurisdiction. Whether universal jurisdiction for serious human rights violations is exercised is however within the competence of every single Member State of the EU. Yet, at the level of the EU, efforts are underway to enhance cooperation between the Member States in the prosecution of serious crimes, such as those against humanity and war crimes. The need for more cooperation on this matter was recognised by the EU in the Framework Decision setting up a network of contact points in respect of persons responsible for genocide, crimes against humanity and war crimes.[49] The Framework Decision is aimed at facilitating contacts between professionals specialised in the investigation and prosecution of international crimes and at increasing the cooperation and exchange of information between them.

### 5.4 The Parliament (the 'democratic voice of the people')

So far, the European Parliament (EP) has held various hearings on the issue of transitional justice. Relevant examples to consider here are the public hearing on transitional justice which opened the fall session of the Sub-Committee on Human

[47] Under the crisis preparedness component of the Instrument for Stability (Art. 4.3), the European Commission has established the Peacebuilding Partnership (PbP) to develop the capacity of its potential partners to respond to crisis situations worldwide. The Peacebuilding Partnership envisages building the capacities of relevant organisations in pre-crisis situations, for instance, to develop early-warning systems, to provide mediation and reconciliation services and to address inter-community tensions. It also involves measures to improve post-conflict and post-disaster recovery.

[48] Article 9(4) of the Cotonou Agreement: 'The Partnership shall actively support the promotion of human rights, processes of democratisation, consolidation of the rule of law, and good governance.' Article 11: 'The Parties shall pursue an active, comprehensive and integrated policy of peacebuilding and conflict prevention and resolution within the framework of the Partnership.'

[49] Council Decision 2002/494/JHA of 13 June 2002, available at: <http://eurocrim.jura.unituebingen.de/cms/en/doc/265.pdf>.

Rights (August 2006).[50] In similar vein, other EP committees and sub-committees occasionally explore transitional justice issues. At present, however, this is only done in an *ad hoc* fashion. Transitional justice is also mentioned in the Annual Report on Human Rights in the World 2006, where the EP 'calls on the Council and the Commission to encourage third countries to promote transitional justice mechanisms on their territory as a step towards securing justice for victims of grave violations of human rights.'[51]

The EP has, however, made it clear that the fight against impunity is a key priority for the Union. On 16 March 2006, the European Parliament passed a resolution on impunity in Africa and in particular the case of Hissène Habré, reiterating that the fight against impunity is one of the cornerstones of the Union's human rights policy and calling 'on the Commission, the Council and the Member States of the African Union to continue to pay attention to this issue.' Furthermore, the resolution called on Member States 'to do whatever they can to ensure that (…) victims of such crimes [committed in Africa or developing countries] receive compensation.'[52] In its resolution on the proceedings against Rios Montt, on 26 October 2006, the European Parliament 'welcomes the progress made in the application of the principle of universal jurisdiction in respect of crimes against humanity, genocide and torture (...) the same procedure should be followed under similar circumstances in taking action against dictators and persons responsible for mass human rights violations.'[53] It is hoped that the EP will also in the future be the engine calling for concrete actions in the area of fighting impunity, including transitional justice.

## 6. Possible future directions for the EU on transitional justice

There is a clear, albeit indirect, EU practice on transitional justice. It appears to be scattered and undertaken in an *ad hoc* fashion. Below are some recommendations for possible future directions the EU could take as regards transitional justice to remedy current shortcomings. The recommendations seek to provide concrete operational solutions both for the EU as a whole, and individually for different institutions.

(i) *Recommendations for the EU as a whole*

- The EU could consider creating a framework to inform and guide the EU's transitional justice policies in order to avoid that actions are taken in an *ad hoc* fashion. A transitional justice framework will give the EU the ability to evaluate the quality of transitional justice interventions at national level and to propose evidence-based and viable transitional justice policy choices at

50 Other transitional justice hearings at DROI: Morocco (February 2007) and general (March 2006).

51 *Report of the EP on the Annual Report on HR in the World 2006 and EU's policy on the matter* (10 April 2007), A6-0128/2007.

52 Impunity in Africa and in particular the case of Hissène Habré, P6_TA(2006)0101.

53 Case against Rios Montt, P6_TA(2006)0466.

international and national levels. A framework will also ensure coherence and consistency in the EU's transitional justice engagements.

- In parallel, it is recommended to establish a working group on transitional justice composed of staff members of the Council and the Commission, to ensure institutional follow-up to an established transitional justice framework. The working group could draw from existing rule of law staff in the different institutions or establish specialised transitional justice focal points in the Commission and Council.

(ii) *Recommendations to the Council*

- *Transitional justice checklist and handbook*: A transitional justice checklist for CSDP missions could be developed with a requirement to be consulted in the course of designing and carrying out any CSDP mission. In addition to the checklist, a transitional justice field handbook for CSDP missions (as well as for the EU's in-country delegations) should be developed in order to put theory into concrete terms of operation and to ensure effective implementation on the ground.
- *Transitional justice training*: The Council should further implement regular pre-deployment training on transitional justice, in coordination with EU Member States, and offer in-mission transitional justice training modules and courses.
- *Transitional justice experts*: The Council could establish a roster of available EU and non-governmental experts in the transitional justice field. This could be a sub-category of any existing EU 'rule of law' experts roster. At the mission level, the creation of a transitional justice focal point for relevant CSDP missions could be considered. There are already some proposals that this should be done in the context of the EU mission in Kosovo. In the context of Kosovo, transitional justice is listed as a formal element of the Ahtisaari plan.
- *Enlargement*: The Council should consider, after the closure of the ICTY,[54] replacing the ICTY conditionality for accession countries of the Balkans with an incentive-based scheme that builds support for the next crucial phase of dealing with the legacy of abuse in the region: regional truth recovery and reconciliation through a regional truth commission (RECOM) as well as domestic prosecutions in the different countries of the former Yugoslavia.
- *Transitional justice as an agenda item in EU human rights dialogues with third states*: The EU undertakes over thirty human rights dialogues with third states, among which countries or regions where transitional justice is relevant (e.g., Colombia, AU). A discussion and exchange of good practices on transitional justice could contribute to building confidence and ensuring that the EU is seen as a partner in finding sustainable solutions for complex issues. Linked to this is a coherent approach within the different EU Member States to address transitional justice questions.

---

[54] It is expected that the ICTY will complete its work by 2013.

(iii) *Recommendations to the Commission*

- *Expert paper on the link between transitional justice and development*: Development policies are often seen to stand in contradiction to efforts to address the legacy of the past. New studies show, however, that development and transitional justice complement each other.[55] In order to undertake transitional justice-friendly development policies, the Commission could work on a possible expert paper regarding the link between TJ and development.
- *Survey of lessons learned in the area of transitional justice*: The Commission could undertake a possible survey of TJ 'lessons learned' and 'best practices' through consultations with EU Delegations in countries where TJ processes are underway. These surveys could also be made available in dialogues which the EU is leading with third states.
- *Mainstreaming of transitional justice at DG AIDCO*: The Europe Aid Coordination Office (AIDCO) is responsible for implementing the external aid instruments of the EU.[56] Transitional justice should be better mainstreamed into the work of AIDCO.

(iv) *Recommendation to the Parliament*

- TJ should be formally 'situated' as a responsibility within a relevant subcommittee of the Committee on Foreign Affairs (AFET).

## 7. Conclusions

For now, the priority remains to continue to raise the level of awareness and understanding of what transitional justice is and why it is relevant to the EU, especially in the area of peacebuilding. As has been shown, there are several entry points for transitional justice to be taken up in the work of the EU, at the policy as well as the operational level. An EU policy framework on transitional justice together with measures to strengthen EU institutions with transitional justice expertise should enhance the future work of the EU on this important matter. The following benchmarks could be considered in order to evaluate the success of an EU transitional justice policy in the future:

- *Council*: More transitional justice-sensitive mandates for CSDP missions and EUSRs. Transitional justice should be a key priority for the new President of the European Council and within the Council Secretariat as well as for the High Representative of the Union who, after the entry into force of the Lisbon Treaty, has a stronger role especially in the area of CSDP (right to set initiatives, coordination role, special hierarchical status in certain situations vis-à-vis the PSC).

---

[55] P. de Greiff and R. Duthie, eds., *Transitional Justice and Development: Making Connections* (The Social Science Research Council 2009).

[56] The main instruments are the European Instrument for Democracy and Human Rights (EIDHR), the Instrument for Stability (IfS), the European Neighbourhood and Partnership Instrument (ENPI), the Instrument for Pre-Accession Assistance (IPA) and the Development Cooperation Instrument (DCI).

- *Commission*: Quality transitional justice policies are developed, and significant expenditures on quality transitional justice actors and processes are made.
- *Parliament*: Significant political support for quality transitional justice actors and processes is expressed on a regular basis.

Overall, there is a need to make sure that TJ is not conceived as merely a foreign policy priority. Just as Europe needs to ensure that its foreign policies on HR are matched by effective domestic human rights policies, so it has to guarantee that its foreign policies on transitional justice are matched by effective domestic policies. There is still some 'unfinished business' in the area of transitional justice in Europe which needs to be addressed. To take a pro-active stance on these issues will also potentially help in countering attacks against EU efforts to promote the International Criminal Court and rebut the claim of double standards.

Whatever TJ policies and practices are ultimately adopted, it would be beneficial for the EU to have a strong relationship with local and international civil society (TJ expert) institutions in order to guarantee that its actions reflect best practices and local knowledge and ownership.

# Part V
# *Good governance and economic development*

# Chapter 18
# INTERNATIONAL TRUSTEESHIP AND DEMOCRATIC PEACEBUILDING: THE EU IN THE BALKANS

**Tonny Brems Knudsen* and Christian Axboe Nielsen****

## 1. INTRODUCTION

In the second half of the 1990s, the peacebuilding ambitions of the international community culminated in a revival of *de facto* international trusteeship arrangements such as those in Bosnia and Herzegovina, Kosovo and East Timor. By then, such 'interim' or 'transitional' administrations had become a high priority for the United Nations (UN) and the European Union (EU) which also turned out to be a very demanding one, especially in the troublesome cases in the former Yugoslavia.

While the resort to informal trusteeship arrangements is probably an indispensable option in the toolbox of comprehensive peacebuilding, it is also one that seems to involve some very serious dilemmas. Two of these will be given special attention in this study. First, the initial goal of bringing a state from a situation of governmental failure, civil war and military intervention into domestic order, peace and prosperity almost inevitably means that democracy must be imposed from the outside. Consequently, the international administrators must live or come to terms with the dilemma of democratisation by means of pressure, dictate or coercion. Second, this extensive and intrusive form of international administration means that the sovereignty of the former authorities is not merely overruled in a dramatic moment of humanitarian intervention or peace enforcement. It is also suspended, annulled or changed over longer periods of time, as in the cases of Kosovo and East Timor. Such arrangements therefore also raise delicate questions pertaining to the future political status of the territory and society under temporary international administration. In some cases, the endpoint is clear and uncontested from the beginning (as in the case of East Timor), but in other cases the constitutional framework and the international legal status will long remain unclear or contested by local and international actors (as in Bosnia and Herzegovina and Kosovo).

---

* Associate Professor of International Relations, Department of Political Science, Aarhus University.

** Assistant Professor of Southeast European Studies, Department of History and Areas Studies, Aarhus University.

*S. Blockmans, J. Wouters & T. Ruys, eds., The European Union and Peacebuilding*

The challenges of international trusteeship have been highly evident in recent years, not least in the European cases of Bosnia and Herzegovina and Kosovo, where the international community has been struggling with the promotion of democracy and the solution of constitutional and political problems since the formal ending of the wars. As of 2009, success is still not guaranteed. Kosovo confronts a situation of contested independence while Bosnia and Herzegovina remains a divided and unstable democracy. At a more fundamental level, such trusteeship arrangements even raise questions about the flexibility and future development of international order. On the one hand, they seem to be at odds with fundamental principles of the Westphalian international order, which is based on a clear division of political authority between fully recognised sovereign states. On the other hand, this order has time and again demonstrated that it cannot function according to any reasonable modern standards of order and justice without occasional international intervention and a temporary assumption of responsibility over territory and people.[1] This implies that international trusteeship arrangements are a problematic but necessary element in contemporary international society.

Consequently, the challenges and dilemmas of international trusteeship administration must be dealt with. This is the academic task to which this chapter will try to contribute on the basis of theoretical analysis and the nearly 15 years of experience from international and European trusteeship administration in the Balkans. The research questions are as follows:

(1) What are the democratic and constitutional challenges of contemporary international trusteeship arrangements?
(2) How have the international community and its primary agents in the Balkans, the EU and the UN dealt with these challenges in Bosnia and Herzegovina and Kosovo, and what have been the consequences of the chosen strategies?

We begin with a discussion of the concept of international trusteeship and the challenges involved in this radical form of international intervention (section 2). We then turn to the lessons learned in Bosnia and Herzegovina (section 3) and Kosovo (section 4), focusing on the dilemmas of imposed democracy, constitutional design and international legal status. This analysis will proceed on the basis of a combination of analyses of the means and strategies chosen by the external administrators as representatives of the international community and analyses of the internal consequences of these policies, especially for the political elites, the population and local society. Finally, we point to a number of lessons to be learned for international trusteeship administration in general and for the ongoing attempt to transform the negative peace in Bosnia and Herzegovina and Kosovo into positive peace in particular (section 5).

---

[1] This dilemma falls under the pluralist-solidarist debate about international trusteeship. See R. Jackson, *The Global Covenant: Human Conduct in a World of States* (Oxford, Oxford University Press 2000), at 294-315, and T. Knudsen and C. Laustsen, 'The Politics of International Trusteeship', in T. Knudsen and C. Laustsen, eds., *Kosovo between War and Peace: Nationalism, Peacebuilding and International Trusteeship* (London, Routledge 2007) 1-18.

## 2. International trusteeship: The concept and the challenge

The tendency of international organisations, NGOs and states acting in the name of international society to take on far-reaching responsibility for war-torn societies can be traced back at least to UN Secretary-General Boutros-Ghali's ambitious plan for a comprehensive reconstruction of Somalia of 3 March 1993 and the ensuing UN Security Council (UNSC) Resolution 814 of 26 March.[2] The latter defined a number of tasks for the UN operation, including humanitarian relief, the maintenance of peace, stability, law and order, and assistance with respect to political reconciliation and the re-establishment of a national police force and civil administration throughout the country.

Although the humanitarian intervention in Somalia has generally been seen as a failure, the UN and its partners were soon engaged in other comprehensive peacebuilding activities, some of them amounting to *de facto* international trusteeships. The clearest examples include Bosnia and Herzegovina (1995) and Eastern Slavonia (1996) following the wars in the former Yugoslavia, East Timor following the choice for independence in the 1999 referendum, and Kosovo following the uprising, the atrocities and the NATO intervention in 1999.[3] Furthermore, the US and international efforts to stabilise Iraq and Afghanistan have been treated by some observers as variants of international trusteeship.[4]

### 2.1 Conceptual clarification

Given the diverse manifestations of the revived trusteeship institution in recent years and the malleability of the term, some preliminary clarifications are required. First, it is helpful to distinguish between military trusteeships (or governorships), in which the governance and reconstruction of the society in question is dominated by (formally or *de facto*) occupying powers, as in the case of Iraq following the war in 2003, and UN trusteeships, where these tasks are in the hands of UN administrators and their partners, as in the cases of Bosnia and Herzegovina, Eastern Slavonia, Kosovo and East Timor.

Second, it should be noted that in their ideal forms both of these models are unlikely to be found very often in reality. On the one hand, great powers are likely

---

[2] See B. Boutros-Ghali, *Report of the Secretary-General*, 3 March 1993 (S/25354), and UN Security Council Resolution 814, 26 March 1993.

[3] For analyses of these cases as examples of a *de facto* revival of the 19th and 20th century protectorate and trusteeship institutions, see W. Bain, *Between Anarchy and Society: Trusteeship and the Obligations of Power* (Oxford, Oxford University Press 2003), at 140-154; R. Caplan, *International Governance of War-Torn Territories: Rule and Reconstruction* (Oxford, Oxford University Press 2005), esp. at 16-41; J. Chopra, 'The UN's Kingdom of East Timor', 42 *Survival* (2000) 27-39; International Crisis Group, *The New Kosovo Protectorate*, ICG Balkans Report No. 69 (Sarajevo, 20 June 1999), Crisis Webnews, available at: <http://www.crisisweb.org>; and Jackson, *supra* n. 1, at 294-315. See also M. Berdal and R. Caplan, eds., 'Special Issue on the Politics of International Administration', 10 *Global Governance* (2004).

[4] See C. Freeman, 'Liberal Trusteeship: The Convergence of Interest and Ideology in International Administration', in Knudsen and Laustsen, eds., *supra* n. 1, 168-186.

to play a central role in UN trusteeship arrangements, as evident from the cases of Kosovo and Bosnia and Herzegovina. On the other hand, great powers will rarely want to do completely without the expertise, resources and legitimacy of the UN in the administration of war-torn or contested societies. This has become clear even in the divisive case of Iraq, where the US asked the UN to take part in the reconstruction of the country in spite of the fact that the invasion had been widely deplored in the UN Security Council and the General Assembly and by Secretary-General Annan as well.

Third, although each case is unique, most academic and political observers would presumably agree that, all other things being equal, the legitimacy of an international trusteeship will be higher, the higher the involvement of the UN, the clearer the original legal case for interventionist measures and the clearer the concerns for security and humanitarian standards.

A number of terms have been applied and suggested for the resort to international administration of war torn-societies since the early 1990s. Some scholars prefer the terms used by the UN itself in cases like Kosovo, namely 'interim administration' and 'transitional administration'[5] referring to the temporary assumption of governmental functions by the UN and its partners over territories and peoples that have been left in a potentially fatal political vacuum, for instance, because of civil war, crimes against humanity, state failure, territorial disputes or outside military intervention.[6]

Others refer to 'comprehensive peacebuilding' which, following Boutros-Ghali's 1992 *Agenda for Peace*, can be defined as 'efforts to identify and support structures which will tend to consolidate peace and advance a sense of confidence and well-being among people.'[7] This term captures a number of the activities involved in subsequent examples of ambitious administration of war-torn and contested territories, such as Bosnia and Herzegovina, Kosovo and East Timor, including the reforming of governmental institutions as suggested already by Boutros-Ghali in 1992. Comprehensive peacebuilding might also be seen as the logical endpoint of a process in which the international community has gone from traditional peacekeeping to wider peacekeeping, peace enforcement, humanitarian intervention and, ultimately, the civil, political, social and economic reconstruction of entire societies.[8]

However, some observers find that there is more to it than the assumption of growing responsibilities in the pursuit of peace. Peacebuilding means that the UN takes on far-reaching responsibilities for the society in question, but it does so by

---

[5] See UN Security Council Resolution 1244 (esp. paragraph 10) of 10 June 1999, which provided for the establishment of the United Nations Interim Administration Mission in Kosovo (UNMIK).

[6] See for instance Caplan, *supra* n. 3, at 16-17, where the term 'international administration' is explicitly preferred to 'trusteeship' and 'protectorate'. 'International administration' is also preferred by Berdal and Caplan, eds., *supra* n. 3.

[7] B. Boutros-Ghali, *An Agenda for Peace,* 2nd edn. (New York, The United Nations 1995), at 61. R. Paris prefers the term peacebuilding as well, see his book *At War's end: Building Peace after Civil Conflict* (Cambridge, Cambridge University Press 2004).

[8] On this development, see M. Pugh, ed., *The UN, Peace and Force* (London, Frank Cass 1997).

working with the government. In cases like Kosovo, the UN *becomes* the government, as evident from UN Security Council Resolution 1244 of 10 June 1999. This Resolution provided for the establishment of the 'United Nations Interim Administration Mission in Kosovo' (UNMIK) with responsibility for promoting substantial autonomy, carrying out basic civilian administration, organising the establishment of democratic institutions, supporting the reconstruction of infrastructure and the provision of humanitarian aid, maintaining law and order, protecting human rights and assuring the safe return of refugees.[9]

Clearly, the assumption of such powers by representatives of the international community amounts to a qualification or cancellation of state sovereignty, meaning that both its internal and external aspects are affected.[10] Internally, the supreme right of a state to govern itself is temporarily annulled. Externally, the mutual recognition of state sovereignty becomes less clear-cut, since the outside administration temporarily brings a hybrid political actor into play. Furthermore, judging from recent examples, this typically happens as a consequence of a military intervention which the former sovereign authorities would, at a minimum, have preferred to avoid. At the same time, arrangements like those in Kosovo and East Timor inevitably re-open sensitive questions concerning national self-determination and the potentially super-national authority of the UN. The political, legal and institutional machinery of international society is, in other words, affected at a fundamental level and in ways that go beyond peacebuilding.

Such radical solutions to the problems of state failure and contested territories are not without historical precedents. These include the international protectorates of the League of Nations which were administrated (and prepared for independence) by advanced states,[11] and the early trusteeships of the UN which were prepared for self-government or independence by a state entrusted with this task under the supervision of the UN.[12]

Arguably, these precedents are to varying degrees burdened with colonial connotations. However, they seem to capture the institutionalised element of present-day governing arrangements as the UN (or its various organs) has taken it upon itself to authorise, establish, run and oversee such arrangements on an *ad hoc* basis. This element of supervision and accountability is further strengthened by the participation of a range of other international and non-governmental organisations whose presence increases the likelihood that misrule and failures will come to the critical attention of the international public. Kosovo, for instance, has been administrated by a veritable network of international organisations based on the four Pillars of

---

[9] Arguably, the administration of East Timor from 1999 to 2002 is an even clearer example of the temporary assumption by the UN of full sovereign authority (and legal personality) over a territory and its population. See Chopra, *supra* n. 3.

[10] On the institutional aspects of sovereignty, see M. Wight, *Systems of States* (Leicester, Leicester University Press 1977), at 129-136, and A. James, *Sovereign Statehood: The Basis of International Society* (London, Allen and Unwin 1986).

[11] J. Murray Jr., *The United Nations Trusteeship System* (Urbana, The University of Illinois Press 1957), at 7-19.

[12] Ibid., at 43-45.

UNMIK.[12a] For all its shortcomings, stemming from its incremental evolution and pragmatic nature, the potential of the current informal trusteeship machinery might not be as weak as one might think. At the same time, the temporary nature of contemporary trusteeship arrangements and the focus on rapid and effective preparation for self-government make any charges of neo-colonialism less convincing.

Terms like 'international protectorates' and 'international trusteeship' particularly capture the exceptional decision by representatives of international society to resort to institutional arrangements which part with the strict Westphalian model of international order and its clear distinction between sovereign and non-sovereign actors. Furthermore, the temporary assumption of full responsibility over a territory and its population which is then prepared for self-government echoes the means and goals of the formal UN trusteeship system. It is not least in these respects that present-day governing arrangements amount to 'an international trusteeship in everything but name' as the one in Kosovo has – with concern and a call for caution – been identified by Jackson.[13]

Consequently, the most extensive forms of transitional international administration are best seen as instances of contemporary international trusteeship arrangements. Based on the conceptual analysis above, our definition of such contemporary trusteeship arrangements contains three key elements: first, we refer to the temporary assumption of governmental authority over a territory and its population by the UN or other representatives of the international community; second, this international assumption of governmental authority is based on a relatively stable and institutionalised set of habits and practices shaped towards the comprehensive reconstruction of war-torn societies and the management of contested territories; third, the purposes of such contemporary trusteeship arrangements include the (re-)establishment of orderly and just affairs in domestic society, a progression to self-rule or, sometimes, independence from the former sovereign authorities, and the normalisation of the international relations of the territory in question. It is exactly the full assumption of governmental authority by international organisations and the possibility of recasting the sovereignty of the former authorities in various ways that makes the institution of international trusteeship qualitatively different from the practice of peacebuilding.

Following the vocabulary of Bull, international trusteeship can thus be seen as a fundamental or semi-fundamental institution of international society: a set of principles, practices and habits 'shaped towards the realization of common goals'.[14] International trusteeship may not be as indispensable to international society as the historical and sociological institutions mentioned by Bull, including diplomacy, international law and balance of power. However, in the critical situation where earlier governmental authorities have manifestly failed while alternative ones are not materialising, the possibility of resorting to international trusteeship may be of

---

12a See the contribution by Keukeleire and Thiers to this volume.

13 Jackson, *supra* n. 1, at 307.

14 H. Bull, *The Anarchical Society* (London, Macmillan 1977), at 74. See also B. Buzan, *From International to World Society? English School Theory and the Social Structure of Globalisation* (Cambridge, Cambridge University Press 2004).

critical importance to the international community. In the cases of Bosnia and Herzegovina, Kosovo and East Timor, the former sovereign authorities had demonstrated a lack of will and ability to provide for orderly and just conditions. At the same time, atrocities, civil war, outside intervention and territorial disputes had left a fatal political vacuum which could hardly be dealt with by any other means than a temporary international governance of these areas. In such circumstances, international trusteeship is first of all a pragmatic and institutionalised response to the breakdown of domestic society.

The critics of such arrangements may point to the violations of sovereignty, the risk of abuse and the pitfalls of paternalism. Clearly, such charges are not without empirical foundations. However, in the world of today, domestic disorder typically also means international disorder. For both domestic and international reasons – the reasons of order, justice and solidarity – it would therefore be a serious loss for international society if such recurrent menaces as great-power ambitions, value imperialism or a lack of resources (menaces that have been particularly associated with the first years of the so-called 'war on terror') should eventually once again lead to an abandonment of this institution.

## 2.2 The problems of contemporary trusteeship arrangements

The institutional value and legal basis of contemporary trusteeship arrangements are not, however, the only aspects of the academic and political debate on this subject. A number of practical problems must be dealt with as well, including not least those relating to the creation of democracy and the settlement of the political status of the territory under international administration, including the highly controversial decisions on the territory's constitution, political system and international legal status. These may be called the democratic problem and the constitutional problem, respectively.

The *democratic problem* follows from the fact that decisions taken by nationally elected leaders may be overruled by international administrators. Put sharply, this is a policy of imposed democracy, and imposition and control from the outside does not fit well into the logic of representative democracy. According to this logic, the government is supposed to rule and to be held accountable by an assembly – the representatives of the people – and, in turn, the assembly is supposed to be held accountable by the people at elections. This is the democratic chain of delegation and accountability.[15]

Unfortunately, trusteeship administration involves interference with this logic. International administration can hardly work if the administrators do not have both the power and the will to intervene and to overrule nationally elected leaders when they take decisions that run counter to the goals of reconstruction and peaceful

---

[15] See W. Müller, T. Bergman, and K. Strøm, 'Parliamentary Democracy: Promise and Problems', in K. Strøm, W. Müller and T. Bergman, eds., *Delegation and Accountability in Parliamentary Democracies* (Oxford, Oxford University Press 2006) 3-32.

coexistence. The question is what this does to the faith of the people in their politicians. Does it undermine the authority, credibility and legitimacy of nationally elected leaders, or does it provide them with a convenient opportunity to blame a lack of results on the international community and their 'custodians'? Clearly, the democratic chain of delegation and accountability which runs from the voters at elections to parliament, government and bureaucracy is undermined when the constituents do not have the possibility of removing some of their rulers (namely the administrators) from power at national elections, and when they have reason to believe that their own politicians cannot really be held accountable for the national state of affairs since they can always refer to demands and interferences coming from outsiders beyond their control.[16] This is not democratically healthy. Voters lose their influence and politicians are likely to lose their legitimacy. If, on the other hand, local nationalist constituencies continue to back nationalist leaders at the elections, these leaders will have the possibility of confronting the international community and their representatives on the basis of a strong popular backing. This is evidently not a desirable scenario for international trusteeship arrangements either. These problems can be seen as a reflection of the more basic and general, but not necessarily correct, prediction by Dahl that democracy cannot work at the international level.[17]

It is also clear, however, that the international community can hardly deal with these democratic problems simply by deciding that the territory in question will be governed solely from the outside until the day the trusteeship is dismantled. In order to maintain a degree of legitimacy and provide for the consolidation of peace and democracy, there has to be a gradual transfer to locally and nationally elected representatives. Local and national elections are, in any case, an important asset when it comes to the maintenance of legitimacy, the cultivation of political participation and the promotion of a sense of *empowerment*: the belief among the people that it matters that they engage in the social and political life of their country. As stressed by Baskin, local governance is the tier of public authority that citizens look to first to solve their immediate social problems.[18] It is also the level of democracy at which the citizen has the most effective opportunity to actively and directly participate in decisions made for all of society. However, in ethnically divided societies like Bosnia and Herzegovina and Kosovo, local elections are bound to confirm the ethnic distribution of the given community and to transform such patterns into legitimate structures of authority: majorities dominating minorities on a democratic

[16] This might fall under what Jackson (*supra* n. 1, at 294-315) has called the problem of paternalism in his sceptical account of the post-Cold War revival of this international institution.

[17] See R. Dahl, 'Can International Organizations Be Democratic? A Sceptic's View', in I. Shapiro and C. Hacker-Cordón, eds., *Democracy's Edges* (Cambridge, Cambridge University Press 1999) 19-37. For a more optimistic view on international democracy, see J. Nye, 'Globalization's Democratic Deficit', 80 *Foreign Affairs* (2001) and A. McGrew, 'Democracy beyond Borders?', in D. Held and A. McGrew, eds., *The Global Transformations Reader,* 1st edn. (Polity Press/Blackwell 2000) 405-419.

[18] See M. Baskin, 'Local Governance in Kosovo: A Link to Democratic Development', in Knudsen and Laustsen, eds., *supra* n. 1, 76-95. Baskin refers to a report by the International Institute for Democracy and Electoral Assistance (see at 76).

mandate. Simultaneously, the hegemonic role of ethnically based politics favours collective concepts of rights. This makes it unlikely that dissenting voices will challenge elected officials, even when they belong to the same ethnicity. To this day in Bosnia and Herzegovina, ethnically based parties dominate the political spectrum instead of the issue-based parties that are more commonly dominant in mature democracies. Hence, even the most simple and innocuous issues such as local sanitation regulations are portrayed in ethnic rather than pragmatic terms. In ethnically divided societies, local democratic governance is thus a double-edged sword, just like the powers of international administrators to overrule national and local authorities.

As for the *constitutional problem*, it has two aspects: first, whether the trusteeship is going to gain independence or not, and second, whether its constitution and political system should be built on national and ethnic divisions or not. These questions are not always easy to answer at the end of war. In order to gain the acceptance of the opposed parties, it is tempting to build the constitution on the existing ethnical, national or religious divisions of society, so that all parties can be assured that they will be represented in parliament, that they will have degrees of autonomy and minimum rights and privileges, and that there will generally be strong checks and balances in the state that comes after international administration. This is the so-called consociational model which has famously been defended by Lijphart and which has dominated the political settlement for Bosnia and Herzegovina as initially set out in the 1995 Dayton Peace Agreement.[19] This approach is strong when it comes to the goal of obtaining a peace agreement and as a basis for building a negative peace in which the parties are no longer close to war but possibly not close to democratic integration and a positive peace either. The model has been criticised for being static and inflexible, and for incorporating and strengthening rather than moderating ethnic and other divisions of society.[20] Although the contexts are radically different, this may be said to be the key problem in both Bosnia and Herzegovina after 1995 and Iraq after 2003.

The alternative is the so-called integrative model which has been promoted by Horowitz, its essence being the attempt to build a democratic system in which politicians will need votes from outside their own ethnic, national or religious groups, meaning that they will have to rely on cross-community appeals.[21] This is the model that the UN, the EU and other relevant actors have increasingly wanted to work towards in Bosnia and Herzegovina. It was probably also this vision of political and constitutional integration that they were hoping to promote in Kosovo while they were delaying the settlement of the future status of the province. Finally, the idea of integration by means of institutional design was evident in the framework for Kosovo proposed by UN negotiator Ahtisaari, before it was toppled by a stalemate in the positions of the parties, followed by Kosovo's unilateral declaration of indepen-

---

[19] See A. Lijphart, *Democracy in Plural Societies* (New Haven, Yale University Press 1977).

[20] N. Caspersen, 'Good Fences Make Good Neighbours? A Comparison of Conflict-Regulation Strategies in Postwar Bosnia', 41 *Journal of Peace Research* (2004) 569-588.

[21] D. Horowitz, *Ethnic Groups in Conflict* (Berkeley, University of California Press 1985).

dence.[22] The force of this model is clearly the long-term potential for the creation of a genuine integrative democracy and a positive peace transcending ethnic boundaries. Its weakness is that it is not very popular in divided societies. This has been evident several times in Bosnia and Herzegovina in the rejections of proposed changes to the post-conflict status quo. The parties are more interested in preserving their ethnically based constitutional privileges than in taking a chance on changes that might lead to the virtues of positive peace (and maybe EU membership) in the long run. The rejection of the Ahtisaari framework by the Serb side in Kosovo may be explained in the same way, although the prospects for the Serbs there were arguably better under that framework than under the present situation of contested independence.[23]

It follows from this that the key question of international trusteeship arrangements of the sort practised in Bosnia and Herzegovina and Kosovo is how to work out a constitutional framework that provides for short-term stability (the static impulse) and long-term progress (the dynamic impulse) at the same time. If the constitutional framework is too inflexible and static and too tied to national and ethnic divisions, as has arguably been the case in Bosnia and Herzegovina, this may hamper democratic development, political compromise and multi-ethnic integration. If the constitution is too loose and if the future status of the territory (or the future balance of power between the opposed parties) is too uncertain, there is a risk that such progress will be prevented by counterproductive strategic behaviour, as was arguably the case at the outset of the international administration of Kosovo.

Having discussed the concept of international trusteeship as well as the problems that such arrangements are likely to give rise to, we now turn to a closer study of the lessons learned in Bosnia and Herzegovina and Kosovo: how did the international administrators try to deal with the democratic and constitutional problems, what was the impact of these strategies on the national and local societies, including the peoples and the politicians, and where has this left the two trusteeships – or, rather, the two young states – today?

## 3. Democratic and constitutional problems: Lessons from Bosnia and Herzegovina

In December 1995, after over three and a half years of brutal warfare and countless serious violations of international humanitarian law, the United States brokered a peace agreement ending the war in Bosnia and Herzegovina. Representatives of the US, together with European diplomats and representatives of the three warring parties in Bosnia and Herzegovina and the neighbouring states of Croatia and the Federal Republic of Yugoslavia (Serbia and Montenegro), negotiated this agreement at

[22] On the proposed framework, see *Comprehensive Proposal for the Kosovo Status Settlement*, UN Security Council (S/2007/168/Add.1).

[23] On this point, see also the proposals in T. Knudsen, 'From UNMIK to Self-Determination? The Puzzle of Kosovo's Future Status', in Knudsen and Laustsen, eds., *supra* n. 1, 156-167.

the Wright-Patterson Air Force Base in Dayton, Ohio.[24] They accepted a divided state structure, with 51% of Bosnian territory to be put under the jurisdiction of the Muslim-Croat Federation of Bosnia and Herzegovina (FBiH) and 49% under the control of the Bosnian Serb Republika Srpska (RS) and with the status of the contested city of Brčko – currently known as the Brčko District – left unresolved.[25] Both entities and the District were to be legally subordinate to the central authorities of the state of Bosnia and Herzegovina. A massive international military and civilian presence, headed by NATO and the United Nations, was responsible for imposing and maintaining the peace.

Formally known as the General Framework for Peace in Bosnia and Herzegovina, the Dayton Peace Accords (DPA) succeeded in putting an end to the war in Bosnia and Herzegovina.[26] Although the country has remained fragile and tense, no further large-scale armed ethnic violence has occurred since 1995. Still, a broad and heterogeneous chorus of international and former Yugoslav observers have criticised the Dayton Accords for establishing an unwieldy institutional framework which, to a considerable extent, freezes in place the ethnic divisions and factions that contributed to the outbreak of conflict.[27] In other words, the critics claim that, while the Dayton Accords have a near-perfect record in maintaining a negative peace, they present a structural obstacle to the establishment of a positive peace.

In recounting the most important developments in Bosnia and Herzegovina since the war, this section will focus on two controversial aspects of the 'Dayton dictate', both relating to the democratic and constitutional problems as discussed above: (1) the extensive powers of the Office of the High Representative, which have been described as neo-colonial by some observers, and the effects thereof on the development of democratic governance in Bosnia and Herzegovina, and (2) the impact

---

[24] On the Dayton Accords, see R. Holbrooke, *To End a War* (New York, Random House 1998); I. Daalder, *Getting to Dayton: The Making of America's Bosnia Policy* (Washington, DC, Brookings Institution Press 2000); D. Chollet, *The Road to the Dayton Accords: A Study of American Statecraft* (New York, Palgrave Macmillan 2007).

[25] The Brčko District was created in 1997 after repeated unsuccessful attempts to resolve the issue of Brčko's status. Elizabeth Pond and Valery Perry have, in separate studies, written admiringly of the very robust international role in Brčko. While Pond implicitly holds Brčko forth as a model to be emulated, Perry is more sceptical, pointing to the problems in Mostar, where the international community also invested huge resources. E. Pond, *Endgame in the Balkans: Regime Change, European Style* (Washington, DC, Brookings Institution Press 2006); V. Perry, 'Democratic Ends, (Un)democratic Means? Reflections on Democratization Strategies in Brčko and in Bosnia-Herzegovina', in M. Innes, ed., *Bosnian Security after Dayton: New Perspectives* (New York, Routledge 2006) 23-50.

[26] See: <http://www.ohr.int/dpa/default.asp?content_id=379>.

[27] M. Fischer, *Peacebuilding and Civil Society in Bosnia-Herzegovina: Ten Years after Dayton* (Berlin, Lit 2006); Pond, *supra* n. 25; G. Nystuen, *Achieving Peace or Protecting Human Rights? Conflicts between Norms Regarding Ethnic Discrimination in the Dayton Peace Agreement* (Leiden, Martinus Nijhoff Publishers 2005); C. Solioz and T. Vogel, eds., *Dayton and Beyond: Perspectives on the Future of Bosnia and Herzegovina* (Baden-Baden, Nomos 2004); S. Bose, *Bosnia after Dayton: Nationalist Partition and International Intervention* (New York, Oxford University Press 2002); Caspersen, *supra* n. 20; E. Cousens and C. Cater, eds., *Toward Peace in Bosnia: Implementing the Dayton Accords* (Boulder, Lynne Riener Publishers 2001); D. Chandler, *Bosnia: Faking Democracy after Dayton* (London, Pluto Press 2000).

of the Dayton architecture on politics in Bosnia and Herzegovina, with a particular focus on the enduring power struggle between the two entities (in particular the RS) and the central state. The emphasis will be on examining the external strategies and the internal debates provoked by them.

### 3.1 The democratic challenge: The long shadow of Dayton

The role and performance of the Office of the High Representative (OHR) of Bosnia and Herzegovina figure centrally in the debate on the Dayton legacy. Annex 10 of the Accords covers the *Agreement on Civilian Implementation of the Peace Settlement.*[28] This Annex calls for the

> 'designation of a High Representative, to be appointed consistent with relevant United Nations Security Council resolutions, to facilitate the Parties' own efforts and to mobilize and, as appropriate, coordinate the activities of the organizations and agencies involved in the civilian aspects of the peace settlement.'

Article 2 of Annex 10 describes the mandate of the OHR.[29]

The High Representative is appointed by the Steering Board of the Peace Implementation Council (PIC). The PIC represents several dozen countries and international organisations, of which the following are on the Steering Board: Canada, France, Germany, Italy, Japan, Russia, the United Kingdom, the United States, the Presidency of the European Union, the European Commission and the Organisation of the Islamic Conference.[30] Since 1995, Bosnia and Herzegovina has had seven High Representatives.[31] The current incumbent (since March 2009) is the Austrian career diplomat Valentin Inzko.

In the first two years of its operation, the OHR was overshadowed by the NATO command structure. Notably, though, in December 1997, the PIC Conference decided at its meeting in Bonn to strengthen the OHR by authorising the High Representative to remove Bosnian officials, including elected officials, if they were deemed to be obstacles to the implementation of the Dayton Accords. In addition, the High Representative could promulgate crucial legislation by decree if the elected officials of Bosnia and Herzegovina proved unwilling or incapable of doing so. In sum, the High Representative had the legal authority of a colonial viceroy.[32] As stated in a 1998 report by the International Crisis Group (ICG):

---

[28] See: <http://www.ohr.int/dpa/default.asp?content_id=380>.

[29] See: <http://www.ohr.int/ohr-info/gen-info/default.asp?content_id=38612>.

[30] See: <http://www.ohr.int/pic/default.asp?content_id=38563>.

[31] See: <http://www.ohr.int/ohr-info/hrs-dhrs/>.

[32] High Representative Wolfgang Petritsch (1999-2002) later wrote that 'the introduction of the so-called "Bonn Powers" in December 1997 shifted the equation of the international presence in favour of the civilian implementation efforts and brought Bosnia closer to a protectorate-like status. (...) Eight years after their introduction, the jury is still out on the "Bonn Powers".' Petritsch's preface to Solioz and Vogel, eds., *supra* n. 27, at 12.

> 'As it became clear that Bosnia's rival ethnic leaders would never live up to their DPA commitments of their own accord, the international community changed tack. The new approach has effectively involved taking over the running of the country. It has also meant taking on the three ruling ethnically-based parties.'[33]

Nearly a year later, the ICG criticised the disparity between the sweeping authority granted to the OHR and the lack of executive power to enforce its decisions.[34] Nevertheless, external powers have never taken the most drastic available step, that of declaring Bosnia and Herzegovina an international protectorate.[35]

These 'Bonn Powers' became a point of intense debate in Bosnia and Herzegovina, with Bosnian Serb politicians, generally speaking, opposed, Bosnian Muslim politicians consistently supportive, and Bosnian Croats more agnostic on the issue. Since the inception, international observers have argued about whether the Bonn Powers have a salutary or inhibiting effect on the development of democratic governance in Bosnia and Herzegovina.[36] Probably the most robust use of these powers came during the tenure of Paddy Ashdown as High Representative, from May 2002 to May 2006. Ashdown dismissed a large number of elected officials from their offices and imposed bans on their future participation in public life. One year into his tenure, the International Crisis Group noted that 'the terminal phase of the international community's belated effort to build a self-sustaining state will be replete with paradox. In order to get out, the country's foreign guardians will have to get in more deeply.'[37]

At the core of this paradox stood the conundrum that Bosnian politicians demonstrated neither maturity nor a willingness to promulgate and implement (sometimes painful) reforms. As High Representative Ashdown curtly told the Bosnian parliament in 2003, 'The more you reform, the less I will have to. The less you reform, the more I will have to.'[38] Through a series of confrontations the international community imposed reforms by decree, which to an extent absolved the country's politicians from accountability. It could therefore be argued that the Bonn Powers, rather than consolidating the democratisation process and contributing to the construction of a viable Bosnian state, undermined the process instead.

---

33 International Crisis Group, *Doing Democracy a Disservice: 1998 Elections in Bosnia and Herzegovina*, 9 September 1998, at 5, available at: <http://www.crisisgroup.org/library/documents/report_archive/A400165_09091998.pdf>.

34 See International Crisis Group, *Is Dayton Failing?: Bosnia Four Years After the Peace Agreement*, 28 October 1999, at 42-43, available at: <http://www.crisisgroup.org/library/documents/report_archive/A400058_28101999.pdf>.

35 In 1999, the International Crisis Group considered this as one policy option. International Crisis Group, *Is Dayton Failing?*, *supra* n. 34.

36 For a critical view, see G. Knaus and F. Martin, 'Travails of the European Raj', *European Stability Initiative*, 3 July 2003, available at: <http://www.esiweb.org/index.php?lang=en&id=156&document_ID=59>.

37 International Crisis Group, *Bosnia's Nationalist Governments: Paddy Ashdown and the Paradoxes of State Building*, 22 July 2003, at ii.

38 Paddy Ashdown cited in A. Kuperman, 'Power-Sharing or Partition? History's Lessons for Keeping the Peace in Bosnia', in Innes, ed., *supra* n. 25, 41.

In addition, although Bosnian politicians were slow to realise this possibility, the OHR's use of the Bonn Powers handed its opponents a useful cudgel. In the early phases of post-war Bosnia and Herzegovina, local politicians, particularly Bosnian Serb and Bosnian Croat hard-liners, regularly confronted the OHR with blatant 'anti-Dayton' opposition grounded firmly and explicitly in nationalist arguments. This resulted in the removal from office of a considerable number of high-ranking politicians and, arguably, in a gradual erosion of their power in favour of politicians perceived at least initially as being more pliable. Yet these politicians, exemplified by the current RS Prime Minister Milorad Dodik, grounded their political legitimacy in the democratic backing of their constituents, making it much more difficult for the OHR to challenge them, even when they adopted stances or policies that were dissonant with the Dayton Accords. From the point of view of Dodik and other Bosnian Serb politicians, it was highly hypocritical for the international community simultaneously to preach democratic standards of governance and then remove politicians elected in internationally monitored and approved elections.

Looking back at the full duration of the international presence in Bosnia and Herzegovina, the OHR's ability to dismiss and appoint officials has led to some interesting developments. In January 1998, as part of the OHR's efforts to break the monopoly of the hard-line nationalist Serb Democratic Party (SDS), founded by Radovan Karadžić, the OHR 'engineered the appointment of the moderate Serb Milorad Dodik.'[39] Likewise, international diplomats at this point in time perceived Bosniak politician Haris Silajdžić to be a useful alternative to the Bosniak nationalist Alija Izetbegović.[40]

Eleven years later, in 2009, foreign diplomats and international organisations perceive Dodik and Silajdžić as major obstacles to reform in Bosnia and Herzegovina. Dodik, who enjoys massive popular support in the RS, opposes any further attempts to transfer power from the entities to the central Bosnian state.[41] He makes no secret of his desire to see the OHR leave Bosnia and Herzegovina as soon as possible. Dodik does not shirk from nationalist rhetoric and has repeatedly flirted with the explosive idea of holding a referendum on independence in the RS, and he has provocatively and derisively referred to Sarajevo as 'Teheran'.[42] This has put

---

[39] International Crisis Group, *Doing Democracy a Disservice*, *supra* n. 33, at 11.

[40] Silajdžić has played a controversial role in Bosnian politics. In 2000, the ICG lauded him as 'the first Bosnian politician to hold the international community to account for its share of the responsibility for the non-implementation of Dayton and to challenge it to meet specific time deadlines to implement certain portions of the Accords as the price for his participation in a SDP [Social Democratic Party]-led coalition.'

[41] International Crisis Group, *Bosnia's Incomplete Transition: Between Dayton and Europe*, 9 March 2009, at 8.

[42] G. Berić, 'Šta je novo u Teheranu', *Oslobođenje*, 24 August 2006. A number of observers believe that Dodik plays the referendum card instrumentally and that he is, in fact, not interested in independence or union with Serbia. Serbia supports the territorial integrity of Bosnia and Herzegovina. A loose union with the Federation of Bosnia and Herzegovina in which the RS leadership enjoys broad powers and autonomy seems to be the preferred solution for Dodik, and is certainly more attractive to him than being reduced to a minor role in an RS merged with Serbia.

him on a collision course with the international community, with Dodik virtually daring the OHR to remove him despite his democratic legitimacy. Moreover, despite serious and credible allegations of corruption in the RS, Dodik can, with good reason, point to the bloated bureaucracy and governing structure of the Federation, compared to which the RS operates rather efficiently.[43] This has allowed him to portray ongoing investigations of corruption in the RS, in which he and his allies figure as potential targets, as a campaign against the RS and, by implication, Bosnian Serbs as a whole.[44] The OHR is portrayed in the RS media as being consistently pro-Bosniak in its decisions, a charge that is easy to sustain given that the OHR is involved in strengthening the state institutions of Bosnia and Herzegovina.[45] On the Bosniak side, Haris Silajdžić at times seems trapped in a wartime mentality. Whatever their factual merits, Silajdžić's references to the 'genocidal foundation' of the RS do not present a constructive criticism of the RS' opposition to reform. On the contrary, the deployment of such politically and nationally sensitive rhetoric drastically reduces the scope for any compromise. Meanwhile on the periphery of the major Bosniak-Serb axis of disagreement, the Bosnian Croats waver between constructive engagement and idle fantasies about a third, Bosnian Croat, entity.[46] This concoction of mutually incompatible views – 'the Dayton blues' – resulted in a situation in which the nationalist elites 'had the least interest in reconciliation, because the maintenance of tensions and feelings of endangerment also maintain their privileges.'[47]

Here it is worth noting the evolution of the Bosnian Serb attitude towards the Dayton Accords since 1995. During the negotiations in Dayton, Ohio, Serbian President Slobodan Milošević kept a muzzle on Radovan Karadžić and the rest of the Bosnian Serb leadership. The Bosnian Serbs were extremely dissatisfied with the result and more or less openly resisted the Dayton Accords until 1997, when a more pliable leadership took the scene. A decade later, Bosnian Serb politicians personified by Milorad Dodik embraced 'Dayton' as the guarantor of the status of the

---

[43] Unlike the Federation, RS is not hamstrung by an unwieldy and expensive cantonal structure.

[44] On the investigations against Dodik, see International Crisis Group, *Bosnia's Incomplete Transition, supra* n. 41, at 3. The State Court of Bosnia and Herzegovina is to a considerable extent a success, as it internalises the prosecution of war criminals commenced at the international level at the International Tribunal for the Former Yugoslavia. It cooperates with similar special courts in Croatia and Serbia. Yet the aspect of the Court's work that focuses on prosecution of serious cases of corruption and organised crime is more controversial. For an example of Dodik's use of categorical and inflammatory rhetoric on the removal of Bosnian Serb officials by the OHR, see D. Šajinović, 'Smjena Jovičića neprihvatljiva', *Nezavisne novine*, 9 June 2009, available at: <http://www.nezavisne.com/dogadjaji/vijesti/41990/Smjena-Jovicica-neprihvatljiva.html>.

[45] D. Jerinić, 'Bečki valcer', *Nezavisne novine*, 9 June 2009, available at: <http://www.nezavisne.com/kolumne/vijesti/42016/Becki-valcer.html>.

[46] In recent years, mainstream politicians in Croatia have repeatedly endorsed the territorial integrity of Bosnia and Herzegovina and exhibit no appetite for the destabilising option of a third, Bosnian Croat entity.

[47] Z. Panović, 'Dejton bluz', *Danas*, 26 November 2005, available at: <http://www.b92.net/info/vesti/pregled_stampe.php?yyyy=2005&mm=11&dd=26&nav_id=181213>.

Republika Srpska within Bosnia and Herzegovina.[48] As such, Dodik completely dismisses any 'activist' reading of the Dayton Accords amounting to a gradually expanding and strong central state.[49]

These divisions are also apparent in the disparate views on the continued presence of the OHR. Since the appointment of the fifth HR, the German diplomat Christian Schwarz-Schilling, in 2006, the international community has made no secret of its desire to conclude the OHR's mission. The attempts to establish a closure date for the OHR and its strong powers to intervene in Bosnian politics has had a strong effect. On the one hand, both international and domestic advocates of continued reform fear that opponents of change need merely persevere until the last HR leaves Sarajevo. On the other hand, as the country lurches from crisis to crisis, the international community has continuously postponed the closing date and has appointed a new HR, the latest taking office in March 2009. The key question remains whether the politicians of Bosnia and Herzegovina can lead their country to EU membership without the OHR, and, indeed, whether the country can demonstrate its viability as a candidate as long as it remains under international custodianship.[50]

As of the spring of 2009, the negative dynamic created and sustained by Dodik and Silajdžić resulted in yet another postponement in the shutting down of the OHR.[51] The PIC has signalled its intentions not to close the OHR until the situation stabilises and Bosnia and Herzegovina's politicians meet specific objectives. These include a law on the disposition of state property, a resolution of the status of the contested Brčko District and full compliance with the Dayton Accords. Ideally, the OHR will then be replaced by a high-ranking EU Special Representative, whose mandate will enable him or her to guide Bosnia and Herzegovina to EU membership.[52] The sticking point will be whether the EU Special Representative will retain the 'Bonn Powers'.

Illustrating the paradoxical nature of the situation, High Representative Inzko has stated that those forces blocking mandatory reforms are responsible for delaying the OHR's departure. Dodik, meanwhile, seems determined to prove that he can outlast the OHR and that any decisions or policies implemented by the OHR will simply be repealed by the RS after the departure of the OHR. On 14 May 2009, the RS Assembly passed a controversial resolution calling not only for the suspension of the Bonn Powers but also for the reversal of previous decisions taken by the

[48] Interview with Milorad Dodik, *Politika*, 16 June 2009, available at: <http://www.politika.rs/rubrike/tema-dana/Amerika-podrzava-Dejton-i-RS.sr.html>.

[49] Indeed, the debate between Bosnian Serb and Bosniak politicians about Dayton's 'true' meaning can at times seem very familiar to connoisseurs of the American debate between judicial conservatives and those whom they accuse of 'judicial activism'. Perhaps more appropriately in a former socialist country, there are also undertones of the Marxist-Leninist debate about the gradual 'withering away of the state' – with the entities taking the place of the state.

[50] International Crisis Group, *Bosnia's Nationalist Governments*, *supra* n. 37.

[51] International Crisis Group, *Bosnia's Incomplete Transition*, *supra* n. 41.

[52] In fact, the High Representative has been 'double-hatted' as the EU Special Representative since 2002.

OHR. This attempt to roll back recent changes in Bosnia and Herzegovina has met with a demand from the OHR to annul the resolution.[53] Officials of the RS counter that the OHR is the institution stalling the transition towards European integration. As stated by Igor Radojčić, the President of the RS Assembly:

> 'The reactivation of the Bonn Powers would push Bosnia and Herzegovina backwards. (…) This should be some other time, in which the OHR is transforming itself into the special mission of the EU. I hope that this will not mean a return to 2004, because Bosnia and Herzegovina would be pushed back a bunch of years.'[54]

In the meantime, Inzko has for the first time used the Bonn Powers to remove one Bosniak and one Bosnian Serb official.[55] And the OHR and the RS are locked in a protracted struggle over the expiration of the mandate for foreign judges and employees at the State Court in Sarajevo, which prosecutes war crimes and serious organised crime. As of the writing of this chapter, the EU and the United States seem to have reached a consensus to shut down the OHR, but it remains very unclear how they will persuade the two largest groups in the country, the Bosnian Serbs and the Bosniaks, to compromise. Bosnia and Herzegovina seems stuck in a protracted constitutional crisis, and the time for overt externally imposed changes has passed.

It is thus plain to see how the long shadow of Dayton has produced dynamics that run counter to the goals of national integration and democratisation, not least with respect to accountability.

### 3.2 The constitutional challenge: From entities to statehood?

Consolidating democratic governance and achieving the cooperation of the three major ethnic groups in Bosnia and Herzegovina has been the main focus of the OHR. At the same time, the international community has, since 1995, consistently advocated the preservation of the territorial integrity of Bosnia and Herzegovina despite strong pressure from both Croatia and Serbia (until the regime changes in those countries in 1999-2000) and weak popular support among Bosnian Croat and Bosnian Serbs for Bosnian statehood. Indeed, at the international level, the recognition of Bosnian statehood dates back to April 1992. Today, Bosnian Serb politicians, in particular, occasionally flirt with the notion of a referendum on the

---

53 'PIC Meets over Bosnian Serb Challenge', *Balkaninsight.com*, 5 June 2009, available at: <http://www.balkaninsight.com/en/main/news/19935/>.

54 V. Popović, 'Zaključci bi mogli postati deklaracija', *Nezavisne novine*, 9 June 2009, available at: <http://www.nezavisne.com/dogadjaji/vijesti/41992/Zakljucci-bi-mogli-postati-deklaracija.html>.

55 M. Čubro, 'Moguća istraga protiv Radoslava Jovičića', *Nezavisne novine*, 9 June 2009, available at: <http://www.nezavisne.com/dogadjaji/vijesti/41991/Moguca-istraga-protiv-Radoslava-Jovicica.html>; J. Gudelj, 'Incko smijenio komesara MUP-a HNK', *Nezavisne novine*, 8 June 2009, available at: <http://www.nezavisne.com/dogadjaji/hronikagradova/41930/Incko-smijenio-komesara-MUP-a-HNK.html>.

independence of the RS. However, while the yearning for independence may be real, such flirtations are more likely to be tactical than strategic. Certainly, as of 2009, both Croatia and Serbia have repeatedly reiterated their support for the territorial integrity of Bosnia and Herzegovina.[56] Regardless of the internal tribulations of the Bosnian state, the fact remains, the two neighbouring states – which are simultaneously the metropoles of the Bosnian Croats and Bosnian Serbs – recognise that challenges to its territorial integrity would have a destabilising effect on the entire region. This is a crucial difference compared to the situation in the early 1990s.

As seen above, after nearly a decade and a half, the Western assumption that Bosnian citizens would, over time, turn away from nationalist politicians seems false. To a considerable degree, this is because the Dayton architecture itself reinforces the ethnic segregation which it seeks to dismantle. Even absenting nationalist sentiments and the historical wounds of ethnic strife, it is an entirely rational, albeit short-sighted, course of action for Bosnian politicians of all ethnicities at the entity level to pursue a strategy of preserving their own political power base. Yet one should also keep in mind that the first multi-party elections held in the then Socialist Republic of Bosnia and Herzegovina in November 1990 already resulted in electoral triumphs for the three nationalist parties.[57] Dayton can therefore not be blamed for everything, as High Representative Inzko has observed.[58] Moreover, there are some indications that the majority of the population, however begrudgingly, accepts the need to coexist and interact with neighbours of other ethnicities.[59]

The international community has notched up certain successes in Bosnia and Herzegovina, but the country remains deeply torn by internal disagreements.[60] The three mutually hostile armies present in Bosnia and Herzegovina in 1995 have been replaced by a single armed force. Other central institutions include a central bank, a

---

[56] In the case of Serbia, such declarations are invariably coupled with unequivocal emphasis on RS' status as one of two entities in Bosnia and Herzegovina. D.R., 'Dejton garant mira', *Večernje novosti*, 25 May 2009, available at: <http://www.novosti.rs/code/navigate.php?Id=1&status=jedna&vest=146530&title_add=Dejton%20garant%20mira&kword_add=bih,%20Boris%20Tadić>. For a statement of Croatian support for Bosnian territorial integrity, see, 'Mesić: BiH mora opstati', *RTS*, 26 May 2009, available at: <http://www.rts.rs/page/stories/sr/story/11/Region/63817/Mesić:+BiH+mora+opstati.html>.

[57] 'Furthermore, as virtually all Western postmortems of the Bosnian experience point out, if elections and other democratic forms are brought in too early, they can serve to polarize a conflicted society rather than move it toward urgently needed commonality, tolerance, and compromise.' Pond, *supra* n. 25, at 141.

[58] N. Krsman, 'Dejtonski sporazum nije izvor svih problema BiH', 17 May 2009, available at: <http://www.nezavisne.com/dogadjaji/vijesti/40915/Dejtonski-sporazum-nije-izvor-svih-problema-BiH.html>.

[59] A. Omeragić, 'Istraživanje UNDP: Srbi, Bošnjaci i Hrvati su za suživot u BiH', *Oslobođenje*, 8 September 2006.

[60] For an overview of the achievements seen from the perspective of a former HR, see P. Ashdown, *State-Building in a Post-Conflict Environment: Lessons Learned in Bosnia and Herzegovina*, lecture held at the European Studies Centre of St. Antony's College, 26 April 2006, available at: <http://www.sant.ox.ac.uk/esc/docs/AshdownLecture26April06.pdf>. See also P. Ashdown, *Swords and Ploughshares: Building Peace in the 21st Century* (London, Weidenfeld & Nicholson 2007).

customs service, a state court and a national investigative agency function, though the latter two are often the focus of bitter polemics along ethnic lines. Despite major efforts and considerable pressure applied by the international community, in particular the US and the EU, the Republika Srpska has successfully resisted attempts to dismantle its police force.[61] This is particularly significant given the crucial role that the dissolution of the police played in the lead-up to the war.[62]

In the end, four positions can be discerned with respect to the establishment of a centralist state. The US and the EU view the creation and maintenance of multiethnic institutions as a key prerequisite for the viability of Bosnia and Herzegovina and hence its candidacy for EU membership. From the perspective of the Republika Srpska, these same efforts appear as an attempt to dismantle the entity, the existence of which is the Bosnian Serbs' main triumph from the war and the *raison d'être* of their political leadership. From the Bosniak nationalist side, the mere existence of the RS is an unacceptable mockery of the Bosniaks who were killed and displaced during the formative phase of the Bosnian Serb republic. Given the very considerable problems apparent in the functioning of the Federation of Bosnia and Herzegovina, it often appears that the Bosniak nationalists are not so much interested in the establishment of a functioning state as they are in settling scores with the Republika Srpska. Indeed, politicians in the RS have a legitimate point when they observe that the RS is a comparatively more efficient entity. Finally, the Bosnian Croats, the least numerous of the three main ethnicities in Bosnia and Herzegovina, tend to go along with the Federation's politics, although they try to maximise their position within the Federation and still occasionally float suggestions for the establishment of a third, ethnically Croat, entity.[63]

Hovering over all of this are two questions: (1) should or could the Dayton structure be renegotiated?; and (2) could such a negotiation possibly be affected by the leaders of the three ethnic groups, who tend to perceive any changes to the status quo in zero-sum terms?[64]

Over time, the carrot of EU membership has come to function as the main incentive for reforms in Bosnia and Herzegovina. To date, however, it appears not to be sufficient to induce major reform.[65] While all indications are that Bosnian citizens, regardless of ethnicity, covet the dream of EU membership – and particularly the

---

[61] International Crisis Group, *Bosnia's Stalled Police Reform: No Progress, No EU*, 6 September 2005; T. Donais, 'The Limits of Post-Conflict Police Reform', in Innes, ed., *supra* n. 25, 173-190.

[62] C. Nielsen, *The Bosnian Serb Ministry of Internal Affairs: Genesis, Performance and Command and Control, 1990-1992*, United Nations International Criminal Tribunal for the Former Yugoslavia, Expert Report in Prosecutor v. Momčilo Krajišnik (IT-00-39), 2004 (revised 2008).

[63] Bosnian Croat yearnings for a third entity receive tactical support from Bosnian Serb politicians, whose interest in a weak Federation is obvious.

[64] Paddy Ashdown and Richard Holbrooke, the Balkan veteran who serves as the United States Special Envoy for Afghanistan and Pakistan in the Obama Administration, have argued that the disbandment of the two entities in Bosnia and Herzegovina or the creation of new entities would provoke renewed conflict. P. Ashdown and R. Holbrooke, 'Sleepwalking in the Balkans', *Project Syndicate*, 4 November 2008, available at: <http://www.project-syndicate.org/commentary/holbrooke6>.

[65] F. Kovačević, 'Šta je nama Brisel', *Oslobođenje*, 14 January 2009.

ability to travel and work in the EU without a visa – the potential real benefits of such membership do not inspire change at home. Very little substantial progress has been made on the vast array of technical and legal prerequisites for the accession process.[66] As the ICG laconically observed already in 2000: 'If Bosnians appreciated either the extent to which some of their free and easy ways will have to change or the Herculean effort that will be required to secure EU membership, many might conclude that drowning now is preferable to swimming for years. As it is, ignorance is bliss.'[67] Seen in this context, the EU's decision in 2008 to sign a Stabilisation and Association Agreement (SAA),[68] a critical stepping stone on the path to EU membership – despite serious problems with internal reforms in Bosnia and Herzegovina –, sent a very troubling signal.

The EU in Bosnia and Herzegovina seems stuck between two mutually unsatisfactory positions. On the one hand, EU and other European officials do not hesitate to warn the Bosnian public and their politicians that Bosnia and Herzegovina lags far behind other (potential) candidates for EU membership in South-Eastern Europe.[69] On the other hand, the EU appears concerned that overly robust action against obstructionist forces might destabilise the country. From this vantage point, it can often seem that the EU's main concern is to keep a decrepit and dysfunctional vehicle moving forwards rather than incur the potential risks of confrontation and structural reform. Sensing the limited appetite of the EU for confrontation, Bosnian politicians know that irresponsible or recalcitrant behaviour will go unpunished. If, as is the current assumption, an EU special envoy replaces the OHR, then the EU must think very carefully about the powers that will be vested in this person, as well as about the degree of flexibility that will be permitted in the policy of conditionality and negotiations for EU membership.[70] Already some have criticised the EU's July 2009 decision to omit Bosnia and Herzegovina from the visa liberalisation extended to Macedonia, Montenegro and Serbia.[71]

The Dayton model of a state of entities has only produced modest and hard-won progress towards real statehood, but the EU and the UN may not be ready to risk a renegotiation of Dayton. As of 2009, the state of Bosnia and Herzegovina remains in limbo not least due to its wartime constitution. Put simply, the predominantly consociational model has supported the nationalist policies of the entities, and this

---

66 European Commission, *Bosnia and Herzegovina 2008 Progress Report*, 5 November 2008, available at: <http://ec.europa.eu/enlargement/pdf/press_corner/key-documents/reports_nov_2008/bosnia_herzegovina_progress_report_en.pdf>.

67 International Crisis Group, *Thessaloniki and After (II): The EU and Bosnia*, 20 June 2003, at 1-2.

68 Council of the EU, 'EU Signs Stabilization and Association Agreement with Bosnia and Herzegovina', 16 June 2008, available at: <http://www.consilium.europa.eu/uedocs/cms_Data/docs/pressdata/en/gena/101234.pdf>.

69 See, for example, the interview with Karolina Ravu, the chief of the Council of Europe delegation in Bosnia and Herzegovina, in *Nezavisne novine*, 9 June 2009.

70 See S. Blockmans, *Tough Love: The European Union's Relations with the Western Balkans* (The Hague, T.M.C. Asser Press 2007), at 68.

71 S. Latal, 'EU Visa Plan Leaves Bosnia "Isolated"', 16 July 2009, *Balkaninsight.com*, available at: <http://www.balkaninsight.com/en/main/news/21110/>.

has forced the international administrators in the PIC and the OHR to continue an interventionist policy which runs counter to the logic of representative democracy.

## 4. Democratic and constitutional problems: Lessons from Kosovo

On 9 June 1999, NATO and the Federal Republic of Yugoslavia signed the Kumanovo Treaty (formally known as the Military Technical Agreement)[72] ending NATO's aerial bombardment of the Federal Republic of Yugoslavia which had commenced on 24 March 1999.[73] Owing to the dramatic changes caused by the armed conflict, most analysts of Kosovo quickly forgot that the Rambouillet conference in March 1999 had created a constitutional framework for the administration of Kosovo.[74] This framework was scrapped in favour of UN Security Council Resolution 1244 (1999), which foresaw a five-stage process for the stabilisation of Kosovo:[75]

> Phase I: The Mission would set up administrative structures, deploy international civilian police, provide emergency assistance for returning refugees and displaced people, restore public services, and train local police and judiciary. It would also develop a phased economic recovery plan and seek to establish a self-sustaining economy;
>
> Phase II: The focus would be on administration of social services and utilities and consolidation of the rule of law. Administration of such sectors as health and education would be transferred to local, and possibly regional, authorities. Preparation for elections would begin;
>
> Phase III: UNMIK would finalise preparations and conduct elections for a Kosovo Transitional Authority;
>
> Phase IV: UNMIK would help Kosovo's elected representatives organise and set up provisional institutions for democratic and autonomous self-government and transfer its remaining administrative responsibilities, while supporting the consolidation of Kosovo's provisional institutions; and
>
> Phase V: The concluding phase would depend on a final settlement of the status of Kosovo. UNMIK would oversee the transfer of authority from Kosovo's provisional institutions to institutions established under a political settlement.

---

[72] See: <http://www.nato.int/KFOR/docu/docs/pdf/mta.pdf>.

[73] See: <http://www.nato.int/kosovo/docu/a990609a.htm>. For the background, a useful primer for non-experts on the complex Kosovo issue is T. Judah, *Kosovo: What Everyone Needs to Know* (New York, Oxford University Press 2008).

[74] M. Weller, 'The Rambouillet Conference on Kosovo', 75 *International Affairs* (1999) 163-203. Weller was an advisor to the Kosovo delegation during the Rambouillet Conference.

[75] UNSC Press Release, 17 November 2001, available at: <http://www.un.org/News/Press/docs/2001/SC7203.doc.htm>. Serbia, with support from Russia, has insisted from the outset that UNSCR 1244 guarantees territorial integrity of the Federal Republic of Yugoslavia (later Serbia and Montenegro), thus including Kosovo, while Kosovo Albanians and Western diplomats have interpreted the Resolution as leaving the final status of Kosovo to be determined at a later date.

As in the case of Bosnia and Herzegovina, the international effort was composed of military and civilian components, led respectively by NATO and the UN.[76]

Resolution 1244 recognised that Kosovo was still formally part of the Federal Republic of Yugoslavia and made no determination on the future status of Kosovo. In practice, however, full authority for Kosovo was transferred to the United Nations Interim Administration Mission in Kosovo (UNMIK) and other international civilian and military organisations. This mission was widely perceived – both by its supporters and detractors, as well as by the majority Kosovo Albanian population – as laying the groundwork for the establishment of a viable and functioning independent state of Kosovo. Indeed, it can be argued that the history of the international interim administration of Kosovo has been a case study in how difficult it is to disentangle post-conflict reconstruction and reforms from state building, particularly when the majority of the population desires independence. Hence, as in the previous case of Bosnia and Herzegovina, the international community was from the outset struggling with the challenge of creating or imposing a real democracy and confronting a fundamental disagreement as to the basic political settlement in which this democracy was supposed to evolve. Moreover, Bosnia and Herzegovina and Kosovo shared similar security challenges: 'organized crime, corruption, and ethnic bias'.[77]

### 4.1 The democratic challenge: The long shadow of Resolution 1244

Both the international and internal administration of Kosovo evolved in the transitional period from 1999 to 2008.[78] In the early stages of UNMIK, a Joint Interim Administrative Structure and an Interim Administrative Council existed as an intermediary between UNMIK and Kosovo's leaders. In May 2001, this was replaced by the Constitutional Framework for Provisional Self-Government,[79] which was designed to foster the creation of a viable indigenous governing structure. In effect, the Framework functioned as a government coordinating the work of incipient ministries. Conceived as a way to push forward self-governance, the structure could act as long as it moved within the guidelines imposed by UNMIK, which could veto the Framework government's decisions. In practice, the relationship between UNMIK and the Framework proved to be turbulent at times.

---

[76] For an overview of the international system in Kosovo, see S. Jones, et al., *Establishing Law and Order after Conflict* (Santa Monica, CA, RAND Corporation 2005), at 27-60.

[77] Ibid., at 28.

[78] Writing in June 2005, the Serb sociologist Dušan Janjić outlined four phases from 1999 to 2005: 1. May-December 1999: the end of war and the creation of an international military and civilian administration, accompanied by ethnic Albanian returns and a Serb exodus; 2. 2000-2002: the construction of the international interim administration, 'standards without status'; 3. 2003-March 2004: the transformation of the UN mission into a mission of building of a Kosovan state, accompanied by an escalation of ethnic Albanian extremism, 'standards before status'; and 4. March 2004-June 2005: the renovation and strengthening of international institutions in Kosovo and the beginning of the process of defining the final status of Kosovo, 'standards and status'. D. Janjić, *Ogledi o Kosovu* (Belgrade, Draslar partner 2007) at 341.

[79] See: <http://www.unmikonline.org/pub/misc/FrameworkPocket_ENG_Dec2002.pdf>.

At the outset of the international administration of Kosovo, Kosovo Albanians were profoundly grateful for the international intervention which had expelled Federal Yugoslav (Serbian) military and police forces from Kosovo. Yet, as the International Crisis Group observed as early as December 1999, the 'honeymoon' quickly ended:

> 'Many Kosovars' frustration has been aggravated by the feeling that they are not being sufficiently consulted by the international community and that, after a decade of disenfranchisement and apartheid instituted by the Serbs, they are again being shut out of the process of rebuilding their homeland.'[80]

The sweeping nature of the UNMIK and NATO mandates created false expectations that the 'internationals' would solve anything. Attempts by locals to take initiatives were rebuffed, creating a damaging gap that inhibited transfer of responsibility to the local population.

In Kosovo, the first post-war elections were held in October 2000, a little over a year after the end of armed conflict.[81] This meant that the international administrators confronted some of the same problems seen in Bosnia and Herzegovina. Most notably, the elections took place in an extremely tense security atmosphere and resulted in a resounding victory for nationalist parties.

In some ways, though, Kosovo presented a less complex situation. Instead of having to cope with three mutually antagonistic ethnic groups, as was the case in Bosnia and Herzegovina, Kosovo after the war featured only two major groups. The Kosovo Liberation Army (UÇK), the armed faction of the majority Kosovo Albanian population, disbanded within approximately a year of the end of the war.[82] The Serb minority remaining in Kosovo was, with the exception of a few enclaves, concentrated in the northern portion of Kosovo, north of the Ibar river.[83] Although far from desirable, the stark separation of the two populations made administration easier and reduced the risk of violence. At the same time, the geographically concentrated nature of the Serb minority also created the risk of a *de facto* territorial division of Kosovo, an option actively encouraged by Belgrade, which maintained and financed parallel structures.[84]

---

80 International Crisis Group, *Starting from Scratch in Kosovo: The Honeymoon Is Over*, 10 December 1999.

81 Kosovo Serbs boycotted the elections. During the early stages of UNMIK's existence, the Serbs in Kosovo tended, on the whole, to boycott the Kosovo Albanian or international structures, fearing that engagement could be construed as implicit recognition of the separation of Kosovo from Serbia.

82 Covert weapons caches and splinter groups remained a problem, however. The ethnic Albanian guerrilla movement in Kosovo also spawned a similar group in Macedonia which played an important role in the brief low-intensity armed conflict in Macedonia in 2001.

83 Several other minorities such as Roma and Turks shared experiences with the Serb minority as victims of discrimination and ethnically motivated violent attacks.

84 Janjić, *Ogledi o Kosovu*, *supra* n. 78, at 94-95.

### 4.2 The constitutional challenge: From postponement to contested independence

The vast majority of Serbs both in Kosovo and in Serbia proper have consistently opposed the independence of Kosovo. Seen from the vantage point of Serb nationalism, Kosovo and Metohija, as the Serbs call the region, holds a sacred spot as the cradle of Serb civilisation.[85] Simply put, Serbia without Kosovo could never be considered complete. The ouster of Slobodan Milošević, who had served as Serbian and Yugoslav president in the 1990s, did not produce any palpable improvement in Serbian-Albanian relations. Rather, Serbian politics under President (former Prime Minister) Vojislav Koštunica were considerably more principled in their nationalism in comparison to the opportunistic use of nationalism during the Milošević era.[86] The Federal Republic of Yugoslavia did, in 2001, establish a Coordination Centre for Kosovo and Metohija, which was charged with liaising with UNMIK. However, the Federal Yugoslav (later Serbian) institutions designated to deal with Kosovo suffered from internal political strife and a palpable lack of interest in the human plight of Kosovo's Serbs strikingly at odds with their rhetorical commitment to a 'Serb Kosovo'.[87]

A political and intellectual minority among Serbs and Kosovo Albanians has for some time argued consistently that both Serbs and Albanians would be better off if a stable relationship could be established between the two groups.[88] On the Serbian side, liberal intellectuals, and even 'the father of the Serb nation', the writer Dobrica Ćosić, have argued that Kosovo presents a dangerous cancer that prevents a recuperation of the Serbian polity as well as the possibility of discussing any of the other critical issues affecting the Serbian state and society.[89] They argue that only a Serbia without Kosovo can create a viable functioning democratic state and prepare for European Union membership. Or, as paraphrased by the ICG, 'Democracy in Serbia is incompatible with absorbing a province most of whose population (comprising as much as 20 per cent of Serbia's total) wants nothing to do with a Serbian or Yugoslav state.'[90] On the Albanian side, the liberal minority recognises that violence against ethnic minorities necessarily begets crime and violence in Kosovan society as a whole. Already in 1999, Kosovo Albanian journalists 'warned that the violence against Serbs would have consequences for the Albanians themselves.'[91]

---

[85] A vast literature exists on this topic. See N. Malcolm, *Kosovo: A Short History* (New York, New York University Press 1998), V. Jovičić, M. Petrović and O. Popović, *Kosovo u svesti i nadahnuću srpskoga naroda* (Šabac, Glas podrinja 1988) and D. Bataković, *Kosovo i Metohija u srpsko-arbanaškim odnosima* (Belgrade, Čigoja štampa 2006).

[86] Even as of 2009, only one political party of any significance in Serbia openly supports Kosovo's independence.

[87] International Crisis Group, *Kosovo toward Final Status*, 24 January 2005, at 16; Janjić, *Ogledi o Kosovu, supra* n. 78.

[88] On alternative proposals for a solution of the Kosovo conflict in the 1990s, see F. Bieber, *Nationalismus in Serbien vom Tode Titos bis zum Ende der Ära Milošević* (Wien, Lit Verlag 2005), at 436-453.

[89] Janjić, *Ogledi o Kosovu, supra* n. 78; D. Ćosić, *Kosovo* (Belgrade, Novosti 2004).

[90] International Crisis Group, *A Kosovo Roadmap (I): Addressing Final Status*, 1 March 2002, at ii.

[91] International Crisis Group, *Kosovo Report Card*, 28 August 2000, at 18.

Lurking in the background was the perceived double standard of permitting the Kosovo Albanians to exercise their right to self-determination while denying this right to the Bosnian Serbs. Indeed, some Serb politicians at times seemed to float the idea of a *quid pro quo* in which Serbia would agree to the independence of Kosovo in exchange for gaining the Republika Srpska. The Western powers did not accept this idea, not least because it was based on a superficial analysis of the two cases. Most significantly, proponents of such a trade did not differentiate between Kosovo – which had a strong legal and constitutional status in the Socialist Federal Republic of Yugoslavia from 1974 to 1990 – and the Republika Srpska, which was created through warfare.

The question of the final territorial status of Kosovo dominated the post-war landscape throughout the period from 1999 to 2008.[92] Given the lack of international unanimity (strong Russian and Chinese dissension) and the absolute opposition of Serbia to the independence of Kosovo, as well as the shattered economy and polity, the reluctance to tackle the status question was perhaps understandable.[93] Yet prolonging the status quo was intensely problematic for at least three reasons. First, it was unrealistic to ignore the strong preference of the Kosovo Albanians for independence, which quickly manifested itself through impatience with international administration. Second, the deferral of status decisions based itself on an equally naïve assumption that Belgrade would eventually 'come around' to an acceptance of Kosovan statehood. This view both ignored the centrality of Kosovo to Serbia's self-image and denied the possibility that unresolved status would feed optimism in Belgrade for partition or other solutions short of independence. Third, and perhaps most crucially, the deferral of a status determination arguably discouraged reforms. In an attempt to counter this, the international administrators, in 2002, devised the phrase 'standards before status'. This policy aimed to communicate to the Kosovo Albanians that they could not expect to achieve independence until they lived up to internationally accepted standards of governance and, in particular, minority rights. From the perspective of the UN, a substantial risk also existed of using an unrealistic benchmark for mission success and therefore being forced to keep the mission going indefinitely.[94] It is therefore somewhat astonishing that it took over a year for UNMIK to decide on what these standards actually were, and then proceed to formulate them in a technocratic manner that proved difficult for local decision-makers to comprehend.[95]

---

[92] In September 2002, the Serb sociologist Dušan Janjić quipped that 'Kosovo is an exceptionally difficult task for the authorities in Belgrade. Generally, Kosovo is not a bit easier for UNMIK or the international community respectively'. See Janjić, *Ogledi*, *supra* n. 78, at 123.

[93] Here, the international element of the Kosovo status question should be noted. Leaving aside the very fragile internal structure of Kosovo, all international partners were conscious of (and feared) the precedent that recognising Kosovo might set.

[94] See United Nations Report of the Secretary-General, *No Exit without a Strategy: Security Council Decision-Making and the Closure or Transition of UN Peacekeeping Operations* (S/2001/394), 20 April 2001.

[95] Marc Weller helpfully notes the gap between the first use of the 'standards before status' in 2002 and the development of eight standards announced in December 2003. M. Weller, *Negotiating the Final Status of Kosovo*, Chaillot Paper No. 114 (Paris, Institute for Security Studies 2008), at 18-19.

In considering the question of status, the International Crisis Group helpfully differentiated between an 'external' and an 'internal' dimension.

> 'The "external" dimension involves devising a process to address final status, including all of the different actors with a stake in Kosovo's future. The "internal" dimension concerns the development of Kosovo's own democratic institutions, the rule of law and human rights, so as to prepare Kosovo for whatever final status may eventually be agreed.'[96]

Seen from this perspective, 'standards before status' meant prioritising the internal over the external dimension. Yet, insofar as the standards included the building of sustainable institutions, it proved impossible to separate or differentiate this from the construction of an independent state, particularly given the majority's preference for independence.

The events of March 2004 demonstrated just how quickly the situation could deteriorate in a territory under interim administration and highlighted the bankruptcy of the 'standards before status' strategy. In a period lasting several days, angry ethnic Albanians carried out a series of attacks on the residences, places of worship and businesses of minorities – in particular those of the Serb minority. Both KFOR and UNMIK 'almost completely lost control' and proved abjectly incapable of maintaining public order or guaranteeing the security of non-Albanians.[97] The failure of the international community to investigate these events and to hold those responsible for the violence accountable destroyed any nascent trust that Kosovo's Serbs had in the interim administration or the local ethnic Albanian administration.[98] The March 2004 crisis also highlighted the conundrum that the ethnic Albanian majority's treatment of ethnic minorities was far removed from internationally acceptable standards, but that the situation might continue to deteriorate as long as the final status question was not resolved. The solution therefore seemed to point towards a decision favouring Kosovan independence in exchange for draft constitutions and laws that would ensure the protection of minority rights in an independent Kosovo.

The official UN study on the March 2004 riots criticised the 'standards before status' policy and instead recommended moving towards a resolution of Kosovo's status.[99] In response to this quandary, the UN, in October 2005, finally gave the green light for status negotiations and the following month appointed former Finnish President Martti Ahtisaari as the UN special envoy to devise a plan for the final status of Kosovo.[100] This phase is typically called 'standards with status'.[101]

---

96 International Crisis Group, *A Kosovo Roadmap (I)*, *supra* n. 90, at i.

97 Human Rights Watch, *Failure to Protect: Anti-Minority Violence in Kosovo, March 2004*, 25 July 2004, available at: <http://www.hrw.org/en/reports/2004/07/25/failure-protect>.

98 Human Rights Watch, *Not on the Agenda: The Continuing Failure to Address Accountability in Kosovo Post-March 2004*, 29 May 2006, available at: <http://www.hrw.org/en/reports/2006/05/29/not-agenda-0>.

99 Report of SRSG Kai Eide (S/2004/613), 30 July 2004.

100 Report of SRSG Kai Eide, *A Comprehensive Review of the Situation in Kosovo* (S/2005/635), 7 October 2005.

101 Weller, *supra* n. 95, at 82.

Starting in February 2006, Ahtisaari supervised negotiations between delegations representing the Kosovo Albanians and Serbia.[102] To no one's surprise, these negotiations did not produce any breakthrough but were rather stuck in a permanent impasse as the independence question was perceived by both sides as a zero-sum issue – as indeed it was.[103] Although willing to permit certain limited concessions on the extent of self-governance in Kosovo, Serbia did not wish to yield on its territorial integrity. The Kosovo Albanians felt assured of strong backing from the West, in particular from the US. The EU and the US directed their main pressure on the Kosovo Albanians towards the prevention of a unilateral declaration of independence and not towards a compromise solution with Serbia.[104] More subtly, the Kosovo Serbs felt that their particular interests were not always respected or accurately represented by Belgrade.[105] Yet all parties shared a common interest in not being perceived as being so recalcitrant as to sabotage the talks.[106] Unfortunately, as frustration mounted on the Serbian side, Serb officials launched a number of personal attacks on Ahtisaari.[107]

Once the negotiations of Kosovo's status finally commenced, Serbia began to produce some interesting creative legal solutions designed to show that options short of full independence were possible. Yet after years of boycotts and obstructionism from Belgrade, this had an unconvincing air about it. As the ICG had argued in 2005: 'Perhaps Belgrade's biggest problem is that its consistent unwillingness to cooperate with UNMIK and the international community on issues ranging from car license plates to war crimes has painted it into a corner from which it is unable to affect Kosovo policy positively.'[108]

In his detailed analysis of the final status negotiations, Marc Weller observes that both sides were well aware of the precedent set by the Dayton Accords in Bosnia and Herzegovina. From the Serbian side, this meant seeking assurances that

---

102 Ibid., at 26.

103 While constructive criticism of the negotiations is certainly possible and legitimate, the zero-sum nature of the status question cannot be ignored.

104 Weller observes that 'during the Ahtisaari talks, the European actors appeared to focus more on the need to maintain their own unity, than on the substance of the negotiations.' Weller, *supra* n. 95, at 94.

105 Both Oliver Jovanović, an erstwhile representative of moderate Kosovo Serbs and later Serbian State Secretary for Kosovo and Metohija, and sociologist Dušan Janjić have pointed to this problem. Janjić, *Ogledi o Kosovu, supra* n. 78, at 94-95. In Bosnia and Herzegovina, Ivan Lovrenović has argued analogously that the Bosnian Croats, particularly moderates living in enclaves in central Bosnia, suffered from the extreme nationalist positions adopted by Herzegovinian Croats and official Croatia in the 1990s. I. Lovrenović, *Bosanski hrvati: Esej o agoniji jedne evropsko-orijentalne mikrokulture* (Zagreb, Durieux 2002).

106 Weller, *supra* n. 95, at 30-31.

107 Weller, *supra* n. 95, at 43. These verbal barbs paled in comparison to the rhetoric in Serbian tabloids, which accused Ahtisaari, among other things, of being paid by 'the Albanian mafia'. Kurir, 'Ahtisari je albanski plaćenik', 16 July 2007, available at: <http://www.naslovi.net/2007-07-16/kurir/ahtisari-je-albanski-placenik/410160>.

108 International Crisis Group, *Kosovo toward Final Status*, *supra* n. 87, at 18. In this respect, however, a notable shift occurred after Kosovo's independence. UNMIK, which had hitherto been the object of Serb ire, was transformed into a desirable partner when juxtaposed with the new European Union mission to Kosovo.

municipalities could associate with each other and enjoy substantial local autonomy – with an eye to the formation of a regional entity. For precisely the same reasons, the Kosovo Albanians, while willing to entertain substantial concessions on minority rights and the protection of cultural heritage sites, 'were more hesitant when it came to power-sharing issues. The experience of Bosnia and Herzegovina taught the Kosovo delegation to be wary of short-term concessions in this area that would make the territory ungovernable in practice.'[109]

In March 2007, Ahtisaari unveiled his *Comprehensive Proposal for the Kosovo Status Settlement* (henceforth 'the Ahtisaari Plan')[110] and recommended that Kosovo be granted independence. In order to salve concerns about a potential 'Kosovo precedent', Ahtisaari and the UN Secretary-General referred repeatedly to the uniqueness of Kosovo.[111] The Ahtisaari Plan included strong and permanent guarantees for minority rights and, while refraining from declaring Kosovan independence to be a fact, bestowed all the institutions associated with an independent state upon Kosovo.[112]

Serbia, with strong support from Russia as a permanent member of the UN Security Council, discarded the Ahtisaari Plan. Serbia and Russia called instead for new negotiations which would take as a point of departure the pre-Ahtisaari status quo. The EU and the US instead pressed for the UN Security Council to endorse the Plan.[113] In late 2007, a new round of negotiations did take place under the leadership of the German diplomat Wolfgang Ischinger. The context of these negotiations was, if anything, less promising than the 'Ahtisaari round'. All along, the events of March 2004 lingered in the minds of the participants, and 'the UN Secretary-General warned that the present impasse might lead to events on the ground taking on a "momentum of their own, putting at serious risk the achievements and legacy of the United Nations in Kosovo".'[114]

At the beginning of 2008, it became clear to all concerned that the proclamation of Kosovo's independence was a matter of time. On 17 February 2008, Kosovo declared its independence and almost immediately received the recognition of the three Western permanent members of the UN Security Council, the US, the UK and France. Serbia, with full Russian support, of course refused to recognise Kosovo. As of October 2009, 62 UN members (among which 22 out of 27 EU Member States) have recognised Kosovo.

Kosovo achieved legally contested statehood in 2008, but this meant the entry onto the international stage of a state with severe internal political, economic, cul-

---

[109] Weller, *supra* n. 95, at 36-37.

[110] See: <http://www.unosek.org/unosek/en/statusproposal.html>.

[111] Weller, *supra* n. 95, at 44.

[112] The Ahtisaari Plan also prohibited Kosovo from entering into a state union with any other state (presumably Albania). Although consistently raised as a probable scenario by Serb opponents of Kosovan statehood, most experts on the area heavily discount the possibility of a union between Albania and Kosovo, pointing out the mutual disinterest in this option. J. Batt, ed., *Is There an Albanian Question?* Chaillot Paper No. 107 (Paris, Institute for Security Studies 2008).

[113] Weller, *supra* n. 95, at 57.

[114] Weller, *supra* n. 95, at 66.

tural and environmental problems. A year after the promulgation of Kosovo's constitution, the International Steering Group representing the international community claimed that 'the people of Kosovo have made significant progress in building a democratic, multi-ethnic State on the principles of democracy and human rights in accordance with its European perspective.'[115] Kosovo was also admitted to a number of important international organisations, in particular the International Monetary Fund and the World Bank. Nonetheless, in September 2008, the International Crisis Group observed a myriad of difficulties, most crucially that 'divisions between Albanian and Serb areas have widened, and prospects for a unitary state are evaporating.'[116] Serbia continued to resist the EU's and the US' desire to implement the Ahtisaari Plan and in particular the planned transition from UNMIK to an EU mission (known as European Union Rule of Law Mission in Kosovo, EULEX).[117] In general, however, Priština and Belgrade seemed to be converging towards the policy articulated by US Vice-President Joseph Biden when he visited the region in May 2009: let us agree to disagree, but work together pragmatically to resolve shared problems.[118]

With the move to independence, Kosovo's international status has finally been settled, but not on the basis of national and international consensus, and not in a way that has solved the internal constitutional disagreements between Albanians and Serbs.

## 5. The EU solution: From Dayton and Kumanovo to Brussels?

In conclusion, it is evident that the problems of international trusteeship have indeed presented themselves with full force in Bosnia and Herzegovina as well as in Kosovo. To recapitulate, these problems include (1) the risk of undermining the democratic chain of delegation and accountability which runs from the voters at elections to parliament, government and bureaucracy, and (2) the risk that constitutional or governing arrangements imposed from the outside will either be too attached to ethnic divisions and therefore too static, or too uncertain with respect to the sharing of power and the settlement of international status to provide for democratic development. Judging from the lessons from Bosnia and Herzegovina and Kosovo, the ultimate questions regarding the management of international trusteeships are more precisely as follows: first, should the international administrators

---

115 Statement of the International Steering Group, quoted in *VIP Daily News Report*, Issue No. 4210, 16 June 2009.

116 International Crisis Group, *Kosovo's Fragile Transition*, 25 September 2008, at i.

117 See the contribution by Keukeleire and Thiers to this volume.

118 'Serbia Seeks New Ties With U.S. During Biden Visit', *Radio Free Europe / Radio Liberty*, 21 May 2009, available at: <http://www.rferl.org/content/Serbia_Seeks_New_Ties_With_US_During_Biden_Visit/1736350.html>. See also the interview with David Harland of the UN Department of Peacekeeping Operations in which he suggests that Kosovo Serbs can pretend to act in accordance with UNSCR 1244, while the Kosovo Albanians can implement the Ahtisaari Plan. 'Srbi po 1244, Albanci po Ahtisariju', *Politika*, 15 June 2009, available at: <http://www.politika.rs/rubrike/Politika/Srbi-po-1244-Albanci-po-Ahtisariju.sr.html>.

have the authority to remove democratically elected officials, and if so, how should they wield this authority? Second, should the international administrators go for standards before status or rather the other way round in cases when delaying status proves directly detrimental to the implementation of standards? These two conundrums can be seen as the two 'chicken and egg' problems of international trusteeship administration.

Beginning with the dilemmas of imposed democracy, key international decision-makers in Bosnia and Herzegovina as well as Kosovo perceived quick elections to be the key to discarding obstructionist politicians and to begin the transfer of authority to the local population. The international administrators began, in other words, with the heart of democracy, namely the rule of the people. In both cases, however, the rapid holding of elections after a traumatic war empowered the wartime leaderships and failed to produce an atmosphere of democratic accountability. Instead, it generated an atmosphere of nationalism and mutual fear. The international community also tended to ignore the local population's lacking experience with the democratic process and elections. In addition, the international organisations responsible for organising the elections underestimated the logistical and demographic difficulties of holding elections in societies in which a large percentage of the population was displaced or lived as refugees in other countries.

Moreover the continuing powers of the administrators to overrule national decisions and an increasing will to use such powers have, by all indications, undermined the belief that accountability rests with the people. Instead, the standards of government have been drafted by outsiders, and decisions whether and when to hold the elected representatives accountable on the basis of these standards have also been taken by them, probably even on an arbitrary basis, at least in the eyes of the local population. Finally, the whole point of democratic delegation of power and decisions from voters to parliament, from parliament to government and from government to bureaucracy has hardly been convincing to the leaders and their constituents as long as outside administrators have reserved a part of the decision-making competences to themselves. However, the main consequence of these democratic problems has not been a loss of confidence in local (and nationalist) representatives in Kosovo and the entities of Bosnia and Herzegovina. Instead, these representatives have to a considerable extent been able to exploit the disturbances in the democratic chain of accountability and delegation to their own advantage, meaning that they have been able to blame the administrators for poor results and to present themselves as the indispensable counterweight to outside interference and threats from rival nationalities and states. But this does not mean that there has been no democratic development in these two countries at all. Furthermore, democratic theory indicates that democratic accountability and political responsiveness may improve with the full return of political power to the national authorities.

Judging from the two cases under investigation, democratic progress is also closely linked to the second dilemma of international trusteeship, namely the settlement of political status including the choice of political system and the determination of international legal status. Apparently, one cannot create real democracy in the absence of a clear and viable solution to the question of political status. The Dayton Peace Agreement and UN Security Council Resolution 1244 were both compromise solutions born out of political necessity, rather than master plans for the accomplishment of a long-term democratic ideal.

The generally agreed lesson from Kosovo seems to be that the cultivation of democracy is very difficult or impossible in the absence of a constitution and a clear international status. Following the declaration of independence and the contested recognition of this country, answers to these problems have materialised, but only to lead to new challenges including the difficult position of the minorities and the governance of the Serb part of the country to the north of the Ibar river.

As for the stability of Bosnia and Herzegovina, all parties have to understand that the territorial integrity of the state itself is non-negotiable. However, the larger crises in this country tend to emerge when the existence of the entities, and in particular the RS, is questioned. Consequently, the political structure of Bosnia and Herzegovina militates against certain needed reforms. The international community therefore needs to decide whether the reform of Dayton is worth a short-term destabilisation that could include a major crisis. An ambitious pursuit of standards might involve a high risk of political setbacks even today, almost 15 years after the drafting of Dayton. As it is, the 1995 peace agreement has left a seemingly permanent division of the Bosnian state into three major ethnic groups and territories. The Bosnian dilemma seems to persist in so far that there will probably be no viable federal state *without* the Dayton framework, but *with* it there will probably be no viable and unified democracy. The more likely choice for the international community, the UN and the EU might therefore be a policy of a gradual transformation towards higher standards of governance as a condition of EU membership in order to consolidate the negative peace provided for by Dayton and gradually transform it into a positive one.[119]

Such a policy of gradual and slow progress towards standards of governance before EU membership seems to be less vulnerable than the seemingly related one of standards before status in Kosovo, in so far that membership of the EU does not involve as serious a set-back for the Serbs in the RS as the accomplishment of *de facto* statehood for Kosovo did for the Serbs of Kosovo. However, a defensive strategy of slow change and limited interference with domestic authorities is likely to lead to a situation in which very little happens over long periods of time. In this scenario, the EU must either close the door to the former trusteeship states (in that case presumably by means of a kind of 'Turkish solution' where membership is delayed endlessly) or move towards inclusion in spite of a lack of progress. It seems, in other words, that the game of 'standards before status or the other way round' is now about to be played out once again, only this time as 'standards before EU membership or the other way round'.

---

[119] The US (and UN) preference for this solution, to be obtained not least through the hard work of the EU, was clearly indicated by US Vice-President Joseph Biden's visit to the Balkans in May 2009.

The EU has wagered heavily that the tremendous potential benefits of membership would eventually prove sufficiently enticing to provoke the necessary reforms. If only Bosnia and Herzegovina can reform itself sufficiently to attain membership, its citizens will eventually come to exist in a borderless community spanning most of the European continent, with enormous potential political and socio-economic benefits. Assuming that Serbia and Croatia also become EU members, the question of national citizenship and ethnic identity should then, ideally, recede in importance.[120] So runs the argument of EU membership. In practice, though, the 'carrot effect' seems to be limited, at least for Bosnia and Herzegovina. Kosovo has the advantage that the EU as midwife is in any case forced to care about its well-being and progressive development. This is the political logic of contemporary European integration and ambition and not least of the heavy political investments that the EU has put into the country by its share in UNMIK (Pillar IV) and by its attempt to take the lead in the solution of the problem of future status before Kosovo's unilateral declaration of independence.

For these reasons, the EU and the international community are likely to cling on to the old belief in the integrative and progressive force of the Union: the closer a country gets to real membership, the closer it gets to real peace and development, either during the process or after a formal entry.

[120] The example of Belgium, one of the original founding members of the European Union, provides a cautionary tale and reason for scepticism.

# Chapter 19
# A MISSED OPPORTUNITY: STATE BUILDING IN BOSNIA AND HERZEGOVINA (OCTOBER 2002 TO OCTOBER 2006)

**Michael Humphreys* and Jasna Jelesić****

## 1. Introduction

Bosnia and Herzegovina provides one of the first examples of a united international approach to peacemaking, peacebuilding and ultimately state building following the end of the Cold War. It also set the scene for the first deployment of the EU civilian actions under the European Security and Defence Policy (ESDP), for the largest EU military action and for the possibility – not yet achieved – of a high-profile EU Special Representative (EUSR) role.

The break-up of Yugoslavia led to the wars in Croatia as well as Bosnia from 1992 to 1995. Peace was only achievable through the Dayton-Paris Agreement (DPA) of November/December 1995,[1] following a committed political and military intervention by the US, supported by the EU and with the acquiescence of Russia. It is now widely acknowledged that Dayton (together with the earlier Washington Agreement establishing the Federation of BiH) provided a political and institutional structure for peace but no clear structure for the development of effective and efficient political, administrative and economic institutions or for the development of a modern, democratic civil society.

Despite the inherent weaknesses of the constitutional and institutional structures, BiH made substantial progress. Peace was assured and became embedded in society; not a single soldier of the NATO or EU military forces was killed or injured in combat; the previous warring factions managed (albeit inefficiently and with tension) to have minimal cooperation; and the economy developed.

---

* Michael Humphreys: former European Commission official and Head of the European Commission Delegation in Bosnia and Herzegovina (2002-2006). The views expressed in the chapter are his own and do not represent the official position of any organisation or institution.

** Jasna Jelisić has worked in Bosnia and Herzegovina since 1997 as a journalist, political advisor and analyst. The views expressed in the chapter are her own and do not represent official positions of any organisation with which she is affiliated. The authors are grateful to the comments from Renzo Daviddi (Head of the EU Commission Office in Pristina), Osman Topčagić (BiH Ambassador to the EU), Stefan Simosas (Head Political Department in the OHR/EUSR) and Reinhard Priebe (former Director for the Western Balkans in the European Commission).

[1] The DPA is reproduced in 35 *International Legal Materials* (1996) 75.

*S. Blockmans, J. Wouters & T. Ruys, eds., The European Union and Peacebuilding*

The period October 2002 to October 2006 marked the first four-year election term for post-Dayton BiH – and thus the first opportunity to have governments at all levels with a mandate long enough to establish a track record in developing and implementing a substantial government programme targeted at building the institutions of the country and preparing BiH for its Euro-Atlantic ambitions – joining NATO and the EU.

The EU as well as the international community as a whole – both in their different ways – were strongly promoting a state-building process. In May 2002, Lord Paddy Ashdown took up the posts of High Representative (HR)[2] for Bosnia and Herzegovina and EU Special Representative in BiH (EUSR).[3] On his arrival, Lord Ashdown noted: 'Peace and stability was not going to be my problem – that had been basically assured by the time I got there. My problem, rather, was going to be state-building.'[4] The major ambition was to move Bosnia from its 'Dayton' to its 'Brussels' phase.

Due to a confluence of both domestic and international circumstances, very substantial progress started to be made in the early part of the 2002-2006 electoral mandate. In the latter period, however, for a variety of reasons the progress was halted, and in the following electoral mandate in part reversed. This chapter will attempt to provide a summary of the background related to the re-creation of BiH with its short-sighted time frame for implementation, of the ethnicised election process that followed, of the brief period of a positive state-building process and of the ultimate freezing of this process.

## 2. Background

### 2.1 The Dayton Peace Agreement and its aftermath

Following the March 1992 Declaration of Independence, BiH was plunged into a three-and-a-half-year war, which saw the worst atrocities in Europe since the Second World War. The war was eventually brought to an end by the biggest military

---

[2] Endorsed by the UNSC, the High Representative is appointed by the Peace Implementation Council (PIC), an *ad hoc* grouping of 55 countries with a Steering Board composed of the most active and interested countries and organisations: Canada, France, Germany, Italy, Japan, Russia, United Kingdom, United States, the Presidency of the European Union, the European Commission and the Organisation of the Islamic Conference (OIC), which is represented by Turkey.

[3] Council Joint Action 2002/211/CFSP of 11 March 2002 on the appointment of the EU Special Representative in Bosnia and Herzegovina, *OJ* 2002 L 70/7, repealed by Council Joint Action 2004/569/CFSP of 12 July 2004 on the mandate of the European Union Special Representative in Bosnia and Herzegovina and repealing Council Joint Action 2002/211/CFSP, *OJ* 2004 L 252/7, amended by Council Joint Action 2006/49/CFSP of 30 January 2006 appointing the European Union Special Representative in Bosnia and Herzegovina, *OJ* 2006 L 26/21.

[4] P. Ashdown, *Swords and Ploughshares: Building Peace in the 21st Century* (London, Phoenix 2008), at 222.

action of NATO in its 45-year-long history, targeted at the Bosnian Serb forces, which helped to push the respective parties to the negotiating table in Dayton, Ohio.

The tailoring of the Dayton set-up of Bosnia was a result of international engineering that started in 1992. At its core, the DPA relied on its fruitless forerunners – the Vance-Owen Peace Plan (1993) and the Contact Group Plan (1994) – that had introduced the idea of ethnic division as a solution to the conflict.[5]

The Bosnian state was re-created in Dayton within the same borders of the Yugoslav Socialist Republic of BiH, divided along ethnic lines, and made extremely decentralised and weak – a main reason for both the initial peacebuilding and later state-building difficulties.[6] The DPA was in fact an agreement that reintroduced the idea of partition as a solution to ethnic conflict – a solution which had fallen into disuse in diplomatic activities since the 1970s[7] but was revived for Bosnia in 1995 and, in 2008, as an option for Kosovo. Officials of the international community appeared to think that once some sort of internal partition was stabilised, the international community would be able to exit the crisis. In fact, a choice between partition and reintegration of the country was left to the 'scattered and terrorized Bosnian civil society'.[8]

In the lead-up to and the follow-on from Dayton, the international community – notably the Europeans – misinterpreted Yugoslav civil society. Many of those who had been in contact with parts of the intellectual elite of the country failed to understand the capacity of the political and intellectual elite to use the instruments of a quasi-totalitarian state to manipulate the political scene and the limited representativeness of this elite. In the absence of consolidated mechanisms of accountability, opposition to war and ethnic cleansing was left to non-political means.

The DPA created a sort of asymmetrical federal structure consisting primarily of two entities – the Serb-dominated and centralised Republika Srpska (RS) and the Bosniak and Croat-dominated decentralised Federation of BiH (FBiH) – and also including the separate Brčko District as a self-governing administrative unit under the sovereignty of Bosnia. The state designed at Dayton had limited competences, primarily related to foreign affairs, foreign trade, monetary policy, refugees and

---

[5] For facts, backgrounds and analysis, see, e.g., D. Owen, *Balkan Odyssey* (New York, Harcourt, Brace & Co. 1995); S. Woodward, *Balkan Tragedy: Chaos and Dissolution after the Cold War* (Washington, Brookings Institution 1995); L. Silber and A. Little, *The Death of Yugoslavia*, rev. edn. (London, Penguin Books 1996); M. Glenny, *The Fall of Yugoslavia*, 3rd edn. (London, Penguin Books 1996); R. Hayden, *Blueprints for a House Divided: The Constitutional Logic of the Yugoslav Conflicts* (Ann Arbor, The University of Michigan Press 2000); M. Glenny, *The Balkans: Nationalism, War, and the Great Powers, 1804-1999* (London, Penguin Books 2001); and R. Bideleux and I. Jeffries, *The Balkans: A Post-Communist History* (London, Routledge 2007).

[6] Bosnia, which in many ways was the centre of the former Yugoslavia, both geographically and culturally, was home to 4.36 million people, 44% of whom declared themselves Bosniak ('Muslim'), 31% Serb and 17% Croat, while there were also significant numbers of Jews, Roma, Albanians, Yugoslavs and others. The country's ethnic diversity before the war did not entail territorial division. There was a high proportion of intermarriage among the various groups (1991 Census figure).

[7] R. Kumar, *Divide and Fall? Bosnia in the Annals of Partition* (New York, Verso 1997).

[8] Ibid., at 1

asylum, but also left open the possibility of additional responsibilities being assigned to the state if agreed by the entities.

The Bosnian political system has been based on ethnic power sharing[9] – a system which has proved to be prone to stalemate and has manifested all its weaknesses,[10] while at the same time delaying execution of 'exit strategies' of peacemakers and state builders in Bosnia. The institutions of Bosnia can be made to work if there is political will but they can and have been misused for political purposes. The nationalist political elites, the dominant political forces during the war, which established themselves at the first post-war elections in 1996, have been able to use the ethnic power-sharing arrangement to block reforms that threatened their interests and their political survival.[11]

In his testimony before the UN Security Council in October 2000, then HR Wolfgang Petritsch stated that 'the main Bosnia and Herzegovina State institutions were still dominated by ethnic rather than State interests.' However, he testified how '"Europeanization" was the one thing that nearly all sides aspired to and the one factor used to drive reform in Bosnia.'[12] From the economic perspective, the World Bank stated that 'different constituent communities' ability to reach consensus on the implementation of the reform agenda has always been problematic', and represented an 'overriding risk to the success of the World Bank program in BiH.'[13]

Processes favouring and supporting intercommunity cooperation are often seen as a condition for stability in divided societies. This did not happen in the case of Bosnia. In addition, the process of creating provisional and later permanent elec-

---

[9] See A. Liphart, *Democracy in Plural Societies* (New Haven, Yale University Press 1977).

[10] Woodward, for example, points out that many diplomats and scholars favoured the power-sharing concept as an apparatus for harmonising war-shattered societies. However, its successes in generating functioning governments and sustainable peace have been insignificant. Woodward claims that power sharing in BiH was imposed as a way of satisfying the interests of Bosnia's neighbours and in the cases of Somalia and Bosnia power sharing created *de facto* partitioning of the country among regional spheres of influence. 'The main problem of the peace-building approaches lies in the fact that international community treats Balkan crises in terms of endemic nationalist conflict and ethnic hatred, rather than in terms of its own policy failures.' See S. Woodward, 'Economic Priorities for Successful Peace Implementation', in S. Stedman, D. Rothschild and E. Cousens, eds., *Ending Civil Wars: The Implementation of Peace Agreements* (London, Lynne Rienner Publishers 2002) 183-214, and B. Steil and S. Woodward, 'A European "New Deal" for the Balkans', 78 *Foreign Affairs* (1999) 95-105.

[11] For more on peace spoilers and power sharing, see C. Hartzell, M. Hoddie and D. Rothchild, 'Stabilizing the Peace After Civil War: An Investigation of Some Key Variables', 55 *International Organization* (2001) 183-208; M. Doyle and N. Sambanis, 'International Peacebuilding: A Theoretical and Quantitative Analysis', 94 *American Political Science Review* (2000) 779-801; S. Woodward., 'On War and Peace Building: Unfinished Legacy of the 1990's' (New York, Social Science Research Council 2002; R. Paris, 'Peacebuilding and the Limits of Liberal Internationalism', 22 *International Security* (1997) 54-89; E. Cousens, 'Building Peace in Bosnia', in E. Cousens and C. Kumar, eds., *Peacebuilding As Politics: Cultivating Peace in Fragile Societies* (Boulder, Lynne Rienner Publishers 2001) 113-152; E. Cousens and C. Cater, *Toward Peace in Bosnia: Implementing the Dayton Accords*, International Peace Academy Occasional Paper Series (London, Lynne Rienner Publishers 2001).

[12] UN Security Council, *Report on Bosnia*, 26 October 2000, available at: <http://www.un.org/News/Press/docs/2000/20001026.sc6940.doc.html>.

[13] See *Country Assistance Strategy (CAS) Progress Report of the World Bank Group for Bosnia and Herzegovina*, South East Europe Country Unit (Washington D.C., 24 September 2001).

tion rules in 2001 in practice discouraged rather than promoted intercommunity relations.

Belief that appropriate political engineering can help construct a democratic political system capable of withstanding the centrifugal tendencies that divide societies is an important assumption of power-sharing theory. Noting that there is no single transportable model of successful power sharing, it has been argued that the whole process of power sharing 'may be appropriate as a transitional, confidence-building mechanism but not as a permanent solution to ethnic conflict management through the democratic institutions.'[14]

The Dayton Constitution which refers to 'Bosniaks, Croats and Serbs, as constituent peoples (along with Others)' led to an ethnicisation of the political system.[15] The power-sharing arrangements from the Constitution favoured collective rights rather than individual rights of citizens, while, despite the European Convention on Human Rights being a part of the Bosnian Constitution, the 'Others' lost their position in the electoral system as well as in the administrative structures. Ethnic division, rather than ethnic sharing, has become the general rule in government ministries and institutions. In Bosnia, the power-sharing principle has become a power-dividing arrangement. The divisions have become even deeper as people learned to define themselves in ethnic terms and play the ethnic card out of pure opportunism.

In BiH, the transitional arrangement helped to hijack the process and created a stalemate in democratisation. What could have been a transitional, confidence-building mechanism became a semi-permanent solution.[16]

The frequent elections did not lead to a broader democratic system. At the time when (under OSCE leadership) the Permanent Election Law was being drafted, the international community missed the opportunity to introduce provisions which would give more moderate forces a chance to be elected. The Permanent Election Law, adopted in 2001, continues to separate rather than unite ethnic communities, resulting in independent political spheres incapable of producing a single vision for the country.

Elections, even fully democratic, free and fair, do not necessarily lead to consolidated and functional democracy, with full accountability and rule of law. As Ralf Dahrendorf has pointed out, there are 'lawless democracies and undemocratic "states of law" (*Rechtsstaat*)'.[17] This issue becomes very relevant when trying to answer the question of why BiH citizens' wishes to join the EU have not been

---

[14] See T. Sisk. *Power Sharing and International Mediation in Ethnic Conflict* (Washington D.C., United States Institute for Peace 1996), at 77.

[15] The Constitution of Bosnia and Herzegovina is laid down in Annex 4 of the DPA.

[16] Major difficulties in BiH are deteriorated public services, organised crime and corruption in public institutions. World Bank, *Bosnia and Herzegovina – Local Level Institutions and Social Capital Study, Findings and Recommendations*, Vol. 2, retrieved from: <http://www.worldbank.org/participation/Bosnia_findings.pdf>.

[17] See R. Dahrendorf, 'Elections Are Not Enough', Project Syndicate/Institute for Human Sciences Vienna, November 2005, available at: <http://www.project-syndicate.org>.

directly translated into the election of accountable governments, truly willing to reform and democratise, hence 'Europeanise' the country. Due to ethnicised electoral process, an ethnic logic has become the principal logic of post-war Bosnian politics, with negative effects on its economic recovery, its political stability and its Euro-Atlantic perspective.

A slight expansion of democratisation in the form of political pluralism took place in Bosnia from 2000-2002, but, as has been largely recognised, this was not a result of genuine Bosnian democratisation so much as it was a consequence of external regional changes and influences. Some of these came with the death of Croatian President Franjo Tuđman in December 1999 and Serbian President Slobodan Milošević's departure to the International Tribunal for Former Yugoslavia in The Hague in June 2001 when the support for the Bosnian separatists from the neighbouring countries declined, and opened a small 'window of opportunity' for democratic change in BiH. In addition, a constructive policy shift of Croatia towards Bosnia further reinforced by Croatia's EU membership aspirations significantly diminished one centrifugal force in BiH.

It was generally thought that the window would close in 2002 when ethnic nationalists returned to power. However, that was not the case and in the first part of the 2002-2006 electoral cycle Bosnia made unprecedented state-building progress, commencing highly significant reforms.

## 2.2 The function of external actors in Bosnia

In 1995, at the end of the war, the international community claimed that it had an 'exit strategy' from Bosnia and would leave militarily after one year of the DPA implementation period.[18] This quite unrealistic time frame was one of the major mistakes of the international community in the process of DPA implementation.

The international community has been forced by events over time to transform its 'exit strategy' into what is seen by some as a sort of 'protectorate strategy'. Partly as a consequence of the DPA, Bosnia had – and still has – a domineering international presence led by the HR of the international community.

Initially the HR had a monitoring, advising and supervising role. However, it soon became apparent that stronger powers were necessary and executive powers (including to appoint/remove officials and to enact legislation) were provided at the international conference of the Bosnia Peace Implementation Council, meeting in

[18] President Clinton's National Security Advisor Tony Lake pressed a diplomatic approach called 'The Endgame Strategy', whose goal was to end the war and maintain a single, though divided, state. The exit strategy rested on the establishment of a military balance of power among the warring factions to deter additional fighting and allow for the removal of US troops at the end of one year. 'Neither we nor the international community has either the responsibility or the means to do whatever it takes for as long as it takes to rebuild nations', Tony Lake stated in March 1996. In December 1997, it was obvious that the policy had changed. President Clinton announced that troop withdrawal deadlines would no longer determine the length of US commitment to Bosnia. See J. Mokhiber and R. Young, 'Nation Building in Bosnia', *PBS Frontline*, available at: <http://www.pbs.org/wgbh/pages/frontline/shows/military/etc/peace.html>.

Germany, which conferred executive authority – the so-called 'Bonn powers' – on the HR in 1997.[19]

## 2.3 The role of the European Union

The EC as an organisation and its Member States misunderstood the potential consequences of the dissolution of the Socialist Federal Republic of Yugoslavia (SFRY). The war that followed the implosion in 1991 led to the unilateral suspension of all coordinated assistance to Yugoslavia. For the first time in the history of the European Communities, a cooperation agreement with a third country (the one with the SFRY from 1980) was denounced. In December 1991, the EEC restored trade links, the Generalised System of Preferences and economic and financial aid terms with all Yugoslav republics, except Serbia and Montenegro.

In 1997, the EU established its regional approach for the Western Balkans based on political and economic conditionality.[20] The Feira European Council meeting in June 2000 formally gave BiH and the other Western Balkan countries a European perspective.[21] This was followed up in Zagreb in November 2000 by the first joint meeting of the Heads of State or Government of the European Union and the Western Balkans.[22]

The prospect of accession was offered on the basis of the provisions of the Treaty on European Union, respect for the criteria defined at the Copenhagen European Council in June 1993 and the progress made in implementing the Stabilisation and Association Agreements, in particular on regional cooperation. The Stabilisation and Association Process (SAP) thus offered BiH the prospect of integration into EU structures and ultimately membership of the EU.[23]

In March 2000, the EU Road Map identified the first concrete steps on this journey. Initially foreseen for implementation over an 18-month period, their substantial fulfilment was only deemed to be achieved in September 2002, which opened the way to the assessment – by means of a Feasibility Study – of Bosnia's ability to negotiate and ultimately sign a Stabilisation and Association Agreement.[24]

In the meantime, the Western Balkans – and Bosnia in particular – had served as a crucible for the development of the European Union Common Foreign and Security Policy (CFSP) and the European Security and Defence Policy (ESDP). The

---

[19] See Peace Implementation Council, Summary of Conclusions, 10 December 1997, available at: <http://www.ohr.int/pic/default.asp?content_id=5183>.

[20] Council Conclusions of 29 April 1997 on the principle of conditionality governing the development of the EU's relations with certain countries of South East Europe, in *Bull. EU* 4-1997, point 2.2.1.

[21] *Bull. EU* 6-2000, point I.49.67.

[22] *Bull. EU* 11-2000, point I.6.57.

[23] The SAP was initiated by the European Commission, see COM(1999) 235 final, Brussels, 26 May 1999, and endorsed at subsequent EU-Western Balkans summits, most crucially at Thessaloniki. For the full text of the declaration of the EU-Western Balkans Summit at Thessaloniki, see *Bull. EU* 6-2003, point 1.6.70. For facts, backgrounds and analysis, see S. Blockmans, *Tough Love: The European Union's Relations with the Western Balkans* (The Hague, T.M.C. Asser Press 2007).

[24] See Blockmans, ibid., at 258-259.

first civilian mission under ESDP was launched in Bosnia (the EUPM – EU Police Mission) in January 2003, and the largest-ever EU military mission – EUFOR ALTHEA – launched in December 2004 is still operational (although with reduced numbers) in BiH.[25]

### 2.4 Immediate situation pre- and post-elections

The 2000 elections had – for the first time – brought in a government which was not dominated by the nationalist parties (SDS, HDZ BiH and SDA) that were political wings of the 1990-1995 warring factions. The Alliance for Change government led by SDP BiH, strongly supported and in part brought into office by the international community, had disappointing results.

In the lead-up to the 2002 elections it became clear that the Alliance coalition was unlikely to achieve a government mandate. The international community viewed the prospect of a return of nationalist party government with trepidation. In order to attempt to provide a foundation for continuation of a progressive, pro-European reform agenda, newly appointed HR Paddy Ashdown developed a common reform/ European integration agenda, which all parties agreed on and accepted prior to the elections.

The elections of 5 October 2002 confirmed the post-Dayton voting pattern. The leading Croat, Serb and Bosniak nationalist parties, the HDZ BIH, SDS and SDA, generally preserved their percentage of the overall vote, a combined total of about 45%. The polls showed that the SDP voters did not turn up at the elections, disappointed by the SDP's failure to make a promised change.

Developing a governing coalition with these conflictual parties was not a straightforward proposition. However, the pragmatic stance of the HR – fully supported by the European Commission – was to recognise the reality of the results and clearly state his readiness to cooperate with whatever legitimate government was formed, provided it was committed to the reform process and to the EU path. The pre-election commitment by all parties provided a clear basis for this policy.[26]

## 3. A window of opportunity – 2003 to 2005

### 3.1 Formation of the new government

The establishment of the new government with a four-year mandate provided an opportunity to re-invigorate the reform and European integration process. The first

---

[25] Ibid., at 221-232.

[26] At the start of 2002, the BiH situation was shortly summarised by HR Lord Paddy Ashdown: 'When my mandate started, Bosnia – a country of 3.5 million – had three armies two customs services, effectively three intelligence services, five presidents, twelve prime ministers, thirteen police forces, no effective central government, no state taxation system, no single judicial structure and no single economic space.' See Ashdown, *supra* n. 4, at 222.

challenge was to put in place a government at state level that could function effectively. The law[27] – which expanded the number of ministries from six to nine (four new ministries and the transformation of the Ministry of European Integration into a Directorate reporting directly to the Chairman of the Council of Ministers of BiH) – ultimately required the HR's 'soft' imposition and was the basis for Adnan Terzić, the incoming Chairman of the Council of Ministers, to form the new government.

Unexpectedly, pragmatic political leaders who were committed to building a functioning state capable of acceding to the EU emerged after the October 2002 elections. Mr Terzić's background as a senior but relatively unknown member of the Bosniak SDA party did not lead to strong expectations of a leader who would be prepared to make the compromises necessary. At entity level, the governments were headed, respectively, by Prime Minister Dragan Mikerević in the RS and Prime Minister Ahmed Hadžipašić in the FBiH – both heading governments primarily composed of a coalition of nationalistic parties. In the RS, additionally, the President was Dragan Čavić from the SDS, the ex-Karadžić party, which was still viewed by the international community as a party continuing to provide support and assistance to the ICTY war crime indictees (PIFWCS).

From the start of his mandate, Mr Terzić made it clear that he was fully committed to the European integration agenda.[28] Mr Hadžipašić – despite his very limited political and governmental background – proved a competent leader of the FBiH government and demonstrated willingness to cooperate with the RS. On the RS side, perhaps the most surprising positive outcome was Mr Dragan Čavić, who over the whole period of his mandate – and at considerable political and personal cost – demonstrated a clear commitment to the reform process and the European ambition and, when justification was clearly demonstrated, was willing to support the state-strengthening and centralisation measures essential for Euro-Atlantic integration. Although the ability of the international community to effectively 'blackmail' the SDS was undoubtedly instrumental in moving some of the reforms forward, Mr Čavić's own commitment to these reforms was also clearly demonstrated.

There is no doubt that the joint platform promoted by the OHR prior to the elections was of fundamental importance in providing the basis for cooperative and progressive action, as also was Ashdown's strong, proactive and committed implementation of his programme. However the importance of individual personalities should not be underestimated.

From the international side there were many actors, with the OHR as the leader of the overall reform process and the European Commission, as the executive of the European Union, for European integration issues. However, other significant actors included NATO, the US, Russia, EU Member States, the OSCE, the International Financial Institutions and, though now in a much diminished role, the UN.

---

27 Official Gazette of Bosnia and Herzegovina 05/03.

28 Ashdown recalls Terzić's first words when he met him: 'Look, I am only interested in one thing – getting this country into Europe and improving the lives of its people so my son Tarik can have a good life.' See Ashdown, *supra* n. 4, at 257.

A pragmatic approach by government leaders at state and entity levels, a strong, proactive and target-oriented international community led by the HR/EUSR Ashdown and a substantially enhanced EU perspective provided an opportunity for significant state-building progress. This included the establishment of the High Judicial and Prosecutorial Council, the State Court and state investigation services and the setting up of some 30 bodies/institutions required for the EU integration process. Defence reform, the creation of the Indirect Tax Administration and the attempted police reform were the most complex and high-profile state-building reform activities. The achievement of the Feasibility Study conditions laid a basis both for the European Union integration process and for the building of efficient and effective government and other institutions.

## 3.2 **OHR reform programme**

### 3.2.1 *Defence reform*

Defence reform leading to the creation of state-level command and control of the military forces was perhaps the most fundamental reform. To make 'defence' a state function required a major restructuring of the armed forces and the establishment of new state-level command and control powers and responsibilities. NATO/SFOR intelligence reports indicated that the ORAO aircraft factory, which was under the authority of the RS, was involved in illegal arms transfers to Iraq in clear breach of the UN embargo. The affair became public in 2003.[29] Using this as a lever and outside stimulus, HR Ashdown was able to revive a major reform of the defence services – establishment of state-level command and control structures and creation of a Ministry of Defence at state level.

On the international side, SFOR/NATO provided intelligence on the actual situation and leadership and technical support in the negotiations.

The defence reform in its essence was not an EU integration-related reform, although essential in the long term to meet EU standards. The EU was not institutionally involved, but individual Member States[30] were part of the core NATO involvement, which was – typically – led by the US.

The defence reform illustrated the approach that would be taken in other major OHR-supported reforms (police, indirect taxation, intelligence): guidelines would be established by the OHR, a committee of experts and professionals would be formed, a high-profile chair/head appointed, and a clearly defined timetable for achievement of results set.

In defence reform, the tenuous connection between the OHR's Dayton powers and reform pressure was played upon to full advantage using effective threats of

---

[29] NATO accused the Bosnian Serb authorities of engaging in espionage against the Dayton-authorised SFOR, European Union police and the OHR, as well as Bosnian institutions and individuals. J. Naegele, 'Bosnia: Political Stability in Question Amid Scandals, Espionage Charges', *Radio Free Europe*, 3 April 2003.

[30] Mainly the United Kingdom with its experts.

sanctions in particular against the SDS in the RS. However, in the long term, success was achieved through negotiation as well as through all sides seeing benefits. The US/NATO lead was critical during the negotiations, as was the presence of a well-respected negotiator on the BiH side,[31] who gained the confidence of all sides.

The key attributes of a successful reform could be summarised in clear conception: a consistent and coordinated message from the international community, good technical support and appropriate negotiating ability and a good understanding of the local situation in order to identify weak spots in the positions of the negotiating parties and to develop flexible approaches to match the evolving situation. In the case of the defence reform, good timing and sequencing also significantly contributed as did a well-founded policy framework and significant diplomatic skills. One of the driving elements behind the success of the approach has been the ability to identify and deal with hidden forces opposing the progress.

Equally fundamental has been the international community's capacity to communicate effectively, clearly exposing some of the benefits deriving to specific groups and constituencies and presenting to the public the advantages of the proposed reform.

The defence reform is also an example where the US effectively used its comparative advantages – single voice, adequate funding, reputation and power. In some ways, the defence reform can be seen as the most impressive and fundamental reform in Bosnia. No significant incidents were recorded after the armies of former enemies united under the single command.

### 3.2.2 *Tax reform*

Tax and police structures were seen as major bases of power in the hands of ethnonationalist ruling elites and a major source of the entities' authority. Each entity had its own revenues and fiscal instruments as well as police forces, which served as major pillars of the quasi-statehood awarded to the entities in Dayton. EU integration required that the ruling elites make a significant surrender of their own influence over these 'two pillars' and transfer them to state level.

Under the DPA, the state received no direct tax revenue and was dependent on revenue appropriations from the RS and the Federation of BiH. In fact, the state budget did not even exist in 1996 and 1997. The state did not have authority to set customs duties or ensure their collection. At the entity level, there were two separate taxation systems and, in the Federation, there were also ten separate cantonal taxation systems. The complex tax systems were highly susceptible to fraud, losses and lack of accountability.

In addition to this complex and disorganised structure, the system of sales tax in operation was not compatible with the EU *acquis*. Tax reform through the implementation of an EU standard VAT system was essential. Thus, the principles of state building and meeting EU criteria came together in support of the creation of

[31] The negotiator on the BiH side was Nikola Radovanović, now BiH ambassador to NATO.

the Indirect Tax Administration (ITA). In some ways, the ITA reform resembled the *stramine* of defence reform: critical sector, clear conditionality, well researched, international community speaking with one voice, unity between the principal international actors (OHR and EU supported by US and others) and a very capable and committed chairperson provided through the European Commission.

Perhaps one of the most significant differences between ITA and defence reform was the absence of a 'blackmail' possibility and the danger that the 'united voice' would disintegrate. In particular the IMF, a key player in fiscal matters, was initially only half convinced of the necessity of a state-level VAT system and, in Ashdown's view, even the EU at one stage was in danger of faltering.

However, the 'forces for reform', both internationally and internally (particularly through the Chair of the Council of Ministers of BiH), prevailed and – with a mixture of positive regional dynamic and blunt messages of EU conditionality – the necessary legislation was passed and institutions established.

### 3.2.3 *Police reform*

Under the DPA, there was no responsibility for police or security at state level, although reforms made in 2002 allowed for the creation of a Minister of Security with initial responsibility for the State Border Service (established in 2000) and subsequent responsibility for the newly established State Information and Protection Agency (SIPA). Policing was at entity level in the RS and canton level in the Federation, resulting in thirteen police forces and a similar number of interior/security ministries without any overall controlling institutions. This resulted in a highly political police force capable of tackling petty crime but incapable of addressing organised crime, war crimes or criminal activities linked to the political elite.

For political, technical and professional reasons, police reform was clearly necessary. However, it was not clear how this could be achieved. Seven years of the UN police mission IPTF had cleaned (at least partially) the police forces but had not reformed the policing structures. Established in January 2003, the EUPM did not have a direct mandate for police structural reform.[32] Although properly functioning policing and judiciary institutions must be conditions for EU integration, the EU itself has no single policy on policing. The absence of any responsibility for policing at state level (other than the State Border Service) or for coordination and professional control structures represented a clear deficit.

Following an EUPM internal report and a European Commission-financed external consultancy report, the Police Restructuring Commission (PRC) was estab-

---

[32] See Council Joint Action 2002/210/CFSP of 11 March 2002 on the European Union Police Mission, *OJ* 2002 L 70/1, which applied until 31 December 2005; and Council Joint Action 2005/824/CFSP of 24 November 2005 on the European Union Police Mission (EUPM) in Bosnia and Herzegovina (BiH), *OJ* 2005 L 307/55, applicable from 1 January 2006 to 31 December 2007 (later prolonged and amended). The EUPM was the first civilian ESDP operation for which the EU alone assumed leadership and responsibility. After having been invited thereto in the statement by the President of the Security Council of 12 December 2002 (UN Doc. S/PRST/2002/33), the EU does, however, report to the Security Council on the activities of the EUPM.

lished in July 2004 with the task of elaborating proposals for 'a single structure of policing for BiH under the overall political oversight of a ministry or ministries in the Council of Ministers.'[33] HR Ashdown appointed former Belgian Prime Minister Wilfried Martens as chairman, with a deadline of end December 2004 for the final report.

The timing and extent of police reform was a priority for the OHR more than for the EU – it was particularly targeted at the RS police structures where there was evidence of pervasive political control, obstruction of cooperation with the ICTY and failure to arrest ICTY war crime indictees. However, the OHR as such did not have authority to impose changes in the police structures, which had been established in accordance with Dayton. Only by making police reform a condition for EU integration was it possible to bring pressure on the BiH politicians to commit to the necessary changes. In agreement with HR Ashdown – and partially at his instigation – this obligation was specified in the three EC minimum requirements for police reform, summarised as:

- Exclusive state competency for policing in BiH;
- Local police areas designed on the basis of technical professional criteria;
- A system that protects police from improper political influence.

Over the course of the next six months, the PRC reached agreement on the basic conditions for a police reform, but failed to do so on the size and shape of local police areas. The RS representatives on the PRC were not prepared to accept any proposal that the police regions should cross the Inter-Entity Boundary Line. Accordingly, the final Martens Report presented in December 2004 left open a number of options for police regions, all of which crossed inter-entity boundaries.[34]

In the early months of 2005, political negotiations continued, culminating in a meeting of political and government leaders at the ski resort in Vlašić Mountain in April 2005 where everything was agreed except the police boundaries. Unfortunately, a compromise[35] on this issue, which could have been fully in line with EU practice, was not considered and the meeting ended without political commitment. Over the next months, negotiations continued, resulting in an agreement in September 2005, which enabled the SAA negotiations to commence but was subsequently not honoured, leading to the suspension of signature of the SAA until June 2008.

The weakened police reform, finally agreed in November 2007, is now under slow and uncertain implementation. Handling of this reform sent a wrong message that EU conditions can be re-negotiated and, in general, negatively affected the credibility of EU conditionality.

---

[33] HR Decision Establishing the Police Restructuring Commission of 5 July 2004.

[34] PRC 2004, Final Report on the work of the Police Restructuring Commission of Bosnia and Herzegovina, Sarajevo, December 2004.

[35] Wilfried Martens' recommendation (in the cover letter to the PRC report) for flexibility on the issue of police districts was not implemented – 'as for the second level (police districts), while I submitted the three options, I would recommend handling this level with enough flexibility so as not to weaken the large consensus on the first level.'

### 3.3 EU integration process of BiH

Following agreement that the Road Map conditions had been met, the Commission initiated work on the Feasibility Study, publishing it in November 2003.[36] The Study assessed BiH's capacity to implement a future Stabilisation and Association Agreement and concluded that negotiations should start once BiH had made progress on sixteen key priorities.[37] These key priorities[38] included substantial state-building requirements: governance issues targeted at the Council of Ministers and reforms of public administration, rule of law issues including state and entity-level judiciary, prosecutorial and policing functions, improvement of human rights institutions and development of economic and financial institutions.

Implementation of these reform measures was clearly in the hands of the BiH authorities, with regular follow-up and reporting in the context of the Consultative Task Force meetings and the sectoral working groups. A European Commission condition for SAA negotiations was that the HR would not use Bonn powers to impose reforms related to the SAA process – although the HR and the staff of the OHR actively supported the process and brought substantial moral and political pressure to ensure progress.

In principle, it had been hoped that action would have been taken on the priorities identified in the Feasibility Study in the course of 2004. In practice, this timetable was too optimistic and instead of one year, it was nearly two years later (in October 2005) that the Commission was able to judge that 'significant progress in addressing the 16 key priorities identified by the 2003 Feasibility Study'[39] had been achieved and to recommend the opening of SAA negotiations. Negotiations were formally opened on 21 November 2005, the tenth anniversary of the Dayton Peace Agreement, and concluded in December 2006. However, signature was delayed until June 2008 pending agreement on the remaining prior conditions – principally police reform.

### 3.4 Constitutional reform

Defence, police and tax reforms all clearly meant moving beyond Dayton and reforming the Constitution by using Article III, Section 5(a), which provided for additional state-level responsibilities where agreed by the entities. However, in the

---

[36] In March 2003, a questionnaire covering all sectors relevant to a future SAA was given to the BiH Directorate for European Integration (DEI). The Feasibility Study was published as COM(2003) 692 final, Brussels, 18 November 2003.

[37] See COM(2004) 202 final, Brussels, 30 March 2004.

[38] In addition to the priorities related to institutional, democratic and economic development, a key priority was full cooperation with the ICTY, particularly on the part of the RS, notably in bringing indicted war criminals to justice before the international tribunal.

[39] Communication from the Commission to the Council on the progress achieved in implementing the priorities identified in the 'Feasibility Study on the preparedness of Bosnia and Herzegovina to negotiate a Stabilisation and Association Agreement with the EU COM(2003) 692 final', COM(2005) 529 final, at 5.

longer term, it was clear that more fundamental changes to the Constitution would be necessary if BiH were to meet EU integration requirements.

The Dayton Constitution itself has been clearly insufficient for creating functioning political and institutional structures. The first major constitutional reform initiative in this area was led by former Principal Deputy HR Donald Hays working in an NGO capacity, with initial support from Nordic countries and with developing support from the EU and its Member States and from the US. His initiative was very consciously an initiative aimed at support and ownership from political and civil society, with the process chaired and led by the domestic actors.[40]

A series of meetings at local and national level culminating in meetings of the party leaders from all constituent peoples in late 2005 in Brussels and Washington came close to reaching agreement but failed to finalise it. The OHR did not participate formally in these meetings. The EU supported the process – although SG/HR Solana himself did not take part in the meeting in Brussels – and US support strengthened to such an extent that it began to appear that the American judgment was that it was now time for the 'mother of all issues' to be tackled.

In November 2005, the US formally took over from Donald Hayes the international community role in the constitutional reform process and organised a series of meetings with political leaders to finalise a constitutional reform package. The package that was eventually agreed in March 2006 provided for a new format for the election of the Presidency and a reduction of its powers, a strengthened Council of Ministers with two new ministries, a significant increase in the membership of both houses of the Parliamentary Assembly and a reduction in the role and functions of the House of Peoples. Significantly, the April Package would also have ensured that legislation necessary for EU accession was the responsibility of the BiH institutions.

The April Package was agreed by all the Serb Parties, by the Croat HDZ party and by the Bosniak SDA and SDP parties. The only parties rejecting the Package were SBiH and HDZ 1990. At the early stage of the negotiations, SBiH had been an active participant in the discussions and had appeared to be ready to accept the compromises. However, following the return to active politics of Haris Silajdžić with an anti-entity agenda, a compromise solution acceptable to SBiH became impossible. On the Croat side, the HDZ BiH had serious internal problems – perhaps to some extent exacerbated by Dragan Čović's removal from the BiH Presidency in 2005. In March 2006, prior to the parliamentary vote, the party split and a new party, HDZ 1990 was created partially on the platform of opposition to the April Package. Short by two votes of the required two-thirds majority, the April Package failed on 26 April 2006.

---

[40] S. Sebastian, 'Leaving Dayton Behind: Constitutional Reform in Bosnia and Herzegovina', *FRIDE*, Madrid, 16 November 2007.

## 4. Reflections

### 4.1 Turning points

Three principal turning points can be identified, which ultimately led to the freezing of the state-building and European integration process: (i) the resignation in December of the RS Prime Minister Mikerević; (ii) the inability to reach an acceptable compromise on police reform at Vlašić in April 2005; and (iii) the failure of the constitutional reform process in April 2006. Other relevant factors included the removal of President Čović as the Croat member of the BiH Presidency in March 2005, the replacement of the Chairman of the ITA Board in 2006 and the successive appointments of three High Representatives over a 3-year period.

The resignation of Prime Minister Mikerević in December 2004 was triggered by a unilateral action of the US State Department, implemented without prior discussion with its counterparts in the EU Member States (although HR Ashdown was briefed in advance), to impose visa restrictions on the two principal RS government parties – the SDS and the PDP. Mr Mikerević was replaced by Pero Bukejlovic, who took a much less pragmatic or reform-minded approach, effectively blocking further significant reforms and ending the established cooperation and trust between the BiH and entity governments. The SDS-led government was of short duration and was replaced by the SNSD, again as a minority government, headed by Milorad Dodik as Prime Minister. Unfortunately, the SNSD government did not renew the policy of its PDP predecessor, and tensions, distrust and lack of cooperation developed between state and entity governments, effectively freezing the progress that had been made in the previous years.

The failure to conclude an agreement on police reform in 2005 and establish an acceptable compromise resulted in the ultimate failure of police reform, undermining and blocking the European integration process over a three-year period in which positive momentum was lost.

The failure of the constitutional reform process in April 2006 is generally seen by both the national and international community as the key factor leading to the freezing of all significant progress for the next three years. As a compromise package it was not ambitious and did not tackle the more fundamental issue of the entity-blocking mechanisms. However, there is no doubt that if the constitutional reform process had succeeded, it would have provided a new and enormously strengthened impetus to the state-building exercise, and its failure paved the way for the return of nationalist confrontational politics in the lead-up to and aftermath of the October 2006 elections.

### 4.2 Interinstitutional coherence

With the appointment of Ashdown as double-hatted HR and EUSR and the decision to launch a major ESDP mission – the EU Police Mission – in Bosnia, the EU actors on the ground – previously confined to the EU Member States' embassies, the European Commission Delegation and the EU Monitoring Mission – took on the full panoply of the EU institutions – Council and Commission. Relations on an operational level between these institutions have not always been easy. It was a priority both at Brussels level and in Bosnia to ensure that Commission and Council activities would be coherent.

With a direct line to Commissioner Patten and with a former member of Patten's cabinet as his political advisor, HR Ashdown could ensure that the Commission and the HR/EUSR spoke with one voice when it came to BiH policy. This also meant – with both positive and negative connotations – that for policy and judgment, Commissioner Patten could rely on HR Ashdown as 'our man' in Bosnia.

Lord Ashdown was meant to be the last High Representative. In the course of 2005, planning commenced for the closure of the OHR and the passing over of any remaining international responsibilities to a strengthened EU office but without Bonn powers and on the understanding that BiH was irreversibly on the road towards EU integration.

However, towards the end of Ashdown's mandate, it became increasingly doubtful whether it would be possible to close the OHR and whether the BiH structures, institutions and, above all, politicians were yet ready to take over full responsibility. Consideration then needed to be given to either continuing the OHR on the same basis as before, with a new HR, or putting in place a revised structure which would ensure a single EU voice, while maintaining, if necessary, the international community's ability to executively guarantee Dayton. One suggestion made at the time was, on the departure of HR Ashdown, to immediately 'double-hat' an appropriately profiled person as EC Head of Delegation and EU Special Representative in BiH, with the current incumbents both leaving. This would have ensured a single and coordinated voice on EU affairs in BiH. It would have been a politically brave decision – always dangerous in the real world – and would have given a clear message to BiH society of the EU's commitment to Bosnia's European credentials and ultimate prospect of accession to the EU. Although the time was appropriate and the conditions ripe, the proposal fell on deaf ears.

In hindsight (always much easier than foresight), the subsequent decision – maintaining the status quo and appointing a very committed replacement to Ashdown, but one whose vision of the abilities of the local political establishment was in advance of reality – was clearly the wrong one. It is unfortunate that the political vision shown in the NATO to EUFOR change could not have been used for a similar policy on a transition towards a reinforced EUSR/EC Head of Delegation.

### 4.3 Lessons learned – what opens opportunities?

*Society-wide commitment to Euro-Atlantic integration*

In post-Dayton BiH, the notion of 'nationality' is specifically confined to the 'nationality' of the three constituent peoples and is viewed externally and, in part, internally as a negative concept. Consequently, within BiH there are very few shared values, ambitions and dreams. However, one of them is European integration and ultimate membership of the EU. Opinion polls have consistently shown a large majority of all constituent peoples strongly in favour of EU membership. The ambition and desire for European integration has been almost universally shared by all levels of society – all ethnic communities, young and old, business and unions, academics and students – and could be used more as an instrument to promote the reforms essential to build functioning institutions as a prerequisite for moving towards EU accession negotiations. As in Central and Eastern Europe, the prospect of potential EU membership can provide not only conditionality but also a blueprint for the future framework of the country.

*Political commitment to EU integration*

The commitment of the political parties in government and opposition to meeting the conditions for EU integration is a fundamental condition for successful progress on the EU accession process. In Bosnia this was most clearly exemplified by the common platform supporting the SAA-related reforms signed by the Bosnian political parties in February 2004 as well as by the establishment of the (albeit only intermittently functioning) Coordination Board for Economic Development and European Integration.

*Well-placed international appointments*

Lord Ashdown had substantial experience of the country, strong backing from the UK government and close connections with the European Commissioner for External Affairs Lord Patten. He was supported by an exceptionally capable Principal Deputy High Representative[41] provided by the US government and also benefitted from excellent staff assigned through the UK government and from the office of Commissioner Patten.

*Clear strategy*

Ashdown's initial priority was to improve the inefficient state government structures of the Council of Ministers by an enlargement of the number of ministries from 6 to 9 and a reform of complex procedures. The development of this proposal and its legislative passage exemplified what was to become a typical process during Ashdown's mandate – in-depth preparation, extensive discussions with the political parties and leaders involved, strong pressure to reach agreement which could be approved by government and passed by parliament, and ultimate imposition under the Bonn powers by the HR if political party leaders were unwilling or unable to implement.

*Clearly defined actions plans and communication*

The success of the OHR-led reforms was also a result of clearly defined timetables, the definition of basic principles, the establishment of a broad-based commission,

---

[41] Ambassador Donald Hays.

the nomination of an international coordinator/chairman and clear communication to the public, which exposed the spoilers and their motivations.

*One voice of the international community*

An outstanding achievement of HR Ashdown was his success – in particular during the early part of his mandate – in achieving a united international voice with the international organisations (particularly between the OHR and NATO/SFOR where relations had been particularly tense), with the Peace Implementation Council (particularly ensuring that the US, EU Member States, Russia and Turkey, representing the OIC, spoke from the same 'hymn sheet') and with the European institutions.

This united voice was not predetermined. Since 2006, the differences in interests and agendas between Russia, the US and EU Member States are again visible. From the start of his mandate, Ashdown committed himself to ensuring a single united international voice, and his achievement was among the crucial factors for success of the state-building action in BiH.

*Strong and motivated local partners*

For the EU, a strong and permanent local counterpart was essential. The setting up in early 2003 of the Directorate for European Integration under a strongly committed Director[42] provided the essential technical basis for progress on the European integration path.

*Managing differences, gaining trust*

The RS and the Serb political parties were continuously seen as being opposed to, or at least having strong reservations about, the process of state building and ensuring that BiH could become a functioning modern democratic state with the institutions necessary both for its own success and for meeting the requirements of EU integration. During the brief period of cooperation and trust between the state and entity leaders from early 2002 until 2005, the differences were apparent but were managed reasonably efficiently. However, after the fall of the Mikerević government and particularly following the October 2006 elections, the level of cooperation and trust between the BiH state authorities and the RS government plummeted.

## 4.4 What froze the state building?

*Return of populists*

The most significant factor which ultimately led to the freezing of progress in the state-building and EU integration process was the return of non-pragmatic populist leaders in combination with the international community's lack of focus and later disengagement.

---

42 Ambassador Osman Topčagić, currently Ambassador of Bosnia and Herzegovina to the EU.

*Inappropriate or ill-defined conditionality*

The two flagship reforms which failed – police reform and constitutional reform – were linked in one instance (police) to conditions[43] which were difficult to justify and in the second instance (constitutional reform) to unwillingness to make the reform a condition for further progress on the EU integration process.

*Opening gap in the international community's approach*

Police reform and constitutional reform also serve as examples of what were now becoming diverging paths of the OHR and the EC. The OHR has essentially a short-term mandate, both in the concept of the office (although it has already survived for 15 years!) and in terms of the successive appointments of HRs each of which sets his own agenda to be achieved within his mandate. The European Commission, on the other hand, has a much longer vision and agenda and is setting standards and conditions to be met over a longer time frame. However, a failure of the EU is its inability to rally consensus about its fundamentally correct vision – BiH problems are not going to be solved overnight, taking shortcuts, under the leadership of non-European countries.

*Disunited EU institutional voice*

The police reform issue also became an example of a difference between the OHR and the EC at working level (though to a lesser extent, if at all, at political level). From the EC Delegation's view, it became a continuing battle to avoid being committed on the geographical policing structures. From the OHR's viewpoint, the EC appeared to be unable or unwilling to state clearly and bluntly the position implicit in its own conditions. In private meetings, the Commission was accused of undermining the police reform. Regardless of who is to blame, the BiH political community and society saw there was a gap between the OHR and the EC conditions, further exemplified when some EU Member States cast doubt on the overall process.

*Missed opportunities, untimely conditions*

In the context of European integration, the single most strongly held ambition was the desire to be able to secure the free circulation throughout Europe without visas, a visa-free regime which the citizens of the Socialist Yugoslavia enjoyed. If in 2003 the EU had been able to hold out a firm timetable for visa liberalisation, it would have overcome a whole range of obstacles to reform. Both police and constitutional reform would probably have been possible if they had been made conditions for a clear timetable leading to visa-free entry to the EU for citizens of BiH. Unfortunately, there was no political will at the time in either the European Commission or the EU Member States.

---

[43] Unlike tax policy, there is no EU *acquis* on police structures. For police, therefore, conditionality is defined in loose terms, while for tax it can be articulated in a very specific format.

## 4.5 The future

The reform and EU integration process in BiH has effectively been frozen since the elections of October 2006. The effort to break the deadlock through a strong US/EU initiative on constitutional reform through the Butmir process has failed – at least for now. The building of functioning institutions and governments at all levels of society remains a major challenge. Despite – and recently perhaps because of – an intrusive international presence over some fifteen years, BiH has not become a successful, well-established, modern state and faces substantial challenges to its continued existence, including calls for a referendum on secession in the Republika Srpska and dysfunctional institutions in the Federation. The progress on developing effective and cooperative institutions at state and entity levels has been halted, and in the RS it even appears that action is being taken to put in place legislation and institutions which could function independently of the central structures.

From the international perspective, the unified voice, which was apparent for a period between 2002 and 2004, has largely dissipated as well. The EU and the US, the major players in the country and the region, remain united despite some differences. However, two other major international actors – Russia and Turkey – have taken positions which are, at the least, not fully in line with the EU/US approach: Russia seeing itself as the defender of RS interests and Turkey taking on a much more proactive role in defending Bosniak interests. In the same period, the OHR has largely lost its credibility.

A basic issue is that mistakes made in the early stages of peacebuilding create problems which are very hard to fix at a later stage. The very short time frame envisaged for the creation and stabilisation of a redesigned BiH meant that the international community's commitment and involvement was continuously unrealistic. Reform of the dysfunctional structures and institutions cemented by the election process is extremely difficult. A coalition of enlightened elites who at some point realise the danger of the dysfunctional model could lead to such reform. Alternatively – and perhaps more drastically – internal or external shocks could prompt fundamental change.

A principal challenge facing the European Union and Bosnia is how to move forward at this stage, with national politicians facing elections in October 2010, with at least a disinterest in further enlargement within the European Union (both at political and civil society levels) and, on the other hand, with substantial progress potentially in view for the other Western Balkan states: Croatia finalising its accession negotiations, Macedonia soon commencing negotiations and Montenegro, Albania and Serbia having made formal applications for membership.

There appears to be no realistic prospect for a pre-electoral pledge on commitment to the Euro-Atlantic process similar to that engineered by Ashdown in early 2002 before the October 2010 elections. However, this should not mean that Europe turns its attention elsewhere or effectively adopts a 'wait and see' approach. Bosnia and the Western Balkans remain at the heart of Europe as the region whose integration into the Euro-Atlantic structures must be a priority, achievable with well-defined implemented and communicated policies and conditions.

The road forward must be that of European integration. Despite the very substantial state-building progress based on local commitment made during the Ashdown period, the experiment of treating Bosnia as a semi-protectorate has failed. For Croatia, Macedonia, Montenegro, Albania and now Serbia, the European Union has so far successfully followed the more traditional road of the European integration process. A similar process but more robust, proactive and focused should now be followed for Bosnia. It may be impossible to close the OHR before the October 2010 elections, but action should already be taken to provide a single EU presence, dissociated from the OHR, whose role would be to provide an unambiguous message of support and clear conditions for the way ahead.

# Chapter 20
# MEETING THE CHALLENGE OF STATE BUILDING: EU DEVELOPMENT POLICY AND COOPERATION IN POST-CONFLICT COUNTRIES

**Philippe Darmuzey***

## 1. Introduction

The uniqueness of each crisis and post-conflict situation requires a tailored response from the European Union, one that relies on an appropriate mix of policies and instruments based on shared analysis to ensure a coordinated, coherent and comprehensive EU approach.

The EU provides substantial crisis response and development assistance aimed at crisis prevention and (re)building peaceful and stable societies. These EU instruments include diplomacy and political dialogue (e.g., EU-level political action plans); humanitarian, civil protection, stabilisation/recovery, reconstruction, development and cooperation assistance; trade and economic measures (sanctions); security sector support in the broad sense; as well as cooperation with the international community (United Nations, African Union, etc.).

The European Commission contributes to an EU response with a range of external assistance instruments, including those specifically for immediate crisis/disaster responses such as the Instrument for Stability; humanitarian aid; and civil protection in coordination with EU Member States. In the medium to longer term, instruments such as development and other aid (including for reconstruction), macro-financial assistance, and trade and other economic measures are available to target post-conflict countries. In addition, the EU has instruments to address post-conflict and crisis situations under the Common Foreign and Security Policy (CFSP).

* Head of Unit, Pan-African Issues and Institutions, Governance and Migration, DG Development & Relations with African, Caribbean and Pacific States, European Commission. The author wishes to thank David Johnson, member of the same Unit, for his invaluable contribution to this chapter. The views expressed herein are the author's own and do not necessarily represent the official position of any organisation or institution.

*S. Blockmans, J. Wouters & T. Ruys, eds., The European Union and Peacebuilding*

## 2. The rationale for intervention in post-conflict countries

### 2.1 European Consensus on Development

While the Commission's development assistance to post-conflict countries and countries in a state of fragility has been a prominent part of the EU package for some time, 2005 saw an explicit recognition of the key linkage between security and development. The adoption of the European Consensus on Development marked a milestone for a new EU Development Policy including operations in post-conflict countries.[1] It refers explicitly to conflict prevention and work in post-conflict situations as a development activity focused on achieving the Millennium Development Goals (MDGs) and on the economic, social and environmental dimensions of poverty eradication. It sets out an approach to 'addressing state fragility', providing guidance on a comprehensive response to fragility. It specifies that the EU will support assistance in post-conflict environments and prevention of state fragility through governance reforms, rule of law, anti-corruption measures and the building of viable state institutions. Addressing the root causes of violent conflict is mentioned as part of its support for conflict prevention and resolution and for peacebuilding, also covering poverty, degradation, exploitation and unequal distribution of and access to land and natural resources, weak governance, human rights abuses and gender inequality. In addition, it refers to a number of other themes, such as a strengthened role for regional and sub-regional organisations in conflict prevention and limitation of the uncontrolled proliferation of small arms and light weapons. The European Consensus on Development reiterates the wish to have EU interventions take place in the framework of multilateral efforts, including the UN Peacebuilding Commission (PBC), and re-establishes principles of ownership and partnership.

### 2.2 Overview of key objectives

We can distinguish three types of objectives that the Commission pursues providing support in situations of fragility and to post-conflict countries as regards conflict prevention and peacebuilding.

Firstly, the Commission aims to foster sustainable economic and social development of developing countries, their integration into the world economy and the campaign against poverty.[2] The contribution of conflict prevention and peacebuilding to sustainable economic and social development of developing countries has, since 2001, been consistently present in strategic documents (e.g., the European Security Strategy of 2003).[3] Development policy and other cooperation programmes are

---

[1] Joint declaration by the Council and the representatives of the governments of the Member States meeting within the Council, the European Parliament and the Commission on the development policy of the European Union entitled 'The European Consensus', *OJ* 2006 C 46/1.

[2] This is specified in Article 208 TFEU.

[3] *A Secure Europe in a Better World – A European Security Strategy*, adopted by the European Council on 12 December 2003 (available at: <http://www.consilium.europa.eu/uedocs/cmsUpload/

without doubt the most powerful instruments at the Union's disposal for treating the root causes of conflict. In this sense, development and poverty reduction are seen as necessary conditions for preventing conflicts and building peace.

Secondly, the Commission aims to preserve peace, strengthen international security[4] and promote international cooperation.[5] In Article 11, the European Consensus on Development states that

> 'the Parties shall pursue an active, comprehensive and integrated policy of peace-building and conflict prevention and resolution within the framework of the Partnership. It shall in particular focus on building regional, sub-regional and national capacities, and on preventing violent conflicts at an early stage by addressing their root-causes in a targeted manner, and with an adequate combination of all available instruments.'

An example of this is the EU support to security system reform (SSR) in Afghanistan. Several EU actors support security sector reform which is recognised as a crucial element of the support to the Afghan government's state-building effort.[6]

Thirdly, the Commission strives to contribute to the development and consolidation of democracy and the rule of law and to the promotion of respect for human rights and fundamental freedoms.[7] The 2001 Communication on Conflict Prevention acknowledges the need to consolidate democracy and the rule of law, as well as respect for human rights and fundamental freedoms, as components of conflict prevention and peacebuilding.[8] It considers for instance that

> 'countries with conflict potential are usually those where the democratic process is the least advanced and where external support (...) is the most difficult to implement. In such conditions, EC support should aim, through targeted activities, at opening the way to a more favourable democratic environment.'[9]

## 2.3 Situations of fragility

The topic of 'fragility' has gained ground in the international agenda in recent years, emerging as a key issue in international policy and interventions in conflict situations. Situations of fragility exacerbate the challenge of achieving the MDGs and may involve global security risks. OECD-DAC 'Whole of Government Approaches

---

78367.pdf>) and complemented by the High Representative's *Report on the Implementation of the European Security Strategy – Providing Security in a Changing World*, doc. 17104/08 (S407/08), 11 December 2008, as endorsed by the European Council, Presidency Conclusions, doc. 17271/08 (CONCL 5), 12 December 2008, point 30.

[4] In accordance with the principles of the United Nations Charter, as well as those of the Helsinki Final Act and the objectives of the Paris Charter.

[5] A CFSP objective since the 1992 Treaty of Maastricht, Article J.1 TEU.

[6] See the contribution by Gross to this volume.

[7] This objective is specified in Article 208 as well as in Article 212 TFEU.

[8] Commission Communication of 11 April 2001 on Conflict Prevention, COM(2001) 211 final.

[9] Ibid., point 6.

to Fragile States' guidelines were issued in 2006,[10] which required economic, development, diplomatic and security actors to cooperate closely in fragile states. In April 2007, this was followed by OECD-DAC 'Principles for Good International Engagement in Fragile States and Situations': a set of ten principles were defined, ranging from basics such as contextualisation and a 'do no harm' approach, to principles relating to the role of state building and peacebuilding and practicalities.[11] Within the EU policy environment, two specific documents on fragility were issued a few months later. The Commission Communication 'Towards an EU response to situations of fragility engaging in difficult environments for sustainable development, stability and peace' was released in October 2007.[12] The EU response aims at preventing and addressing fragility holistically through a consistent overall response linking peace, security and development. It is built on the existing external intervention framework, including the guidance on a comprehensive response to fragility provided in the 2005 European Consensus on Development. A month later, in the same direction, the Council adopted two sets of conclusions: 'An EU response to situations of fragility'[13] and 'Security and development'.[14] The Council underlined that situations of fragility constitute a major challenge to sustainable development and peace, may exacerbate the risk of failing to reach the Millennium Development Goals, as well as involve regional and global security risks. The Council also stated that in order to contribute to the coherence of EU external action, the nexus between security and development should inform EU strategies and policies. The European Commission and the General Secretariat of the Council, in close cooperation with Member States, were tasked to prepare action plans for implementing the orientations and policy commitments set out in the conclusions. In order to develop plans regarding lessons learnt, studies and pilot exercises were undertaken in a set of countries representing different degrees of insecurity and fragility and levels of development, and with varied ways of EU engagement on the ground.

**The 2009 European Report on Development (ERD)**[15]

In addition to practical improvements, the EU also aims at contributing to the more general debate on the causes, concepts, consequences and policy implications of fragility. The first edition of the European Report on Development was dedicated to the topic 'Overcoming fragility in Africa – forging a new European approach' and brought together a consortium of European researchers under the lead of the European University Institute. A participatory process involving a wide range of scholars, policy makers and

10 Available at: <http://www.oecd.org/dataoecd/15/24/37826256.pdf>.

11 Available at: <http://www.oecd.org/dataoecd/61/45/38368714.pdf>.

12 COM(2007) 643 final of 25.10.2007.

13 See Doc. 15118/07 of 20 November 2007. See also European Parliament Resolution De P6_TA-PROV(2007)0540 of 15 November 2007.

14 See Doc. 15097/07 of 20 November 2007. See also European Parliament Resolution P6_TA-PROV(2008)0639 of 18 December 2008.

15 The ERD is available at: <http://erd.eui.eu>.

civil society representatives, from both Europe and Africa, was at the heart of this ambitious policy research initiative.

The report analyses the structural features and causes of fragility in sub-Saharan Africa, as well as the costs it entails from a human, economic and security perspective, including at regional and global levels. It then explores the complex links between fragility, vulnerability and resilience and describes how fragile African countries in particular have been hit by the succession of crises (food, fuel and financial/economic). In conclusion, the report assesses the EU's current engagement and proposes long-term policy priorities.

## 3. Instruments

The Commission has a number of instruments other than its medium/long-term development assistance to contribute to tackling the immediate challenges facing countries in crisis or in post-conflict situations. These include the Instrument for Stability, the African Peace Facility and humanitarian assistance.

### 3.1 Trends in Commission funding between 2001 and 2008

The section below provides evidence of the increasing focus on the Commission – in both policy and resource allocation – in addressing the specific challenges in conflict, post-conflict and fragile situations. The period since 2001 has seen a significant enhancement of the policy environment, specific tools and human resource allocation for these situations. Resource allocation has increased significantly, especially over the last years because of the economic crisis and the need to address urgently the drivers of conflict and fragility.

*Overview of funding for conflict prevention and peacebuilding (CPPB) assistance*[16]
The Commission contracted a total amount of €6.2bn for CPPB interventions in developing countries in the period 2001-2008. The total amount disbursed was €5.3bn, or 85% of the total amount contracted. 74% of the total amount contracted for these interventions came from the Commission's general budget and 26% from the European Development Fund (EDF).[17] The corresponding disbursements were €4bn (or 86% of the amount contracted from the general budget) and €1.3bn (81% of the amount contracted from the EDF). With regard to the number of contracts, a total of 3,095 were signed during the period 2001-2008, reaching an annual level of 625 contracts for CPPB interventions in 2008.

---

16 See *Thematic Evaluation of the European Commission Support to Conflict Prevention and Peace Building. Preliminary study: scoping and mapping, Final Report for the Preliminary Study, Volume I*, carried out by the Particip-led consortium, EVA 2007/main-pol+strat LOT5, framework contract for multi-country thematic and regional/country-level strategy evaluation studies and synthesis in the area of external co-operation. Ref.: EuropeAid/122888/C/SER/Multi, July 2009, at 38, available at: <http://ec.europa.eu/europeaid/how/evaluation/evaluation_reports/reports/2009/1266_pst_vol1_en.pdf>.

17 See *infra* n. 21.

*Country / regional breakdown*[18]
The Commission intervenes in the field of CPPB in all regions where its external cooperation is implemented. The distribution varies from year to year but between 2001 and 2008 the ACP region (33%) represented the largest share of amounts contracted for CPPB interventions, mainly in support of the APF, interventions in Sudan, and operations in the Democratic Republic of Congo (DRC). The ENP-MEDA region represented 30% of the total amount contracted, mainly relating to interventions in the West Bank and Gaza Strip (€1,793m out of €1,896m for the whole region). The Asia region received 27% of the total amount contracted, most of which (81%) went to Afghanistan (€695m) and Iraq (€668m). The ENP -TACIS region represented 4%, Latin America 4% and the multi-region category 2%.

*Thematic breakdown*[19]
The thematic breakdown of CPPB funding (2001-2008) indicates a broad approach and impact. The main thematic categories are peace consolidation and prevention of future conflict (20.8% or €1,286m ); rapid intervention (19.9% or €1,233m); democracy, rule of law and civil society (14.7% or €911m); population flows and human trafficking (14.5% or €898m); reconstruction and infrastructure (14.4% or €889m); economic support and trade cooperation (5.8% or €357m); security sector (4.8% or €280m); and multi-sector (3% or €177m).

*Partners*[20]
The Commission worked with 1,484 different partners for the implementation of its CPPB interventions in the period 2001-2008. Of these contractors, 48 accounted for €5.1bn or 83% of the total amount contracted and €4.5bn or 86% of the total amount disbursed. These 48 main partners include the following six categories: international organisations, national governments, regional organisations, private companies, non-governmental organisations (NGOs) and development agencies. The main channels, in terms of amount contracted, used by the Commission for CPPB interventions are the international organisations, mainly the UN and the World Bank. Indeed, these two organisations administer reconstruction trust funds through which the Commission channels large amounts of funds such as the IRFFI for the reconstruction of Iraq (€600m) and the LOTFA (€195m) and ARTF (€237m) in Afghanistan. The Commission also contributes to UNRWA's general budget (a total amount of €476m from 2001 to 2008) and to the support of elections, mainly through the UNDP, including €324m for election support in more than 20 countries.

## 3.2 European Development Fund

The medium-term development assistance foreseen for the ACP countries through the European Development Fund (EDF) is an example of a key instrument address-

[18] Ibid., at 41.
[19] Ibid., at 44.
[20] Ibid., at 46.

ing post-conflict countries.[21] The EC General Budget and the EDF provide flexible mechanisms in response to such situations, termed 'crisis situations' (EC General Budget and EDF) and 'emergency and post-emergency assistance' (EDF only). In essence, these mechanisms make it possible to apply quicker and simpler procedures – mainly negotiated procedures for procurement contracts and direct award for grant contracts – once the relevant authority has established that the circumstances for applying these procedures exist in a given country or region.[22]

Article 72 of the Cotonou Agreement defines emergency assistance as aid accorded to the population in ACP states faced with serious economic and social difficulties of an exceptional nature resulting from natural disasters, man-made crises such as wars and other conflicts or extraordinary circumstances having comparable effects.

Article 73 of the Cotonou Agreement provides that post-emergency action, aimed at physical and social rehabilitation, may be undertaken, using effective and flexible mechanisms, to ease the transition from the emergency phase to the development phase, promote the socio-economic reintegration of the populations affected, remove as far as possible the causes of the crisis and strengthen institutions and ownership by local and national actors.

The legal definitions of crisis situations and emergency and post-emergency situations focus on the effects of the situations described in those provisions and do not limit their duration or establish an open-ended list of causes leading to the above-mentioned threats or difficulties. A country or region may suffer from long-term structural instability (or fragility), leading to such threats and difficulties, before it is able to reach a level of stability allowing the implementation of 'normal' structural development aid. These situations of long-term structural crisis also require the use of the afore-mentioned flexible procedures. Flexible procedures can be used in all cases falling under Articles 72 and 73 of the Cotonou Agreement, regardless of the duration of the causes or the effects deriving from the threats and difficulties covered by these provisions.

For example, between 2003 and 2005, the political dialogue in Guinea-Bissau was conducted in the framework of Article 96 of the Cotonou Agreement. At the end of this period, both parties agreed on the need to maintain a sustained and deepened political dialogue. From January 2008 onwards, EU Heads of Mission in Guinea-Bissau conduct a monthly political dialogue with the government of Guinea-Bissau in the framework of Article 8 of the Cotonou Agreement.

---

[21] See Council Regulation (EC) No 617/2007 of 14 May 2007 on the implementation of the 10th European Development Fund under the ACP-EC Partnership Agreement, *OJ* 2007 L 152/1.

[22] Under the EDF, the application of emergency (and post-emergency) assistance is defined in Articles 72 and 73 of the Cotonou Agreement. See the Partnership Agreement APC-EC, signed in Cotonou on 23 June 2000, *OJ* 2000 L 317/3 (revised in Luxembourg on 25 June 2005).

## 3.3 Instrument for Stability

The Instrument for Stability (IfS)[23] contributes to EU crisis responses by addressing 'windows of opportunity' to prevent conflict escalation; addressing direct consequences of violent conflict; supporting diplomatic and peace initiatives, mediation and reconciliation processes, DDR, reconstruction, etc; promoting post-crisis stabilisation through support for good governance; constitutional processes and SSR activities; ensuring that basic needs are addressed again after a crisis: getting the public administration working, ensuring that children can go back to school and reopening health services; creating employment; and securing conditions for a renewal of 'normal' development aid.

The IfS has been shown to be an effective instrument in post-conflict countries. IfS funding for crisis response is €1.3 billion (2007-2013), with over 40 IfS crisis responses in 2008, implemented through over 30 of the Commission's 130+ Delegations. The interventions vary from limited urgent interventions to larger interventions. For example, in 2008: Eastern DR Congo (€10m), Georgia (€15m), Bangladesh (€13m) and Kosovo (€14.2m); and in early 2009: Gaza as a high priority.[24]

## 3.4 African Peace Facility[25]

The African Peace Facility (APF) has been by far the most important Commission source of funding to support the African Peace and Security Agenda and the implementation of the Peace and Security Partnership.[26] Since 2004, the APF allocation has reached €740m, including over €40m provided through an innovative mechanism of Additional Voluntary Contributions of EU Member States. These Contributions have been pooled in the APF framework and managed in accordance with APF rules and procedures.

African-led Peace Support Operations (PSOs) have been the core business of the APF. The Facility has provided funding for the African Union Mission in Sudan (AMIS) – over €305m; the MICOPAX Mission in the Central African Republic led by ECCAS (ex-FOMUC) – €53,2m; the African Union Mission in Somalia (AMISOM) – €95.5m; and the African Union Mission in Comoros (AMISEC) – €8.5m.[27]

---

23 And the Crisis Preparedness – IfS 'Peacebuilding Partnership'. The IfS was introduced by Regulation (EC) No 1717/2006 of the European Parliament and of the Council of 15 November 2006 establishing an Instrument for Stability, *OJ* 2006 L 327/1.

24 Information available at: <http://ec.europa.eu/external_relations/ifs/index_en.htm>.

25 See also the contribution by Vervaeke to this volume.

26 See Council Regulation (EC) No 617/2007 of 14 May 2007 on the implementation of the 10th European Development Fund under the ACP-EC Partnership Agreement, *OJ* 2007 L 152/1, and Decision No 2/2007 of the ACP-EC Council of Ministers of 25 May 2007 allowing additional bilateral contributions, to be managed by the Commission, in support of the objectives of the African Peace Facility, *OJ* 2007 L 175/35.

27 Information available at: <http://ec.europa.eu/europeaid/where/acp/regional-cooperation/peace/peace-support-operations/index_en.htm>.

In terms of support to capacity building, the APF has focused on support to: strengthening capacities of the African Union Commission (€6m); African Standby Force (ASF) workshops (€988,552); and planning capacities of the African Standby Force, including early warning systems and financial management at both sub-regional and continental levels (€20m).

The second-generation APF launched in 2009 as a successor to the first Facility is based on priorities and recommendations jointly developed with the African side, following a broad and comprehensive consultation process that involved the African Union and African sub-regional organisations (SROs). The landmarks of this process included the joint lessons-learned workshop on the implementation of the APF (Djibouti, 2-3 November 2007) and the APF Joint Coordination Committee meeting (Addis Abeba, 4 February 2008) where recommendations for the future African Peace Facility were agreed. The main orientations of the new Facility (€300m for a period of three years) include an enlarged scope of the APF, allowing a more integrated ('continuum') approach to challenges to peace, stability and security in Africa. As a result, the APF has become an instrument with a better balance between crisis management and development/civilian activities. Its programming reflects priorities of the Joint Africa-EU Strategy, namely the Partnership on Peace and Security and its first Action Plan, and responds to the need to ensure greater flexibility of the APF.[28]

## 4. Challenges and ways forward

### 4.1 Introduction

The EU is working on developing practical ways for the EU actors to better address situations of fragility and conflict, including the security and development nexus. These revolve around four main areas:

- firstly, steps to improve the coordinated, coherent and holistic – 'Whole-of-the-Union' – approach including relevant EU actors from different policy communities (in particular security, development, humanitarian assistance and diplomacy);
- secondly, a focus on building peaceful, legitimate and inclusive states as the central objective of external intervention;
- thirdly, the challenge of making EU development assistance and support aimed at reaching the MDGs more effective, responsive and adapted to the challenges posed by fragility and conflict;
- and lastly, the deepening of strategic international partnerships with global, regional as well as sub-regional organisations.

---

[28] Information available at: <http://ec.europa.eu/europeaid/where/acp/regional-cooperation/peace/index_en.htm>.

## 4.2 Towards a 'Whole-of-the-Union' approach

As a global actor, the EU can avail itself of a wide array of instruments to contribute to long-term development and poverty eradication, to the promotion of democracy, the rule of law and human rights, to the prevention and management of conflict and to support for peacebuilding in partner countries. However, the range of EU actors and instruments will only have a real and sustained impact if and when they are coherent, coordinated and complementary. A holistic approach is especially important in situations of fragility and conflict, where unclear messages and uncoordinated action will weaken the role of the international community, including that of the EU, and can do harm on the ground. The EU therefore needs to address challenges related to its internal coherence.[29]

## 4.3 The state building challenge

As noted above, the concept of 'fragility' refers to situations where the social contract between the population and the state structures is broken due to the state's incapacity or unwillingness to perform its basic functions and responsibilities.[30] Countries where this may be the case range from those weakened by conflict to those with strong governments unwilling to provide basic services to the majority and where human rights abuses are widespread. The building of peaceful, legitimate and inclusive states should therefore be at the heart of all efforts in fragile situations.

State building is first and foremost an endogenous process, driven by state-society relationships. The construction or strengthening of state institutions is only one dimension of this wide definition of state building, with equal importance attached to local administration, civil society and the broad range of state-society relations. In many situations, the main providers of basic services, ranging from health to security, are civil society organisations and private sector representatives. Civil society organisations are also indispensable in articulating the concerns and priorities of populations, including of marginalised groups. Media institutions are key in influencing opinions and can thereby either support or undermine peacebuilding efforts.

The EU actors are engaged in supporting various activities of relevance to state-building efforts, but often without an express focus on state building. Yet, the state-building perspective can contribute to a more focused and coherent response in different policy areas by putting people's expectations and needs at the forefront. Providing assistance in regard to political settlements and state institutions should, for instance, not reduce attention for the provision of basic social services such as

---

[29] Communication from the Commission to the Council, the European Parliament, the Economic and Social Committee and the Committee of the Regions, 'Policy Coherence for Development – Establishing the policy framework for a whole-of-the-Union approach', COM(2009) 458 final, Brussels, 15.09.2009.

[30] COM(2007) 643 final of 25.10.2007.

health and education, which correspond to social expectations and needs. Where appropriate, the support should be channelled through state and local institutions in order to strengthen the legitimacy and capacity of the local administration. In other cases, non-state actors, in particular non-governmental organisations, will be the main providers.

Providing security and the rule of law is one of the state's core functions, relating to both personal and state safety. However, a repressive security apparatus can spoil these efforts, and in situations of conflict and post-conflict non-state actors are often the main providers of security. Taking these factors into account, supporting security sector reform can be an important element of state building. Recent years have seen an increasing number of development cooperation actors involved in SSR.[31] At the same time, more traditional military cooperation has been complemented by civilian crisis management. The diversity of actors involved, with sometimes overlapping activities, make the coherence and coordination of activities a challenge. Ensuring local ownership of SSR, including the justice system, is critical for sustainable reform. This requires donors to be willing to scale down donor visibility.[32]

The effects of climate change and recent food and fuel shocks as well as the current financial and economic crisis have underlined states' vulnerability and lack of resilience to external (economic and other) shocks. In that respect, measures to reduce vulnerability and enhance the resilience of states and their populations to external shocks are integral parts of state-building efforts, both from an aid effectiveness and from a security perspective. For people affected by fragility and conflict, ensuring their livelihoods is an important priority. Economic development needs to be at the focus of efforts from early on. Considering the linkage between economic and political stability, the local private sector is an important and interested actor and ally in peacebuilding and state-building efforts.

## 4.4 Rendering EU development assistance more effective and responsive

As agreed in the Paris Declaration and reinforced in the Accra Agenda for Action, aid effectiveness principles apply equally to countries in fragile situations, even if they need to be adapted to environments of weak ownership or capacity.[33] The 2007 OECD 'Principles on Good International Engagement in Fragile States and Situations' guide the way.[34] Countries in fragile situations are often supported only by a limited number of donors, leaving them underfunded when compared to other developing countries.[35] The international community has engaged in efforts to draw

---

[31] See the contribution by Spence to this volume.

[32] This was one of the main findings of in-country SSR consultations which the OECD carried out in Burundi, the Central African Republic, Guinea-Bissau and Bolivia, based on its SSR handbook (December 2007 – October 2008).

[33] Aid effectiveness has accordingly been the focus of all pilot country exercises, such as in Timor Leste, by setting the goal of establishing a joint EU CSP by 2014.

[34] See *supra* n. 10.

[35] See the OECD Report *Ensuring Fragile States Are Not Left Behind* (March 2009).

attention to this challenge of so-called 'donor orphans', e.g., by creating the UN Peacebuilding Commission and Fund.

Adhering to aid effectiveness principles requires special attention in situations of fragility and conflict. In practice, development assistance in such situations has to meet two specific challenges. Firstly, instruments, tools and modalities must be adapted to a fast changing environment with limited capacity and/or ownership on the part of the country concerned. Secondly, there is pressing need for aid to be as effective as possible, and coordination and policy coherence for development are of the essence. Transaction costs can be high, whether donors are working with government, CSOs, the private sector or others, draining scarce resources, particularly human resources and management capacity. This set-up makes it a challenge to choose the appropriate instruments and modalities for development cooperation.

Having a limited number of donors presents an opportunity for donor coordination, making it easier to agree on joint assessments and missions and division of labour. A well-coordinated system can then act as a catalyst for further support if gradually more donors become engaged as the situation turns less fragile. In many countries, EU actors present participate in overall donor coordination and any EU coordination should not duplicate these wider efforts.

Donor arrangements should be aligned to partner country systems as quickly as the situation allows, which can be challenging in fragile and conflict situations. Often capacity development has to be prioritised and technical cooperation used as an aid modality. However, even in these cases local ownership of development efforts is crucial and when parallel project implementation units are set up they need to have appropriate exit strategies in their initial design.

State building and macroeconomic stability require, in certain cases, specific aid modalities including budget support. Eligibility for the latter follows the same guiding principles in fragile and non-fragile environments,[36] but with a nuanced interpretation to adapt to fragility particularities and risks. In order to refine the use and delivery of budget support, the Commission is working on internal guidelines for its modalities in fragile situations, as well as on better coordination with other international actors. These exercises will incorporate budget support in the framework of state-building efforts and macroeconomic stability while encouraging clear and coordinated identification of risks and proposing appropriate mitigation strategies.

## 4.5 Strategic partnerships

In addition to its general engagement as an actor in international fora, the EU has developed strategic partnerships with key international players, addressing both general and specific challenges that can best be tackled in cooperation.

In September 2008, the European Commission, the United Nations Development Group and the World Bank signed a Joint Declaration on Post-Crisis Assessments and Recovery Planning stating their commitment to harmonise and coordinate

---

[36] See in particular Art. 61 of the Cotonou Agreement.

post-crisis response frameworks in order to enhance country resilience to crises.[37] The Declaration sets out a common platform for action, at both headquarters and field level, in the areas of monitoring, planning and developing methodologies for post-conflict and post-disaster needs assessment.

In 2004, the European Commission and UNDP set up a strategic partnership in the field of electoral assistance.[38] This partnership builds on a history of sector experience, specific attention to lessons learned in previous projects and a mutual understanding of each other's approaches, roles and capacities. The partnership is proving to be of increasing value to electoral assistance operations in conflict and fragile environments, as it rationalises interventions and leads to a better and more timely formulation, implementation and monitoring of projects.

The Joint Africa-EU Strategy can be seen as a model for a more strategic approach to engaging with regional organisations.[39] As regards situations of fragility and conflict, the Partnership on Democratic Governance and Human Rights and the Partnership on Peace and Security are of particular importance. In the framework of the latter, the Commission and Member States finance, through the African Peace Facility, efforts to strengthen African capacity (African Union and regional organisations) in conflict management. The APF also funds peace and security operations led by Africans for Africans. For the EU institutions and Member States this regional partnership requires internal coordination and possibly revision of policies and funding instruments. The involvement of civil society is also key to the Joint Africa-EU Strategy.

**The Africa-EU Strategic Partnership: A Joint Africa-EU Partnership**[40]

*Africa-EU Partnership on Peace and Security*[41]
Peace and security lie at the foundation of progress and sustainable development. The objective of the Joint Strategy is cooperation in enhancing the capacity of Africa and EU to respond timely and adequately to security threats, as well as to join efforts in addressing global challenges. In this respect, the Peace and Security Partnership has focused on three priority actions for the period 2008-2010: to enhance dialogue on challenges to peace and security; to ensure full operationalisation of the African Peace and Security Architecture; and to work towards predictable funding for African-led Peace Support Operations.

---

[37] Available at: <http://www.undg.org/docs/9419/trilateral-JD-on-post-crisis-assessments-final.pdf>.

[38] See also the contribution by Gourlay to this volume.

[39] Details are available at: <http://www.africa-eu-partnership.org>. See also the contribution by Vervaeke to this volume.

[40] Council of the European Union, *The Africa-EU Strategic Partnership: A Joint Africa-EU Partnership*, doc. 16344/07 (Presse 291), Lisbon, 9 December 2007.

[41] Information available at: <http://www.africa-eu-partnership.org/partnerships/items/peace_security_en.htm>.

*Africa-EU Partnership on Democratic Governance and Human Rights*[42]
Democratic governance and human rights are key to sustainable development and to cooperation between partners, and form an integral part of both the EU's and the AU's core values. The Africa-EU Partnership on Democratic Governance and Human Rights should enable a comprehensive continent-to-continent dialogue and cooperation on aspects and concepts such as local capacity strengthening, the protection of human rights and fundamental freedoms for all, democratic principles, the rule of law and equitable access to legal systems, management of natural resources, the fight against corruption and fraud, accountable management of public funds, institutional development and reform, global governance, and security sector reform.

Finally, the EU has established several channels of dialogue and cooperation with non-state actors on peace, conflict and security issues, at both headquarters and field levels.[43] It needs to build on existing best practice, ongoing processes and lessons learned to enhance the inclusion and participation of international and local civil society in the planning, implementation and review of its policies and programmes.

## 5. Conclusion

EU political and development strategies in situations of post-conflict and fragility should focus on supporting the building of peaceful, resilient and legitimate states, accountable to and concerned for the welfare of their entire population. By analysing existing state-society relations, including issues relating to legitimacy, transparency, accountability, non-discrimination, gender and drivers of conflict, opportunities for strengthening the legitimacy and promoting the inclusiveness of the state can be identified.

The European Union is developing more coherent ways of addressing conflict, fragility and post-conflict situations in third countries. An EU Action Plan for Situations of Fragility and Conflict – a follow-up to the 2007 Council Conclusions on fragile situations and on security and development – is in the process of elaboration and should be implemented in the near future. It is expected that the forthcoming full operationalisation of the European External Action Service (EEAS) created by the Treaty of Lisbon will enhance the coherence of EU external actions especially in situations of conflict, fragility and post-conflict.

---

42 Information available at: <http://www.africa-eu-partnership.org/partnerships/items/democratic_governance_en.htm>.

43 These include formal and informal consultations, the Peacebuilding Partnership under the Instrument for Stability, funding support, etc.

# Chapter 21
# THE EU AND THE KIMBERLEY PROCESS: A NEW INTERNATIONAL ACTOR FOR NEW INTERNATIONAL RELATIONS*

**Stéphane Chardon****

## 1. Introduction

Conflict diamonds, also known as blood diamonds, are diamonds that are used by rebel groups to fuel conflict and civil wars. They have funded brutal conflicts in Africa that have resulted in the death and displacement of millions of people. The issue of 'conflict diamonds'[1] emerged in the 1990s, as the trade in rough diamonds provided substantial financing for rebel groups in countries such as Angola, Sierra Leone and the Democratic Republic of Congo (DRC). The United Nations had tried to address the problem of conflict diamonds through a series of resolutions applying targeted sanctions against diamond trade from Angola,[2] Sierra Leone[3] and Liberia.[4] Sanctions – even where complemented by national certification schemes – nonetheless lacked effectiveness as 'conflict diamonds' were difficult to identify and easily smuggled through other countries.

NGO media campaigns and recommendations from UN Groups of Experts raised awareness on the issue and prompted an international response. The Security Council issued a report – the 'Fowler report'[5] – in March 2000 and the Kimberley Pro-

* The abbreviation for the 'European Union' is used in this title, though – at the time of writing – formally the European Community (EC) is a Participant in the Kimberley Process Certification Scheme, and the KPCS is implemented through an EC regulation (Regulation (EC) No 2368/2002 of 20 December 2002) adopted under the EC Treaty.

** The author works for the European Commission, DG RELEX/A2: crisis response and peacebuilding, sanctions and Kimberley Process. The views expressed herein are strictly personal and do not necessarily reflect the official position of the European Commission.

[1] The term 'conflict diamonds' was popularised by the 1998 report *A Rough Trade* by Global Witness, exposing the role of conflict diamonds in funding Angola's civil war. Conflict diamonds are officially defined by the UN as 'rough diamonds which are used by rebel movements to finance their military activities, including attempts to undermine or overthrow legitimate governments.' Here, the term 'conflict diamonds' is preferred to the term 'blood diamonds' often used in the media.

[2] S/Res/1173 (1998).

[3] S/Res/1295 (2000).

[4] S/Res/1336 (2001).

[5] After the Canadian diplomat Robert Fowler, UN document S/2000/2003.

*S. Blockmans, J. Wouters & T. Ruys, eds., The European Union and Peacebuilding*

cess was launched in May 2000, while the General Assembly called, in Resolution 55/56 of 1 December 2000, for the development and implementation of an international certification scheme for rough diamonds.[6] The G8 meetings in Okinawa in July 2000 and Kananaskis in July 2002 expressed support for the Kimberley Process (KP) in their final communiqués.[7] In UNSCR 1459 (2003) of 28 January 2003, the UNSC strongly supported the Kimberley Process Certification Scheme (KPCS) as a valuable contribution against the trafficking in conflict diamonds. At the request of KP members, the WTO granted a waiver with respect to the measures taken to implement the KPCS that effectively restrict trade in rough diamonds.[8] Thus, from the outset, the KP has enjoyed wide support from the United Nations and other international organisations, thereby conferring it authority and legitimacy.

The Kimberley Process was officially launched in May 2000 when government officials from more than 30 diamond-producing and trading countries came together along with representatives from the diamond industry and NGOs in the South African city of Kimberley – where South African diamonds were first discovered towards the end of the nineteenth century – and initiated a dialogue to break the link between diamond trade and devastating conflicts in Africa. Two years later, with the Interlaken Declaration of 5 November 2002, 52 countries adopted the Kimberley Process Certification Scheme (KPCS), under which all countries commit to comply with certification requirements for rough diamond trade.[9] The KPCS became effective in January 2003.

From the very beginning, in particular due to its prominent position in rough diamond trade, the EU was at the heart of efforts to fight conflict diamonds.[10] The EU's commitment to conflict prevention and peacebuilding played a major role in its support to the Kimberley Process. In June 2001, in Göteborg, the European Council adopted a programme for the prevention of violent conflicts, which highlighted in particular the fight against conflict diamonds as a factor in conflict prevention.[11]

The UN sanctions that preceded the KPCS were mostly implemented directly by EU Member States as members of the United Nations, and though sanctions were increasingly addressed at EU level under the newly created Common Foreign and Security Policy (CFSP), EU Member States were originally involved in the Kimberley Process negotiations directly. However, inasmuch as the KPCS was to operate as an international trade regulation for rough diamonds and therefore fell under EC competence, the Council authorised the Commission, on 29 October 2001,

---

6 The UNGA has regularly reiterated support through its Resolutions 56/263 of 13 March 2002, 57/302 of 15 April 2003, 58/290 of 14 April 2004, 59/144 of 15 December 2004, 60/182 of 20 December 2005, 61/28 of 4 December 2006, 62/11 of 26 November 2007 and 63/11 of 11 December 2008.

7 See: <http://www.g7.utoronto.ca/summit/2000okinawa/finalcom.htm>.

8 See General Council Decisions of 15 May 2003 (Document WT/L/518) and of 17 November 2006 (Document G/C/W/559/rev.1).

9 See: <http://www.kimberleyprocess.com/download/getfile/11>.

10 It is estimated that over 80% of rough diamonds pass through Antwerp and, moreover, De Beers operations were then centred in London.

11 See: <http://ec.europa.eu/external_relations/cfsp/conflict_prevention/docs/index_en.htm>.

to negotiate an international certification scheme in the framework of a binding international agreement.[12] The European Community thus became a single Participant in the KPCS, represented by the European Commission.

In the first years of its operation, the KP has proved remarkably successful, to the point that the vast majority of international rough diamond trade moves through official Kimberley channels. All significant diamond-producing, manufacturing and trading centres implement the KPCS that today brings together 49 Participants representing 75 countries, including the 27 members of the European Union. The KP contributed to curbing the flows of conflict diamonds from an estimated 4 to 15% at the end of the 1990s down to less than 0.2 % in 2008.[13] The KP also serves as a 'warning' or deterrent and contributes to the prevention of future diamonds-related conflict.

The Kimberley Process has thus emerged as a uniquely innovative international arrangement (section 2). It has developed into a remarkable conflict prevention and peacebuilding instrument (section 3) and has demonstrated its capacity to operate effectively in situations of crisis (section 4) in spite of challenges arising from a rapidly changing economic and political environment (section 5), to the point that it has become a reference in discussions involving 'conflict resources'. The EU has played an active role in the creation and operation of the Kimberley Process, and the KP's development coincided with the emergence of the EU as an international actor. This illustrates how a new international issue has been addressed through an innovative international instrument with the support of an emerging international actor (section 6).

## 2. The Kimberley process: An innovative international instrument

The Kimberley Process emerged on the international scene as a uniquely innovative instrument as regards its legal status, its institutional set-up as well as its original tripartite composition and informal working methods. It has demonstrated a capacity to operate efficiently with a flexible and pragmatic approach, based on the principle of burden sharing and voluntary commitments by Participants and Observers. For its part, the EU has held key institutional positions in the KP, culminating in the 2007 KP Chairmanship.

### 2.1 The legal status of the Kimberley Process: An international scheme based on national laws

The Kimberley Process is founded on a basic 'KPCS document' accepted by the parties at the Interlaken meeting. This 'basic document' falls short of meeting the

[12] Common Position 2001/758/CFSP of 29 October 2001 on combating the illicit traffic in conflict diamonds, as a contribution to prevention and settlement of conflicts.

[13] In 2009, only diamonds from Côte d'Ivoire are still officially classified as 'conflict diamonds'. The KP estimates that about 114,000 to 188,000 cts were produced in Côte d'Ivoire in 2008.

standard of an international agreement: it has not been signed by governments and is not legally binding as an international treaty. It thus appears as an intergovernmental functional mechanism operating with the support of industry and civil society. The preamble to the KPCS Document clarifies that the KP is a 'simple (...) *international* scheme based on *national* laws (...)' [emphasis added]. In fact, Participants are required to enact legislation to enter 'the club' and it is their domestic legislation that actually provides the legal basis for implementing the KPCS. The legal force and effectiveness of this international scheme thus derives formally from the requisite national legislations.

The flexible and *ad hoc* approach so characteristic of KP working methods has led to the adoption of a number of Administrative Decisions, Technical Guidelines and other documents, whose legal status remains unclear. The 'proliferation' of such technical documents resulted in a need for consolidation, highlighted by the KPCS review in 2006.[14] The EC decided, under its Chairmanship the following year, to incorporate all KP documents into a 'Compilation' available for all Participants on the KP website,[15] which operates as the central repository for KP documents and files.

### 2.2 The KP's innovative organisational set-up: Flexibility and burden sharing

The KP has no permanent organisational structure: when it comes to logistics, human and budgetary resources, it operates on the basis of burden sharing and voluntary commitments and depends on the contributions from Participants and Observers. The increasing complexity of the KP has at times prompted calls for the creation of a dedicated and funded administrative body, but the KP has thus far developed along its original innovative principles, steering clear of any 'institutionalisation' or 'bureaucratisation'.

#### 2.2.1 *The Chair*

The central element in the KP's flexible structure is the rotating KP Chair that holds extensive duties of a political and administrative nature and requires substantial financial and political commitment. South Africa, Canada, Russia, Botswana, the EC, India and Namibia have held this position, and Israel has been selected as the Chair for 2010.

The position of the KP Chair is traditionally held by a high-level official,[16] as KP Chairs may be required to undertake high-level political consultations, as was the case in 2007-2008 under the EC and Indian chairmanships, when the KP held protracted and heated discussions on Venezuela's compliance with KPCS require-

---

14 See: <http://www.kimberleyprocess.com/documents/third_year_view_en.html?>.

15 See: <http://www.kimberleyprocess.com/>.

16 The EC appointed Mr Karel Kovanda, Deputy Director-General of its External Relations Directorate. The current KP Chair, Mr Berhnard Esau, is Namibia's Vice-Minister of Mines.

ments.[17] In 2009, again, the KP Chair held high-level consultations with the political leadership in Zimbabwe to express KP concerns regarding smuggling and violence in Marange (see section 5).

The Chair is also responsible for funding and managing the KP Secretariat, whose operational and administrative support is essential to the operation of the KP. The KP Secretariat coordinates the activity of KP working groups, ensures communication with all Participants and is in charge of organising the two main yearly meetings: the Intersessional Meeting, traditionally held in June for Working Group members, and the Plenary Meeting, traditionally in November for all Participants. The Chair also operates the KP website,[18] which contains a public section as well as a section restricted to Participants, where documentation is made available to KP Participants and Observers. The website plays a key role in ensuring the continuity of the KP's operations while the Chairs rotate.

The EC assumed the KP Chairmanship in 2007 and strove to enhance the efficiency of the KP Chair's steering and coordinating function through an Action Programme which outlined the main activities and objectives of the KP in 2007 and provided a 'roadmap' for all Participants.[19] The EC Chairmanship provided a rare opportunity for the European Commission to lead an international scheme.

### 2.2.2 *Working groups*

The flexible structure of the KP also involves devolution of considerable responsibilities to working groups, with specific mandates and membership. The Participation Committee (chaired by the previous KP Chair and in charge of accession and compliance),[20] the Monitoring Working group (WGM, chaired by the EC and in charge of monitoring implementation), the Working Group on Statistics (WGS, chaired by the US and responsible for statistical transparency) and the Working Group of Diamond Experts (chaired by the World Diamond Council (WDC) and in charge of technical issues). New working groups have been created over the years to address specific issues, such as the Working Group of Alluvial Diamond Producers (chaired by Angola) and the Committee on Rules and Procedures (chaired by the Russian Federation). The composition of working groups illustrates the diversified leadership in the Kimberley Process. As a concrete application of the tripartite principle underlying the KP, NGOs and industry representatives actively participate in all working groups.

The 'Rules of Procedures' provide a basic framework for the operation of KP working groups and meetings. Working groups operate throughout the year, essentially through informal or electronic exchanges and frequent teleconferences ensur-

---

[17] See: <http://www.kimberleyprocess.com/documents/plenary_intersessional_meeting_en.html>.

[18] See: <http://www.kimberleyprocess.com/>.

[19] See: <http://ec.europa.eu/external_relations/blood_diamonds/index_en.htm>.

[20] The Participation Committee is chaired by the outgoing KP Chair as part of a system designed to ensure continuity of KP activities. The EC – C. Berger, Head of Unit, Crisis Response and Peacebuilding – chaired the Participation Committee in 2008.

ing rapid and cost-effective implementation of their respective mandates. The KP makes use of traditional diplomatic forms only occasionally: more usual working methods include specific KP tools, such as the annual reporting process, peer reviews, guidelines for the collection of statistics, questionnaires for applicants, etc.

### 2.3 Tripartite composition and consensual decision-making

The KP recognises the importance of state sovereignty and accordingly requires decisions to be adopted by consensus. This principle has proved effective, ensuring a continuous search for mutually acceptable solutions on the basis of mutual respect and trust. Consensus is key to ensure the confidence of Participants and a sense of shared ownership and legitimacy.

At the same time, the KP's decision-making process proves to be innovative insofar as it relies on the working collaboration of governments, industry and NGOs at all levels. NGOs and industry representatives (WDC) are formally recognised by the KPCS as 'observers', and their interaction with governments in working groups has contributed to the flexibility and responsiveness of the KP. The role of civil society and industry in the creation of the KP thus continues in the operation of the KP, through their membership in KP working groups and participation in review visits, meetings, etc. This has contributed to the development of a decision-making process marked by what might be called 'dynamic consensus'.

## 3. From Kimberley to Windhoek – the maturity of the KP (2003-2009)

As stated in the preamble of the 'KPCS basic document', the KP was essentially conceived as a 'simple' certification scheme founded on 'minimum' standards, operated through a limited number of international trade controls without being unduly onerous. The KPCS basically requires that all diamond shipments must be accompanied by a formal KPCS certificate and that participating governments implement import/export controls, ensure statistical transparency, and ensure 'internal control systems' regulating their private sectors.

At the mercy of Participants' agreement for every single decision, the basic KPCS document provided an uncertain basis for the fight against conflict diamonds. Yet, though the document has never been amended and remains the foundation for the Scheme, the KPCS has developed a remarkable array of instruments to fulfil its mandate. Along with others, the EU initiated or promoted a number of key initiatives and the KP certainly looks very different today from what was originally conceived.

### 3.1 KP 'inclusiveness' – an attractive club

In line with the General Assembly's mandate, the KP has remained open on a global, non-discriminatory basis and has maintained an inclusive approach to all applicants 'willing and able' to fulfil its requirements. The Kimberley Process represents diamond-producing as well as manufacturing and trading countries from all parts of the world, and in spite of the removal of some countries from the list of KPCS Participants (see *infra*), the list has continued to steadily increase, most recently with the accession of Mexico, the Republic of Congo (RoC, Brazzaville) and Liberia. Inclusiveness has been a key ingredient for success, with each type of actor bringing its respective interests, expertise and knowledge to the table. There is no end in sight to the expanding membership of the KP, with interest coming in from places as diverse as Swaziland, Panama and Greenland.

The principle of inclusiveness also applies to the diamond industry and NGOs. As regards NGOs, Global Witness and Partnership Africa Canada have been particularly active in the KP, and created, in 2007, a coalition of civil society organisations to enhance the participation of southern civil society in the KP. As for industry, the World Diamond Centre represents virtually all major players in the industry – producers such as De Beers and Rio Tinto, but also traders, jewellers and consumers.

### 3.2 KP statistics – transparency in the diamond sector

*Statistical transparency* is one of the cornerstones of the Kimberley Process, and the regular collection and publication of statistical data is a key requirement under the Scheme. The Working Group on Statistics is in charge of managing the KPCS database and dedicated website, which has matured into an effective tool for the collection and dissemination of data, thereby ensuring unprecedented transparency. This represents no small feat in an area where secrecy – or at least discretion – had long prevailed, and publication of data was forbidden as being 'state secret' by some Participants until the KP came into effect. Virtually all Participants now submit statistical reports on a timely basis and the WGS has developed a user manual to ensure that all Participants can effectively access the statistics website, notwithstanding the diversity of their technical capabilities and infrastructures. Participants failing to meet the transparency requirements for two consecutive periods (in spite of reminders) are subject to a 'name and shame' procedure before the issue is referred to the Participation Committee for consideration of their compliance with minimum requirements.

The reliability or relevance of KP statistics has at times been questioned, with NGOs and some Participants calling for the creation of a fund or specialised bodies to analyse the data. The WGS has therefore gradually shifted the emphasis to the analysis and accuracy of data and WGS members have committed the necessary financial and human resources so that the collective capacity of the KP to conduct complex and resource-intensive statistical analysis has improved considerably. Where WGS statistical experts discover statistical anomalies, the WGS informs the WGM for follow-up under the annual reporting process and during review visits and other monitoring actions.

Statistical data bring an important contribution to the credibility of the KP. In some cases, statistical analysis can lead KP officials to the detection of irregularities or instances of non-compliance. Statistical anomalies showing that the Republic of Congo's production and trade data were highly inconsistent prompted the KP to dispatch a Review Mission to Brazzaville to verify KPCS implementation. The Review Mission confirmed that exports were approximately a hundred times greater than the estimated production: the RoC appeared to serve as a conduit for smuggling diamonds mainly originating in the DRC. Local authorities were unable to account for this massive discrepancy and the KP Chair proposed to remove the RoC from the list of KPCS Participants, which was accepted by all members through a written procedure in June 2004.[21]

The increasing capacity to cross-check and analyse statistical data has provided the KP with a powerful tool to identify statistical discrepancies and detect diversions of trade flows that may reveal problems with KPCS implementation, thus contributing to the effectiveness and credibility of the KP. As a WGS member, the EC is providing a major contribution to the KP's statistical effort, through the mobilisation of statistical expertise from its 'Joint Research Centre'.[22]

### 3.3 Monitoring KP implementation – the KP's 'investigative arm'?

*The KP's Peer Review System*. The KP's Peer Review System, adopted through the Sun City Administrative Decision,[23] is one of the most remarkable features of the KP and a key element for its credibility and effectiveness. It is operated by the Monitoring Working Group, which has been chaired by the EC since its inception. It originally comprised two 'pillars', namely annual reports, which provide a regular overview of KPCS implementation by all Participants, and review visits conducted by KP experts to assess in-depth KPCS implementation in a given country. Full compliance with the annual reporting requirement has been achieved, and annual reports have turned into a tool for regular dialogue with Participants on specific implementation issues. A first round of review visits to all Participants was completed in 2007, and a second round of review visits is currently underway.[24] Other monitoring tools and 'enhanced monitoring arrangements' have moreover been developed to strengthen the KP's monitoring capacity, to the point that the WGM has been described by some as the KP's 'investigative arm'.[25]

*Strengthening Participants' internal controls: the heart of the matter?* As it started to review Participants' implementation of KPCS requirements, the WGM soon came to the conclusion that the strengthening of internal controls – e.g., controls de-

21 The Republic of Congo was readmitted in November 2007.

22 See: <http://ec.europa.eu/dgs/jrc/index.cfm>.

23 See: <http://www.kimberleyprocess.com/structure/working_group_en.html#2>.

24 For its part, the EC received a first review visit in 2004, led by Botswana, and a second review visit in 2009, led by the USA.

25 *Diamonds in the Rough*, Human Rights Watch Report, 26 June 2009.

signed to eliminate the presence of conflict diamonds in the chain of production and/or trade from the point of mining or import to the point of export – was key to effectiveness: the KP would only be as strong as its weakest link. Over the years, the KP has made remarkable progress on this issue of internal controls that is so central to the traceability of diamonds.

The KPCS Document, under Section IV, requests Participants to 'establish a system of internal controls' and contains standard optional measures in Annex II as guidance for Participants to act at the national level. Thus, even though it provides for mandatory internal control systems, there is no harmonised approach as regards detailed control standards. This was justified by the considerable differences in producing and trading practices, as well as by various institutional and legal issues. Nevertheless, as it came of age, the Kimberley Process increasingly had to recognise that its credibility hinges on domestic systems of internal controls. Thus, the emphasis in the KP eventually shifted from legal and institutional issues to the complex issue of internal controls. Indeed, internal controls go the heart of the KP: the pledge of provenance on the KP certificate requires traceability. Controls over production activities and internal trade up to the first point of export are crucial for ensuring conflict-free diamond trade.

The consensual identification and definition of standards of control are a key part of this challenge. In this respect, the KP has progressively developed instruments to assist Participants in devising effective chains of control providing for an auditable paper trail. This effort resulted in the adoption, at the Gaborone Plenary in 2006,[26] of the Administrative Decision on Internal Controls, which provides a framework of reference and outlines recommendations for all Participants in the KP. The Brussels Plenary in 2007 shifted the focus to trading and manufacturing centres, highlighting the specific complex challenges they face in ensuring traceability of rough diamonds, especially as huge amounts of diamonds from all origins are mixed and moved around.[27]

Apart from the dissemination of best practices and the identification of common standards, proper implementation of controls on the ground remains a major challenge. This is particularly true for diamonds mined artisanally in vast alluvial diamond fields. Unlike those mined in the deep kimberlite pipes, these are spread over vast areas of territory often only centimetres under the surface. Poor or badly enforced controls are most evident in countries where alluvial diamonds are produced by artisanal miners, outside the formal sector. Fragile countries most vulnerable to conflict diamonds are thus often the least able to implement appropriate controls. The KP recognised this challenge and the 2004 Gatineau Plenary mandated the WGM to establish an *ad hoc* sub-group to address the challenges facing artisanal alluvial producers – including regulation of artisanal diamond mining, traceability from mine to export, illicit cross-border trade, etc. This organ was formally transformed into the Working Group of Alluvial Artisanal Producers at the Gaborone Plenary in 2006.

---

26 See: <http://www.kimberleyprocess.com/documents/plenary_intersessional_meeting_en.html>.
27 Ibid.

*Ghana's internal controls and Ivorian diamonds*. The Action Plan adopted at the Gaborone Plenary in order to enhance the effectiveness of Ghana's internal controls provides a vivid illustration of the efforts undertaken in this respect. Ghana's flawed internal controls were exposed by the UN Group of Experts on Sanctions against Côte d'Ivoire, and Ghana was suspected of serving as a conduit for Ivorian diamonds under sanctions. The Gaborone Plenary suspended Ghana's exports and requested that Ghana implement an Action Plan to strengthen its internal control chain (e.g., registration of informal miners, production estimate, auditing, security of the certification process, etc.). The UN Group of Experts then recognised Ghana's progress and the 2007 Brussels Plenary decided to apply risk-based monitoring arrangements to Ghana's exports, whereby all exports can be controlled *a posteriori* by the KP and a 'footprint' (a sort of ID card) for Ghana's diamonds could be progressively constituted. In 2009, the Windhoek Intersessional discussed the possible lifting of specific monitoring arrangements in light of further progress and the completion of the footprint that can henceforth be used by Ghana itself to monitor its own exports and to ensure that no suspicious shipments are laundered through its certification scheme.[28]

*KP monitoring tools and crisis reaction capacity*. Apart from the central issue of internal controls, the KP has, over the years, developed a 'toolbox' with innovative instruments in support of its monitoring and crisis reaction capacity.

The KP's monitoring capacity has benefited from scientific and technological support provided by some Participants, notably the EC. For instance, satellite imagery has been used to monitor or detect illicit diamond production sites, open source analysis has contributed to the understanding of situations, and statistical research has helped detect trade anomalies.

Moreover, the KP is actively developing additional tools to support the traceability of diamonds through 'footprinting' and 'fingerprinting' and thus complement this administrative traceability. Since its inception, the KP operates as a paper-based tracking system: it relies on a chain of supporting documentation to ensure traceability of the goods from production to export. KP diamond experts[29] have invested considerable resources in the development of 'footprints', which map the physical characteristics of diamonds from certain origins, as the most advanced tool. Footprints have thus been developed for Côte d'Ivoire, Ghana and Zimbabwe in particular. In addition, the KP has promoted scientific experiments to 'fingerprint' diamonds based on trace elements. The EC convened an international seminar on this issue in 2007, but research on 'fingerprinting' has not yet advanced to the stage of practical application.

Government oversight constitutes the 'teeth' of the certification scheme and therefore the KP has recently devoted increasing attention to cooperation on enforcement. The need for enforcement was highlighted when in 2006 a wave of arrests by

[28] Ibid.

[29] The Working Group of Diamond Experts, chaired by Mr Mark Van Bockstael (Antwerp World Diamond Centre), developed the footprinting methodology.

the Brazilian police confirmed the indications of weak internal controls previously exposed by NGOs, and again, in 2007, with the seizures by the Belgian police of approximately USD 20 mln linked to the smuggling of Ivorian diamonds. The seizures of irregular shipments and prosecutions for infringements of KPCS regulations demonstrate an increased awareness among customs and law enforcement officials, but also bring to the fore the need for increased international cooperation among KP Participants. The KP has recognised this development and initiated discussions on 'cooperation on KP implementation and enforcement' at the 2008 Delhi Plenary, at the initiative of the EC.

### 3.4 From conflict prevention towards peacebuilding

*KP technical assistance and 'crisis management' – a shared interest.* From the very outset, the KP recognised that some countries would need technical assistance to effectively implement the certification scheme. Antwerp's HRD[30] actively supported the efforts of some countries to draft legislation in order to become KP Participants. The KP further responded to this perceived need by setting up, at the 2005 Moscow Plenary, a technical assistance (TA) mechanism under the aegis of the Monitoring Working Group to coordinate the efforts of KP Participants and other organisations in addressing the needs identified through review visits and raised by Participants. The US chairs this mechanism and regularly updates lists of relevant projects and needs, especially expressed during review visits, in annual reports and at KP meetings. This has proved invaluable to ensure KP effectiveness, especially in case of crisis. Thus, when weaknesses in Ghana's internal controls were evidenced at the end of 2006, Ghana immediately benefited from technical assistance from various KP Participants as well as industry[31] to support implementation of its Action Plan to strengthen its internal controls and remain part of the KP. This joint effort corresponds to a shared interest and is not merely a demonstration of solidarity of the KP 'family' but an essential step to protect the credibility of the KP. Thus, though the KP is not a technical assistance instrument, it integrates technical assistance as a means to strengthen KPCS implementation.

*KP technical assistance and peacebuilding: the case of Liberia.* The technical assistance provided by KP Participants in post-crisis or post-conflict situations highlights the particular contribution of the 'KP community' to peacebuilding. Liberia's accession to the Kimberley Process was thus supported through technical assistance from certain Participants as a long-term commitment to peacebuilding in that country devastated by conflict diamonds. The EC continues to fund the project 'Strengthening the Implementation of the Kimberley Process in Liberia' that supports the Ministry of Lands, Mines and Energy's efforts to ensure that the legal

---

[30] *Hoge Raad voor Diamanten*, now Antwerp World Diamond Centre.

[31] The US, the EC and South Africa, in particular, joined forces with De Beers to monitor Ghana's exports and strengthen its internal controls.

system, trading conditions and diamond industry governance, as well as enforcement, meet KP standards.

*From conflict diamonds to peacebuilding: the case of Sierra Leone.* The KP's contribution to the settlement of conflicts and the consolidation of peace in Angola, the Democratic Republic of Congo, Liberia and Sierra Leone are largely recognised, but the KP's benefits for producing countries are broader, since legitimate diamond trade, which is 'protected' by the KP, makes a critical contribution to the economies of developing countries. The KP only certifies legal diamonds and this has created an incentive for producers and traders to process their diamonds through legal channels in order for them to obtain a certificate. Compliance with KP and transparent controls over diamond production and trading has generated government revenues through the imposition of licensing fees and duties. The value of revenue collected, together with improved employment conditions, has had a direct impact upon the availability of funds for potential development purposes and has thus brought developmental benefits in previously war-torn areas.

In the case of Sierra Leone, the total value of exports increased from USD 26 mln in 2001 to 141 mln in 2007, and revenues from diamond trade were partly allocated to a Sierra Leone diamond area community fund. A concept for the redistribution of diamond export proceeds was adopted in 2001 as part of post-war policies in Sierra Leone. Under the so-called 'Diamond Area Community Development Fund' (DACDF), one quarter of diamond export royalties is returned to diamond-producing areas for development purposes. As diamond exports in Sierra Leone increased, the values released to communities under the DACDF scheme rose dramatically. Close to USD 4.5 mln was released from diamond export royalties to diamond-producing areas for community development projects during the period 2002-2007. In parallel, KP members and industry supported the creation of a diamond export certification scheme in Sierra Leone. During the period 2003-2007 miners, chiefs, government officials, community women and NGO leaders were trained in basic diamond valuation. Mined-out land was reclaimed for agriculture, while attempts were made to form mining cooperatives bringing together artisanal miners. The success of the Sierra Leone model in ensuring that some of the diamond revenue is returned to producing communities for development purposes thus owes much to the demands for KP compliance and related increases in declared revenues – though clearly it is national policies, not the KP process itself, that determine local development.

*The KP and EU conflict prevention and peacebuilding activities.* Over the last years, the EU has intensified its work in the area of conflict prevention, crisis management and peacebuilding. Since 2007, the Instrument for Stability (IfS) has been used to finance a large number of crisis response projects worldwide, such as the Peacebuilding Partnership which, like the KP, draws on civil society expertise for peacebuilding activities.

The Kimberley Process appears as a key instrument in the EU's toolbox to deliver effective responses to emerging and actual external crises. In certain crises, synergies are developed and EU actions in the KP benefit from the support of other tools. For instance, since 2005, the EU implements a specific project, funded under the IfS, to monitor illicit production and trade of diamonds from northern Côte d'Ivoire. The interpretation of satellite imagery, the analysis of statistical data and open source information enable the EU – and the KP – to access reliable information and take appropriate decisions on an informed basis. The information is also shared with the UN Sanctions Committee and Group of Experts to assist them in their investigations, in line with Security Council Resolution 1842 (2008).[32] In 2009, the EU also initiated a similar project to detect and monitor illicit production and trade in Marange (Zimbabwe) and thus support implementation of the vigilance measures decided by the KP (see below). This clearly shows that the KP machinery has developed a real capacity to operate in concrete crises.

## 4. The KP's operations in crises

Although its *raison d'être* consists in the prevention of conflict, the KP operates primarily as a certification scheme – a trade instrument. It was implemented against the backdrop of a changing security environment. Today, the issue of 'conflict diamonds' is admittedly not as acute as it was when rough diamonds were fuelling wars in Africa. Nevertheless, the continuing conflict in Côte d'Ivoire and the fragility of a number of diamond-producing countries means that conflict diamonds remain topical from a conflict prevention and peacebuilding perspective. Moreover, the KP was soon confronted with concrete crises affecting the diamond sectors of Participants and had to deal with situations that were not originally envisaged in their full complexity at the time of its creation but could no longer be ignored. It rapidly had to develop and demonstrate a 'crisis reaction capacity' (see also under section 3.3: 'KP monitoring tools and crisis reaction capacity').

### 4.1 Côte d'Ivoire: UN and KP united in the fight against conflict diamonds

The biggest test to the KP's credibility came from the Côte d'Ivoire and the larger West Africa region. Following the eruption of hostilities in September 2002, the *Forces Nouvelles* rebels took control of the country's two main mining areas – Bobi-Séguéla and Tortiya – in northern Côte d'Ivoire, estimated to produce about 200,000 cts per year. The KP undertook to assess the situation through a field visit by the KP Chair, and his report to the Security Council alerted the international community. The 2005 Moscow Plenary adopted a nine-point KP resolution urging all Participants to 'undertake all possible efforts (...) to ensure that illicit Côte d'Ivoire diamonds cannot be introduced into the legitimate trade.' Shortly thereafter, the UN

---

[32] See: <http://www.un.org/french/sc/committees/1572/index.shtml>.

imposed sanctions[33] on trade in Ivorian diamonds. The KP then initiated monitoring of illicit production in diamond-mining areas, and the EC funded satellite imagery to support the KP's evaluation of the situation. The KP also enhanced cooperation with the UN Groups of Experts through regular exchange of information and joint field visits, as well as recourse to KP expertise on specific occasions. The 2007 Brussels Plenary[34] consolidated KP action and adopted an 'Initiative' calling for a concerted approach at national, regional and international level. The KP also reinforced controls in neighbouring countries (e.g., Ghana) and readmitted Liberia in 2007, with a view to setting up a 'first line of defence' against illicit flows of Ivorian diamonds. The UN continues to benefit from KP support to its diamond sanctions programmes, as acknowledged most recently by UNSCR 1842 (2008), and the Security Council has mandated the KP to pursue its actions. Significant seizures by KP Participants – notably the EC, where some USD 20 mln worth of Ivorian diamonds have been seized – demonstrate that vigilance is applied and the flow of illicit diamonds from Côte d'Ivoire is contained. The Ivorian crisis also illustrates that close coordination with the UN Sanctions Committee and the Groups of Experts is mutually beneficial.

## 4.2 Marange diamonds: 'Blood diamonds' or 'conflict diamonds'?

More recently, developments in the Marange area, in Zimbabwe, have confronted the KP with a new type of crisis, in which no classical 'conflict diamonds' are involved, but where underlying principles of the KP are nonetheless at stake. Towards the end of 2006, tens of thousands of diggers invaded the diamond fields in Marange (Manicaland Province). Confronted with this diamond rush, the government stepped in and imposed wide-ranging security measures, such as fencing off the core production area, cordoning off the region, police patrols and customs checks. In spite of these measures, the ability of the government to maintain effective control of the area came under question as mounting evidence of wide-spread smuggling and reports about the possible involvement of corrupt and high-level officials in illicit mining and smuggling were given. Zimbabwe thus became a country of particular concern for the KP and was subjected by the KP to enhanced monitoring measures in the form of an *ad hoc* review visit in June 2007 and regular reports to the KP on the implementation of the review's recommendations.

At the end of 2008, things went from bad to worse as the government launched Operation Hakudzwoki ('no return') and deployed considerable military resources – including a surveillance helicopter – to prevent diggers from entering the fields. Operation Hakudzwoki was quickly associated with reports of violence and human rights abuses – including the extra-judicial killing of dozens of diamond diggers. The government denied any killing.

In response to these events, the KP released a public statement[35] expressing 'growing concerns at the reports of violence and indications of smuggling in the

33 See: <http://www.un.org/french/docs/sc/2005/cs2005.htm>.

34 See: <http://www.kimberleyprocess.com/documents/plenary_intersessional_meeting_en.html>.

35 See: <http://www.kimberleyprocess.com/>.

Marange mining area', and a KP high-level envoy visited the country in March 2009 to convey the KP message at political level. The KP also launched research into the situation with a view to providing a solid information basis for any further decision on Zimbabwe's status in the KP. Moreover, the KP also developed specific measures to contain the flow of illicit diamonds and stepped up international efforts to counter the laundering of those diamonds, in particular with a call for vigilance and reporting of suspicious transactions based on footprint, as well as regional co-operation. In June 2009, after the Windhoek Intersessional Meeting decided to send a 'review mission' to assess compliance with KP requirements and to investigate reports of violence and smuggling, the government agreed, as a first step, to withdraw the army from the mining areas.

## 5. Challenges to the KP's future

In spite of the nearly unanimous agreement that the KP has achieved remarkable success in a short time, the KP is not, of course, an iron-clad deterrent and its actions have not 'eradicated' the trade in conflict diamonds or the smuggling of rough diamonds. By and large, however, the KP has demonstrated its effectiveness and has evolved rapidly, developing new instruments, addressing new challenges and adapting to changing circumstances – a rapid evolution facilitated by a flexible and non-formalistic approach. This evolution has brought the KP to maturity, but has also brought new, more fundamental challenges to the fore, which touch on the very foundations of the Kimberley Process.

### 5.1 Too narrow a mandate?

There is perhaps no issue more sensitive than that of the KP's 'mandate'. The official mandate of the Kimberley Process is to prevent 'conflict diamonds' from entering the legitimate international diamond markets, but this mandate – and the very notion of 'conflict diamonds' – has been a regular subject of debate. The United Nations define 'conflict diamonds' as 'rough diamonds which are used by rebel movements to finance their military activities, including attempts to undermine or overthrow legitimate governments.'[36] The reference to the UN definition, however, strictly links KP action to UN decisions and provides too tight a jacket for the KP in the real world. Indeed, the KP is a multilateral scheme whose credibility hinges on its effective implementation by all Participants – including those with no conflict diamonds: inasmuch as Participants with weak internal controls pose a risk to the system by possibly offering a conduit for conflict diamonds.

The central issue of internal controls has thus provided a basis for a more dynamic interpretation of the KP mandate that would extend, *de facto*, to smuggling, since weak internal controls are often revealed by large-scale smuggling. The tradi-

[36] UN Resolution by the General Assembly, A/Res/55/56.

tionally secretive diamond sector, that operated largely on a cash basis with few formal contracts, has long defied effective government regulation and was used to going underground to escape corrupt and predatory government and high taxes or to hide and export profits. By introducing a clear distinction between legal and illegal markets, the KP has increased the 'cost' of illicit production and trade, thus contributing to a remarkable increase in diamond production and trade using legal channels and to a corresponding reduction of illicit diamond mining and trade. Reputable traders would nowadays think twice before entering into illicit transactions. Nevertheless, though illicit diamond mining and trading is less attractive than in the past, a parallel market for diamonds continues to exist and illicit trade is thought to remain significant in some countries. Smuggling, though not central to its mandate, has thus become a matter of attention for the Kimberley Process. In this sense, the 'separation' of Venezuela[37] from the KPCS marks a milestone in the KP's history: Venezuela, a small alluvial diamond producer, was not accused of directly producing or trading conflict diamonds, but rather of not complying with KPCS requirements, especially in terms of internal controls. Venezuela was accused of 'having dropped off the KPCS radar'[38] as lax controls allowed dealers to smuggle most of its production out of the country. The EU and Indian Chairs spared no efforts to promote KPCS implementation in Venezuela, but in October 2008 a KP Chair mission eventually confirmed Venezuela's difficulties in meeting KPCS requirements. Venezuela subsequently 'separated' from the KPCS and was removed from the list of Participants in the certification scheme at the Delhi Plenary, though it remains formally part of the Kimberley Process as such.

Recent events in Zimbabwe have focused attention on the question of human rights, with NGOs calling for the KP to broaden its mandate and include this concern. Here again, there is little doubt that the KP was not conceived as an instrument for the promotion of human rights. At the same time, there is also a recognition that respect for fundamental rights constitutes one of the underlying principles of the KP, as is stated in the preamble to the KPCS document.

## 5.2 Strong international rules *v.* weak national implementation

KP effectiveness ultimately depends on the institutional and administrative capacity of Participants – lack of capacity, poor governance and porous borders will continue to offer opportunities for conflict diamonds to move into the legal trade. KP rules, as any other rule, require efficient administration to implement them and are of little value in the hands of corrupt officials or ineffective administrations. The 'laundering' of conflict diamonds through KP Participants with limited institu-

---

[37] Under the terms of the Delhi Plenary decision concerning Venezuela's 'separation' from the KPCS Venezuela remains a member of the Kimberley Process but stops trading in rough diamonds under its certification scheme until it can establish that it is compliant with KPCS requirements.

[38] *The Lost World – Diamond Mining and Smuggling in Venezuela*, Partnership Africa Canada, November 2006.

tional and administrative capacity represents a major challenge to the KP, especially in post-conflict situations or situations of fragility.

Conversely, some NGOs in particular have argued that the current KP organisation and working methods – in a word, its limited institutional and administrative capacity – hamper its ability to fulfil its mandate and cause concern as to its sustainability over the long term. As demonstrated in section 3, however, the KP's flexible structure has served it well so far.

### 5.3 Adaptation and evolution

The KP was born out of specific political and economic situations – in particular the hold that De Beers and Antwerp had on rough diamond production and trade – and its introduction provoked important changes in the diamond scene. For example, before the KP, Liberia exported diamonds – essentially of foreign origin – worth billions of dollars, and then had to cease official exports completely until 2007. Before the KP, the EC recorded imports from a number of non-producing countries, such as Zambia and Rwanda, which have not joined the KP and have ceased exporting diamonds.

Today, the economic crisis and the dramatic evolution of the diamond industry bring new challenges to the KP. The structure of the diamond industry is changing. 'Beneficiation' – the cutting and polishing of diamonds in diamond-producing countries – in particular implies that the KP will capture an ever-smaller share of rough diamonds produced worldwide. The KP risks losing some of its relevance, as the multiplication of cutting and polishing centres will make controls more problematic. The evolving security situation also brings new challenges: while the volume of 'conflict diamonds' has been greatly reduced, other 'blood diamonds' are 'discovered' in relation to human rights violations.

### 5.4 A Kimberley Process for all 'conflict resources'?

The KP is often cited as an example of a renewed interest in conflict resources. In 2008, the UN Security Council held regular discussions on conflict resources and in relation to the fighting in eastern DRC, where illegal exploitation and trade of abundant natural resources appears to be one of the root causes of the conflict. Other international initiatives, e.g., the G8 Heiligendam Summit,[39] have highlighted the need to address the link between natural resources and security.

The replicability of the Kimberley Process to other conflict resources remains a subject of debate, and many factors that contributed to the emergence of the KP should be considered when addressing this issue. The characteristics of the goods can, at first sight, hardly explain the KP's success – quite the contrary: arguably, diamonds are perhaps among the most difficult commodities to regulate. The most

[39] See: <http://www.canadainternational.gc.ca/g8/summit-sommet/2007/index.aspx?lang=fra&menu_id=41&menu=L>.

concentrated form of wealth, diamonds are small stones produced in immense quantities; they can be easily transported and concealed. Differences between diamonds from various origins are often small. Moreover, diamonds are traditionally 'mixed and sorted' so that it becomes impossible for the best '*diamantaire*' to positively recognise their origin. However, for all those characteristics explaining why the underground trade in diamonds has always been so attractive, there is another characteristic that has played a crucial role in the emergence of the KPCS: diamonds are the luxury product *par excellence* and have no intrinsic value, except in the eyes of customers 'educated' by decades of intensive advertising campaigns.

The structure of the diamond industry at the end of the 1990s also helped considerably, as a few major players became concerned that the legitimate diamond industry could be tarnished and would seriously suffer from the consumer campaigns led by NGOs. Under the pressure of NGOs, they decided to engage actively in the process and assumed leadership of the diamond sector through the creation of the World Diamond Council, a coalition of diamond-mining companies, trading firms and jewellery industry representatives created to engage with the KP. Thus, under sustained NGO pressure, the active engagement of the diamond industry coincided with the determination of some governments in Africa and Europe with high stakes in the diamond industry as well as strong UN support, and laid the foundations for the creation of the Kimberley Process. To replicate such a combination of factors to other resources will be no easy task, though it may not be impossible.

## 6. Conclusion – a new instrument for a new century

The Kimberley Process appeared on the international scene at the turn of the century as a consensual, innovative effort of industry, NGOs and governments to tackle the new issue of conflict diamonds and is now widely recognised as a success. It has demonstrated a capacity to operate effectively and although the letter of its founding Document has been left untouched, it has evolved and adapted through the adoption of numerous decisions, the expanding operations of its working groups and the development of a broad range of instruments. It has fulfilled its formal mandate to the extent that its contribution to the 'reduction' of conflict is undisputed. This, however, also points to its (obviously) limited ability to utterly 'eradicate' conflict diamonds *in situ*. Furthermore, the constraints on KP effectiveness caused by poor governance and limited institutional capacity as well as growing demands placed upon it with respect to smuggling and human rights, question its continued ability to respond to growing expectations for which it is, arguably, ill-qualified.

The Kimberley Process itself emerged from a reflection about the limitations of more traditional and 'tested' international instruments, viz. UN sanctions. It was conceived with a view to facilitating the implementation of sanctions through a dedicated system of control, and, in a way, represents an extension of those sanctions in reach, time and intensity. The KP demonstrates that certification systems can be viewed, politically, as a constructive alternative to export bans on natural resources that are difficult to enforce effectively, and, economically, as a viable instrument to ensure traceability of the trading chain. The KP also illustrates that certification systems offer a potential for increasing transparency and good governance in the extraction and commercialisation of natural resources.

The KP may thus appear as a 'pioneer' for a new generation of international instruments, combining the capacity to react 'against' a perceived international threat with the potential to contribute 'positively' to stability and development, the capacity to operate at the 'technical' level and the pursuit of highly political objectives of international peace and security. With its innovative legal and institutional set-up, its flexible and informal functioning, and the mixture of technical and political issues it deals with, the KP perhaps illustrates a new way to deal with international issues in a new century – this 'functional approach' resembles that of other recent international processes, such as the Financial Action Task Force (FATF) in the area of money laundering and terrorism financing.

The creation of the Kimberley Process as an international instrument thus coincides with the increasing emergence of the European Union as an international actor on the world stage. In this sense, the EU and the KP, which both emerge at the turn of the century as 'innovative and consensual' efforts to tackle new challenges in a constructive way, reflect this fundamental trend. The KP instrument was perfectly suited for the EU as an actor well anchored in international trade issues but making its *debut* on the international political scene and showing great interest in conflict prevention issues. The KP corresponds ideally to the EU's objective to promote 'effective multilateralism and a rule-based international order'. The KP Chairmanship epitomised this symbiosis and provided the EU with a rare opportunity to lead an international process.

# LIST OF CONTRIBUTORS

**Fabio Bargiacchi** is a Senior Electoral Assistance Advisor at the UN/UNDP Brussels Office.

**Dr. Steven Blockmans** is Senior Research Fellow in EU law at the T.M.C. Asser Institute in The Hague and academic coordinator of the Centre for the Law of EU External Relations (CLEER).

**Stéphane Chardon** works on crisis response and peacebuilding, sanctions and the Kimberley Process at DG External Relations of the European Commission.

**Aurélie Courtier** is a Junior Research Fellow at the European Institute of Public Administration (EIPA) in Maastricht.

**Philippe Darmuzey** is Head of Unit, Pan-African Issues and Institutions, Governance and Migration at DG Development and Relations with African, Caribbean and Pacific States of the European Commission.

**Justin Davies** is the EU Coordinator/Political Advisor to the European Union Special Representative in Kosovo. Previously, he was the Chief of Staff of the Aceh Monitoring Mission.

**Prof. Dr. Simon Duke** is Senior Research Fellow at the European Institute of Public Administration (EIPA) in Maastricht.

**Patrick Dupont** works on election observation issues at DG External Relations of the European Commission.

**Christophe Gadrey** is a Desk Officer for Chad at DG ECHO of the European Commission.

**Dr. David Galbreath** is Senior Lecturer in International Relations at the Department of Politics and International Relations of the University of Aberdeen.

**Catriona Gourlay** is Research Fellow and Project Manager at the United Nations Institute for Disarmament Research (UNIDIR) in Geneva.

**Dr. Eva Gross** is Senior Research Fellow at the Institute for European Studies of the Vrije Universiteit Brussel.

**Dr. Hadewych Hazelzet** works as an official at the General Secretariat of the Council of the European Union, DG External and Politico-Military Relations, Directorate for Civilian Crisis Management.

**Michael Humphreys** is a former European Commission official and Head of the European Commission Delegation in Bosnia and Herzegovina (2002-2006).

**Jasna Jelisić** works in Bosnia and Herzegovina as a journalist, political advisor and analyst.

**Prof. Dr. Stephan Keukeleire** is Jean Monnet Professor in European Foreign Policy at the Institute for International and European Policy of Leuven University and Visiting Professor at the College of Europe in Bruges.

**Dr. Tonny Brems Knudsen** is Associate Professor of International Relations at the Department of Political Science of Aarhus University.

**Dr. Marta Martinelli** is Research Fellow at the Pôle Bernheim for Peace and Citizenship, Institute of European Studies of the Université Libre de Bruxelles.

**Dr. Michael Merlingen** is Associate Professor at the Central European University in Budapest.

**Dr. Christian Axboe Nielsen** is Assistant Professor of Southeast European Studies at the Department of History and Areas Studies of Aarhus University.

**Cesare Onestini** is First Counsellor, Political Affairs, at the Delegation of the European Union to the United Nations in New York.

**Dr. Rasa Ostrauskaitė** is a former member of the Policy Unit of the EU Council General Secretariat.

**Dr. Tom Ruys** is attorney at law at Stibbe in Brussels and Substitute Lecturer and Senior Member of the Leuven Centre for Global Governance Studies at the University of Leuven.

**David Spence** is First Counsellor at the Delegation of the European Union to the United Nations in Geneva.

**Robin Thiers** is a policy advisor within the Agriculture Department of the Flemish government in the framework of the Belgian EU Presidency.

**Dr. Nathalie Tocci** is a Senior Fellow at the Istituto Affari Internazionali in Rome.

**Stefano Tomat** is First Secretary at the Delegation of the European Union to the United Nations in New York.

**Dr. Francesco Torcoli** works as an Election Specialist/Quality Management Officer at the DG EuropeAid Cooperation Office of the European Commission.

**Thomas Unger** works at the Human Rights Department of the Austrian Foreign Ministry. Previously he was a Senior Associate at the International Center for Transitional Justice.

**Koen Vervaeke** is EU Special Representative and Head of the European Union Delegation to the African Union in Addis Abeba.

**Cees Wittebrood** is Head of Unit for Humanitarian Operations in Africa at DG ECHO of the European Commission.

**Prof. Dr. Jan Wouters** is Jean Monnet Chair EU and Global Governance, Professor of International Law and International Organisations and Director of the Leuven Centre for Global Governance Studies and Institute for International Law at the University of Leuven.

# INDEX

**J**



**K**

MIX
Papier aus verantwortungsvollen Quellen
Paper from responsible sources
FSC® C105338

If you have any concerns about our products,
you can contact us on
**ProductSafety@springernature.com**

In case Publisher is established outside the EU,
the EU authorized representative is:
**Springer Nature Customer Service Center GmbH**
**Europaplatz 3, 69115 Heidelberg, Germany**

Printed by Libri Plureos GmbH
in Hamburg, Germany